THE
MAHABHARATA

THE
MAHABHARATA
of
Krishna–Dwaipayana Vyasa

Translated into English Prose from the Original Sanskrit
Text
by
Kisari Mohan Ganguli

pac ps
Pacific Publishing Studio

Published in the United States by Madison Park, an imprint of Pacific Publishing Studio.

www.PacPS.com

ISBN is 1453771964

EAN-13 is 9781453771969

TRANSLATOR'S PREFACE

The object of a translator should ever be to hold the mirror upto his author. That being so, his chief duty is to represent so far as practicable the manner in which his author's ideas have been expressed, retaining if possible at the sacrifice of idiom and taste all the peculiarities of his author's imagery and of language as well. In regard to translations from the Sanskrit, nothing is easier than to dish up Hindu ideas, so as to make them agreeable to English taste. But the endeavour of the present translator has been to give in the following pages as literal a rendering as possible of the great work of Vyasa. To the purely English reader there is much in the following pages that will strike as ridiculous. Those unacquainted with any language but their own are generally very exclusive in matters of taste. Having no knowledge of models other than what they meet with in their own tongue, the standard they have formed of purity and taste in composition must necessarily be a narrow one. The translator, however, would ill-discharge his duty, if for the sake of avoiding ridicule, he sacrificed fidelity to the original. He must represent his author as he is, not as he should be to please the narrow taste of those entirely unacquainted with him. Mr. Pickford, in the preface to his English translation of the Mahavira Charita, ably defends a close adherence to the original even at the sacrifice of idiom and taste against the claims of what has been called 'Free Translation,' which means dressing the author in an outlandish garb to please those to whom he is introduced.

In the preface to his classical translation of Bhartrihari's Niti Satakam and Vairagya Satakam, Mr. C.H. Tawney says, "I am sensible that in the present attempt I have retained much local colouring. For instance, the ideas of worshipping the feet of a god of great men, though it frequently occurs in Indian literature, will undoubtedly move the laughter of Englishmen unacquainted with Sanskrit, especially if they happen to belong to that class of readers who revel their attention on the accidental and remain blind to the essential. But a certain measure of fidelity to the original even at the risk of making oneself ridiculous, is better than the studied dishonesty which characterises so many translations of oriental poets."

We fully subscribe to the above although, it must be observed, the censure conveyed to the class of translators last indicated is rather undeserved, there being nothing like a 'studied dishonesty' in their efforts which proceed only from a mistaken view of their duties and as such betray only an error of the head but not of the heart. More than twelve years ago when Babu Pratapa Chandra Roy, with Babu Durga Charan Banerjee, went to my retreat at Seebpore, for engaging me to translate the Mahabharata into English, I was amazed with the grandeur of the scheme. My first question to him was,—whence was the money to come, supposing my competence for the task. Pratapa then unfolded to me the details of his plan, the hopes he could legitimately cherish of assistance from different quarters. He was full of enthusiasm. He showed me Dr. Rost's letter, which, he said, had suggested to him the undertaking. I had known Babu Durga Charan for many years and I had the highest opinion of his scholarship and practical good sense. When he warmly took Pratapa's side for convincing me of the practicability of the scheme, I listened to him patiently. The two were for completing all arrangements with me the very day. To this I did not agree. I took a week's time to consider. I consulted some of my literary friends, foremost among whom was the late lamented Dr. Sambhu C. Mookherjee. The latter, I found, had been waited upon by Pratapa. Dr. Mookherjee spoke to me of Pratapa as a man of indomitable energy and perseverance. The result of my conference with Dr. Mookherjee was that I wrote to Pratapa asking him to see me again. In this second interview estimates were drawn up, and everything was arranged as far as my portion of the work was concerned. My friend left with me a specimen of translation which he had received from Professor Max Muller. This I began to study, carefully comparing it sentence by sentence with the original. About its literal character there could be no doubt, but it had no flow and, therefore, could not be perused with pleasure by the general reader. The translation had been executed thirty years ago by a young German friend of the great Pundit. I had to touch up every sentence. This I did without at all impairing faithfulness to the original. My first 'copy' was set up in type and a dozen sheets were struck off. These were submitted to the judgment of a number of eminent writers, European and native. All of them, I was glad to see, approved of the specimen, and then the task of translating the Mahabharata into English seriously began.

Before, however, the first fasciculus could be issued, the question as to whether the authorship of the translation should be publicly owned, arose. Babu Pratapa Chandra Roy was against anonymity. I was for it. The reasons I adduced were chiefly founded upon the impossibility of one person translating the whole of the gigantic work. Notwithstanding my resolve to discharge to the fullest extent the duty that I took up, I might not live to carry it out. It would take many years before the end could be reached. Other circumstances than death might arise in consequence of which my connection with the work might cease. It could not be desirable to issue successive fasciculus with the names of a succession of translators appearing on the title pages. These and other considerations convinced my friend that, after all, my view was correct. It was, accordingly, resolved to withhold the name of the translator. As a compromise, however, between the two views, it was resolved to issue the first fasciculus with two prefaces, one over the signature of the publisher and the other headed— 'Translator's Preface.' This, it was supposed, would effectually guard against misconceptions of every kind. No careful reader would then confound the publisher with the author.

Although this plan was adopted, yet before a fourth of the task had been accomplished, an influential Indian journal came down upon poor Pratapa Chandra Roy and accused him openly of being a party to a great literary imposture, viz., of posing before the world as the translator of Vyasa's work when, in fact, he was only the publisher. The charge came upon my friend as a surprise, especially as he had never made a secret of the authorship in his correspondence with Oriental scholars in every part of the world. He promptly wrote to the journal in question, explaining the reasons there were for anonymity, and pointing to the two prefaces with which the first fasciculus had been given to the world. The editor readily admitted his mistake and made a satisfactory apology.

Now that the translation has been completed, there can no longer be any reason for withholding the name of the translator. The entire translation is practically the work of one hand. In portions of the Adi and the Sabha Parvas, I was assisted by Babu Charu Charan Mookerjee. About four forms of the Sabha Parva were done by Professor Krishna Kamal Bhattacharya, and about half a fasciculus during my illness, was done by another hand. I should however state that before passing to the printer the copy received from these gentlemen I carefully compared every sentence with the original, making such alterations as were needed for securing a uniformity of style with the rest of the work.

I should here observe that in rendering the Mahabharata into English I have derived very little aid from the three Bengali versions that are supposed to have been executed with care. Every one of these is full of inaccuracies and blunders of every description. The Santi in particular which is by far the most difficult of the eighteen Parvas, has been made a mess of by the Pundits that attacked it. Hundreds of ridiculous blunders can be pointed out in both the Rajadharma and the Mokshadharma sections. Some of these I have pointed out in footnotes.

I cannot lay claim to infallibility. There are verses in the Mahabharata that are exceedingly difficult to construe. I have derived much aid from the great commentator Nilakantha. I know that Nilakantha's authority is not incapable of being challenged. But when it is remembered that the interpretations given by Nilakantha came down to him from preceptors of olden days, one should think twice before rejecting Nilakantha as a guide.

About the readings I have adopted, I should say that as regards the first half of the work, I have generally adhered to the Bengal texts; as regards the latter half, to the printed Bombay edition. Sometimes individual sections, as occurring in the Bengal editions, differ widely, in respect of the order of the verses, from the corresponding ones in the Bombay edition. In such cases I have adhered to the Bengal texts, convinced that the sequence of ideas has been better preserved in the Bengal editions than the Bombay one.

I should express my particular obligations to Pundit Ram Nath Tarkaratna, the author of 'Vasudeva Vijayam' and other poems, Pundit Shyama Charan Kaviratna, the learned editor of Kavyaprakasha with the commentary of Professor Mahesh Chandra Nayaratna, and Babu Aghore Nath Banerjee, the manager of the Bharata Karyalaya. All these scholars were my referees on all points of difficulty. Pundit Ram Nath's solid scholarship is known to them that have come in contact with him. I never referred to him a difficulty that he could not clear up. Unfortunately, he was not always at hand to consult. Pundit Shyama Charan Kaviratna, during my residence at Seebpore, assisted me in going over the Mokshadharma sections of the Santi Parva. Unostentatious in the extreme, Kaviratna is truly the type of a learned Brahman of ancient India. Babu Aghore Nath Banerjee also has from time to time, rendered me valuable assistance in clearing my difficulties.

Gigantic as the work is, it would have been exceedingly difficult for me to go on with it if I had not been encouraged by Sir Stuart Bayley, Sir Auckland Colvin, Sir Alfred Croft, and among Oriental scholars, by the late lamented Dr. Reinhold Rost, and Mons. A. Barth of Paris. All these eminent men know from the beginning that the translation was proceeding from my pen. Notwithstanding the enthusiasm, with which my poor friend, Pratapa Chandra Roy, always endeavoured to fill me. I am sure my energies would have flagged and patience exhausted but for the encouraging words which I always received from these patrons and friends of the enterprise.

Lastly, I should name my literary chief and friend, Dr. Sambhu C. Mookherjee. The kind interest he took in my labours, the repeated exhortations he addressed to me inculcating patience, the care with which he read every fasciculus as it came out, marking all those passages which threw light upon topics of antiquarian interest, and the words of praise he uttered when any expression particularly happy met his eyes, served to stimulate me more than anything else in going on with a task that sometimes seemed to me endless.

Kisari Mohan Ganguli
Calcutta

THE MAHABHARATA ADI PARVA

SECTION I

Om! Having bowed down to Narayana and Nara, the most exalted male being, and also to the goddess Saraswati, must the word Jaya be uttered.

Ugrasrava, the son of Lomaharshana, surnamed Sauti, well-versed in the Puranas, bending with humility, one day approached the great sages of rigid vows, sitting at their ease, who had attended the twelve years' sacrifice of Saunaka, surnamed Kulapati, in the forest of Naimisha. Those ascetics, wishing to hear his wonderful narrations, presently began to address him who had thus arrived at that recluse abode of the inhabitants of the forest of Naimisha. Having been entertained with due respect by those holy men, he saluted those Munis (sages) with joined palms, even all of them, and inquired about the progress of their asceticism. Then all the ascetics being again seated, the son of Lomaharshana humbly occupied the seat that was assigned to him. Seeing that he was comfortably seated, and recovered from fatigue, one of the Rishis beginning the conversation, asked him, 'Whence comest thou, O lotus-eyed Sauti, and where hast thou spent the time? Tell me, who ask thee, in detail.'

Accomplished in speech, Sauti, thus questioned, gave in the midst of that big assemblage of contemplative Munis a full and proper answer in words consonant with their mode of life.

"Sauti said, 'Having heard the diverse sacred and wonderful stories which were composed in his Mahabharata by Krishna-Dwaipayana, and which were recited in full by Vaisampayana at the Snake-sacrifice of the high-souled royal sage Janamejaya and in the presence also of that chief of Princes, the son of Parikshit, and having wandered about, visiting many sacred waters and holy shrines, I journeyed to the country venerated by the Dwijas (twice-born) and called Samantapanchaka where formerly was fought the battle between the children of Kuru and Pandu, and all the chiefs of the land ranged on either side. Thence, anxious to see you, I am come into your presence. Ye reverend sages, all of whom are to me as Brahma; ye greatly blessed who shine in this place of sacrifice with the splendour of the solar fire: ye who have concluded the silent meditations and have fed the holy fire; and yet who are sitting—without care, what, O ye Dwijas (twice-born), shall I repeat, shall I recount the sacred stories collected in the Puranas containing precepts of religious duty and of worldly profit, or the acts of illustrious saints and sovereigns of mankind?"

"The Rishi replied, 'The Purana, first promulgated by the great Rishi Dwaipayana, and which after having been heard both by the gods and the Brahmarshis was highly esteemed, being the most eminent narrative that exists, diversified both in diction and division, possessing subtle meanings logically combined, and gleaned from the Vedas, is a sacred work. Composed in elegant language, it includeth the subjects of other books. It is elucidated by other Shastras, and comprehendeth the sense of the four Vedas. We are desirous of hearing that history also called Bharata, the holy composition of the wonderful Vyasa, which dispelleth the fear of evil, just as it was cheerfully recited by the Rishi Vaisampayana, under the direction of Dwaipayana himself, at the snake-sacrifice of Raja Janamejaya?'

"Sauti then said, 'Having bowed down to the primordial being Isana, to whom multitudes make offerings, and who is adored by the multitude; who is the true incorruptible one, Brahma, perceptible, imperceptible, eternal; who is both a non-existing and an existing-non-existing being; who is the universe and also distinct from the existing and non-existing universe; who is the creator of high and low; the ancient, exalted, inexhaustible one; who is Vishnu, beneficent and the beneficence itself, worthy of all preference, pure and immaculate; who is Hari, the ruler of the faculties, the guide of all things moveable and immoveable; I will declare the sacred thoughts of the illustrious sage Vyasa, of marvellous deeds and worshipped here by all. Some bards have already published this history, some are now teaching it, and others, in like manner, will hereafter promulgate it upon the earth. It is a great source of knowledge, established throughout the three regions of the world. It is possessed by the twice-born both in detailed and compendious forms. It is the delight of the learned for being embellished with elegant expressions, conversations human and divine, and a variety of poetical measures."'

In this world, when it was destitute of brightness and light, and enveloped all around in total darkness, there came into being, as the primal cause of creation, a mighty egg, the one inexhaustible seed of all created beings. It is called Mahadivya, and was formed at the beginning of the Yuga, in which we are told, was the true light Brahma, the eternal one, the wonderful and inconceivable being present alike in all places; the invisible and subtle cause, whose nature partaketh of entity and non-entity. From this egg came out the lord Pitamaha Brahma, the one only Prajapati; with Suraguru and Sthanu. Then appeared the twenty-one Prajapatis, viz., Manu, Vasishtha and Parameshthi; ten Prachetas, Daksha, and the seven sons of Daksha. Then appeared the man of inconceivable nature whom all the Rishis know and so the Viswe-devas, the Adityas, the Vasus, and the twin Aswins; the Yakshas, the Sadhyas, the Pisachas, the Guhyakas, and the Pitris. After these were produced the wise and most holy Brahmarshis, and the numerous Rajarshis distinguished by every noble quality. So the water, the heavens, the earth, the air, the sky, the points of the heavens, the years, the seasons, the months, the fortnights, called Pakshas, with day and night in due succession. And thus were produced all things which are known to mankind.

And what is seen in the universe, whether animate or inanimate, of created things, will at the end of the world, and after the expiration of the Yuga, be again confounded. And, at the commencement of other Yugas, all things will be renovated, and, like the various fruits of the earth, succeed each other in the due order of their seasons. Thus continueth perpetually to revolve in the world, without beginning and without end, this wheel which causeth the destruction of all things.

The generation of Devas, in brief, was thirty-three thousand, thirty-three hundred and thirty-three. The sons of Div were Brihadbhanu, Chakshus, Atma Vibhavasu, Savita, Richika, Arka, Bhanu, Asavaha, and Ravi. Of these Vivaswans of old, Mahya was the youngest whose son was Deva-vrata. The latter had for his son, Su-vrata who, we learn, had three sons,—Dasa-jyoti, Sata-jyoti, and Sahasra-jyoti, each of them producing numerous offspring. The illustrious Dasa-jyoti had ten thousand, Sata-jyoti ten times that number, and Sahasra-jyoti ten times the number of Sata-jyoti's offspring. From these are descended the family of the Kurus, of the Yadus, and of Bharata; the family of Yayati and of Ikshwaku; also of all the Rajarshis. Numerous also were the generations produced, and very abundant were the creatures and their places of abode. The mystery which is threefold—the Vedas, Yoga, and Vijnana Dharma, Artha, and Kama—also various books upon the subject of Dharma, Artha, and Kama; also rules for the conduct of mankind; also histories and discourses with various srutis; all of which having been seen by the Rishi Vyasa are here in due order mentioned as a specimen of the book.

The Rishi Vyasa published this mass of knowledge in both a detailed and an abridged form. It is the wish of the learned in the world to possess the details and the abridgement. Some read the Bharata beginning with the initial mantra (invocation), others with the story of Astika, others with Uparichara, while some Brahmanas study the whole. Men of learning display their various knowledge of the institutes in commenting on the composition. Some are skilful in explaining it, while others, in remembering its contents.

The son of Satyavati having, by penance and meditation, analysed the eternal Veda, afterwards composed this holy history, when that learned Brahmarshi of strict vows, the noble Dwaipayana Vyasa, offspring of Parasara, had finished this greatest of narrations, he began to consider how he might teach it to his disciples. And the possessor of the six attributes, Brahma, the world's preceptor, knowing of the anxiety of the Rishi Dwaipayana, came in person to the place where the latter was, for gratifying the saint, and benefiting the people. And when Vyasa, surrounded by all the tribes of Munis, saw him, he was surprised; and, standing with joined palms, he bowed and ordered a seat to be brought. And Vyasa having gone round him who is called Hiranyagarbha seated on that distinguished seat stood near it; and being commanded by Brahma Parameshthi, he sat down near the seat, full of affection and smiling in joy. Then the greatly glorious Vyasa, addressing Brahma Parameshthi, said, "O divine Brahma, by me a poem hath been composed which is greatly respected. The mystery of the Veda, and what other subjects have been explained by me; the various rituals of the Upanishads with the Angas; the compilation of the Puranas and history formed by me and named after the three divisions of time, past, present, and future; the determination of the nature of decay, fear, disease, existence, and non-existence, a description of creeds and of the various modes of life; rule for the four castes, and the import of all the Puranas; an account of asceticism and of the duties of a religious student; the dimensions of the sun and moon, the planets, constellations, and stars, together with the duration of the four ages; the Rik, Sama and Yajur Vedas; also the Adhyatma; the sciences called Nyaya, Orthphy and Treatment of diseases; charity and Pasupatadharma; birth celestial and human, for particular purposes; also a description of places of pilgrimage and other holy places of rivers, mountains,, forests, the ocean, of heavenly cities and the kalpas; the art of war; the different kinds of nations and languages: the nature of the manners of the people; and the all-pervading spirit;—all these have been represented. But, after all, no writer of this work is to be found on earth.'

"Brahma said. 'I esteem thee for thy knowledge of divine mysteries, before the whole body of celebrated Munis distinguished for the sanctity of their lives. I know thou hast revealed the divine word, even from its first utterance, in the language of truth. Thou hast called thy present work a poem, wherefore it shall be a poem. There shall be no poets whose works may equal the descriptions of this poem, even, as the three other modes called Asrama are ever unequal in merit to the domestic Asrama. Let Ganesa be thought of, O Muni, for the purpose of writing the poem.'

"Sauti said, 'Brahma having thus spoken to Vyasa, retired to his own abode. Then Vyasa began to call to mind Ganesa. And Ganesa, obviator of obstacles, ready to fulfil the desires of his votaries, was no sooner thought of, than he repaired to the place where Vyasa was seated. And when he had been saluted, and was seated, Vyasa addressed him thus, 'O guide of the Ganas! be thou the writer of the Bharata which I have formed in my imagination, and which I am about to repeat."

"Ganesa, upon hearing this address, thus answered, 'I will become the writer of thy work, provided my pen do not for a moment cease writing." And Vyasa said unto that divinity, 'Wherever there be anything thou dost not comprehend, cease to continue writing.' Ganesa having signified his assent, by repeating the word Om! proceeded to write; and Vyasa began; and by way of diversion, he knit the knots of composition exceeding close; by doing which, he dictated this work according to his engagement.

I am (continued Sauti) acquainted with eight thousand and eight hundred verses, and so is Suka, and perhaps Sanjaya. From the mysteriousness of their meaning, O Muni, no one is able, to this day, to penetrate those closely knit difficult slokas. Even the omniscient Ganesa took a moment to consider; while Vyasa, however, continued to compose other verses in great abundance.

The wisdom of this work, like unto an instrument of applying collyrium, hath opened the eyes of the inquisitive world blinded by the darkness of ignorance. As the sun dispelleth the darkness, so doth the Bharata by its discourses on religion, profit, pleasure and final release, dispel the ignorance of men. As the full-moon by its mild light expandeth the buds of the water-lily, so this Purana, by exposing the light of the Sruti hath expanded the human intellect. By the lamp of history, which destroyeth the darkness of ignorance, the whole mansion of nature is properly and completely illuminated.

This work is a tree, of which the chapter of contents is the seed; the divisions called Pauloma and Astika are the root; the part called Sambhava is the trunk; the books called Sabha and Aranya are the roosting perches; the books called Arani is the knitting knots; the books called Virata and Udyoga the pith; the book named Bhishma, the main branch; the book called Drona, the leaves; the book called Karna, the fair flowers; the book named Salya, their sweet smell; the books entitled Stri and Aishika, the refreshing shade; the book called Santi, the mighty fruit; the book called Aswamedha, the immortal sap; the denominated Asramavasika, the spot where it groweth; and the book called Mausala, is an epitome of the Vedas and held in great respect by the virtuous Brahmanas. The tree of the Bharata, inexhaustible to mankind as the clouds, shall be as a source of livelihood to all distinguished poets."

"Sauti continued, 'I will now speak of the undying flowery and fruitful productions of this tree, possessed of pure and pleasant taste, and not to be destroyed even by the immortals. Formerly, the spirited and virtuous Krishna-Dwaipayana, by the injunctions of Bhishma, the wise son of Ganga and of his own mother, became the father of three boys who were like the three fires by the two wives of Vichitra-virya; and having thus raised up Dhritarashtra, Pandu and Vidura, he returned to his recluse abode to prosecute his religious exercise.

It was not till after these were born, grown up, and departed on the supreme journey, that the great Rishi Vyasa published the Bharata in this region of mankind; when being solicited by Janamejaya and thousands of Brahmanas, he instructed his disciple Vaisampayana, who was seated near him; and he, sitting together with the Sadasyas, recited the Bharata, during the intervals of the ceremonies of the sacrifice, being repeatedly urged to proceed.

Vyasa hath fully represented the greatness of the house of Kuru, the virtuous principles of Gandhari, the wisdom of Vidura, and the constancy of Kunti. The noble Rishi hath also described the divinity of Vasudeva, the rectitude of the sons of Pandu, and the evil practices of the sons and partisans of Dhritarashtra.

Vyasa executed the compilation of the Bharata, exclusive of the episodes originally in twenty-four thousand verses; and so much only is called by the learned as the Bharata. Afterwards, he composed an epitome in one hundred and fifty verses, consisting of the introduction with the chapter of contents. This he first taught to his son Suka; and afterwards he gave it to others of his disciples who were possessed of the same qualifications. After that he executed another compilation, consisting of six hundred thousand verses. Of those, thirty hundred thousand are known in the world of the Devas; fifteen hundred thousand in the world of the Pitris: fourteen hundred thousand among the Gandharvas, and one hundred thousand in the regions of mankind. Narada recited them to the Devas, Devala to the Pitris, and Suka published them to the Gandharvas, Yakshas, and Rakshasas: and in this world they were recited by Vaisampayana, one of the disciples of Vyasa, a man of just principles and the first among all those acquainted with the Vedas. Know that I, Sauti, have also repeated one hundred thousand verses.

Yudhishthira is a vast tree, formed of religion and virtue; Arjuna is its trunk; Bhimasena, its branches; the two sons of Madri are its full-grown fruit and flowers; and its roots are Krishna, Brahma, and the Brahmanas.

Pandu, after having subdued many countries by his wisdom and prowess, took up his abode with the Munis in a certain forest as a sportsman, where he brought upon himself a very severe misfortune for having killed a stag coupling with its mate, which served as a warning for the conduct of the princes of his house as long as they lived. Their mothers, in order that the ordinances of the law might be fulfilled, admitted as substitutes to their embraces the gods Dharma, Vayu, Sakra, and the divinities the twin Aswins. And when their offspring grew up, under the care of their two mothers, in the society of ascetics, in the midst of sacred groves and holy recluse-abodes of religious men, they were conducted by Rishis into the presence of Dhritarashtra and his sons, following as students in the habit of Brahmacharis, having their hair tied in knots on their heads. 'These our pupils', said they, 'are as your sons, your brothers, and your friends; they are Pandavas.' Saying this, the Munis disappeared.

When the Kauravas saw them introduced as the sons of Pandu, the distinguished class of citizens shouted exceedingly for joy. Some, however, said, they were not the sons of Pandu; others said, they were; while a few asked how they could be his offspring, seeing he had been so long dead. Still on all sides voices were heard crying, 'They are on all accounts welcome! Through divine Providence we behold the family of Pandu! Let their welcome be proclaimed!' As these acclamations ceased, the plaudits of invisible spirits, causing every point of the heavens to resound, were tremendous. There were showers of sweet-scented flowers, and the sound of shells and kettle-drums. Such were the wonders that happened on the arrival of the young princes. The joyful noise of all the citizens, in expression of their satisfaction on the occasion, was so great that it reached the very heavens in magnifying plaudits.

Having studied the whole of the Vedas and sundry other shastras, the Pandavas resided there, respected by all and without apprehension from any one.

The principal men were pleased with the purity of Yudhishthira, the courage of Arjuna, the submissive attention of Kunti to her superiors, and the humility of the twins, Nakula and Sahadeva; and all the people rejoiced in their heroic virtues.

After a while, Arjuna obtained the virgin Krishna at the swayamvara, in the midst of a concourse of Rajas, by performing a very difficult feat of archery. And from this time he became very much respected in this world among all bowmen; and in fields of battle also, like the sun, he was hard to behold by foe-men. And having vanquished all the neighbouring princes and every considerable tribe, he accomplished all that was necessary for the Raja (his eldest brother) to perform the great sacrifice called Rajasuya.

Yudhishthira, after having, through the wise counsels of Vasudeva and by the valour of Bhimasena and Arjuna, slain Jarasandha (the king of Magadha) and the proud Chaidya, acquired the right to perform the grand sacrifice of Rajasuya abounding in provisions and offering and fraught with transcendent merits. And Duryodhana came to this sacrifice; and when he beheld the vast wealth of the Pandavas scattered all around, the offerings, the precious stones, gold and jewels; the wealth in cows, elephants, and horses; the curious textures, garments, and mantles; the precious shawls and furs and carpets made of the skin of the Ranku; he was filled with envy and became exceedingly displeased. And when he beheld the hall of assembly elegantly constructed by Maya (the Asura architect) after the fashion of a celestial court, he was inflamed with rage. And having started in confusion at certain architectural deceptions within this building, he was derided by Bhimasena in the presence of Vasudeva, like one of mean descent.

And it was represented to Dhritarashtra that his son, while partaking of various objects of enjoyment and diverse precious things, was becoming meagre, wan, and pale. And Dhritarashtra, some time after, out of affection for his son, gave his consent to their playing (with the Pandavas) at dice. And Vasudeva coming to know of this, became exceedingly wroth. And being dissatisfied, he did nothing to prevent the disputes, but overlooked the gaming and sundry other horried unjustifiable transactions arising therefrom: and in spite of Vidura, Bhishma, Drona, and Kripa, the son of Saradwan, he made the Kshatriyas kill each other in the terrific war that ensued.'

"And Dhritarashtra hearing the ill news of the success of the Pandavas and recollecting the resolutions of Duryodhana, Karna, and Sakuni, pondered for a while and addressed to Sanjaya the following speech:—

'Attend, O Sanjaya, to all I am about to say, and it will not become thee to treat me with contempt. Thou art well-versed in the shastras, intelligent and endowed with wisdom. My inclination was never to war, not did I delight in the destruction of my race. I made no distinction between my own children and the children of Pandu. My own sons were prone to wilfulness and despised me because I am old. Blind as I am, because of my miserable plight and through paternal affection, I bore it all. I was foolish after the thoughtless Duryodhana ever growing in folly. Having been a spectator of the riches of the mighty sons of Pandu, my son was derided for his awkwardness while ascending the hall. Unable to bear it all and unable himself to overcome the sons of Pandu in the field, and though a soldier, unwilling yet to obtain good fortune by his own exertion, with the help of the king of Gandhara he concerted an unfair game at dice.

'Hear, O Sanjaya, all that happened thereupon and came to my knowledge. And when thou hast heard all I say, recollecting everything as it fell out, thou shall then know me for one with a prophetic eye. When I heard that Arjuna, having bent the bow, had pierced the curious mark and brought it down to the ground, and bore away in triumph the maiden Krishna, in the sight of the assembled princes, then, O Sanjaya I had no hope of success. When I heard that Subhadra of the race of Madhu had, after forcible seizure been married by Arjuna in the city of Dwaraka, and that the two heroes of the race of Vrishni (Krishna and Balarama the brothers of Subhadra) without resenting it had entered Indraprastha as friends, then, O Sanjaya, I had no hope of success. When I heard that Arjuna, by his celestial arrow preventing the downpour by Indra the king of the gods, had gratified Agni by making over to him the forest of Khandava, then, O Sanjaya, I had no hope of success. When I heard that the five Pandavas with their mother Kunti had escaped from the house of lac, and that Vidura was engaged in the accomplishment of their designs, then, O Sanjaya, I had no hope of success. When I heard that Arjuna, after having pierced the mark in the arena had won Draupadi, and that the brave Panchalas had joined the Pandavas, then, O Sanjaya, I had no hope of success. When I heard that Jarasandha, the foremost of the royal line of Magadha, and blazing in the midst of the Kshatriyas, had been slain by Bhima with his bare arms alone, then, O Sanjaya, I had no hope of success. When I heard that in their general campaign the sons of Pandu had conquered the chiefs of the land and performed the grand sacrifice of the Rajasuya, then, O Sanjaya, I had no hope of success. When I heard that Draupadi, her voice choked with tears and heart full of agony, in the season of impurity and with but one raiment on, had been dragged into court and though she had protectors, she had been treated as if she had none, then, O Sanjaya, I had no hope of success. When I heard that the wicked wretch Duhsasana, was striving to strip her of that single garment, had only drawn from her person a large heap of cloth without being able to arrive at its end, then, O Sanjaya, I had no hope of success. When I heard that Yudhishthira, beaten by Saubala at the game of dice and deprived of his kingdom as a consequence thereof, had still been attended upon by his brothers of incomparable prowess, then, O Sanjaya, I had no hope of success. When I heard that the virtuous Pandavas weeping with affliction had followed their elder brother to the wilderness and exerted themselves variously for the mitigation of his discomforts, then, O Sanjaya, I had no hope of success.

'When I heard that Yudhishthira had been followed into the wilderness by Snatakas and noble-minded Brahmanas who live upon alms, then, O Sanjaya, I had no hope of success. When I heard that Arjuna, having, in combat, pleased the god of gods, Tryambaka (the three-eyed) in the disguise of a hunter, obtained the great weapon Pasupata, then O Sanjaya, I had no hope of success. When I heard that the just and renowned Arjuna after having been to the celestial regions, had there obtained celestial weapons from Indra himself then, O Sanjaya, I had no hope of success. When I heard that afterwards Arjuna had vanquished the Kalakeyas and the Paulomas proud with the boon they had obtained and which had rendered them invulnerable even to the celestials, then, O Sanjaya, I had no hope of success. When I heard that Arjuna, the chastiser of enemies, having gone to the regions of Indra for the destruction of the Asuras, had returned thence successful, then, O Sanjaya, I had no hope of success. When I heard that Bhima and the other sons of Pritha (Kunti) accompanied by Vaisravana had arrived at that country which is inaccessible to man then, O Sanjaya, I had no hope of success. When I heard that my sons, guided by the counsels of Karna, while on their journey of Ghoshayatra, had been taken prisoners by the Gandharvas and were set free by Arjuna, then, O Sanjaya, I had no hope of success. When I heard that Dharma (the god of justice) having come under the form of a Yaksha had proposed certain questions to Yudhishthira then, O Sanjaya, I had no hope of success. When I heard that my sons had failed to discover the Pandavas under their disguise while residing with Draupadi in the dominions of Virata, then, O Sanjaya, I had no hope of success. When I heard that the principal men of my side had all been vanquished by the noble Arjuna with a single chariot while residing in the dominions of Virata, then, O Sanjaya, I had no hope of success. When I heard that Vasudeva of the race of Madhu, who covered this whole earth by one foot, was heartily interested in the welfare of the Pandavas, then, O Sanjaya, I had no hope of success. When I heard that the king of Matsya, had offered his virtuous daughter Uttara to Arjuna and that Arjuna had accepted her for his son, then, O Sanjaya, I had no hope of success. When I heard that Yudhishthira, beaten at dice, deprived of wealth, exiled and separated from his connections, had assembled yet an army of seven Akshauhinis, then, O Sanjaya, I had no hope of success. When I heard Narada, declare that Krishna and Arjuna were Nara and Narayana and he (Narada) had seen them together in the regions of Brahma, then, O Sanjaya, I had no hope of success. When I heard that Krishna, anxious to bring about peace, for the welfare of mankind had repaired to the Kurus, and went away without having been able to effect his purpose, then, O Sanjaya, I had no hope of success. When I heard that Karna and Duryodhana resolved upon imprisoning Krishna displayed in himself the whole universe, then, O Sanjaya, I had no hope of success. Then I heard that at the time of his departure, Pritha (Kunti) standing, full of sorrow, near his chariot received consolation from Krishna, then, O Sanjaya, I had no hope of success. When I heard that Vasudeva and Bhishma the son of Santanu were the counsellors of the Pandavas and Drona the son of Bharadwaja pronounced blessings on them, then, O Sanjaya, I had no hope of success. When Karna said unto Bhishma—I will not fight when thou art fighting—and, quitting the army, went away, then, O Sanjaya, I had no hope of success. When I heard that Vasudeva and Arjuna and the bow Gandiva of immeasurable prowess, these three of dreadful energy had come together, then, O Sanjaya, I had no hope of success. When I heard that upon Arjuna having been seized with compunction on his chariot and ready to sink, Krishna showed him all the worlds within his body, then, O Sanjaya, I had no hope of success. When I heard that Bhishma, the desolator of foes, killing ten thousand charioteers every day in the field of battle, had not slain any amongst the Pandavas then, O Sanjaya, I had no hope of success. When I heard that Bhishma, the righteous son of Ganga, had himself indicated the means of his defeat in the field of battle and that the same were accomplished by the Pandavas with joyfulness, then, O Sanjaya, I had no hope of success. When I heard that Arjuna, having placed Sikhandin before himself in his chariot, had wounded Bhishma of infinite courage and invincible in battle, then, O Sanjaya, I had no hope of success. When I heard that the aged hero Bhishma, having reduced the numbers of the race of shomaka to a few, overcome with various wounds was lying on a bed of arrows, then, O Sanjaya, I had no hope of success. When I heard that upon Bhishma's lying on the ground with thirst for water, Arjuna, being requested, had pierced the ground and allayed his thirst, then, O Sanjaya, I had no hope of success. When Bayu together with Indra and Suryya united as allies for the success of the sons of Kunti, and the beasts of prey (by their inauspicious presence) were putting us in fear, then, O Sanjaya, I had no hope of success. When the wonderful warrior Drona, displaying various modes of fight in the field, did not slay any of the superior Pandavas, then, O Sanjaya, I had no hope of success. When I heard that the Maharatha Sansaptakas of our army appointed for the overthrow of Arjuna were all slain by Arjuna himself, then, O Sanjaya, I had no hope of success. When I heard that our disposition of forces, impenetrable by others, and defended by Bharadwaja himself well-armed, had been singly forced and entered by the brave son of Subhadra, then, O Sanjaya, I had no hope of success. When I heard that our Maharathas, unable to overcome Arjuna, with jubilant faces after having jointly surrounded and slain the boy Abhimanyu, then, O Sanjaya, I had no hope of success. When I heard that the blind Kauravas were shouting for joy after having slain Abhimanyu and that thereupon Arjuna in anger made his celebrated speech referring to Saindhava, then, O Sanjaya, I had no hope of success. When I heard that Arjuna had vowed the death of Saindhava and fulfilled his vow in the presence of his enemies, then, O Sanjaya, I had no hope of success. When I heard that upon the horses of Arjuna being fatigued, Vasudeva releasing them made them drink water and bringing them back and reharnessing them continued to guide them as before, then, O Sanjaya, I had no hope of success. When I heard that while his horses were fatigued, Arjuna staying in his chariot checked all his assailants, then, O Sanjaya, I had no hope of success. When I heard that Yuyudhana of the race of Vrishni, after having thrown into confusion the army of Drona rendered unbearable in prowess owing to the presence of elephants, retired to where Krishna and Arjuna were, then, O Sanjaya, I had no hope of success. When I heard that Karna even though he had got Bhima within his power allowed him to escape after only addressing him in contemptuous terms and dragging him with the end of his bow, then, O Sanjaya, I had no hope of success. When I heard that Drona, Kritavarma, Kripa, Karna, the son of Drona, and the valiant king of Madra (Salya) suffered Saindhava to be slain, then, O Sanjaya, I had no hope of success. When I heard that the celestial Sakti given by Indra (to Karna) was by Madhava's machinations caused to be hurled upon Rakshasa Ghatotkacha of frightful countenance, then, O Sanjaya, I had no hope of success. When I heard that in the encounter between Karna and Ghatotkacha, that Sakti was hurled against Ghatotkacha by Karna, the same which was certainly to have slain Arjuna in battle, then, O Sanjaya. I had no hope of success. When I heard that Dhristadyumna, transgressing the laws of battle, slew Drona while alone in his chariot and resolved on death, then, O Sanjaya, I had no hope of success. When I heard that Nakula. the son of Madri, having in the presence of the whole army engaged in single combat with the son of Drona and showing himself equal to him drove his chariot in circles around, then, O Sanjaya, I had no hope of success. When upon the death of Drona, his son misused the weapon called Narayana but failed to achieve the destruction of the Pandavas, then, O Sanjaya, I had no hope of success. When I heard that Bhimasena drank the blood of his brother Duhsasana in the field of battle without anybody being able to prevent him, then, O Sanjaya, I had no hope of success. When I heard that the infinitely brave Karna, invincible in battle, was slain by Arjuna in that war of brothers mysterious even to the gods, then, O Sanjaya, I had no hope of success. When I heard that Yudhishthira, the Just, overcame the heroic son of Drona, Duhsasana, and the fierce Kritavarman, then, O Sanjaya, I had no hope of success. When I heard that the brave king of Madra who ever dared Krishna in battle was slain by Yudhishthira, then, O Sanjaya, I had no hope of success. When I heard that the wicked Suvala of magic power, the root of the gaming and the feud, was slain in battle by Sahadeva, the son of Pandu, then, O Sanjaya, I had no hope of success. When I heard that Duryodhana, spent with fatigue, having gone to a lake and made a refuge for himself within its waters, was lying there alone, his strength gone and without a chariot, then, O Sanjaya, I had no hope of success. When I heard that the Pandavas having gone to that lake accompanied by Vasudeva and standing on its beach began to address contemptuously my son who was incapable of putting up with affronts, then, O Sanjaya, I had no hope of success. When I heard that while, displaying in circles a variety of curious modes (of attack and defence) in an encounter with clubs, he was unfairly slain according to the counsels of Krishna, then, O Sanjaya, I had no hope of success. When I heard the son of Drona and others by slaying the Panchalas and the sons of Draupadi in their sleep, perpetrated a horrible and infamous deed, then, O Sanjaya, I had no hope of success. When I heard that Aswatthaman while being pursued by Bhimasena had discharged the first of weapons called Aishika, by which the embryo in the womb (of Uttara) was wounded, then, O Sanjaya, I had no hope of success. When I heard that the weapon Brahmashira (discharged by Aswatthaman) was repelled by Arjuna with another weapon over which he had pronounced the word "Sasti" and that Aswatthaman had to give up the jewel-like excrescence on his head, then, O Sanjaya, I had no hope of success. When I heard that upon the embryo in the womb of Virata's daughter being wounded by Aswatthaman with a mighty weapon, Dwaipayana and Krishna pronounced curses on him, then, O Sanjaya, I had no hope of success.

'Alas! Gandhari, destitute of children, grand-children, parents, brothers, and kindred, is to be pitied. Difficult is the task that hath been performed by the Pandavas: by them hath a kingdom been recovered without a rival.

'Alas! I have heard that the war hath left only ten alive: three of our side, and the Pandavas, seven, in that dreadful conflict eighteen Akshauhinis of Kshatriyas have been slain! All around me is utter darkness, and a fit of swoon assaileth me: consciousness leaves me, O Suta, and my mind is distracted."

"Sauti said, 'Dhritarashtra, bewailing his fate in these words, was overcome with extreme anguish and for a time deprived of sense; but being revived, he addressed Sanjaya in the following words.

"After what hath come to pass, O Sanjaya, I wish to put an end to my life without delay; I do not find the least advantage in cherishing it any longer."

"Sauti said, 'The wise son of Gavalgana (Sanjaya) then addressed the distressed lord of Earth while thus talking and bewailing, sighing like a serpent and repeatedly tainting, in words of deep import.

"Thou hast heard, O Raja, of the greatly powerful men of vast exertions, spoken of by Vyasa and the wise Narada; men born of great royal families, resplendent with worthy qualities, versed in the science of celestial arms, and in glory emblems of Indra; men who having conquered the world by justice and performed sacrifices with fit offerings (to the Brahmanas), obtained renown in this world and at last succumbed to the sway of time. Such were Saivya; the valiant Maharatha; Srinjaya, great amongst conquerors. Suhotra; Rantideva, and Kakshivanta, great in glory; Valhika, Damana, Saryati, Ajita, and Nala; Viswamitra the destroyer of foes; Amvarisha, great in strength; Marutta, Manu, Ikshaku, Gaya, and Bharata; Rama the son of Dasaratha; Sasavindu, and Bhagiratha; Kritavirya, the greatly fortunate, and Janamejaya too; and Yayati of good deeds who performed sacrifices, being assisted therein by the celestials themselves, and by whose sacrificial altars and stakes this earth with her habited and uninhabited regions hath been marked all over. These twenty-four Rajas were formerly spoken of by the celestial Rishi Narada unto Saivya when much afflicted for the loss of his children. Besides these, other Rajas had gone before, still more powerful than they, mighty charioteers noble in mind, and resplendent with every worthy quality. These were Puru, Kuru, Yadu, Sura and Viswasrawa of great glory; Anuha, Yuvanaswu, Kakutstha, Vikrami, and Raghu; Vijava, Virihorta, Anga, Bhava, Sweta, and Vripadguru; Usinara, Sata-ratha, Kanka, Duliduha, and Druma; Dambhodbhava, Para, Vena, Sagara, Sankriti, and Nimi; Ajeya, Parasu, Pundra, Sambhu, and holy Deva-Vridha; Devahuya, Supratika, and Vrihad-ratha; Mahatsaha, Vinitatma, Sukratu, and Nala, the king of the Nishadas; Satyavrata, Santabhaya, Sumitra, and the chief Subala; Janujangha, Anaranya, Arka, Priyabhritya, Chuchi-vrata, Balabandhu, Nirmardda, Ketusringa, and Brhidbala; Dhrishtaketu, Brihatketu, Driptaketu, and Niramaya; Abikshit, Chapala, Dhurta, Kritbandhu, and Dridhe-shudhi; Mahapurana-sambhavya, Pratyanga, Paraha and Sruti. These, O chief, and other Rajas, we hear enumerated by hundreds and by thousands, and still others by millions, princes of great power and wisdom, quitting very abundant enjoyments met death as thy sons have done! Their heavenly deeds, valour, and generosity, their magnanimity, faith, truth, purity, simplicity and mercy, are published to the world in the records of former times by sacred bards of great learning. Though endued with every noble virtue, these have yielded up their lives. Thy sons were malevolent, inflamed with passion, avaricious, and of very evil- disposition. Thou art versed in the Sastras, O Bharata, and art intelligent and wise; they never sink under misfortunes whose understandings are guided by the Sastras. Thou art acquainted, O prince, with the lenity and severity of fate; this anxiety therefore for the safety of thy children is unbecoming. Moreover, it behoveth thee not to grieve for that which must happen: for who can avert, by his wisdom, the decrees of fate? No one can leave the way marked out for him by Providence. Existence and non-existence, pleasure and pain all have Time for their root. Time createth all things and Time destroyeth all creatures. It is Time that burneth creatures and it is Time that extinguisheth the fire. All states, the good and the evil, in the three worlds, are caused by Time. Time cutteth short all things and createth them anew. Time alone is awake when all things are asleep: indeed, Time is incapable of being overcome. Time passeth over all things without being retarded. Knowing, as thou dost, that all things past and future and all that exist at the present moment, are the offspring of Time, it behoveth thee not to throw away thy reason.'

"Sauti said, 'The son of Gavalgana having in this manner administered comfort to the royal Dhritarashtra overwhelmed with grief for his sons, then restored his mind to peace. Taking these facts for his subject, Dwaipayana composed a holy Upanishad that has been published to the world by learned and sacred bards in the Puranas composed by them.

"The study of the Bharata is an act of piety. He that readeth even one foot, with belief, hath his sins entirely purged away. Herein Devas, Devarshis, and immaculate Brahmarshis of good deeds, have been spoken of; and likewise Yakshas and great Uragas (Nagas). Herein also hath been described the eternal Vasudeva possessing the six attributes. He is the true and just, the pure and holy, the eternal Brahma, the supreme soul, the true constant light, whose divine deeds wise and learned recount; from whom hath proceeded the non-existent and existent-non-existent universe with principles of generation and progression, and birth, death and re- birth. That also hath been treated of which is called Adhyatma (the superintending spirit of nature) that partaketh of the attributes of the five elements. That also hath been described who is purusha being above such epithets as 'undisplayed' and the like; also that which the foremost yatis exempt from the common destiny and endued with the power of meditation and Tapas behold dwelling in their hearts as a reflected image in the mirror.

"The man of faith, devoted to piety, and constant in the exercise of virtue, on reading this section is freed from sin. The believer that constantly heareth recited this section of the Bharata, called the Introduction, from the beginning, falleth not into difficulties. The man repeating any part of the introduction in the two twilights is during such act freed from the sins contracted during the day or the night. This section, the body of the Bharata, is truth and nectar. As butter is in curd, Brahmana among bipeds, the Aranyaka among the Vedas, and nectar among medicines; as the sea is eminent among receptacles of water, and the cow among quadrupeds; as are these (among the things mentioned) so is the Bharata said to be among histories.

"He that causeth it, even a single foot thereof, to be recited to Brahmanas during a Sradha, his offerings of food and drink to the manes of his ancestors become inexhaustible.

"By the aid of history and the Puranas, the Veda may be expounded; but the Veda is afraid of one of little information lest he should it. The learned man who recites to other this Veda of Vyasa reapeth advantage. It may without doubt destroy even the sin of killing the embryo and the like. He that readeth this holy chapter of the moon, readeth the whole of the Bharata, I ween. The man who with reverence daily listeneth to this sacred work acquireth long life and renown and ascendeth to heaven.

"In former days, having placed the four Vedas on one side and the Bharata on the other, these were weighed in the balance by the celestials assembled for that purpose. And as the latter weighed heavier than the four Vedas with their mysteries, from that period it hath been called in the world Mahabharata (the great Bharata). Being esteemed superior both in substance and gravity of import it is denominated Mahabharata on account of such substance and gravity of import. He that knoweth its meaning is saved from all his sins.

"'Tapa is innocent, study is harmless, the ordinance of the Vedas prescribed for all the tribes are harmless, the acquisition of wealth by exertion is harmless; but when they are abused in their practices it is then that they become sources of evil.'"

SECTION II

"The Rishis said, 'O son of Suta, we wish to hear a full and circumstantial account of the place mentioned by you as Samanta-panchaya.'

"Sauti said, 'Listen, O ye Brahmanas, to the sacred descriptions I utter O ye best of men, ye deserve to hear of the place known as Samanta-panchaka. In the interval between the Treta and Dwapara Yugas, Rama (the son of Jamadagni) great among all who have borne arms, urged by impatience of wrongs, repeatedly smote the noble race of Kshatriyas. And when that fiery meteor, by his own valour, annihilated the entire tribe of the Kshatriyas, he formed at Samanta-panchaka five lakes of blood. We are told that his reason being overpowered by anger he offered oblations of blood to the manes of his ancestors, standing in the midst of the sanguine waters of those lakes. It was then that his forefathers of whom Richika was the first having arrived there addressed him thus, 'O Rama, O blessed Rama, O offspring of Bhrigu, we have been gratified with the reverence thou hast shown for thy ancestors and with thy valour, O mighty one! Blessings be upon thee. O thou illustrious one, ask the boon that thou mayst desire.'

"Rama said, 'If, O fathers, ye are favourably disposed towards me, the boon I ask is that I may be absolved from the sins born of my having annihilated the Kshatriyas in anger, and that the lakes I have formed may become famous in the world as holy shrines.' The Pitris then said, 'So shall it be. But be thou pacified.' And Rama was pacified accordingly. The region that lieth near unto those lakes of gory water, from that time hath been celebrated as Samanta-panchaka the holy. The wise have declared that every country should be distinguished by a name significant of some circumstance which may have rendered it famous. In the interval between the Dwapara and the Kali Yugas there happened at Samanta-panchaka the encounter between the armies of the Kauravas and the Pandavas. In that holy region, without ruggedness of any kind, were assembled eighteen Akshauhinis of soldiers eager for battle. And, O Brahmanas, having come thereto, they were all slain on the spot. Thus the name of that region, O Brahmanas, hath been explained, and the country described to you as a sacred and delightful one. I have mentioned the whole of what relateth to it as the region is celebrated throughout the three worlds.'

"The Rishis said, 'We have a desire to know, O son of Suta, what is implied by the term Akshauhini that hath been used by thee. Tell us in full what is the number of horse and foot, chariots and elephants, which compose an Akshauhini for thou art fully informed.'

"Sauti said, 'One chariot, one elephant, five foot-soldiers, and three horses form one Patti; three pattis make one Sena-mukha; three sena-mukhas are called a Gulma; three gulmas, a Gana; three ganas, a Vahini; three vahinis together are called a Pritana; three pritanas form a Chamu; three chamus, one Anikini; and an anikini taken ten times forms, as it is styled by those who know, an Akshauhini. O ye best of Brahmanas, arithmeticians have calculated that the number of chariots in an Akshauhini is twenty-one thousand eight hundred and seventy. The measure of elephants must be fixed at the same number. O ye pure, you must know that the number of foot- soldiers is one hundred and nine thousand, three hundred and fifty, the number of horse is sixty-five thousand, six hundred and ten. These, O Brahmanas, as fully explained by me, are the numbers of an Akshauhini as said by those acquainted with the principles of numbers. O best of Brahmanas, according to this calculation were composed the eighteen Akshauhinis of the Kaurava and the Pandava army. Time, whose acts are wonderful assembled them on that spot and having made the Kauravas the cause, destroyed them all. Bhishma acquainted with choice of weapons, fought for ten days. Drona protected the Kaurava Vahinis for five days. Karna the desolator of hostile armies fought for two days; and Salya for half a day. After that lasted for half a day the encounter with clubs between Duryodhana and Bhima. At the close of that day, Aswatthaman and Kripa destroyed the army of Yudishthira in the night while sleeping without suspicion of danger.

"'O Saunaka, this best of narrations called Bharata which has begun to be repeated at thy sacrifice, was formerly repeated at the sacrifice of Janamejaya by an intelligent disciple of Vyasa. It is divided into several sections; in the beginning are Paushya, Pauloma, and Astika parvas, describing in full the valour and renown of kings. It is a work whose description, diction, and sense are varied and wonderful. It contains an account of various manners and rites. It is accepted by the wise, as the state called Vairagya is by men desirous of final release. As Self among things to be known, as life among things that are dear, so is this history that furnisheth the means of arriving at the knowledge of Brahma the first among all the sastras. There is not a story current in this world but doth depend upon this history even as the body upon the foot that it taketh. As masters of good lineage are ever attended upon by servants desirous of preferment so is the Bharata cherished by all poets. As the words constituting the several branches of knowledge appertaining to the world and the Veda display only vowels and consonants, so this excellent history displayeth only the highest wisdom.

"'Listen, O ye ascetics, to the outlines of the several divisions (parvas) of this history called Bharata, endued with great wisdom, of sections and feet that are wonderful and various, of subtle meanings and logical connections, and embellished with the substance of the Vedas.

"'The first parva is called Anukramanika; the second, Sangraha; then Paushya; then Pauloma; the Astika; then Adivansavatarana. Then comes the Sambhava of wonderful and thrilling incidents. Then comes Jatugrihadaha (setting fire to the house of lac) and then Hidimbabadha (the killing of Hidimba) parvas; then comes Baka-badha (slaughter of Baka) and then Chitraratha. The next is called Swayamvara (selection of husband by Panchali), in which Arjuna by the exercise of Kshatriya virtues, won Draupadi for wife. Then comes Vaivahika (marriage). Then comes Viduragamana (advent of Vidura), Rajyalabha (acquirement of kingdom), Arjuna-banavasa (exile of Arjuna) and Subhadra-harana (the carrying away of Subhadra). After these come Harana-harika, Khandava-daha (the burning of the Khandava forest) and Maya-darsana (meeting with Maya the Asura architect). Then come Sabha, Mantra, Jarasandha, Digvijaya (general campaign). After Digvijaya come Raja-suyaka, Arghyaviharana (the robbing of the Arghya) and Sisupala-badha (the killing of Sisupala). After these, Dyuta (gambling), Anudyuta (subsequent to gambling), Aranyaka, and Krimira- badha (destruction of Krimira). The Arjuna-vigamana (the travels of Arjuna), Kairati. In the last hath been described the battle between Arjuna and Mahadeva in the guise of a hunter. After this Indra- lokavigamana (the journey to the regions of Indra); then that mine of religion and virtue, the highly pathetic Nalopakhyana (the story of Nala). After this last, Tirtha-yatra or the pilgrimage of the wise prince of the Kurus, the death of Jatasura, and the battle of the Yakshas. Then the battle with the Nivata-kavachas, Ajagara, and Markandeya-Samasya (meeting with Markandeya). Then the meeting of Draupadi and Satyabhama, Ghoshayatra, Mirga-Swapna (dream of the deer). Then the story of Brihadaranyaka and then Aindradrumna. Then Draupadi-harana (the abduction of Draupadi), Jayadratha-bimoksana (the release of Jayadratha). Then the story of 'Savitri' illustrating the great merit of connubial chastity. After this last, the story of 'Rama'. The parva that comes next is called 'Kundala- harana' (the theft of the ear-rings). That which comes next is 'Aranya' and then 'Vairata'. Then the entry of the Pandavas and the fulfilment of their promise (of living unknown for one year). Then the destruction of the 'Kichakas', then the attempt to take the kine (of Virata by the Kauravas). The next is called the marriage of Abhimanyu with the daughter of Virata. The next you must know is the most wonderful parva called Udyoga. The next must be known by the name of 'Sanjaya-yana' (the arrival of Sanjaya). Then comes 'Prajagara' (the sleeplessness of Dhritarashtra owing to his anxiety). Then Sanatsujata, in which are the mysteries of spiritual philosophy. Then 'Yanasaddhi', and then the arrival of Krishna. Then the story of 'Matali' and then of 'Galava'. Then the stories of 'Savitri', 'Vamadeva', and 'Vainya'. Then the story of 'Jamadagnya and Shodasarajika'. Then the arrival of Krishna at the court, and then Bidulaputrasasana. Then the muster of troops and the story of Sheta. Then, must you know, comes the quarrel of the high-souled Karna. Then the march to the field of the troops of both sides. The next hath been called numbering the Rathis and Atirathas. Then comes the arrival of the messenger Uluka which kindled the wrath (of the Pandavas). The next that comes, you must know, is the story of Amba. Then comes the thrilling story of the installation of Bhishma as commander-in-chief. The next is called the creation of the insular region Jambu; then Bhumi; then the account about the formation of islands. Then comes the 'Bhagavat-gita'; and then the death of Bhishma. Then the installation of Drona; then the destruction of the 'Sansaptakas'. Then the death of Abhimanyu; and then the vow of Arjuna (to slay Jayadratha). Then the death of Jayadratha, and then of Ghatotkacha. Then, must you know, comes the story of the death of Drona of surprising interest. The next that comes is called the discharge of the weapon called Narayana. Then, you know, is Karna, and then Salya. Then comes the immersion in the lake, and then the encounter (between Bhima and Duryodhana) with clubs. Then comes Saraswata, and then the descriptions of holy shrines, and then genealogies. Then comes Sauptika describing incidents disgraceful (to the honour of the Kurus). Then comes the 'Aisika' of harrowing incidents. Then comes 'Jalapradana' oblations of water to the manes of the deceased, and then the wailings of the women. The next must be known as 'Sraddha' describing the funeral rites performed for the slain Kauravas. Then comes the destruction of the Rakshasa Charvaka who had assumed the disguise of a Brahmana (for deceiving Yudhishthira). Then the coronation of the wise Yudhishthira. The next is called the 'Grihapravibhaga'. Then comes 'Santi', then 'Rajadharmanusasana', then 'Apaddharma', then 'Mokshadharma'. Those that follow are called respectively 'Suka-prasna-abhigamana', 'Brahma- prasnanusana', the origin of 'Durvasa', the disputations with Maya. The next is to be known as 'Anusasanika'. Then the ascension of Bhishma to heaven. Then the horse-sacrifice, which when read purgeth all sins away. The next must be known as the 'Anugita' in which are words of spiritual philosophy. Those that follow are called 'Asramvasa', 'Puttradarshana' (meeting with the spirits of the deceased sons), and the arrival of Narada. The next is called 'Mausala' which abounds with terrible and cruel incidents. Then comes 'Mahaprasthanika' and ascension to heaven. Then comes the Purana which is called Khilvansa. In this last are contained 'Vishnuparva', Vishnu's frolics and feats as a child, the destruction of 'Kansa', and lastly, the very wonderful 'Bhavishyaparva' (in which there are prophecies regarding the future).

The high-souled Vyasa composed these hundred parvas of which the above is only an abridgement: having distributed them into eighteen, the son of Suta recited them consecutively in the forest of Naimisha as follows:

'In the Adi parva are contained Paushya, Pauloma, Astika, Adivansavatara, Samva, the burning of the house of lac, the slaying of Hidimba, the destruction of the Asura Vaka, Chitraratha, the Swayamvara of Draupadi, her marriage after the overthrow of rivals in war, the arrival of Vidura, the restoration, Arjuna's exile, the abduction of Subhadra, the gift and receipt of the marriage dower, the burning of the Khandava forest, and the meeting with (the Asura-architect) Maya. The Paushya parva treats of the greatness of Utanka, and the Pauloma, of the sons of Bhrigu. The Astika describes the birth of Garuda and of the Nagas (snakes), the churning of the ocean, the incidents relating to the birth of the celestial steed Uchchaihsrava, and finally, the dynasty of Bharata, as described in the Snake-sacrifice of king Janamejaya. The Sambhava parva narrates the birth of various kings and heroes, and that of the sage, Krishna Dwaipayana: the partial incarnations of deities, the generation of Danavas and Yakshas of great prowess, and serpents, Gandharvas, birds, and of all creatures; and lastly, of the life and adventures of king Bharata—the progenitor of the line that goes by his name—the son born of Sakuntala in the hermitage of the ascetic Kanwa. This parva also describes the greatness of Bhagirathi, and the births of the Vasus in the house of Santanu and their ascension to heaven. In this parva is also narrated the birth of Bhishma uniting in himself portions of the energies of the other Vasus, his renunciation of royalty and adoption of the Brahmacharya mode of life, his adherence to his vows, his protection of Chitrangada, and after the death of Chitrangada, his protection of his younger brother, Vichitravirya, and his placing the latter on the throne: the birth of Dharma among men in consequence of the curse of Animondavya; the births of Dhritarashtra and Pandu through the potency of Vyasa's blessings (?) and also the birth of the Pandavas; the plottings of Duryodhana to send the sons of Pandu to Varanavata, and the other dark counsels of the sons of Dhritarashtra in regard to the Pandavas; then the advice administered to Yudhishthira on his way by that well-wisher of the Pandavas—Vidura—in the mlechchha language—the digging of the hole, the burning of Purochana and the sleeping woman of the fowler caste, with her five sons, in the house of lac; the meeting of the Pandavas in the dreadful forest with Hidimba, and the slaying of her brother Hidimba by Bhima of great prowess. The birth of Ghatotkacha; the meeting of the Pandavas with Vyasa and in accordance with his advice their stay in disguise in the house of a Brahmana in the city of Ekachakra; the destruction of the Asura Vaka, and the amazement of the populace at the sight; the extra-ordinary births of Krishna and Dhrishtadyumna; the departure of the Pandavas for Panchala in obedience to the injunction of Vyasa, and moved equally by the desire of winning the hand of Draupadi on learning the tidings of the Swayamvara from the lips of a Brahmana; victory of Arjuna over a Gandharva, called Angaraparna, on the banks of the Bhagirathi, his contraction of friendship with his adversary, and his hearing from the Gandharva the history of Tapati, Vasishtha and Aurva. This parva treats of the journey of the Pandavas towards Panchala, the acquisition of Draupadi in the midst of all the Rajas, by Arjuna, after having successfully pierced the mark; and in the ensuing fight, the defeat of Salya, Karna, and all the other crowned heads at the hands of Bhima and Arjuna of great prowess; the ascertainment by Balarama and Krishna, at the sight of these matchless exploits, that the heroes were the Pandavas, and the arrival of the brothers at the house of the potter where the Pandavas were staying; the dejection of Drupada on learning that Draupadi was to be wedded to five husbands; the wonderful story of the five Indras related in consequence; the extraordinary and divinely-ordained wedding of Draupadi; the sending of Vidura by the sons of Dhritarashtra as envoy to the Pandavas; the arrival of Vidura and his sight to Krishna; the abode of the Pandavas in Khandava-prastha, and then their rule over one half of the kingdom; the fixing of turns by the sons of Pandu, in obedience to the injunction of Narada, for connubial companionship with Krishna. In like manner hath the history of Sunda and Upasunda been recited in this. This parva then treats of the departure of Arjuna for the forest according to the vow, he having seen Draupadi and Yudhishthira sitting together as he entered the chamber to take out arms for delivering the kine of a certain Brahmana. This parva then describes Arjuna's meeting on the way with Ulupi, the daughter of a Naga (serpent); it then relates his visits to several sacred spots; the birth of Vabhruvahana; the deliverance by Arjuna of the five celestial damsels who had been turned into alligators by the imprecation of a Brahmana, the meeting of

Madhava and Arjuna on the holy spot called Prabhasa; the carrying away of Subhadra by Arjuna, incited thereto by her brother Krishna, in the wonderful car moving on land and water, and through mid- air, according to the wish of the rider; the departure for Indraprastha, with the dower; the conception in the womb of Subhadra of that prodigy of prowess, Abhimanyu; Yajnaseni's giving birth to children; then follows the pleasure-trip of Krishna and Arjuna to the banks of the Jamuna and the acquisition by them of the discus and the celebrated bow Gandiva; the burning of the forest of Khandava; the rescue of Maya by Arjuna, and the escape of the serpent,—and the begetting of a son by that best of Rishis, Mandapala, in the womb of the bird Sarngi. This parva is divided by Vyasa into two hundred and twenty-seven chapters. These two hundred and twenty- seven chapters contain eight thousand eight hundred and eighty-four slokas.

The second is the extensive parva called Sabha or the assembly, full of matter. The subjects of this parva are the establishment of the grand hall by the Pandavas; their review of their retainers; the description of the lokapalas by Narada well-acquainted with the celestial regions; the preparations for the Rajasuya sacrifice; the destruction of Jarasandha; the deliverance by Vasudeva of the princes confined in the mountain-pass; the campaign of universal conquest by the Pandavas; the arrival of the princes at the Rajasuya sacrifice with tribute; the destruction of Sisupala on the occasion of the sacrifice, in connection with offering of arghya; Bhimasena's ridicule of Duryodhana in the assembly; Duryodhana's sorrow and envy at the sight of the magnificent scale on which the arrangements had been made; the indignation of Duryodhana in consequence, and the preparations for the game of dice; the defeat of Yudhishthira at play by the wily Sakuni; the deliverance by Dhritarashtra of his afflicted daughter-in-law Draupadi plunged in the sea of distress caused by the gambling, as of a boat tossed about by the tempestuous waves. The endeavours of Duryodhana to engage Yudhishthira again in the game; and the exile of the defeated Yudhishthira with his brothers. These constitute what has been called by the great Vyasa the Sabha Parva. This parva is divided into seventh-eight sections, O best of Brahmanas, of two thousand, five hundred and seven slokas.

Then comes the third parva called Aranyaka (relating to the forest) This parva treats of the wending of the Pandavas to the forest and the citizens, following the wise Yudhishthira, Yudhishthira's adoration of the god of day; according to the injunctions of Dhaumya, to be gifted with the power of maintaining the dependent Brahmanas with food and drink: the creation of food through the grace of the Sun: the expulsion by Dhritarashtra of Vidura who always spoke for his master's good; Vidura's coming to the Pandavas and his return to Dhritarashtra at the solicitation of the latter; the wicked Duryodhana's plottings to destroy the forest-ranging Pandavas, being incited thereto by Karna; the appearance of Vyasa and his dissuasion of Duryodhana bent on going to the forest; the history of Surabhi; the arrival of Maitreya; his laying down to Dhritarashtra the course of action; and his curse on Duryodhana; Bhima's slaying of Kirmira in battle; the coming of the Panchalas and the princes of the Vrishni race to Yudhishthira on hearing of his defeat at the unfair gambling by Sakuni; Dhananjaya's allaying the wrath of Krishna; Draupadi's lamentations before Madhava; Krishna's cheering her; the fall of Sauva also has been here described by the Rishi; also Krishna's bringing Subhadra with her son to Dwaraka; and Dhrishtadyumna's bringing the son of Draupadi to Panchala; the entrance of the sons of Pandu into the romantic Dwaita wood; conversation of Bhima, Yudhishthira, and Draupadi; the coming of Vyasa to the Pandavas and his endowing Yudhishthira with the power of Pratismriti; then, after the departure of Vyasa, the removal of the Pandavas to the forest of Kamyaka; the wanderings of Arjuna of immeasurable prowess in search of weapons; his battle with Mahadeva in the guise of a hunter; his meeting with the lokapalas and receipt of weapons from them; his journey to the regions of Indra for arms and the consequent anxiety of Dhritarashtra; the wailings and lamentations of Yudhishthira on the occasion of his meeting with the worshipful great sage Brihadaswa. Here occurs the holy and highly pathetic story of Nala illustrating the patience of Damayanti and the character of Nala. Then the acquirement by Yudhishthira of the mysteries of dice from the same great sage; then the arrival of the Rishi Lomasa from the heavens to where the Pandavas were, and the receipt by these high-souled dwellers in the woods of the intelligence brought by the Rishi of their brother Arjuna staving in the heavens; then the pilgrimage of the Pandavas to various sacred spots in accordance with the message of Arjuna, and their attainment of great merit and virtue consequent on such pilgrimage; then the pilgrimage of the great sage Narada to the shrine Putasta; also the pilgrimage of the high-souled Pandavas. Here is the deprivation of Karna of his ear-rings by Indra. Here also is recited the sacrificial magnificence of Gaya; then the story of Agastya in which the Rishi ate up the Asura Vatapi, and his connubial connection with Lopamudra from the desire of offspring. Then the story of Rishyasringa who adopted Brahmacharya mode of life from his very boyhood; then the history of Rama of great prowess, the son of Jamadagni, in which has been narrated the death of Kartavirya and the Haihayas; then the meeting between the Pandavas and the Vrishnis in the sacred spot called Prabhasa; then the story of Su-kanya in which Chyavana, the son of Bhrigu, made the twins, Aswinis, drink, at the sacrifice of king Saryati, the Soma juice (from which they had been excluded by the other gods), and in which besides is shown how Chyavana himself acquired perpetual youth (as a boon from the grateful Aswinis). Then hath been described the history of king Mandhata; then the history of prince Jantu; and how king Somaka by offering up his only son (Jantu) in sacrifice obtained a hundred others; then the excellent history of the hawk and the pigeon; then the examination of king Sivi by Indra, Agni, and Dharma; then the story of Ashtavakra, in which occurs the disputation, at the sacrifice of Janaka, between that Rishi and the first of logicians, Vandi, the son of Varuna; the defeat of Vandi by the great Ashtavakra, and the release by the Rishi of his father from the depths of the ocean. Then the story of Yavakrita, and then that of the great Raivya: then the departure (of the Pandavas) for Gandhamadana and their abode in the asylum called Narayana; then Bhimasena's journey to Gandhamadana at the request of Draupadi (in search of the sweet-scented flower). Bhima's meeting on his way, in a grove of bananas, with Hanuman, the son of Pavana of great prowess; Bhima's bath in the tank and the destruction of the flowers therein for obtaining the sweet-scented flower (he was in search of); his consequent battle with the mighty Rakshasas and the Yakshas of great prowess including Hanuman; the destruction of the Asura Jata by Bhima; the meeting (of the Pandavas) with the royal sage Vrishaparva; their departure for the asylum of Arshtishena and abode therein: the incitement of Bhima (to acts of vengeance) by Draupadi. Then is narrated the ascent on the hills of Kailasa by Bhimasena, his terrific battle with the mighty Yakshas headed by Hanuman; then the meeting of the Pandavas with Vaisravana (Kuvera), and the meeting with Arjuna after he had obtained for the purpose of Yudhishthira many celestial weapons; then Arjuna's terrible encounter with the Nivatakavachas dwelling in Hiranyaparva, and also with the Paulomas, and the Kalakeyas; their destruction at the hands of Arjuna; the commencement of the display of the celestial weapons by Arjuna before Yudhishthira, the prevention of the same by Narada; the descent of the Pandavas from Gandhamadana; the seizure of Bhima in the forest by a mighty serpent huge as the mountain; his release from the coils of the snake, upon Yudhishthira's answering certain questions; the return of the Pandavas to the Kamyaka woods. Here is described the reappearance of Vasudeva to see the mighty sons of Pandu; the arrival of Markandeya, and various recitals, the history of Prithu the son of Vena recited by the great Rishi; the stories of Saraswati and the Rishi Tarkhya. After these, is the story of Matsya; other old stories recited by Markandeya; the stories of Indradyumna and Dhundhumara; then the history of the chaste wife; the history of Angira, the meeting and conversation of Draupadi and Satyabhama; the return of the Pandavas to the forest of Dwaita; then the procession to see the calves and the captivity of Duryodhana; and when the wretch was being carried off, his rescue by Arjuna; here is Yudhishthira's dream of the deer; then the re-entry of the Pandavas into the Kamyaka forest, here also is the long story of Vrihidraunika. Here also is recited the story of Durvasa; then the abduction by Jayadratha of Draupadi from the asylum; the pursuit of the ravisher by Bhima swift as the air and the ill-shaving of Jayadratha's crown at Bhima's hand. Here is the long history of Rama in which is shown how Rama by his prowess slew Ravana in battle. Here also is narrated the story of Savitri; then Karna's deprivation by Indra of his ear-rings; then the presentation to Karna by the gratified Indra of a Sakti (missile weapon) which had the virtue of killing only one person against whom it might be hurled; then the story called Aranya in which Dharma (the god of justice) gave advice to his son (Yudhishthira); in which, besides is recited how the Pandavas after having obtained a boon went towards the west. These are all included in the third Parva called Aranyaka, consisting of two hundred and sixty-nine sections. The number of slokas is eleven thousand, six hundred and sixty-four.

"The extensive Parva that comes next is called Virata. The Pandavas arriving at the dominions of Virata saw in a cemetery on the outskirts of the city a large shami tree whereon they kept their weapons. Here hath been recited their entry into the city and their stay there in disguise. Then the slaying by Bhima of the wicked Kichaka who, senseless with lust, had sought Draupadi; the appointment by prince Duryodhana of clever spies; and their despatch to all sides for tracing the Pandavas; the failure of these to discover the mighty sons of Pandu; the first seizure of Virata's kine by the Trigartas and the terrific battle that ensued; the capture of Virata by the enemy and his rescue by Bhimasena; the release also of the kine by the Pandava (Bhima); the seizure of Virata's kine again by the Kurus; the defeat in battle of all the Kurus by the single-handed Arjuna; the release of the king's kine; the bestowal by Virata of his daughter Uttara for Arjuna's acceptance on behalf of his son by Subhadra—Abhimanyu —the destroyer of foes. These are the contents of the extensive fourth Parva—the Virata. The great Rishi Vyasa has composed in these sixty-seven sections. The number of slokas is two thousand and fifty.

"Listen then to (the contents of) the fifth Parva which must be known as Udyoga. While the Pandavas, desirous of victory, were residing in the place called Upaplavya, Duryodhana and Arjuna both went at the same time to Vasudeva, and said, "You should render us assistance in this war." The high-souled Krishna, upon these words being uttered, replied, "O ye first of men, a counsellor in myself who will not fight and one Akshauhini of troops, which of these shall I give to which of you?" Blind to his own interests, the foolish Duryodhana asked for the troops; while Arjuna solicited Krishna as an unfighting counsellor. Then is described how, when the king of Madra was coming for the assistance of the Pandavas, Duryodhana, having deceived him on the way by presents and hospitality, induced him to grant a boon and then solicited his assistance in battle; how Salya, having passed his word to Duryodhana, went to the Pandavas and consoled them by reciting the history of Indra's victory (over Vritra). Then comes the despatch by the Pandavas of their Purohita (priest) to the Kauravas. Then is described how king Dhritarashtra of great prowess, having heard the word of the purohita of the Pandavas and the story of Indra's victory decided upon sending his purohita and ultimately despatched Sanjaya as envoy to the Pandavas from desire for peace. Here hath been described the sleeplessness of Dhritarashtra from anxiety upon hearing all about the Pandavas and their friends, Vasudeva and others. It was on this occasion that Vidura addressed to the wise king Dhritarashtra various counsels that were full of wisdom. It was here also that Sanat-sujata recited to the anxious and sorrowing monarch the excellent truths of spiritual philosophy. On the next morning Sanjaya spoke, in the court of the King, of the identity of Vasudeva and Arjuna. It was then that the illustrious Krishna, moved by kindness and a desire for peace, went himself to the Kaurava capital, Hastinapura, for bringing about peace. Then comes the rejection by prince Duryodhana of the embassy of Krishna who had come to solicit peace for the benefit of both parties. Here hath been recited the story of Damvodvava; then the story of the high-souled Matuli's search for a husband for his daughter: then the history of the great sage Galava; then the story of the training and discipline of the son of Bidula. Then the exhibition by Krishna, before the assembled Rajas, of his Yoga powers upon learning the evil counsels of Duryodhana and Karna; then Krishna's taking Karna in his chariot and his tendering to him of advice, and Karna's rejection of the same from pride. Then the return of Krishna, the chastiser of enemies from Hastinapura to Upaplavya, and his narration to the Pandavas of all that had happened. It was then that those oppressors of foes, the Pandavas, having heard all and consulted properly with each other, made every preparation for war. Then comes the march from Hastinapura, for battle, of foot-soldiers, horses, charioteers and elephants. Then the tale of the troops by both parties. Then the despatch by prince Duryodhana of Uluka as envoy to the Pandavas on the day previous to the battle. Then the tale of charioteers of different classes. Then the story of Amba. These all have been described in the fifth Parva called Udyoga of the Bharata, abounding with incidents appertaining to war and peace. O ye ascetics, the great Vyasa hath composed one hundred and eighty-six sections in this Parva. The number of slokas also composed in this by the great Rishi is six thousand, six hundred and ninety-eight.

"Then is recited the Bhishma Parva replete with wonderful incidents. In this hath been narrated by Sanjaya the formation of the region known as Jambu. Here hath been described the great depression of Yudhishthira's army, and also a fierce fight for ten successive days. In this the high-souled Vasudeva by reasons based on the philosophy of final release drove away Arjuna's compunction springing from the latter's regard for his kindred (whom he was on the eve of slaying). In this the magnanimous Krishna, attentive to the welfare of Yudhishthira, seeing the loss inflicted (on the Pandava army), descended swiftly from his chariot himself and ran, with dauntless breast, his driving whip in hand, to effect the death of Bhishma. In this, Krishna also smote with piercing words Arjuna, the bearer of the Gandiva and the foremost in battle among all wielders of weapons. In this, the foremost of bowmen, Arjuna, placing Shikandin before him and piercing Bhishma with his sharpest arrows felled him from his chariot. In this, Bhishma lay stretched on his bed of arrows. This extensive Parva is known as the sixth in the Bharata. In this have been composed one hundred and seventeen sections. The number of slokas is five thousand, eight hundred and eighty-four as told by Vyasa conversant with the Vedas.

"Then is recited the wonderful Parva called Drona full of incidents. First comes the installation in the command of the army of the great instructor in arms, Drona: then the vow made by that great master of weapons of seizing the wise Yudhishthira in battle to please Duryodhana; then the retreat of Arjuna from the field before the Sansaptakas, then the overthrow of Bhagadatta like to a second Indra in the field, with the elephant Supritika, by Arjuna; then the death of the hero Abhimanyu in his teens, alone and unsupported, at the hands of many Maharathas including Jayadratha; then after the death of Abhimanyu, the destruction by Arjuna, in battle of seven Akshauhinis of troops and then of Jayadratha; then the entry, by Bhima of mighty arms and by that foremost of warriors-in-chariot, Satyaki, into the Kaurava ranks impenetrable even to the gods, in search of Arjuna in obedience to the orders of Yudhishthira, and the destruction of the remnant of the Sansaptakas. In the Drona Parva, is the death of Alambusha, of Srutayus, of Jalasandha, of Shomadatta, of Virata, of the great warrior-in-chariot Drupada, of Ghatotkacha and others; in this Parva, Aswatthaman, excited beyond measure at the fall of his father in battle, discharged the terrible weapon Narayana. Then the glory of Rudra in connection with the burning (of the three cities). Then the arrival of Vyasa and recital by him of the glory of Krishna and Arjuna. This is the great seventh Parva of the Bharata in which all the heroic chiefs and princes mentioned were sent to their account. The number of sections in this is one hundred and seventy. The number of slokas as composed in the Drona Parva by Rishi Vyasa, the son of Parasara and the possessor of true knowledge after much meditation, is eight thousand, nine hundred and nine.

"Then comes the most wonderful Parva called Karna. In this is narrated the appointment of the wise king of Madra as (Karna's) charioteer. Then the history of the fall of the Asura Tripura. Then the application to each other by Karna and Salya of harsh words on their setting out for the field, then the story of the swan and the crow recited in insulting allusion: then the death of Pandya at the hands of the high-souled Aswatthaman; then the death of Dandasena; then that of Darda; then Yudhishthira's imminent risk in single combat with Karna in the presence of all the warriors; then the mutual wrath of Yudhishthira and Arjuna; then Krishna's pacification of Arjuna. In this Parva, Bhima, in fulfilment of his vow, having ripped open Dussasana's breast in battle drank the blood of his heart. Then Arjuna slew the great Karna in single combat. Readers of the Bharata call this the eighth Parva. The number of sections in this is sixty-nine and the number of slokas is four thousand, nine hundred and sixty-tour.

"Then hath been recited the wonderful Parva called Salya. After all the great warriors had been slain, the king of Madra became the leader of the (Kaurava) army. The encounters one after another, of charioteers, have been here described. Then comes the fall of the great Salya at the hands of Yudhishthira, the Just. Here also is the death of Sakuni in battle at the hands of Sahadeva. Upon only a small remnant of the troops remaining alive after the immense slaughter, Duryodhana went to the lake and creating for himself room within its waters lay stretched there for some time. Then is narrated the receipt of this intelligence by Bhima from the fowlers: then is narrated how, moved by the insulting speeches of the intelligent Yudhishthira, Duryodhana ever unable to bear affronts, came out of the waters. Then comes the encounter with clubs, between Duryodhana and Bhima; then the arrival, at the time of such encounter, of Balarama: then is described the sacredness of the Saraswati; then the progress of the encounter with clubs; then the fracture of Duryodhana's thighs in battle by Bhima with (a terrific hurl of) his mace. These all have been described in the wonderful ninth Parva. In this the number of sections is fifty-nine and the number of slokas composed by the great Vyasa—the spreader of the fame of the Kauravas—is three thousand, two hundred and twenty.

"Then shall I describe the Parva called Sauptika of frightful incidents. On the Pandavas having gone away, the mighty charioteers, Kritavarman, Kripa, and the son of Drona, came to the field of battle in the evening and there saw king Duryodhana lying on the ground, his thighs broken, and himself covered with blood. Then the great charioteer, the son of Drona, of terrible wrath, vowed, 'without killing all the Panchalas including Drishtadyumna, and the Pandavas also with all their allies, I will not take off armour.' Having spoken those words, the three warriors leaving Duryodhana's side entered the great forest just as the sun was setting. While sitting under a large banian tree in the night, they saw an owl killing numerous crows one after another. At the sight of this, Aswatthaman, his heart full of rage at the thought of his father's fate, resolved to slay the slumbering Panchalas. And wending to the gate of the camp, he saw there a Rakshasa of frightful visage, his head reaching to the very heavens, guarding the entrance. And seeing that Rakshasa obstructing all his weapons, the son of Drona speedily pacified by worship the three-eyed Rudra. And then accompanied by Kritavarman and Kripa he slew all the sons of Draupadi, all the Panchalas with Dhrishtadyumna and others, together with their relatives, slumbering unsuspectingly in the night. All perished on that fatal night except the five Pandavas and the great warrior Satyaki. Those escaped owing to Krishna's counsels, then the charioteer of Dhrishtadyumna brought to the Pandavas intelligence of the slaughter of the slumbering Panchalas by the son of Drona. Then Draupadi distressed at the death of her sons and brothers and father sat before her lords resolved to kill herself by fasting. Then Bhima of terrible prowess, moved by the words of Draupadi, resolved, to please her; and speedily taking up his mace followed in wrath the son of his preceptor in arms. The son of Drona from fear of Bhimasena and impelled by the fates and moved also by anger discharged a celestial weapon saying, 'This is for the destruction of all the Pandavas'; then Krishna saying. 'This shall not be', neutralised Aswatthaman's speech. Then Arjuna neutralised that weapon by one of his own. Seeing the wicked Aswatthaman's destructive intentions, Dwaipayana and Krishna pronounced curses on him which the latter returned. Pandava then deprived the mighty warrior-in-chariot Aswatthaman, of the jewel on his head, and became exceedingly glad, and, boastful of their success, made a present of it to the sorrowing Draupadi. Thus the tenth Parva, called Sauptika, is recited. The great Vyasa hath composed this in eighteen sections. The number of slokas also composed (in this) by the great reciter of sacred truths is eight hundred and seventy. In this Parva has been put together by the great Rishi the two Parvas called Sauptika and Aishika.

"After this hath been recited the highly pathetic Parva called Stri, Dhritarashtra of prophetic eye, afflicted at the death of his children, and moved by enmity towards Bhima, broke into pieces a statue of hard iron deftly placed before him by Krishna (as substitute of Bhima). Then Vidura, removing the distressed Dhritarashtra's affection for worldly things by reasons pointing to final release, consoled that wise monarch. Then hath been described the wending of the distressed Dhritarashtra accompanied by the ladies of his house to the field of battle of the Kauravas. Here follow the pathetic wailings of the wives of the slain heroes. Then the wrath of Gandhari and Dhritarashtra and their loss of consciousness. Then the Kshatriya ladies saw those heroes,—their unreturning sons, brothers, and fathers,—lying dead on the field. Then the pacification by Krishna of the wrath of Gandhari distressed at the death of her sons and grandsons. Then the cremation of the bodies of the deceased Rajas with due rites by that monarch (Yudhishthira) of great wisdom and the foremost also of all virtuous men. Then upon the presentation of water of the manes of the deceased princes having commenced, the story of Kunti's acknowledgment of Karna as her son born in secret. Those have all been described by the great Rishi Vyasa in the highly pathetic eleventh Parva. Its perusal moveth every feeling heart with sorrow and even draweth tears from the eyes. The number of sections composed is twenty-seven. The number of slokas is seven hundred and seventy-five.

"Twelfth in number cometh the Santi Parva, which increaseth the understanding and in which is related the despondency of Yudhishthira on his having slain his fathers, brothers, sons, maternal uncles and matrimonial relations. In this Parva is described how from his bed of arrows Bhishma expounded various systems of duties worth the study of kings desirous of knowledge; this Parva expounded the duties relative to emergencies, with full indications of time and reasons. By understanding these, a person attaineth to consummate knowledge. The mysteries also of final emancipation have been expatiated upon. This is the twelfth Parva the favourite of the wise. It consists of three hundred and thirty-nine sections, and contains fourteen thousand, seven hundred and thirty-two slokas.

"Next in order is the excellent Anusasana Parva. In it is described how Yudhishthira, the king of the Kurus, was reconciled to himself on hearing the exposition of duties by Bhishma, the son of Bhagirathi. This Parva treats of rules in detail and of Dharma and Artha; then the rules of charity and its merits; then the qualifications of donees, and the supreme ride-regarding gifts. This Parva also describes the ceremonials of individual duty, the rules of conduct and the matchless merit of truth. This Parva showeth the great merit of Brahmanas and kine, and unraveleth the mysteries of duties in relation to time and place. These are embodied in the excellent Parva called Anusasana of varied incidents. In this hath been described the ascension of Bhishma to Heaven. This is the thirteenth Parva which hath laid down accurately the various duties of men. The number of sections, in this is one hundred and forty-six. The number of slokas is eight thousand.

"Then comes the fourteenth Parva Aswamedhika. In this is the excellent story of Samvarta and Marutta. Then is described the discovery (by the Pandavas) of golden treasuries; and then the birth of Parikshit who was revived by Krishna after having been burnt by the (celestial) weapon of Aswatthaman. The battles of Arjuna the son of Pandu, while following the sacrificial horse let loose, with various princes who in wrath seized it. Then is shown the great risk of Arjuna in his encounter with Vabhruvahana the son of Chitrangada (by Arjuna) the appointed daughter of the chief of Manipura. Then the story of the mongoose during the performance of the horse-sacrifice. This is the most wonderful Parva called Aswamedhika. The number of sections is one hundred and three. The number of slokas composed (in this) by Vyasa of true knowledge is three thousand, three hundred and twenty.

"Then comes the fifteenth Parva called Asramvasika. In this, Dhritarashtra, abdicating the kingdom, and accompanied by Gandhari and Vidura went to the woods. Seeing this, the virtuous Pritha also, ever engaged in cherishing her superiors, leaving the court of her sons, followed the old couple. In this is described the wonderful meeting through the kindness of Vyasa of the king (Dhritarashtra) with the spirits of his slain children, grand- children, and other princes, returned from the other world. Then the monarch abandoning his sorrows acquired with his wife the highest fruit of his meritorious actions. In this Parva, Vidura after having leaned on virtue all his life attaineth to the most meritorious state.

"The learned son of Gavalgana, Sanjaya, also of passions under full control, and the foremost of ministers, attained, in the Parva, to the blessed state. In this, Yudhishthira the just met Narada and heard from him about the extinction of the race of Vrishnis. This is the very wonderful Parva called Asramvasika. The number of sections in this is forty-two, and the number of slokas composed by Vyasa cognisant of truth is one thousand five hundred and six.

"After this, you know, comes the Maushala of painful incidents. In this, those lion-hearted heroes (of the race of Vrishni) with the scars of many a field on their bodies, oppressed with the curse of a Brahmana, while deprived of reason from drink, impelled by the fates, slew each other on the shores of the Salt Sea with the Eraka grass which (in their hands) became (invested with the fatal attributes of the) thunder. In this, both Balarama and Kesava (Krishna) after causing the extermination of their race, their hour having come, themselves did not rise superior to the sway of all-destroying Time. In this, Arjuna the foremost among men, going to Dwaravati (Dwaraka) and seeing the city destitute of the Vrishnis was much affected and became exceedingly sorry. Then after the funeral of his maternal uncle Vasudeva the foremost among the Yadus (Vrishnis), he saw the heroes of the Yadu race lying stretched in death on the spot where they had been drinking. He then caused the cremation of the bodies of the illustrious Krishna and Balarama and of the principal members of the Vrishni race. Then as he was journeying from Dwaraka with the women and children, the old and the decrepit—the remnants of the Yadu race—he was met on the way by a heavy calamity. He witnessed also the disgrace of his bow Gandiva and the unpropitiousness of his celestial weapons. Seeing all this, Arjuna became despondent and, pursuant to Vyasa's advice, went to Yudhishthira and solicited permission to adopt the Sannyasa mode of life. This is the sixteenth Parva called Maushala. The number of sections is eight and the number of slokas composed by Vyasa cognisant of truth is three hundred and twenty.

"The next is Mahaprasthanika, the seventeenth Parva.

"In this, those foremost among men the Pandavas abdicating their kingdom went with Draupadi on their great journey called Mahaprasthana. In this, they came across Agni, having arrived on the shore of the sea of red waters. In this, asked by Agni himself, Arjuna worshipped him duly, returned to him the excellent celestial bow called Gandiva. In this, leaving his brothers who dropped one after another and Draupadi also, Yudhishthira went on his journey without once looking back on them. This the seventeenth Parva is called Mahaprasthanika. The number of sections in this is three. The number of slokas also composed by Vyasa cognisant of truth is three hundred and twenty.

"The Parva that comes after this, you must know, is the extraordinary one called Svarga of celestial incidents. Then seeing the celestial car come to take him, Yudhishthira moved by kindness towards the dog that accompanied him, refused to ascend it without his companion. Observing the illustrious Yudhishthira's steady adherence to virtue, Dharma (the god of justice) abandoning his canine form showed himself to the king. Then Yudhishthira ascending to heaven felt much pain. The celestial messenger showed him hell by an act of deception. Then Yudhishthira, the soul of justice, heard the heart-rending lamentations of his brothers abiding in that region under the discipline of Yama. Then Dharma and Indra showed Yudhishthira the region appointed for sinners. Then Yudhishthira, after leaving the human body by a plunge in the celestial Ganges, attained to that region which his acts merited, and began to live in joy respected by Indra and all other gods. This is the eighteenth Parva as narrated by the illustrious Vyasa. The number of slokas composed, O ascetics, by the great Rishi in this is two hundred and nine.

"The above are the contents of the Eighteen Parvas. In the appendix (Khita) are the Harivansa and the Vavishya. The number of slokas contained in the Harivansa is twelve thousand."

These are the contents of the section called Parva-sangraha. Sauti continued, "Eighteen Akshauhinis of troops came together for battle. The encounter that ensued was terrible and lasted for eighteen days. He who knows the four Vedas with all the Angas and Upanishads, but does not know this history (Bharata), cannot be regarded as wise. Vyasa of immeasurable intelligence, has spoken of the Mahabharata as a treatise on Artha, on Dharma, and on Kama. Those who have listened to his history can never bear to listen to others, as, indeed, they who have listened to the sweet voice of the male Kokila can never hear the dissonance of the crow's cawing. As the formation of the three worlds proceedeth from the five elements, so do the inspirations of all poets proceed from this excellent composition. O ye Brahman, as the four kinds of creatures (viviparous, oviparous, born of hot moisture and vegetables) are dependent on space for their existence, so the Puranas depend upon this history. As all the senses depend for their exercise upon the various modifications of the mind, so do all acts (ceremonials) and moral qualities depend upon this treatise. There is not a story current in the world but doth depend on this history, even as body upon the food it taketh. All poets cherish the Bharata even as servants desirous of preferment always attend upon masters of good lineage. Even as the blessed domestic Asrama can never be surpassed by the three other Asramas (modes of life) so no poets can surpass this poem.

"Ye ascetics, shake off all inaction. Let your hearts be fixed on virtue, for virtue is the one only friend of him that has gone to the other world. Even the most intelligent by cherishing wealth and wives can never make these their own, nor are these possessions lasting. The Bharata uttered by the lips of Dwaipayana is without a parallel; it is virtue itself and sacred. It destroyeth sin and produceth good. He that listeneth to it while it is being recited hath no need of a bath in the sacred waters of Pushkara. A Brahmana, whatever sins he may commit during the day through his senses, is freed from them all by reading the Bharata in the evening. Whatever sins he may commit also in the night by deeds, words, or mind, he is freed from them all by reading Bharata in the first twilight (morning). He that giveth a hundred kine with horns mounted with gold to a Brahmana well-posted up in the Vedas and all branches of learning, and he that daily listeneth to the sacred narrations of the Bharata, acquireth equal merit. As the wide ocean is easily passable by men having ships, so is this extensive history of great excellence and deep import with the help of this chapter called Parva sangraha."

Thus endeth the section called Parva-sangraha of the Adi Parva of the blessed Mahabharata.

SECTION III
(Paushya Parva)

Sauti said, "Janamejaya, the son of Parikshit, was, with his brothers, attending his long sacrifice on the plains of Kurukshetra. His brothers were three, Srutasena, Ugrasena, and Bhimasena. And as they were sitting at the sacrifice, there arrived at the spot an offspring of Sarama (the celestial bitch). And belaboured by the brothers of Janamejaya, he ran away to his mother, crying in pain. And his mother seeing him crying exceedingly asked him, 'Why criest thou so? Who hath beaten thee?' And being thus questioned, he said unto his mother, 'I have been belaboured by the brothers of Janamejaya.' And his mother replied, 'Thou hast committed some fault for which hast thou been beaten!' He answered, 'I have not committed any fault. I have not touched the sacrificial butter with my tongue, nor have I even cast a look upon it.' His mother Sarama hearing this and much distressed at the affliction of her son went to the place where Janamejaya with his brothers was at his long-extending sacrifice. And she addressed Janamejaya in anger, saying, 'This my son hath committed no fault: he hath not looked upon your sacrificial butter, nor hath he touched it with his tongue. Wherefore hath he been beaten?' They said not a word in reply; whereupon she said, 'As ye have beaten my son who hath committed no fault, therefore shall evil come upon ye, when ye least expect it.'

"Janamejaya, thus addressed by the celestial bitch, Sarama, became exceedingly alarmed and dejected. And after the sacrifice was concluded returned to Hastinapura, and began to take great pains in searching for a Purohita who could by procuring absolution for his sin, neutralise the effect of the curse.

"One day Janamejaya, the son of Parikshit, while a-hunting, observed in a particular part of his dominions a hermitage where dwelt a certain Rishi of fame, Srutasrava. He had a son named Somasrava deeply engaged in ascetic devotions. Being desirous of appointing that son of the Rishi as his Purohita, Janamejaya, the son of Parikshit, saluted the Rishi and addressed him, saying, 'O possessor of the six attributes, let this thy son be my purohita.' The Rishi thus addressed, answered Janamejaya, 'O Janamejaya, this my son, deep in ascetic devotions, accomplished in the study of the Vedas, and endued with the full force of my asceticism, is born of (the womb of) a she-snake that had drunk my vital fluid. He is able to absolve thee from all offences save those committed against Mahadeva. But he hath one particular habit, viz. he would grant to any Brahmana whatever might be begged of him. If thou canst put up with it, then thou take him.' Janamejaya thus addressed replied to the Rishi, 'It shall be even so.' And accepting him for his Purohita, he returned to his capital; and he then addressed his brothers saying, 'This is the person I have chosen for my spiritual master; whatsoever he may say must be complied with by you without examination.' And his brothers did as they were directed. And giving these directions to his brothers, the king marched towards Takshyashila and brought that country under his authority.

"About this time there was a Rishi, Ayoda-Dhaumya by name. And Ayoda- Dhaumya had three disciples, Upamanyu, Aruni, and Veda. And the Rishi bade one of these disciples, Aruni of Panchala, to go and stop up a breach in the water-course of a certain field. And Aruni of Panchala, thus ordered by his preceptor, repaired to the spot. And having gone there he saw that he could not stop up the breach in the water-course by ordinary means. And he was distressed because he could not do his preceptor's bidding. But at length he saw a way and said, 'Well, I will do it in this way.' He then went down into the breach and lay down himself there. And the water was thus confined.

"And some time after, the preceptor Ayoda-Dhaumya asked his other disciples where Aruni of Panchala was. And they answered, 'Sir, he hath been sent by yourself saying, 'Go, stop up the breach in the water-course of the field,' Thus reminded, Dhaumya, addressing his pupils, said, 'Then let us all go to the place where he is.'

"And having arrived there, he shouted, 'Ho Aruni of Panchala! Where art thou? Come hither, my child.' And Aruni hearing the voice of his preceptor speedily came out of the water-course and stood before his preceptor. And addressing the latter, Aruni said, 'Here I am in the breach of the water- course. Not having been able to devise any other means, I entered myself for the purpose of preventing the water running out. It is only upon hearing thy voice that, having left it and allowed the waters to escape, I have stood before thee. I salute thee, Master; tell me what I have to do.'

"The preceptor, thus addressed, replied, 'Because in getting up from the ditch thou hast opened the water-course, thenceforth shalt thou be called Uddalaka as a mark of thy preceptor's favour. And because my words have been obeyed by thee, thou shalt obtain good fortune. And all the Vedas shall shine in thee and all the Dharmasastras also.' And Aruni, thus addressed by his preceptor, went to the country after his heart.

"The name of another of Ayoda-Dhaumya's disciples was Upamanyu. And Dhaumya appointed him saying, 'Go, my child, Upamanyu, look after the kine.' And according to his preceptor's orders, he went to tend the kine. And having watched them all day, he returned in the evening to his preceptor's house and standing before him he saluted him respectfully. And his preceptor seeing him in good condition of body asked him, 'Upamanyu, my child, upon what dost thou support thyself? Thou art exceedingly plump.' And he answered, 'Sir, I support myself by begging.' And his preceptor said, 'What is obtained in alms should not be used by thee without offering it to me.' And Upamanyu, thus told, went away. And having obtained alms, he offered the same to his preceptor. And his preceptor took from him even the whole. And Upamanyu, thus treated, went to attend the cattle. And having watched them all day, he returned in the evening to his preceptor's abode. And he stood before his preceptor and saluted him with respect. And his preceptor perceiving that he still continued to be of good condition of body said unto him, 'Upamanyu, my child, I take from thee even the whole of what thou obtainest in alms, without leaving anything for thee. How then dost thou, at present, contrive to support thyself?' And Upamanyu said unto his preceptor, 'Sir, having made over to you all that I obtain in alms, I go a-begging a second time for supporting myself.' And his preceptor then replied, 'This is not the way in which thou shouldst obey the preceptor. By this thou art diminishing the support of others that live by begging. Truly having supported thyself so, thou hast proved thyself covetous.' And Upamanyu, having signified his assent to all that his preceptor said, went away to attend the cattle. And having watched them all day, he returned to his preceptor's house. And he stood before his preceptor and saluted him respectfully. And his preceptor observing that he was still fat, said again unto him, 'Upamanyu, my child, I take from thee all thou obtainest in alms and thou dost not go a-begging a second time, and yet art thou in healthy condition. How dost thou support thyself?' And Upamanyu, thus questioned, answered, 'Sir, I now live upon the milk of these cows.' And his preceptor thereupon told him, 'It is not lawful for thee to appropriate the milk without having first obtained my consent.' And Upamanyu having assented to the justice of these observations, went away to tend the kine. And when he returned to his preceptor's abode, he stood before him and saluted him as usual. And his preceptor seeing that he was still fat, said, 'Upamanyu, my child, thou eatest no longer of alms, nor dost thou go a-begging a second time, not even drinkest of the milk; yet art thou fat. By what means dost thou contrive to live now? And Upamanyu replied, 'Sir, I now sip the froth that these calves throw out, while sucking their mother's teats.' And the preceptor said, 'These generous calves, I suppose, out of compassion for thee, throw out large quantities of froth. Wouldst thou stand in the way of their full meals by acting as thou hast done? Know that it is unlawful for thee to drink the froth.' And Upamanyu, having signified his assent to this, went as before to tend the cows. And restrained by his preceptor, he feedeth not on alms, nor hath he anything else to eat; he drinketh not of the milk, nor tasteth he of the froth!

"And Upamanyu, one day, oppressed by hunger, when in a forest, ate of the leaves of the Arka (Asclepias gigantea). And his eyes being affected by the pungent, acrimonious, crude, and saline properties of the leaves which he had eaten, he became blind. And as he was crawling about, he fell into a pit. And upon his not returning that day when the sun was sinking down behind the summit of the western mountains, the preceptor observed to his disciples that Upamanyu was not yet come. And they told him that he had gone out with the cattle.

"The preceptor then said, 'Upamanyu being restrained by me from the use of everything, is, of course, and therefore, doth not come home until it be late. Let us then go in search of him.' And having said this, he went with his disciples into the forest and began to shout, saying, 'Ho Upamanyu, where art thou?' And

Upamanyu hearing his preceptor's voice answered in a loud tone, 'Here I am at the bottom of a well.' And his preceptor asked him how he happened to be there. And Upamanyu replied, 'Having eaten of the leaves of the Arka plant I became blind, and so have I fallen into this well.' And his preceptor thereupon told him, 'Glorify the twin Aswins, the joint physicians of the gods, and they will restore thee thy sight.' And Upamanyu thus directed by his preceptor began to glorify the twin Aswins, in the following words of the Rig Veda:

'Ye have existed before the creation! Ye first-born beings, ye are displayed in this wondrous universe of five elements! I desire to obtain you by the help of the knowledge derived from hearing, and of meditation, for ye are Infinite! Ye are the course itself of Nature and intelligent Soul that pervades that course! Ye are birds of beauteous feathers perched on the body that is like to a tree! Ye are without the three common attributes of every soul! Ye are incomparable! Ye, through your spirit in every created thing, pervade the Universe!

'Ye are golden Eagles! Ye are the essence into which all things disappear! Ye are free from error and know no deterioration! Ye are of beauteous beaks that would not unjustly strike and are victorious in every encounter! Ye certainly prevail over time! Having created the sun, ye weave the wondrous cloth of the year by means of the white thread of the day and the black thread of the night! And with the cloth so woven, ye have established two courses of action appertaining respectively to the Devas and the Pitris. The bird of Life seized by Time which represents the strength of the Infinite soul, ye set free for delivering her unto great happiness! They that are in deep ignorance, as long as they are under delusions of their senses, suppose you, who are independent of the attributes of matter, to be gifted with form! Three hundred and sixty cows represented by three hundred and sixty days produce one calf between them which is the year. That calf is the creator and destroyer of all. Seekers of truth following different routes, draw the milk of true knowledge with its help. Ye Aswins, ye are the creators of that calf!

'The year is but the nave of a wheel to which is attached seven hundred and twenty spokes representing as many days and nights. The circumference of this wheel represented by twelve months is without end. This wheel is full of delusions and knows no deterioration. It affects all creatures whether to this or of the other worlds. Ye Aswins, this wheel of time is set in motion by you!

'The wheel of Time as represented by the year has a nave represented by the six seasons. The number of spokes attached to that nave is twelve as represented by the twelve signs of the Zodiac. This wheel of Time manifests the fruits of the acts of all things. The presiding deities of Time abide in that wheel. Subject as I am to its distressful influence, ye Aswins, liberate me from that wheel of Time. Ye Aswins, ye are this universe of five elements! Ye are the objects that are enjoyed in this and in the other world! Make me independent of the five elements! And though ye are the Supreme Brahma, yet ye move over the Earth in forms enjoying the delights that the senses afford.

'In the beginning, ye created the ten points of the universe! Then have ye placed the Sun and the Sky above! The Rishis, according to the course of the same Sun, perform their sacrifices, and the gods and men, according to what hath been appointed for them, perform their sacrifices also enjoying the fruits of those acts!

'Mixing the three colours, ye have produced all the objects of sight! It is from these objects that the Universe hath sprung whereon the gods and men are engaged in their respective occupations, and, indeed, all creatures endued with life!

'Ye Aswins, I adore you! I also adore the Sky which is your handiwork! Ye are the ordainers of the fruits of all acts from which even the gods are not free! Ye are yourselves free from the fruits of your acts!

'Ye are the parents of all! As males and females it is ye that swallow the food which subsequently develops into the life creating fluid and blood! The new-born infant sucks the teat of its mother. Indeed it is ye that take the shape of the infant! Ye Aswins, grant me my sight to protect my life!"

"The twin Aswins, thus invoked, appeared and said, 'We are satisfied. Here is a cake for thee. Take and eat it.' And Upamanyu thus addressed, replied, 'Your words, O Aswins, have never proved untrue. But without first offering this cake to my preceptor I dare not take it.' And the Aswins thereupon told him, 'Formerly, thy preceptor had invoked us. We thereupon gave him a cake like this; and he took it without offering it to his master. Do thou do that which thy preceptor did.' Thus addressed, Upamanyu again said unto them, 'O Aswins, I crave your pardon. Without offering it to my preceptor I dare not apply this cake.' The Aswins then said, 'O, we are pleased with this devotion of thine to thy preceptor. Thy master's teeth are of black iron. Thine shall be of gold. Thou shall be restored to sight and shall have good fortune.'

"Thus spoken to by the Aswins he recovered his sight, and having gone to his preceptor's presence he saluted him and told him all. And his preceptor was well-pleased with him and said unto him, 'Thou shalt obtain prosperity even as the Aswins have said. All the Vedas shall shine in thee and all the Dharma-sastras.' And this was the trial of Upamanyu.

"Then Veda the other disciple of Ayoda-Dhaumya was called. His preceptor once addressed him, saying, 'Veda, my child, tarry some time in my house and serve thy preceptor. It shall be to thy profit.' And Veda having signified his assent tarried long in the family of his preceptor mindful of serving him. Like an ox under the burthens of his master, he bore heat and cold, hunger and thirst, at all times without a murmur. And it was not long before his preceptor was satisfied. And as a consequence of that satisfaction, Veda obtained good fortune and universal knowledge. And this was the trial of Veda.

"And Veda, having received permission from his preceptor, and leaving the latter's residence after the completion of his studies, entered the domestic mode of life. And while living in his own house, he got three pupils. And he never told them to perform any work or to obey implicitly his own behests; for having himself experienced much woe while abiding in the family of his preceptor, he liked not to treat them with severity.

"After a certain time, Janamejaya and Paushya, both of the order of Kshatriyas, arriving at his residence appointed the Brahman, Veda, as their spiritual guide (Upadhyaya). And one day while about to depart upon some business related to a sacrifice, he employed one of his disciples, Utanka, to take charge of his household. 'Utanka', said he, 'whatsoever should have to be done in my house, let it be done by thee without neglect.' And having given these orders to Utanka, he went on his journey.

"So Utanka always mindful of the injunction of his preceptor took up his abode in the latter's house. And while Utanka was residing there, the females of his preceptor's house having assembled addressed him and said, 'O Utanka, thy mistress is in that season when connubial connection might be fruitful. The preceptor is absent; then stand thou in his place and do the needful.' And Utanka, thus addressed, said unto those women, 'It is not proper for me to do this at the bidding of women. I have not been enjoined by my preceptor to do aught that is improper.'

"After a while, his preceptor returned from his journey. And his preceptor having learnt all that had happened, became well-pleased and, addressing Utanka, said, 'Utanka, my child, what favour shall I bestow on thee? I have been served by thee duly; therefore hath our friendship for each other increased. I therefore grant thee leave to depart. Go thou, and let thy wishes be accomplished!'

"Utanka, thus addressed, replied, saying, 'Let me do something that you wish, for it hath been said, "He who bestoweth instruction contrary to usage and he who receiveth it contrary to usage, one of the two dieth, and enmity springeth up between the two." I, therefore, who have received thy leave to depart, am desirous of bringing thee some honorarium due to a preceptor.' His master, upon hearing this, replied, 'Utanka, my child, wait a while.' Sometime after, Utanka again addressed his preceptor, saying, 'Command me to bring that for honorarium, which you desire.' And his preceptor then said, 'My dear Utanka, thou hast often told me of your desire to bring something by way of acknowledgment for the instruction thou hast received. Go then in and ask thy mistress what thou art to bring. And bring thou that which she directs.' And thus directed by his preceptor Utanka addressed his preceptress, saying, 'Madam, I have obtained my master's leave to go home, and I am desirous of bringing something agreeable to thee as honorarium for the instruction I have received, in order that I may not depart as his debtor. Therefore, please command me what I am to bring.' Thus addressed, his preceptress replied, 'Go unto King Paushya and beg of him the pair of ear-rings worn by his Queen, and bring them hither. The fourth day hence is a sacred day when I wish to appear before the Brahmanas (who may dine at my house) decked with these ear-rings. Then accomplish this, O Utanka! If thou shouldst succeed, good fortune shall attend thee; if not, what good canst thou expect?'

"Utanka thus commanded, took his departure. And as he was passing along the road he saw a bull of extraordinary size and a man of uncommon stature mounted thereon. And that man addressed Utanka and said, 'Eat thou of the dung of this bull.' Utanka, however, was unwilling to comply. The man said again, 'O Utanka, eat of it without scrutiny. Thy master ate of it before.' And Utanka signified his assent and ate of the dung and drank of the urine of that bull, and rose respectfully, and washing his hands and mouth went to where King Paushya was.

'On arriving at the palace, Utanka saw Paushya seated (on his throne). And approaching him Utanka saluted the monarch by pronouncing blessings and said, 'I am come as a petitioner to thee.' And King Paushya, having returned Utanka's salutations, said, 'Sir, what shall I do for thee?' And Utanka said, 'I came to beg of thee a pair of ear-rings as a present to my preceptor. It behoveth thee to give me the ear-rings worn by the Queen.'

"King Paushya replied, 'Go, Utanka, into the female apartments where the Queen is and demand them of her.' And Utanka went into the women's apartments. But as he could not discover the Queen, he again addressed the king, saying, 'It is not proper that I should be treated by thee with deceit. Thy Queen is not in the private apartments, for I could not find her.' The king thus addressed, considered for a while and replied, 'Recollect, Sir, with attention whether thou art not in a state of defilement in consequence of contact with the impurities of a repast. My Queen is a chaste wife and cannot be seen by any one who is impure owing to contact with the leavings of a repast. Nor doth she herself appear in sight of any one who is defiled.'

"Utanka, thus informed, reflected for a while and then said, 'Yes, it must be so. Having been in a hurry I performed my ablutions (after meal) in a standing posture.' King Paushya then said, 'Here is a transgression, purification is not properly effected by one in a standing posture, not by one while he is going along.' And Utanka having agreed to this, sat down with his face towards the east, and washed his face, hands, and feet thoroughly. And he then, without a noise, sipped thrice of water free from scum and froth, and not warm, and just sufficient to reach his stomach and wiped his face twice. And he then touched with water the apertures of his organs (eyes, ears, etc.). And having done all this, he once more entered the apartments of the women. And this time he saw the Queen. And as the Queen perceived him, she saluted him respectfully and said, 'Welcome, Sir, command me what I have to do.' And Utanka said unto her, 'It behoveth thee to give me those ear-rings of thine. I beg them as a present for my preceptor.' And the Queen having been highly pleased with Utanka's conduct and, considering that Utanka as an object of charity could not be passed over, took off her ear-rings and gave them to him. And she said, 'These ear-rings are very much sought after by Takshaka, the King of the serpents. Therefore shouldst thou carry them with the greatest care.'

"And Utanka being told this, said unto the Queen, 'Lady, be under no apprehension. Takshaka, Chief of the serpents, is not able to overtake me.' And having said this, and taking leave of the Queen, he went back into the presence of Paushya, and said, 'Paushya, I am gratified.' Then Paushya said to Utanka, 'A fit object of charity can only be had at long intervals. Thou art a qualified guest, therefore do I desire to perform a sraddha. Tarry thou a little. And Utanka replied, 'Yes, I will tarry, and beg that the clean provisions that are ready may be soon brought in.' And the king having signified his assent, entertained Utanka duly. And Utanka seeing that the food placed before him had hair in it, and also that it was cold, thought it unclean. And he said unto Paushya, 'Thou givest me food that is unclean, therefore shalt thou lose thy sight.' And Paushya in answer said, 'And because dost thou impute uncleanliness to food that is clean, therefore shalt thou be without issue.' And Utanka thereupon rejoined, 'It behoveth thee not, after having offered me unclean food, to curse me in return. Satisfy thyself by ocular proof.'

"And Paushya seeing the food alleged to be unclean satisfied himself of its uncleanliness. And Paushya having ascertained that the food was truly unclean, being cold and mixed with hair, prepared as it was by a woman with unbraided hair, began to pacify the Rishi Utanka, saying, 'Sir, the food placed before thee is cold, and doth contain hair, having been prepared without sufficient care. Therefore I pray thee pardon me. Let me not become blind.' And Utanka answered, 'What I say must come to pass. Having become blind, thou mayst, however, recover the sight before long. Grant that thy curse also doth not take effect on me.' And Paushya said unto him, 'I am unable to revoke my curse. For my wrath even now hath not been appeased. But thou knowest not this. For a Brahmana's heart is soft as new-churned butter, even though his words bear a sharp-edged razor. It is otherwise in respect of these with the Kshatriya. His words are soft as new-churned butter, but his heart is like a sharp-edged tool, such being the case, I am unable, because of the hardness of my heart, to neutralise my curse. Then go thou thy own way.' To this Utanka made answer, 'I showed thee the uncleanliness of the food offered to me, and I was even now pacified by thee. Besides, saidst thou at first that because I imputed uncleanliness to food that was clean I should be without issue. But the food truly unclean, thy curse cannot affect me. Of this I am sure.' And Utanka having said this departed with the ear-rings.

"On the road Utanka perceived coming towards him a naked idle beggar sometimes coming in view and sometimes disappearing. And Utanka put the ear-rings on the ground and went for water. In the meantime the beggar came quickly to the spot and taking up the ear-rings ran away. And Utanka having completed his ablutions in water and purified himself and having also reverently bowed down to the gods and his spiritual masters pursued the thief with the utmost speed. And having with great difficulty overtaken him, he seized him by force. But at that instant the person seized, quitting the form of a beggar and assuming his real form, viz., that of Takshaka, speedily entered a large hole open in the ground. And having got in, Takshaka proceeded to his own abode, the region of the serpents.

"Now, Utanka, recollecting the words of the Queen, pursued the Serpent, and began to dig open the hole with a stick but was unable to make much progress. And Indra beholding his distress sent his thunder-bolt (Vajra) to his assistance. Then the thunder-bolt entering that stick enlarged that hole. And Utanka began to enter the hole after the thunder-bolt. And having entered it, he beheld the region of the serpents infinite in extent, filled with hundreds of palaces and elegant mansions with turrets and domes and gate-ways, abounding with wonderful places for various games and entertainments. And Utanka then glorified the serpents by the following slokas:

'Ye Serpents, subjects of King Airavata, splendid in battle and showering weapons in the field like lightning-charged clouds driven by the winds! Handsome and of various forms and decked with many coloured ear-rings, ye children of Airavata, ye shine like the Sun in the firmament! On the northern banks of the Ganges are many habitations of serpents. There I constantly adore the great serpents. Who except Airavata would desire to move in the burning rays of the Sun? When Dhritarashtra (Airavata's brother) goes out, twenty-eight thousand and eight serpents follow him as his attendants. Ye who move near him and ye who stay at a distance from him, I adore all of you that have Airavata for your elder brother.

'I adore thee also, to obtain the ear-rings, O Takshaka, who formerly dwelt in Kurukshetra and the forest of Khandava! Takshaka and Aswasena, ye are constant companions who dwell in Kurukshetra on the banks of the Ikshumati! I also adore the illustrious Srutasena, the younger brother of Takshaka, who resided at the holy place called Mahadyumna with a view to obtaining the chiefship of the serpents.

"The Brahmana Rishi Utanka having saluted the chief serpents in this manner, obtained not, however, the ear-rings. And he thereupon became very thoughtful. And when he saw that he obtained not the ear-rings even though he had adored the serpents, he then looked about him and beheld two women at a loom weaving a piece of cloth with a fine shuttle; and in the loom were black and white threads. And he likewise saw a wheel, with twelve spokes, turned by six boys. And he also saw a man with a handsome horse. And he began to address them the following mantras:

'This wheel whose circumference is marked by twenty-four divisions representing as many lunar changes is furnished with three hundred spokes! It is set in continual motion by six boys (the seasons)! These damsels representing universal nature are weaving without intermission a cloth with threads black and white, and thereby ushering into existence the manifold worlds and the beings that inhabit them! Thou wielder of the thunder, the protector of the universe, the slayer of Vritra and Namuchi, thou illustrious one who wearest the black cloth and displayest truth and untruth in the universe, thou who ownest for thy carrier the horse which was received from the depths of the ocean, and which is but another form of Agni (the god of fire), I bow to thee, thou supreme Lord, thou Lord of the three worlds, O Purandara!'

"Then the man with the horse said unto Utanka, 'I am gratified by this thy adoration. What good shall I do to thee?' And Utanka replied, 'Even let the serpents be brought under my control.' Then the man rejoined, 'Blow into this horse.' And Utanka blew into that horse. And from the horse thus blown into, there issued, from every aperture of his body, flames of fire with smoke by which the region of the Nagas was about to be consumed. And Takshaka, surprised beyond measure and terrified by the heat of the fire, hastily came out of his abode taking the ear-rings with him, and said unto Utanka, 'Pray, Sir, take back the ear-rings.' And Utanka took them back.

"But Utanka having recovered his ear-rings thought, 'O, this is that sacred day of my preceptress. I am at a distance. How can I, therefore, show my regard for her? And when Utanka was anxious about this, the man addressed him and said, 'Ride this horse, Utanka, and he will in a moment carry thee to thy master's abode.' And Utanka having signified his assent, mounted the horse and presently reached his preceptor's house.

"And his preceptress that morning after having bathed was dressing her hair sitting, thinking of uttering a curse on Utanka if he should not return within time. But, in the meantime, Utanka entered his preceptor's abode and paid his respects to his preceptress and presented her the ear- rings. 'Utanka', said she, 'thou hast arrived at the proper time at the proper place. Welcome, my child; thou art innocent and therefore I do not curse thee! Good fortune is even before thee. Let thy wishes be crowned with success!'

"Then Utanka waited on his preceptor. And his preceptor said, 'Thou art welcome! What hath occasioned thy long absence?' And Utanka replied to his preceptor, 'Sir, in the execution of this my business obstruction was offered by Takshaka, the King of serpents. Therefore I had to go to the region of the Nagas. There I saw two damsels sitting at a loom, weaving a fabric with black and white threads. Pray, what is that? There likewise I beheld a wheel with twelve spokes ceaselessly turned by six boys. What too doth that import? Who is also the man that I saw? And what the horse of extraordinary size likewise beheld by me? And when I was on the road I also saw a bull with a man mounted thereon, by whom I was endearingly accosted thus, 'Utanka, eat of the dung of this bull, which was also eaten by thy master?' So I ate of the dung of that bull according to his words. Who also is he? Therefore, enlightened by thee, I desire to hear all about them.'

"And his preceptor thus addressed said unto him, 'The two damsels thou hast seen are Dhata and Vidhata; the black and white threads denote night and day; the wheel of twelve spokes turned by the six boys signified the year comprising six seasons. The man is Parjanya, the deity of rain, and the horse is Agni, the god of fire. The bull that thou hast seen on the road is Airavata, the king of elephants; the man mounted thereon is Indra; and the dung of the bull which was eaten by thee was Amrita. It was certainly for this (last) that thou hast not met with death in the region of the Nagas; and Indra who is my friend having been mercifully inclined showed thee favour. It is for this that thou returnest safe, with the ear- rings about thee. Then, O thou amiable one, I give thee leave to depart. Thou shall obtain good fortune.'

"And Utanka, having obtained his master's leave, moved by anger and resolved to avenge himself on Takshaka, proceeded towards Hastinapura. That excellent Brahmana soon reached Hastinapura. And Utanka then waited upon King Janamejaya who had some time before returned victorious from Takshashila. And Utanka saw the victorious monarch surrounded on all sides by his ministers. And he pronounced benedictions on him in a proper form. And Utanka addressed the monarch at the proper moment in speech of correct accent and melodious sounds, saying, 'O thou the best of monarchs! How is it that thou spendest thy time like a child when there is another matter that urgently demandeth thy attention?'"

Sauti said, "The monarch Janamejaya, thus addressed, saluting that excellent Brahmana replied unto him, 'In cherishing these my subjects I do discharge the duties of my noble tribe. Say, what is that business to be done by me and which hath brought thee hither.'

"The foremost of Brahmanas and distinguished beyond all for good deeds, thus addressed by the excellent monarch of large heart, replied unto him, 'O King! the business is thy own that demandeth thy attention; therefore do it, please. O thou King of kings! Thy father was deprived of life by Takshaka; therefore do thou avenge thy father's death on that vile serpent. The time hath come, I think, for the act of vengeance ordained by the Fates. Go then avenge the death of thy magnanimous father who, being bitten without cause by that vile serpent, was reduced to five elements even like a tree stricken by thunder. The wicked Takshaka, vilest of the serpent race, intoxicated with power committed an unnecessary act when he bit the King, that god-like father, the protector of the race of royal saints. Wicked in his deeds, he even caused Kasyapa (the prince of physicians) to run back when he was coming for the relief of thy father. It behoveth thee to burn the wicked wretch in the blazing fire of a snake- sacrifice. O King! Give instant orders for the sacrifice. It is thus thou canst avenge the death of thy father. And a very great favour shall have also been shown to me. For by that malignant wretch, O virtuous Prince, my business also was, on one occasion, obstructed, while proceeding on account of my preceptor."

Sauti continued, "The monarch, having heard these words, was enraged with Takshaka. By the speech of Utanka was inflamed the prince, even as the sacrificial fire with clarified butter. Moved by grief also, in the presence of Utanka, the prince asked his ministers the particulars of his father's journey to the regions of the blessed. And when he heard all about the circumstances of his father's death from the lips of Utanka, he was overcome with pain and sorrow.

And thus endeth the section called Paushya of the Adi Parva of the blessed Mahabharata."

SECTION IV
(Pauloma Parva)

Ugrasrava Sauti, the son of Lomaharshana, versed in the Puranas, while present in the forest of Naimisha, at the twelve years' sacrifice of Saunaka, surnamed Kulapati, stood before the Rishis in attendance. Having studied Puranas with meticulous devotion and thus being thoroughly acquainted with them, he addressed them with joined hands thus, "I have graphically described to you the history of Utanka which is one of the causes of King Janamejaya's Snake-sacrifice. What, revered Sirs, do ye wish to hear now? What shall I relate to you?" The holy men replied, "O son of Lomaharshana, we shall ask thee about what we are anxious to hear and thou wilt recount the tales one by one. Saunaka, our revered master, is at present attending the apartment of the holy fire. He is acquainted with those divine stories which relate to the gods and asuras. He adequately knoweth the histories of men, serpents, and Gandharvas. Further, O Sauti, in this sacrifice that learned Brahmana is the chief. He is able, faithful to his vows, wise, a master of the Sastras and the Aranyaka, a speaker of truth, a lover of peace, a mortifier of the flesh, and an observer of the penances according to the authoritative decrees. He is respected by us all. It behoveth us therefore to wait for him. And when he is seated on his highly respected seat, thou wilt answer what that best of Dwijas shall ask of thee."

Sauti said, "Be it so. And when the high-souled master hath been seated I shall narrate, questioned by him, sacred stories on a variety of subjects." After a while that excellent Brahmana (Saunaka) having duly finished all his duties, and having propitiated the gods with prayers and the manes with oblations of water, came back to the place of sacrifice, where with Sauti seated before was the assembly of saints of rigid vows sitting at ease. And when Saunaka was seated in the midst of the Ritwiks and Sadhyas, who were also in their seats, he spake as followeth.

SECTION V
(Pauloma Parva continued)

"Saunaka said, 'Child, thy father formerly read the whole of the Puranas, O son of Lomaharshana, and the Bharata with Krishna-Dwaipayana. Hast thou also made them thy study? In those ancient records are chronicled interesting stories and the history of the first generations of the wise men, all of which we heard being rehearsed by thy sire. In the first place, I am desirous of hearing the history of the race of Bhrigu. Recount thou that history, we shall attentively listen to thee."

"Sauti answered, 'By me hath been acquired all that was formerly studied by the high-souled Brahmanas including Vaisampayana and repeated by them; by me hath been acquired all that had been studied by my father. O descendant of the Bhrigu race, attend then to so much as relateth to the exalted race of Bhrigu, revered by Indra and all the gods, by the tribes of Rishis and Maruts (Winds). O great Muni, I shall first properly recount the story of this family, as told in the Puranas.

"The great and blessed saint Bhrigu, we are informed, was produced by the self-existing Brahma from the fire at the sacrifice of Varuna. And Bhrigu had a son, named Chyavana, whom he dearly loved. And to Chyavana was born a virtuous son called Pramati. And Pramati had a son named Ruru by Ghritachi (the celestial dancer). And to Ruru also by his wife Pramadvara, was born a son, whose name was Sunaka. He was, O Saunaka, thy great ancestor exceedingly virtuous in his ways. He was devoted to asceticism, of great reputation, proficient in law, and eminent among those having a knowledge of the Vedas. He was virtuous, truthful, and of well-regulated fare.'

"Saunaka said, 'O son of Suta, I ask thee why the illustrious son of Bhrigu was named Chyavana. Do tell me all.'

"Sauti replied, 'Bhrigu had a wife named Puloma whom he dearly loved. She became big with child by Bhrigu. And one day while the virtuous continent Puloma was in that condition, Bhrigu, great among those that are true to their religion, leaving her at home went out to perform his ablutions. It was then that the Rakshasa called Puloma came to Bhrigu's abode. And entering the Rishi's abode, the Rakshasa saw the wife of Bhrigu, irreproachable in everything. And seeing her he became filled with lust and lost his senses. The beautiful Puloma entertained the Rakshasa thus arrived, with roots and fruits of the forest. And the Rakshasa who burnt with desire upon seeing her, became very much delighted and resolved, O good sage, to carry her away who was so blameless in every respect.

'My design is accomplished,' said the Rakshasa, and so seizing that beautiful matron he carried her away. And, indeed, she of agreeable smiles, had been betrothed by her father himself, to him, although the former subsequently bestowed her, according to due rites, on Bhrigu. O thou of the Bhrigu race, this wound rankled deep in the Rakshasa's mind and he thought the present moment very opportune for carrying the lady away.

"And the Rakshasa saw the apartment in which the sacrificial fire was kept burning brightly. The Rakshasa then asked the flaming element 'Tell me, O Agni, whose wife this woman rightfully is. Thou art the mouth of gods; therefore thou art bound to answer my question. This lady of superior complexion had been first accepted by me as wife, but her father subsequently bestowed her on the false Bhrigu. Tell me truly if this fair one can be regarded as the wife of Bhrigu, for having found her alone, I have resolved to take her away by force from the hermitage. My heart burneth with rage when I reflect that Bhrigu hath got possession of this woman of slender waist, first betrothed to me.'"

"Sauti continued, 'In this manner the Rakshasa asked the flaming god of fire again and again whether the lady was Bhrigu's wife. And the god was afraid to return an answer. 'Thou, O god of fire,' said he, 'residest constantly within every creature, as witness of her or his merits and demerits. O thou respected one, then answer my question truly. Has not Bhrigu appropriated her who was chosen by me as my wife? Thou shouldst declare truly whether, therefore, she is my wife by first choice. After thy answer as to whether she is the wife of Bhrigu, I will bear her away from this hermitage even in sight of thee. Therefore answer thou truly.'"

"Sauti continued, 'The Seven flamed god having heard these words of the Rakshasa became exceedingly distressed, being afraid of telling a falsehood and equally afraid of Bhrigu's curse. And the god at length made answer in words that came out slowly. 'This Puloma was, indeed, first chosen by thee, O Rakshasa, but she was not taken by thee with holy rites and invocations. But this far-famed lady was bestowed by her father on Bhrigu as a gift from desire of blessing. She was not bestowed on thee O Rakshasa, this lady was duly made by the Rishi Bhrigu his wife with Vedic rites in my presence. This is she—I know her. I dare not speak a falsehood. O thou best of the Rakshasas, falsehood is never respected in this world.'"

SECTION VI
(Pauloma Parva continued)

"Sauti said, 'O Brahmana, having heard these words from the god of fire, the Rakshasa assumed the form of a boar, and seizing the lady carried her away with the speed of the wind—even of thought. Then the child of Bhrigu lying in her body enraged at such violence, dropped from his mother's womb, for which he obtained the name of Chyavana. And the Rakshasa perceiving the infant drop from the mother's womb, shining like the sun, quitted his grasp of the woman, fell down and was instantly converted into ashes. And the beautiful Pauloma, distracted with grief, O Brahmana of the Bhrigu race, took up her offspring Chyavana, the son of Bhrigu and walked away. And Brahma, the Grandfather of all, himself saw her, the faultless wife of his son, weeping. And the Grandfather of all comforted her who was attached to her son. And the drops of tears which rolled down her eyes formed a great river. And that river began to follow the foot-steps of the wife of the great ascetic Bhrigu. And the Grandfather of the worlds seeing that river follow the path of his son's wife gave it a name himself, and he called it Vadhusara. And it passeth by the hermitage of Chyavana. And in this manner was born Chyavana of great ascetic power, the son of Bhrigu.

"And Bhrigu saw his child Chyavana and its beautiful mother. And the Rishi in a rage asked her, 'By whom wast thou made known to that Rakshasa who resolved to carry thee away? O thou of agreeable smiles, the Rakshasa could not know thee as my wife. Therefore tell me who it was that told the Rakshasa so, in order that I may curse him through anger.' And Pauloma replied, 'O possessor of the six attributes! I was identified to the Rakshasa by Agni (the god of fire). And he (the Rakshasa) bore me away, who cried like the Kurari (female osprey). And it was only by the ardent splendour of this thy son that I was rescued, for the Rakshasa (seeing this infant) let me go and himself falling to the ground was turned into ashes.'

"Sauti continued, 'Bhrigu, upon hearing this account from Pauloma, became exceedingly enraged. And in excess of passion the Rishi cursed Agni, saying, 'Thou shalt eat of all things.'"

So ends the sixth section called "the curse on Agni" in the Adi Parva.

SECTION VII
(Pauloma Parva continued)

"Sauti said, 'the god of fire enraged at the curse of Bhrigu, thus addressed the Rishi, 'What meaneth this rashness, O Brahmana, that thou hast displayed towards me? What transgression can be imputed to me who was labouring to do justice and speak the truth impartially? Being asked I gave the true answer. A witness who when interrogated about a fact of which he hath knowledge, representeth otherwise than it is, ruineth his ancestors and descendants both to the seventh generation. He, too, who, being fully cognisant of all the particulars of an affair, doth not disclose what he knoweth, when asked, is undoubtedly stained with guilt. I can also curse thee, but Brahmanas are held by me in high respect. Although these are known to thee, O Brahmana, I will yet speak of them, so please attend! Having, by ascetic power, multiplied myself, I am present in various forms, in places of the daily homa, at sacrifices extending for years, in places where holy rites are performed (such as marriage, etc.), and at other sacrifices. With the butter that is poured upon my flame according to the injunctions prescribed in the Vedas, the Devas and the Pitris are appeased. The Devas are the waters; the Pitris are also the waters. The Devas have with the Pitris an equal right to the sacrifices called Darshas and Purnamasas. The Devas therefore are the Pitris and the Pitris, the Devas. They are identical beings, worshipped together and also separately at the changes of the moon. The Devas and the Pitris eat what is poured upon me. I am therefore called the mouth of the Devas and the Pitris. At the new moon the Pitris, and at the full moon the Devas, are fed through my mouth, eating of the clarified butter that is poured on me. Being, as I am, their mouth, how am I to be an eater of all things (clean and unclean)?'

"Then Agni, after reflecting for a while, withdrew himself from all places; from places of the daily homa of the Brahmanas, from all long-extending sacrifices, from places of holy rites, and from other ceremonies. Without their Oms and Vashats, and deprived of their Swadhas and Swahas (sacrificial mantras during offerings), the whole body of creatures became much distressed at the loss of their (sacrificial) fire. The Rishis in great anxiety went to the gods and addressed them thus, 'Ye immaculate beings! The three regions of the universe are confounded at the cessation of their sacrifices and ceremonies in consequence of the loss of fire! Ordain what is to be done in this matter, so that there may be no loss of time.' Then the Rishis and the gods went together to the presence of Brahma. And they represented to him all about the curse on Agni and the consequent interruption of all ceremonies. And they said, 'O thou greatly fortunate! Once Agni hath been cursed by Bhrigu for some reason. Indeed, being the mouth of the gods and also the first who eateth of what is offered in sacrifices, the eater also of the sacrificial butter, how will Agni be reduced to the condition of one who eateth of all things promiscuously?' And the creator of the universe hearing these words of theirs summoned Agni to his presence. And Brahma addressed Agni, the creator of all and eternal as himself, in these gentle words, 'Thou art the creator of the worlds and thou art their destroyer! Thou preserves the three worlds and thou art the promoter of all sacrifices and ceremonies! Therefore behave thyself so that ceremonies be not interrupted. And, O thou eater of the sacrificial butter, why dost thou act so foolishly, being, as thou art, the Lord of all? Thou alone art always pure in the universe and thou art its stay! Thou shall not, with all thy body, be reduced to the state of one who eateth of all things promiscuously. O thou of flames, the flame that is in thy viler parts shall alone eat of all things alike. The body of thine which eateth of flesh (being in the stomach of all carnivorous animals) shall also eat of all things promiscuously. And as every thing touched by the sun's rays becometh pure, so shall everything be pure that shall be burnt by thy flames. Thou art, O fire, the supreme energy born of thy own power. Then, O Lord, by that power of thine make the Rishi's curse come true. Continue to receive thy own portion and that of the gods, offered at thy mouth.'

Sauti continued, "Then Agni replied to the Grandfather, 'So be it.' And he then went away to obey the command of the supreme Lord. The gods and the Rishis also returned in delight to the place whence they had come. And the Rishis began to perform as before their ceremonies and sacrifices. And the gods in heaven and all creatures of the world rejoiced exceedingly. And Agni too rejoiced in that he was free from the prospect of sin.

"Thus, O possessor of the six attributes, had Agni been cursed in the days of yore by Bhrigu. And such is the ancient history connected with the destruction of the Rakshasa, Pauloma and the birth of Chyavana.'"

Thus endeth the seventh section of the Pauloma Parva of the Adi Parva of the blessed Mahabharata.

SECTION VIII
(Pauloma Parva continued)

"Sauti said, 'O Brahmana, Chyavana, the son of Bhrigu, begot a son in the womb of his wife Sukanya. And that son was the illustrious Pramati of resplendent energy. And Pramati begot in the womb of Ghritachi a son called Ruru. And Ruru begot on his wife Pramadvara a son called Sunaka. And I shall relate to you in detail, O Brahmana, the entire history of Ruru of abundant energy. O listen to it then in full!

"Formerly there was a great Rishi called Sthulakesa possessed of ascetic power and learning and kindly disposed towards all creatures. At that time, O Brahmana sage, Viswavasu, the King of the Gandharvas, it is said, had intimacy with Menaka, the celestial dancing-girl. And the Apsara, Menaka, O thou of the Bhrigu race, when her time was come, brought forth an infant near the hermitage of Sthulakesa. And dropping the newborn infant on the banks of the river, O Brahmana, Menaka, the Apsara, being destitute of pity and shame, went away. And the Rishi, Sthulakesa, of great ascetic power, discovered the infant lying forsaken in a lonely part of the river- side. And he perceived that it was a female child, bright as the offspring of an Immortal and blazing, as it were, with beauty: And the great Brahmana, Sthulakesa, the first of Munis, seeing that female child, and filled with compassion, took it up and reared it. And the lovely child grew up in his holy habitation, the noble-minded and blessed Rishi Sthulakesa performing in due succession all the ceremonies beginning with that at birth as ordained by the divine law. And because she surpassed all of her sex in goodness, beauty, and every quality, the great Rishi called her by the name of Pramadvara. And the pious Ruru having seen Pramadvara in the hermitage of Sthulakesa became one whose heart was pierced by the god of love. And Ruru by means of his companions made his father Pramati, the son of Bhrigu, acquainted with his passion. And Pramati demanded her of the far-famed Sthulakesa for his son. And her foster-father betrothed the virgin Pramadvara to Ruru, fixing the nuptials for the day when the star Varga-Daivata (Purva-phalguni) would be ascendant.

"Then within a few days of the time fixed for the nuptials, the beautiful virgin while at play with companions of her own sex, her time having come, impelled by fate, trod upon a serpent which she did not perceive as it lay in coil. And the reptile, urged to execute the will of Fate, violently darted its envenomed fangs into the body of the heedless maiden. And stung by that serpent, she instantly dropped senseless on the ground, her colour faded and all the graces of her person went off. And with dishevelled hair she became a spectacle of woe to her companions and friends. And she who was so agreeable to behold became on her death what was too painful to look at. And the girl of slender waist lying on the ground like one asleep—being overcome with the poison of the snake—once more became more beautiful than in life. And her foster-father and the other holy ascetics who were there, all saw her lying motionless upon the ground with the splendour of a lotus. And then there came many noted Brahmanas filled with compassion, and they sat around her. And Swastyatreya, Mahajana, Kushika, Sankhamekhala, Uddalaka, Katha, and Sweta of great renown, Bharadwaja, Kaunakutsya, Arshtishena, Gautama, Pramati, and Pramati's son Ruru, and other inhabitants of the forest, came there. And when they saw that maiden lying dead on the ground overcome with the poison of the reptile that had bitten her, they all wept filled with compassion. But Ruru, mortified beyond measure, retired from the scene.'"

So ends the eighth section of the Pauloma Parva of the Adi Parva of the blessed Mahabharata.

SECTION IX
(Pauloma Parva continued)

"Sauti said, 'While those illustrious Brahmanas were sitting around the dead body of Pramadvara, Ruru, sorely afflicted, retired into a deep wood and wept aloud. And overwhelmed with grief he indulged in much piteous lamentation. And, remembering his beloved Pramadvara, he gave vent to his sorrow in the following words, 'Alas! The delicate fair one that increaseth my affliction lieth upon the bare ground. What can be more deplorable to us, her friends? If I have been charitable, if I have performed acts of penance, if I have ever revered my superiors, let the merit of these arts restore to life my beloved one! If from my birth I have been controlling my passions, adhered to my vows, let the fair Pramadvara rise from the ground.'

"And while Ruru was indulging in these lamentations for the loss of his bride, a messenger from heaven came to him in the forest and addressed him thus, 'The words thou utterest, O Ruru, in thy affliction are certainly ineffectual. For, O pious man, one belonging to this world whose days have run out can never come back to life. This poor child of a Gandharva and Apsara has had her days run out! Therefore, O child, thou shouldst not consign thy heart to sorrow. The great gods, however, have provided beforehand a means of her restoration to life. And if thou compliest with it, thou mayest receive back thy Pramadvara.'

"And Ruru replied, 'O messenger of heaven! What is that which the gods have ordained. Tell me in full so that (on hearing) I may comply with it. It behoveth thee to deliver me from grief!' And the celestial messenger said unto Ruru, 'Resign half of thy own life to thy bride, and then, O Ruru of the race of Bhrigu, thy Pramadvara shall rise from the ground.' 'O best of celestial messengers, I most willingly offer a moiety of my own life in favour of my bride. Then let my beloved one rise up once more in her dress and lovable form.'

"Sauti said, 'Then the king of Gandharvas (the father of Pramadvara) and the celestial messenger, both of excellent qualities, went to the god Dharma (the Judge of the dead) and addressed him, saying, 'If it be thy will, O Dharmaraja, let the amiable Pramadvara, the betrothed wife of Ruru, now lying dead, rise up with a moiety of Ruru's life.' And Dharmaraja answered, 'O messenger of the gods, if it be thy wish, let Pramadvara, the betrothed wife of Ruru, rise up endued with a moiety of Ruru's life.'

"Sauti continued, 'And when Dharmaraja had said so, that maiden of superior complexion, Pramadvara, endued with a moiety of Ruru's life, rose as from her slumber. This bestowal by Ruru of a moiety of his own span of life to resuscitate his bride afterwards led, as it would be seen, to a curtailment of Ruru's life.

"And on an auspicious day their fathers gladly married them with due rites. And the couple passed their days, devoted to each other. And Ruru having obtained such a wife, as is hard to be found, beautiful and bright as the filaments of the lotus, made a vow for the destruction of the serpent-race. And whenever he saw a serpent he became filled with great wrath and always killed it with a weapon.

"One day, O Brahmana, Ruru entered an extensive forest. And there he saw an old serpent of the Dundubha species lying stretched on the ground. And Ruru thereupon lifted up in anger his staff, even like to the staff of Death, for the purpose of killing it. Then the Dundubha, addressing Ruru, said, 'I have done thee no harm, O Brahmana! Then wherefore wilt thou slay me in anger?'"

So ends the ninth section of the Pauloma Parva of the Adi Parva of the blessed Mahabharata.

SECTION X
(Pauloma Parva continued)

"Sauti said, 'And Ruru, on hearing those words, replied, 'My wife, dear to me as life, was bit by a snake; upon which, I took, O snake, a dreadful vow, viz., that I would kill every snake that I might come across. Therefore shall I smite thee and thou shalt be deprived of life.'

"And the Dundubha replied, 'O Brahmana, the snakes that bite man are quite different in type. It behoveth thee not to slay Dundubhas who are serpents only in name. Subject like other serpents to the same calamities but not sharing their good fortune, in woe the same but in joy different, the Dundubhas should not be slain by thee under any misconception.'

"Sauti continued, 'And the Rishi Ruru hearing these words of the serpent, and seeing that it was bewildered with fear, albeit a snake of the Dundubha species, killed it not. And Ruru, the possessor of the six attributes, comforting the snake addressed it, saying, 'Tell me fully, O snake, who art thou thus metamorphosed?' And the Dundubha replied, 'O Ruru! I was formerly a Rishi by name Sahasrapat. And it is by the curse of a Brahmana that I have been transformed into a snake.' And Ruru asked, 'O thou best of snakes, for what wast thou cursed by a Brahmana in wrath? And how long also will thy form continue so?'"

And so ends the tenth section of the Pauloma Parva of the Adi Parva.

SECTION XI
(Pauloma Parva continued)

"Sauti continued 'The Dundubha then said, 'In former times, I had a friend Khagama by name. He was impetuous in his speech and possessed of spiritual power by virtue of his austerities. And one day when he was engaged in the Agni-hotra (Fire-sacrifice), I made a mock snake of blades of grass, and in a frolic attempted to frighten him with it. And anon he fell into a swoon. On recovering his senses, that truth-telling and vow-observing ascetic, burning with wrath, exclaimed, 'Since thou hast made a powerless mock snake to frighten me, thou shalt be turned even into a venomless serpent thyself by my curse.' O ascetic, I well knew the power of his penances; therefore with an agitated heart, I addressed him thus, bending low with joined hands, 'Friend, I did this by way of a joke, to excite thy laughter. It behoveth thee to forgive me and revoke thy curse.' And seeing me sorely troubled, the ascetic was moved, and he replied, breathing hot and hard.

'What I have said must come to pass. Listen to what I say and lay it to thy heart. O pious one! when Ruru the pure son of Pramati, will appear, thou shall be delivered from the curse the moment thou seest him. Thou art the very Ruru and the son of Pramati. On regaining my native form, I will tell thee something for thy good.'

"And that illustrious man and the best of Brahmanas then left his snake- body, and attained his own form and original brightness. He then addressed the following words to Ruru of incomparable power, 'O thou first of created beings, verily the highest virtue of man is sparing the life of others. Therefore a Brahmana should never take the life of any creature. A Brahmana should ever be mild. This is the most sacred injunction of the Vedas. A Brahmana should be versed in the Vedas and Vedangas, and should inspire all creatures with belief in God. He should be benevolent to all creatures, truthful, and forgiving, even as it is his paramount duty to retain the Vedas in his memory. The duties of the Kshatriya are not thine. To be stern, to wield the sceptre and to rule the subjects properly are the duties of the Kshatriya. Listen, O Ruru, to the account of the destruction of snakes at the sacrifice of Janamejaya in days of yore, and the deliverance of the terrified reptiles by that best of Dwijas, Astika, profound in Vedic lore and might in spiritual energy.'"

And so ends the eleventh section of the Pauloma Parva of the Adi Parva.

SECTION XII
(Pauloma Parva continued)

"Sauti continued, 'Ruru then asked, 'O best of Dwijas, why was king Janamejaya bent upon destroying the serpents?—And why and how were they saved by the wise Astika? I am anxious to hear all this in detail.'

"The Rishi replied, 'O Ruru, the important history of Astika you will learn from the lips of Brahmanas.' Saying this, he vanished.

"Sauti continued, 'Ruru ran about in search of the missing Rishi, and having failed to find him in all the woods, fell down on the ground, fatigued. And revolving in his mind the words of the Rishi, he was greatly confounded and seemed to be deprived of his senses. Regaining consciousness, he came home and asked his father to relate the history in question. Thus asked, his father related all about the story.'"

So ends the twelfth section in the Pauloma Parva of the Adi Parva.

SECTION XIII
(Astika Parva)

"Saunaka said, 'For what reason did that tiger among kings, the royal Janamejaya, determine to take the lives of the snakes by means of a sacrifice? O Sauti, tell us in full the true story. Tell us also why Astika, that best of regenerate ones, that foremost of ascetics, rescued the snakes from the blazing fire. Whose son was that monarch who celebrated the snake-sacrifice? And whose son also was that best of regenerate ones?'

"Sauti said, 'O best of speakers, this story of Astika is long. I will duly relate it in full, O listen!'

"Saunaka said, 'I am desirous of hearing at length the charming story of that Rishi, that illustrious Brahmana named Astika.'

"Sauti said, 'This history (first) recited by Krishna-Dwaipayana, is called a Purana by the Brahmanas. It was formerly narrated by my wise father, Lomaharshana, the disciple of Vyasa, before the dwellers of the Naimisha forest, at their request. I was present at the recital, and, O Saunaka, since thou askest me, I shall narrate the history of Astika exactly as I heard it. O listen, as I recite in full that sin-destroying story.

"The father of Astika was powerful like Prajapati. He was a Brahma-charin, always engaged in austere devotions. He ate sparingly, was a great ascetic, and had his lust under complete control. And he was known by the name of Jaratkaru. That foremost one among the Yayavaras, virtuous and of rigid vows, highly blessed and endued with great ascetic power, once undertook a journey over the world. He visited diverse places, bathed in diverse sacred waters, and rested where night overtook him. Endued with great energy, he practised religious austerities, hard to be practised by men of unrestrained souls. The sage lived upon air only, and renounced sleep for ever. Thus going about like a blazing fire, one day he happened to see his ancestors, hanging heads down in a great hole, their feet pointing upwards. On seeing them, Jaratkaru addressed them, saying:

'Who are you thus hanging heads down in this hole by a rope of virana fibres that is again secretly eaten into on all sides by a rat living here?'

"The ancestors said, 'We are Rishis of rigid vows, called Yayavaras. We are sinking low into the earth for want of offspring. We have a son named Jaratkaru. Woe to us! That wretch hath entered upon a life of austerities only! The fool doth not think of raising offspring by marriage! It is for that reason, viz., the fear of extinction of our race, that we are suspended in this hole. Possessed of means, we fare like unfortunates that have none! O excellent one, who art thou that thus sorrowest as a friend on our account? We desire to learn, O Brahmana, who thou art that standest by us, and why, O best of men, thou sorrowest for us that are so unfortunate.'

"Jaratkaru said, 'Ye are even my sires and grandsires; I am that Jaratkaru! O, tell me, how I may serve you.'

"The fathers then answered, 'Try thy best, O child, to beget a son to extend our line. Thou wilt then, O excellent one, have done a meritorious art for both thyself and us. Not by the fruits of virtue, not by ascetic penances well hoarded up, acquireth the merit which one doth by becoming a father. Therefore, O child, by our command, set thy heart upon marriage and offspring. Even this is our highest good.'

"Jaratkaru replied, 'I shall not marry for my sake, nor shall I earn wealth for enjoyment, but I shall do so for your welfare only. According to this understanding, I shall, agreeably to the Sastric ordinance, take a wife for attaining the end. I shall not act otherwise. If a bride may be had of the same name with me, whose friends would, besides, willingly give her to me as a gift in charity, I shall wed her duly. But who will give his daughter to a poor man like me for wife. I shall, however, accept any daughter given to me as alms. I shall endeavour, ye sires, even thus to wed a girl! Having given my word, I will not act otherwise. Upon her I will raise offspring for your redemption, so that, ye fathers, ye may attain to eternal regions (of bliss) and may rejoice as ye like.'"

So ends the thirteenth section in the Astika Parva of the Adi Parva.

SECTION XIV
(Astika Parva continued)

"Sauti said, 'That Brahmana of rigid vows then wandered over the earth for a wife but a wife found he not. One day he went into the forest, and recollecting the words of his ancestors, he thrice prayed in a faint voice for a bride. Thereupon Vasuki rose and offered his sister for the Rishi's acceptance. But the Brahmana hesitated to accept her, thinking her not to be of the same name with himself. The high-souled Jaratkaru thought within himself, 'I will take none for wife who is not of the same name with myself.' Then that Rishi of great wisdom and austere penances asked him, saying, 'Tell me truly what is the name of this thy sister, O snake.'

"Vasuki replied, 'O Jaratkaru, this my younger sister is called Jaratkaru. Given away by me, accept this slender-waisted damsel for thy spouse. O best of Brahmanas, for thee I reserved her. Therefore, take her.' Saying this, he offered his beautiful sister to Jaratkaru who then espoused her with ordained rites."

So ends the thirteenth section in the Astika Parva of the Adi Parva.

SECTION XV
(Astika Parva continued)

"Sauti said, 'O foremost of persons acquainted with Brahma, the mother of the snakes had cursed them of old, saying, 'He that hath the Wind for his charioteer (viz., Agni) shall burn you all in Janamejaya's sacrifice!' It was to neutralise that curse that the chief of the snakes married his sister to that high-souled Rishi of excellent vows. The Rishi wedded her according to the rites ordained (in the scriptures), and from them was born a high-souled son called Astika. An illustrious ascetic; versed in the Vedas and their branches, he regarded all with an even eye, and removed the fears of both his parents.

"Then, after a long space of time, a king descending from the Pandava line celebrated a great sacrifice known as the Snake-sacrifice, After that sacrifice had commenced for the destruction of the snakes, Astika delivered the Nagas, viz., his brothers and maternal uncles and other snakes (from a fiery death). And he delivered his fathers also by begetting offspring. And by his austerities, O Brahmana, and various vows and study of the Vedas, he freed himself from all his debts. By sacrifices, at which various kinds of offerings were made, he propitiated the gods. By practising the Brahmacharya mode of life he conciliated the Rishis; and by begetting offspring he gratified his ancestors.

"Thus Jaratkaru of rigid vows discharged the heavy debt he owed to his sires who being thus relieved from bondage ascended to heaven. Thus having acquired great religious merit, Jaratkaru, after a long course of years, went to heaven, leaving Astika behind. There is the story of Astika that I have related duly Now, tell me, O tiger of Bhrigu's race, what else I shall narrate."

So ends the fifteenth section in the Astika Parva of the Adi Parva.

SECTION XVI
(Astika Parva continued)

"Saunaka said, 'O Sauti, relate once more in detail this history of the learned and virtuous Astika. Our curiosity for hearing it is great. O amiable one, thou speakest sweetly, with proper accent and emphasis; and we are well-pleased with thy speech. Thou speakest even as thy father. Thy sire was ever ready to please us. Tell us now the story as thy father had related it.'

"Sauti said, 'O thou that art blest with longevity, I shall narrate the history of Astika as I heard it from my father. O Brahmana, in the golden age, Prajapati had two daughters. O sinless one, the sisters were endowed with wonderful beauty. Named Kadru and Vinata, they became the wives of Kasyapa. Kasyapa derived great pleasure from his two wedded wives and being gratified he, resembling Prajapati himself, offered to give each of them a boon. Hearing that their lord was willing to confer on them their choice blessings, those excellent ladies felt transports of joy. Kadru wished to have for sons a thousand snakes all of equal splendour. And Vinata wished to bring forth two sons surpassing the thousand offsprings of Kadru in strength, energy, size of body, and prowess. Unto Kadru her lord gave that boon about a multitude of offspring. And unto Vinata also, Kasyapa said, 'Be it so!' Then Vinata, having obtained her prayer, rejoiced greatly. Obtaining two sons of superior prowess, she regarded her boon fulfilled. Kadru also obtained her thousand sons of equal splendour. 'Bear the embryos carefully,' said Kasyapa, and then he went into the forest, leaving his two wives pleased with his blessings.'

"Sauti continued, 'O best of regenerate ones, after a long time, Kadru brought forth a thousand eggs, and Vinata two. Their maid-servants deposited the eggs separately in warm vessels. Five hundred years passed away, and the thousand eggs produced by Kadru burst and out came the progeny. But the twins of Vinata did not appear. Vinata was jealous, and therefore she broke one of the eggs and found in it an embryo with the upper part developed but the lower one undeveloped. At this, the child in the egg became angry and cursed his mother, saying. 'Since thou hast prematurely broken this egg, thou shall serve as a slave. Shouldst thou wait five hundred years and not destroy, or render the other egg half- developed, by breaking it through impatience, then the illustrious child within it will deliver thee from slavery! And if thou wouldst have the child strong, thou must take tender care of the egg for all this time!' Thus cursing his mother, the child rose to the sky. O Brahmana, even he is the charioteer of Surya, always seen in the hour of morning!

"Then at the expiration of the five hundred years, bursting open the other egg, out came Garuda, the serpent-eater. O tiger of Bhrigu's race, immediately on seeing the light, that son of Vinata left his mother. And the lord of birds, feeling hungry, took wing in quest of the food assigned to him by the Great Ordainer of all.".

So ends the sixteenth section in the Astika Parva of the Adi Parva.

SECTION XVII
(Astika Parva continued)

"Sauti said, 'O ascetic, about this time the two sisters saw approaching near, that steed of complacent appearance named Uchchaihsravas who was worshipped by the gods, that gem of steeds, who arose at the churning of the Ocean for nectar. Divine, graceful, perpetually young, creation's master-piece, and of irresistible vigour, it was blest with every auspicious mark.'

"Saunaka asked, 'Why did the gods churn the Ocean for nectar, and under what circumstances and when as you say, did that best of steeds so powerful and resplendent spring?'

"Sauti said, 'There is a mountain named Meru, of blazing appearance, and looking like a heap of effulgence. The rays of the Sun falling on its peaks of golden lustre are dispersed by them. Decked with gold and exceedingly beautiful, that mountain is the haunt of the gods and the Gandharvas. It is immeasurable and unapproachable by men of manifold sins. Dreadful beasts of prey wander over its breasts, and it is illuminated by many divine life-giving herbs. It stands kissing the heavens by its height and is the first of mountains. Ordinary people cannot even think of ascending it. It is graced with trees and streams, and resounds with the charming melody of winged choirs. Once the celestials sat on its begemmed peak—in conclave. They who had practised penances and observed excellent vows for amrita now seemed to be eager seekers after amrita (celestial ambrosia). Seeing the celestial assembly in anxious mood Nara-yana said to Brahman, 'Do thou churn the Ocean with the gods and the Asuras. By doing so, amrita will be obtained as also all drugs and gems. O ye gods, churn the Ocean, ye will discover amrita.'"

So ends the seventeenth section in the Astika Parva of the Adi Parva.

SECTION XVIII
(Astika Parva continued]

"Sauti said, 'There is a mountain called Mandara adorned with cloud-like peaks. It is the best of mountains, and is covered all over with intertwining herbs. There countless birds pour forth their melodies, and beasts of prey roam about. The gods, the Apsaras and the Kinnaras visit the place. Upwards it rises eleven thousand yojanas, and descends downwards as much. The gods wanted to tear it up and use it as a churning rod but failing to do so came to Vishnu and Brahman who were sitting together, and said unto them, 'Devise some efficient scheme, consider, ye gods, how Mandara may be dislodged for our good.'

"Sauti continued, 'O son of Bhrigu! Vishnu with Brahman assented to it. And the lotus-eyed one (Vishnu) laid the hard task on the mighty Ananta, the prince of snakes. The powerful Ananta, directed thereto both by Brahman and Narayana, O Brahmana, tore up the mountain with the woods thereon and with the denizens of those woods. And the gods came to the shore of the Ocean with Ananta and addressed the Ocean, saying, 'O Ocean; we have come to churn thy waters for obtaining nectar.' And the Ocean replied, 'Be it so, as I shall not go without a share of it. I am able to bear the prodigious agitation of my waters set up by the mountain.' The gods then went to the king of tortoises and said to him, 'O Tortoise-king, thou wilt have to hold the mountain on thy back!' The Tortoise-king agreed, and Indra contrived to place the mountain on the former's back.

"And the gods and the Asuras made of Mandara a churning staff and Vasuki the cord, and set about churning the deep for amrita. The Asuras held Vasuki by the hood and the gods held him by the tail. And

Ananta, who was on the side of the gods, at intervals raised the snake's hood and suddenly lowered it. And in consequence of the stretch Vasuki received at the hands of the gods and the Asuras, black vapours with flames issued from his mouth. These, turned into clouds charged with lightning, poured showers that refreshed the tired gods. And flowers that also fell on all sides of the celestials from the trees on the whirling Mandara, refreshed them.

"Then, O Brahmana, out of the deep came a tremendous roar like unto the roar of the clouds at the Universal Dissolution. Diverse aquatic animals being crushed by the great mountain gave up the ghost in the salt waters. And many denizens of the lower regions and the world of Varuna were killed. Large trees with birds on the whirling Mandara were torn up by the roots and fell into the water. The mutual friction of those trees also produced fires that blazed up frequently. The mountain thus looked like a mass of dark clouds charged with lightning. O Brahmana, the fire spread, and consumed the lions, elephants and other creatures that were on the mountain. Then Indra extinguished that fire by pouring down heavy showers.

"After the churning, O Brahmana, had gone on for some time, gummy exudations of various trees and herbs vested with the properties of amrita mingled with the waters of the Ocean. And the celestials attained to immortality by drinking of the water mixed with those gums and with the liquid extract of gold. By degrees, the milky water of the agitated deep turned into clarified butter by virtue of those gums and juices. But nectar did not appear even then. The gods came before the boon-granting Brahman seated on his seat and said, 'Sire, we are spent up, we have no strength left to churn further. Nectar hath not yet arisen so that now we have no resource save Narayana.'

"On hearing them, Brahman said to Narayana, 'O Lord, condescend to grant the gods strength to churn the deep afresh.'

"Then Narayana agreeing to grant their various prayers, said, 'Ye wise ones, I grant you sufficient strength. Go, put the mountain in position again and churn the water.'

"Re-established thus in strength, the gods recommenced churning. After a while, the mild Moon of a thousand rays emerged from the Ocean. Thereafter sprung forth Lakshmi dressed in white, then Soma, then the White Steed, and then the celestial gem Kaustubha which graces the breast of Narayana. Then Lakshmi, Soma and the Steed, fleet as the mind, all came before the gods on high. Then arose the divine Dhanwantari himself with the white vessel of nectar in his hand. And seeing him, the Asuras set up a loud cry, saying, 'It be ours.'

"And at length rose the great elephant, Airavata, of huge body and with two pair of white tusks. And him took Indra the wielder of the thunderbolt. But with the churning still going on, the poison Kalakuta appeared at last. Engulfing the Earth it suddenly blazed up like a fire attended with fumes. And by the scent of the fearful Kalakuta, the three worlds were stupefied. And then Siva, being solicited by Brahman, swallowed that poison for the safety of the creation. The divine Maheswara held it in his throat, and it is said that from that time he is called Nilakantha (blue-throated). Seeing all these wondrous things, the Asuras were filled with despair, and got themselves prepared for entering into hostilities with the gods for the possession of Lakshmi and Amrita. Thereupon Narayana called his bewitching Maya (illusive power) to his aid, and assuming the form of an enticing female, coquetted with the Danavas. The Danavas and the Daityas charmed with her exquisite beauty and grace lost their reason and unanimously placed the Amrita in the hands of that fair damsel.'"

So ends the eighteenth section in the Astika Parva of the Adi Parva.

SECTION XIX
(Astika Parva continued)

"Sauti said, 'Then the Daityas and the Danavas equipped with first-class armours and various weapons attacked the gods. In the meantime the valiant Lord Vishnu in the form of an enchantress accompanied by Nara deceived the mighty Danavas and took away the Amrita from their hands.

"And all the gods at that time of great fright drank the Amrita with delight, receiving it from Vishnu. And while the gods were partaking of it, after which they had so much hankered, a Danava named Rahu was also drinking it among them in the guise of a god. And when the Amrita had reached Rahu's throat only, Surya and Soma (recognised him and) intimated the fact to the gods. And Narayana instantly cut off with his discus the well-adorned head of the Danava who was drinking the Amrita without permission. And the huge head of the Danava, cut off by the discus and resembling a mountain peak, then rose up to the sky and began to utter dreadful cries. And the Danava's headless trunk, falling upon the ground and rolling thereon, made the Earth tremble with her mountains, forests and islands. And from that time there is a long-standing quarrel between Rahu's head and Surya and Soma. And to this day it swalloweth Surya and Soma (during solar and lunar eclipses).

"Then Narayana quitting his enchanting female form and hurling many terrible weapons at the Danavas, made them tremble. And thus on the shores of the salt-water sea, commenced the dreadful battle of the gods and the Asuras. And sharp-pointed javelins and lances and various weapons by thousands began to be discharged on all sides. And mangled with the discus and wounded with swords, darts and maces, the Asuras in large numbers vomited blood and lay prostrate on the earth. Cut off from the trunks with sharp double-edged swords, heads adorned with bright gold, fell continually on the field of battle. Their bodies drenched in gore, the great Asuras lay dead everywhere. It seemed as if red-dyed mountain peaks lay scattered all around. And when the Sun rose in his splendour, thousands of warriors struck one another with weapons. And cries of distress were heard everywhere. The warriors fighting at a distance from one another brought one another down by sharp iron missiles, and those fighting at close quarters slew one another with blows of their fists. And the air was filled with shrieks of distress. Everywhere were heard the alarming sounds,—'cut', 'pierce', 'at them', 'hurl down', 'advance'.

"And when the battle was raging fiercely, Nara and Narayana entered the field. And Narayana seeing the celestial bow in the hand of Nara, called to mind his own weapon, the Danava-destroying discus. And lo! the discus, Sudarsana, destroyer of enemies, like to Agni in effulgence and dreadful in battle, came from the sky as soon as thought of. And when it came, Narayana of fierce energy, possessing arms like the trunk of an elephant, hurled with great force that weapon of extraordinary lustre, effulgent as blazing fire, dreadful and capable of destroying hostile towns. And that discus blazing like the fire that consumeth all things at the end of Yuga, hurled with force from the hands of Narayana, and falling constantly everywhere, destroyed the Daityas and the Danavas by thousands. Sometimes it blazed like fire and consumed them all; sometimes it struck them down as it coursed through the sky; and sometimes, falling on the earth, it drank their life-blood like a goblin.

"On the other hand, the Danavas, white as the clouds from which the rain hath dropped, possessing great strength and bold hearts, ascended the sky, and by hurling down thousands of mountains, continually harassed the gods. And those dreadful mountains, like masses of clouds, with their trees and flat tops, falling from the sky, collided with one another and produced a tremendous roar. And when thousands of warriors shouted without intermission in the field of battle and mountains with the woods thereon began to fall around, the earth with her forests trembled. Then the divine Nara appeared at the scene of the dreadful conflict between the Asuras and the Ganas (the followers of Rudra), and reducing to dust those rocks by means of his gold-headed arrows, he covered the heavens with dust. Thus discomfited by the gods, and seeing the furious discus scouring the fields of heaven like a blazing flame, the mighty Danavas entered the bowels of the earth, while others plunged into the sea of salt-waters.

"And having gained the victory, the gods offered due respect to Mandara and placed him again on his own base. And the nectar-bearing gods made the heavens resound with their shouts, and went to their own abodes. And the gods, on returning to the heavens, rejoiced greatly, and Indra and the other deities made over to Narayana the vessel of Amrita for careful keeping.'"

And so ends the nineteenth section in the Astika Parva of the Adi Parva.

SECTION XX
(Astika Parva continued)

"Sauti said, 'Thus have I recited to you the whole story of how Amrita was churned out of the Ocean, and the occasion on which the horse Uchchaihsravas of great beauty and incomparable prowess was obtained. It was this horse about which Kadru asked Vinata, saying, 'Tell me, amiable sister, without taking much time, of what colour Uchchaishravas is.' And Vinata answered, 'That prince of steeds is certainly white. What dost thou think, sister? Say thou what is its colour. Let us lay a wager upon it.' Kadru replied, then, 'O thou of sweet smiles. I think that horse is black in its tail. Beauteous one, bet with me that she who loseth will become the other's slave.'

'Sauti continued, 'Thus wagering with each other about menial service as a slave, the sisters went home, and resolved to satisfy themselves by examining the horse next day. And Kadru, bent upon practising a deception, ordered her thousand sons to transform themselves into black hair and speedily cover the horse's tail in order that she might not become a slave. But her sons, the snakes, refusing to do her bidding, she cursed them, saying, 'During the snake-sacrifice of the wise king Janamejaya of the Pandava race, Agni shall consume you all.' And the Grandsire (Brahman) himself heard this exceedingly cruel curse pronounced by Kadru, impelled by the fates. And seeing that the snakes had multiplied exceedingly, the Grandsire, moved by kind consideration for his creatures, sanctioned with all the gods this curse of Kadru. Indeed, as the snakes were of virulent poison, great prowess and excess of strength, and ever bent on biting other creatures, their mother's conduct towards them—those persecutors of all creatures,—was very proper for the good of all creatures. Fate always inflicts punishment of death on those who seek the death of other creatures. The gods, having exchanged such sentiments with one another, supported Kadru's action (and went away). And Brahman, calling Kasyapa to him, spake unto him these words, 'O thou pure one who overcomest all enemies, these snakes begotten by you, who are of virulent poison and huge bodies, and ever intent on biting other creatures, have been cursed by their mother. O son, do not grieve for it in the least. The destruction of the snakes in the sacrifice hath, indeed, been ordained long ago.' Saying this, the divine Creator of the Universe comforted Kasyapa and imparted to that illustrious one the knowledge of neutralising poison."

And so ends the twentieth section in the Astika Parva of the Adi Parva.

SECTION XXI
(Astika Parva continued)

"Sauti said, 'Then when the night had passed away and the sun had risen in the morning, O thou whose wealth is asceticism, the two sisters Kadru and Vinata, having laid a wager about slavery, went with haste and impatience to view the steed Uchchaishravas from a near point. On their way they saw the Ocean, that receptacle of waters, vast and deep, rolling and tremendously roaring, full of fishes large enough to swallow the whale, and abounding with huge makaras and creatures of various forms by thousands, and rendered inaccessible by the presence of other terrible, monster-shaped, dark, and fierce aquatic animals, abounding with tortoises and crocodiles, the mine of all kinds of gems, the home of Varuna (the water-God), the excellent and beautiful residence of the Nagas, the lord of all rivers, the abode of the subterranean fire, the friend (or asylum) of the Asuras, the terror of all creatures, the grand reservoir of water, and ever immutable. It is holy, beneficial to the gods, and is the great source of nectar; without limits, inconceivable, sacred, and highly wonderful. It is dark, terrible with the sound of aquatic creatures, tremendously roaring, and full of deep whirl-pools. It is an object of terror to all creatures. Moved by the winds blowing from its shores and heaving high, agitated and disturbed, it seems to dance everywhere with uplifted hands represented by its surges. Full of swelling billows caused by the waxing and waning of the moon the parent of Vasudeva's great conch called Panchajanya, the great mine of gems, its waters were formerly disturbed in consequence of the agitation caused within them by the Lord Govinda of immeasurable prowess when he had assumed the form of a wild boar for raising the (submerged) Earth. Its bottom, lower than the nether regions, the vow observing regenerate Rishi Atri could not fathom after (toiling for) a hundred years. It becomes the bed of the lotus-naveled Vishnu when at the termination of every Yuga that deity of immeasurable power enjoys yoga-nidra, the deep sleep under the spell of spiritual meditation. It is the refuge of Mainaka fearful of falling thunder, and the retreat of the Asuras overcome in fierce encounters. It offers water as sacrificial butter to the blazing fire issuing from the mouth of Varava (the Ocean-mare). It is fathomless and without limits, vast and immeasurable, and the lord of rivers.

"And they saw that unto it rushed mighty rivers by thousands with proud gait, like amorous competitors, each eager for meeting it, forestalling the others. And they saw that it was always full, and always dancing in its waves. And they saw that it was deep and abounding with fierce whales and makaras. And it resounded constantly with the terrible sounds of aquatic creatures. And they saw that it was vast, and wide as the expanse of space, unfathomable, and limitless, and the grand reservoir of water.'"

SECTION XXII
(Astika Parva continued)

"Sauti said, 'The Nagas after consultation arrived at the conclusion that they should do their mother's bidding, for if she failed in obtaining her desire she might withdraw her affection and burn them all. If, on the other hand, she were graciously inclined, she might free them from her curse. They said, 'We will certainly render the horse's tail black.' And it is said that they then went and became hairs in the horse's tail.

"Now the two co-wives had laid the wager. And having laid the wager, O best of Brahmanas, the two sisters Kadru and Vinata, the daughters of Daksha, proceeded in great delight along the sky to see the other side of the Ocean. And on their way they saw the Ocean, that receptacle of waters, incapable of being easily disturbed, mightily agitated all of a sudden by the wind, and roaring tremendously; abounding with fishes capable of swallowing the whale and full of makaras; containing also creatures of diverse forms counted by thousands; frightful from the presence of horrible monsters, inaccessible, deep, and terrible, the mine of all kinds of gems, the home of Varuna (the water-god), the wonderful habitations of the Nagas, the lord of rivers, the abode of the subterranean fire; the residence of the Asuras and of many dreadful creatures; the reservoir of water, not subject to decay, aromatic, and wonderful, the great source of the amrita of the celestials; immeasurable and inconceivable, containing waters that are holy, filled to the brim by many thousands of great rivers, dancing as it were in waves. Such was the Ocean, full of rolling waves, vast as the expanse of the sky, deep, of body lighted with the flames of subterranean fire, and roaring, which the sisters quickly passed over.'"

And so ends the twenty-second section in the Astika Parva of the Adi Parva.

SECTION XXIII
(Astika Parva continued)

"Sauti said, 'Having crossed the Ocean, Kadru of swift speed, accompanied by Vinata, soon alighted near the horse. They then both beheld that foremost of steeds of great speed, with body white as the rays of the moon but having black hairs (in the tail). And observing many black hairs in the tail, Kadru put Vinata, who was deeply dejected, into slavery. And thus Vinata having lost the wager, entered into a state of slavery and became exceedingly sorry.

"In the meantime, when his time came, burst forth from the egg without (the help of his) mother, Garuda of great splendour, enkindling all the points of the universe, that mighty being endued with strength, that bird capable of assuming at will any form, of going at will everywhere, and of calling to his aid at will any measure of energy. Effulgent like a heap of fire, he shone terribly. Of lustre equal to that of the fire at the end of the Yuga, his eyes were bright like the lightning-flash. And soon after birth, that bird grew in size and increasing his body ascended the skies. Fierce and vehemently roaring, he looked as terrible as second Ocean-fire. And all the deities seeing him, sought the protection of Vibhavasu (Agni). And they bowed down to that deity of manifold forms seated on his seat and spake unto him these words, 'O Agni, extend not thy body! Wilt thou consume us? Lo, this huge heap of thy flames is spreading wide!' And Agni replied, 'O, ye persecutors of the Asuras, it is not as ye imagine. This is Garuda of great strength and equal to me in splendour, endued with great energy, and born to promote the joy of Vinata. Even the sight of this heap of effulgence hath caused this delusion in you. He is the mighty son of Kasyapa, the destroyer of the Nagas, engaged in the well-being of the gods, and the foe of the Daityas and the Rakshasas. Be not afraid of it in the least. Come with me and see.' Thus addressed, the gods from a distance.

"The gods said, 'Thou art a Rishi (i.e., one cognisant of all mantras), share of the largest portion in sacrifices, ever resplendent, the controller along with the Rishi wended their way towards Garuda and adored him of birds, the presiding spirit of the animate and the inanimate universe. Thou art the destroyer of all, the creator of all; thou art the very Hiranyagarbha; thou art the progenitor of creation in the form of Daksha and the other Prajapatis; thou art Indra (the king of the gods), thou art Hayagriva the steed necked incarnation of Vishnu; thou art the arrow (Vishnu himself, as he became such in the hands of Mahadeva at the burning of Tripura); thou art the lord of the universe; thou art the mouth of Vishnu; thou art the four-faced Padmaja; thou art the Brahmana (i.e., wise), thou art Agni, Pavana, etc. (i.e., the presiding deity of every object in the universe). Thou art knowledge, thou art the illusion to which we are all subject; thou art the all-pervading spirit; thou art the lord of the gods; thou art the great Truth; thou art fearless; thou art ever unchanged; thou art Brahma without attributes; thou art the energy of the Sun; thou art the intellectual functions; thou art our great protector; thou art the ocean of holiness; thou art purity; thou art bereft of the attributes of darkness; thou art the possessor of the six high attributes; thou art he who cannot be withstood in contest. From thee have emanated all things; thou art of excellent deeds; thou art all that hath not been and all that hath been. Thou art pure knowledge; thou displayest to us, as Surya does by his rays, this animate and inanimate universe; thou darkenest the splendour of Surya at every moment, and thou art the destroyer of all; thou art all that is perishable and all that is imperishable. O thou resplendent as Agni, thou burnest all even as Surya in his anger burneth all creatures. O terrible one, thou resistest even as the fire that destroys everything at the time of the Universal Dissolution. O mighty Garuda who movest in the skies, we seek thy protection. O lord of birds thy energy is extraordinary, thy splendour is that of fire, thy brightness is like that of the lightning that no darkness can approach. Thou reachest the very clouds, and art both the cause and the effect; the dispenser of boons and invincible in prowess. O Lord, this whole universe is rendered hot by thy splendour, bright as the lustre of heated gold. Protect these high-souled gods, who overcome by thee and terrified withal, are flying along the heavens in different directions on their celestial cars. O thou best of birds, thou Lord of all, thou art the son of the merciful and high-souled Rishi Kasyapa; therefore, be not wroth but have mercy on the universe. Thou art Supreme. O pacify thy anger and preserve us. At thy voice, loud as the roar of the thunder, the ten points, the skies, the heavens, the Earth and our hearts, O bird, thou art continuously shaking. O, diminish this thy body resembling Agni. At the sight of the splendour resembling that of Yama when in wrath, our hearts lose all equanimity and quake. O thou lord of birds, be propitious to us who solicit thy mercy! O illustrious one, bestow on us good fortune and joy.'

'And that bird of fair feathers, thus adored by the deities and diverse sections of Rishis, reduced his own energy and splendour.'"

And thus ends the twenty-third section in the Astika Parva of the Adi Parva.

SECTION XXIV
(Astika Parva continued)

"Sauti said, 'Then hearing of and beholding his own body, that bird of beautiful feathers diminished its size.'

"And Garuda said, 'Let no creature be afraid; as ye are in a fright at the sight of my terrible form, I shall diminish my energy.'

"Sauti continued, 'Then that bird capable of going everywhere at will, that ranger of the skies capable of calling to his aid any measure of energy, bearing Aruna on his back, wended from his father's home and arrived at his mother's side on the other shore of the great ocean. And he placed Aruna of great splendour in the eastern regions, just at a time when Surya had resolved to burn the worlds with his fierce rays.'

"Saunaka said, 'When did the revered Surya resolve at the time to burn the worlds? What wrong was done to him by the gods that provoked his ire?'

"Sauti said, 'O sinless one, when Rahu was drinking nectar among the gods at the time of the churning of the ocean he was pointed out to the gods by Surya and Soma, and from that time he conceived an enmity towards those deities. And upon this Rahu sought to devour his afflictor (Surya), became wroth, and thought, 'Oh, this enmity of Rahu towards me hath sprung from my desire of benefiting the gods. And this dire consequence I alone have to sustain. Indeed, at this pass help I obtain not. And before the very eyes of the denizens of heaven I am going to be devoured and they brook it quietly. Therefore, for the destruction of the worlds must I strive.' And with this resolution he went to the mountains of the west.

"And from that place he began to radiate his heat around for the destruction of the world. And then the great Rishis, approaching the gods, spake unto them, 'Lo, in the middle of the night springeth a great heat striking terror into every heart, and destructive of the three worlds.' Then the gods, accompanied by the Rishis, wended to the Grandsire, and said unto him, 'O what is this great heat today that causeth such panic? Surya hath not yet risen, still the destruction (of the world) is obvious. O Lord, what will happen when he

41

doth rise?' The Grandsire replied, 'Indeed, Surya is prepared to rise today for the destruction of the world. As soon as he will appear he will burn everything into a heap of ashes. By me, however, hath the remedy been provided beforehand. The intelligent son of Kasyapa is known to all by the name of Aruna. He is huge of body and of great splendour; he shall stay in front of Surya, doing the duty of his charioteer and taking away all the energy of the former. And this will ensure the welfare of the worlds, of the Rishis, and of the dwellers in heaven.'

"Sauti continued, 'Aruna, at the behest of the Grandsire, did all that he was ordered to do. And Surya rose veiled by Aruna's person. I have told thee now why Surya was in wrath, and how Aruna, the brother of Garuda, was appointed as his charioteer. Hear next of that other question asked by thee a little while ago.'"

And so ends the twenty-fourth section in the Astika Parva of the Adi Parva.

SECTION XXV
(Astika Parva continued)

"Sauti said, 'Then that bird of great strength and energy and capable of going at will to every place repaired to his mother's side on the other shore of the great ocean. Thither lived Vinata in affliction, defeated in wager and put into a state of slavery. Once Kadru calling Vinata who had prostrated herself before the former, addressed her these words in the presence of her son, 'O gentle Vinata, there is in the midst of the ocean, in a remote quarter, a delightful and fair region inhabited by the Nagas. Bear me thither!' At this that mother of the bird of fair feathers bore (on her shoulders) the mother of the snakes. And Garuda also, directed by his mother's words, carried (on his back) the snakes. And that ranger of the skies born of Vinata began to ascend towards the Sun. And thereupon the snakes, scorched by the rays of the Sun, swooned away. And Kadru seeing her sons in that state prayed to Indra, saying, 'I bow to thee, thou Lord of all the gods! I bow to thee, thou slayer of Vritra! I bow to thee, thou slayer of Namuchi! O thou of a thousand eyes, consort of Sachi! By thy showers, be thou the protector of the snakes scorched by the Sun. O thou best of the deities, thou art our great protector. O Purandara, thou art able to grant rain in torrents. Thou art Vayu (the air), the clouds, fire, and the lightning of the skies. Thou art the propeller of the clouds, and hast been called the great cloud (i.e., that which will darken the universe at the end of Yuga). Thou art the fierce and incomparable thunder, and the roaring clouds. Thou art the Creator of the worlds and their Destroyer. Thou art unconquered. Thou art the light of all creatures, Aditya, Vibhavasu, and the wonderful elements. Thou art the ruler of all the gods. Thou art Vishnu. Thou hast a thousand eyes. Thou art a god, and the final resource. Thou art, O deity, all amrita, and the most adored Soma. Thou art the moment, the lunar day, the bala (minute), thou art the kshana (4 minutes). Thou art the lighted fortnight, and also the dark fortnight. Thou art kala, thou kashtha, and thou Truti. Thou art the year, the seasons, the months, the nights, and the days. Thou art the fair Earth with her mountains and forests. Thou art also the firmament, resplendent with the Sun. Thou art the great Ocean with heaving billows and abounding with whales, swallowers of whales, and makaras, and various fishes. Thou art of great renown, always adored by the wise and by the great Rishis with minds rapt in contemplation. Thou drinkest, for the good of all creatures, the Soma juice in sacrifices and the clarified butter offered with sacred invocation. Thou art always worshipped at sacrifices by Brahmanas moved by desire of fruit. O thou of incomparable mass of strength, thou art sung in the Vedas and Vedangas. It is for that reason that learned Brahmanas bent upon performing sacrifices, study the Vedas with every care.'"

And so ends the twenty-fifth section in the Astika Parva of the Adi Parva.

SECTION XXVI
(Astika Parva continued)

THE MAHABHARATA

"Sauti said, 'And then Indra, the king of gods, having the best of horses for his bearer, thus adored by Kadru, covered the entire firmament with masses of blue clouds. And he commanded the clouds, saying, Pour ye, your vivifying and blessed drops!' And those clouds, luminous with lightning, and incessantly roaring against each other in the welkin, poured abundant water. And the sky, in consequence of those wonderful and terribly-roaring clouds that were incessantly begetting vast quantities of water, looked as if the end of Yuga had come. And in consequence of the myriads of waves caused in the falling torrents, the deep roar of the clouds, the flashes of lightning, the violence of the wind, and the general agitation, the sky looked as if dancing in madness. The sky became overcast, and the rays of the Sun and the Moon totally disappeared in consequence of that incessant downpour.

"And upon Indra's causing that downpour, the Nagas became exceedingly delighted. And the Earth was filled with water all around. And the cool, clear water reached even the nether regions. And there were countless waves of water all over the Earth. And the snakes with their mother reached (in safety) the island called Ramaniyaka."

And so ends the twenty-sixth section in the Astika Parva of the Adi Parva.

SECTION XXVII
(Astika Parva continued)

"Sauti said, 'And then the Nagas drenched by that shower, became exceedingly glad. And borne by that bird of fair feathers, they soon arrived at the island. That island had been fixed by the Creator of the Universe as the abode of the makaras. There they saw the terrible Lavana Samudra (ocean of salt). On arriving there with Garuda, they saw there a beautiful forest washed by the waters of the sea and resounding with the music of winged choirs. And there were clusters of trees all around laden with various fruits and flowers. And there were also fair mansions all around; and many tanks full of lotuses. And it was also adorned with many lakes of pure water. And if was refreshed with pure incense-breathing breezes. And it was adorned with many a tree that grew only on the hills of Malaya, and seemed by their tallness to reach the very heavens. And there were also various other trees whose flowers were scattered all around by the breeze. And that forest was charming and dear to the Gandharvas and always gave them pleasure. And it was full of bees maddened with the honey they sucked. And the sight of all this was exceedingly delightful. And in consequence of many things there, capable of charming everybody, that forest was fair, delightful, and holy. And, echoing with the notes of various birds, it delighted greatly the sons of Kadru.

"And the snakes, after arriving at that forest, began to enjoy themselves. And they commanded the lord of birds, viz., Garuda, of great energy, saying, 'Convey us to some other fair island with pure water. Thou ranger of the skies, thou must have seen many fair regions while coursing (through the air).' Garuda, after reflecting for a few moments, asked his mother Vinata, saying, 'Why, mother, have I to do the bidding of the snakes?' Vinata thus questioned by him spake unto that ranger of the skies, her son, invested with every virtue, of great energy, and great strength, as follows: "Vinata said, 'O thou best of birds, I have become, from misfortune, the slave of my co-wife. The snakes, by an act of deception, caused me to lose my bet and have made me so.' When his mother had told him the reason, that ranger of the skies, dejected with grief, addressed the snakes, saying, 'Tell me, ye snakes, by bringing what thing, gaining a knowledge of what thing, or doing what act of prowess, we may be freed from this state of bondage to you.'" Sauti continued, 'The snakes, hearing him, said, 'Bring thou amrita by force. Then O bird, shall you be freed from bondage.'" And so ends the twenty-seventh section in the Astika Parva of the Adi Parva.

SECTION XXVIII
(Astika Parva continued)

"Sauti said, 'Garuda, thus addressed by the snakes, then said unto his mother, 'I shall go to bring amrita, I desire to eat something in the way. Direct me to it.' Vinata replied, 'In a remote region in the midst of the ocean, the Nishadas have their fair home. Having eaten the thousands of Nishadas that live there, bring thou amrita. But let not thy heart be ever set on taking the life of a Brahmana. Of all creatures a Brahmana must not be slain. He is, indeed, like fire. A Brahmana, when angry, becomes like fire or the Sun, like poison or an edged weapon. A Brahmana, it has been said, is the master of all creatures. For these and other reasons, a Brahmana is the adored of the virtuous. O child, he is never to be slain by thee even in anger. Hostility with Brahmanas, therefore, would not be proper under any circumstances. O sinless one, neither Agni nor Surya truly can consume so much as does a Brahmana of rigid vows, when angry. By these various indications must thou know a good Brahmana. Indeed, a brahmana is the first-born of all creatures, the foremost of the four orders, the father and the master of all.' Garuda then asked, 'O mother, of what form is a Brahmana, of what behaviour, and of what prowess? Doth he shine like fire, or is he of tranquil mien? And, O mother, it behoveth thee to tell my inquiring self, those auspicious signs by which I may recognise a Brahmana.' Vinata replied, saying, 'O child, him shouldst thou know as the best amongst Brahmanas who having entered thy throat would torture thee as a fish-hook or burn thee as blazing charcoal. A Brahmana must never be slain by thee even in anger.' And Vinata out of affection for her son, again told him these words, 'Him shouldst thou know as a good Brahmana who would not be digested in thy stomach.' Although she knew the incomparable strength of her son, yet she blessed him heartily, for, deceived by the snakes, she was very much afflicted by woe. And she said. 'Let Marut (the god of the winds) protect thy wings, and Surya and Soma thy vertebral regions; let Agni protect thy head, and the Vasus thy whole body. I also, O child (engaged in beneficial ceremonies), shall sit here for your welfare. Go then, O child, in safety to accomplish thy purpose.'

"Sauti continued, 'Then Garuda, having heard the words of his mother, stretched his wings and ascended the skies. And endued with great strength, he soon fell upon the Nishadas, hungry and like another Yama. And bent upon slaying the Nishadas, he raised a great quantity of dust that overspread the firmament, and sucking up water from amid the ocean, shook the trees growing on the adjacent mountains. And then that lord of birds obstructed the principal thoroughfares of the town of the Nishadas by his mouth, increasing its orifice at will. And the Nishadas began to fly in great haste in the direction of the open mouth of the great serpent-eater. And as birds in great affliction ascend by thousand into the skies when the trees in a forest are shaken by the winds, so those Nishadas blinded by the dust raised by the storm entered the wide-extending cleft of Garuda's mouth open to receive them. And then the hungry lord of all rangers of the skies, that oppressor of enemies, endued with great strength, and moving with greatest celerity to achieve his end, closed his mouth, killing innumerable Nishadas following the occupation of fishermen.'"

So ends the twenty-eighth section in the Astika Parva of Adi Parva.

SECTION XXIX
(Astika Parva continued)

"Sauti continued, 'A certain Brahmana with his wife had entered the throat of that ranger of the skies. The former began to burn the bird's throat like a piece of flaming charcoal. Him Garuda addressed, saying, 'O best of Brahmanas, come out soon from my mouth which I open for thee. A Brahmana must never be slain by me, although he may be always engaged in sinful practices.' Unto Garuda who had thus addressed him that Brahmana said, 'O, let this woman of the Nishada caste, who is my wife, also come out with me.' And Garuda said, 'Taking the woman also of the Nishada caste with thee, come out soon. Save thyself without delay since thou hast not yet been digested by the heat of my stomach.'

"Sauti continued, 'And then that Brahmana, accompanied by his wife of the Nishada caste, came out, and praising Garuda wended whatever way he liked. And when that Brahmana had come out with his wife, that lord of birds, fleet as the mind, stretching his wings ascended the skies. He then saw his father, and, hailed by him, Garuda, of incomparable prowess made proper answers. And the great Rishi (Kasyapa) then asked him, 'O child, is it well with thee? Dost thou get sufficient food every day? Is there food in plenty for thee in the world of men?'

"Garuda replied, 'My mother is ever well. And so is my brother, and so am I. But, father, I do not always obtain plenty of food, for which my peace is incomplete. I am sent by the snakes to fetch the excellent amrita. Indeed, I shall fetch it today for emancipating my mother from her bondage. My mother command me, saying, 'Eat thou the Nishadas.' I have eaten them by thousands, but my hunger is not appeased. Therefore, O worshipful one, point out to me some other food, by eating which, O master, I may be strong enough to bring away amrita by force. Thou shouldst indicate some food wherewith I may appease my hunger and thirst.'

"Kasyapa replied, 'This lake thou seest is sacred. It hath been heard, of even in the heavens. There is an elephant, with face downwards, who continually draggeth a tortoise, his elder brother. I shall speak to you in detail of their hostility in former life. Just listen as I tell you why they are here.

"There was of old a great Rishi of the name of Vibhavasu. He was exceedingly wrathful. He had a younger brother of the name of Supritika. The latter was averse to keeping his wealth jointly with his brother's. And Supritika would always speak of partition. After some time his brother Vibhavasu told Supritika, 'It is from great foolishness that persons blinded by love of wealth always desire to make a partition of their patrimony. After effecting a partition they fight with each other, deluded by wealth. Then again, enemies in the guise of friends cause estrangements between ignorant and selfish men alter they become separated in wealth, and pointing out faults confirm their quarrels, so that the latter soon fall one by one. Absolute ruin very soon overtakes the separated. For these reasons the wise never speak approvingly of partition amongst brothers who, when divided, do not regard the most authoritative Sastras and live always in fear of each other. But as thou, Supritika, without regarding my advice impelled by desire of separation, always wishest to make an arrangement about your property, thou shall become an elephant.' Supritika, thus cursed, then spake unto Vibhavasu, 'Thou also shall become a tortoise moving in the midst of the waters.'

"And thus on account of wealth those two fools, Supritika and Vibhavasu, from each other's curse, have become an elephant and a tortoise respectively. Owing to their wrath, they have both become inferior animals. And they are engaged in hostilities with each other, proud of their excessive strength and the weight of their bodies. And in this lake those two beings of huge bodies are engaged in acts according to their former hostility. Look here, one amongst them, the handsome elephant of huge body, is even now approaching. Hearing his roar, the tortoise also of huge body, living within the waters, cometh out, agitating the lake violently. And seeing him the elephant, curling his trunk, rusheth into the water. And endued with great energy, with motion of his tusks and fore-part of his trunk and tail and feet, he agitates the water of the lake abounding with fishes. And the tortoise also of great strength, with upraised head, cometh forward for an encounter. And the elephant is six yojanas in height and twice that measure in circumference. And the height of the tortoise also is three yojanas and his circumference ten. Eat thou up both of them that are madly engaged in the encounter and bent upon slaying each other, and then accomplish the task that thou desirest. Eating that fierce elephant which looketh like a huge mountain and resembleth a mass of dark clouds, bring thou amrita.'

"Sauti continued, 'Having said so unto Garuda, he (Kasyapa) blessed him, saying, 'Blest be thou when thou art in combat with the gods. Let water pitchers filled to the brim, Brahmanas, kine, and other auspicious objects, bless thee, thou oviparous one. And, O thou of great strength, when thou art engaged with the gods in combat, let the Riks, the Yajus, the Samas, the sacred sacrificial butter, all the mysteries (Upanishads), constitute thy strength.'

"Garuda, thus addressed by his father, wended to the side of that lake. He saw that expanse of clear water with birds of various kinds all around. And remembering the words of his father, that ranger of the skies possessed of great swiftness of motion, seized the elephant and the tortoise, one in each claw. And that bird then soared high into the air. And he came upon a sacred place called Alamva and saw many divine trees. And struck by the wind raised by his wings, those trees began to shake with fear. And those divine trees having golden boughs feared that they would break. And the ranger of the skies seeing that those trees capable of granting every wish were quaking with fear, went to other trees of incomparable appearance. And those gigantic trees were adorned with fruits of gold and silver and branches of precious gems. And they were washed with the water of the sea. And there was a large banian among them, which had grown into gigantic proportions, that spoke unto that lord of bird coursing towards it with the fleetness of the mind, 'Sit thou on this large branch of mine extending a hundred yojanas and eat the elephant and the tortoise.' When that best of birds, of great swiftness and of body resembling a mountain, quickly alighted upon a bough of that banian tree, the resort of thousands of winged creatures—that bough also full of leaves shook and broke down.'"

So ends the twenty-ninth section in the Astika Parva of the Adi Parva.

SECTION XXX
(Astika Parva continued)

"Sauti said, 'At the very touch by Garuda of great might with his feet, the branch of the tree broke as it was caught by Garuda. Casting his eyes around in wonder he saw Valakhilya Rishis hanging therefrom with heads downwards and engaged in ascetic penances. Reflecting that if that bough fell down, the Rishis would be slain, the mighty one held the elephant and the tortoise still more firmly with his claws. And from fear of slaying the Rishis and desire of saving them, held that bough in his beaks, and rose on his wings. The great Rishis were struck with wonder at the sight of that act of his which was beyond even the power of the gods, and gave that mighty bird a name. And they said, 'As this ranger of the skies rises on its wings bearing a heavy burden, let this foremost of birds having snakes for his food be called Garuda (bearer of heavy weight).'

"And shaking the mountains by his wings, Garuda leisurely coursed through the skies. And as he soared with the elephant and the tortoise (in his claws), he beheld various regions underneath. Desiring as he did to save the Valakhilyas, he saw not a spot whereon to sit. At last he went to that foremost of mountains called Gandhamadana. There he saw his father Kasyapa engaged in ascetic devotions. Kasyapa also saw his son, that ranger of the skies, of divine form, possessed of great splendour, and energy and strength, and endued with the speed of the wind or the mind, huge as a mountain peak, a ready smiter like the curse of a Brahmana, inconceivable, indescribable, frightful to all creatures, possessed of great prowess, terrible, of the splendour of Agni himself, and incapable of being overcome by the deities, Danavas, and invincible Rakshasas, capable of splitting mountain summits and sucking the ocean itself and destroying the three worlds, fierce, and looking like Yama himself. The illustrious Kasyapa, seeing him approach and knowing also his motive, spoke unto him these words:

"Kasyapa said, 'O child, do not commit a rash act, for then thou wouldst have to suffer pain. The Valakhilyas, supporting themselves by drinking the rays of the sun, might, if angry, blast thee.'

"Sauti continued, 'Kasyapa then propitiated, for the sake of his son, the Valakhilyas of exceeding good fortune and whose sins had been destroyed by ascetic penances.' And Kasyapa said, 'Ye whose wealth is asceticism, the essay of Garuda is for the good of all creatures. The task is great that he is striving to accomplish. It behoveth you to accord him your permission.'

"Sauti continued, 'Those ascetics thus addressed by the illustrious Kasyapa, abandoned that bough and went to the sacred mountain of Himavat for purposes of ascetic penances. After those Rishis had gone away, the son of Vinata, with voice obstructed by the bough in his beaks, asked his father Kasyapa saying, 'O illustrious one, where shall I throw this arm of the tree? O illustrious one, indicate to me some region without human beings.' Then Kasyapa spoke of a mountain without human beings with caves and dales always covered with snow and incapable of approach by ordinary creatures even in thought. And the great bird bearing that branch, that elephant, and that tortoise, proceeded with great speed towards that mountain. The great arm of the tree with which that bird of huge body flew away could not be girt round with a cord made of a hundred (cow) hides. Garuda, the lord of birds, then flew away for hundreds of thousand of yojanas within—the shortest time. And going according to the directions of his father to that mountain almost in a moment, that ranger of the skies let fall the gigantic bough. And it fell with a great noise. And that Prince of mountains shook, struck with the storm raised by Garuda's wings. And the trees thereon dropped showers of flowers. And the peaks decked with gems and gold adorning that great mountain itself, were loosened and tell down on all sides. And the falling bough struck down numerous trees which, with golden flowers amid dark foliage, shone there like clouds charged with lightning. And those trees, bright as gold, falling down upon the ground and, dyed with mountain metals, shone as if they were bathed in the rays of the sun.

"Then that best of birds, Garuda, perching on the summit of that mountain, ate both the elephant and the tortoise, rose on his wings with great speed from the top of the mountain.

"And various omens began to appear among the gods foreboding fear. Indra's favourite thunderbolt blazed up in a fright. Meteors with flames and smoke, loosened from the welkin, shot down during the day. And the weapons of the Vasus, the Rudras, the Adityas, the Sabhyas, the Maruts, and other gods, began to spend their force against one another. Such a thing had never happened even during the war between the gods and the Asuras. And the winds blew accompanied with thunder, and meteors fell by thousands. And the sky, though cloudless, roared tremendously. And even he who was the god of gods shed showers of blood. And the flowery garlands on the necks of the gods faded and their prowess suffered diminution. And terrible masses of clouds dropped thick showers of blood. And the dust raised by the winds darkened the splendour of the very coronets of the gods. And He of a thousand sacrifices (Indra), with the other gods, perplexed with fear at the sight of those dark forebodings spoke unto Vrihaspati thus, 'Why, O worshipful one, have these natural disturbances suddenly arisen? No foe do I behold who would oppress us in war.' Vrihaspati answered, 'O chief of the gods, O thou of a thousand sacrifices, it is from thy fault and carelessness, and owing also to the ascetic penance of the high-souled great Rishis, the Valakhilyas, that the son of Kasyapa and Vinata, a ranger of the skies endued with great strength and possessing the capacity of assuming at will any form, is approaching to take away the Soma. And that bird, foremost among all endued with great strength, is able to rob you of the Soma. Everything is possible with him; the unachievable he can achieve.'

"Sauti continued, 'Indra, having heard these words, then spoke unto those that guarded the amrita, saying, 'A bird endued with great strength and energy has set his heart on taking away the amrita. I warn you beforehand so that he may not succeed in taking it away by force. Vrihaspati has told me that his strength is immeasurable.' And the gods hearing of it were amazed and took precautions. And they stood surrounding the amrita and Indra also of great prowess, the wielder of the thunder, stood with them. And the gods wore curious breastplates of gold, of great value, and set with gems, and bright leathern armour of great toughness. And the mighty deities wielded various sharp-edged weapons of terrible shapes, countless in number, emitting, even all of them, sparks of fire with smoke. And they were also armed with many a discus and iron mace furnished with spikes, and trident, battle-axe, and various kinds of sharp-pointed missiles and polished swords and maces of terrible form, all befitting their respective bodies. And decked with celestial ornaments and resplendent with those bright arms, the gods waited there, their fears allayed. And the gods, of incomparable strength, energy, and splendour, resolved to protect the amrita. Capable of splitting the towns of the Asuras, all displayed themselves in forms resplendent as the fire. And in consequence of the gods standing there, that (would be) battle-field, owing to hundreds of thousands of maces furnished with iron spikes, shone like another firmament illumined by the rays of the Sun.'"

So ends the thirtieth section in the Astika Parva of the Adi Parva.

SECTION XXXI
(Astika Parva continued)

"Saunaka said, 'O son of Suta, what was Indra's fault, what his act of carelessness? How was Garuda born in consequence of the ascetic penances of the Valakhilyas? Why also Kasyapa—a Brahman—had the king of birds for a son? Why, too, was he invincible of all creatures and unslayable of all? Why also was that ranger of the skies capable of going into every place at will and of mustering at will any measure of energy? If these are described in the Purana, I should like to hear them.'

"Sauti said, 'What thou askest me is, indeed, the subject of the Purana. O twice-born one, listen as I briefly recite it all.

"Once upon a time, when the lord of creation, Kasyapa, was engaged in a sacrifice from desire of offspring, the Rishis, the gods, and the Gandharvas, all gave him help. And Indra was appointed by Kasyapa to bring the sacrificial fuel; and with him those ascetics the Valakhilyas, and all the other deities. And the lord Indra, taking up according to his own strength, a weight that was mountain-like, brought it without any fatigue. And he saw on the way some Rishis, of bodies of the measure of the thumb, all together carrying one single stalk of a Palasa (Butea frondosa) leaf. And those Rishis were, from want of food, very lean and almost merged in their own bodies. And they were so weak that they were much afflicted when sunk in the water that collected in an indentation on the road produced by the hoof of a cow. And Purandara, proud of his strength, beheld them with surprise, and laughing at them in derision soon left them behind insulting them, besides, by passing over their heads. And those Rishis being thus insulted were filled with rage and sorrow. And they made preparations for a great sacrifice at which Indra was terrified. Hear, O Saunaka, of the wish for accomplishment of which those vow-observing wise, and excellent ascetics poured clarified butter of the sacrificial fire with loudly uttered mantras, 'There shall be another Indra of all gods, capable of going everywhere at will, and of mustering at will any measure of energy, and striking tear into the (present) king of the gods. By the fruit of our ascetic penance, let one arise, fleet as the mind, and fierce withal.' And the lord of the celestials of a hundred sacrifices, having come to know of this, became very much alarmed and sought the protection of the vow- observing Kasyapa. And the Prajapati Kasyapa, hearing everything from Indra, went to the Valakhilyas and asked them if their sacrifice had been successful. And those truth-speaking Rishis replied to him, saying, 'Let it be as thou sayest!' And the Prajapati Kasyapa pacifying them, spake unto them as follows, 'By the word of Brahman, this one (Indra) hath been made the Lord of the three worlds. Ye ascetics, ye also are striving to create another Indra! Ye excellent ones, it behoveth you not to falsify the word of Brahman. Let not also this purpose, for (accomplishing) which ye are striving, be rendered futile. Let there spring an Indra (Lord) of winged creatures, endued with excess of strength! Be gracious unto Indra who is a suppliant before you.' And the Valakhilyas, thus addressed by Kasyapa, after offering reverence to that first of the Munis, viz., the Prajapati Kasyapa, spake unto him:

"The Valakhilyas said, 'O Prajapati, this sacrifice of us all is for an Indra! Indeed this hath also been meant for a son being born unto thee! Let this task be now left to thee. And in this matter do whatsoever thou seest to be good and proper.'

"Sauti continued, 'Meanwhile, moved by the desire of offspring, the good daughter of Daksha, the vow-observing, amiable, and fortunate Vinata, her ascetic penances over, having purified herself with a bath in that season when connubial companionship might prove fruitful, approached her lord. And Kasyapa spake unto her, 'Respected one, the sacrifice commenced by me hath borne fruit. What hath been desired by thee shall come to pass. Two heroic sons, shall be born unto thee, who shall be the lords of the three worlds. By the penances of the Valakhilyas and by virtue of the desire with which I commenced my sacrifice, those sons shall be of exceedingly good fortune and worshipped in the three worlds!' And the illustrious Kasyapa spake unto her again, 'Bear thou these auspicious seeds with great care. These two will be the lords of all winged creatures. These heroic rangers of the skies will be respected in all the worlds, and capable of assuming any form at will.'

"And the Prajapati, gratified with all that took place, then addressed Indra of a hundred sacrifices, saying, 'Thou shalt have two brothers of great energy and prowess, who shall be to thee even as the helpmates. From them no injury shall result unto thee. Let thy sorrow cease; thou shalt continue as the lord of all. Let not, however, the utterers of the name of Brahma be ever again slighted by thee. Nor let the very wrathful ones, whose words are even the thunderbolt, be ever again insulted by thee.' Indra, thus addressed, went to heaven, his fears dispelled. And Vinata also, her purpose fulfilled, was exceedingly glad. And she gave birth to two sons, Aruna and Garuda. And Aruna, of undeveloped body, became the fore-runner of the Sun. And Garuda was vested with the lordship over the birds. O thou of Bhrigu's race, hearken now to the mighty achievement of Garuda.'"

So ends the thirty-first section in the Astika Parva of the Adi Parva.

SECTION XXXII
(Astika Parva continued)

"Sauti said, 'O foremost of Brahmanas, the gods having prepared for battle in that way, Garuda, the king of birds, soon came upon those wise ones. And the gods beholding him of excessive strength began to quake with fear, and strike one another with all their weapons. And amongst those that guarded the Soma was Brahmana (the celestial architect), of measureless might, effulgent as the electric fire and of great energy. And after a terrific encounter lasting only a moment, managed by the lord of birds with his talons, beak, and wings, he lay as dead on the fields. And the ranger of the skies making the worlds dark with the dust raised by the hurricane of his wings, overwhelmed the celestials with it. And the latter, overwhelmed with that dust, swooned away. And the immortals who guarded the amrita, blinded by that dust, could no longer see

THE MAHABHARATA

Garuda. Even thus did Garuda agitate the region of the heavens. And even thus he mangled the gods with the wounds inflicted by his wings and beak.

"Then the god of a thousand eyes commanded Vayu (the god of wind), saying, 'Dispel thou this shower of dust soon. O Maruta, this is indeed, thy task. Then the mighty Vayu soon drove away that dust. And when the darkness had disappeared, the celestials attacked Garuda. And as he of great might was attacked by the gods, he began to roar aloud, like the great cloud that appeareth in the sky at the end of the Yuga, frightening every creature. And that king of birds, of great energy, that slayer of hostile heroes, then rose on his wings. All the wise ones (the celestials) with Indra amongst them armed with double-edged broad swords, iron maces furnished with sharp spikes, pointed lances, maces, bright arrows, and many a discus of the form of the sun, saw him over head. And the king of birds, attacked them on all sides with showers of various weapons and fought exceedingly hard without wavering for a moment. And the son of Vinata, of great prowess blazing in the sky, attacked the gods on all sides with his wings and breast. And blood began to flow copiously from the bodies of the gods mangled by the talons and the beak of Garuda. Overcome by the lord of birds, the Sadhyas with the Gandharvas fled eastwards, the Vasus with the Rudras towards the south, the Adityas towards the west, and the twin Aswins towards the north. Gifted with great energy, they retreated fighting, looking back every moment on their enemy.

"And Garuda had encounters with the Yakshas, Aswakranda of great courage, Rainuka, the bold Krathanaka, Tapana, Uluka, Swasanaka, Nimesha, Praruja, and Pulina. And the son of Vinata mangled them with his wings, talons, and beak, like Siva himself, that chastiser of enemies, and the holder of Pinaka in rage at the end of the Yuga. And those Yakshas of great might and courage, mangled all over by that ranger of the skies, looked like masses of black clouds dropping thick showers of blood.

"And Garuda, depriving them of life, and then went to where the amrita was. And he saw that it was surrounded on all sides by fire. And the terrible flames of that fire covered the entire sky. And moved by violent winds, they seemed bent on burning the Sun himself. The illustrious Garuda then assumed ninety times ninety mouths and quickly drinking the waters of many rivers with those mouths and returning with great speed, that chastiser of enemies, having wings for his vehicle extinguished that fire with that water. And extinguishing that fire, he assumed a very small form, desirous of entering into (the place where the Soma was)."

So ends the thirty-second section in the Astika Parva of the Adi Parva.

SECTION XXXIII
(Astika Parva continued)

"Santi said, 'And that bird, assuming a golden body bright as the rays of the Sun, entered with great force (the region where the Soma was), like a torrent entering the ocean. And he saw, placed near the Soma, a wheel of steel keen-edged, and sharp as the razor, revolving incessantly. And that fierce instrument, of the splendour of the blazing sun and of terrible form, had been devised by the gods for cutting in pieces all robbers of the Soma. Garuda, seeing a passage through it, stopped there for a moment. Diminishing his body, in an instant he passed through the spokes of that wheel. Within the line of the wheel, he beheld, stationed there for guarding the Soma two great snakes of the effulgence of blazing fire, with tongues bright as the lightning-flash, of great energy, with mouth emitting fire, with blazing eyes, containing poison, very terrible, always in anger, and of great activity. Their eyes were ceaselessly inflamed with rage and were also winkless. He who may be seen by even one of the two would instantly be reduced to ashes. The bird of fair feathers suddenly covered their eyes with dust. And unseen by them he attacked them from all sides. And the son of Vinata, that ranger of the skies, attacking their bodies, mangled them into pieces. He then approached the Soma without loss of time. Then the mighty son of Vinata, taking up the Amrita from the place where it was kept, rose on his wings with great speed, breaking into pieces the machine that had surrounded it. And the bird soon came out, taking the Amrita but without drinking it himself. And he then wended on his way without the least fatigue, darkening the splendour of the Sun.

"And the son of Vinata then met Vishnu on his way along the sky. And Narayana was gratified at that act of self-denial on the part of Garuda. And that deity, knowing no deterioration, said unto the ranger of the skies, 'O, I am inclined to grant thee a boon.' The ranger of the skies thereupon said, 'I shall stay above thee.'

And he again spake unto Narayana these words, 'I shall be immortal and free from disease without (drinking) Amrita.' Vishnu said unto the son of Vinata, 'Be it so.' Garuda, receiving those two boons, told Vishnu, 'I also shall grant thee a boon; therefore, let the possessor of the six attributes ask of me.' Vishnu then asked the mighty Garuda to become his carrier. And he made the bird sit on the flagstaff of his car, saying, 'Even thus thou shalt stay above me.' And the ranger of the skies, of great speed, saying unto Narayana, 'Be it so,' swiftly wended on his way, mocking the wind with his fleetness.

"And while that foremost of all rangers of the skies, that first of winged creatures, Garuda, was coursing through the air after wresting the Amrita, Indra hurled at him his thunderbolt. Then Garuda, the lord of birds, struck with thunderbolt, spake laughingly unto Indra engaged in the encounter, in sweet words, saying, 'I shall respect the Rishi (Dadhichi) of whose bone the Vajra hath been made. I shall also respect the Vajra, and thee also of a thousand sacrifices. I cast this feather of mine whose end thou shalt not attain. Struck with thy thunder I have not felt the slightest pain.' And having said this, the king of birds cast a feather of his. And all creatures became exceedingly glad, beholding that excellent feather of Garuda so cast off. And seeing that the feather was very beautiful, they said, 'Let this bird be called Suparna (having fair feathers).' And Purandara of a thousand eyes, witnessing this wonderful incident, thought that bird to be some great being and addressed him thus.

"And Indra said, 'O best of birds, I desire to know the limit of thy great strength. I also desire eternal friendship with thee.'"

So ends the thirty-third section in the Astika Parva of the Adi Parva.

SECTION XXXIV
(Astika Parva continued)

"Sauti continued, 'Garuda then said, 'O Purandara, let there be friendship between thee and me as thou desirest. My strength, know thou, is hard to bear. O thou of a thousand sacrifices, the good never approve of speaking highly of their own strength, nor do they speak of their own merits. But being made a friend, and asked by thee, O friend, I will answer thee, although self-praise without reason is ever improper. I can bear, on a single feather of mine, O Sakra, this Earth, with her mountains and forests and with the waters of the ocean, and with thee also stationed thereon. Know thou, my strength is such that I can bear without fatigue even all the worlds put together, with their mobile and immobile objects.'

"Sauti continued, 'O Saunaka, after Garuda of great courage had thus spoken, Indra the chief of the gods, the wearer of the (celestial) crown, ever bent upon the good of the worlds, replied, saying, 'It is as thou sayest. Everything is possible in thee. Accept now my sincere and hearty friendship. And if thou hast no concern with the Soma, return it to me. Those to whom thou wouldst give it would always oppose us.' Garuda answered, 'There is a certain reason for which the Soma is being carried by me. I shall not give the Soma to any one for drink. But, O thou of a thousand eyes, after I have placed it down, thou, O lord of the heavens, canst then, taking it up, instantly bring it away.' Indra then said, 'O oviparous one, I am highly gratified with these words now spoken by thee. O best of all rangers of the skies; accept from me any boon that thou desirest.'

"Sauti continued, 'Then Garuda, recollecting the sons of Kadru and remembering also the bondage of his mother caused by an act of deception owing to the well-known reason (viz., the curse of Aruna), said, 'Although I have power over all creatures, yet I shall do your bidding. Let, O Sakra, the mighty snakes become my food.' The slayer of the Danavas having said unto him, 'Be it so,' then went to Hari, the god of gods, of great soul, and the lord of Yogins. And the latter sanctioned everything that had been said by Garuda. And the illustrious lord of heaven again said unto Garuda, 'I shall bring away the Soma when thou placest it down.' And having said so, he bade farewell to Garuda. And the bird of fair feathers then went to the presence of his mother with great speed.

"And Garuda in joy then spake unto all the snakes, 'Here have I brought the Amrita. Let me place it on some Kusa grass. O ye snakes, sitting here, drink of it after ye have performed your ablutions and religious rites. As said by you, let my mother become, from this day, free, for I have accomplished your bidding.' The snakes having said unto Garuda, 'Be it so,' then went to perform their ablutions. Meanwhile, Sakra taking up the Amrita, wended back to heaven. The snakes after performing their ablutions, their daily devotions, and other sacred rites, returned in joy, desirous of drinking the Amrita. They saw that the bed of kusa grass whereon the Amrita had been placed was empty, the Amrita itself having been taken away by a counter-act of deception. And they began to lick with their tongues the kusa grass, as the Amrita had been placed thereon. And the tongues of the snakes by that act became divided in twain. And the kusa grass, too, from the contact with Amrita, became sacred thenceforth. Thus did the illustrious Garuda bring Amrita (from the heavens) for the snakes, and thus were the tongues of snakes divided by what Garuda did.

"Then the bird of fair feathers, very much delighted, enjoyed himself in those woods accompanied by his mother. Of grand achievements, and deeply revered by all rangers of the skies, he gratified his mother by devouring the snakes.

"That man who would listen to this story, or read it out to an assembly of good Brahmanas, must surely go to heaven, acquiring great merit from the recitation of (the feats of) Garuda.'"

And so ends the thirty-fourth section in the Astika Parva of the Adi Parva.

SECTION XXXV
(Astika Parva continued)

"Saunaka said, 'O son of Suta, thou hast told us the reason why the snakes were cursed by their mother, and why Vinata also was cursed by her son. Thou hast also told us about the bestowal of boons, by their husband, on Kadru and Vinata. Thou hast likewise told us the names of Vinata's sons. But thou hast not yet recited to us the names of the snakes. We are anxious to hear the names of the principal ones.'

"Sauti said, O thou whose wealth is asceticism, from fear of being lengthy, I shall not mention the names of all the snakes. But I will recite the names of the chief ones. Listen to me!

"Sesha was born first, and then Vasuki. (Then were born) Airavata,
Takshaka, Karkotaka, Dhananjaya, Kalakeya, the serpent Mani, Purana,
Pinjaraka, and Elapatra, Vamana, Nila, Anila, Kalmasha, Savala, Aryaka,
Ugra, Kalasapotaka, Suramukha, Dadhimukha, Vimalapindaka, Apta, Karotaka,
Samkha, Valisikha, Nisthanaka, Hemaguha, Nahusha, Pingala, Vahyakarna,
Hastipada, Mudgarapindaka, Kamvala Aswatara, Kaliyaka, Vritta, Samvartaka,
Padma, Mahapadma, Sankhamukha, Kushmandaka, Kshemaka, Pindaraka, Karavira,
Pushpadanshtraka, Vilwaka, Vilwapandara, Mushikada, Sankhasiras,
Purnabhadra, Haridraka, Aparajita, Jyotika, Srivaha, Kauravya,
Dhritarashtra, Sankhapinda, Virajas, Suvahu, Salipinda, Prabhakara,
Hastipinda, Pitharaka, Sumuksha, Kaunapashana, Kuthara, Kunjara, Kumuda,
Kumudaksha, Tittri, Halika, Kardama, Vahumulaka, Karkara, Akarkara,
Kundodara, and Mahodara.

"Thus, O best of regenerate ones, have I said the names of the principal serpents. From fear of being tedious I do not give names of the rest. O thou whose wealth is asceticism, the sons of these snakes, with their grandsons, are innumerable. Reflecting upon this, I shall not name them to thee. O best ascetics, in this world the number of snakes baffles calculation, there being many thousands and millions of them."

So ends the thirty-fifth section in the Astika Parva of the Adi Parva.

SECTION XXXVI
(Astika Parva continued)

"Saunaka said, 'O child, thou hast named many of the serpents gifted with great energy and incapable of being easily overcome. What did they do after hearing of that curse?'

"Sauti said, 'The illustrious Sesha amongst them, of great renown, leaving his mother practised hard penances, living upon air and rigidly observing his vows. He practised these ascetic devotions, repairing to Gandhamadana, Vadri, Gokarna, the woods of Pushkara, and the foot of Himavat. And he passed his days in those sacred regions, some of which were sacred for their water and others for their soil in the rigid observance of his vows, with singleness of aim, and his passions under complete control. And the Grandsire of all, Brahma, saw that ascetic with knotted hair, clad in rags, and his flesh, skin, and sinews dried up owing to the hard penances he was practising. And the Grandsire addressing him, that penance-practising one of great fortitude, said, 'What is that thorn doest, O Sesha? Let the welfare of the creatures of the worlds also engage thy thoughts. O sinless one, thou art afflicting all creatures by thy hard penances. O Sesha, tell me the desire implanted in thy breast.'

"And Sesha replied, 'My uterine brothers are all of wicked hearts. I do not desire to live amongst them. Let this be sanctioned by thee. Like enemies they are always jealous of one another. I am, therefore, engaged in ascetic devotions. I will not see them even. They never show any kindness for Vinata and her son. Indeed, Vinata's son capable of ranging through the skies, is another brother of ours. They always envy him. And he, too, is much stronger owing to the bestowal of that boon by our father, the high-souled Kasyapa. For these, I engaged in ascetic penances, and I will cast off this body of mine, so that I may avoid companionship with them, even in another state of life.'

"Unto Sesha who had said so, the Grandsire said, 'O Sesha, I know the behaviour of all thy brothers and their great danger owing to their offence against their mother. But O Snake, a remedy (for this) hath been provided by me even beforehand. It behoveth thee not to grieve for thy brothers. O Sesha, ask of me the boon thou desirest. I have been highly gratified with thee and I will grant thee today a boon. O best of snakes, it is fortunate that thy heart hath been set on virtue. Let thy heart be more and more firmly set on virtue.'

"Then Sesha replied, 'O divine Grandsire, this is the boon desired by me; viz., may my heart always delight in virtue and in blessed ascetic penances, O Lord of all!'

"Brahman said, 'O Sesha, I am exceedingly gratified with this thy self- denial and love of peace. But, at my command, let this act be done by thee for the good of my creatures. Bear thou, O Sesha, properly and well this Earth so unsteady with her mountains and forests, her seas and towns and retreats, so that she may be steady.'

"Sesha said, 'O divine Lord of all creatures, O bestower of boons, O lord of the Earth, lord of every created thing, lord of the universe, I will, even as thou sayest hold the Earth steady. Therefore, O lord of all creatures, place her on my head.'

"Brahman said, 'O best of snakes, go underneath the Earth. She will herself give thee a crevice to pass through. And, O Sesha, by holding the Earth, thou shalt certainly do what is prized by me very greatly.'

"Sauti continued, 'Then the elder brother of the king of the snakes, entering a hole, passed to the other side of the Earth, and holding her, supported with his head that goddess with her belt of seas passing all round.'

"Brahman said, 'O Sesha, O best of snakes, thou art the god Dharma, because alone, with thy huge body, thou supportest the Earth with everything on her, even as I myself, or Valavit (Indra), can.'

"Sauti continued, 'The snake, Sesha, the lord Ananta, of great prowess, lives underneath the Earth, alone supporting the world at the command of Brahman. And the illustrious Grandsire, the best of the immortals, then gave unto Ananta the bird of fair feathers, viz., the son of Vinata, for Ananta's help.'"

So ends the thirty-sixth section in the Astika Parva of the Adi Parva.

SECTION XXXVII
(Astika Parva continued)

"Sauti said, 'That best of snakes, viz., Vasuki, hearing the curse of his mother, reflected how to render it abortive. He held a consultation with all his brothers, Airavata and others, intent upon doing what they deemed best for themselves.'

"And Vasuki said, 'O ye sinless ones, the object of this curse is known to you. It behoveth us to strive to neutralise it. Remedies certainly exist for all curses, but no remedy can avail those cursed by their mother. Hearing that this curse hath been uttered in the presence of the Immutable, the Infinite, and the True one, my heart trembleth. Surely, our annihilation hath come. Otherwise why should not the Immutable Lord prevent our mother while uttering the curse? Therefore, let us consult today how we may secure the safety of the snakes. Let us not waste time. All of you are wise and discerning. We will consult together and find out the means of deliverance as (did) the gods of yore to regain lost Agni who had concealed himself within a cave, so that Janamejaya's sacrifice for the destruction of the snakes may not take place, and so that we may not meet with destruction.'

"Sauti continued, 'Thus addressed all the offspring of Kadru assembled together, and, wise in counsels, submitted their opinions to one another. One party of the serpents said, 'We should assume the guise of superior Brahmanas, and beseech Janamejaya, saying, 'This (intended) sacrifice of yours ought not to take place.' Other snakes thinking themselves wise, said, 'We should all become his favourite counsellors. He will then certainly ask for our advice in all projects. And we will then give him such advice that the sacrifice may be obstructed. The king, the foremost of wise men, thinking us of sterling worth will certainly ask us about his sacrifice. We will say, 'It must not be!' And pointing to many serious evils in this and the next worlds, we will take care that the sacrifice may not take place. Or, let one of the snakes, approaching, bite the person who, intending the monarch's good, and well-acquainted with the rites of the snake-sacrifice, may be appointed as the sacrificial priest, so that he will die. The sacrificial priest dying, the sacrifice will not be completed. We will also bite all those who, acquainted with the rites of the snake-sacrifice, may be appointed Ritwiks of the sacrifice, and by that means attain our object.' Other snakes, more virtuous and kind, said, 'O, this counsel of yours is evil. It is not meet to kill Brahmanas. In danger, that remedy is proper, which is blessed on the practices of the righteous. Unrighteousness finally destroyeth the world.' Other serpents said, 'We will extinguish the blazing sacrificial fire by ourselves becoming clouds luminous with lightning and pouring down showers.' Other snakes, the best of their kind, proposed, 'Going, by night, let us steal away the vessel of Soma juice. That will disturb the rite. Or, at that sacrifice, let the snakes, by hundreds and thousands, bite the people, and spread terror around. Or, let the serpents defile the pure food with their food-defiling urine and dung.' Others said, 'Let us become the king's Ritwiks, and obstruct his sacrifice by saying at the outset, 'Give us the sacrificial fee.' He (the king), being placed in our power, will do whatever we like.' Others there said, 'When the king will sport in the waters, we will carry him to our home and bind him, so that that sacrifice will not take place!' Other serpents who deemed themselves wise, said, 'Approaching the king, let us bite him, so that our object will be accomplished. By his death the root of all evil will be torn up. This is the final deliberation of us all, O thou who hearest with thy eyes! Then, do speedily what thou deemest proper.' Having said this, they looked intently at Vasuki, that best of snakes. And Vasuki also, after reflecting, answered saying, 'Ye snakes, this final determination of you doth not seem worthy of adoption. The advice of you all is not to my liking. What shall I say which would be for your good? I think the grace of the illustrious Kasyapa (our father) can alone do us good. Ye snakes, my heart doth not know which of all your suggestions is to be adopted for the welfare of my race as also of me. That must be done by me which would be to your weal. It is this that makes me so anxious, for the credit or the discredit (of the measure) is mine alone.'"

So ends the thirty-seventh section in the Astika Parva of the Adi Parva.

SECTION XXXVIII
(Astika Parva continued)

"Sauti said, 'Hearing the respective speeches of all the snakes, and hearing also the words of Vasuki, Elapatra began to address them, saying, 'That sacrifice is not one that can be prevented. Nor is king Janamejaya of the Pandava race from whom this fear proceedeth, such that he can be hindered. The person, O king, who is afflicted by fate hath recourse to fate alone; nothing else can be his refuge. Ye best of snakes, this fear of ours hath fate for its root. Fate alone must be our refuge in this. Listen to what I say. When that curse was uttered, ye best of snakes, in fear I lay crouching on the lap of our mother. Ye best of snakes, and O lord (Vasuki) of great splendour, from that place I heard the words the sorrowing gods spake unto the Grandsire. The gods said, 'O Grandsire, thou god of gods who else than the cruel Kadru could thus, after getting such dear children, curse them so, even in thy presence? And, O Grandsire, by thee also hath been spoken, with reference to those words of hers, 'Be it so.' We wish to know the reason why thou didst not prevent her.' Brahman replied, 'The snakes have multiplied. They are cruel, terrible in form and highly poisonous. From desire of the good of my creatures, I did not prevent Kadru then. Those poisonous serpents and others who are sinful, biting others for no faults, shall, indeed, be destroyed, but not they who are harmless and virtuous. And hear also, how, when the hour comes, the snakes may escape this dreadful calamity. There shall be born in the race of the Yayavaras a great Rishi known by the name of Jaratkaru, intelligent, with passions under complete control. That Jaratkaru shall have a son of the name of Astika. He shall put a stop to that sacrifice. And those snakes who shall be virtuous shall escape therefrom.' The gods said, 'O thou truth-knowing one, on whom will Jaratkaru, that foremost Muni, gifted with great energy and asceticism, beget that illustrious son?' Brahma answered, 'Gifted with great energy, that best Brahmana shall beget a son possessed of great energy on a wife of the same name as his. Vasuki, the king of the snakes, hath a sister of the name of Jaratkaru; the son, of whom I speak, shall be born of her, and he shall liberate the snakes.'

"Elapatra continued, 'The gods then said unto the Grandsire, 'Be it so.' And the lord Brahman, having said so unto the gods, went to heaven. O Vasuki, I see before me that sister of thine known by the name of Jaratkaru. For relieving us from fear, give her as alms unto him (i.e., the Rishi), Jaratkaru, of excellent vows, who shall roam abegging for a bride. This means of release hath been heard of by me!'"

SECTION XXXIX
(Astika Parva continued)

"Sauti said, 'O best of regenerate ones, hearing these words of Elapatra, all the serpents, in great delight, exclaimed, 'Well said, well said!' And from that time Vasuki set about carefully bringing up that maiden, viz., his sister Jaratkaru. And he took great delight in rearing her.

"And much time did not elapse from this, when the gods and the Asuras, assembling together, churned the abode of Varuna. And Vasuki, the foremost of all gifted with strength, became the churning-cord. And directly the work was over, the king of the snakes presented himself before the Grandsire. And the gods, accompanied by Vasuki, addressed the Grandsire, saying, 'O lord, Vasuki is suffering great affliction from fear of (his mother's curse). It behoveth thee to root out the sorrow, begotten of the curse of his mother, that hath pierced the heart of Vasuki desirous of the weal of his race. The king of the snakes is ever our friend and benefactor. O Lord of the gods, be gracious unto him and assuage his mind's fever.'

"Brahman replied, 'O ye immortals, I have thought, in my mind, of what ye have said. Let the king of the snakes do that which hath been communicated to him before by Elapatra. The time hath arrived. Those only shall be destroyed that are wicked, not those that are virtuous. Jaratkaru hath been born, and that Brahmana is engaged in hard ascetic penances. Let Vasuki, at the proper time, bestow on him his sister. Ye gods, what hath been spoken by the snake Elapatra for the weal of the snakes is true and not otherwise.'

"Sauti continued, 'Then the king of the snakes, Vasuki, afflicted with the curse of his mother, hearing these words of the Grandsire, and intending to bestow his sister of the Rishi Jaratkaru, commanded all the serpents, a large numbers of whom were ever attentive to their duties, to watch the Rishi Jaratkaru, saying,

'When the lord Jaratkaru will ask for a wife, come immediately and inform me of it. The weal of our race depends upon it.'"

SECTION XL
(Astika Parva continued)

"Saunaka said, 'O son of Suta, I desire to know the reason why the illustrious Rishi whom thou hast named Jaratkaru came to be so called on earth. It behoveth thee to tell us the etymology of the name Jaratkaru.'

"Sauti said, 'Jara is said to mean waste, and Karu implies huge. This Rishi's body had been huge, and he gradually reduced it by severe ascetic penances. For the same reason, O Brahmanas, the sister of Vasuki was called Jaratkaru.'

The virtuous Saunaka, when he heard this, smiled and addressing Ugrasravas said, 'It is even so.'

Saunaka then said, 'I have heard all that thou hast before recited. I desire to know how Astika was born.'

Sauti, on hearing these words, began to relate according to what was written in the Sastras.

"Sauti said, 'Vasuki, desirous of bestowing his sister upon the Rishi Jaratkaru, gave the snakes (necessary) orders. But days went on, yet that wise Muni of rigid vows, deeply engaged in ascetic devotions, did not seek for a wife. That high-souled Rishi, engaged in studies and deeply devoted to asceticism, his vital seed under full control, fearlessly wandered over the whole earth and had no wish for a wife.

"Afterwards, once upon a time, there was a king, O Brahmana, of the name of Parikshit, born in the race of the Kauravas. And, like his great- grandfather Pandu of old, he was of mighty arms, the first of all bearers of bows in battle, and fond of hunting. And the monarch wandered about, hunting deer, and wild boars, and wolves, and buffaloes and various other kinds of wild animals. One day, having pierced a deer with a sharp arrow and slung his bow on his back, he penetrated into the deep forest, searching for the animal here and there, like the illustrious Rudra himself of old pursuing in the heavens, bow in hand, the deer which was Sacrifice, itself turned into that shape, after the piercing. No deer that was pierced by Parikshit had ever escaped in the wood with life. This deer, however wounded as before, fled with speed, as the (proximate) cause of the king's attainment to heaven. And the deer that Parikshit—that king of men—had pierced was lost to his gaze and drew the monarch far away into the forest. And fatigued and thirsty, he came across a Muni, in the forest, seated in a cow-pen and drinking to his fill the froth oozing out of the mouths of calves sucking the milk of their dams. And approaching him hastily, the monarch, hungry and fatigued, and raising his bow, asked that Muni of rigid vows, saying, 'O Brahmana, I am king Parikshit, the son of Abhimanyu. A deer pierced by me hath been lost. Hast thou seen it?' But that Muni observing then the vow of silence, spoke not unto him a word. And the king in anger thereupon placed upon his shoulder a dead snake, taking it up with the end of his bow. The Muni suffered him to do it without protest. And he spoke not a word, good or bad. And the king seeing him in that state, cast off his anger and became sorry. And he returned to his capital but the Rishi continued in the same state. The forgiving Muni, knowing that the monarch who was a tiger amongst kings was true to the duties of his order, cursed him not, though insulted. That tiger amongst monarchs, that foremost one of Bharata's race, also did not know that the person whom he had so insulted was a virtuous Rishi. It was for this that he had so insulted him.

"That Rishi had a son by name Sringin, of tender years, gifted with great energy, deep in ascetic penances, severe in his vows, very wrathful, and difficult to be appeased. At times, he worshipped with great attention and respect his preceptor seated with ease on his seat and ever engaged in the good of creatures.

"And commanded by his preceptor, he was coming home when, O best of Brahmanas, a companion of his, a Rishi's son named Krisa in a playful mood laughingly spoke unto him. And Sringin, wrathful and like unto poison itself, hearing these words in reference to his father, blazed up in rage.

"And Krisa said, 'Be not proud, O Sringin, for ascetic as thou art and possessed of energy, thy father bears on his shoulders a dead snake. Henceforth speak not a word to sons of Rishis like ourselves who have knowledge of the truth, are deep in ascetic penances, and have attained success. Where is that manliness of thine, those high words of thine begotten of pride, when thou must have to behold thy father bearing a dead snake? O best of all the Munis, thy father too had done nothing to deserve this treatment, and it is for this that I am particularly sorry as if the punishment were mine.'"

SECTION XLI
(Astika Parva continued)

"Sauti said, 'Being thus addressed, and hearing that his sire was bearing a dead snake, the powerful Sringin burned with wrath. And looking at Krisa, and speaking softly, he asked him, 'Pray, why doth my father bear today a dead snake?' And Krisa replied, 'Even as king Parikshit was roving, for purpose of hunting, O dear one, he placed the dead snake on the shoulder of thy sire.'

"And Sringin asked, 'What wrong was done to that wicked monarch by my father? O Krisa, tell me this, and witness the power of my asceticism.'

"And Krisa answered, 'King Parikshit, the son of Abhimanyu, while hunting, had wounded a fleet stag with an arrow and chased it alone. And the king lost sight of the animal in that extensive wilderness. Seeing then thy sire, he immediately accosted him. Thy sire was then observing the vow of silence. Oppressed by hunger, thirst and labour, the prince again and again asked thy sire sitting motionless, about the missing deer. The sage, being under the vow of silence, returned no reply. The king thereupon placed the snake on thy sire's shoulder with the end of his bow. O Sringin, thy sire engaged in devotion is in the same posture still. And the king also hath gone to his capital which is named after the elephant!'

"Sauti continued, 'Having heard of a dead snake placed upon his (father's) shoulders, the son of the Rishi, his eyes reddened with anger, blazed up with rage. And possessed by anger, the puissant Rishi then cursed the king, touching water and overcome with wrath.'

"And Sringin said, 'That sinful wretch of a monarch who hath placed a dead snake on the shoulders of my lean and old parent, that insulter of Brahmanas and tarnisher of the fame of the Kurus, shall be taken within seven nights hence to the regions of Yama (Death) by the snake Takshaka, the powerful king of serpents, stimulated thereto by the strength of my words!'

"Sauti continued, 'And having thus cursed (the king) from anger, Sringin went to his father, and saw the sage sitting in the cow-pen, bearing the dead snake. And seeing his parent in that plight, he was again inflamed with ire. And he shed tears of grief, and addressed his sire, saying, 'Father, having been informed of this thy disgrace at the hands of that wicked wretch, king Parikshit, I have from anger even cursed him; and that worst of Kurus hath richly deserved my potent curse. Seven days hence, Takshaka, the lord of snakes, shall take the sinful king to the horrible abode of Death.' And the father said to the enraged son, 'Child, I am not pleased with thee. Ascetics should not act thus. We live in the domains of that great king. We are protected by him righteously. In all he does, the reigning king should by the like of us forgiven. If thou destroy Dharma, verily Dharma will destroy thee. If the king do not properly protect us, we fare very ill; we cannot perform our religious rites according to our desire. But protected by righteous sovereigns, we attain immense merit, and they are entitled to a share thereof. Therefore, reigning royalty is by all means to be forgiven. And Parikshit like unto his great-grandsire, protecteth us as a king should protect his subjects. That penance- practising monarch was fatigued and oppressed with hunger. Ignorant of my vow (of silence) he did this. A kingless country always suffereth from evils. The king punisheth offenders, and fear of punishments to peace; and people do their duties and perform their rites undisturbed. The king establisheth religion—establisheth the kingdom of heaven. The king protecteth sacrifices from disturbance, and sacrifices to please the gods. The gods cause rain, and rain produceth grains and herbs, which are always useful to man. Manu sayeth, a ruler of the destinies of men is equal (in dignity) to ten Veda-studying priests. Fatigued and oppressed with hunger, that penance-practising prince hath done this through ignorance of my vow. Why then hast thou rashly done this unrighteous action through childishness? O son, in no way doth the king deserve a curse from us.'"

SECTION XLII
(Astika Parva continued)

"Sauti said, 'And Sringin then replied to his father, saying, 'Whether this be an act of rashness, O father, or an improper act that I have done, whether thou likest it or dislikest it, the words spoken by me shall never be in vain. O father, I tell thee (a curse) can never be otherwise. I have never spoken a lie even in jest.'

"And Samika said, 'Dear child, I know that thou art of great prowess, and truthful in speech. Thou hast never spoken falsehood before, so that thy curse shall never be falsified. The son, even when he attaineth to age, should yet be always counselled by the father, so that crowned with good qualities he may acquire great renown. A child as thou art, how much more dost thou stand in need of counsel? Thou art ever engaged in ascetic penances. The wrath of even the illustrious ones possessing the six attributes increaseth greatly. O thou foremost of ordinance-observing persons, seeing that thou art my son and a minor too, and beholding also thy rashness, I see that I must counsel thee. Live thou, O son, inclined to peace and eating fruits and roots of the forest. Kill this thy anger and destroy not the fruit of thy ascetic acts in this way. Wrath surely decreaseth the virtue that ascetics acquire with great pains. And then for those deprived of virtue, the blessed state existeth not. Peacefulness ever giveth success to forgiving ascetics. Therefore, becoming forgiving in thy temper and conquering thy passions, shouldst thou always live. By forgiveness shalt thou obtain worlds that are beyond the reach of Brahman himself. Having adopted peacefulness myself, and with a desire also for doing good as much as lies in my power, I must do something; even must I send to that king, telling him, 'O monarch, thou hast been cursed by my son of tender years and undeveloped intellect, in wrath, at seeing thy act of disrespect towards myself.'

"Sauti continued, 'And that great ascetic, observer of vows, moved by kindness, sent with proper instructions a disciple of his to king Parikshit. And he sent his disciple Gaurmukha of good manners and engaged also in ascetic penances, instructing him to first enquire about the welfare of the king and then to communicate the real message. And that disciple soon approached that monarch, the head of the Kuru race. And he entered the king's palace having first sent notice of his arrival through the servant in attendance at the gate.

"And the twice-born Gaurmukha was duly worshipped by the monarch. And after resting for a while, he detailed fully to the king, in the presence of his ministers, the words of Samika, of cruel import, exactly as he had been instructed.'

"And Gaurmukha said, 'O king of kings, there is a Rishi, Samika, by name, of virtuous soul, his passions under control, peaceful, and given up to hard ascetic devotions, living in thy dominions! By thee, O tiger among men, was placed on the shoulders of that Rishi observing at present the vow of silence, a dead snake, with the end of thy bow! He himself forgave thee that act. But his son could not. And by the latter hast thou today been cursed, O king of kings, without the knowledge of his father, to the effect that within seven nights hence, shall (the snake) Takshaka cause thy death. And Samika repeatedly asked his son to save thee, but there is none to falsify his son's curse. And because he hath been unable to pacify his son possessed by anger, therefore have I been sent to thee, O king, for thy good!'

"And that king of the Kuru race, himself engaged in ascetic practices, having heard these cruel words and recollecting his own sinful act, became exceedingly sorry. And the king, learning that foremost of Rishis in the forest had been observing the vow of silence, was doubly afflicted with sorrow and seeing the kindness of the Rishi Samika, and considering his own sinful act towards him, the king became very repentant. And the king looking like a very god, did not grieve so much for hearing of his death as for having done that act to the Rishi.'

"And then the king sent away Gaurmukha, saying, 'Let the worshipful one (Samika) be gracious to me!' And when Gaurmukha had gone away, the king, in great anxiety, without loss of time, consulted his ministers. And having consulted them, the king, himself wise in counsels, caused a mansion to be erected upon one solitary column. It was well-guarded day and night. And for its protection were placed there physicians and medicines, and Brahmanas skilled in mantras all around. And the monarch, protected on all sides, discharged his kingly duties from that place surrounded by his virtuous ministers. And no one could approach that best of kings there. The air even could not go there, being prevented from entering.

"And when the seventh day had arrived, that best of Brahmanas, the learned Kasyapa was coming (towards the king's residence), desirous of treating the king (after the snake-bite). He had heard all that had taken place, viz., that Takshaka, that first of snakes, would send that best of monarchs to the presence of Yama (Death). And he thought, I would cure the monarch after he is bit by that first of snakes. By that I may have wealth and may acquire virtue also.' But that prince of snakes, Takshaka, in the form of an old Brahmana, saw Kasyapa approaching on his way, his heart set upon curing the king. And the prince of snakes then spake unto that bull among Munis, Kasyapa, saying, 'Whither dost thou go with such speed? What, besides, is the business upon which thou art intent?'

"And Kasyapa, thus addressed, replied, 'Takshaka, by his poison, will today burn king Parikshit of the Kuru race, that oppressor of all enemies. I go with speed, O amiable one, to cure, without loss of time, the king of immeasurable prowess, the sole representative of the Pandava race, after he is bit by the same

Takshaka like to Agni himself in energy.' And Takshaka answered, 'I am that Takshaka, O Brahmana, who shall burn that lord of the earth. Stop, for thou art unable to cure one bit by me.' And Kasyapa rejoined, 'I am sure that, possessed (that I am) of the power of learning, going thither I shall cure that monarch bit by thee.'"

SECTION XLIII
(Astika Parva continued)

"Sauti said, 'And Takshaka, after this, answered, 'If, indeed, thou art able to cure any creature bitten by me, then, O Kasyapa, revive thou this tree bit by me. O best of Brahmanas, I burn this banian in thy sight. Try thy best and show me that skill in mantras of which thou hast spoken.'

"And Kasyapa said, If thou art so minded, bite thou then, O king of snakes, this tree. O snake, I shall revive it, though bit by thee.

"Sauti continued, 'That king of snakes, thus addressed by the illustrious Kasyapa, bit then that banian tree. And that tree, bit by the illustrious snake, and penetrated by the poison of the serpent, blazed up all around. And having burnt the banian so, the snake then spake again unto Kasyapa, saying, 'O first of Brahmanas, try thy best and revive this lord of the forest.'

"Sauti continued, 'The tree was reduced to ashes by the poison of that king of snakes. But taking up those ashes, Kasyapa spoke these words. 'O king of snakes, behold the power of my knowledge as applied to this lord of the forest! O snake, under thy very nose I shall revive it.' And then that best of Brahmanas, the illustrious and learned Kasyapa, revived, by his vidya, that tree which had been reduced to a heap of ashes. And first he created the sprout, then he furnished it with two leaves, and then he made the stem, and then the branches, and then the full-grown tree with leaves and all. And Takshaka, seeing the tree revived by the illustrious Kasyapa, said unto him, 'It is not wonderful in thee that thou shouldst destroy my poison or that of any one else like myself. O thou whose wealth is asceticism, desirous of what wealth, goest thou thither? The reward thou hopest to have from that best of monarchs, even I will give thee, however difficult it may be to obtain it. Decked with fame as thou art, thy success may be doubtful on that king affected by a Brahmana's curse and whose span of life itself hath been shortened. In that case, this blazing fame of thine that hath overspread the three worlds will disappear like the Sun when deprived of his splendour (on the occasion of the eclipse).'

"Kasyapa said, 'I go there for wealth, give it unto me, O snake, so that taking thy gold. I may return.' Takshaka replied, 'O best of regenerate ones, even I will give thee more than what thou expectest from that king. Therefore do not go.'

"Sauti continued, 'That best of Brahmanas, Kasyapa, of great prowess and intelligence, hearing those words of Takshaka, sat in yoga meditation over the king. And that foremost of Munis, viz., Kasyapa, of great prowess and gifted with spiritual knowledge, ascertaining that the period of life of that king of the Pandava race had really run out, returned, receiving from Takshaka as much wealth as he desired.

"And upon the illustrious Kasyapa's retracing his steps, Takshaka at the proper time speedily entered the city of Hastinapura. And on his way he heard that the king was living very cautiously, protected by means of poison-neutralising mantras and medicines.'

"Sauti continued, 'The snake thereupon reflected thus, 'The monarch must be deceived by me with power of illusion. But what must be the means?' Then Takshaka sent to the king some snakes in the guise of ascetics taking with them fruits, kusa grass, and water (as presents). And Takshaka, addressing them, said, 'Go ye all to the king, on the pretext of pressing business, without any sign of impatience, as if to make the monarch only accept the fruits and flowers and water (that ye shall carry as presents unto him).'

"Sauti continued, 'Those snakes, thus commanded by Takshaka, acted accordingly. And they took to the king, Kusa grass and water, and fruits. And that foremost of kings, of great prowess, accepted those offerings. And after their business was finished, he said upto them, 'Retire.' Then after those snakes disguised as ascetics had gone away, the king addressed his ministers and friends, saying, 'Eat ye, with me, all these fruits of excellent taste brought by the ascetics.' Impelled by Fate and the words of the Rishi, the king, with his ministers, felt the desire of eating those fruits. The particular fruit, within which Takshaka had entered, was taken by the king himself for eating. And when he was eating it, there appeared, O Saunaka, an ugly insect out of it, of shape scarcely discernible, of eyes black, and of coppery colour. And that foremost of kings, taking that insect, addressed his councillors, saying, 'The sun is setting; today I have no more fear from poison. Therefore, let this insect become Takshaka and bite me, so that my sinful act may be expiated and the words of the ascetic rendered true.' And those councillors also, impelled by Fate, approved of that speech. And then the monarch smiled, losing his senses, his hour having come. And he quickly placed that insect on his neck. And as the king was smiling, Takshaka, who had (in the form of that insect) come out of the fruit that had been offered to the king, coiled himself round the neck of the monarch. And quickly coiling round the king's neck and uttering a tremendous roar, Takshaka, that lord of snakes, bit that protector of the earth.'"

SECTION XLIV
(Astika Parva continued)

"Sauti said, 'Then the councillors beholding the king in the coils of Takshaka, became pale with fear and wept in exceeding grief. And hearing the roar of Takshaka, the ministers all fled. And as they were flying away in great grief, they saw Takshaka, the king of snakes, that wonderful serpent, coursing through the blue sky like a streak of the hue of the lotus, and looking very much like the vermilion-coloured line on a woman's crown dividing the dark masses of her hair in the middle.

"And the mansion in which the king was living blazed up with Takshaka's poison. And the king's councillors, on beholding it, fled away in all directions. And the king himself fell down, as if struck by lightning.

"And when the king was laid low by Takshaka's poison, his councillors with the royal priest—a holy Brahmana—performed all his last rites. All the citizens, assembling together, made the minor son of the deceased monarch their king. And the people called their new king, that slayer of all enemies, that hero of the Kuru race, by the name of Janamejaya. And that best of monarchs, Janamejaya, though a child, was wise in mind. And with his councillors and priest, the eldest son Parikshita, that bull amongst the Kurus, ruled the kingdom like his heroic great-grand-father (Yudhishthira). And the ministers of the youthful monarch, beholding that he could now keep his enemies in check, went to Suvarnavarman, the king of Kasi, and asked him his daughter Vapushtama for a bride. And the king of Kasi, after due inquiries, bestowed with ordained rites, his daughter Vapushtama on that mighty hero of Kuru race. And the latter, receiving his bride, became exceedingly glad. And he gave not his heart at any time to any other woman. And gifted with great energy, he wandered in pursuit of pleasure, with a cheerful heart, on expanses of water and amid woods and flowery fields. And that first of monarchs passed his time in pleasure as Pururavas of old did, on receiving the celestial damsel Urvasi. Herself fairest of the fair, the damsel Vapushtama too, devoted to her lord and celebrated for her beauty having gained a desirable husband, pleased him by the excess of her affection during the period he spent in the pursuit of pleasure.'"

SECTION XLV
(Astika Parva continued)

"Meanwhile the great ascetic Jaratkaru wandered over the whole earth making the place where evening fell his home for the night. And gifted with ascetic power, he roamed, practising various vows difficult to be practised by the immature, and bathing also in various sacred waters. And the Muni had air alone for his food and was free from desire of worldly enjoyment. And he became daily emaciated and grew lean-fleshed. And one day he saw the spirits of his ancestors, heads down, in a hole, by a cord of virana roots having only one thread entire. And that even single thread was being gradually eaten away by a large rat dwelling in that hole. And the Pitris in that hole were without food, emaciated, pitiable, and eagerly desirous of salvation. And Jaratkaru, approaching the pitiable one, himself in humble guise, asked them, 'Who are ye hanging by this cord of virana roots? The single weak root that is still left in this cord of virana roots already eaten away by the rat, dwelling in this hole, is itself being gradually eaten away by the same rat with his sharp teeth. The little that remains of that single thread will soon be cut away. It is clear ye shall then have to fall down into this pit with faces downwards. Seeing you with faces downwards, and overtaken by this great calamity, my pity hath been excited. What good can I do to you. Tell me quickly whether this calamity can be averted by a fourth, a third, or even by the sacrifice of a half of this my asceticism, O, relieve yourselves even with the whole of my asceticism. I consent to all this. Do ye as ye please.'

"The Pitris said, 'Venerable Brahmacharin, thou desirest to relieve us. But, O foremost of Brahmanas, thou canst not dispel our affliction by thy asceticism. O child, O first of speakers, we too have the fruits of our asceticism. But, O Brahmana, it is for the loss of children that we are falling down into this unholy hell. The grandsire himself hath said that a son is a great merit. As we are about to be cast in this hole, our ideas are no longer clear. Therefore, O child, we know thee not, although thy manhood is well-known on earth. Venerable thou art and of good fortune, thou who thus from kindness grievest for us worthy of pity and greatly afflicted. O Brahmana, listen, who we are. We are Rishis of the Yayavara sect, of rigid vows. And, O Muni, from loss of children, we have fallen down from a sacred region. Our severe penances have not been destroyed; we have a thread yet. But we have only one thread now. It matters little, however, whether he is or is not. Unfortunate as we are, we have a thread in one, known as Jaratkaru. The unfortunate one has gone through the Vedas and their branches and is practising asceticism alone. He being one with soul under complete control, desires set high, observant of vows, deeply engaged in ascetic penances, and free from greed for the merits or asceticism, we have been reduced to this deplorable state. He hath no wife, no son, no relatives. Therefore, do we hang in this hole, our consciousness lost, like men having none to take care of them. If thou meetest him, O, tell him, from thy kindness to ourselves, Thy Pitris, in sorrow, are hanging with faces downwards in a hole. Holy one, take a wife and beget children. O thou of ascetic wealth, thou art, O amiable one, the only thread that remaineth in the line of thy ancestors. O Brahmana, the cord of virana roots that thou seest we are hanging by, is the cord representing our multiplied race. And, O Brahmana, these threads of the cord of virana roots that thou seest as eaten away, are ourselves who have been eaten up by Time. This root thou seest hath been half-eaten and by which we are hanging in this hole is he that hath adopted asceticism alone. The rat that thou beholdest is Time of infinite strength. And he (Time) is gradually weakening the wretch Jaratkaru engaged in ascetic penances tempted by the merits thereof, but wanting in prudence and heart. O excellent one, his asceticism cannot save us. Behold, our roots being torn, cast down from higher regions, deprived of consciousness by Time, we are going downwards like sinful wretches. And upon our going down into this hole with all our relatives, eaten up by Time, even he shall sink with us into hell. O child, whether it is asceticism, or sacrifice, or whatever else there be of very holy acts, everything is inferior. These cannot count with a son. O child, having seen all, speak unto that Jaratkaru of ascetic wealth. Thou shouldst tell him in detail everything that thou hast beheld. And, O Brahmana, from thy kindness towards us, thou shouldst tell him all that would induce him to take a wife and beget children. Amongst his friends, or of our own race, who art thou, O excellent one, that thus grievest for us all like a friend? We wish to hear who thou art that stayest here.'"

SECTION XLVI
(Astika Parva continued)

"Sauti said. 'Jaratkaru, hearing all this, became excessively dejected. And from sorrow he spoke unto those Pitris in words obstructed by tears.' And Jaratkaru said, 'Ye are even my fathers and grand-fathers gone before. Therefore, tell me what I must do for your welfare. I am that sinful son of yours, Jaratkaru! Punish me for my sinful deeds, a wretch that I am.'

"The Pitris replied, saying, 'O son, by good luck hast thou arrived at this spot in course of thy rambles. O Brahmana, why hast thou not taken a wife?'

"Jaratkaru said. 'Ye Pitris, this desire hath always existed in my heart that I would, with vital seed drawn up, carry this body to the other world. My mind hath been possessed with the idea that I would not take a wife. But ye grandsires, having seen you hanging like birds, I have diverted my mind from the Brahmacharya mode of life. I will truly do what you like. I will certainly marry, if ever I meet with a maiden of my own name. I shall accept her who, bestowing herself of her own accord, will be as aims unto me, and whom I shall not have to maintain. I shall marry if I get such a one; otherwise, I shall not. This is the truth, ye grandsires! And the offspring that will be begot upon her shall be your salvation. And ye Pitris of mine, ye shall live for ever in blessedness and without fear.'

'Sauti continued, 'The Muni, having said so unto the Pitris, wandered over the earth again. And, O Saunaka, being old, he obtained no wife. And he grieved much that he was not successful. But directed (as before) by his ancestors, he continued the search. And going into the forest, he wept loudly in great grief. And having gone into the forest, the wise one, moved by the desire of doing good to his ancestors, said, 'I will ask for a bride,' distinctly repeating these words thrice. And he said, 'Whatever creatures are here, mobile and immobile, so whoever there be that are invisible, O, hear my words! My ancestors, afflicted with grief, have directed me that am engaged in the most severe penances, saying, 'Marry thou for (the acquisition of) a son.' 'O ye, being directed by my ancestors, I am roaming in poverty and sorrow, over the wide world for wedding a maiden that I may obtain as alms. Let that creature, amongst those I have addressed, who hath a daughter, bestow on me that am roaming far and near. Such a bride as is of same name with me, to be bestowed on me as alms, and whom, besides, I shall not maintain, O bestow on me!' Then those snakes that had been set upon Jaratkaru track, ascertaining his inclination, gave information to Vasuki. And the king of the snakes, hearing their words, took with him that maiden decked with ornaments, and went into the forest unto that Rishi. And, O Brahmana, Vasuki, the king of the snakes, having gone there, offered that maiden as alms unto that high-souled Rishi. But the Rishi did not at once accept her. And the Rishi, thinking her not to be of the same name with himself, and seeing that the question of her maintenance also was unsettled, reflected for a few moments, hesitating to accept her. And then, O son of Bhrigu, he asked Vasuki the maiden's name, and also said unto him, 'I shall not maintain her.'"

SECTION XLVII
(Astika Parva continued)

"Sauti said, 'Then Vasuki spake unto the Rishi Jaratkaru these words, 'O best of Brahmanas, this maiden is of the same name with thee. She is my sister and hath ascetic merit. I will maintain thy wife; accept her. O thou of ascetic wealth, I shall protect her with all my ability. And, O foremost of the great Munis, she hath been reared by me for thee.' And the Rishi replied, 'This is agreed between us that I shall not maintain her; and she shall not do aught that I do not like. If she do, I leave her!'

"Sauti continued, 'When the snake had promised, saying, 'I shall maintain my sister,' Jaratkaru then went to the snake's house. Then that first of mantra-knowing Brahmanas, observing rigid vows, that virtuous and veteran ascetic, took her hand presented to him according to shastric rites. And taking his bride with him, adored by the great Rishi, he entered the delightful chamber set apart for him by the king of the snakes. And in that chamber was a bed-stead covered with very valuable coverlets. And Jaratkaru lived there with his wife. And the excellent Rishi made an agreement with his wife, saying, 'Nothing must ever be done or said by thee that is against my liking. And in case of thy doing any such thing, I will leave thee and no longer continue to stay in thy house. Bear in mind these words that have been spoken by me.'

"And then the sister of the king of the snakes in great anxiety and grieving exceedingly, spoke unto him, saying, 'Be it so.' And moved by the desire of doing good to her relatives, that damsel, of unsullied reputation, began to attend upon her lord with the wakefulness of a dog, the timidity of a deer, and knowledge of signs possessed by the crow. And one day, after the menstrual period, the sister of Vasuki, having purified herself by a bath according to custom, approached her lord the great Muni. And thereupon she conceived. And the embryo was like unto a flame of fire, possessed of great energy, and resplendent as fire itself. And it grew like the moon in the bright fortnight.

"And one day, within a short time, Jaratkaru of great fame, placing his head on the lap of his wife, slept, looking like one fatigued. And as he was sleeping, the sun entered his chambers in the Western mountain and was about to set. And, O Brahmana, as the day was fading, she, the excellent sister of Vasuki, became thoughtful, fearing the loss of her husband's virtue. And she thought, 'What should I now do? Shall I wake my husband or not? He is exacting and punctilious in his religious duties. How can I act as not to offend him? The alternatives are his anger and the loss of virtue of a virtuous man. The loss of virtue, I ween, is the greater of the two evils. Again, if I wake him, he will be angry. But if twilight passeth away without his prayers being said, he shall certainly sustain loss of virtue.'

'And having resolved at last, the sweet-speeched Jaratkaru, the sister of Vasuki, spake softly unto that Rishi resplendent with ascetic penances, and lying prostrate like a flame of fire, 'O thou of great good fortune, awake, the sun is setting. O thou of rigid vows, O illustrious one, do your evening prayer after purifying yourself with water and uttering the name of Vishnu. The time for the evening sacrifice hath come. Twilight, O lord, is even now gently covering the western side.'

"The illustrious Jaratkaru of great ascetic merit, thus addressed, spake unto his wife these words, his upper lip quivering in anger, 'O amiable one of the Naga race, thou hast insulted me. I shall no longer abide with thee, but shall go where I came from. O thou of beautiful thighs, I believe in my heart that the sun hath no power to set in the usual time, if I am asleep. An insulted person should never live where he hath met with the insult, far less should I, a virtuous person, or those that are like me.' Jaratkaru, the sister of Vasuki, thus addressed by her lord, began to quake with terror, and she spake unto him, saying, 'O Brahmana, I have not waked thee from desire of insult; but I have done it so that thy virtue may not sustain any loss.'

"The Rishi Jaratkaru, great in ascetic merit, possessed with anger and desirous of forsaking his spouse, thus addressed, spake unto his wife, saying, O thou fair one, never have I spoken a falsehood. Therefore, go I shall. This was also settled between ourselves. O amiable one, I have passed the time happily with thee. And, O fair one, tell thy brother, when I am gone, that I have left thee. And upon my going away, it behoveth thee not to grieve for me.'

"Thus addressed Jaratkaru, the fair sister of Vasuki, of faultless features, filled with anxiety and sorrow, having mustered sufficient courage and patience, though her heart was still quaking, then spake unto Rishi Jaratkaru. Her words were obstructed with tears and her face was pale with fear. And the palms of her hands were joined together, and her eyes were bathed in tears. And she said, 'It behoveth thee not to leave me without a fault. Thou treadest over the path of virtue. I too have been in the same path, with heart fixed on the good of my relatives. O best of Brahmanas, the object for which I was bestowed on thee hath not been accomplished yet. Unfortunate that I am, what shall Vasuki say unto me? O excellent one, the offspring desired of by my relatives afflicted by a mother's curse, do not yet appear! The welfare of my relatives dependeth on the acquisition of offspring from thee. And in order that my connection with thee may not be fruitless, O illustrious Brahmana, moved by the desire of doing good to my race do I entreat thee. O excellent one, high- souled thou art; so why shall thou leave me who am faultless? This is what is not just clear to me.'

"Thus addressed, the Muni of great ascetic merit spake unto his wife Jaratkaru these words that were proper and suitable to the occasion. And he said, 'O fortunate one, the being thou hast conceived, even like unto Agni himself is a Rishi of soul highly virtuous, and a master of the Vedas and their branches.'

"Having said so, the great Rishi, Jaratkaru of virtuous soul, went away, his heart firmly fixed on practising again the severest penances.'"

SECTION XLVIII
(Astika Parva continued)

"Sauti said, 'O thou of ascetic wealth, soon after her lord had left her, Jaratkaru went to her brother. And she told him everything that had happened. And the prince of snakes, hearing the calamitous news, spake unto his miserable sister, himself more miserable still.'

"And he said, 'Thou knowest, O amiable one, the purpose of thy bestowal, the reason thereof. If, from that union, for the welfare of the snakes, a son be born, then he, possessed of energy, will save us all from the snake- sacrifice. The Grandsire had said so, of old, in the midst of the gods. O fortunate one, hast thou conceived from thy union with that best of Rishis? My heart's desire is that my bestowal of thee on that wise one may not be fruitless. Truly, it is not proper for me to ask thee about this. But from the gravity of the interests I ask thee this. Knowing also the obstinacy of thy lord, ever engaged in severe penances, I shall not follow him, for he may curse me. Tell me in detail all that thy lord, O amiable one, hath done, and extract that terribly afflicting dart that lies implanted for a long time past in my heart.'

"Jaratkaru, thus addressed, consoling Vasuki, the king of the snakes, at length replied, saying, 'Asked by me about offspring, the high-souled and mighty ascetic said, 'There is,'—and then he went away. I do not remember him to have ever before speak even in jest aught that is false. Why should he, O king, speak a falsehood on such a serious occasion? He said, 'Thou shouldst not grieve, O daughter of the snake race, about the intended result of our union. A son shall be born to thee, resplendent as the blazing sun.' O brother, having said this to me, my husband of ascetic wealth went away—Therefore, let the deep sorrow cherished in thy heart disappear.'

"Sauti continued, 'Thus addressed, Vasuki, the king of the snakes, accepted those words of his sister, and in great joy said, 'Be it so!' And the chief of the snakes then adored his sister with his best regards, gift of wealth, and fitting eulogies. Then, O best of Brahmanas, the embryo endued with great splendour, began to develop, like the moon in the heavens in the bright fortnight.

"And in due time, the sister of the snakes, O Brahmana, gave birth to a son of the splendour of a celestial child, who became the reliever of the fears of his ancestors and maternal relatives. The child grew up there in the house of the king of the snakes. He studied the Vedas and their branches with the ascetic Chyavana, the son of Bhrigu. And though but a boy, his vows were rigid. And he was gifted with great intelligence, and with the several attributes of virtue, knowledge, freedom from the world's indulgences, and saintliness. And the name by which he was known to the world was Astika. And he was known by the name of Astika (whoever is) because his father had gone to the woods, saying. 'There is', when he was in the womb. Though but a boy, he had great gravity and intelligence. And he was reared with great care in the palace of the snakes. And he was like the illustrious lord of the celestials, Mahadeva of the golden form, the wielder of the trident. And he grew up day by day, the delight of all the snakes.'"

SECTION XLIX
(Astika Parva continued)

"Saunaka said, 'Tell me again, in detail,—all that king Janamejaya had asked his ministers about his father's ascension to heaven.'

'Sauti said, 'O Brahmana, hear all that the king asked his ministers, and all that they said about the death of Parikshit.'

"Janamejaya asked, 'Know ye all that befell my father. How did that famous king, in time, meet with his death? Hearing from you the incidents of my father's life in detail, I shall ordain something, if it be for the benefit of the world. Otherwise, I shall do nothing.'

'The minister replied, 'Hear, O monarch, what thou hast asked, viz., an account of thy illustrious father's life, and how also that king of kings left this world. Thy father was virtuous and high-souled, and always protected his people. O, hear, how that high-souled one conducted himself on earth. Like unto an impersonation of virtue and justice, the monarch, cognisant of virtue, virtuously protected the four orders, each engaged in the discharge of their specified duties. Of incomparable prowess, and blessed with fortune, he protected the goddess Earth. There was none who hated him and he himself hated none. Like unto Prajapati (Brahma) he was equally disposed towards all creatures. O monarch, Brahmanas and Kshatriyas and Vaisyas and Sudras, all engaged contentedly in the practice of their respective duties, were impartially protected by that king. Widows and orphans, the maimed and the poor, he maintained. Of handsome features, he was unto all creatures like a second Soma. Cherishing his subjects and keeping them contented, blessed with good fortune, truth- telling, of immense prowess, he was the disciple of Saradwat in the science of arms. And, O Janamejaya, thy father was dear unto Govinda. Of great fame, he was loved by all men. And he was born in the womb of Uttara when the Kuru race was almost extinct. And, therefore, the mighty son of Abhimanyu came to be called Parikshit (born in an extinct line). Well- versed in the interpretation of treatises on the duties of kings, he was gifted with every virtue. With passions under complete control, intelligent, possessing a retentive memory, the practiser of all virtues, the conqueror of his six passions of powerful mind, surpassing all, and fully acquainted with the science of morality and political science, the father had ruled over these subjects for sixty years. And he then died, mourned by all his subjects. And, after him, O first of men, thou hast acquired this hereditary kingdom of the Kurus for the last thousand years. Thou wast installed while a child, and art thus protecting every creature.'

"Janamejaya said, 'There hath not been born in our race a king who hath not sought the good of his subjects or been loved by them. Behold especially the conduct of my grandsires ever engaged in great achievements. How did my father, blessed with many virtues, meet with his death? Describe everything to me as it happened. I am desirous of hearing it from you!'

"Sauti continued, 'Thus directed by the monarch, those councillors, ever solicitous of the good of the king, told him everything exactly as it had occurred.'

'And the councillors said, 'O king, that father of thine, that protector of the whole earth, that foremost of all persons obedient to the scriptures, became addicted to the sports of the field, even as Pandu of mighty arms, that foremost of all bearers of the bow in battle. He made over to us all the affairs of state from the most trivial to the most important. One day, going into the forest, he pierced a deer with an arrow. And having pierced it he followed it quickly on foot into the deep woods, armed with sword and quiver. He could not, however, come upon the lost deer. Sixty years of age and decrepit, he was soon fatigued and became hungry. He then saw in the deep woods a high-souled Rishi. The Rishi was then observing the vow of silence. The king asked him about the deer, but, though asked, he made no reply. At last the king, already tired with exertion and hunger, suddenly became angry with that Rishi sitting motionless like a piece of wood in observance of his vow of silence. Indeed, the king knew not that he was a Muni observing the vow of silence. Swayed by anger, thy father insulted him. O excellent one of the Bharata race, the king, thy father taking up from the ground with the end of his bow a dead snake placed it on the shoulders of that Muni of pure soul. But the Muni spake not a word good or bad and was without anger. He continued in the same posture, bearing the dead snake.'"

SECTION L
(Astika Parva continued)

'Sauti continued, 'The ministers said, 'That king of kings then, spent with hunger and exertion, and having placed the snake upon the shoulders of that Muni, came back to his capital. The Muni had a son, born of a cow, of the name of Sringin. He was widely known, possessed of great prowess and energy, and very wrathful. Going (every day) to his preceptor he was in the habit of worshipping him. Commanded by him, Sringin was returning home, when he heard from a friend of his about the insult of his father by thy parent. And, O tiger among kings, he heard that his father, without having committed any fault, was bearing, motionless like a statue, upon his shoulders a dead snake placed thereon. O king, the Rishi insulted by thy father was severe in ascetic penances, the foremost of Munis, the controller of passions, pure, and ever engaged in wonderful acts. His soul was enlightened with ascetic penances, and his organs and their functions were under complete control. His practices and his speech were both very nice. He was contented and without avarice. He was without meanness of any kind and without envy. He was old and used to observe the vow of silence. And he was the refuge whom all creatures might seek in distress.

"Such was the Rishi insulted by thy father. The son, however, of that Rishi, in wrath, cursed thy father. Though young in years, the powerful one was old in ascetic splendour. Speedily touching water, he spake, burning as it were with spiritual energy and rage, these words in allusion to thy father, 'Behold the power of my asceticism! Directed by my words, the snake Takshaka of powerful energy and virulent poison, shall, within seven nights hence, burn, with his poison the wretch that hath placed the dead snake upon my un-offending father.' And having said this, he went to where his father was. And seeing his father he told him of his curse. The tiger among Rishis thereupon sent to thy father a disciple of his, named Gaurmukha, of amiable manners and possessed of every virtue. And having rested a while (after arrival at court) he told the king everything, saying in the words of his master, 'Thou hast been cursed, O king, by my son. Takshaka shall burn thee with his poison! Therefore, O king, be careful.' O Janamejaya, hearing those terrible words, thy father took every precaution against the powerful snake Takshaka.

"And when the seventh day had arrived, a Brahmana Rishi, named Kasyapa, desired to come to the monarch. But the snake Takshaka saw Kasyapa. And the prince of snakes spake unto Kasyapa without loss of time, saying, 'Where dost thou go so quickly, and what is the business on which thou goest?' Kasyapa replied, saying, 'O Brahmana, I am going whither king Parikshit, that best of the Kurus, is. He shall today be burnt by the poison of the snake Takshaka. I go there quickly in order to cure him, in fact, in order that, protected by me, the snake may not bite him to death.' Takshaka answered, saying, 'Why dost thou seek to revive the king to be bitten by me? I am that Takshaka. O Brahmana, behold the wonderful power of my poison. Thou art incapable of reviving that monarch when bit by me.' So saying, Takshaka, then and there, bit a lord of the forest (a banian tree). And the banian, as soon as it was bit by the snake, was converted into ashes. But Kasyapa, O king, revived it. Takshaka thereupon tempted him, saying, 'Tell me thy desire.' And Kasyapa, too, thus addressed, spake again unto Takshaka, saying, 'I go there from desire of wealth.' And Takshaka, thus addressed, then spake unto the high-souled Kasyapa in these soft words, 'O sinless one, take from me more wealth than what thou expectest from that monarch, and go back!' And Kasyapa, that foremost of men, thus addressed by the snake, and receiving from him as much wealth as he desired, wended his way back.

"And Kasyapa going back, Takshaka, approaching in disguise, blasted, with the fire of his poison, thy virtuous father, the first of kings, then staying in his mansion with all precautions. And after that, thou hast, O tiger among men, been installed (on the throne). And, O best of monarchs, we have thus told thee all that we have seen and heard, cruel though the account is. And hearing all about the discomfiture of thy royal father, and of the insult to the Rishi Utanka, decide thou that which should follow!'

'Sauti continued, 'King Janamejaya, that chastiser of enemies, then spake upto all his ministers. And he said, 'When did ye learn all that happened upon that, banian reduced to ashes by Takshaka, and which, wonderful as it is, was afterwards revived by Kasyapa? Assuredly, my father could not have died, for the poison could have been neutralised by Kasyapa with his mantras. That worst of snakes, of sinful soul, thought within his mind that if Kasyapa resuscitated the king bit by him, he, Takshaka, would be an object of ridicule in the world owing to the neutralisation of his poison. Assuredly, having thought so, he pacified the Brahmana. I have devised a way, however, of inflicting punishment upon him. I like to know, however, what ye saw or heard, what happened in the deep solitude of the forest,—viz., the words of Takshaka and the speeches of Kasyapa. Having known it, I shall devise the means of exterminating the snake race.'

"The ministers said, 'Hear, O monarch of him who told us before of the meeting between that foremost Brahmana and that prince of snakes in the woods. A certain person, O monarch, had climbed up that tree containing some dry branches with the object of breaking them for sacrificial fuel. He was not perceived either by the snake or by the Brahmana. And, O king, that man was reduced to ashes along with the tree itself. And, O king of kings, he was revived with the tree by the power of the Brahmana. That man, a Brahmana's menial, having come to us, represented fully everything as it happened between Takshaka and the Brahmana. Thus have we told thee, O king, all that we have seen and heard. And having heard it, O tiger among kings, ordain that which should follow.'

"Sauti continued, 'King Janamejaya, having listened to the words of his ministers, was sorely afflicted with grief, and began to weep. And the monarch began to squeeze his hands. And the lotus-eyed king began to breathe a long and hot breath, shed tears, and shrieked aloud. And possessed with grief and sorrow, and shedding copious tears, and touching water according to the form, the monarch spake. And reflecting for a moment, as if settling something in his mind, the angry monarch, addressing all ministers, said these words.

'I have heard your account of my father's ascension to heaven. Know ye now what my fixed resolve is. I think no time must be lost in avenging this injury upon the wretch Takshaka that killed my father. He burnt my father making Sringin only a secondary cause. From malignity alone he made Kasyapa return. If that Brahmana had arrived, my father assuredly would have lived. What would he have lost if the king had revived by the grace of Kasyapa and the precautionary measures of his ministers? From ignorance of the effects of my wrath, he prevented Kasyapa—that excellent of Brahmanas—whom he could not defeat, from coming to my father with the desire of reviving him. The act of aggression is great on the part of the wretch Takshaka who gave wealth unto that Brahmana in order that he might not revive the king. I must now avenge myself on my father's enemy to please myself, the Rishi Utanka and you all.'"

SECTION LI
(Astika Parva continued)

'Sauti said, 'King Janamejaya having said so, his ministers expressed their approbation. And the monarch then expressed his determination to perform a snake-sacrifice. And that lord of the Earth—that tiger of the Bharata race—the son of Parikshit, then called his priest and Ritwiks. And accomplished in speech, he spake unto them these words relating to the accomplishment of his great task. 'I must avenge myself on the wretch Takshaka who killed my father. Tell me what I must do. Do you know any act by which I may cast into the blazing fire the snake Takshaka with his relatives? I desire to burn that wretch even as he burnt, of yore, by the fire of his poison, my father.'

"The chief priest answered, 'There is, O king, a great sacrifice for thee devised by the gods themselves. It is known as the snake-sacrifice, and is read of in the Puranas. O king, thou alone canst accomplish it, and no one else. Men versed in the Puranas have told us, there is such a sacrifice.'

"Sauti continued, 'Thus addressed, the king, O excellent one, thought Takshaka to be already burnt and thrown into the blazing mouth of Agni, the eater of the sacrificial butter. The king then said unto those Brahmanas versed in mantras, 'I shall make preparations for that sacrifice. Tell me the things that are necessary.' And the king's Ritwiks, O excellent Brahmana, versed in the Vedas and acquainted with the rites of that sacrifice measured, according to the scriptures, the land for the sacrificial platform. And the platform was decked with valuable articles and with Brahmanas. And it was full of precious things and paddy. And the Ritwika sat upon it at ease. And after the sacrificial platform had been thus constructed according to rule and as desired, they installed the king at the snake-sacrifice for the attainment of its object. And before the commencement of the snake-Sacrifice that was to come, there occurred this very important incident foreboding obstruction to the sacrifice. For when the sacrificial platform was being constructed, a professional builder of great intelligence and well-versed in the knowledge of laying foundations, a Suta by caste, well-acquainted with the Puranas, said, 'The soil upon which and the time at which the measurement for the sacrificial platform has been made, indicate that this sacrifice will not be completed, a Brahmana becoming the reason thereof.' Hearing this, the king, before his installation, gave orders to his gate-keepers not to admit anybody without his knowledge."

SECTION LII
(Astika Parva continued)

"Sauti said, 'The snake-sacrifice then commenced according to due form. And the sacrificial priests, competent in their respective duties according to the ordinance, clad in black garments and their eyes red from contact with smoke, poured clarified butter into the blazing fire, uttering the appropriate mantras. And causing the hearts of all the snakes to tremble with fear, they poured clarified butter into the mouth of Agni uttering the names of the snakes. And the snakes thereupon began to fall into the blazing fire, benumbed and piteously calling upon one another. And swollen and breathing hard, and twining each other with their heads and tails, they came in large numbers and fell into the fire. The white, the black, the blue, the old and the young—all fell alike into the fire, uttering various cries. Those measuring a krosa, and those measuring a yojana, and those of the measure of a gokarna, fell continuously with great violence into that first of all fires. And hundreds and thousands and tens of thousands of snakes, deprived of all control over their limbs, perished on that occasion. And amongst those that perished, there were some that were like horses, other like trunks of elephants, and others of huge bodies and strength like maddened elephants Of various colours and virulent poison, terrible and looking like maces furnished with iron- spikes, of great strength, ever inclined to bite, the snakes, afflicted with their mother's curse, fell into the fire.'"

SECTION LIII
(Astika Parva continued)

"Saunaka asked, 'What great Rishis became the Ritwiks at the snake- sacrifice of the wise king Janamejaya of the Pandava line? Who also became the Sadasyas in that terrible snake-sacrifice, so frightful to the snakes, and begetting such sorrow in them? It behoveth thee to describe all these in detail, so that, O son of Suta, we may know who were acquainted with the rituals of the snake-sacrifice.'

"Sauti replied, 'I will recite the names of those wise ones who became the monarch's Ritwiks and Sadasyas. The Brahmana Chandabhargava became the Hotri in that sacrifice. He was of great reputation, and was born in the race of Chyavana and was the foremost of those acquainted with the Vedas. The learned old Brahmana, Kautsa, became the Udgatri, the chanter of the Vedic hymns. Jaimini became the Brahmana, and Sarngarva and Pingala the Adhvaryus, Vyasa with his son and disciples, and Uddalaka, Pramataka, Swetaketu, Pingala, Asita, Devala, Narada, Parvata, Atreya, Kundajathara, the Brahmana Kalaghata, Vatsya, old Srutasravas ever engaged in japa and the study of the Vedas. Kohala Devasarman, Maudgalya, Samasaurava, and many other Brahmanas who had got through the Vedas became the Sadasyas at that sacrifice of the son of Parikshit.

"When the Ritwiks in that snake-sacrifice began to pour clarified butter into the fire, terrible snakes, striking fear into every creature, began to fall into it. And the fat and the marrow of the snakes thus falling into the fire began to flow in rivers. And the atmosphere was filled with an insufferable stench owing to the incessant burning of the snakes. And incessant also were the cries of the snakes fallen into the fire and those in the air about to fall into it.

'Meanwhile, Takshaka, that prince of snakes, as soon as he heard that king Janamejaya was engaged in the sacrifice, went to the palace of Purandara (Indra). And that best of snakes, having represented all that had taken place, sought in terror the protection of Indra after having acknowledged his fault. And Indra, gratified, told him, 'O prince of snakes, O Takshaka, here thou hast no fear from that snake-sacrifice. The Grandsire was pacified by me for thy sake. Therefore, thou hast no fear. Let this fear of thy heart be allayed.'

"Sauti continued, 'Thus encouraged by him, that best of snakes began to dwell in Indra's abode in joy and happiness. But Vasuki, seeing that the snakes were incessantly falling into the fire and that his family was reduced to only a few, became exceedingly sorry. And the king of the snakes was afflicted with great grief, and his heart was about to break. And summoning his sister, he spake unto her, saying, 'O amiable one, my limbs are burning and I no longer see the points of the heavens. I am about to fall down from loss of consciousness. My mind is turning, my sight is falling and my heart is breaking. Benumbed, I may fall today into that blazing fire! This sacrifice of the son of Parikshit is for the extermination of our race. It is evident I also shall have to go to the abode of the king of the dead. The time is come, O my sister, on account of which thou wert bestowed by me on Jaratkaru to protect us with our relatives. O best of the women of the snake race, Astika will put an end to the sacrifice that is going on. The Grandsire told me this of old. Therefore, O child, solicit thy dear son who is fully conversant with the Vedas and regarded even by the old, for the protection of myself and also of those dependent on me.'"

SECTION LIV
(Astika Parva continued)

"Sauti said, 'Then the snake-dame Jaratkaru, calling her own son, told him the following words according to the directions of Vasuki, the king of the snakes. 'O son, the time is come for the accomplishment of that object for which I was bestowed on thy father by my brother. Therefore, do thou that which should be done.'

"Astika asked, 'Why wert thou, O mother, bestowed on my father by my uncle? Tell me all truly so that on hearing it, I may do what is proper.'

"Then Jaratkaru, the sister of the king of the snakes, herself unmoved by the general distress, and even desirous of the welfare of her relatives, said unto him, 'O son, it is said that the mother of all the snakes is Kadru. Know thou why she cursed in anger her sons.' Addressing the snakes she said, 'As ye have refused to falsely represent Uchchaihsravas, the prince of horses, for bringing about Vinata's bondage according to the wager, therefore, shall he whose charioteer is Vayu burn you all in Janamejaya's sacrifice. And perishing in that sacrifice, ye shall go to the region of the unredeemed spirits.' The Grandsire of all the worlds spake unto her while uttering this curse, 'Be it so,' and thus approved of her speech. Vasuki, having heard that curse and then the words of the Grandsire, sought the protection of the gods, O child, on the occasion when the amrita was being churned for. And the gods, their object fulfilled, for they had obtained the excellent amrita, with Vasuki ahead, approached the Grandsire. And all the gods, with king Vasuki, sought to incline Him who was born of the lotus to be propitious, so that the curse might be made abortive.'

"And the gods said, 'O Lord, Vasuki, the king of the snakes, is sorry on account of his relatives. How may his mother's curse prove abortive?'

"Brahman thereupon replied, saying, 'Jaratkaru will take unto himself a wife of the name of Jaratkaru; the Brahmana born of her will relieve the snakes.'

"Vasuki, the best of snakes, hearing those words, bestowed me, O thou of godlike looks, on thy high-souled father some time before the commencement of the sacrifice. And from that marriage thou art born of me. That time has come. It behoveth thee to protect us from this danger. It behoveth thee to protect my brother and myself from the fire, so that the object, viz., our relief, for which I was bestowed on thy wise father, may not be unfulfilled. What dost thou think, O son?'

"Sauti continued, 'Thus addressed, Astika said unto his mother, 'Yes, I will.' And he then addressed the afflicted Vasuki, and as if infusing life into him, said, 'O Vasuki, thou best of snakes, thou great being, truly do I say, I shall relieve thee from that curse. Be easy, O snake! There is no fear any longer. I shall strive earnestly so that good may come! Nobody hath ever said that my speech, even in jest, hath proved false. Hence on serious occasions like this, I need not say anything more, O uncle, going thither today I shall gratify, with words mixed with blessings, the monarch Janamejaya installed at the sacrifice, so that, O excellent one, the sacrifice may stop. O highminded one, O king of the snakes, believe all that I say. Believe me, my resolve can never be unfulfilled.'

"And Vasuki then said, 'O Astika, my head swims and my heart breaks. I cannot discern the points of the earth, as I am afflicted with a mother's curse.'

"And Astika said, 'Thou best of snakes, it behoveth thee not to grieve any longer. I shall dispel this fear of thine from the blazing fire. This terrible punishment, capable of burning like the fire at the end of the Yuga, I shall extinguish. Nurse not thy fear any longer.'

"Sauti continued, 'Then that best of Brahmanas, Astika, quelling the terrible fear of the Vasuki's heart, and taking it, as it were, on himself, wended, for the relief of the king of the snakes, with speed to Janamejaya's sacrifice blessed with every merit. And Astika having gone thither, beheld the excellent sacrificial compound with numerous Sadasyas on it whose splendour was like unto that of the Sun or Agni. But that best of Brahmanas was refused admittance by the door-keepers. And the mighty ascetic gratified them, being desirous of entering the sacrificial compound. And that best of Brahmanas, that foremost of all virtuous men, having entered the excellent sacrificial compound, began to adore the king of infinite achievements, Ritwiks, the Sadasyas, and also the sacred fire.'"

SECTION LV
(Astika Parva continued)

"Astika said, 'Soma and Varuna and Prajapati performed sacrifices of old in Prayaga. But thy sacrifice, O foremost one of Bharata's race, O son of Parikshit, is not inferior to any of those. Let those dear unto us be blessed! Sakra performed a hundred sacrifices. But this sacrifice of thine, O foremost one of Bharata's race, O son of Parikshit, is fully equal to ten thousand sacrifices of Sakra. Let those dear unto us be blessed! Like the sacrifice of Yama, of Harimedha, or of king Rantideva, is the sacrifice of thine, O foremost one of Bharata's race, O son of Parikshit. Let those dear unto us be blessed! Like the sacrifice of Maya, of king Sasavindu, or of king Vaisravana, is this sacrifice of thine, O foremost one of Bharata's race, O son of Satyavati, in which he himself was the chief priest, is this sacrifice of Nriga, of Ajamida, of the son of Dasaratha, is this sacrifice of thine, O foremost one of Bharata's race, O son of Parikshit. Let those dear unto us be blessed! Like the sacrifice of king Yudhishthira, the son of a god and belonging to Ajamida race, heard of (even) in the heavens, is this sacrifice of thine. O foremost one of Bharata's race, O son of Parikshit, let those dear unto us be blessed! Like the sacrifice of Krishna (Dwaipayana), the son of Satyavati, in which he himself was the chief priest, is this sacrifice of thine, O foremost one of Bharata's race, O son of Parikshit. Let those dear unto us be blessed! These (Ritwiks and Sadasyas) that are here engaged in making thy sacrifice, like unto that of the slayer of Vritra, are of splendour equal to that of the sun. There now remains nothing for them to know, and gifts made to them become inexhaustible (in merit). It is my conviction that there is no Ritwik in all the worlds who is equal to thy Ritwik, Dwaipayana. His disciples, becoming Ritwiks, competent for their duties, travel over the earth. The high-souled bearer of libation (viz., Agni), called also Vibhavasu and Chitrabhanu, having gold for his vital seed and having his path, marked by black smoke, blazing up with flames inclined to the right, beareth these thy libations of clarified butter to the gods. In this world of men there is no other monarch equal to thee in the protection of subjects. I am ever well-pleased with thy abstinence. Indeed, thou art either Varuna, or Yama, the god of Justice. Like Sakra himself, thunderbolt in hand, thou art, in this world, the protector of all creatures. In this earth there is no man so great as thou and no monarch who is thy equal in sacrifice. Thou art like Khatwanga, Nabhaga, and Dilipa. In prowess thou art like Yayati and Mandhatri. In splendour equal to the sun, and of excellent vows, thou art O monarch, like Bhishma! Like Valmiki thou art of energy concealed. Like Vasishtha thou hast controlled thy wrath. Like Indra is thy lordship. Thy splendour also shines like that of Narayana. Like Yama art thou conversant with the dispensation of justice. Thou art like Krishna adorned with every virtue. Thou art the home of the good fortune that belongs to the Vasus. Thou art also the refuge of the sacrifices. In strength thou art equal to Damvodbhava. Like Rama (the son of Jamadagni) thou art conversant with the scriptures and arms. In energy thou art equal to Aurva and Trita. Thou inspirest terror by thy looks like Bhagiratha.'

"Sauti said, 'Astika, having thus adored them, gratified them all, viz., the king, the Sadasyas, the Ritwiks and the sacrificial fire. And king Janamejaya beholding the signs and indications manifested all around, addressed them as follows.'"

SECTION LVI
(Astika Parva continued)

"Janamejaya said, 'Though this one is but a boy, he speaks yet like a wise old man. He is not a boy but one wise and old. I think, I desire to bestow on him a boon. Therefore, ye Brahmanas, give me the necessary permission.'

"The Sadasyas said, 'A Brahmana, though a boy, deserves the respect of kings. The learned ones do more so. This boy deserves every desire of his being fulfilled by thee, but not before Takshaka comes with speed.'

"Sauti continued, 'The king, being inclined to grant the Brahmana a boon, said 'Ask thou a boon.' The Hotri, however, being rather displeased, said, 'Takshaka hath not come as yet into this sacrifice.'

"Janamejaya replied, 'Exert ye to the best of your might, so that this sacrifice of mine may attain completion, and Takshaka also may soon come here. He is my enemy.'

"The Ritwiks replied, 'As the scriptures declare unto us, and as the fire also saith, O monarch, (it seems that) Takshaka is now staying in the abode of Indra, afflicted with fear.'

"Sauti continued, 'The illustrious Suta named Lohitaksha also, conversant with the Puranas, had said so before.

"Asked by the king on the present occasion he again told the monarch, 'Sire, it is even so as the Brahmanas have said—Knowing the Puranas, I say, O monarch, that Indra hath granted him this boon, saying, 'Dwell with me in concealment, and Agni shall not burn thee.'

"Sauti continued, 'Hearing this, the king installed in the sacrifice became very sorry and urged the Hotri to do his duty. And as the Hotri, with mantras, began to pour clarified butter into the fire Indra himself appeared on the scene. And the illustrious one came in his car, adorned by all the gods standing around, followed by masses of clouds, celestial singers, and the several bevies of celestial dancing girls. And Takshaka anxious with fear, hid himself in the upper garment of Indra and was not visible. Then the king in his anger again said unto his mantra-knowing Brahmanas these words, bent upon the destruction of Takshaka, 'If the snake Takshaka be in the abode of Indra, cast him into the fire with Indra himself.'

"Sauti continued, 'Urged thus by the king Janamejaya about Takshaka, the Hotri poured libations, naming that snake then staying there. And even as the libations were poured, Takshaka, with Purandara himself, anxious and afflicted, became visible in a moment in the skies. Then Purandara, seeing that sacrifice, became much alarmed, and quickly casting Takshaka off, went back to his own abode. After Indra had gone away, Takshaka, the prince of snakes, insensible with fear, was by virtue of the mantras, brought near enough the flames of the sacrificial fire.'

"The Ritwiks then said, 'O king of kings, the sacrifice of thine is being performed duly. It behoveth thee, O Lord, to grant a boon now to this first of Brahmanas.'

"Janamejaya then said, 'Thou immeasurable one of such handsome and child- like features, I desire to grant thee a worthy boon. Therefore, ask thou that which thou desirest in thy heart. I promise thee, that I will grant it even if it be ungrantable.'

"The Ritwiks said, 'O monarch, behold, Takshaka is soon coming under thy control! His terrible cries, and loud roar is being heard. Assuredly, the snake hath been forsaken by the wielder of thunder. His body being disabled by your mantras, he is falling from heaven. Even now, rolling in the skies, and deprived of consciousness, the prince of snakes cometh, breathing loudly.'

"Sauti continued, 'While Takshaka, the prince of snakes was about to fall into the sacrificial fire, during those few moments Astika spoke as follows, 'O Janamejaya, if thou wouldst grant me a boon, let this sacrifice of thine come to an end and let no more snakes fall into the fire.'

"O Brahmana, the son of Parikshit, being thus addressed by Astika, became exceedingly sorry and replied unto Astika thus, 'O illustrious one, gold, silver, kine, whatever other possessions thou desirest I shall give unto thee. But let not my sacrifice come to an end.'

"Astika thereupon replied, 'Gold, silver or kine, I do not ask of thee, O monarch! But let thy sacrifice be ended so that my maternal relations be relieved.'

"Sauti continued, 'The son of Parikshit, being thus addressed by Astika, repeatedly said this unto that foremost of speakers, 'Best of the Brahmanas, ask some other boon. O, blessed be thou!' But, O thou of Bhrigu's race, he did not beg any other boon. Then all the Sadasyas conversant with the Vedas told the king in one voice, 'Let the Brahmana receive his boon!'"

SECTION LVII
(Astika Parva continued)

"Saunaka said, 'O son of a Suta, I desire to hear the names of all those snakes that fell into the fire of this snake-sacrifice!'

"Sauti replied, 'Many thousands and tens of thousands and billions of snakes fell into the fire. O most excellent Brahmana, so great is the number that I am unable to count them all. So far, however, as I remember, hear the names I mention of the principal snakes cast into the fire. Hear first the names of the principal ones of Vasuki's race alone, of colour blue, red and white of terrible form and huge body and deadly poison. Helpless and miserable and afflicted with their mother's curse, they fell into the sacrificial fire like libations of butter.

"Kotisa, Manasa, Purna, Cala, Pala Halmaka, Pichchala, Kaunapa, Cakra, Kalavega, Prakalana, Hiranyavahu, Carana, Kakshaka, Kaladantaka—these snakes born of Vasuki, fell into the fire. And, O Brahmana, numerous other snakes well-born, and of terrible form and great strength, were burnt in the blazing fire. I shall now mention those born in the race of Takshaka. Hear thou their names. Puchchandaka, Mandalaka, Pindasektri, Ravenaka; Uchochikha, Carava, Bhangas, Vilwatejas, Virohana; Sili, Salakara, Muka, Sukumara, Pravepana, Mudgara and Sisuroman, Suroman and Mahahanu. These snakes born of Takshaka fell into the fire. And Paravata, Parijata, Pandara, Harina, Krisa, Vihanga, Sarabha, Meda, Pramoda, Sauhatapana— these born in the race of Airavata fell into the fire. Now hear, O best of Brahmanas, the names of the snakes I mention born in the race of Kauravya: Eraka, Kundala Veni, Veniskandha, Kumaraka, Vahuka, Sringavera, Dhurtaka, Pratara and Astaka. There born in the race of Kauravya fell into the fire. Now hear the names I mention, in order, of those snakes endued with the speed of the wind and with virulent poison, born in the race of Dhritarashtra: Sankukarna, Pitharaka, Kuthara, Sukhana, and Shechaka; Purnangada, Purnamukha, Prahasa, Sakuni, Dari, Amahatha, Kumathaka, Sushena, Vyaya, Bhairava, Mundavedanga, Pisanga, Udraparaka, Rishabha, Vegavat, Pindaraka; Raktanga, Sarvasaranga, Samriddha, Patha and Vasaka; Varahaka, Viranaka, Suchitra, Chitravegika, Parasara, Tarunaka, Maniskandha and Aruni.

"O Brahmana, thus I have recited the names of the principal snakes known widely for their achievements—I have not been able to name all, the number being countless. The sons of these snakes, the sons of those sons, that were burnt having fallen into the fire, I am unable to mention. They are so many! Some of three heads, some of seven, others of ten, of poison like unto the fire at the end of the yuga and terrible in form,—they were burnt by thousands!

"Many others, of huge bodies, of great speed, tall as mountain summits, of the length of a yama, of a yojana, and of two yojanas, capable of assuming at will any form and of mastering at will any degree of strength, of poison like unto blazing fire, afflicted by the curse of a mother, were burnt in that great 'sacrifice.'"

SECTION LVIII
(Astika Parva, continued)

"Sauti said, 'Listen now to another very wonderful incident in connection with Astika. When king Janamejaya was about to gratify Astika by granting the boon, the snake (Takshaka), thrown off Indra's hands, remained in mid without actually falling. King Janamejaya thereupon became curious, for Takshaka, afflicted with fear, did not at once fall into the fire although libations were poured in proper form into the blazing sacrificial Agni in his name.'

"Saunaka said, 'Was it, O Suta, that the mantras of those wise Brahmanas were not potent; since Takshaka did not fall into the fire?'

"Sauti replied, 'Unto the unconscious Takshaka, that best of snakes, after he had been cast off Indra's hands, Astika had thrice said, 'Stay,' 'Stay,' 'Stay.' And he succeeded in staying in the skies, with afflicted heart, like a person somehow staying between the welkin and the earth.

"The king then, on being repeatedly urged by his Sadasyas, said, 'Let it be done as Astika hath said. Let the sacrifice be ended, let the snakes be safe, let this Astika also be gratified, O Suta, thy words also be true.' When the boon was granted to Astika, plaudits expressive of joy rang through the air. Thus the sacrifice of the son of Parikshit—that king of the Pandava race—came to an end. The king Janamejaya of the Bharata race was himself pleased, and on the Ritwiks with the Sadasyas, and on all who had come there, the king, bestowed money by hundreds and thousands. And unto Suta Lohitaksha—conversant with the rules of building and foundations—who had at the commencement said that a Brahmana would be the cause of the interruption of the snake-sacrifice, the king gave much wealth. The king, of uncommon kindness, also gave him various things, with food and wearing apparel, according to his desire, and became very much pleased. Then he concluded his sacrifice according to the prescribed rites, and after treating him with every respect, the king in joy sent home the wise Astika exceedingly gratified, for he had attained his object. And the king said unto him, 'Thou must come again to become a Sadasya in my great Horse-sacrifice.' And Astika said, 'yes' and then returned home in great joy, having achieved his great end after gratifying the monarch. And returning in joy to his uncle and mother and touching their feet, he recounted to them everything as it had happened.'

"Sauti continued, 'Hearing all he had said, the snakes that had come thither became very much delighted, and their fears were allayed. They were much pleased with Astika and asked him to solicit a boon, saying, 'O learned one, what good shall we do unto thee? We have been very much gratified, having been all saved by thee. What shall we accomplish for thee, O child!'

"Astika said, 'Let those Brahmanas, and other men, who shall, in the morning or in the evening, cheerfully and with attention, read the sacred account of this my act, have no fear from any of you.' And the snakes in joy thereupon said, 'O nephew, in the nature of thy boon, let it be exactly as thou sayest. That which thou askest we all shall cheerfully do, O nephew! And those also that call to mind Astika, Artiman and Sunitha, in the day or in the night, shall have no fear of snakes. He again shall have no fear of snakes who will say, 'I call to mind the famous Astika born of Jaratkaru, that Astika who saved the snakes from the snake-sacrifice. Therefore, ye snakes of great good fortune, it behoveth you not to bite me. But go ye away, blessed be ye, or go away thou snake of virulent poison, and remember the words of Astika after the snake sacrifice of Janamejaya. That snake who does not cease from biting after hearing such mention of Astika, shall have his hood divided a hundredfold like the fruit of Sinsa tree.'

"Sauti continued, 'That first of Brahmanas, thus addressed by the foremost of the chief snakes assembled together, was very much gratified. And the high-souled one then set his heart upon going away.

"And that best of Brahmanas, having saved the snakes from the snake- sacrifice, ascended to heaven when his time came, leaving sons and grandsons behind him.

'Thus have I recited to thee this history of Astika exactly as it happened. Indeed, the recitation of this history dispelleth all fear of snakes.'

'Sauti continued, 'O Brahmanas, O foremost one of Bhrigu's race, as thy ancestor Pramati had cheerfully narrated unto his inquiring son Ruru, and as I had heard it, thus have I recited this blessed history, from the beginning, of the learned Astika. And, O Brahmana, O oppressor of all enemies, having heard this holy history of Astika that increaseth virtue, and which thou hadst asked me about after hearing the story of the Dundubha, let thy ardent curiosity be satisfied.'"

SECTION LIX
(Adivansavatarana Parva)

"Saunaka said, 'O son, thou hast narrated to me this extensive and great history commencing from the progeny of Bhrigu. O son of Suta, I have been much gratified with thee. I ask thee again, to recite to me, O son of a Suta, the history composed by Vyasa. The varied and wonderful narrations that were recited amongst those illustrious Sadasyas assembled at the sacrifice, in the intervals of their duties of that long-extending ceremony, and the objects also of those narrations, I desire to hear from thee, O son of a Suta! Recite therefore, all those to me fully.'

"Sauti said, 'The Brahmanas, in the intervals of the duties, spoke of many things founded upon the Vedas. But Vyasa recited the wonderful and great history called the Bharata.'

"Saunaka said, 'That sacred history called the Mahabharata, spreading the fame of the Pandavas, which Krishna-Dwaipayana, asked by Janamejaya, caused to be duly recited after the completion of the sacrifice. I desire to hear duly. That history hath been born of the ocean-like mind of the great Rishi of soul purified by yoga. Thou foremost of good men, recite it unto me, for, O son of a Suta, my thirst hath not been appeased by all thou hast said.'

"Sauti said, 'I shall recite to thee from the beginning of that great and excellent history called the Mahabharata composed by Vyasa. O Brahmana, listen to it in full, as I recite it. I myself feel a great pleasure in reciting it.'"

SECTION LX
(Adivansavatarana Parva continued)

"Sauti said, 'Hearing that Janamejaya was installed in the snake-sacrifice, the learned Rishi Krishna-Dwaipayana went thither on the occasion. And he, the grand-father of the Pandavas, was born in an island of the Yamuna, of the virgin Kali by Sakti's son, Parasara. And the illustrious one developed by his will alone his body as soon as he was born, and mastered the Vedas with their branches, and all the histories. And he readily obtained that which no one could obtain by asceticism, by the study of the Vedas, by vows, by fasts, by progeny, and by sacrifice. And the first of Veda-knowing ones, he divided the Vedas into four parts. And the Brahmana Rishi had knowledge of the supreme Brahma, knew the past by intuition, was holy, and cherished truth. Of sacred deeds and great fame, he begot Pandu and Dhritarashtra and Vidura in order to continue the line of Santanu.

"And the high-souled Rishi, with his disciples all conversant with the Vedas and their branches, entered the sacrificial pavilion of the royal sage, Janamejaya. And he saw that the king Janamejaya was seated in the sacrificial region like the god Indra, surrounded by numerous Sadasyas, by kings of various countries whose coronal locks had undergone the sacred bath, and by competent Ritwiks like unto Brahman himself. And that foremost one of Bharata's race, the royal sage Janamejaya, beholding the Rishi come, advanced quickly with his followers and relatives in great joy. And the king with the approval of his Sadasyas, gave the Rishi a golden seat as Indra did to Vrihaspati. And when the Rishi, capable of granting boons and adored by the celestial Rishis themselves, had been seated, the king of kings worshipped him according to the rites of the scriptures. And the king then offered him—his grandfather Krishna—who fully deserved them, water to wash his feet and mouth, and the Arghya, and kine. And accepting those offerings from the Pandava Janamejaya and ordering the kine also not to be slain, Vyasa became much gratified. And the king, after those adorations bowed to his great-grandfather, and sitting in joy asked him about his welfare. And the illustrious Rishi also, casting his eyes upon him and asking him about his welfare, worshipped the Sadasyas, having been before worshipped by them all. And after all this, Janamejaya with all his Sadasyas, questioned that first of Brahmanas, with joined palms as follows:

'O Brahmana, thou hast seen with thy own eyes the acts of the Kurus and the Pandavas. I am desirous of hearing thee recite their history. What was the cause of the disunion amongst them that was fruitful of such extraordinary deeds? Why also did that great battle, which caused the death of countless creatures occur between all my grandfathers—their clear sense over-clouded by fate? O excellent Brahmana, tell me all this in full as everything had happened.'

"Hearing those words of Janamejaya, Krishna-Dwaipayana directed his disciple Vaisampayana seated by his side, saying, 'The discord that happened between the Kurus and the Pandavas of old, narrate all to the king even as thou hast heard from me.'

"Then that blessed Brahmana, at the command of his preceptor recited the whole of that history unto the king, the Sadasyas, and all the chieftains there assembled. And he told them all about the hostility and the utter extinction of the Kurus and the Pandavas.'"

SECTION LXI
(Adivansavatarana Parva continued)

"Vaisampayana said, 'Bowing down in the first place to my preceptor with the eight parts of my body touching the ground, with devotion and reverence, and with all my heart, worshipping the whole assembly of Brahmanas and other learned persons, I shall recite in full what I have heard from the high-souled and great Rishi Vyasa, the first of intelligent men in the three worlds. And having got it within thy reach, O monarch, thou also art a fit person to hear the composition called Bharata. Encouraged by the command of my preceptor my heart feeleth no fear.

"Hear, O monarch, why that disunion occurred between the Kurus and the Pandavas, and why also that exile into the woods immediately proceeding from the game at dice prompted by the desire (of the Kurus) for rule. I shall relate all to thee who askest it thou best of the Bharata race!

"On the death of their father those heroes (the Pandavas) came to their own home. And within a short time they became well-versed in archery. And the Kurus beholding the Pandavas gifted with physical strength, energy, and power of mind, popular also with the citizens, and blessed with good fortune, became very jealous. Then the crookedminded Duryodhana, and Karna, with (the former's uncle) the son of Suvala began to persecute them and devise means for their exile. Then the wicked Duryodhana, guided by the counsels of Sakuni (his maternal uncle), persecuted the Pandavas in various ways for the acquirement of undisputed sovereignty. The wicked son of Dhritarashtra gave poison to Bhima, but Bhima of the stomach of the wolf digested the poison with the food. Then the wretch again tied the sleeping Bhima on the margin of the Ganges and, casting him into the water, went away. But when Bhimasena of strong arms, the son of Kunti woke, he tore the strings with which he had been tied and came up, his pains all gone. And while asleep and in the water black snakes of virulent poison bit him in every part of his body. But that slayer of foes did not still perish. And in all those persecutions of the Pandavas by their cousins, the Kurus, the high-minded Vidura attentively engaged himself neutralising those evil designs and rescuing the persecuted ones. And as Sakra from the heavens keeps in happiness the world of men, so did Vidura always keep the Pandavas from evil.

"When Duryodhana, with various means, both secret and open, found himself incapable of destroying the Pandavas who were protected by the fates and kept alive for grave future purposes (such as the extermination of the Kuru race), then called together his counsellors consisting of Vrisha (Karna), Duhsasana and others, and with the knowledge of Dhritarashtra caused a house of lac to be constructed. And king Dhritarashtra, from affection for his children, and prompted by the desire of sovereignty, sent the Pandavas tactfully into Varanavata. And the Pandavas then went away with their mother from Hastinapura. And when they were leaving the city, Vidura gave them some idea of impending danger and how they could come out of it.

"The sons of Kunti reached the town of Varanavata and lived there with their mother. And, agreeably to the command of Dhritarashtra, those illustrious slayers of all enemies lived in the palace of lac, while in that town. And they lived in that place for one year, protecting themselves from Purochana very wakefully. And causing a subterranean passage to be constructed, acting according to the directions of Vidura, they set fire to that house of lac and burnt Purochana (their enemy and the spy of Duryodhana) to death. Those slayers of all enemies, anxious with fear, then fled with their mother. In the woods beside a fountain they saw a Rakshasa. But, alarmed at the risk they ran of exposure by such an act the Pandavas fled in the darkness, out of fear from the sons of Dhritarashtra. It was here that Bhima gained Hidimva (the sister of the Rakshasa he slew) for a wife, and it was of her that Ghatotkacha was born. Then the Pandavas, of rigid vows, and conversant with the Vedas wended to a town of the name of Ekachakra and dwelt there in the guise of Brahmacharins. And those bulls among men dwelt in that town in the house of a Brahmana for some time, with temperance and abstinence. And it was here that Bhima of mighty arms came upon a hungry and mighty and man- eating Rakshasa of the name of Vaka. And Bhima, the son of Pandu, that tiger among men, slew him speedily with the strength of his arms and made the citizens safe and free from fear. Then they heard of Krishna (the princess of Panchala) having become disposed to select a husband from among the assembled princes. And, hearing of it, they went to Panchala, and there they obtained the maiden. And having obtained Draupadi (as their common wife) they then dwelt there for a year. And after they became known, those chastisers of all enemies went back to Hastinapura. And they were then told by king Dhritarashtra and the son of Santanu (Bhishma) as follows: 'In order, O dear ones, dissensions may not take place between you and your cousins, we have settled that Khandavaprastha should be your abode. Therefore, go ye, casting off all jealousy, to Khandavaprastha which contains many towns served by many broad roads, for dwelling there.' And accordingly the Pandavas went, with all their friends and followers, to Khandavaprastha taking with them many jewels and precious stones. And the sons of Pritha dwelt there for many years. And they brought, by force of arms, many a prince under their subjection. And thus, setting their hearts on virtue and firmly adhering to truth, unruffled by affluence, calm in deportment, and putting down numerous evils, the Pandavas gradually rose to power. And Bhima of great reputation subjugated the East, the heroic Arjuna, the North, Nakula, the West; Sahadeva that slayer of all hostile heroes, the South. And this having been done, their domination was spread over the whole world. And with the five Pandavas, each like unto the Sun, the Earth looked as if she had six Suns.

"Then, for some reason, Yudhishthira the just, gifted with great energy and prowess, sent his brother Arjuna who was capable of drawing the bow with the left hand, dearer unto him than life itself, into the woods. And Arjuna, that tiger among men, of firm soul, and gifted with every virtue, lived in the woods for eleven years and months. And during this period, on a certain occasion, Arjuna went to Krishna in Dwaravati. And Vibhatsu (Arjuna) there obtained for a wife the lotus-eyed and sweet-speeched younger sister of Vasudeva, Subhadra by name. And she became united, in gladness, with Arjuna, the son of Pandu, like Sachi with the great Indra, or Sri with Krishna himself. And then, O best of monarchs, Arjuna, the son of Kunti, with Vasudeva, gratified Agni; the carrier of the sacrificial butter, in the forest of Khandava (by burning the medicinal plants in that woods to cure Agni of his indigestion). And to Arjuna, assisted as he was by Kesava, the task did not at all appear heavy even as nothing is heavy to Vishnu with immense design and resources in the matter of destroying his enemies. And Agni gave unto the son of Pritha the excellent bow Gandiva and a quiver that was inexhaustible, and a war-chariot bearing the figure of Garuda on its standard. And it was on this occasion that Arjuna relieved the great Asura (Maya) from fear (of being consumed in the fire). And Maya, in gratitude, built (for the Pandavas) a celestial palace decked with every sort of jewels and precious stones. And the wicked Duryodhana, beholding that building, was tempted with the desire of possessing it. And deceiving Yudhishthira by means of the dice played through the hands of the son of Suvala, Duryodhana sent the Pandavas into the woods for twelve years and one additional year to be passed in concealment, thus making the period full thirteen.

"And the fourteenth year, O monarch, when the Pandavas returned and claimed their property, they did not obtain it. And thereupon war was declared, and the Pandavas, after exterminating the whole race of Kshatriyas and slaying king Duryodhana, obtained back their devastated kingdom.

"This is the history of the Pandavas who never acted under the influence of evil passions; and this the account, O first of victorious monarchs of the disunion that ended in the loss of their kingdom by the Kurus and the victory of the Pandavas.'"

THE MAHABHARATA

SECTION LXII
(Adivansavatarana Parva continued)

"Janamejaya said, 'O excellent Brahmana, thou hast, indeed, told me, in brief, the history, called Mahabharata, of the great acts of the Kurus. But, O thou of ascetic wealth, recite now that wonderful narration fully. I feel a great curiosity to hear it. It behoveth thee to recite it, therefore, in full. I am not satisfied with hearing in a nutshell the great history. That could never have been a trifling cause for which the virtuous ones could slay those whom they should not have slain, and for which they are yet applauded by men. Why also did those tigers among men, innocent and capable of avenging themselves upon their enemies, calmly suffer the persecution of the wicked Kurus? Why also, O best of Brahmanas, did Bhima of mighty arms and of the strength of ten thousand elephants, control his anger, though wronged? Why also did the chaste Krishna, the daughter of Drupada, wronged by those wretches and able to burn them, not burn the sons of Dhritarashtra with her wrathful eyes? Why also did the two other sons of Pritha (Bhima and Arjuna) and the two sons of Madri (Nakula and Sahadeva), themselves injured by the wretched Kurus, follow Yudhishthira who was greatly addicted to the evil habit of gambling? Why also did Yudhishthira, that foremost of all virtuous men, the son of Dharma himself, fully acquainted with all duties, suffer that excess of affliction? Why also did the Pandava Dhananjaya, having Krishna for his charioteer, who by his arrows sent to the other world that dauntless host of fighting men (suffer such persecution)? O thou of ascetic wealth, speak to me of all these as they took place, and everything that those mighty charioteers achieved.'

"Vaisampayana said, 'O monarch, appoint thou a time for hearing it. This history told by Krishna-Dwaipayana is very extensive. This is but the beginning. I shall recite it. I shall repeat the whole of the composition in full, of the illustrious and great Rishi Vyasa of immeasurable mental power, and worshipped in all the worlds. This Bharata consists of a hundred thousand sacred slokas composed by the son of Satyavati, of immeasurable mental power. He that reads it to others, and they that hear it read, attain to the world of Brahman and become equal to the very gods. This Bharata is equal unto the Vedas, is holy and excellent; is the worthiest of all to be listened to, and is a Purana worshipped by the Rishis. It contains much useful instruction on Artha and Kama (profit and pleasure). This sacred history maketh the heart desire for salvation. Learned persons by reciting this Veda of Krishna-Dwaipayana to those that are liberal, truthful and believing, earn much wealth. Sins, such as killing the embryo in the womb, are destroyed assuredly by this. A person, however cruel and sinful, by hearing this history, escapes from all his sins like the Sun from Rahu (after the eclipse is over). This history is called Jaya. It should be heard by those desirous of victory. A king by hearing it may bring the whole world under subjection and conquer all his foes. This history in itself is a mighty act of propitiation, a mighty sacrifice productive of blessed fruit. It should always be heard by a young monarch with his queen, for then they beget a heroic son or a daughter to occupy a throne. This history is the high and sacred science of Dharma, Artha, and also of Moksha; it hath been so said by Vyasa himself of mind that is immeasurable. This history is recited in the present age and will be recited in the future. They that hear it, read, have sons and servants always obedient to them and doing their behests. All sins that are committed by body, word, or mind, immediately leave them that hear this history. They who hear, without the spirit of fault finding, the story of the birth of the Bharata princes, can have no fear of maladies, let alone the fear of the other world.

"For extending the fame of the high-souled Pandavas and of other Kshatriyas versed in all branches of knowledge, high spirited, and already known in the world for their achievements, Krishna-Dwaipayana, guided also by the desire of doing good to the world, hath composed this work. It is excellent, productive of fame, grants length of life, is sacred and heavenly. He who, from desire of acquiring religious merit, causeth this history to be heard by sacred Brahmanas, acquireth great merit and virtue that is inexhaustible. He that reciteth the famous generation of the Kurus becometh immediately purified and acquireth a large family himself, and becometh respected in the world. That Brahmana who regularly studies this sacred Bharata for the four months of the rainy season, is cleansed from all his sins. He that has read the Bharata may be regarded as one acquainted with the Vedas.

"This work presents an account of the gods and royal sages and sacred regenerate Rishis, the sinless Kesava; the god of gods, Mahadeva and the goddess Parvati; the birth of Kartikeya who sprang from union of Parvati with Mahadeva and was reared by many mothers; the greatness of Brahmanas and of kine. This Bharata is a collection of all the Srutis, and is fit to be heard by every virtuous person. That learned man who reciteth it to Brahmanas during the sacred lunations, becometh cleansed of all sins, and, not caring for heaven as it were, attaineth to a union with Brahma. He that causeth even a single foot of this poem to be heard by Brahmanas during the performance of a Sraddha, maketh that Sraddha inexhaustible, the Pitris becoming ever gratified with the articles once presented to them. The sins that are committed daily by our senses or the mind, those that are committed knowingly or unknowingly by any man, are all destroyed by hearing the Mahabharata. The history of the exalted birth of the Bharata princes is called the Mahabharata. He who knoweth this etymology of the name is cleansed of all his sins. And as this history of the Bharata race is so wonderful, that, when recited, it assuredly purifieth mortals from all sins. The sage Krishna-Dwaipayana completed his work in three years. Rising daily and purifying himself and performing his ascetic devotions, he composed this Mahabharata. Therefore, this should be heard by Brahmanas with the formality of a vow. He who reciteth this holy narration composed by Krishna (Vyasa) for the hearing of others, and they who hear it, in whatever state he or they may be, can never be affected by the fruit of deeds, good or bad. The man desirous of acquiring virtue should hear it all. This is equivalent to all histories, and he that heareth it always attaineth to purity of heart. The gratification that one deriveth from attaining to heaven is scarcely equal to that which one deriveth from hearing this holy history. The virtuous man who with reverence heareth it or causeth it to be heard, obtaineth the fruit of the Rajasuya and the horse-sacrifice. The Bharata is said to be as much a mine of gems as the vast Ocean or the great mountain Meru. This history is sacred and excellent, and is equivalent to the Vedas, worthy of being heard, pleasing to the ear, sin-cleansing, and virtue-increasing. O monarch, he that giveth a copy of the Bharata to one that asketh for it doth indeed make a present of the whole earth with her belt of seas. O son of Parikshit, this pleasant narration that giveth virtue and victory I am about to recite in its entirety: listen to it. The sage Krishna-Dwaipayana regularly rising for three years, composed this wonderful history called Mahabharata. O bull amongst the Bharata monarchs, whatever is spoken about virtue, wealth, pleasure, and salvation may be seen elsewhere; but whatever is not contained in this is not to be found anywhere.'"

SECTION LXIII
(Adivansavatarana Parva continued)

"Vaisampayana said, 'There was a king of the name of Uparichara. That monarch was devoted to virtue. He was very much addicted also to hunting. That king of the Paurava race, called also Vasu, conquered the excellent and delightful kingdom of Chedi under instructions from Indra. Some time after, the king gave up the use of arms and, dwelling in a secluded retreat, practised the most severe austerities. The gods with Indra at their head once approached the monarch during this period, believing that he sought the headship of the gods, by those severe austerities of his. The celestials, becoming objects of his sight, by soft speeches succeeded in winning him away from his ascetic austerities.'

"The gods said, 'O lord of the earth, thou shouldst take care so that virtue may not sustain a diminution on earth! Protected by thee, virtue itself will in return protect the universe.' And Indra said, 'O king, protect virtue on earth attentively and rigidly. Being virtuous, thou shalt, for all time, behold (in after life) many sacred regions. And though I am of Heaven, and thou art of earth, yet art thou my friend and dear to me. And, O king of men, dwell thou in that region on earth which is delightful, and aboundeth in animals, is sacred, full of wealth and corn, is well-protected like heaven, which is of agreeable climate, graced with every object of enjoyment, and blessed with fertility. And, O monarch of Chedi, this thy dominion is full of riches, of gems and precious stones, and containeth, besides, much mineral wealth. The cities and towns of this region are all devoted to virtue; the people are honest and contented; they never lie even in jest. Sons never divide their wealth with their fathers and are ever mindful of the welfare of their parents. Lean cattle are never yoked to the plough or the cart or engaged in carrying merchandise; on the other hand, they are well-fed and fattened. In Chedi the four orders are always engaged in their respective vocations. Let nothing be unknown to thee that happens in the three worlds. I shall give thee a crystal car such as the celestials alone are capable of carrying the car through mid air. Thou alone, of all mortals on earth, riding on that best of cars, shall course through mid-air like a celestial endued with a physical frame. I shall also give thee a triumphal garland of unfading lotuses, with which on, in battle, thou shall not be wounded by weapons. And, O king, this blessed and incomparable garland, widely known on earth as Indra's garland, shall be thy distinctive badge.'"

"The slayer of Vritra (Indra) also gave the king, for his gratification, a bamboo pole for protecting the honest and the peaceful. After the expiry of a year, the king planted it in the ground for the purpose of worshipping the giver thereof, viz., Sakra. From that time forth, O monarch, all kings, following Vasu's example, began to plant a pole for the celebration of Indra's worship. After erecting the pole they decked it with golden cloth and scents and garlands and various ornaments. And the god Vasava is worshipped in due form with such garlands and ornaments. And the god, for the gratification of the illustrious Vasu, assuming the form of a swan, came himself to accept the worship thus offered. And the god, beholding the auspicious worship thus made by Vasu, that first of monarchs, was delighted, and said unto him, 'Those men, and kings also, who will worship me and joyously observe this festival of mine like the king of Chedi, shall have glory and victory for their countries and kingdom. Their cities also shall expand and be ever in joy.'

"King Vasu was thus blessed by the gratified Maghavat, the high-souled chief of the gods. Indeed, those men who cause this festivity of Sakra to be observed with gifts of land, of gems and precious stones, become the respected of the world. And king Vasu, the lord of Chedis bestowing boons and performing great sacrifices and observing the festivity of Sakra, was much respected by Indra. And from Chedi he ruled the whole world virtuously. And for the gratification of Indra, Vasu, the lord of the Chedis, observed the festivity of Indra.

"And Vasu had five sons of great energy and immeasurable prowess. And the emperor installed his sons as governors of various provinces.

"And his son Vrihadratha was installed in Magadha and was known by the name of Maharatha. Another son of his was Pratyagraha; and another, Kusamva, who was also called Manivahana. And the two others were Mavella, and Yadu of great prowess and invincible in battle.

"These, O monarch, were the sons of that royal sage of mighty energy. And the five sons of Vasu planted kingdoms and towns after their own names and founded separate dynasties that lasted for long ages.

"And when king Vasu took his seat in that crystal car, with the gift of Indra, and coursed through the sky, he was approached by Gandharvas and Apsaras (the celestial singers and dancers). And as he coursed through the upper regions, he was called Uparichara. And by his capital flowed a river called Suktimati. And that river was once attacked by a life-endued mountain called Kolahala maddened by lust. And Vasu, beholding the foul attempt, struck the mountain with his foot. And by the indentation caused by Vasu's stamp, the river came out (of the embraces of Kolahala). But the mountain begat on the river two children that were twins. And the river, grateful to Vasu for his having set her free from Kolahala's embraces, gave them both to Vasu. And the son was made the generalissimo to his forces by Vasu, that best of royal sages and giver of wealth and punisher of enemies. And the daughter called Girika, was wedded by Vasu.

"And Girika, the wife of Vasu, after her menstrual course, purifying herself by a bath, represented her state unto her lord. But that very day the Pitris of Vasu came unto that best of monarchs and foremost of wise men, and asked him to slay deer (for their Sraddha). And the king, thinking that the command of the Pitris should not be disobeyed, went a-hunting thinking of Girika alone who was gifted with great beauty and like unto another Sri herself. And the season being the spring, the woods within which the king was roaming, had become delightful like unto the gardens of the king of the Gandharvas himself. There were Asokas and Champakas and Chutas and Atimuktas in abundance: and there were Punnagas and Karnikaras and Vakulas and Divya Patalas and Patalas and Narikelas and Chandanas and Arjunas and similar other beautiful and sacred trees resplendent with fragrant flowers and sweet fruits. And the whole forest was maddened by the sweet notes of the kokila and echoed with the hum of maddened bees. And the king became possessed with desire, and he saw not his wife before him. Maddened by desire he was roaming hither and thither, when he saw a beautiful Asoka decked with dense foliage, its branches covered with flowers. And the king sat at his ease in the shade of that tree. And excited by the fragrance of the season and the charming odours of the flowers around, and excited also by the delicious breeze, the king could not keep his mind away from the thought of the beautiful Girika. And beholding that a swift hawk was resting very near to him, the king, acquainted with the subtle truths of Dharma and Artha, went unto him and said, 'Amiable one, carry thou this seed (semen) for my wife Girika and give it unto her. Her season hath arrived.'

"The hawk, swift of speed, took it from the king and rapidly coursed through the air. While thus passing, the hawk was seen by another of his species. Thinking that the first one was carrying meat, the second one flew at him. The two fought with each other in the sky with their beaks. While they were fighting, the seed fell into the waters of the Yamuna. And in those waters dwelt an Apsara of the higher rank, known by the name of Adrika, transformed by a Brahmana's curse into a fish. As soon as Vasu's seed fell into the water from the claws of the hawk, Adrika rapidly approached and swallowed it at once. That fish was, some time after, caught by the fishermen. And it was the tenth month of the fish's having swallowed the seed. From the stomach of that fish came out a male and a female child of human form. The fishermen wondered much, and wending unto king Uparichara (for they were his subjects) told him all. They said, 'O king, these two beings of human shape have been found in the body of a fish!' The male child amongst the two was taken by Uparichara. That child afterwards became the virtuous and truthful monarch Matsya.

"After the birth of the twins, the Apsara herself became freed from her curse. For she had been told before by the illustrious one (who had cursed her) that she would, while living in her piscatorial form, give birth to two children of human shape and then would be freed from the curse. Then, according to these words, having given birth to the two children, and been killed by the fishermen, she left her fish-form and assumed her own celestial shape. The Apsara then rose up on the path trodden by the Siddhas, the Rishis and the Charanas.

"The fish-smelling daughter of the Apsara in her piscatorial form was then given by the king unto the fishermen, saying, 'Let this one be thy daughter.' That girl was known by the name of Satyavati. And gifted with great beauty and possessed of every virtue, she of agreeable smiles, owing to contact with fishermen, was for some time of the fishy smell. Wishing to serve her (foster) father she plied a boat on the waters of the Yamuna.

"While engaged in this vocation, Satyavati was seen one day by the great Rishi Parasara, in course of his wanderings. As she was gifted with great beauty, an object of desire even with an anchorite, and of graceful smiles, the wise sage, as soon as he beheld her, desired to have her. And that bull amongst Munis addressed the daughter of Vasu of celestial beauty and tapering thighs, saying, 'Accept my embraces, O blessed one!' Satyavati replied, 'O holy one, behold the Rishis standing on either bank of the river. Seen by them, how can I grant thy wish?'

"Thus addressed by her, the ascetic thereupon created a fog (which existed not before and) which enveloped the whole region in darkness. And the maiden, beholding the fog that was created by the great Rishi wondered much. And the helpless one became suffused with the blushes of bashfulness. And she said, 'O holy one, note that I am a maiden under the control of my father. O sinless one, by accepting your embraces my virginity will be sullied. O best of Brahmanas, my virginity being sullied, how shall I, O Rishi, be able to return home? Indeed, I shall not then be able to bear life. Reflecting upon all this, O illustrious one, do that which should be done.' That best of Rishis, gratified with all she said, replied, 'Thou shall remain a virgin even if thou grantest my wish. And, O timid one, O beauteous lady, solicit the boon that thou desirest. O thou of fair smiles, my grace hath never before proved fruitless.' Thus addressed, the maiden asked for the boon that her body might emit a sweet scent (instead of the fish-odour that it had). And the illustrious Rishi thereupon granted that wish of her heart.

"Having obtained her boon, she became highly pleased, and her season immediately came. And she accepted the embraces of that Rishi of wonderful deeds. And she thenceforth became known among men by the name of Gandhavati (the sweet-scented one). And men could perceive her scent from the distance of a yojana. And for this she was known by another name which was Yojanagandha (one who scatters her scent for a yojana all around). And the illustrious Parasara, after this, went to his own asylum.

"And Satyavati gratified with having obtained the excellent boon in consequence of which she became sweet-scented and her virginity remained unsullied conceived through Parasara's embraces. And she brought forth the very day, on an island in the Yamuna, the child begot upon her by Parasara and gifted with great energy. And the child, with the permission of his mother, set his mind on asceticism. And he went away saying, 'As soon as thou rememberest me when occasion comes, I shall appear unto thee.'

"And it was thus that Vyasa was born of Satyavati through Parasara. And because he was born in an island, he was called Dwaipayana (Dwaipa or islandborn). And the learned Dwaipayana, beholding that virtue is destined to become lame by one leg each yuga (she having four legs in all) and that the period of life and the strength of men followed the yugas, and moved by the desire of obtaining the favour of Brahman and the Brahmanas, arranged the Vedas. And for this he came to be called Vyasa (the arranger or compiler). The boon-giving great one then taught Sumanta, Jaimini, Paila, his son Suka, and Vaisampayana, the Vedas having the Mahabharata for their fifth. And the compilation of the Bharata was published by him through them separately.

"Then Bhishma, of great energy and fame and of immeasurable splendour, and sprung from the component parts of the Vasus, was born in the womb of Ganga through king Santanu. And there was a Rishi of the name of Animandavya of great fame. And he was conversant with the interpretations of the Vedas, was illustrious, gifted with great energy, and of great reputation. And, accused of theft, though innocent, the old Rishi was impaled. He thereupon summoned Dharma and told him these words, 'In my childhood I had pierced a little fly on a blade of grass, O Dharma! I recollect that one sin: but I cannot call to mind any other.

I have, however, since practised penances a thousandfold. Hath not that one sin been conquered by this my asceticism? And because the killing of a Brahmana is more heinous than that of any other living thing, therefore, hast thou, O Dharma, been sinful. Thou shalt, therefore, be born on earth in the Sudra order.' And for that curse Dharma was born a Sudra in the form of the learned Vidura of pure body who was perfectly sinless. And the Suta was born of Kunti in her maidenhood through Surya. And he came out of his mother's womb with a natural coat of mail and face brightened by ear-rings. And Vishnu himself, of world-wide fame, and worshipped of all the worlds, was born of Devaki through Vasudeva, for the benefit of the three worlds. He is without birth and death, of radiant splendour, the Creator of the universe and the Lord of all! Indeed, he who is the invisible cause of all, who knoweth no deterioration, who is the all-pervading soul, the centre round which everything moveth, the substance in which the three attributes of Sattwa, Rajas and Tamas co-inhere, the universal soul, the immutable, the material out of which hath been created this universe, the Creator himself, the controlling lord, the invisible dweller in every object, progenitor of this universe of five elements, who is united with the six high attributes, is the Pranava or Om of the Vedas, is infinite, incapable of being moved by any force save his own will, illustrious, the embodiment of the mode of life called Sannyasa, who floated on the waters before the creation, who is the source whence hath sprung this mighty frame, who is the great combiner, the uncreate, the invisible essence of all, the great immutable, bereft of those attributes that are knowable by the senses, who is the universe itself, without beginning, birth, and decay,—is possessed of infinite wealth, that Grandsire of all creatures, became incarnate in the race of the Andhaka-Vrishnis for the increase of virtue.

"And Satyaki and Kritavarma, conversant with (the use of) weapons possessed of mighty energy, well-versed in all branches of knowledge, and obedient to Narayana in everything and competent in the use of weapons, had their births from Satyaka and Hridika. And the seed of the great Rishi Bharadwaja of severe penances, kept in a pot, began to develop. And from that seed came Drona (the pot-born). And from the seed of Gautama, fallen upon a clump of reeds, were born two that were twins, the mother of Aswatthaman (called Kripi), and Kripa of great strength. Then was born Dhrishtadyumna, of the splendour of Agni himself, from the sacrificial fire. And the mighty hero was born with bow in hand for the destruction of Drona. And from the sacrificial altar was born Krishna (Draupadi) resplendent and handsome, of bright features and excellent beauty. Then was born the disciple of Prahlada, viz., Nagnajit, and also Suvala. And from Suvala was born a son, Sakuni, who from the curse of the gods became the slayer of creatures and the foe of virtue. And unto him was also born a daughter (Gandhari), the mother of Duryodhana. And both were well-versed in the arts of acquiring worldly profits. And from Krishna was born, in the soil of Vichitravirya, Dhritarashtra, the lord of men, and Pandu of great strength. And from Dwaipayana also born, in the Sudra caste, the wise and intelligent Vidura, conversant with both religion and profit, and free from all sins. And unto Pandu by his two wives were born five sons like the celestials. The eldest of them was Yudhishthira. And Yudhishthira was born (of the seed) of Dharma (Yama, the god of justice); and Bhima of the wolf's stomach was born of Marut (the god of wind), and Dhananjaya, blessed with good fortune and the first of all wielders of weapons, was born of Indra; and Nakula and Sahadeva, of handsome features and ever engaged in the service of their superiors, were born of the twin Aswins. And unto the wise Dhritarashtra were born a hundred sons, viz., Duryodhana and others, and another, named Yuyutsu, who was born of a vaisya woman. And amongst those hundred and one, eleven, viz., Duhsasana, Duhsaha, Durmarshana, Vikarna, Chitrasena, Vivinsati, Jaya, Satyavrata, Purumitra, and Yuyutsu by a Vaisya wife, were all Maharathas (great car-warriors). And Abhimanyu was born of Subhadra, the sister of Vasudeva through Arjuna, and was, therefore, the grandson of the illustrious Pandu. And unto the five Pandavas were born five sons by (their common wife) Panchali. And these princes were all very handsome and conversant with all branches of knowledge. From Yudhishthira was born Pritivindhya; from Vrikodara, Sutasoma; from Arjuna, Srutakirti; from Nakula, Satanika; and from Sahadeva, Srutasena of great prowess; and Bhima, in the forest begot on Hidimva a son named Ghatotkacha. And from Drupada was born a daughter Sikhandin who was afterwards transformed into a male child. Sikhandini was so transformed into a male by Yaksha named Sthuna from the desire of doing her good.

"In that great battle of the Kurus came hundreds of thousands of monarchs for fighting against one another. The names of the innumerable host I am unable to recount even in ten thousand years. I have named, however, the principal ones who have been mentioned in this history.'"

SECTION LXIV
(Adivansavatarana Parva continued)

"Janamejaya said, 'O Brahmana, those thou hast named and those thou hast not named, I wish to hear of them in detail, as also of other kings by thousands. And, O thou of great good fortune, it behoveth thee to tell me in full the object for which those Maharathas, equal unto the celestials themselves, were born on earth.'

"Vaisampayana said, 'It hath been heard by us, O monarch, that what thou askest is a mystery even to the gods. I shall, however, speak of it unto thee, after bowing down (to the self-born). The son of Jamadagni (Parasurama), after twenty-one times making the earth bereft of Kshatriyas wended to that best of mountains Mahendra and there began his ascetic penances. And at that time when the earth was bereft of Kshatriyas, the Kshatriya ladies, desirous of offspring, used to come, O monarch, to the Brahmanas and Brahmanas of rigid vows had connection with them during the womanly season alone, but never, O king, lustfully and out of season. And Kshatriya ladies by thousands conceived from such connection with Brahmanas. Then, O monarch, were born many Kshatriyas of greater energy, boys and girls, so that the Kshatriya race, might thrive. And thus sprang the Kshatriya race from Kshatriya ladies by Brahmanas of ascetic penances. And the new generation, blessed with long life, began to thrive in virtue. And thus were the four orders having Brahmanas at their head re-established. And every man at that time went in unto his wife during her season and never from lust and out of season. And, O bull of the Bharata race, in the same way, other creatures also, even those born in the race of birds went in unto their wives during the season alone. And, O protector of the earth, hundreds of thousands of creatures were born, and all were virtuous and began to multiply in virtue, all being free from sorrow and disease. And, O thou of the elephant's tread, this wide earth having the ocean for her boundaries, with her mountains and woods and towns, was once more governed by the Kshatriyas. And when the earth began to be again governed virtuously by the Kshatriyas, the other orders having Brahmanas for their first were filled with great joy. And the kings giving up all vices born of lust and anger and justly awarding punishments to those that deserved them protected the earth. And he of a hundred sacrifices, possessed also of a thousand eyes, beholding that the Kshatriya monarchs ruled so virtuously, poured down vivifying showers at proper times and places and blessed all creatures. Then, O king, no one of immature years died, and none knew a woman before attaining to age. And thus, O bull of the Bharata race, the earth, to the very coasts of the ocean, became filled with men that were all long-lived. The Kshatriyas performed great sacrifices bestowing much wealth. And the Brahmanas also all studied the Vedas with their branches and the Upanishads. And, O king, no Brahmana in those days ever sold the Vedas (i.e., taught for money) or ever read aloud the Vedas in the presence of a Sudra. The Vaisyas, with the help of bullocks, caused the earth to be tilled. And they never yoked the cattle themselves. And they fed with care all cattle that were lean. And men never milked kine as long as the calves drank only the milk of their dams (without having taken to grass or any other food). And no merchant in those days ever sold his articles by false scales. And, O tiger among men, all persons, holding to the ways of virtue, did everything with eyes set upon virtue. And, O monarch, all the orders were mindful of their own respective duties. Thus, O tiger among men, virtue in those days never sustained any diminution. And, O bull of the Bharata race, both kine and women gave birth to their offspring at the proper time. And trees bore flowers and fruit duly according to the seasons. And thus, O king, the krita age having then duly set in, the whole earth was filled with numerous creatures.

"And, O bull of the Bharata race, when such was the blessed state of the terrestrial world, the Asuras, O lord of men, began to be born in kingly lines. And the sons of Diti (Daityas) being repeatedly defeated in war by the sons of Aditi (celestials) and deprived also of sovereignty and heaven, began to be incarnated on the earth. And, O king, the Asuras being possessed of great powers, and desirous of sovereignty began to be born on earth amongst various creatures, such as kine, horses, asses, camels, buffaloes, among creatures such as Rakshasas and others, and among elephants and deer. And, O protector of the earth, owing to those already born and to those that were being born, the earth became incapable of supporting herself. And amongst the sons of Diti and of Danu, cast out of heaven, some were born on the earth as kings of great pride and insolence. Possessed of great energy, they covered the earth in various shapes. Capable of oppressing all foes, they filled the earth having the ocean for its boundaries. And by their strength they began to oppress Brahmanas and Kshatriyas and Vaisyas and Sudras and all other creatures also. Terrifying and killing all creatures, they traversed the earth, O king, in bands of hundreds and thousands. Devoid of truth and virtue, proud of their strength, and intoxicated with (the wine of) insolence, they even insulted the great Rishis in their hermitages.

"And the earth, thus oppressed by the mighty Asuras endued with great strength and energy and possessed of abundant means, began to think of waiting on Brahman. The united strength of the creatures (such as Sesha, the Tortoise, and the huge Elephant), and of many Seshas too, became capable of supporting the earth with her mountains, burdened as she was with the weight of the Danavas. And then, O king, the earth, oppressed with weight and afflicted with fear, sought the protection of the Grandsire of all creatures. And she beheld the divine Brahman—the Creator of the worlds who knoweth no deterioration—surrounded by the gods, Brahmanas, and great Rishis, of exceeding good fortune, and adored by delighted Gandharvas and Apsaras always engaged in the service of the celestials. And the Earth, desirous of protection, then represented everything to him, in the presence, O Bharata, of all the Regents of the worlds. But, O king, the Earth's object had been known beforehand to the Omniscient, Self-create, and Supreme Lord. And, O Bharata, Creator as he is of the universe, why should he not know fully what is in the minds of his creatures including the very gods and the Asuras? O king, the Lord of the Earth, the Creator of all creatures, also called Isa, Sambhu, Prajapati, then spake unto her. And Brahman said, 'O holder of wealth, for the accomplishment of the object for which thou hast approached me, I shall appoint all the dwellers in the heavens.'

"Vaisampayana continued, 'Having said so unto the Earth, O king, the divine Brahman bade her farewell. And the Creator then commanded all the gods saying, 'To ease the Earth of her burden, go ye and have your births in her according to your respective parts and seek ye strife (with the Asuras already born there)'. And the Creator of all, summoning also all the tribes of the Gandharvas and the Apsaras, spake unto them these words of deep import, 'Go ye and be born amongst men according to your respective parts in forms that ye like.'

"And all the gods with Indra, on hearing these words of the Lord of the celestials—words that were true, desirable under the circumstances, and fraught with benefit,—accepted them. And they all having resolved to come down on earth in their respected parts, then went to Narayana, the slayer of all foes, at Vaikunth—the one who has the discus and the mace in his hands, who is clad in purple, who is of great splendour, who hath the lotus on his navel, who is the slayer of the foes of the gods, who is of eyes looking down upon his wide chest (in yoga attitude), who is the lord of the Prajapati himself, the sovereign of all the gods, of mighty strength, who hath the mark of the auspicious whirl on his breast, who is the mover of every one's faculties and who is adored by all the gods. Him, Indra the most exalted of persons, addressed, saying, 'Be incarnate.' And Hari replied,—'Let it be.'"

SECTION LXV
(Sambhava Parva)

"Vaisampayana said, 'Then Indra had a consultation with Narayana about the latter's descent on the earth from heaven with all the gods according to their respective parts. And, having commanded all the dwellers in heaven, Indra returned from the abode of Narayana. And the dwellers in heaven gradually became incarnate on earth for the destruction of the Asuras and for the welfare of the three worlds. And then, O tiger among kings, the celestials had their births, according as they pleased, in the races of Brahmarshis and royal sages. And they slew the Danavas, Rakshasas, Gandharvas and Snakes, other man-eaters, and many other creatures. And, O bull in the Bharata race, the Danavas, Rakshasas and Gandharvas and Snakes, could not slay the incarnate celestials even in their infancy, so strong they were.'

"Janamejaya said, 'I desire to hear from the beginning of the births of the gods, the Danavas, the Gandharvas, the Apsaras, men, Yakshas and Rakshasas. Therefore, it behoveth thee to tell me about the births of all creatures.'

"Vaisampayana said, 'Indeed, I shall, having bowed down to the Self-create, tell thee in detail the origin of the celestials and other creatures. It is known that Brahman hath six spiritual sons, viz., Marichi, Atri, Angiras, Pulastya, Pulaha and Kratu. And Marichi's son is Kasyapa, and from Kasyapa have sprung these creatures. Unto Daksha (one of the Prajapatis) were born thirteen daughters of great good fortune. The daughters of Daksha are, O tiger among men and prince of the Bharata race, Aditi, Diti, Danu, Kala, Danayu, Sinhika, Krodha, Pradha, Viswa, Vinata, Kapila, Muni, and Kadru. The sons and grandsons of these, gifted with great energy, are countless. From Aditi have sprung the twelve Adityas who are the lords of the universe. And, O Bharata, as they are according to their names, I shall recount them to thee. They are Dhatri,

Mitra, Aryaman, Sakra, Varuna, Ansa, Vaga, Vivaswat, Usha, Savitri, Tvashtri, and Vishnu. The youngest, however, is superior to them all in merit. Diti had one son called Hiranyakasipu. And the illustrious Hiranyakasipu had five sons, all famous throughout the world. The eldest of them all was Prahlada, the next was Sahradha; the third was Anuhrada; and after him were Sivi and Vashkala. And, O Bharata, it is known everywhere that Prahlada had three sons. They were Virochana, Kumbha, and Nikumbha. And unto Virochana was born a son, Vali, of great prowess. And the son of Vali is known to be the great Asura, Vana. And blessed with good fortune, Vana was a follower of Rudra, and was known also by the name of Mahakala. And Danu had forty sons, O Bharata! The eldest of them all was Viprachitti of great fame Samvara, and Namuchi and Pauloman; Asiloman, and Kesi and Durjaya; Ayahsiras, Aswasiras, and the powerful Aswasanku; also Gaganamardhan, and Vegavat, and he called Ketumat; Swarbhanu, Aswa, Aswapati, Vrishaparvan, and then Ajaka; and Aswagriva, and Sukshama, and Tuhunda of great strength, Ekapada, and Ekachakra, Virupaksha, Mahodara, and Nichandra, and Nikumbha, Kupata, and then Kapata; Sarabha, and Sulabha, Surya, and then Chandramas; these in the race of Danu are stated to be well-known. The Surya and Chandramas (the Sun and the Moon) of the celestials are other persons, and not the sons of Danu as mentioned above. The following ten, gifted with great strength and vigour, were also, O king, born in the race of Danu;—Ekaksha, Amritapa of heroic courage, Pralamva and Naraka, Vatrapi, Satrutapana, and Satha, the great Asura; Gavishtha, and Vanayu, and the Danava called Dirghajiva. And, O Bharata, the sons and the grandsons of these were known to be countless. And Sinhika gave birth to Rahu, the persecutor of the Sun and the Moon, and to three others, Suchandra, Chandrahantri, and Chandrapramardana. And the countless progeny of Krura (krodha) were as crooked and wicked as herself. And the tribe was wrathful, of crooked deeds, and persecutors of their foes. And Danayu also had four sons who were bulls among the Asuras. They were Vikshara, Vala, Vira, and Vritra the great Asura. And the sons of Kala were all like Yama himself and smiter of all foes. And they were of great energy, and oppressors of all foes. And the sons of Kala were Vinasana and Krodha, and then Krodhahantri, and Krodhasatru. And there were many others among the sons of Kala. And Sukra, the son of a Rishi, was the chief priest of the Asuras. And the celebrated Sukra had four sons who were priests of the Asuras. And they were Tashtadhara and Atri, and two others of fierce deeds. They were like the Sun himself in energy, and set their hearts on acquiring the regions of Brahman.

"Thus hath been recited by me, as heard in the Purana, of progeny of the gods and the Asuras, both of great strength and energy. I am incapable, O king, of counting the descendants of these, countless as they are, are not much known to fame.

"And the sons of Vinata were Tarkhya and Arishtanemi, and Garuda and Aruna, and Aruni and Varuni. And Sesha of Ananta, Vasuki, Takshaka, Kumara, and Kulika are known to be the sons of Kadru; and Bhimasena, Ugrasena, Suparna, Varuna, Gopati, and Dhritarashtra, and Suryavarchas the seventh, Satyavachas, Arkaparna, Prayuta, Bhima, and Chitraratha known to fame, of great learning, and a controller of his passions, and then Kalisiras, and, O king, Parjanya, the fourteenth in the list, Kali, the fifteenth, and Narada, the sixteenth—these Devas and Gandharvas are known to be the sons of Muni (Daksha's daughter as mentioned before). I shall recount many others, O Bharata! Anavadya Manu, Vansa, Asura, Marganapria, Anupa, Subhaga, Vasi, were the daughters brought forth by Pradha, Siddha, and Purna, and Varhin, and Purnayus of great fame, Brahmacharin, Ratiguna, and Suparna who was the seventh; Viswavasu, Bhanu, and Suchandra who was the tenth, were also the sons of Pradha. All these were celestial Gandharvas. And it is also known that this Pradha of great fortune, through the celestial Rishi (Kasyapa, her husband), brought forth the sacred of the Apsaras, Alamvusha, Misrakesi, Vidyutparna, Tilottama, Aruna, Rakshita, Rambha, Manorama, Kesini, Suvahu, Surata, Suraja, and Supria were the daughters, and Ativahu and the celebrated Haha and Huhu, and Tumvuru were the sons—the best of Gandharvas—of Pradha and Amrita. The Brahmanas, kine, Gandharvas, and Apsaras, were born of Kapila as stated in the Purana.

"Thus hath been recited to thee by me the birth of all creatures duly—of Gandharvas and Apsaras, of Snakes, Suparnas, Rudras, and Maruts; of kine and of Brahmanas blessed with great good fortune, and of sacred deeds. And this account (if read) extendeth the span of life, is sacred, worthy of all praise, and giveth pleasure to the ear. It should be always heard and recited to others, in a proper frame of mind.

"He who duly readeth this account of the birth of all high-souled creatures in the presence of the gods and Brahmanas, obtaineth large progeny, good fortune, and fame, and attaineth also to excellent worlds hereafter.'"

SECTION LXVI
(Sambhava Parva continued)

"Vaisampayana said, 'It is known that the spiritual sons of Brahman were the six great Rishis (already mentioned). There was another of the name of Sthanu. And the sons of Sthanu, gifted with great energy, were, it is known, eleven. They were Mrigavayadha, Sarpa, Niriti of great fame: Ajaikapat, Ahivradhna, and Pinaki, the oppressor of foes; Dahana and Iswara, and Kapali of great splendour; and Sthanu, and the illustrious Bharga. These are called the eleven Rudras. It hath been already said, that Marichi, Angiras, Atri, Pulastya, Pulaha, and Kratu—these six great Rishis of great energy—are the sons of Brahman. It is well-known in the world that Angiras's sons are three,—Vrihaspati, Utathya, and Samvarta, all of rigid vows. And, O king, it is said that the sons of Atri are numerous. And, being great Rishis, they are all conversant with the Vedas, crowned with ascetic success, and of souls in perfect peace. And, O tiger among kings, the sons of Pulastya of great wisdom are Rakshasas, Monkeys, Kinnaras (half-men and half-horses), and Yakshas. And, O king, the son of Pulaha were, it is said, the Salabhas (the winged insects), the lions, the Kimpurushas (half-lions and half-men), the tigers, bears, and wolves. And the sons of Kratu, sacred as sacrifices, are the companions of Surya, the Valikhilyas, known in three worlds and devoted to truth and vows. And, O protector of the Earth, the illustrious Rishi Daksha, of soul in complete peace, and of great asceticism, sprung from the right toe of Brahman. And from the left toe of Brahman sprang the wife of the high-souled Daksha. And the Muni begat upon her fifty daughters; and all those daughters were of faultless features and limbs and of eyes like lotus-petals. And the lord Daksha, not having any sons, made those daughters his Putrikas (so that their sons might belong both to himself and to their husbands). And Daksha bestowed, according to the sacred ordinance, ten of his daughters on Dharma, twenty-seven on Chandra (the Moon), and thirteen on Kasyapa. Listen as I recount the wives of Dharma according to their names. They are ten in all—Kirti, Lakshmi, Dhriti, Medha, Pushti, Sraddha, Kria, Buddhi, Lajja, and Mali. These are the wives of Dharma as appointed by the Self- create. It is known also throughout the world that the wives of Soma (Moon) are twenty-seven. And the wives of Soma, all of sacred vows, are employed in indicating time; and they are the Nakshatras and the Yoginis and they became so for assisting the courses of the worlds.

"And Brahman had another son named Manu. And Manu had a son of the name of Prajapati. And the sons of Prajapati were eight and were called Vasus whom I shall name in detail. They were Dhara, Dhruva, Soma, Aha, Anila, Anala, Pratyusha, and Prabhasa. These eight are known as the Vasus. Of these, Dhara and the truth-knowing Dhruva were born of Dhumra; Chandramas (Soma) and Swasana (Anila) were born of the intelligent Swasa; Aha was the son of Rata; and Hutasana (Anala) of Sandilya; and Pratyusha and Prabhasa were the sons of Prabhata. And Dhara had two sons, Dravina and Huta-havya-vaha. And the son of Dhruva is the illustrious Kala (Time), the destroyer of the worlds. And Soma's son is the resplendent Varchas. And Varchas begot upon his wife Manohara three sons—Sisira, and Ramana. And the son of Aha were Jyotih, Sama, Santa, and also Muni. And the son of Agni is the handsome Kumara born in a forest of reeds. And, he is also called Kartikeya because he was reared by Krittika and others. And, after Kartikeya, there were born his three brothers Sakha, Visakha, Naigameya. And the wife of Anila is Siva, and Siva's son were Manojava and Avijnataagati. These two were the sons of Anila. The son of Pratyusha, you must know, is the Rishi named Devala; and Devala had two sons who were both exceedingly forgiving and of great mental power. And the sister of Vrihaspati, the first of women, uttering the sacred truth, engaged in ascetic penances, roamed over the whole earth; and she became the wife of Prabhasa, the eighth Vasu. And she brought forth the illustrious Viswakarman, the founder of all arts. And he was the originator of a thousand arts, the engineer of the immortals, the maker of all kinds of ornaments, and the first of artists. And he it was who constructed the celestial cars of the gods, and mankind are enabled to live in consequence of the inventions of that illustrious one. And he is worshipped, for that reason, by men. And he is eternal and immutable, this Viswakarman.

"And the illustrious Dharma, the dispenser of all happiness, assuming a human countenance, came out through the right breast of Brahman. And Ahasta (Dharma) hath three excellent sons capable of charming every creature. And they are Sama, Kama, Harsha (Peace, Desire, and Joy). And by their energy they are supporting the worlds. And the wife of Kama is Rati, of Sama is Prapti; and the wife of Harsha is Nanda. And upon them, indeed, are the worlds made to depend.

"And the son of Marichi is Kasyapa. And Kasyapa's offspring are the gods and the Asuras. And, therefore, is Kasyapa, the Father of the worlds. And Tvashtri, of the form of Vadava (a mare), became the wife of Savitri. And she gave birth, in the skies, to two greatly fortunate twins, the Aswins. And, O king, the sons of

Aditi are twelve with Indra heading them all. And the youngest of them all was Vishnu upon whom the worlds depend.

"These are the thirty-three gods (the eight Vasus, the eleven Rudras, the twelve Adityas, Prajapati, and Vashatkara). I shall now recount their progeny according to their Pakshas, Kulas, and Ganas. The Rudras, the Saddhyas, the Maruts, the Vasus, the Bhargavas, and the Viswedevas are each reckoned as a Paksha. Garuda the son of Vinata and the mighty Aruna also, and the illustrious Vrihaspati are reckoned among the Adityas. The twin Aswins, all annual plants, and all inferior animals, are reckoned among the Guhyakas.

"These are the Ganas of the gods recited to thee, O king! This recitation washes men of all sins.

"The illustrious Bhrigu came out, ripping open the breast of Brahman. The learned Sukra is Bhrigu's son. And the learned Sukra becoming a planet and engaged according to the command of the Self-existent in pouring and withholding rain, and in dispensing and remitting calamities, traverses, for sustaining the lives of all the creatures in the three worlds, through the skies. And the learned Sukra, of great intelligence and wisdom, of rigid vows, leading the life of a Brahmacharin, divided himself in twain by power of asceticism, and became the spiritual guide of both the Daityas and the gods. And after Sukra was thus employed by Brahman in seeking the welfare (of the gods and the Asuras), Bhrigu begot another excellent son. This was Chyavana who was like the blazing sun, of virtuous soul, and of great fame. And he came out of his mother's womb in anger and became the cause of his mother's release, O king (from the hands of the Rakshasas). And Arushi, the daughter of Manu, became the wife of the wise Chyavana. And, on her was begotten Aurva of great reputation. And he came out, ripping open the thigh of Arushi. And Aurva begot Richika. And Richika even in his boyhood became possessed of great power and energy, and of every virtue. And Richika begot Jamadagni. And the high-souled Jamadagni had four sons. And the youngest of them all was Rama (Parasurama). And Rama was superior to all his brothers in the possession of good qualities. And he was skilful in all weapons, and became the slayer of the Kshatriyas. And he had his passions under complete control. And Aurva had a hundred sons with Jamadagni the eldest. And these hundred sons had offspring by thousands spread over this earth.

"And Brahman had two other sons, viz., Dhatri and Vidhatri who stayed with Manu. Their sister is the auspicious Lakshmi having her abode amid lotuses. And the spiritual sons of Lakshmi are the sky-ranging horses. And the daughter born of Sukra, named Divi, became the eldest wife of Varuna. Of her were born a son named Vala and a daughter named Sura (wine), to the joy of the gods. And Adharma (Sin) was born when creatures (from want of food) began to devour one another. And Adharma always destroys every creature. And Adharma hath Niriti for his wife, whence the Rakshasas who are called Nairitas (offspring of Niriti). And she hath also three other cruel sons always engaged in sinful deeds. They are Bhaya (fear), Mahabhaya (terror), and Mrityu (Death) who is always engaged in slaying every created thing. And, as he is all-destroying, he hath no wife, and no son. And Tamra brought forth five daughters known throughout the worlds. They are Kaki (crow), Syeni (hawk), Phasi (hen), Dhritarashtri (goose), and Suki (parrot). And Kaki brought forth the crows; Syeni, the hawks, the cocks and vultures; Dhritarashtri, all ducks and swans; and she also brought forth all Chakravakas; and the fair Suki, of amiable qualities, and possessing all auspicious signs brought forth all the parrots. And Krodha gave birth to nine daughters, all of wrathful disposition. And their names were Mrigi, Mrigamanda, Hari, Bhadramana, Matangi, Sarduli, Sweta, Surabhi, and the agreeable Surasa blessed with every virtue. And, O foremost of men, the offspring of Mrigi are all animals of the deer species. And the offspring of Mrigamanda are all animals of the bear species and those called Srimara (sweet-footed). And Bhadramana begot the celestial elephants, Airavata. And the offspring of Hari are all animals of the simian species endued with great activity, so also all the horses. And those animals also, that are called Go-langula (the cow-tailed), are said to be the offspring of Hari. And Sarduli begot lions and tigers in numbers, and also leopards and all other strong animals. And, O king, the offspring of Matangi are all the elephants. And Sweta begat the large elephant known by the name of Sweta, endued with great speed. And, O king, Surabhi gave birth to two daughters, the amiable Rohini and the far-famed Gandharvi. And, O Bharata, she had also two other daughters named Vimala and Anala. From Rohini have sprung all kine, and from Gandharvi all animals of the horse species. And Anala begat the seven kinds of trees yielding pulpy fruits. (They are the date, the palm, the hintala, the tali, the little date, the nut, and the cocoanut.) And she had also another daughter called Suki (the mother of the parrot species). And Surasa bore a son called Kanka (a species of long-feathered birds). And Syeni, the wife of Aruna, gave birth to two sons of great energy and strength, named Sampati and the mighty Jatayu. Surasa also bore the Nagas, and Kadru, the Punnagas (snakes). And Vinata had two sons Garuda and Aruna, known far and wide. And, O king of men, O foremost of intelligent persons, thus hath the genealogy of all the principal creatures been fully described by me. By listening to this, a man is fully cleansed of all his sins, and acquireth great knowledge, and finally attaineth to the first of states in after- life!'"

SECTION LXVII
(Sambhava Parva continued)

"Janamejaya said, 'O worshipful one, I wish to hear from thee in detail about the birth, among men, of the gods, the Danavas, the Gandharvas, the Rakshasas, the lions, the tigers, and the other animals, the snakes, the birds, and in fact, of all creatures. I wish also to hear about the acts and achievements of those, in due order, after they became incarnate in human forms.'

"Vaisampayana said, 'O king of men, I shall first tell thee all about those celestials and Danavas that were born among men—The first of Danavas, who was known by the name of Viprachitti, became that bull among men, noted as Jarasandha. And, O king, that son of Diti, who was known as Hiranyakasipu, was known in this world among men as the powerful Sisupala. He who had been known as Samhlada, the younger brother of Prahlada, became among men the famous Salya, that bull amongst Valhikas. The spirited Anuhlada who had been the youngest became noted in the world as Dhrishtaketu. And, O king, that son of Diti who had been known as Sivi became on earth the famous monarch Druma. And he who was known as the great Asura Vashkala became on earth the great Bhagadatta. The five great Asuras gifted with great energy, Ayahsira, Aswasira, the spirited Aysanku, Gaganamurdhan, and Vegavat, were all born in the royal line of Kekaya and all became great monarchs. That other Asura of mighty energy who was known by the name of Ketumat became on earth the monarch Amitaujas of terrible deeds. That great Asura who was known as Swarbhanu became on earth the monarch Ugrasena of fierce deeds. That great Asura who was known as Aswa became on earth the monarch Asoka of exceeding energy and invincible in battle. And, O king, the younger brother of Aswa who was known as Aswapati, a son of Diti, became on earth the mighty monarch Hardikya. The great and fortunate Asura who was known as Vrishaparvan became noted on earth as king Dirghaprajna. And, O king, the younger brother of Vrishaparvan who was known by the name of Ajaka became noted on earth as king Salwa. The powerful and mighty Asura who was known as Aswagriva became noted on earth as king Rochamana. And, O king, the Asura who was known as Sukshma, endued with great intelligence and whose achievements also were great, became on earth the famous king Vrihadratha. And that first of Asuras who was known by the name of Tuhunda, became noted on earth as the monarch, Senavindu. That Asura of great strength who was known as Ishupa became the monarch Nagnajita of famous prowess. The great Asura who was known as Ekachakra became noted on earth as Pritivindhya. The great Asura Virupaksha capable of displaying various modes of fight became noted on earth as king Chitravarman. The first of Danavas, the heroic Hara, who humbled the pride of all foes became on earth the famous and fortunate Suvahu. The Asura Suhtra of great energy and the destroyer of foemen, became noted on earth as the fortunate monarch, Munjakesa. That Asura of great intelligence called Nikumbha, who was never vanquished in battle was born on earth as king Devadhipa, the first among monarchs. That great Asura known amongst the sons of Diti by the name of Sarabha became on earth the royal sage called Paurava. And, O king, the great Asura of exceeding energy, the fortunate Kupatha, was born on earth as the famous monarch Suparswa. The great Asura, O king, who was called Kratha, was born on earth as the royal sage Parvateya of form resplendent like a golden mountain. He amongst the Asura who was known as Salabha the second, became on earth the monarch Prahlada in the country of the Valhikas. The foremost, among the sons of Diti known by the name of Chandra and handsome as the lord of the stars himself, became on earth noted as Chandravarman, the king of the Kamvojas. That bull amongst the Danavas who was known by the name of Arka became on earth, O king, the royal sage Rishika. That best of Asuras who was known as Mritapa became on earth, O best of kings, the monarch, Pascimanupaka. That great Asura of surpassing energy known as Garishtha became noted on earth as king Drumasena. The great Asura who was known as Mayura became noted on earth as the monarch Viswa. He who was the younger brother of Mayura and called Suparna became noted on earth as the monarch, Kalakirti. The mighty Asura who was known as Chandrahantri became on earth the royal sage Sunaka. The great Asura who was called Chandravinasana became noted on earth as the monarch, Janaki. That bull amongst the Danavas, O prince of the Kuru race, who was called Dhirghajihva, became noted on earth as Kasiraja. The Graha who was brought forth by Sinhika and who persecuted the Sun and the Moon became noted on earth as the monarch Kratha. The eldest of the four sons of Danayu, who was known by the name of Vikshara, became known on earth the spirited monarch, Vasumitra. The second brother of Vikshara, the great Asura, was born on earth as the king of the country, called Pandya. That best of Asuras who was known by the name of Valina became on earth the monarch Paundramatsyaka. And, O king, that great Asura who was known as Vritra became on earth the royal sage known by the name of Manimat. That Asura who was the younger brother of Vritra and known as Krodhahantri became noted on earth as king Danda. That other Asura who was known by the name Krodhavardhana became noted on earth as the monarch, Dandadhara. The eight sons of the Kaleyas that were born on earth all became great kings endued with the prowess of tigers. The eldest of them all became king Jayatsena in Magadha. The second of them, in prowess, like Indra, became noted on earth as Aparajita. The third of them, endued with great energy and power of producing deception, was born on earth as the king of the Nishadas gifted with great prowess. That other amongst them who was known as the fourth was noted on earth as Srenimat, that best of royal sages. That great Asura amongst them who was the fifth, became noted on earth as king Mahanjas, the oppressor of enemies. That great Asura possessing great intelligence who was the sixth of them became noted on earth as Abhiru, that best of royal sages. The seventh of them became known throughout earth, from the centre to the sea, as king Samudrasena well acquainted with the truths of the scriptures. The eighth of the Kaleyas known as Vrihat became on earth a virtuous king ever engaged in the good of all creatures. The mighty Danava known by the name of Kukshi became on earth as Parvatiya from his brightness as of a golden mountain. The mighty Asura Krathana gifted with great energy became noted on earth as the monarch Suryaksha. The great Asura of handsome features known by the name of Surya, became on earth the monarch of the Valhikas by name Darada, that foremost of all kings. And, O king, from the tribe of Asuras called Krodhavasa, of whom I have already spoken to thee, were born many heroic kings on earth. Madraka, and Karnaveshta, Siddhartha, and also Kitaka; Suvira, and Suvahu, and Mahavira, and also Valhika, Kratha, Vichitra, Suratha, and the handsome king Nila; and Chiravasa, and Bhumipala; and Dantavakra, and he who was called Durjaya; that tiger amongst kings named Rukmi; and king Janamejaya, Ashada, and Vayuvega, and also Bhuritejas; Ekalavya, and Sumitra, Vatadhana, and also Gomukha; the tribe of kings called the Karushakas, and also Khemadhurti; Srutayu, and Udvaha, and also Vrihatsena; Kshema, Ugratirtha, the king of the Kalingas; and Matimat, and he was known as king Iswara; these first of kings were all born of the Asura class called Krodhavasa.

"There was also born on earth a mighty Asura known amongst the Danavas by the name of Kalanemi, endued with great strength, of grand achievements, and blessed with a large share of prosperity. He became the mighty son of Ugrasena and was known on earth by the name of Kansa. And he who was known among the Asuras by the name of Devaka and was besides in splendour like unto Indra himself, was born on earth as the foremost king of the Gandharvas. And, O monarch, know thou that Drona, the son of Bharadwaja, not born of any woman, sprung from a portion of the celestial Rishi Vrihaspati of grand achievements. And he was the prince of all bowmen, conversant with all weapons, of mighty achievements, of great energy. Thou shouldst know he was also well-acquainted with the Vedas and the science of arms. And he was of wonderful deeds and the pride of his race. And, O king, his son the heroic Aswatthaman, of eyes like the lotus-petals, gifted with surpassing energy, and the terror of all foes, the great oppressor of all enemies, was born on earth, of the united portions of Mahadeva, Yama, Kama, and Krodha. And from the curse of Vasishtha and the command also of Indra, the eight Vasus were born of Ganga by her husband Santanu. The youngest of them was Bhishma, the dispeller of the fears of the Kurus, gifted with great intelligence, conversant with the Vedas, the first speakers, and the thinner of the enemy's ranks. And possessed of mighty energy and the first of all persons acquainted with weapons, he encountered the illustrious Rama himself, the son of Jamadagni of the Bhrigu race. And, O king, that Brahman sage who, on earth, was known by the name of Kripa and was the embodiment of all manliness was born of the tribe of the Rudras. And the mighty chariot-fighter and king who on earth was known by the name of Sakuni, that crusher of foes, thou shouldst know, O king, was Dwapara himself (the third yuga). And he who was Satyaki of sure aim, that upholder of the pride of Vrishni race, that oppressor of foes, begotten of the portion of gods called the Maruts. And that royal sage Drupada who on earth was a monarch, the first among all persons bearing arms, was also born of the same tribe of the celestials. And, O king, thou shouldst also know that Kritavarman, that prince among men, of deeds unsurpassed by any one, and the foremost of all bulls amongst Kshatriyas, was born of the portion of the same celestials. And that royal sage also, Virata by name, the scorcher of the kingdoms of others, and the great oppressor of all foes, was born of the portion of the same gods. That son of Arishta who was known by the name of Hansa, was born in the Kuru race and became the monarch of the Gandharvas. He who was known as Dhritarashtra born of the seed of Krishna-Dwaipayana, and gifted with long arms and great energy, also a monarch, of the prophetic eye, became blind in consequence of the fault of his mother and the wrath of the Rishi. His younger brother who was possessed of great strength and was really a great being known as Pandu, devoted to truth and virtue, was Purity's self. And, O king, thou shouldst know that he who was known on earth as Vidura, who was the first of all virtuous men, who was the god of Justice himself, was the excellent and greatly fortunate son of the Rishi Atri. The evil-minded and wicked king Duryodhana, the destroyer of the fair fame of the Kurus, was born of a portion of Kali on earth. It was who caused all creatures to be slain and the earth to be wasted; and he it was who fanned the flame of hostility that ultimately consumed all. They who had been the sons of Pulastya (the Rakshasas) were born on earth among men of Duryodhana's brothers, that century of wicked individuals commencing with Duhasasana as their first. And, O bull among the Bharata princes, Durmukha, Duhsaha, and others whose names I do not mention, who always supported Duryodhana (in all his schemes), were, indeed, the sons of Pulastya. And over and above these hundred, Dhritarashtra had one son named Yuyutsu born of a Vaisya wife.'

"Janamejaya said, 'O illustrious one, tell me the names of Dhritarashtra's sons according to the order of their birth beginning from the eldest.'

"Vaisampayana said, 'O king, they are as follows: Duryodhana, and Yuyutsu, and also Duhsasana; Duhsaha and Duhshala, and then Durmukha; Vivinsati, and Vikarna, Jalasandha, Sulochna, Vinda and Anuvinda, Durdharsha, Suvahu, Dushpradharshana; Durmarshana, and Dushkarna, and Karna; Chitra and Vipachitra, Chitraksha, Charuchitra, and Angada, Durmada, and Dushpradharsha, Vivitsu, Vikata, Sama; Urananabha, and Padmanabha, Nanda and Upanandaka; Sanapati, Sushena, Kundodara; Mahodara; Chitravahu, and Chitravarman, Suvarman, Durvirochana; Ayovahu, Mahavahu, Chitrachapa and Sukundala, Bhimavega, Bhimavala, Valaki, Bhimavikrama, Ugrayudha, Bhimaeara, Kanakayu, Dridhayudha, Dridhavarman, Dridhakshatra Somakirti, Anadara; Jarasandha, Dridhasandha, Satyasandha, Sahasravaeh; Ugrasravas, Ugrasena, and Kshemamurti; Aprajita, Panditaka, Visalaksha, Duradhara, Dridhahasta, and Suhasta, Vatavega, and Suvarchasa; Adityaketu, Vahvasin, Nagadatta and Anuyaina; Nishangi, Kuvachi, Dandi, Dandadhara, Dhanugraha; Ugra, Bhimaratha, Vira, Viravahu, Alolupa; Abhaya, and Raudrakarman, also he who was Dridharatha; Anadhrishya, Kundaveda, Viravi, Dhirghalochana; Dirghavahu; Mahavahu; Vyudhoru, Kanakangana; Kundaja and Chitraka. There was also a daughter named Duhsala who was over and above the hundred. And Yuyutsu who was Dhritarashtra's son by a Vaisya wife, was also over and above the hundred. Thus, O king, have I recited the names of the hundred sons and also that of the daughter (of Dhritarashtra). Thou hast now known their names according to the order of their births. All of them were heroes and great car-warriors, and skilled in the art of warfare. Besides, all of them were versed in the Vedas, and, O king, all of them had got through the scriptures. All of them were mighty in attack and defence, and all were graced with learning. And, O monarch, all of them had wives suitable to them in grace and accomplishments. And, O king, when the time came, the Kaurava monarch bestowed his daughter Duhsala on Jayadratha, the king of the Sindhus, agreeably to the counsels of Sakuni.

"And, O monarch, learn that king Yudhishthira was a portion of Dharma; that Bhimasena was of the deity of wind; that Arjuna was of Indra, the chief of the celestials; and that Nakula and Sahadeva, the handsomest beings among all creatures, and unrivalled for beauty on earth, were similarly portions of the twin Aswins. And he who was known as the mighty Varchas, the son of Soma, became Abhimanyu of wonderful deeds, the son of Arjuna. And before his incarnation, O king, the god Soma had said these words to the celestials, 'I cannot give (part with) my son. He is dearer to me than life itself. Let this be the compact and let it be not transgressed. The destruction of the Asuras on earth is the work of the celestials, and, therefore, it is our work as well. Let this Varchas, therefore, go thither, but let him not stay there long. Nara, whose companion is Narayana, will be born as Indra's son and indeed, will be known as Arjuna, the mighty son of Pandu. This boy of mine shall be his son and become a mighty car-warrior in his boyhood. And let him, ye best of immortals, stay on earth for sixteen years. And when he attaineth to his sixteenth year, the battle shall take place in which all who are born of your portions shall achieve the destruction of mighty warriors. But a certain encounter shall take place without both Nara and Narayana (taking any part in it). And, indeed, your portions, ye celestials, shall fight, having made that disposition of the forces which is known by the name of the Chakra-vyuha. And my son shall compel all foes to retreat before him. The boy of mighty arms having penetrated the impenetrable array, shall range within it fearlessly and send a fourth part of the hostile force, in course of half a day, unto the regions of the king of the dead. Then when numberless heroes and mighty car-warriors will return to the charge towards the close of the day, my boy of mighty arms, shall reappear before me. And he shall beget one heroic son in his line, who shall continue the almost extinct Bharata race.' Hearing these words of Soma, the dwellers in heaven replied, 'So be it.' And then all together applauded and worshipped (Soma) the king of stars. Thus, O king, have I recited to thee the (particulars of the) birth of thy father's father.

"Know also, O monarch, that the mighty car-warrior Dhrishtadyumna was a portion of Agni. And know also that Sikhandin, who was at first a female, was (the incarnation of) a Rakshasa. And, O bull in Bharata's race, they who became the five sons of Draupadi, those bulls amongst the Bharata princes, were the celestials known as the Viswas. Their names were Pritivindhya, Sutasoma, Srutakirti, Satanika, Nakula, and Srutasena, endued with mighty energy.

"Sura, the foremost of the Yadus, was the father of Vasudeva. He had a daughter called Pritha, who for her beauty, was unrivalled on earth. And Sura, having promised in the presence of fire that he would give his firstborn child to Kuntibhoja, the son of his paternal aunt, who was without offspring, gave his daughter unto the monarch in expectation of his favours. Kuntibhoja thereupon made her his daughter. And she became, thenceforth, in the house of her (adoptive) father, engaged in attending upon Brahmanas and guests. One day she had to wait upon the wrathful ascetic of rigid vows, Durvasa by name, acquainted with truth and fully conversant with the mysteries of religion. And Pritha with all possible care gratified the wrathful Rishi with soul under complete control. The holy one, gratified with the attentions bestowed on him by the maiden, told her, 'I am satisfied, O fortunate one, with thee! By this mantra (that I am about to give thee), thou shall be able to summon (to thy side) whatever celestials thou likest. And, by their grace, shall thou also obtain children.' Thus addressed, the girl (a little while after), seized with curiosity, summoned, during the period of her maiden-hood, the god Surya. And the lord of light thereupon made her conceive and begot on her a son who became the first of all wielders of weapons. From fear of relatives she brought forth in secrecy that child who had come out with ear-rings and coat of mail. And he was gifted with the beauty of a celestial infant, and in splendour was like unto the maker of day himself. And every part of his body was symmetrical and well-adorned. And Kunti cast the handsome child into the water. But the child thus thrown into the water was taken up by the excellent husband of Radha and given by him to his wife to be adopted by her as their son. And the couple gave him the name of Vasusena, by which appellation the child soon became known all over the land. And, as he grew up, he became very strong and excelled in all weapons. The first of all successful persons, he soon mastered the sciences. And when the intelligent one having truth for his strength recited the Vedas, there was nothing he would not then give to the Brahmanas. At that time Indra, the originator of all things, moved by the desire of benefiting his own son Arjuna, assumed the guise of a Brahmana, came to him, and begged of the hero his ear-rings and natural armour. And the hero taking off his ear-rings and armour gave them unto the Brahmana. And Sakra (accepting the gift) presented to the giver a dart, surprised (at his open handedness), and addressed him in these words, 'O invincible one, amongst the celestials, Asuras, men, Gandharvas, Nagas, and Rakshasas, he at whom thou hurlest (this weapon), that one shall certainly be slain.' And the son of Surya was at first known in the world by the name of Vasusena. But, for his deeds, he subsequently came to be called Karna. And because that hero of great fame had taken off his natural armour, therefore was he—the first son of Pritha—called Karna. And, O best of kings, the hero began to grow up in the Suta caste. And, O king, know thou that Karna—the first of all exalted men—the foremost of all wielders of weapons—the slayer of foes—and the best portion of the maker of day— was the friend and counsellor of Duryodhana. And he, called Vasudeva, endued with great valour, was among men a portion of him called Narayana—the god of gods—eternal. And Valadeva of exceeding strength was a portion of the Naga, Sesha. And, O monarch, know that Pradyumna of great energy was Sanatkumara. And in this way the portion of various other dwellers in heaven became exalted men in the race of Vasudeva, increasing the glory thereof. And, O king, the portions of the tribe of Apsaras which I have mentioned already, also became incarnate on earth according to Indra's commands—And sixteen thousand portions of those goddesses became, O king, in this world of men, the wives of Vasudeva. And a portion of Sri herself became incarnate on earth, for the gratification of Narayana, in the line of Bhishmaka. And she was by name the chaste Rukmini. And the faultless Draupadi, slender-waisted like the wasp, was born of a portion of Sachi (the queen of the celestials), in the line of Drupada. And she was neither low nor tall in stature. And she was of the fragrance of the blue lotus, of eyes large as lotus-petals, of thighs fair and round, of dense masses of black curly hair. And endued with every auspicious feature and of complexion like that of the emerald, she became the charmer of the hearts of five foremost of men. And the two goddesses Siddhi and Dhriti became the mothers of those five, and were called Kunti and Madri. And she who was Mati became the daughter (Gandhari) of Suvala.

"Thus, O king, have I recited to thee all about the incarnation, according to their respective portions, of the gods, the Asuras, the Gandharvas, the Apsaras, and of the Rakshasas. They who were born on earth as monarchs invincible in battle, those high-souled ones who were born in the wide extended line of the Yadus, they who were born as mighty monarchs in other lines, they who were born as Brahmanas and Kshatriyas and Vaisyas, have all been recited by me duly. And this account of the incarnation (of superior beings according to their respective portions) capable of bestowing wealth, fame, offspring, long life, and success, should always be listened to in a proper frame of mind. And having listened to this account of incarnation, according to their portions, of gods, Gandharvas, and Rakshasas, the hearer becoming acquainted with the creation, preservation, and destruction of the universe and acquiring wisdom, is never cast down even under the most engrossing sorrows.'"

SECTION LXVIII
(Sambhava Parva continued)

"Janamejaya said, 'O Brahmana, I have, indeed, heard from thee this account of the incarnation, according to their portions, of the gods, the Danavas, the Rakshasas, and also of the Gandharvas and the Apsaras. I however, again desire to hear of the dynasty of the Kurus from the very beginning. Therefore, O Brahmana, speak of this in the presence of all these regenerate Rishis.'

"Vaisampayana said, 'O exalted one of Bharata's race, the founder of the Paurava line was Dushmanta gifted with great energy. And he was the protector of the earth bounded by the four seas. And that king had full sway over four quarters of this world. And he was the lord also of various regions in the midst of the sea. And that great oppressor of all foes had sway over the countries even of the Mlechchhas.

"And during his rule there were no men of mixed castes, no tillers of the soil (for the land, of itself, yielded produce), no workers of mines (for the surface of the earth yielded in abundance), and no sinful men. All were virtuous, and did everything from virtuous motives, O tiger among men. There was no fear of thieves, O dear one, no fear of famine, no fear of disease. And all four orders took pleasure in doing their respective duties and never performed religious acts for obtaining fruition of desires. And his subjects, depending upon him, never entertained any fear. And Parjanya (Indra) poured showers at the proper time, and the produce of the fields was always pulpy and juicy. And the earth was full of all kinds of wealth and all kinds of animals. And the Brahmanas were always engaged in their duties and they were always truthful. And the youthful monarch was endued with wonderful prowess and a physical frame hard as the thunderbolt, so that he could, taking up the mountain Mandara with its forests and bushes, support it on his arms. And he was well-skilled in four kinds of encounters with the mace (hurling it at foes at a distance, striking at those that are near, whirling it in the midst of many, and driving the foe before). And he was skilled also in the use of all kinds of weapons and in riding elephants and horses. And in strength he was like unto Vishnu, in splendour like unto the maker of day, in gravity like unto the ocean, and in patience, like unto the earth. And the monarch was loved by all his subjects, and he ruled his contented people virtuously.'"

SECTION LXIX
(Sambhava Parva continued)

"Janamejaya said, 'I desire to hear from thee about the birth and life of the high-souled Bharata and of the origin of Sakuntala. And, O holy one, I also desire to hear all about Dushmanta—that lion among men—and how the hero obtained Sakuntala. It behoveth thee, O knower of truth and the first of all intelligent men, to tell me everything.'

"Vaisampayana said, 'Once on a time (king Dushmanta) of mighty arms, accompanied by a large force, went into the forest. And he took with him hundreds of horses and elephants. And the force that accompanied the monarch was of four kinds (foot-soldiers, car-warriors, cavalry, and elephants)—heroes armed with swords and darts and bearing in their hands maces and stout clubs. And surrounded by hundreds of warriors with lances and spears in their hands, the monarch set out on his journey. And with the leonine roars of the warriors and the notes of conchs and sound of drums, with the rattle of the car-wheels and shrieks of huge elephants, all mingling with the neighing of horses and the clash of weapons of the variously armed attendants in diverse dresses, there arose a deafening tumult while the king was on his march. And ladies gifted with great beauty beheld from the terraces of goodly mansions that heroic monarch, the achiever of his own fame. And the ladies saw that he was like unto Sakra, the slayer of his enemies, capable of repulsing the elephants of foes—And they believed that he was the wielder of the thunderbolt himself. And they said, 'This is that tiger among men who in battle is equal unto the Vasus in prowess, and in consequence of the might of whose arms no foes are left.' And saying this, the ladies from affection gratified the monarch by showering flowers on his head. And followed by foremost of Brahmanas uttering blessings all the way, the king in great gladness of heart went towards the forest, eager for slaying the deer. And many Brahmanas, Kshatriyas, Vaisyas, and Sudras, followed the monarch who was like unto the king of the celestials seated on the back of a proud elephant. The citizens and other classes followed the monarch for some distance. And they at last refrained from going farther at the command of the king. And the king, then, ascending his chariot of winged speed, filled the whole earth and even the heavens, with the rattle of his chariot wheels. And, as he went, he saw around him a forest like unto Nandana itself (the celestial garden). And it was full of Vilwa, Arka, Khadira (catechu), Kapittha (wood-apple) and Dhava trees. And he saw that the soil was uneven and scattered over with blocks of stone loosened from the neighbouring cliffs. And he saw that it was without water and without human beings and lay extended for many Yojanas around. And it was full of deer, and lions, and other terrible beasts of prey.

"And king Dushmanta, that tiger among men, assisted by his followers and the warriors in his train, agitated that forest, killing numerous animals. And Dushmanta, piercing them with his arrows, felled numerous tigers that were within shooting range. And the king wounded many that were too distant, and killed many that were too near with his heavy sword. And that foremost of all wielders of darts killed many by hurling his darts at them. And well-conversant with the art of whirling the mace, the king of immeasurable prowess fearlessly wandered over the forest. And the king roamed about, killing the denizens of the wilderness sometimes with his sword and sometimes by fast-descending blows of his mace and heavy club.

"And when the forest was so disturbed by the king possessed of wonderful energy and by the warriors in his train delighting in warlike sports, the lions began to desert it in numbers. And herds of animals deprived of their leaders, from fear and anxiety began to utter loud cries as they fled in all directions. And fatigued with running, they began to fall down on all sides, unable to slake their thirst, having reached river-beds that were perfectly dry. And many so falling were eaten up by the hungry warriors. While others were eaten up after having been duly quartered and roasted in fires lit up by them. And many strong elephants, maddened with the wounds they received and alarmed beyond measure, fled with trunks raised on high. And those wild elephants, betraying the usual symptoms of alarm by urinating and ejecting the contents of their stomachs and vomiting blood in large quantities, trampled, as they ran, many warriors to death. And that forest which had been full of animals, was by the king with his bands of followers and with sharp weapons soon made bereft of lions and tigers and other monarchs of the wilderness.'"

SECTION LXX
(Sambhava Parva continued)

"Vaisampayana said, 'Then the king with his followers, having killed thousands of animals, entered another forest with a view to hunting. And attended by a single follower and fatigued with hunger and thirst, he came upon a large desert on the frontiers of the forest. And having crossed this herbless plain, the king came upon another forest full of the retreats of ascetics, beautiful to look at, delightful to the heart and of cool agreeable breezes. And it was full of trees covered with blossoms, the soil overgrown with the softest and greenest grass, extending for many miles around, and echoing with the sweet notes of winged warblers. And it resounded with the notes of the male Kokila and of the shrill cicala. And it was full of magnificent trees with outstretched branches forming a shady canopy overhead. And the bees hovered over flowery creepers all around. And there were beautiful bowers in every place. And there was no tree without fruits, none that had prickles on it, none that had no bees swarming around it. And the whole forest resounded with the melody of winged choristers. And it was decked with the flowers of every season. And there were refreshing shades of blossoming trees.

"Such was the delicious and excellent forest that the great bowman entered. And trees with branches beautified with clusters began to wave gently at the soft breeze and rain their flowers over the monarch's head. And the trees, clad in their flowery attires of all colours, with sweet-throated warblers perched on them, stood there in rows with heads touching the very heavens. And around their branches hanging down with the weight of flowers the bees tempted by the honey hummed in sweet chorus. And the king, endued with great energy, beholding innumerable spots covered with bowers of creepers decked with clusters of flowers, from excess of gladness, became very much charmed. And the forest was exceedingly beautiful in consequence of those trees ranged around with flowery branches twining with each other and looking like so many rainbows for gaudiness and variety of colour. And it was the resort of bands of Siddhas, of the Charanas, of tribes of Gandharvas, and Apsaras, of monkeys and Kinnaras drunk with delight. Delicious cool, and fragrant breezes, conveying the fragrance from fresh flowers, blew in all directions as if they had come there to sport with the trees. And the king saw that charming forest gifted with such beauties. And it was situated in a delta of the river, and the cluster of high trees standing together lent the place the look of a gaudy pole erected to Indra's honour.

"And in that forest which was the resort of ever cheerful birds, the monarch saw a delightful and charming retreat of ascetics. And there were many trees around it. And the sacred fire was burning within it. And the king worshipped that unrivalled retreat. And he saw seated in it numerous Yotis, Valakhilyas and other Munis. And it was adorned with many chambers containing sacrificial fire. And the flowers dropping from the trees had formed a thick carpet spread over the ground. And the spot looked exceedingly beautiful with those tall trees of large trunks. And by it flowed, O king, the sacred and transparent Malini with every species of water-fowl playing on its bosom. And that stream infused gladness into the hearts of the ascetics who resorted to it for purposes of ablutions. And the king beheld on its banks many innocent animals of the deer species and was exceedingly delighted with all that he saw.

"And the monarch, the course of whose chariot no foe could obstruct, then entered that asylum which was like unto the region of the celestials, being exceedingly beautiful all over. And the king saw that it stood on the margin of the sacred stream which was like the mother of all the living creatures residing in its vicinage. And on its bank sported the Chakravaka, and waves of milkwhite foam. And there stood also the habitations of Kinnaras. And monkeys and bears too disported themselves in numbers. And there lived also holy ascetics engaged in studies and meditation. And there could be seen also elephants and tigers and snakes. And it was on the banks of that stream that the excellent asylum of the illustrious Kasyapa stood, offering a home to numerous Rishis of great ascetic merit. And beholding that river, and also the asylum washed by that river which was studded with many islands and which possessed banks of so much beauty,— an asylum like unto that of Nara and Narayana laved by the water of the Ganga—the king resolved to enter into that sacred abode. And that bull among men, desirous of beholding the great Rishi of ascetic wealth, the illustrious Kanwa of the race of Kasyapa, one who possessed every virtue and who, for his splendour, could be gazed at with difficulty, approached that forest resounding with the notes of maddened peacocks and like unto the gardens of the great Gandharva, Chitraratha, himself. And halting his army consisting of flags, cavalry, infantry, and elephants at the entrance of the forest, the monarch spoke as follows, 'I shall go to behold the mighty ascetic of Kasyapa's race, one who is without darkness. Stay ye here until my return!'

"And the king having entered that forest which was like unto Indra's garden, soon forgot his hunger and thirst. And he was pleased beyond measure. And the monarch, laying aside all signs of royalty, entered that excellent asylum with but his minister and his priest, desirous of beholding that Rishi who was an indestructible mass of ascetic merit. And the king saw that the asylum was like unto the region of Brahman. Here were bees sweetly humming and there were winged warblers of various species pouring forth their melodies. At particular places that tiger among men heard the chanting of Rik hymns by first-rate Brahmanas according to the just rules of intonation. Other places again were graced with Brahmanas acquainted with ordinances of sacrifice, of the Angas and of the hymns of the Yajurveda. Other places again were filled with the harmonious strains of Saman hymns sung by vow-observing Rishis. At other places the asylum was decked with Brahmanas learned in the Atharvan Veda. At other places again Brahmanas learned in the Atharvan Veda and those capable of chanting the sacrificial hymns of the Saman were reciting the Samhitas according to the just rules of voice. And at other places again, other Brahmanas well-acquainted with the science of orthoepy were reciting mantras of other kinds. In fact, that sacred retreat resounding with these holy notes was like unto a second region of Brahman himself. And there were many Brahmanas skilled in the art of making sacrificial platforms and in the rules of Krama in sacrifices, conversant with logic and the mental sciences, and possessing a complete knowledge of the Vedas. There were those also who were fully acquainted with the meanings of all kinds of expressions; those that were conversant with all special rites, those also that were followers of Moksha-Dharma; those again that were well-skilled in establishing propositions; rejecting superfluous causes, and drawing right conclusions. There were those having a knowledge of the science of words (grammar), of prosody, of Nirukta; those again that were conversant with astrology and learned in the properties of matter and the fruits of sacrificial rites, possessing a knowledge of causes and effects, capable of understanding the cries of birds and monkeys, well-read in large treatises, and skilled in various sciences. And the king, as he proceeded, heard their voices. And the retreat resounded also with voice of men capable of charming human hearts. And the slayer of hostile heroes also saw around him learned Brahmanas of rigid vows engaged in Japa (the repeated muttering of the names of gods) and Homa (burnt-offering). And the king wondered much on beholding the beautiful carpets which those Brahmanas offered to him respectfully. And that best of monarchs, at the sight of the rites with which those Brahmanas worshipped the gods and the great Rishis, thought within himself that he was in the region of Brahman. And the more the king saw that auspicious and sacred asylum of Kasyapa protected by that Rishi's ascetic virtues and possessing all the requisites of a holy retreat, the more he desired to see it. In fact, he was not satisfied with his short survey. And the slayer of heroes at last, accompanied by his minister and his priest, entered that charming and sacred retreat of Kasyapa inhabited all around by Rishis of ascetic wealth and exalted vows.'"

SECTION LXXI
(Sambhava Parva continued)

"Vaisampayana said, 'The monarch then, as he proceeded, left even his reduced retinue at the entrance of the hermitage. And entering quite alone he saw not the Rishi (Kanwa) of rigid vows. And not seeing the Rishi and finding that the abode was empty, he called loudly, saying, 'What ho, who is here?' And the sound of his voice was echoed back. And hearing the sound of his voice, there came out of the Rishi's abode a maiden beautiful as Sri herself but dressed as an ascetic's daughter. And the black-eyed fair one, as she saw king Dushmanta, bade him welcome and received him duly. And, showing him due respect by the offer of a seat, water to wash his feet, and Arghya, she enquired about the monarch's health and peace. And having worshipped the king and asked him about his health and peace, the maiden reverentially asked, 'What must be done, O king! I await your commands.' The king, duly worshipped by her, said unto that maiden of faultless features and sweet speech, 'I have come to worship the highly- blessed Rishi Kanwa. Tell me, O amiable and beautiful one, where has the illustrious Rishi gone?'

"Sakuntala then answered, 'My illustrious father hath gone away from the asylum to fetch fruit. Wait but a moment and thou wilt see him when he arrives.'

"Vaisampayana continued, 'The king not seeing the Rishi and addressed thus by her, beheld that the maiden was exceedingly beautiful and endued with perfect symmetry of shape. And he saw that she was of sweet smiles. And she stood decked with the beauty of her faultless features, her ascetic penances, and her humility. And he saw that she was in the bloom of youth. He therefore asked her, 'Who art thou? And whose daughter, O beautiful one? Why hast thou come into the woods also? O handsome one, gifted with so much beauty and such virtues, whence hast thou come? O charming one, at the very first glance hast thou stolen my heart! I desire to learn all about thee; therefore tell me all.' And thus addressed by the monarch, the maiden smilingly replied in these sweet words, 'O Dushmanta, I am the daughter of the virtuous, wise, high-souled, and illustrious ascetic Kanwa.'

"Dushmanta, hearing this, replied, 'The universally-worshipped and highly- blessed Rishi is one whose seed hath been drawn up. Even Dharma himself might fall off from his course but an ascetic of rigid vows can never fall off so. Therefore, O thou of the fairest complexion, how hast thou been born as his daughter? This great doubt of mine it behoveth thee to dispel.'

"Sakuntala then replied, 'Hear, O king, what I have learnt regarding all that befell me of old and how I became the daughter of the Muni. Once on a time, a Rishi came here and asked about my birth. All that the illustrious one (Kanwa) told him, hear now from me, O king!

"My father Kanwa, in answer to that Rishi's enquiries, said, 'Viswamitra, of old, having been engaged in the austerest penances alarmed Indra, the chief of the celestials, who thought that the mighty ascetic of blazing energy would, by his penances, hurl him down from his high seat in heaven. Indra, thus alarmed, summoned Menaka and told her, 'Thou, O Menaka, art the first of celestial Apsaras. Therefore, O amiable one, do me this service. Hear what I say. This great ascetic Viswamitra like unto the Sun in splendour, is engaged in the most severe of penances. My heart is trembling with fear. Indeed, O slender-waisted Menaka, this is thy business. Thou must see that Viswamitra of soul rapt in contemplation and engaged in the austerest penances, who might hurl me down from my seat. Go and tempt him and frustrating his continued austerities accomplish my good. Win him away from his penances, O beautiful one, by tempting him with thy beauty, youth, agreeableness, arts, smiles and speech.' Hearing all this, Menaka replied, 'The illustrious Viswamitra is endued with great energy and is a mighty ascetic. He is very short-tempered too, as is known to thee. The energy, penances, and wrath of the high-souled one have made even thee anxious. Why should I not also be anxious? He it was who made even the illustrious Vasishtha bear the pangs of witnessing the premature death of his children. He it was who, though at first born as Kshatriya, subsequently became a Brahmana by virtue of his ascetic penances. He it was who, for purposes of his ablutions, created a deep river that can with difficulty be forded, and which sacred stream is known by the name of the Kausiki. It was Viswamitra whose wife, in a season of distress, was maintained by the royal sage Matanga (Trisanku) who was then living under a father's curse as a hunter. It was Viswamitra who, on returning after the famine was over, changed the name of the stream having his asylum from Kausik into Para. It was Viswamitra who in return for the services of Matanga, himself became the latter's priest for purposes of a sacrifice. The lord of the celestials himself went through fear to drink the Soma juice. It was Viswamitra who in anger created a second world and numerous stars beginning with Sravana. He it was who granted protection to Trisanku smarting under a superior's curse. I am frightened to approach him of such deeds. Tell me, O Indra, the means that should be adopted so that I may not be burnt by his wrath. He can burn the three worlds by his splendour, can, by a stamp (of his foot), cause the earth to quake. He can sever the great Meru from the earth and hurl it to any distance. He can go round the ten points of the earth in a moment. How can a woman like me even touch such a one full of ascetic virtues, like unto a blazing fire, and having his passions under complete control? His mouth is like unto a blazing fire; the pupils of his eyes are like the Sun and the Moon; his tongue is like unto Yama himself. How shall, O chief of the celestials, a woman like me even touch him? At the thought of his prowess Yama, Soma, the great Rishis, the Saddhyas, the Viswas, Valakhilyas, are terrified! How can a woman like me gaze at him without alarm? Commanded, however, by thee, O king of the celestials, I shall somehow approach that Rishi. But, O chief of the gods, devise thou some plan whereby protected by thee, I may safely move about that Rishi. I think that when I begin to play before the Rishi, Marut (the god of wind) had better go there and rob me of my dress, and Manmatha (the god of love) had also, at thy command, better help me then. Let also Marut on that occasion bear thither fragrance from the woods to tempt the Rishi.' Saying this and seeing that all she had spoken about had been duly provided, Menaka went to the retreat of the great Kausika."

SECTION LXXII
(Sambhava Parva continued)

"Kanwa continued, 'And Sakra, thus addressed by her, then commanded him who could approach every place (viz., the god of the wind) to be present with Menaka at the time she would be before the Rishi. And the timid and beautiful Menaka then entered the retreat and saw there Viswamitra who had burnt, by his penances, all his sins, and was engaged still in ascetic penances. And saluting the Rishi, she then began to sport before him. And just at that time Marut robbed her of her garments that were white as the Moon. And she thereupon ran, as if in great bashfulness, to catch hold of her attire, and as if she was exceedingly annoyed with Marut. And she did all this before the very eyes of Viswamitra who was endued with energy like that of fire. And Viswamitra saw her in that attitude. And beholding her divested of her robes, he saw that she was of faultless feature. And that best of Munis saw that she was exceedingly handsome, with no marks of age on her person. And beholding her beauty and accomplishments that bull amongst Rishis was possessed with lust and made a sign that he desired her companionship. And he invited her accordingly, and she also of faultless features expressed her acceptance of the invitation. And they then passed a long time there in each other's company. And sporting with each other, just as they pleased, for a long time as if it were only a single day, the Rishi begat on Menaka a daughter named Sakuntala. And Menaka (as her conception advanced) went to the banks of the river Malini coursing along a valley of the charming mountains of Himavat. And there she gave birth to that daughter. And she left the new-born infant on the bank of that river and went away. And beholding the new-born infant lying in that forest destitute of human beings but abounding with lions and tigers, a number of vultures sat around to protect it from harm. No Rakshasas or carnivorous animals took its life. Those vultures protected the daughter of Menaka. I went there to perform my ablution and beheld the infant lying in the solitude of the wilderness surrounded by vultures. Bringing her hither I have made her my daughter. Indeed, the maker of the body, the protector of life, the giver of food, are all three, fathers in their order, according to the scriptures. And because she was surrounded in the solitude of the wilderness, by Sakuntas (birds), therefore, hath she been named by me Sakuntala (bird-protected). O Brahman, learn that it is thus that Sakuntala hath become my daughter. And the faultless Sakuntala also regards me as her father.'

"This is what my father had said unto the Rishi, having been asked by him.
O king of men, it is thus that thou must know I am the daughter of Kanwa.
And not knowing my real father, I regard Kanwa as my father. Thus have I
told thee, O king, all that hath been heard by me regarding my birth!'"

SECTION LXXIII
(Sambhava Parva continued)

"Vaisampayana continued, 'King Dushmanta, hearing all this, said, 'Well- spoken, O princess, this that thou hast said! Be my wife, O beautiful one! What shall I do for thee? Golden garlands, robes, ear-rings of gold, white and handsome pearls, from various countries, golden coins, finest carpets, I shall present thee this very day. Let the whole of my kingdom be thine today, O beautiful one! Come to me, O timid one, wedding me, O beautiful one, according to the Gandharva form. O thou of tapering thighs, of all forms of marriage, the Gandharva one is regarded as the first.'

"Sakuntala, hearing this, said, 'O king, my father hath gone away from this asylum to bring fruit. Wait but a moment; he will bestow me on thee.'

"Dushmanta replied, 'O beautiful and faultless one, I desire that thou shouldst be my life's companion. Know thou that I exist for thee, and my heart is in thee. One is certainly one's own friend, and one certainly may depend upon one's own self. Therefore, according to the ordinance, thou canst certainly bestow thyself. There are, in all, eight kinds of marriages. These are Brahma, Daiva, Arsha, Prajapatya, Asura, Gandharva, Rakshasa, and Paisacha, the eighth. Manu, the son of the self-create, hath spoken of the appropriateness of all these forms according to their order. Know, O faultless one, that the first four of these are fit for Brahmanas, and the first six for Kshatriyas. As regards kings, even the Rakshasa form is permissible. The Asura form is permitted to Vaisyas and Sudras. Of the first five the three are proper, the other two being improper. The Paisacha and the Asura forms should never be practised. These are the institutes of religion, and one should act according to them. The Gandharva and the Rakshasa form are consistent with the practices of Kshatriyas. Thou needst not entertain the least fear. There is not the least doubt that either according to any one of these last-mentioned forms, or according to a union of both of them, our wedding may take place. O thou of the fairest complexion, full of desire I am, thou also in a similar mood mayst become my wife according to the Gandharva form.'

"Sakuntala, having listened to all this, answered, 'If this be the course sanctioned by religion, if, indeed, I am my own disposer, hear, O thou foremost one of Puru's race, what my terms are. Promise truly to give me what I ask thee. The son that shall be begotten on me shall become thy heir-apparent. This, O king, is my fixed resolve. O Dushmanta, if thou grant this, then let our union take place.'

"Vaisampayana continued, 'The monarch, without taking time to consider at once told her, 'Let it be so. I will even take thee, O thou of agreeable smiles, with me to my capital. I tell thee truly. O beautiful one, thou deservest all this.' And so saying, that first of kings wedded the handsome Sakuntala of graceful gait, and knew her as a husband. And assuring her duly, he went away, telling her repeatedly, 'I shall send thee, for thy escort, my troops of four classes. Indeed, it is even thus that I shall take thee to my capital, O thou of sweet smiles!"

"Vaisampayana continued, 'O Janamejaya, having promised so unto her, the king went away. And as he retraced his way homewards, he began to think of Kasyapa. And he asked himself, 'What will the illustrious ascetic say, after he has known all?' Thinking of this, he entered his capital.

"The moment the king had left, Kanwa arrived at his abode. But Sakuntala, from a sense of shame, did not go out to receive her father. That great ascetic, however, possessed of spiritual knowledge, knew all. Indeed beholding everything with his spiritual eye, the illustrious one was pleased, and addressing her, said, 'Amiable one, what hath been done by thee today in secret, without, having waited for me—viz., intercourse with a man—hath not been destructive of thy virtue. Indeed, union according to the Gandharva form, of a wishful woman with a man of sensual desire, without mantras of any kind, it is said, is the best for Kshatriyas. That best of men, Dushmanta, is also high-souled and virtuous. Thou hast, O Sakuntala, accepted him for thy husband. The son that shall be born of thee shall be mighty and illustrious in this world. And he shall have sway over the sea. And the forces of that illustrious king of kings, while he goeth out against his foes shall be irresistible.'

"Sakuntala then approached her fatigued father and washed his feet. And taking down the load he had with him and placing the fruits in proper order, she told him, 'It behoveth thee to give thy grace to that Dushmanta whom I have accepted for my husband, as well as his ministers!'

"Kanwa replied, 'O thou of the fairest complexion, for thy sake I am inclined to bless him. But receive from me, O blessed one, the boon that thou desirest.'

"Vaisampayana continued, 'Sakuntala, thereupon, moved by desire of benefiting Dushmanta, asked the boon that the Paurava monarchs might ever be virtuous and never deprived of their thrones.'"

SECTION LXXIV
(Sambhava Parva continued)

"Vaisampayana said, 'After Dushmanta had left the asylum having made those promises unto Sakuntala, the latter of tapering thighs brought forth a boy of immeasurable energy. And when the child was three years old, he became in splendour like the blazing fire. And, O Janamejaya, he was possessed of beauty and magnanimity and every accomplishment. And that first of virtuous men, Kanwa, caused all the rites of religion to be performed in respect of that intelligent child thriving day by day. And the boy gifted with pearly teeth and shining locks, capable of slaying lions even then, with all auspicious signs on his palm, and broad expansive forehead, grew up in beauty and strength. And like unto a celestial child in splendour, he began to grow up rapidly. And when he was only six years of age, endued with great strength he used to seize and bind to the trees that stood around that asylum, lions and tigers and bears and buffaloes and elephants. And he rode on some animals, and pursued others in sportive mood. The dwellers at Kanwa's asylum thereupon bestowed on him a name. And they said, because he seizes and restrains an animals however strong, let him, be called Sarvadamana (the subduer of all). And it was thus that the boy came to be named Sarvadamana, endued as he was with prowess, and energy and strength. And the Rishi seeing the boy and marking also his extraordinary acts, told Sakuntala that the time had come for his installation as the heir-apparent. And beholding the strength of the boy, Kanwa commanded his disciples, saying, 'Bear ye without delay this Sakuntala with her son from this abode to that of her husband, blessed with every auspicious sign. Women should not live long in the houses of their paternal or maternal relations. Such residence is destructive of their reputation, their good conduct, their virtue. Therefore, delay not in bearing her hence.' These disciples of the Rishi thereupon, saying 'So be it,' went towards the city named after an elephant (Hastinapura) with Sakuntala and her son ahead of them. And then she of fair eye-brows, taking with her that boy of celestial beauty, endued with eyes like lotus petals, left the woods where she had been first known by Dushmanta. And having approached the king, she with her boy resembling in splendour the rising sun was introduced to him. And the disciples of the Rishi having introduced her, returned to the asylum. And Sakuntala having worshipped the king according to proper form, told him, 'This is thy son, O king! Let him be installed as thy heir-apparent. O king, this child, like unto a celestial, hath been begotten by thee upon me. Therefore, O best of men, fulfil now the promise thou gavest me. Call to mind, O thou of great good fortune, the agreement thou hadst made on the occasion of thy union with me in the asylum of Kanwa.'

"The king, hearing these her words, and remembering everything said, 'I do not remember anything. Who art thou, O wicked woman in ascetic guise? I do not remember having any connection with thee in respect of Dharma, Kama and Arthas. Go or stay or do as thou pleasest.' Thus addressed by him, the fair-coloured innocent one became abashed. Grief deprived her of consciousness and she stood for a time like an wooden post. Soon, however, her eyes became red like copper and her lips began to quiver. And the glances she now and then cast upon the king seemed to burn the latter. Her rising wrath however, and the fire of her asceticism, she extinguished within herself by an extraordinary effort. Collecting her thoughts in a moment, her heart possessed with sorrow and rage, she thus addressed her lord in anger, looking at him, 'Knowing everything, O monarch, how thou, like an inferior person, thus say that thou knowest it not? Thy heart is a witness to the truth or falsehood of this matter. Therefore, speak truly without degrading thyself. He who being one thing representeth himself as another thing to others, is like a thief and a robber of his own self. Of what sin is he not capable? Thou thinkest that thou alone hast knowledge of thy deed. But knowest thou not that the Ancient, Omniscient one (Narayana) liveth in thy heart? He knoweth all thy sins, and thou sinnest in His presence. He that sins thinks that none observes him. But he is observed by the gods and by Him also who is in every heart. The Sun, the Moon, the Air, the Fire, the Earth, the Sky, Water, the heart, Yama, the day, the night, both twilights, and Dharma, all witness the acts of man. Yama, the son of Surya, takes no account of the sins of him with whom Narayana the witness of all acts, is gratified. But he with whom Narayana is not gratified is tortured for his sins by Yama. Him who degradeth himself by representing his self falsely, the gods never bless. Even his own soul blesseth him not. I am a wife devoted to my husband. I have come of my own accord, it is true. But do not, on that account, treat me with disrespect. I am thy wife and, therefore, deserve to be treated respectfully. Wilt thou not treat me so, because I have come hither of my own accord? In the presence of so many, why dost thou treat me like an ordinary woman? I am not certainly crying in the wilderness. Dost thou not hear me? But if thou refuse to do what I supplicate thee for, O Dushmanta, thy head this moment shall burst into a hundred pieces! The husband entering the womb of the wife cometh out himself in the form of the son. Therefore is the wife called by those cognisant of the Vedas as Jaya (she of whom one is born). And the son that is so born unto persons cognisant of the Vedic Mantras rescueth the spirits of deceased ancestors. And because the son rescueth ancestors from the hell called Put, therefore, hath he been called by the Self-create himself as Puttra (the rescuer from Put). By a son one conquereth the three worlds. By a son's son, one enjoyeth eternity. And by a grandson's son great-grand-fathers enjoy everlasting happiness. She is a true wife who is skilful in household affairs. She is a true wife who hath borne a son. She is a true wife whose heart is devoted to her lord. She is a true wife who knoweth none but her lord. The wife is a man's half. The wife is the first of friends. The wife is the root of religion, profit, and desire. The wife is the root of salvation. They that have wives can perform religious acts. They that have wives can lead domestic lives. They that have wives have the means to be cheerful. They that have wives can achieve good fortune. Sweet-speeched wives are friends on occasions of joy. They are as fathers on occasions of religious acts. They are mothers in sickness and woe. Even in the deep woods to a traveller a wife is his refreshment and solace. He that hath a wife is trusted by all. A wife, therefore, is one's most valuable possession. Even when the husband leaving this world goeth into the region of Yama, it is the devoted wife that accompanies him thither. A wife going before waits for the husband. But if the husband goeth before, the chaste wife followeth close. For these reasons, O king, doth marriage exist. The husband enjoyeth the companionship of the wife both in this and in the other worlds. It hath been said by learned persons that one is himself born as one's son. Therefore, a man whose wife hath borne a son should look upon her as his mother. Beholding the face of the son one hath begotten upon his wife, like his own face in a mirror, one feeleth as happy as a virtuous man, on attaining to heaven. Men scorched by mental grief, or suffering under bodily pain, feel as much refreshed in the companionship of their wives as a perspiring person in a cool bath. No man, even in anger, should ever do anything that is disagreeable to his wife, seeing that happiness, joy, and virtue,—everything dependeth on the wife. A wife is the sacred field in which the husband is born himself. Even Rishis cannot create creatures without women. What happiness is greater than what the father feeleth when the son running towards him, even though his body be covered with dust, claspeth his limbs? Why then dost thou treat with indifference such a son, who hath approached thee himself and who casteth wistful glances towards thee for climbing thy knees? Even ants support their own eggs without destroying them; then why shouldst not thou, a virtuous man that thou art, support thy own child? The touch of soft sandal paste, of women, of (cool) water is not so agreeable as the touch of one's own infant son locked in one's embrace. As a Brahmana is the foremost of all bipeds, a cow, the foremost of all quadrupeds, a protector, the foremost of all superiors, so is the son the foremost of all objects, agreeable to the touch. Let, therefore, this handsome child touch thee in embrace. There is nothing in the world more agreeable to the touch than the embrace of one's son. O chastiser of foes, I have brought forth this child, O monarch, capable of dispelling all thy sorrows after bearing him in my womb for full three years. O monarch of Puru's race, 'He shall perform a hundred horse-sacrifices'—these were the words uttered from the sky when I was in the lying-in room. Indeed, men going into places remote from their homes take up there others' children on their laps and smelling their heads feel great happiness. Thou knowest that Brahmanas repeat these Vedic mantras on the occasion of the consecrating rites of infancy.—Thou art born, O son, of my body! Thou art sprung from my heart. Thou art myself in the form of a son. Live thou to a hundred years! My life dependeth on thee, and the continuation of my race also, on thee. Therefore, O son, live thou in great happiness to a hundred years. He hath sprung from thy body, this second being from thee! Behold thyself in thy son, as thou beholdest thy image in the clear lake. As the sacrificial fire is kindled from the domestic one, so hath this one sprung from thee. Though one, thou hast divided thyself. In course of hunting while engaged in pursuit of the deer, I was approached by thee, O king, I who was then a virgin in the asylum of my father. Urvasi, Purvachitti, Sahajanya, Menaka, Viswachi and Ghritachi, these are the six foremost of Apsaras. Amongst them again, Menaka, born of Brahman, is the first. Descending from heaven on Earth, after intercourse with Viswamitra, she gave birth to me. That celebrated Apsara, Menaka, brought me forth in a valley of Himavat. Bereft of all affection, she went away, cast me there as if I were the child of somebody else. What sinful act did I do, of old, in some other life that I was in infancy cast away by my parents and at present am cast away by thee! Put away by thee, I am ready to return to the refuge of my father. But it behoveth thee not to cast off this child who is thy own.'

"Hearing all this, Dushmanta said, 'O Sakuntala, I do not know having begot upon thee this son. Women generally speak untruths. Who shall believe in thy words? Destitute of all affection, the lewd Menaka is thy mother, and she cast thee off on the surface of the Himavat as one throws away, after the worship is over, the flowery offering made to his gods. Thy father too of the Kshatriya race, the lustful Viswamitra, who was tempted to become a Brahmana, is destitute of all affection. However, Menaka is the first of Apsaras, and thy father also is the first of Rishis. Being their daughter, why dost thou speak like a lewd woman? Thy words deserve no credit. Art thou not ashamed to speak them, especially before me? Go hence, O wicked woman in ascetic guise. Where is that foremost of great Rishis, where also is that Apsara Menaka? And why art thou, low as thou art, in the guise of an ascetic? Thy child too is grown up. Thou sayest he is a boy, but he is very strong. How hath he soon grown like a Sala sprout? Thy birth is low. Thou speakest like a lewd woman. Lustfully hast thou been begotten by Menaka. O woman of ascetic guise, all that thou sayest is quite unknown to me. I don't know thee. Go withersoever thou choosest.'

"Sakuntala replied, 'Thou seest, O king, the fault of others, even though they be as small as a mustard seed. But seeing, thou noticest not thy own faults even though they be as large as the Vilwa fruit. Menaka is one of the celestials. Indeed, Menaka is reckoned as the first of celestials. My birth, therefore, O Dushmanta, is far higher than thine. Thou walkest upon the Earth, O king, but I roam in the skies! Behold, the difference between ourselves is as that between (the mountain) Meru and a mustard seed! Behold my power, O king! I can repair to the abodes of Indra, Kuvera, Yama, and Varuna! The saying is true which I shall refer to before thee, O sinless one! I refer to it for example's sake and not from evil motives. Therefore, it behoveth thee to pardon me after thou hast heard it. An ugly person considereth himself handsomer than others until he sees his own face in the mirror. But when he sees his own ugly face in the mirror, it is then that he perceiveth the difference between himself and others. He that is really handsome never taunts anybody. And he that always talketh evil becometh a reviler. And as the swine always look for dirt and filth even when in the midst of a flower-garden, so the wicked always choose the evil out of both evil and good that others speak. Those, however, that are wise, on hearing the speeches of others that are intermixed with both good and evil, accept only what is good, like geese that always extract the milk only, though it be mixed with water. As the honest are always pained at speaking ill of others, so do the wicked always rejoice in doing the same thing. As the honest always feel pleasure in showing regard for the old, so do the wicked always take delight in aspersing the good. The honest are happy in not seeking for faults. The wicked are happy in seeking for them. The wicked ever speak ill of the honest. But the latter never injure the former, even if injured by them. What can be more ridiculous in the world than that those that are themselves wicked should represent the really honest as wicked? When even atheists are annoyed with those that have fallen off from truth and virtue and who are really like angry snakes of virulent poison, what shall I say of myself who am nurtured in faith? He that having begotten a son who is his own image, regardeth him not, never attaineth to the worlds he coveteth, and verily the gods destroy his good fortune and possessions. The Pitris have said that the son continueth the race and the line and is, therefore, the best of all religious acts. Therefore, none should abandon a son. Manu hath said that there are five kinds of sons; those begotten by one's self upon his own wife, those obtained (as gift) from others, those purchased for a consideration, those reared with affection and those begotten upon other women than upon wedded wives. Sons support the religion and achievements of men, enhance their joys, and rescue deceased ancestors from hell. It behoveth thee not, therefore, O tiger among kings, to abandon a son who is such. Therefore, O lord of Earth, cherish thy own self, truth, and virtue by cherishing thy son. O lion among monarchs, it behoveth thee not to support this deceitfulness. The dedication of a tank is more meritorious than that of a hundred wells. A sacrifice again is more meritorious than the dedication of a tank. A son is more meritorious than a sacrifice. Truth is more meritorious than a hundred sons. A hundred horse-sacrifices had once been weighed against Truth, and Truth was found heavier than a hundred horse-sacrifices. O king, Truth, I ween, may be equal to the study of, the entire Vedas and ablutions in all holy places. There is no virtue equal to Truth: there is nothing superior to Truth. O king, Truth is God himself; Truth is the highest vow. Therefore, violate not thy pledge, O monarch! Let Truth and thee be even united. If thou placest no credit in my words, I shall of my own accord go hence. Indeed, thy companionship should be avoided. But thou, O Dushmanta, that when thou art gone, this son of mine shall rule the whole Earth surrounded by the four seas and adorned with the king of the mountains.'

"Vaisampayana continued, 'Sakuntala having spoken to the monarch in this wise, left his presence. But as soon as she had left, a voice from the skies, emanating from no visible shape, thus spoke unto Dushmanta as he was sitting surrounded by his occasional and household priests, his preceptors, and ministers. And the voice said, 'The mother is but the sheath of flesh; the son sprung from the father is the father himself. Therefore, O Dushmanta, cherish thy son, and insult not Sakuntala. O best of men, the son, who is but a form of one's own seed, rescueth (ancestors) from the region of Yama. Thou art the progenitor of this boy. Sakuntala hath spoken the truth. The husband, dividing his body in twain, is born of his wife in the form of son. Therefore, O Dushmanta, cherish, O monarch, thy son born of Sakuntala. To live by forsaking one's living son is a great misfortune. Therefore, O thou of Puru's race, cherish thy high- souled son born of Sakuntala—And because this child is to be cherished by thee even at our word, therefore shall this thy son be known by the name of Bharata (the cherished).' Hearing these words uttered by the dwellers in heaven, the monarch of Puru's race became overjoyed and spoke as follows unto his priests and ministers, 'Hear ye these words uttered by the celestial messenger? I myself know this one to be my son. If I had taken him as my son on the strength of Sakuntala's words alone, my people would have been suspicious and my son also would not have been regarded as pure.'

"Vaisampayana continued, 'The monarch, then, O thou of Bharata's race, seeing the purity of his son established by the celestial messenger, became exceedingly glad. And he took unto him that son with joy. And the king with a joyous heart then performed all those rites upon his son that a father should perform. And the king smelt his child's head and hugged him with affection. And the Brahmanas began to utter blessings upon him and the bards began to applaud him. And the monarch then experienced the great delight that one feeleth at the touch of one's son. And Dushmanta also received that wife of his with affection. And he told her these words, pacifying her affectionately, 'O goddess, my union with thee took place privately. Therefore, I was thinking of how best to establish thy purity. My people might think that we were only lustfully united and not as husband and wife, and therefore, this son that I would have installed as my heir apparent would only have been regarded as one of impure birth. And dearest, every hard word thou hast uttered in thy anger, have I, O large-eyed one, forgiven thee. Thou art my dearest!' And the royal sage Dushmanta, having spoken thus unto his dear wife, O Bharata, received her with offerings of perfume, food, and drink. And king Dushmanta, then, bestowed the name of Bharata upon his child, and formally installed him as the heir apparent. And the famous and bright wheels of Bharata's car, invincible and like unto the wheels of the cars owned by the gods, traversed every region, filling the whole Earth with their rattle. And the son of Dushmanta reduced to subjection all kings of the Earth. And he ruled virtuously and earned great fame. And that monarch of great prowess was known by the titles of Chakravarti and Sarvabhauma. And he performed many sacrifices like Sakra, the lord of the Maruts. And Kanwa was the chief priest at those sacrifices, in which the offerings to Brahmanas were great. And the blessed monarch performed both the cow and the horse- sacrifices. And Bharata gave unto Kanwa a thousand gold coins as the sacerdotal fee. It is that Bharata from whom have emanated so many mighty achievements. It is from him that the great race called after him in his race are called after him. And in the Bharata race there have been born many godlike monarchs gifted with great energy, and like unto Brahman himself. Their number cannot be counted. But, O thou of Bharata's race, I shall name the principal ones that were blessed with great good fortune, like unto the gods, and devoted to truth and honesty.'"

SECTION LXXV
(Sambhava Parva continued)

"Vaisampayana said, 'Hear now, as I recite the recorded genealogy, that is sacred and subservient to religion, profit and pleasure, of these royal sages—Daksha, the lord of creation, Manu, the son of Surya, Bharata, Ruru, Puru, and Ajamidha. I shall also recite to thee, O sinless one, the genealogies of the Yadavas and of the Kurus and of the king of the Bharata line. These genealogies are sacred and their recitation is a great act of propitiation. That recitation conferreth wealth, fame and long life. And, O sinless one, all these I have named shone in their splendour and were equal unto the great Rishis in energy.

"Prachetas had ten sons who were all devoted to asceticism and possessed of every virtue. They burnt, of old, by the fire emanating from their mouths, several plants of poisonous and innumerable large trees that had covered the Earth and became a source of great discomfort to man. After these ten, was born another named Daksha. It is from Daksha that all creatures have sprung. Therefore is he, O tiger among men, called the Grandfather. Born of Prachetas the Muni Daksha, uniting himself with Virini, begat a thousand sons of rigid vows, all like himself. And Narada taught these thousand sons of Daksha the excellent philosophy of Sankhya as a means of salvation. And, O Janamejaya, the lord of creation, Daksha, then, from the desire of making creatures, begat fifty daughters. And he made all of them his appointed daughters (so that their sons might be his sons also for the performance of all religious acts). And he bestowed ten of his daughters on Dharma, and thirteen on Kasyapa. And he gave twenty- seven to Chandra, who are all engaged in indicating time. And Kasyapa, the son of Marichi, begat on the eldest of his thirteen wives, the Adityas, the celestials endued with great energy and having Indra as their head and also Vivaswat (the Sun). And of Vivaswat was born the lord Yama. And Martanda (Vivaswat) also begat another son after Yama, gifted with great intelligence and named Manu. And Manu was endued with great wisdom and devoted to virtue. And he became the progenitor of a line. And in Manu's race have been born all human beings, who have, therefore, been called Manavas. And it is of Manu that all men including Brahmanas, Kshatriyas, and others have been descended, and are, therefore, all called Manavas. Subsequently, O monarch, the Brahmanas became united with the Kshatriyas. And those sons of Manu that were Brahmanas devoted themselves to the study of the Vedas. And Manu begat ten other children named Vena, Dhrishnu, Narishyan, Nabhaga, Ikshvaku, Karusha, Saryati, the eighth, a daughter named Ila, Prishadhru the ninth, and Nabhagarishta, the tenth. They all betook themselves to the practices of Kshatriyas. Besides these, Manu had fifty other sons on Earth. But we heard that they all perished, quarrelling with one another. The learned Pururavas was born of Ila. It hath been heard by us that Ila was both his mother and father. And the great Pururavas had sway over thirteen islands of the sea. And, though a human being, he was always surrounded by companions that were superhuman. And Pururavas intoxicated with power quarrelled with the Brahmanas and little caring for their anger robbed them of their wealth. Beholding all this Sanatkumara came from the region of Brahman and gave him good counsel, which was, however, rejected by Pururavas. Then the wrath of the great Rishis was excited, and the avaricious monarch, who intoxicated with power, had lost his reason, was immediately destroyed by their curse.

"It was Pururavas who first brought from the region of the Gandharvas the three kinds of fire (for sacrificial purpose). And he brought thence, the Apsara Urvasi also. And the son of Ila begat upon Urvasi six sons who were called Ayus, Dhimat, Amavasu and Dhridhayus, and Vanayus, and Satayus. And it is said that Ayus begat four sons named Nahusha, Vriddhasarman, Rajingaya, and Anenas, on the daughter of Swarbhanu. And, O monarch, Nahusha, of all the sons of Ayus, being gifted with great intelligence and prowess ruled his extensive kingdom virtuously. And king Nahusha supported evenly the Pitris, the celestials, the Rishis, the Brahmanas, the Gandharvas, the Nagas, the Rakshasas, the Kshatriyas, and the Vaisyas. And he suppressed all robber-gangs with a mighty hand. But he made the Rishis pay tribute and carry him on their backs like bests of burden. And, conquering the very gods by the beauty of his person, his asceticism, prowess, and energy, he ruled as if he were Indra himself. And Nahusha begat six sons, all of sweet speech, named Yati, Yayati, Sanyati, Ayati, and Dhruva. Yati betaking himself to asceticism became a Muni like unto Brahman himself. Yayati became a monarch of great prowess and virtue. He ruled the whole Earth, performed numerous sacrifices, worshipped the Pitris with great reverence, and always respected the gods. And he brought the whole world under his sway and was never vanquished by any foe. And the sons of Yayati were all great bowmen and resplendent with every virtue. And, O king, they were begotten upon (his two wives) Devayani and Sarmishtha. And of Devayani were born Yadu and Turvasu, and of Sarmishtha were born Drahyu, Anu, and Puru. And, O king, having virtuously ruled his subjects for a long time, Yayati was attacked with a hideous decrepitude destroying his personal beauty. And attacked by decrepitude, the monarch then spoke, O Bharata, unto his sons Yadu and Puru and Turvasu and Drahyu and Anu these words, 'Ye dear sons, I wish to be a young man and to gratify my appetites in the company of young women. Do you help me therein.' To him his eldest son born of Devayani then said, 'What needest thou, O king? Dost thou want to have your youth?' Yayati then told him, 'Accept thou my decrepitude, O son! With thy youth I would enjoy myself. During the time of a great sacrifice I have been cursed by the Muni Usanas (Sukra). O son, I would enjoy myself with your youth. Take any of you this my decrepitude and with my body rule ye my kingdom. I would enjoy myself with a renovated body. Therefore, ye my sons, take ye my decrepitude.' But none of his sons accepted his decrepitude. Then his youngest son Puru said unto him, 'O king, enjoy thyself thou once again with a renovated body and returned youth! I shall take thy decrepitude and at thy command rule thy kingdom.' Thus addressed, the royal sage, by virtue of his ascetic power then transferred his own decrepitude unto that high-souled son of his and with the youth of Puru became a youth; while with the monarch's age Puru ruled his kingdom.

"Then, after a thousand years had passed away, Yayati, that tiger among kings, remained as strong and powerful as a tiger. And he enjoyed for a long time the companionship of his two wives. And in the gardens of Chitraratha (the king of Gandharvas), the king also enjoyed the company of the Apsara Viswachi. But even after all this, the great king found his appetites unsatiated. The king, then recollected the following truths contained in the Puranas, 'Truly, one's appetites are never satiated by enjoyment. On the other hand, like sacrificial butter poured into the fire, they flame up with indulgence. Even if one enjoyed the whole Earth with its wealth, diamonds and gold, animals and women, one may not yet be satiated. It is only when man doth not commit any sin in respect of any living thing, in thought, deed, or speech, it is then that he attaineth to purity as that of Brahman. When one feareth nothing, when one is not feared by anything, when one wisheth for nothing, when one injureth nothing, it is then that one attaineth to the purity of Brahman.' The wise monarch seeing this and satisfied that one's appetites are never satiated, set his mind at rest by meditation, and took back from his son his own decrepitude. And giving him back his youth, though his own appetites were unsatiated, and installing him on the throne, he spoke unto Puru thus, 'Thou art my true heir, thou art my true son by whom my race is to be continued. In the world shall my race be known by thy name.'

"Vaisampayana continued, 'Then that tiger among kings, having installed his son Puru on the throne, went away to the mount of Bhrigu for devoting himself to asceticism. And, having acquired great ascetic merit, after long years, he succumbed to the inevitable influence of Time. He left his human body by observing the vow of fasting, and ascended to heaven with his wives.'"

SECTION LXXVI
(Sambhava Parva continued)

"Janamejaya said, 'O thou of the wealth of asceticism, tell me how our ancestor Yayati, who is the tenth from Prajapati, obtained for a wife the unobtainable daughter of Sukra. I desire to hear of it in detail. Tell me also, one after another, of those monarchs separately who were the founders of dynasties.'

"Vaisampayana said, 'The monarch Yayati was in splendour like unto Indra himself. I will tell thee, in reply to thy question, O Janamejaya, how both Sukra and Vrishaparvan bestowed upon him, with due rites, their daughters, and how his union took place with Devayani in special.

"Between the celestials and the Asuras, there happened, of yore, frequent encounters for the sovereignty of the three worlds with everything in them. The gods, then, from desire of victory, installed the son of Angiras (Vrihaspati) as their priest to conduct their sacrifices; while their opponents installed the learned Usanas as their priest for the same purpose. And between those two Brahmanas there are always much boastful rivalry. Those Danavas assembled for encounter that were slain by the gods were all revived by the seer Sukra by the power of his knowledge. And then starting again, into life,—these fought with the gods. The Asuras also slew on the field of battle many of the celestials. But the open-minded Vrihaspati could not revive them, because he knew not the science called Sanjivani (re-vivification) which Kavya endued with great energy knew so well. And the gods were, therefore, in great sorrow. And the gods, in great anxiety of heart and entertaining a fear of the learned Usanas, then went to Kacha, the eldest son of Vrihaspati, and spoke unto him, saying, 'We pay court to thee, be kind to us and do us a service that we regard as very great.

That knowledge which resides in Sukra, that Brahmana of immeasurable prowess, make thy own as soon as thou canst. Thou shalt find the Brahmana in the court of Vrishaparvan. He always protects the Danavas but never us, their opponents. Thou art his junior in age, and, therefore, capable of adoring him with reverence. Thou canst also adore Devayani, the favourite daughter of that high-souled Brahmana. Indeed, thou alone art capable of propitiating them both by worship. There is none else that can do so. By gratifying Devayani with thy conduct, liberality, sweetness, and general behaviour, thou canst certainly obtain that knowledge.' The son of Vrihaspati, thus solicited by the gods, said 'So be it,' and went to where Vrishaparvan was. Kacha, thus sent by the gods, soon went to the capital of the chief of the Asuras, and beheld Sukra there. And beholding him, he thus spoke unto him, 'Accept me as thy disciple. I am the grandson of the Rishi Angiras and son of Vrihaspati. By name I am known as Kacha. Thyself becoming my preceptor, I shall practise the Brahmacharya mode of life for a thousand years. Command me, then, O Brahmana!'

"Sukra (hearing this) said, 'Welcome art thou, O Kacha! I accept thy speech. I will treat thee with regard; for by so doing, it is Vrihaspati who will be regarded.'

"Vaisampayana continued, 'Kacha commanded by Kavya or Usanas himself, called also Sukra, then said, 'So be it,' and took the vow he had spoken of. And, O Bharata, accepting the vow of which he had spoken, at the proper time, Kacha began to conciliate regardfully both his preceptor and (his daughter) Devayani. Indeed, he began to conciliate both. And as he was young, by singing and dancing and playing on different kinds of instruments, he soon gratified Devayani who was herself in her youth. And, O Bharata, with his whole heart set upon it, he soon gratified the maiden Devayani who was then a young lady, by presents of flowers and fruits and services rendered with alacrity. And Devayani also with her songs and sweetness of manners used, while they were alone, to attend upon that youth carrying out his vow. And when five hundred years had thus passed of Kacha's vow, the Danavas came to learn his intention. And having no compunctions about slaying a Brahmana, they became very angry with him. And one day they saw Kacha in a solitary part of the woods engaged in tending (his preceptor's) kine. They then slew Kacha from their hatred of Vrihaspati and also from their desire of protecting the knowledge of reviving the dead from being conveyed by him. And having slain him, they hacked his body into pieces and gave them to be devoured by jackals and wolves. And (when twilight came) the kine returned to the fold without him who tended them. And Devayani, seeing the kine returned from the woods without Kacha, spoke, O Bharata, unto her father thus:

'Thy evening-fire hath been kindled. The Sun also hath set, O father! The kine have returned without him who tendeth them. Kacha is, indeed, not to be seen. It is plain that Kacha hath been lost, or is dead. Truly do I say, O father, that without him I will not live.'

"Sukra hearing this said, I will revive him by saying, 'Let this one come.' Then having recourse to the science of reviving the dead, Sukra summoned Kacha. And summoned by his preceptor, Kacha appeared before him in the gladness of heart tearing by virtue of his preceptor's science the bodies of the wolves (that had devoured him). And asked about the cause of his delay, he thus spoke unto Bhargava's daughter. Indeed, asked by that Brahman's daughter, he told her, 'I was dead. O thou of pure manners, burdened with sacrificial fuel, Kusa grass, and logs of wood, I was coming towards our abode. I sat under a banian tree. The kine also, having been brought together, were staying under the shade of that same banian tree. The Asuras, beholding me, asked 'Who art thou?' They heard me answer, 'I am the son of Vrihaspati.' As soon as I said this, the Danavas slew me, and hacking my body into pieces gave my remains to jackals and wolves. And they then went home in the gladness of heart. O amiable one, summoned by the high-souled Bhargava, I after all come before thee fully revived.'

"On another occasion, asked by Devayani, the Brahmana Kacha went into the woods. And as he was roving about for gathering flowers, the Danavas beheld him. They again slew him, and pounding him into a paste they mixed it with the water of the ocean. Finding him long still (in coming), the maiden again represented the matter unto her father. And summoned again by the Brahmana with the aid of his science, Kacha appearing before his preceptor and his daughter told everything as it had happened. Then slaying him for the third time and burning him and reducing him to ashes, the Asuras gave those ashes to the preceptor himself, mixing them with his wine. And Devayani again spoke unto her father, saying, 'O father, Kacha was sent to gather flowers. But he is not to be seen. It is plain he hath been lost, or has died. I tell thee truly, I would not live without him.'

"Sukra hearing this said, 'O daughter, the son of Vrihaspati hath gone to the region of the dead. Though revived by my science, he is thus slain frequently. What, indeed, am I to do? O Devayani, do not grieve, do not cry. One like thee should not grieve for one that is mortal. Thou art indeed, O daughter, in consequence of my prowess, worshipped thrice a day during the ordained hours of prayer, by Brahmanas, the gods with

Indra, the Vasus, the Aswins, the Asuras, in fact, by the whole universe. It is impossible to keep him alive, for revived by me he is often killed.' To all this Devayani replied, 'Why shall I, O father, not grieve for him whose grandfather is old Angiras himself, whose father is Vrihaspati who is an ocean of ascetic merit, who is the grandson of a Rishi and the son also of a Rishi? He himself too was a Brahmacharin and an ascetic; always wakeful and skilled in everything. I will starve and follow the way Kacha has gone. The handsome Kacha is, O father, dear unto me.'

"Vaisampayana continued, 'The great Rishi Kavya, then, afflicted by what Devayani said, cried in anger, 'Certainly, the Asuras seek to injure me, for they slay my disciple that stayeth with me. These followers of Rudra desire to divest me of my character as a Brahmana by making me participate in their crime. Truly, this crime hath a terrible end. The crime of slaying a Brahmana would even burn Indra himself.' Having said this, the Brahmana Sukra, urged by Devayani, began to summon Kacha who had entered the jaws of Death. But Kacha, summoned with the aid of science, and afraid of the consequence to his preceptor, feebly replied from within the stomach of his preceptor, saying, 'Be graceful unto me, O lord! I am Kacha that worshippeth thee. Behave unto me as to thy own dearly-loved son.'

"Vaisampayana continued, 'Sukra then said, 'By what path, O Brahmana, hast thou entered my stomach, where thou stayest now? Leaving the Asuras this very moment, I shall go over to the gods.' Kacha replied, 'By thy grace, memory hath not failed me. Indeed, I do recollect everything as it hath happened. My ascetic virtues have not been destroyed. It is, therefore, that I am able to bear this almost insufferable pain. O Kavya, slain by the Asuras and burnt and reduced to powder, I have been given to thee with thy wine. When thou art present, O Brahmana, the art of the Asuras will never be able to vanquish, the science of the Brahmana.'

"Hearing this, Sukra said, 'O daughter, what good can I do to thee? It is with my death that Kacha can get his life back. O Devayani, Kacha is even within me. There is no other way of his coming out except by ripping open my stomach.' Devayani replied, 'Both evils shall, like fire, burn me! The death of Kacha and thy own death are to me the same! The death of Kacha would deprive me of life. If thou also diest, I shall not be able to bear my life.' Then Sukra said, 'O son of Vrihaspati, thou art, indeed, one already crowned with success, because Devayani regards thee so well. Accept the science that I will today impart to thee, if, indeed, thou be not Indra in the form of Kacha. None can come out of my stomach with life. A Brahmana, however, must not be slain, therefore, accept thou the science I impart to thee. Start thou into life as my son. And possessed of the knowledge received from me, and revived by me, take care that, on coming out of my body, thou dost act gracefully.'

"Vaisampayana continued, 'Receiving the science imparted to him by his preceptor the handsome Kacha, ripped open his stomach, came out like the moon at evening on the fifteenth day of the bright fort-night. And beholding the remains of his preceptor lying like a heap of penances, Kacha revived him, aided by the science he had learned. Worshipping him with regard, Kacha said unto his preceptor, 'Him who poureth the nectar of knowledge into one's ears, even as thou hast done into those of myself who was void of knowledge, him do I regard both as my father and mother. And remembering the immense service done by him, who is there so ungrateful as to injure him? They that, having acquired knowledge, injure their preceptor who is always an object of worship, who is the giver of knowledge, who is the most precious of all precious objects on Earth, come to be hated on Earth and finally go to the regions of the sinful.'

"Vaisampayana continued, 'The learned Sukra, having been deceived while under the influence of wine, and remembering the total loss of consciousness that is one of the terrible consequences of drink, and beholding too before him the handsome Kacha whom he had, in a state of unconsciousness, drunk with his wine, then thought of effecting a reform in the manners of Brahmanas. The high-souled Usanas rising up from the ground in anger, then spoke as follows: "The wretched Brahmana who from this day, unable to resist the temptation, will drink wine shall be regarded as having lost his virtue, shall be reckoned to have committed the sin of slaying a Brahmana, shall be hated both in this and the other worlds. I set this limit to the conduct and dignity of Brahmanas everywhere. Let the honest, let Brahmanas, let those with regard for their superiors, let the gods, let the three worlds, listen!' Having said these words that high-souled one, that ascetic of ascetics, then summoning the Danavas who had been deprived by fate of the good sense, told them these words, Ye foolish Danavas, know ye that Kacha hath obtained his wishes. He will henceforth dwell with me. Having obtained the valuable knowledge of reviving the dead, that Brahmana hath, indeed, become in prowess even as Brahman himself!'

"Vaisampayana continued, 'Bhargava having said so much cut short his speech. The Danavas were surprised and went away to their homes. Kacha, too, having stayed with his preceptor for a full thousand years, then prepared to return to the abode of the celestials, after having obtained his preceptor's permission.'"

SECTION LXXVII
(Sambhava Parva continued)

"Vaisampayana said, 'After the expiry of the period of his vow, Kacha, having obtained his preceptor's leave, was about to return to the abode of the celestials, when Devayani, addressing him, said, 'O grandson of the Rishi Angiras, in conduct and birth, in learning, asceticism and humility, thou shinest most brightly. As the celebrated Rishi Angiras is honoured and regarded by my father, so is thy father regarded and worshipped by me. O thou of ascetic wealth, knowing this, listen to what I say. Recollect my conduct towards thee during the period of thy vow (Brahmacharya). Thy vow hath now been over. It behoveth thee to fix thy affections on me. O accept my hand duly with ordained mantras.'

"Kacha replied, 'Thou art to me an object of regard and worship even as thy father! O thou of faultless features, thou art, indeed, even an object of greater reverence! Thou art dearer than life to the high-souled Bhargava, O amiable one! As the daughter of my preceptor, thou art ever worthy of my worship! As my preceptor Sukra, thy father, is ever deserving of my regards, so art thou, O Devayani! Therefore, it behoveth thee not to say so.' Hearing this, Devayani replied, 'Thou, too, art the son of my father's preceptor's son. Therefore, O best of Brahmanas, thou art deserving of my regards and worship. O Kacha, when thou wert slain so many times by the Asuras, recollect today the affection I showed for thee. Remembering my friendship and affection for thee, and, indeed, my devoted regard also, O virtuous one, it behoveth thee not to abandon me without any fault. I am truly devoted to thee.'

"Hearing all this, Kacha said, 'O thou of virtuous vows, do not urge me into such a sinful course. O thou of fair eye-brows, be gracious unto me. Beautiful one, thou art to me an object of greater regard than my preceptor. Full of virtuous resolves, O large-eyed one, of face as handsome, as moon, the place where thou hadst resided, viz., the body of Kavya, hath also been my abode. Thou art truly my sister. Amiable one, happily have we passed the days that we have been together. There is perfect good understanding between us. I ask thy leave to return to my abode. Therefore, bless me so that my journey may be safe. I must be remembered by thee, when thou recallest me in connection with topics of conversation, as one that hath not transgressed virtue. Always attend upon my preceptor with readiness and singleness of heart.' To all this, Devaniya answered, 'Solicited, by me, if, indeed, thou truly refusest to make me thy wife, then, O Kacha, this thy knowledge shall not bear fruit.'

"Hearing this, Kacha said, 'I have refused thy request only because thou art the daughter of my preceptor, and not because thou hast any fault. Nor hath my preceptor in this respect issued any command. Curse me if it please thee. I have told thee what the behaviour should be of a Rishi. I do not deserve thy curse, O Devayani. But yet thou hast cursed me! Thou hast acted under the influence of passion and not from a sense of duty. Therefore, thy desire will not be fulfilled. No Rishi's son shall ever accept thy hand in marriage. Thou hast said that my knowledge shall not bear fruit. Let it be so. But in respect of him it shall bear fruit to whom I may impart it.'

"Vaisampayana continued, 'That first of Brahmanas, Kacha, having said so unto Devayani speedily wended his way unto the abode of the chief of the celestials. Beholding him arrived, the celestials with Indra ahead, having first worshipped him, spoke unto him as follows, 'Thou hast indeed, performed an act of great benefit for us. Wonderful hath been thy achievement! Thy fame shall never die! Thou shall be a sharer with us in sacrificial offerings.'"

SECTION LXXVIII
(Sambhava Parva continued)

"Vaisampayana said, 'The dwellers in heaven became exceedingly glad in welcoming Kacha who had mastered the wonderful science. And, O bull of Bharata's race, the celestials then learnt that science from Kacha and considered their object already achieved. And assembling together, they spoke unto him of a hundred sacrifices, saying, 'The time hath come for showing prowess. Slay thy foes, O Purandara!' And thus addressed, Maghavat, then accompanied by the celestials, set out, saying, 'So be it.' But on his way he saw a number of damsels. These maidens were sporting in a lake in the gardens of the Gandharva Chitraratha. Changing himself into wind, he soon mixed up the garments of those maidens which they had laid on the bank. A little while after, the maidens, getting up from the water, approached their garments that had, indeed, got mixed up with one another. And it so happened that from the intermingled heap, the garments of Devayani were appropriated by Sarmishtha, the daughter of Vrishaparvan, from ignorance that it was not hers. And, O king, thereupon, between them, Devayani and Sarmishtha, then ensued a dispute. And Devayani said, 'O daughter of the Asura (chief), why dost thou take my attire, being, as thou art, my disciple? As thou art destitute of good behaviour, nothing good can happen to thee!' Sarmishtha, however, quickly replied, 'Thy father occupying a lower seat, always adoreth with downcast looks, like a hired chanter of praises, my father, whether he sitteth at his ease or reclineth at full length! Thou art the daughter of one that chanteth the praises of others, of one that accepteth alms. I am the daughter of one who is adored, of one who bestoweth alms instead of ever accepting them! Beggar-woman as thou art, thou art free to strike thy breast, to use ill words, to vow enmity to me, to give way to thy wrath. Acceptress of alms, thou weepest tears of anger in vain! If so minded, I can harm thee, but thou canst not. Thou desirest to quarrel. But know thou that I do not reckon thee as my equal!'

"Vaisampayana continued, 'Hearing these words, Devayani became exceedingly angry and began to pull at her clothes. Sarmishtha thereupon threw her into a well and went home. Indeed, the wicked Sarmishtha believing that Devayani was dead, bent her steps home-wards in a wrathful mood.

"After Sarmishtha had left, Yayati the son of Nahusha soon came to that spot. The king had been out a-hunting. The couple of horses harnessed to his car and the other single horse with him were all fatigued. And the king himself was thirsty. And the son of Nahusha saw a well that was by. And he saw that it was dry. But in looking down into it, he saw a maiden who in splendour was like a blazing fire. And beholding her within it, the blessed king addressed that girl of the complexion of the celestials, soothing her with sweet words. And he said, 'Who art thou, O fair one, of nails bright as burnished copper, and with ear-rings decked with celestial gems? Thou seemest to be greatly perturbed. Why dost thou weep in affliction? How, indeed, hast thou fallen into this well covered with creepers and long grass? And, O slender-waisted girl, answer me truly whose daughter thou art.'

"Devayani then replied, 'I am the daughter of Sukra who brings back into life the Asuras slain by the gods. He doth not know what hath befallen me. This is my right hand, O king, with nails bright as burnished copper. Thou art well-born; I ask thee, to take and raise me up! I know thou art of good behaviour, of great prowess, and of wide fame! It behoveth thee, therefore, to raise me from this well.'

"Vaisampayana continued, 'King Yayati, learning that she was a Brahmana's daughter, raised her from that well by catching hold of her right hand. And the monarch promptly raising her from the pit and squinting to her tapering thighs, sweetly and courteously returned to his capital.

"When the son of Nahusha had gone away, Devayani of faultless features, afflicted with grief, then spoke unto her maid, Ghurnika by name, who met her then. And she said, 'O Ghurnika, go thou quickly and speak to my father without loss of time of everything as it hath happened. I shall not now enter the city of Vrishaparvan.'

"Vaisampayana continued, 'Ghurnika, thus commanded, repaired quickly to the mansion, of the Asura chief, where she saw Kavya and spoke unto him with her perception dimmed by anger. And she said, 'I tell thee, O great Brahmana, that Devayani hath been ill-used, O fortunate one, in the forest by Sarmishtha, the daughter of Vrishaparvan.' And Kavya, hearing that his daughter had been ill-used by Sarmishtha speedily went out with a heavy heart, seeking her in the woods. And when he found her in the woods, he clasped her with affection and spoke unto her with voice choked with grief, 'O daughter, the weal or woe that befalleth people is always due to their own faults. Thou hast therefore some fault, I ween, which hath been expiated thus.' Hearing this Devayani replied, 'Be it a penalty or not, listen to me with attention. O, hear that all Sarmishtha, the daughter of Vrishaparvan, hath said unto me. Really hath she said that thou art only the hired chanter of the praises of the Asura king! Even thus hath she— that Sarmishtha, Vrishaparvan's daughter,—spoken to me, with reddened eyes, these piercing and cruel words, 'Thou art the daughter of one that ever chanteth for hire the praises of others, of one that asketh for charities, of one that accepteth alms; whereas I am the daughter of one that receiveth adorations, of one that giveth, of one that never accepteth anything as gift!' These have been the words repeatedly spoken unto me by the proud Sarmishtha, the daughter of Vrishaparvan, with eyes red with anger. If, O father, I am really the daughter of a hired chanter of praises, of one that accepteth gifts, I must offer my adorations in the hope of obtaining her grace! Oh, of this I have already told her!'

"Sukra replied, 'Thou art, O Devayani, no daughter of a hired adorer, of one that asketh for alms and accepteth gifts. Thou art the daughter of one that adores none, but of one that is adored by all! Vrishaparvan himself knoweth it, and Indra, and king Yayati too. That inconceivable Brahma, that unopposable Godhead, is my strength! The self-create, himself, gratified by me, hath said that I am for aye the lord of that which is in all things on Earth or in Heaven! I tell thee truly that it is I who pour rain for the good of creatures and who nourish the annual plants that sustain all living things!'

"Vaisampayana continued, 'It was by such sweet words of excellent import that the father endeavoured to pacify his daughter afflicted with woe and oppressed by anger.'"

SECTION LXXIX
(Sambhava Parva continued)

"Sukra continued, 'Know, then, O Devayani, that he that mindeth not the evil speeches of others, conquereth everything! The wise say that he is a true charioteer who without slackening holdeth tightly the reins of his horses. He, therefore, is the true man that subdueth, without indulging in his rising wrath. Know thou, O Devayani, that by him is everything conquered, who calmly subdueth his rising anger. He is regarded as a man who by having recourse to forgiveness, shaketh off his rising anger like a snake casting off its slough. He that suppresseth his anger, he that regardeth not the evil speeches of others, he that becometh not angry, though there be cause, certainly acquireth the four objects for which we live (viz., virtue, profit, desire, and salvation). Between him that performeth without fatigue sacrifices every month for a hundred years, and him that never feeleth angry at anything, he that feeleth not wrath is certainly the higher. Boys and girls, unable to distinguish between right and wrong, quarrel with each other. The wise never imitate them.' Devayani, on hearing this speech of her father, said, 'O father, I know, also what the difference is between anger and forgiveness as regards the power of each. But when a disciple behaveth disrespectfully, he should never be forgiven by the preceptor if the latter is really desirous of benefiting the former. Therefore, I do not desire to live any longer in a country where evil behaviour is at a premium. The wise man desirous of good, should not dwell among those sinfully inclined men who always speak ill of good behaviour and high birth. But there should one live,—indeed, that hath been said to be the best of dwelling places,—where good behaviour and purity of birth are known and respected. The cruel words uttered by Vrishaparvan's daughter burn my heart even as men, desirous of kindling a fire, burn the dry fuel. I do not think anything more miserable for a man in the three worlds than to adore one's enemies blessed with good fortune, himself possessing none. It hath been indeed said by the learned that for such a man even death would be better.'"

SECTION LXXX
(Sambhava Parva continued)

"Vaisampayana said, 'Then Kavya, the foremost of Bhrigu's line, became angry himself. And approaching Vrishaparvan where the latter was seated, began to address him without weighing his words, 'O king,' he said, 'sinful acts do not, like the Earth, bear fruit immediately! But gradually and secretly do they extirpate their doers. Such fruit visiteth either in one's own self, one's son, or one's grandson. Sins must bear their fruit. Like rich food they can never be digested. And because ye slew the Brahmana Kacha, the grandson of Angiras, who was virtuous, acquainted with the precepts of religion, and attentive to his duties, while residing in my abode, even for this act of slaughter—and for the mal-treatment of my daughter too, know, O Vrishaparvan, I shall leave thee and thy relatives! Indeed, O king, for this, I can no longer stay with thee! Dost thou, O Asura chief, think that I am a raving liar? Thou makest light of thy offence without seeking to correct it!'.

"Vrishaparvan then said, 'O son of Bhrigu, never have I attributed want of virtue, of falsehood, to thee. Indeed, virtue and truth ever dwell in thee. Be kind to me! O Bhargava, if, leaving us, thou really goest hence, we shall then go into the depths of the ocean. Indeed, there is nothing else for us to do.'

"Sukra then replied, 'Ye Asuras, whether ye go into the depths of the ocean or fly away to all directions, I care little. I am unable to bear my daughter's grief. My daughter is ever dear to me. My life dependeth on her. Seek ye to please her. As Vrihaspati ever seeketh the good of Indra, so do I always seek thine by my ascetic merits.'

"Vrishaparvan then said, 'O Bhargava, thou art the absolute master of whatever is possessed by the Asura chiefs in this world-their elephants, kine and horses, and even my humble self!'

"Sukra then answered, 'If it is true, O great Asura, that I am the lord of all the wealth of the Asuras, then go and gratify Devayani.'

"Vaisampayana continued, 'when the great Kavya was so addressed by Vrishaparvan, he then went to Devayani and told her all. Devayani, however, quickly replied, 'O Bhargava, if thou art truly the lord of the Asura king himself and of all his wealth, then let the king himself come to me and say so in my presence.' Vrishaparvan then approached Devayani and told her, 'O Devayani of sweet smiles, whatever thou desirest I am willing to give thee, however difficult it may be to grant the same.' Devayani answered, 'I desire Sarmishtha with a thousand maids to wait on me! She must also follow me to where my father may give me away.'

"Vrishaparvan then commanded a maid-servant in attendance on him, saying,
'Go and quickly bring Sarmishtha hither. Let her also accomplish what
Devayani wisheth.'

"Vaisampayana continued, 'The maid-servant then repaired to Sarmishtha and told her, 'O amiable Sarmishtha, rise and follow me. Accomplish the good of thy relatives. Urged by Devayani, the Brahmana (Sukra) is on the point of leaving his disciples (the Asuras). O sinless one, thou must do what Devayani wisheth.' Sarmishtha replied, 'I shall cheerfully do what Devayani wisheth. Urged by Devayani Sukra is calling me. Both Sukra and Devayani must not leave the Asuras through my fault.'

"Vaisampayana continued, 'Commanded by her father, then, Sarmishtha, accompanied by a thousand maidens, soon came, in a palanquin, out of her father's excellent mansion. And approaching Devayani she said, 'With my thousand maids, I am thy waiting-maid! And I shall follow thee where thy father may give thee away.' Devayani replied, 'I am the daughter of one who chanteth the praises of thy father, and who beggeth and accepteth alms; thou, on the other hand, art the daughter of one who is adored. How canst thou be my waiting-maid?'

"Sarmishtha answered, 'One must by all means contribute to the happiness of one's afflicted relatives. Therefore shall I follow thee wherever thy father may give thee away.'

"Vaisampayana continued, 'When Sarmishtha thus promised to be Devayani's waiting-maid the latter, O king, then spoke unto her father thus, 'O best of all excellent Brahmanas, I am gratified. I shall now enter the Asura capital! I now know that thy science and power of knowledge are not futile!'

"Vaisampayana continued, 'That best of Brahmanas, of great reputation, thus addressed by his daughter, then, entered the Asura capital in the gladness of his heart. And the Danavas worshipped him with great reverence.'"

SECTION LXXXI
(Sambhava Parva continued)

Vaisampayana said, 'After some length of time, O best of monarchs, Devayani of the fairest complexion went into the same woods for purposes of pleasure. And accompanied by Sarmishtha with her thousand maids she reached the same spot and began to wander freely. And waited upon by all those companions she felt supremely happy. And sporting with light hearts, they began drinking the honey in flowers, eating various kinds of fruit and biting some. And just at that time, king Yayati, the son of Nahusha, again came there tired and thirsty, in course of his wanderings, in search of deer. And the king saw Devayani and Sarmishtha, and those other maidens also, all decked with celestial ornaments and full of voluptuous languor in consequence of the flower-honey they drank. And Devayani of sweet smiles, unrivalled for beauty and possessed of the fairest complexion amongst them all, was reclining at her ease. And she was waited upon by Sarmishtha who was gently kneading her feet.

"And Yayati seeing all this, said, 'O amiable ones, I would ask you both your names and parentage. It seems that these two thousand maids wait on you two.' Hearing the monarch, Devayani then answered, 'Listen to me, O best of men. Know that I am the daughter of Sukra, the spiritual guide of the Asuras. This my companion is my waiting-maid. She attendeth on me wherever I go. She is Sarmishtha, the daughter of the Asura king Vrishaparvan.'

"Yayati then asked, 'I am curious to know why is this thy companion of fair eye-brows, this maiden of the fairest complexion, the daughter of the Asura chief thy waiting-maid!' Devayani replied, 'O best of king, everything resulteth from Fate. Knowing this also to be the result of Fate, wonder not at it. Thy feature and attire are both like a king's. Thy speech also is fair and correct as that of the Vedas. Tell me thy name, whence thou art and whose son also.'

"The monarch replied, 'During my vow of Brahmacharya, the whole Vedas entered my ears. I am known as Yayati, a king's son and myself a king.' Devayani then enquired, 'O king, what hast thou come here for? Is it to gather lotuses or to angle or to hunt?' Yayati said, 'O amiable one, thirsty from the pursuit of deer, I have come hither in search of water. I am very much fatigued. I await but your commands to leave this spot.'

"Devayani answered, 'With my two thousand damsels and my waiting-maid Sarmishtha, I wait but your commands. Prosperity to thee. Be thou my friend and lord.'

"Yayati, thereupon, replied, 'Beautiful one, I do not deserve thee. Thou art the daughter of Sukra far superior to me. Thy father cannot bestow thee even on a great king.' To this Devayani replied, 'Brahmanas had before this been united with the Kshatriyas, and Kshatriyas with Brahmanas. Thou art the son of a Rishi and thyself a Rishi. Therefore, O son of Nahusha, marry me.' Yayati, however, replied, 'O thou of the handsomest features, the four orders have, indeed, sprung from one body. But their duties and purity are not the same, the Brahmana being truly superior to all.' Devayani answered, 'This hand of mine hath never been touched before by any man save thee. Therefore, do I accept thee for my lord. How, indeed, shall any other man touch my hand which had before been touched by thyself who art a Rishi?' Yayati then said, 'The wise know that a Brahmana is more to be avoided than an angry snake of virulent poison, or a blazing fire of spreading flames.' Devayani then told the monarch, 'O bull amongst men, why dost thou, indeed, say that Brahmana should be more avoided than an angry snake of virulent poison or a blazing fire of spreading flames?' The monarch answered, 'The snake killeth only one. The sharpest weapon slayeth but a single person. The Brahmana, when angry destroyeth whole cities and kingdoms! Therefore, O timid one, do I deem a Brahmana as more to be avoided than either. I cannot hence wed thee, O amiable one, unless thy father bestoweth thee on me.' Devayani then said, 'Thou art, indeed, chosen by me. And, O king, it is understood that thou wilt accept me if my father bestoweth me on thee. Thou needst not fear to accept my poor self bestowed on thee. Thou dost not, indeed, ask for me.'

"Vaisampayana continued, 'After this, Devayani quickly sent a maidservant to her father. The maid represented to Sukra everything as it had happened. And as soon as he had heard all, Bhargava came and saw Yayati. And beholding Bhargava come, Yayati worshipped and adored that Brahmana, and stood with joined palms in expectation of his commands.'

"And Devayani then said, 'This O father, is the son of Nahusha. He took hold of my hand, when I was in distress. I bow to thee. Bestow me upon him. I shall not wed any other person in the world.' Sukra exclaimed, 'O thou of splendid courage, thou hast, indeed, been accepted as her lord by this my dear daughter. I bestow her on thee. Therefore, O son of Nahusha, accept her as thy wife.'

"Yayati then said, 'I solicit the boon, O Brahmana, that by so doing, the sin of begetting a half-breed might not touch me.' Sukra, however, assured him by saying, 'I shall absolve thee from the sin. Ask thou the boon that thou desirest. Fear not to wed her. I grant thee absolution. Maintain virtuously thy wife—the slender-waisted Devayani. Transports of happiness be thine in her company. This other maiden, Vrishaparvan's daughter, Sarmishtha should ever be regarded by thee. But thou shall not summon her to thy bed.'

"Vaisampayana continued, 'Thus addressed by Sukra, Yayati then walked round the Brahmana. And the king then went through the auspicious ceremony of marriage according to the rites of the scriptures. And having received from Sukra this rich treasure of the excellent Devayani with Sarmishtha and those two thousand maidens, and duly honoured also by Sukra himself and the Asuras, the best of monarchs, then, commanded by the high-souled Bhargava, returned to his capital with a joyous heart.'"

SECTION LXXXII
(Sambhava Parva continued)

"Vaisampayana said, 'Yayati then, on returning to his capital which was like unto the city of Indra, entered his inner apartments and established there his bride Devayani. And the monarch, directed by Devayani, established Vrishaparvan's daughter Sarmishtha in a mansion especially erected near the artificial woods of Asokas in his gardens. And the king surrounded Vrishaparvan's daughter Sarmishtha with a thousand maids and honoured her by making every arrangement for her food and garments. But it was with Devayani that the royal son of Nahusha sported like a celestial for many years in joy and bliss. And when her season came, the fair Devayani conceived. And she brought forth as her first child a fine boy. And when a thousand years had passed away, Vrishaparvan's daughter Sarmishtha having attained to puberty saw that her season had come. She became anxious and said to herself, 'My season hath arrived. But I have not yet chosen a husband. O, what hath happened, what should I do? How am I to obtain the fruition of my wishes? Devayani hath become mother. My youth is doomed to pass away in vain. Shall I choose him also for my husband whom Devayani hath chosen? This is, indeed, my resolve: that monarch should give me a son. Will not the virtuous one grant me a private interview?'

"Vaisampayana continued, 'While Sarmishtha was thus busy with her thoughts, the king wandering listlessly came to that very wood of Asokas, and beholding Sarmishtha before him, stood there in silence. Then Sarmishtha of sweet smiles seeing the monarch before her with nobody to witness what might pass, approached him and said with joined palms, 'O son of Nahusha, no one can behold the ladies that dwell in the inner apartments of Soma, of Indra, of Vishnu, of Yama, of Varuna, and of thee! Thou knowest, O king, that I am both handsome and well-born. I solicit thee, O king! My season hath arrived. See that it goeth not in vain.'

"Yayati answered, 'Well do I know that honour of birth is thine, born as thou art in the proud race of the Danavas. Thou art also gifted with beauty. I do not, indeed, see even the speck of a fault in thy feature. But Usanas commanded me, while I was united with Devayani, that never should Vrishaparvan's daughter he summoned to my bed.'

"Sarmishtha then said, 'It hath been said, O king, that it is not sinful to lie on the occasion of a joke, in respect of women sought to be enjoyed, on occasions of marriage, in peril of immediate death and of the loss of one's whole fortune. Lying is excusable on these five occasions. O king, it is not true that he is fallen who speaks not the truth when asked. Both Devayani and myself have been called hither as companions to serve the same purpose. When, therefore, thou hadst said that you wouldst confine thyself to one only amongst as, that was a lie thou hadst spoken.' Yayati replied, 'A king should ever be a model in the eyes of his people. That monarch certainly meets with destruction who speaks an untruth. As for myself, I dare not speak an untruth even if the greatest loss threatens me!' Sarmishtha answered, 'O monarch, one may look upon her friend's husband as her own. One's friend's marriage is the same as one's own. Thou hast been chosen by my friend as her husband. Thou art as much my husband, therefore.' Yayati then said, 'It is, indeed my vow always to grant what one asketh. As thou askest me, tell me then what I am to do.' Sarmishtha then said, 'Absolve me, O king, from sin. Protect my virtue. Becoming a mother by thee, let me practise the highest virtue in this world. It is said, O king, that a wife, a slave, and a son can never earn wealth for themselves. What they earn always belongeth to him who owneth them. I am, indeed, the slave of Devayani. Thou art Devayani's master and lord. Thou art, therefore, O king, my master and lord as much as Devayani's! I solicit thee! O, fulfil my wishes!'

"Vaisampayana continued, 'Thus addressed by Sarmishtha, the monarch was persuaded into the truth of all she spoke. He therefore, honoured Sarmishtha by protecting her virtue. And they passed some time together. And taking affectionate farewell of each other, they then parted, each returning to whence he or she had come.

"And it came to pass that Sarmishtha of sweet smiles and fair eyebrows conceived in consequence of that connection of hers with that best of monarchs. And, O king, that lotus-eyed lady then in due course of time brought forth a son of the splendour of a celestial child and of eyes like lotus-petals.'"

SECTION LXXXIII
(Sambhava Parva continued)

"Vaisampayana said, 'When Devayani of sweet smiles heard of the birth of this child, she became jealous, and O Bharata, Sarmishtha became an object of her unpleasant reflections. And Devayani, repairing to her, addressed her thus, 'O thou of fair eye-brows, what sin is this thou hast committed by yielding to the influence of lust?' Sarmishtha replied, 'A certain Rishi of virtuous soul and fully conversant with the Vedas came to me. Capable of granting boons he was solicited by me to grant my wishes that were based on considerations of virtue. O thou of sweet smiles, I would not seek the sinful fulfilment of my desires. I tell thee truly that this child of mine is by that Rishi!' Devayani answered, 'It is all right if that be the case, O timid one! But if the lineage, name, and family of that Brahmana be known to thee, I should like to hear them.' Sarmishtha replied, 'O thou of sweet smiles, in asceticism and energy, that Rishi is resplendent like the Sun himself. Beholding him, I had not, any need to make these enquiries—' Devayani then said, 'If this is true, if indeed, thou hast obtained thy child from such a superior Brahmana, then, O Sarmishtha, I have no cause of anger.'

"Vaisampayana continued, 'Having thus talked and laughed with each other, they separated, Devayani returning to the palace with the knowledge imparted to her by Sarmishtha. And, O king, Yayati also begot on Devayani two sons called Yadu and Turvasu, who were like Indra and Vishnu. And Sarmishtha, the daughter of Vrishaparvan, became through the royal sage the mother of three sons in all, named Drahyu, Anu, and Puru.

"And, O king, it so came to pass that one day Devayani of sweet smiles, by Yayati, went into a solitary part of the woods, (in the king's extensive park). And there she saw three children of celestial beauty playing with perfect trustfulness. And Devayani asked in surprise, 'Whose children are they, O king, who are so handsome and so like unto the children of the celestials? In splendour and beauty they are like thee, I should think.'

"Vaisampayana continued, 'And Devayani without waiting for a reply from the king, asked the children themselves, 'Ye children, what is your lineage? Who is your father? Answer me truly. I desire to know all.' Those children then pointed at the king (with their forefingers) and spoke of Sarmishtha as their mother.

"And having so said, the children approached the king to clasp his knees. But the king dared not caress them in the presence of Devayani. The boys then left the place, and made towards their mother, weeping in grief. And the king, at this conduct of the boys, became very much abashed. But Devayani, marking the affection of the children for the king learnt the secret and addressing Sarmishtha, said, 'How hast thou dared to do me an injury, being, as thou art, dependent on me? Dost thou not fear to have recourse once more to that Asura custom of thine?'

"Sarmishtha said, 'O thou of sweet smiles, all that I told thee of a Rishi is perfectly true. I have acted rightly and according to the precepts of virtue, and therefore, do I not fear thee. When thou hadst chosen the king for thy husband, I, too, chose him as mine. O beautiful one, a friend's husband is, according to usage, one's own husband as well. Thou art the daughter of a Brahmana and, therefore, deservest my worship and regard. But dost thou not know that this royal sage is held by me in greater esteem still?'

"Vaisampayana said, 'Devayani then, hearing those words of hers, exclaimed, O king, thus, 'Thou hast wronged me, O monarch! I shall not live here any longer.' And saying this, she quickly rose, with tearful eyes, to go to her father. And the king was grieved to see her thus, and alarmed greatly, followed in her foot-steps, endeavouring to appease her wrath. But Devayani, with eyes red with anger, would not desist. Speaking not a word to the king, with eyes bathed in tears, she soon reached the side of her father Usanas, the son of Kavi. And beholding her father, she stood before him, after due salutations. And Yayati also, immediately after, saluted and worshipped Bhargava.'

"And Devayani said, 'O father, virtue hath been vanquished by vice. The low have risen, and the high have fallen. I have been offended again by Sarmishtha, the daughter of Vrishaparvan. Three sons have been begotten upon her by this king Yayati. But, O father, being luckless I have got only two sons! O son of Bhrigu, this king is renowned for his knowledge of the precepts of religion. But, O Kavya, I tell thee that he hath deviated from the path of rectitude.'

"Sukra, hearing all this, said, 'O monarch, since thou hast made vice thy beloved pursuit, though fully acquainted with the precepts of religion, invincible decrepitude shall paralyse thee!' Yayati answered, 'Adorable one, I was solicited by the daughter of the Danava king to fructify her season. I did it from a sense of virtue and not from other motives. That male person, who being solicited by a woman in her season doth not grant her wishes, is called, O Brahmana, by those conversant with the Vedas, a slayer of the embryo. He who, solicited in secret by a woman full of desire and in season, goeth not in unto her, loseth virtue and is called by the learned a killer of the embryo, O son of Bhrigu, for these reasons, and anxious to avoid sin, I went into Sarmishtha.' Sukra then replied, 'Thou art dependent on me. Thou shouldst have awaited my command. Having acted falsely in the matter of thy duty, O son of Nahusha, thou hast been guilty of the sin of theft.'

"Vaisampayana continued, 'Yayati, the son of Nahusha, thus cursed by the angry Usanas, was then divested of his youth and immediately overcome by decrepitude. And Yayati said, 'O son of Bhrigu, I have not yet been satiated with youth or with Devayani. Therefore, O Brahmana, be graceful unto me so that decrepitude might not touch me.' Sukra then answered, 'I never speak an untruth. Even now, O king, art thou attacked by decrepitude. But if thou likest, thou art competent to transfer this thy decrepitude to another.' Yayati said, 'O Brahmana, let it be commanded by thee that that son of mine who giveth me his youth shall enjoy my kingdom, and shall achieve both virtue and fame.' Sukra replied, 'O son of Nahusha, thinking of me thou mayst transfer this thy decrepitude to whomsoever thou likest. That son who shall give thee his youth shall become thy successor to the throne. He shall also have long life, wide fame, and numerous progeny!'"

SECTION LXXXIV
(Sambhava Parva continued)

"Vaisampayana said, 'Yayati, then, overcome with decrepitude, returned to his capital and summoning his eldest son Yadu who was also the most accomplished, addressed him thus, 'Dear child, from the curse of Kavya called also Usanas, decrepitude and wrinkles and whiteness of hair have come over me. But I have not been gratified yet with the enjoyment of youth. Do thou, O Yadu, take this my weakness along with my decrepitude. I shall enjoy with thy youth. And when a full thousand years will have elapsed, returning to thee thy youth, I shall take back my weakness with this decrepitude!'

"Yadu replied, 'There are innumerable inconveniences in decrepitude, in respect of drinking and eating. Therefore, O king, I shall not take thy decrepitude. This is, indeed, my determination. White hair on the head, cheerlessness and relaxation of the nerves, wrinkles all over the body, deformities, weakness of the limbs, emaciation, incapacity to work, defeat at the hands of friends and companions—these are the consequences of decrepitude. Therefore, O king, I desire not to take it. O king, thou hast many sons some of whom are dearer to thee. Thou art acquainted with the precepts of virtue. Ask some other son of thine to take thy decrepitude.

"Yayati replied, 'Thou art sprung from my heart, O son, but thou givest me not thy youth. Therefore, thy children shall never be kings.' And he continued, addressing another son of his, 'O Turvasu, take thou this weakness of mine along with my decrepitude. With thy youth, O son, I like to enjoy the pleasure of life. After the lapse of a full thousand years I shall give back to thee thy youth, and take back from thee my weakness and decrepitude.'

"Turvasu replied, 'I do not like decrepitude, O father, it takes away all appetites and enjoyments, strength and beauty of person, intellect, and even life.' Yayati said to him, 'Thou art sprung from my heart, O son! But thou givest me not thy youth! Therefore, O Turvasu, thy race shall be extinct. Wretch, thou shall be the king of those whose practices and precepts are impure, amongst whom men of inferior blood procreate children upon women of blue blood, who live on meat, who are mean, who hesitate not to appropriate the wives of their superiors, whose practices are those of birds and beasts, who are sinful, and non-Aryan.'

"Vaisampayana said, 'Yayati, having thus cursed his son Turvasu, then, addressed Sarmishtha's son Drahyu thus, 'O Drahyu, take thou for a thousand years my decrepitude destructive of complexion and personal beauty and give me thy youth. When a thousand years have passed away, I shall return thee thy youth and take back my own weakness, and decrepitude.' To this Drahyu replied, 'O king, one that is decrepit can never enjoy elephants and cars and horses and women. Even his voice becometh hoarse. Therefore, I do not desire (to take) thy decrepitude.' Yayati said to him, 'Thou art sprung from my heart, O son! But thou refusest to give me thy youth. Therefore, thy most cherished desires shall never be fulfilled. Thou shalt be king only in name, of that region where there are no roads for (the passage of) horses and cars and elephants, and good vehicles, and asses, and goats and bullocks, and palanquins; where there is swimming only by rafts and floats.' Yayati next addressed Anu and said, 'O Anu, take my weakness and decrepitude. I shall with thy youth enjoy the pleasures of life for a thousand years.' To this Anu replied, 'Those that are decrepit always eat like children and are always impure. They cannot pour libations upon fire in proper times. Therefore, I do not like to take thy decrepitude.' Yayati said to him, 'Thou art sprung from my heart, thou givest not thy youth. Thou findest so many faults in decrepitude. Therefore, decrepitude shall overcome thee! And, O Anu, thy progeny also as soon as they attain to youth, shall die. And thou shalt also not be able to perform sacrifices before fire.'

"Yayati at last turned to his youngest child, Puru, and addressing him said, 'Thou art, O Puru, my youngest son! But thou shall be the first of all! Decrepitude, wrinkles, and whiteness of hair have come over me in consequence of the curse of Kavya called also Usanas. I have not yet however, been satiated with my youth. O Puru, take thou this my weakness and decrepitude! With thy youth I shall enjoy for some years the pleasures of life. And when a thousand years have passed away, I shall give back to thee thy youth and take back my own decrepitude.'

"Vaisampayana said, 'Thus addressed by the king, Puru answered with humility, 'I shall do, O monarch, as thou bidest me. I shall take, O king, thy weakness and decrepitude. Take thou my youth and enjoy as thou listest the pleasures of life. Covered with thy decrepitude and becoming old, I shall, as thou commandest, continue to live, giving thee my youth.' Yayati then said, 'O Puru, I have been gratified with thee. And being gratified, I tell thee that the people in thy kingdom shall have all their desires fulfilled.'

"And having said this, the great ascetic Yayati, then thinking of Kavya, transferred his decrepitude unto the body of the high-souled Puru.'"

SECTION LXXXV
(Sambhava Parva continued)

"Vaisampayana said, 'The excellent monarch Yayati, the son of Nahusha, having received Puru's youth, became exceedingly gratified. And with it he once more began to indulge in his favourite pursuits to the full extent of his desires and to the limit of his powers, according to seasons, so as to derive the greatest pleasure therefrom. And, O king, in nothing that he did, he acted against the precepts of his religion as behoved him well. He gratified the gods by his sacrifices; the pitris, by Sraddhas; the poor, by his charities; all excellent Brahmanas, by fulfilling their desires; all persons entitled to the rites of hospitality, with food and drink; the Vaisyas, by protection; and the Sudras, by kindness. And the king repressed all criminals by proper punishments. And Yayati, gratifying all sections of his subjects, protected them virtuously like another Indra. And the monarch possessed of the prowess of a lion, with youth and every object of enjoyment under control, enjoyed unlimited happiness without transgressing the precepts of religion. And the king became very happy in thus being able to enjoy all the excellent objects of his desires. And he was only sorry when he thought that those thousand years would come to an end. And having obtained youth for a thousand years, the king acquainted with the mysteries of time, and watching proper Kalas and Kashthas sported with (the celestial damsel) Viswachi, sometimes in the beautiful garden of Indra, sometimes in Alaka (the city of Kuvera), and sometimes on the summit of the mountain Meru on the north. And when the virtuous monarch saw that the thousand years were full, he summoned his son, Puru, and addressed him thus, 'O oppressor of foes, with thy youth, O son, I have enjoyed the pleasures of life, each according to its season to the full extent of my desires, to the limit of my powers. Our desires, however, are never gratified by indulgence. On the other hand, with indulgence, they only flame up like fire with libations of sacrificial butter. If a single person were owner of everything on Earth—all her yields of paddy and barley, her silver, gold, and gems, her animals and women, he would not still be content. Thirst of enjoyment, therefore, should be given up. Indeed, true happiness belongeth to them that have cast off their thirst for worldly objects—a thirst which is difficult to be thrown off by the wicked and the sinful, which faileth not with the failing life, and which is truly the fatal disease of man. My heart hath for a full thousand years been fixed upon the objects of desires. My thirst for these, however, increaseth day by day without abating. Therefore, I shall cast it off, and fixing my mind on Brahma I shall pass the rest of my days with the innocent deer in the forest peacefully and with no heart for any worldly objects. And O Puru, I have been exceedingly gratified with thee! Prosperity be thine! Receive back this thy youth! Receive thou also my kingdom. Thou art, indeed, that son of mine who has done me the greatest services.'

"Vaisampayana continued, 'Then Yayati, the son of Nahusha, received back his decrepitude. And his son Puru received back his own youth. And Yayati was desirous of installing Puru, his youngest son, on the throne. But the four orders, with the Brahmanas at their head, then addressed the monarch thus, 'O king, how shall thou bestow thy kingdom on Puru, passing over thy eldest son Yadu born of Devayani, and, therefore, the grandson of the great Sukra? Indeed, Yadu is thy eldest son; after him hath been born Turvasu; and of Sarmishtha's sons, the first is Drahyu, then Anu and then Puru. How doth the youngest deserve the throne, passing all his elder brothers over? This we represent to thee! O, conform to virtuous practice.'

"Yayati then said, 'Ye four orders with Brahmanas at their head, hear my words as to why my kingdom should not be given to my eldest son. My commands have been disobeyed by my eldest son, Yadu. The wise say that he is no son who disobeyeth his father. That son, however, who doth the bidding of his parents, who seeketh their good, who is agreeable to them, is indeed, the best of sons. I have been disregarded by Yadu and by Turvasu, too. Much I have been disregarded by Drahyu and by Anu also. By Puru alone hath my word been obeyed. By him have I been much regarded. Therefore, the youngest shall be my heir. He took my decrepitude. Indeed, Puru is my friend. He did what was so agreeable to me. It hath also been commanded by Sukra himself, the son of Kavi, that, that son of mine who should obey me will become king after me and bring the whole Earth under his sway. I, therefore, beseech thee, let Puru be installed on the throne.'

"The people then said, 'True it is, O king, that, that son who is accomplished and who seeketh the good of his parents, deserveth prosperity even if he be the youngest. Therefore, doth Puru, who hath done the good, deserve the crown. And as Sukra himself hath commanded it, we have nothing to say to it.'

"Vaisampayana continued., 'The son of Nahusha, thus addressed by the contented people, then installed his son, Puru, on the throne. And having bestowed his kingdom on Puru, the monarch performed the initiatory ceremonies for retiring into the woods. And soon after he left his capital, followed by Brahmanas and ascetics.

"The sons of Yadu are known by the name of the Yadavas: while those of Turvasu have come to be called the Yavanas. And the sons of Drahyu are the Bhojas, while those of Anu, the Mlechchhas. The progeny of Puru, however, are the Pauravas, amongst whom, O monarch, thou art born, in order to rule for a thousand years with thy passions under complete control.'"

SECTION LXXXVI
(Sambhava Parva continued)

"Vaisampayana said, 'King Yayati, the son of Nahusha, having thus installed his dear son on the throne, became exceedingly happy, and entered into the woods to lead the life of a hermit. And having lived for some time into forest in the company of Brahmanas, observing many rigid vows, eating fruits and roots, patiently bearing privations of all sorts, the monarch at last ascended to heaven. And having ascended to heaven he lived there in bliss. But soon, however, he was hurled down by Indra. And it hath been heard by me, O king, that, though hurled from heaven, Yayati, without reaching the surface of the Earth, stayed in the firmament. I have heard that some time after he again entered the region of the celestials in company with Vasuman, Ashtaka, Pratarddana, and Sivi.'

"Janamejaya said, 'I desire to hear from thee in detail why Yayati, having first obtained admission into heaven, was hurled therefrom, and why also he gained re-admittance. Let all this, O Brahmana, be narrated by thee in the presence of these regenerate sages. Yayati, lord of Earth, was, indeed, like the chief of the celestials. The progenitor of the extensive race of the Kurus, he was of the splendour of the Sun. I desire to hear in full the story of his life both in heaven and on Earth, as he was illustrious, and of world-wide celebrity and of wonderful achievements.'

"Vaisampayana said, 'Indeed, I shall recite to thee the excellent story of Yayati's adventures on Earth and in heaven. That story is sacred and destroyeth the sins of those that hear it.

"King Yayati, the son of Nahusha, having installed his youngest son, Puru, on the throne after casting his sons with Yadu for their eldest amongst the Mlechchhas, entered the forest to lead the life of a hermit. And the king eating fruits and roots lived for some time in the forest. Having his mind and passions under complete control, the king gratified by sacrifices the Pitris and the gods. And he poured libations of clarified butter upon the fire according to the rites prescribed for those leading the Vanaprastha mode of life. And the illustrious one entertained guests and strangers with the fruit of the forest and clarified butter, while he himself supported life by gleaning scattered corn seeds. And the king led this sort of life for a full thousand years. And observing the vow of silence and with mind under complete control he passed one full year, living upon air alone and without sleep. And he passed another year practising the severest austerities in the midst of four fires around and the Sun overhead. And, living upon air alone, he stood erect upon one leg for six months. And the king of sacred deeds ascended to heaven, covering heaven as well as the Earth (with the fame of his achievements).'"

SECTION LXXXVII
(Sambhava Parva continued)

"Vaisampayana said, 'While that king of kings dwelt in heaven—the home of the celestials, he was reverenced by the gods, the Sadhyas, the Maruts, and the Vasus. Of sacred deeds, and mind under complete control, the monarch used to repair now and then from the abode of the celestials unto the region of Brahman. And it hath been heard by me that he dwelt for a long time in heaven.

"One day that best of kings, Yayati, went to Indra and there in course of conversation the lord of Earth was asked by Indra as follows:

'What didst thou say, O king, when thy son Puru took thy decrepitude on Earth and when thou gavest him thy kingdom?'

"Yayati answered, 'I told him that the whole country between the rivers Ganga and Yamuna was his. That is, indeed, the central region of the Earth, while the out-lying regions are to be the dominions of thy brothers. I also told him that those without anger were ever superior to those under its sway, those disposed to forgive were ever superior to the unforgiving. Man is superior to the lower animals. Among men again the learned are superior to the un-learned. If wronged, thou shouldst not wrong in return. One's wrath, if disregarded, burneth one's own self; but he that regardeth it not taketh away all the virtues of him that exhibiteh it. Never shouldst thou pain others by cruel speeches. Never subdue thy foes by despicable means; and never utter such scorching and sinful words as may torture others. He that pricketh as if with thorns men by means of hard and cruel words, thou must know, ever carrieth in his mouth the Rakshasas. Prosperity and luck fly away at his very sight. Thou shouldst ever keep the virtuous before thee as thy models; thou shouldst ever with retrospective eye compare thy acts with those of the virtuous; thou shouldst ever disregard the hard words of the wicked. Thou shouldst ever make the conduct of the wise the model upon which thou art to act thyself. The man hurt by the arrows of cruel speech hurled from one's lips, weepeth day and night. Indeed, these strike at the core of the body. Therefore the wise never fling these arrows at others. There is nothing in the three worlds by which thou canst worship and adore the deities better than by kindness, friendship, charity and sweet speeches unto all. Therefore, shouldst thou always utter words that soothe, and not those that scorch. And thou shouldst regard those that deserve, thy regards, and shouldst always give but never beg!'"

SECTION LXXXVIII
(Sambhava Parva continued)

"Vaisampayana said, 'After this Indra again asked Yayati, 'Thou didst retire into the woods, O king, after accomplishing all thy duties. O Yayati, son of Nahusha, I would ask thee to whom thou art equal in ascetic austerities.' Yayati answered, 'O Vasava, I do not, in the matter of ascetic austerities, behold my equal among men, the celestials, the Gandharvas, and the great Rishis.' Indra then said, 'O monarch, because thou disregardest those that are thy superiors, thy equals, and even thy inferiors, without, in fact, knowing their real merits, thy virtues have suffered diminution and thou must fall from heaven.' Yayati then said, 'O Sakra, if, indeed, my virtues have really sustained diminution and I must on that account fall down from heaven, I desire, O chief of the celestials, that I may at least fall among the virtuous and the honest.' Indra replied, 'O king, thou shall fall among those that are virtuous and wise, and thou shall acquire also much renown. And after this experience of thine, O Yayati, never again disregard those that are thy superiors or even thy equals.'

"Vaisampayana continued, 'Upon this, Yayati fell from the region of the celestials. And as he was falling, he was beheld by that foremost of royal sages, viz., Ashtaka, the protector of his own religion. Ashtaka beholding him, enquired, 'Who art thou, O youth of a beauty equal to that of Indra, in splendour blazing as the fire, thus falling from on high? Art thou that foremost of sky-ranging bodies—the sun—emerging from, dark masses of clouds? Beholding thee falling from the solar course, possessed of immeasurable energy and the splendour of fire or the sun, every one is curious as to what it is that is so falling, and is, besides, deprived of consciousness! Beholding thee in the path of the celestials, possessed of energy like that of Sakra, or Surya, or Vishnu, we have approached thee to ascertain the truth. If thou hast first asked us who we were, we would never have been guilty of the incivility of asking thee first. We now ask thee who thou art and why thou approachest hither. Let thy fears be dispelled; let thy woes and afflictions cease. Thou art now in the presence of the virtuous and the wise. Even Sakra himself—the slayer of Vala—cannot here do thee any injury. O thou of the prowess of the chief of the celestials, the wise and the virtuous are the support of their brethren in grief. Here there are none but the wise and virtuous like thee assembled together. Therefore, stay thou here in peace. Fire alone hath power to give heat. The Earth alone hath power to infuse life into the seed. The sun alone hath power to illuminate everything. So the guest alone hath power to command the virtuous and the wise.'"

SECTION LXXXIX
(Sambhava Parva continued)

"Yayati said, 'I am Yayati, the son of Nahusha and the father of Puru. Cast off from the region of the celestials and of Siddhas and Rishis for having disregarded every creature, I am falling down, my righteousness having sustained diminution. In years I am older than you; therefore, I have not saluted you first. Indeed, the Brahmanas always reverence him who is older in years or superior in learning or in ascetic merit.'

"Ashtaka then replied, 'Thou sayest, O monarch, that he who is older in years is worthy of regard. But it is said that he is truly worthy of worship who is superior in learning and ascetic merit.'

"Yayati replied to this, 'It is said that sin destroyeth the merits of four virtuous acts. Vanity containeth the element of that which leadeth to hell. The virtuous never follow in the footsteps of the vicious. They act in such a way that their religious merit always increaseth. I myself had great religious merit, but all that, however, is gone. I will scarcely be able to regain it even by my best exertions. Beholding my fate, he that is bent upon (achieving) his own good, will certainly suppress vanity. He who having acquired great performeth meritorious sacrifices, who having acquired all kinds of learning remaineth humble, and who having studied the entire Vedas devoteth himself to asceticism with a heart withdrawn from all mundane enjoyments, goeth to heaven. None should exult in having acquired great wealth. None should be vain of having studied the entire Vedas. In the world men are of different dispositions. Destiny is supreme. Both power and exertion are all fruitless. Knowing Destiny to be all- powerful, the wise, whatever their portions may be, should neither exult nor boast. When creatures know that their weal and woe are dependent on Destiny and not on their own exertion or power, they should neither grieve nor exult, remembering that Destiny is all powerful. The wise should ever live contented, neither grieving at woe nor exulting at weal. When Destiny is supreme, both grief and exultation are one. O Ashtaka, I never suffer myself to be overcome by fear, nor do I ever entertain grief, knowing for certain that I shall be in the world what the great disposer of all hath ordained. Insects and worms, all oviparous creatures, vegetable existences, all crawling animals, vermin, the fish in the water, stones, grass, wood—in fact, all created things, when they are freed from the effects of their acts, are united with the Supreme Soul. Happiness and misery are both transient. Therefore,

O Ashtaka, why should I grieve? We can never know how we are to act in order to avoid misery. Therefore, none should grieve for misery.'

"Possessed of every virtue, king Yayati who was the maternal grandfather of Ashtaka, while staying in the welkin, at the conclusion of his speech, was again questioned by Ashtaka. The latter said, 'O king of kings, tell me, in detail, of all those regions that thou hast visited and enjoyed, as well as the period for which thou hast enjoyed each. Thou speakest of the precepts of religion even like the clever masters acquainted with the acts and sayings of great beings!' Yayati replied, 'I was a great king on Earth, owning the whole world for my dominion. Leaving it, I acquired by dint of religious merit many high regions. There I dwelt for a full thousand years, and then I attained to a very high region the abode of Indra, of extraordinary beauty having a thousand gates, and extending over a hundred yojanas all round. There too, I dwelt a full thousand years and then attained to a higher region still. That is the region of perfect beatitude, where decay never exists, the region, viz., that of the Creator and the Lord of Earth, so difficult of attainment. There also I dwelt for a full thousand years, and then attained to another very high region viz., that of the god of gods (Vishnu) where, too, I had lived in happiness. Indeed, I dwelt in various regions, adored by all the celestials, and possessed of prowess and splendour equal unto those of the celestials themselves. Capable of assuming any form at will, I lived for a million years in the gardens of Nandana sporting with the Apsaras and beholding numberless beautiful trees clad in flowery vesture and sending forth delicious perfume all round. And after many, many years had elapsed, while still residing there in enjoyment of perfect beatitude, the celestial messenger of grim visage, one day, in a loud and deep voice, thrice shouted to me— Ruined! Ruined! Ruined!—O lion among kings, this much do I remember. I was then fallen from Nandana, my religious merits gone! I heard in the skies, O king, the voices of the celestials exclaiming in grief,—Alas! What a misfortune! Yayati, with his religious merits destroyed, though virtuous and of sacred deeds, is falling!—And as I was falling, I asked them loudly, 'Where, ye celestials, are those wise ones amongst whom I am to fall?' They pointed out to me this sacred sacrificial region belonging to you. Beholding the curls of smoke blackening the atmosphere and smelling the perfume of clarified butter poured incessantly upon fire, and guided thereby, I am approaching this region of yours, glad at heart that I come amongst you.'"

SECTION XC
(Sambhava Parva continued)

"Ashtaka said, 'Capable of assuming any form at will, thou hast lived for a million years in the gardens of Nandana. For what cause, O foremost of those that flourished in the Krita age, hast thou been compelled to leave that region and come hither?' Yayati answered, 'As kinsmen, friends, and relatives forsake, in this world, those whose wealth disappears so, in the other world, the celestials with Indra as their chief, forsake him who hath lost his righteousness.' Ashtaka said, 'I am extremely anxious to know how in the other world men can lose virtue. Tell me also, O king, what regions are attainable by what courses of action. Thou art acquainted, I know, with the acts and sayings of great beings.'

"Yayati answered, 'O pious one, they that speak of their own merits are doomed to suffer the hell called Bhauma. Though really emaciated and lean, they appear to grow on Earth (in the shape of their sons and grandsons) only to become food for vultures, dogs, and jackals. Therefore, O king, this highly censurable and wicked vice should be repressed. I have now, O king, told thee all. Tell me what more I shall say.'

"Ashtaka said, 'When life is destroyed with age, vultures, peacocks, insects, and worms eat up the human body. Where doth man then reside? How doth he also come back to life? I have never heard of any hell called Bhauma on Earth!'

"Yayati answered, 'After the dissolution of the body, man, according to his acts, re-entereth the womb of his mother and stayeth there in an indistinct form, and soon after assuming a distinct and visible shape reappeareth in the world and walketh on its surface. This is that Earth- hell (Bhauma) where he falleth, for he beholdeth not the termination of his existence and acteth not towards his emancipation. Some dwell for sixty thousand years, some, for eighty thousand years in heaven, and then they fall. And as they fall, they are attacked by certain Rakshasas in the form of sons, grandsons, and other relatives, that withdraw their hearts from acting for their own emancipation.'

"Ashtaka asked, 'For what sin are beings, when they fall from heaven, attacked by these fierce and sharp-toothed Rakshasas? Why are they not reduced to annihilation? How do they again enter the womb, furnished with senses?'

"Yayati answered, 'After falling from heaven, the being becometh a subtle substance living in water. This water becometh the semen whence is the seed of vitality. Thence entering the mother's womb in the womanly season, it developeth into the embryo and next into visible life like the fruit from the flower. Entering trees, plants, and other vegetable substances, water, air, earth, and space, that same watery seed of life assumeth the quadrupedal or bipedal form. This is the case with all creatures that you see.'

"Ashtaka said, 'O tell me, I ask thee because I have my doubts. Doth a being that hath received a human form enter the womb in its own shape or in some other? How doth it also acquire its distinct and visible shape, eyes and ears and consciousness as well? Questioned by me, O, explain it all! Thou art, O father, one acquainted with the acts and sayings of great beings.' Yayati answered, 'According to the merits of one's acts, the being that in a subtle form co-inheres in the seed that is dropped into the womb is attracted by the atmospheric force for purposes of re-birth. It then developeth there in course of time; first it becomes the embryo, and is next provided with the visible physical organism. Coming out of the womb in due course of time, it becometh conscious of its existence as man, and with his ears becometh sensible of sound; with his eyes, of colour and form; with his nose, of scent; with his tongue, of taste; by his whole body, of touch; and by his mind, of ideas. It is thus, O Ashtaka, that the gross and visible body developeth from the subtle essence.'

"Ashtaka asked, 'After death, the body is burnt, or otherwise destroyed. Reduced to nothing upon such dissolution, by what principle is one revived?' Yayati said, 'O lion among kings, the person that dies assumes a subtil form; and retaining consciousness of all his acts as in a dream, he enters some other form with a speed quicker than that of air itself. The virtuous attain to a superior, and the vicious to an inferior form of existence. The vicious become worms and insects. I have nothing more to say, O thou of great and pure soul! I have told thee how beings are born, after development of embryonic forms, as four-footed, six-footed creatures and others with more feet. What more wilt thou ask me?'

"Ashtaka said, 'How, O father, do men attain to those superior regions whence there is no return to earthly life? Is it by asceticism or by knowledge? How also can one gradually attain to felicitous regions? Asked by me, O answer it in full.'

"Yayati answered, 'The wise say that for men there are seven gates through which admission may be gained into Heaven. There are asceticism, benevolence, tranquillity of mind, self-command, modesty, simplicity, and kindness to all creatures. The wise also say that a person loseth all these in consequence of vanity. That man who having acquired knowledge regardeth himself as learned, and with his learning destroyed the reputation of others, never attaineth to regions of indestructible felicity. That knowledge also doth not make its possessor competent to attain to Brahma. Study, taciturnity, worship before fire, and sacrifices, these four remove all fear. When, however, these are mixed with vanity, instead of removing it, they cause fear. The wise should never exult at (receiving) honours nor should they grieve at insults. For it is the wise alone that honour the wise; the wicked never act like the virtuous. I have given away so much—I have performed so many sacrifices,—I have studied so much,—I have observed these vows,—such vanity is the root of fear. Therefore, thou must not indulge in such feelings. Those learned men who accept as their support the unchangeable, inconceivable Brahma alone that ever showereth blessings on persons virtuous like thee, enjoy perfect peace here and hereafter.'"

SECTION XCI
(Sambhava Parva continued)

"Ashtaka said, 'Those cognisant of the Vedas differ in opinion as to how the followers of each of the four modes of life, viz., Grihasthas, Bhikshus, Brahmacharins, and Vanaprashthas, should conduct themselves in order to acquire religious merit.'

"Yayati answered, 'These are what a Brahmacharin must do. While dwelling in the abode of his preceptor, he must receive lessons only when his preceptor summons him to do so; he must attend to the service of his preceptor without waiting for the latter's command; he must rise from his bed before his preceptor riseth, and go to bed after his preceptor hath gone to bed. He must be humble, must have his passions under complete control, must be patient, vigilant, and devoted to studies. It is then only that he can achieve success. It hath been said in the oldest Upanishad that a grihastha, acquiring wealth by honest means, should perform sacrifices; he should always give something in charity, should perform the rites of hospitality unto all arriving at his abode, and should never use anything without giving a portion thereof to others. A Muni, without search for woods, depending on his own vigour, should abstain from all vicious acts, should give away something in charity, should never inflict pain on any creature. It is then only that he can achieve success. He, indeed, is a true Bhikshu who doth not support himself by any manual arts, who possesseth numerous accomplishments, who hath his passions under complete control, who is unconnected with worldly concerns, who sleepeth not under the shelter of a householder's roof, who is without wife, and who going a little way every day, travelleth over a large extent of the country. A learned man should adopt the Vanaprastha mode of life after performance of the necessary rites, when he hath been able to control his appetites for enjoyment and desire of acquiring valuable possessions. When one dieth in the woods while leading the Vanaprastha mode of life, he maketh his ancestors and the successors, numbering ten generations including himself, mix with the Divine essence.'

"Ashtaka asked, 'How many kinds of Munis are there (observers of the vow of the silence)?'

"Yayati answered, 'He is, indeed, a Muni who, though dwelling in the woods, hath an inhabited place near, or who, though dwelling in an inhabited place, hath the woods near.'

"Ashtaka enquired what is meant by Muni. Yayati replied, 'A Muni withdrawing himself from all worldly objects liveth in the woods. And though he might never seek to surround himself with those objects that are procurable in an inhabited place, he might yet obtain them all by virtue of his ascetic power. He may truly be said to dwell in the woods having an inhabited place near to himself. Again a wise man withdrawn from all earthly objects, might live in a hamlet leading the life of a hermit. He may never exhibit the pride of family, birth or learning. Clad in the scantiest robes, he may yet regard himself as attired in the richest vestments. He may rest content with food just enough for the support of life. Such a person, though dwelling in an inhabited place, liveth yet in the woods.

"The person again, who, with passions under complete control, adopteth the vow of silence, refraining from action and entertaining no desire, achieveth success. Why shouldst thou not, indeed, reverence the man who liveth on clean food, who refraineth from ever injuring others, whose heart is ever pure, who stands in the splendour of ascetic attributes, who is free from the leaden weight of desire, who abstaineth from injury even when sanctioned by religion? Emaciated by austerities and reduced in flesh, marrow and blood, such a one conquereth not only this but the highest world. And when the Muni sits in yoga meditation, becoming indifferent to happiness and misery, honour and insult, he then leaveth the world and enjoyeth communion with Brahma. When the Muni taketh food like wine and other animals, i. e., without providing for it beforehand and without any relish (like a sleeping infant feeding on the mother's lap), then like the all-pervading spirit he becometh identified with the whole universe and attaineth to salvation.'"

SECTION XCII
(Sambhava Parva continued)

"Ashtaka asked, 'Who amongst these, O king, both exerting constantly like the Sun and the Moon, first attaineth to communion with Brahma, the ascetic or the man of knowledge?'

"Yayati answered, 'The wise, with the help of the Vedas and of Knowledge, having ascertained the visible universe to be illusory, instantly realises the Supreme Spirit as the sole existent independent essence. While they that devote themselves to Yoga meditation take time to acquire the same knowledge, for it is by practice alone that these latter divest themselves of the consciousness of quality. Hence the wise attain to salvation first. Then again if the person devoted to Yoga find not sufficient time in one life to attain success, being led astray by the attractions of the world, in his next life he is benefited by the progress already achieved, for he devoteth himself regretfully to the pursuit of success. But the man of knowledge ever beholdeth the indestructible unity, and, is, therefore, though steeped in worldly enjoyments, never affected by them at heart. Therefore, there is nothing to impede his salvation. He, however, who faileth to attain to knowledge, should yet devote himself to piety as dependent on action (sacrifices). But he that devoteth himself to such piety, moved thereto by desire of salvation, can never achieve success. His sacrifices bear no fruit and partake of the nature of cruelty. Piety which is dependent on action that proceedeth not from the desire of fruit, is, in case of such men Yoga itself.'

"Ashtaka said, 'O king, thou lookest like a young man; thou art handsome and decked with a celestial garland. Thy splendour is great! Whence dost thou come and where dost thou go? Whose messenger art thou? Art thou going down into the Earth?'

"Yayati said, 'Fallen from heaven upon the loss of all my religious merits, I am doomed to enter the Earth-hell. Indeed, I shall go there after I have finished my discourse with you. Even now the regents of the points of the universe command me to hasten thither. And, O king, I have obtained it as a boon from Indra that though fall I must upon the earth, yet I should fall amidst the wise and the virtuous. Ye are all wise and virtuous that are assembled here.'

"Ashtaka said, 'Thou art acquainted with everything. I ask thee, O king, are there any regions for myself to enjoy in heaven or in the firmament? If there be, then, thou shalt not fall, though falling.'

"Yayati answered, 'O king, there are as many regions for thee to enjoy in heaven even as the number of kine and horses on Earth with the animals in the wilderness and on the hills.'

"Ashtaka said, 'If there are worlds for me to enjoy, as fruits of my religious merits, in heaven, O king, I give them all unto thee. Therefore, though falling, thou shalt not fall. O, take thou soon all those, wherever they be, in heaven or in the firmament. Let thy sorrow cease.'

"Yayati answered, 'O best of kings, a Brahma-knowing Brahmana alone can take in gift, but not one like ourselves. And, O monarch, I myself have given away to Brahmanas as one should. Let no man who is not a Brahmana and let not the wife of a learned Brahmana ever live in infamy by accepting gifts. While on earth, I ever desired to perform virtuous acts. Having never done so before, how shall I now accept a gift?'

"Pratardana who was amongst them asked, 'O thou of the handsomest form, I am Pratardana by name. I ask thee if there are any worlds for me to enjoy as fruits of my religious merits, in heaven or the firmament? Answer me, thou art acquainted with everything.'

"Yayati said, 'O king, numberless worlds, full of felicity, effulgent like the solar disc, and where woe can never dwell, await thee. If thou dwellest in each but for seven days, they would not yet be exhausted.'

"Pratardana said, 'These then I give unto thee. Therefore, though falling, thou must not fall. Let the worlds that are mine be thine, whether they be in the firmament or heaven. O, soon take them. Let thy woes cease.'

"Yayati answered, 'O monarch, no king of equal energy should ever desire to receive as gift the religious merits of another king acquired by Yoga austerities. And no king who is afflicted with calamity through the fates should, if wise, act in a censurable way. A king keeping his eye fixed for ever on virtue should walk along the path of virtue like myself and, knowing what his duties are, should not act so meanly as thou directest. When others desirous of acquiring religious merits do not accept gifts, how can I do what they themselves do not?' On the conclusion of this speech, that best of kings, Yayati, was then addressed by Vasumat in the following words."

SECTION XCIII
(Sambhava Parva continued)

"Vasumat said, 'I am Vasumat, the son of Oshadaswa. I would ask thee, O king, whether there are any worlds for me to enjoy as fruits of my religious merits, in heaven or the firmament. Thou art, O high-souled one, acquainted with all holy regions.'

"Yayati answered, 'There are as many regions for thee to enjoy in heaven as the number of places in the firmament, the Earth and the ten points of the universe illumined by the Sun.'

"Vasumat then said, 'I give them to thee. Let those regions that are for me be thine. Therefore, though falling, thou shall not fall. If to accept them as gift be improper for thee, then, O monarch, buy them for a straw?'

"Yayati answered, 'I do not remember having ever bought and sold anything unfairly. This has never been done by other kings. How shall I therefore do it?'

THE MAHABHARATA

"Vasumat said, 'If buying them, O king, be regarded by thee as improper, then take them as gift from me. For myself I answer that I will never go to those regions that are for me. Let them, therefore, be thine.'

"Sivi then addressed the king thus, I am, O king, Sivi by name, the son of Usinara. O father, are there in the firmament or in heaven any worlds for me to enjoy as the fruit of his religious merit.'

"Yayati said, 'Thou hast never, by speech or in mind, disregarded the honest and the virtuous that applied to thee. There are infinite worlds for thee to enjoy in heaven, all blazing like lightning.' Sivi then said, 'If thou regardest their purchase as improper, I give them to thee. Take them all, O king! I shall never take them, viz., those regions where the wise never feel the least disquiet.'

Yayati answered, 'O Sivi, thou hast indeed, obtained for thyself, possessed of the prowess of Indra, infinite worlds. But I do not desire to enjoy regions given to me by others. Therefore, I accept not thy gift.'

"Ashtaka then said, 'O king, each of us has expressed his desire to give thee worlds that each of us has acquired by his religious merits. Thou acceptest not them. But leaving them for thee, we shall descend into the Earth-hell.'

"Yayati answered, 'Ye all are truth-loving and wise. Give me that which I deserve. I shall not be able to do what I have never done before.'

"Ashtaka then said, 'Whose are those five golden cars that we see? Do men that repair to these regions of everlasting bliss ride in them?'

"Yayati answered, 'Those five golden cars displayed in glory, and blazing as fire, would indeed, carry you to regions of bliss.'

"Ashtaka said, 'O king, ride on those cars thyself and repair to heaven. We can wait. We follow thee in time.'

"Yayati said, 'We can now all go together. Indeed, all of us have conquered heaven. Behold, the glorious path to heaven becomes visible."

"Vaisampayana continued, 'Then all those excellent monarchs riding in those cars set out for heaven for gaining admittance into it, illuminating the whole firmament by the glory of their virtues.'

"Then Ashtaka, breaking the silence asked, 'I had always thought that Indra was my especial friend, and that I, of all others, should first obtain admittance into heaven. But how is it that Usinara's son, Sivi hath already left us behind?'

"Yayati answered, 'This Usinara's son had given all he possessed for attaining to the region of Brahman. Therefore, is he the foremost among us. Besides, Sivi's liberality, asceticism, truth, virtue, modesty, forgiveness, amiability, desire of performing good acts, have been so great that none can measure them!'

"Vaisampayana continued, 'After this, Ashtaka, impelled by curiosity, again asked his maternal grandfather resembling Indra himself, saying, 'O king, I ask thee, tell me truly, whence thou art, who thou art, and whose son? Is there any other Brahmana or Kshatriya who hath done what thou didst on earth?' Yayati answered, 'I tell thee truly, I am Yayati, the son of Nahusha and the father of Puru. I was lord of all the Earth. Ye are my relatives; I tell thee truly, I am the maternal grandfather of you all. Having conquered the whole earth, I gave clothes to Brahmanas and also a hundred handsome horses fit for sacrificial offering. For such acts of virtue, the gods became propitious to those that perform them. I also gave to Brahmanas this whole earth with her horses and elephants and kine and gold all kinds of wealth, along with a hundred Arbudas of excellent milch cows. Both the earth and the firmament exist owing to my truth and virtue; fire yet burneth in the world of men owing to my truth and virtue. Never hath a word spoken by me been untrue. It is for this that the wise adore Truth. O Ashtaka, all I have told thee, Pratardana, and Vasumat, is Truth itself. I know it for certain that the gods and the Rishis and all the mansions of the blessed are adorable only because of Truth that characteriseth them all. He that will without malice duly read unto good Brahmanas his account of our ascension to heaven shall himself attain to the same worlds with us.'

"Vaisampayana continued, 'It was thus that the illustrious king Yayati of high achievements, rescued by his collateral descendants, ascended to heaven, leaving the earth and covering the three worlds with the fame of his deeds.'"

SECTION XCIV
(Sambhava Parva continued)

"Janamejaya said, 'O adorable one, I desire to hear the histories of those kings who were descended from Puru. O tell me of each as he was possessed of prowess and achievements. I have, indeed, heard that in Puru's line there was not a single one who was wanting in good behaviour and prowess, or who was without sons. O thou of ascetic wealth, I desire to hear the histories in detail of those famous monarchs endued with learning and all accomplishments.'

"Vaisampayana said, 'Asked by thee, I shall tell thee all about the heroic- kings in Puru's line, all equal unto Indra in prowess, possessing great affluence and commanding the respect of all for their accomplishments.

"Puru had by his wife Paushti three sons, Pravira, Iswara, and Raudraswa, all of whom were mighty car-warriors. Amongst them, Pravira was the perpetuator of the dynasty. Pravira had by his wife Suraseni a son named Manasyu. And the latter of eyes like lotus-petals had his sway over the whole Earth bounded by the four seas. And Manasyu had for his wife Sauviri. And he begat upon her three sons called Sakta, Sahana, and Vagmi. And they were heroes in battle and mighty car-warriors. The intelligent and virtuous Kaudraswa begat upon the Apsara Misrakesi ten sons who were all great bowmen. And they all grew up into heroes, performing numerous sacrifices in honour of the gods. And they all had sons, were learned in all branches of knowledge and ever devoted to virtue. They are Richeyu, and Kaksreyu and Vrikeyu of great prowess; Sthandileyu, and Vaneyu, and Jaleyu of great fame; Tejeyu of great strength and intelligence; and Satyeyu of the prowess of Indra; Dharmeyu, and Sannateyu the tenth of the prowess of the celestials. Amongst them all, Richeyu became the sole monarch of the whole earth and was known by the name of Anadhrishti. And in prowess he was like unto Vasava amongst the celestials. And Anadhristi had a son of the name of Matinara who became a famous and virtuous king and performed the Rajasuya and the horse-sacrifice. And Matinara had four sons of immeasurable prowess, viz., Tansu, Mahan, Atiratha, and Druhyu of immeasurable glory. (Amongst them, Tansu of great prowess became the perpetator of Puru's line). And he subjugated the whole earth and acquired great fame and splendour. And Tansu begat a son of great prowess named Ilina. And he became the foremost of all conquerors and brought the whole world under his subjection. And Ilina begat upon his wife Rathantara five sons with Dushmanta at their head, all equal in might unto the five elements. They were Dushmanta, Sura, Bhima, Pravasu, and Vasu. And, O Janamejaya, the eldest of them, Dushmanta, became king. And Dushmanta had by his wife Sakuntala an intelligent son named Bharata who became king. And Bharata gave his name to the race of which he was the founder. And it is from him that the fame of that dynasty hath spread so wide. And Bharata begat upon his three wives nine sons in all. But none of them were like their father and so Bharata was not at all pleased with them. Their mothers, therefore, became angry and slew them all. The procreation of children by Bharata, therefore, became vain. The monarch then performed a great sacrifice and through the grace of Bharadwaja obtained a son named Bhumanyu. And then Bharata, the great descendant of Puru, regarding himself as really possessing a son, installed, O foremost one of Bharata's race, that son as his heir-apparent. And Bhumanyu begat upon his wife, Pushkarini six sons named Suhotra, Suhotri, Suhavih, Sujeya, Diviratha and Kichika. The eldest of them all, Suhotra, obtained the throne and performed many Rajasuyas and horse-sacrifices. And Suhotra brought under his sway the whole earth surrounded by her belt of seas and full of elephants, kine and horses, and all her wealth of gems of gold. And the earth afflicted with the weight of numberless human beings and elephants, horses, and cats, was, as it were, about to sink. And during the virtuous reign of Suhotra the surface of the whole earth was dotted all over with hundreds and thousands, of sacrificial stakes. And the lord of the earth, Suhotra, begat, upon his wife Aikshaki three sons, viz., Ajamidha, Sumidha, and Purumidha. The eldest of them, Ajamidha, was the perpetuator of the royal line. And he begat six sons,— Riksha was born of the womb of Dhumini, Dushmanta and Parameshthin, of Nili, and Jahnu, Jala and Rupina were born in that of Kesini. All the tribes of the Panchalas are descended from Dushmanta and Parameshthin. And the Kushikas are the sons of Jahnu of immeasurable prowess. And Riksha who was older than both Jala and Rupina became king. And Riksha begat Samvarana, the perpetuator of the royal line. And, O king, it hath been heard by us that while Samvarana, the son of Riksha, was ruling the earth, there happened a great loss of people from famine, pestilence, drought, and disease. And the Bharata princes were beaten by the troops of enemies. And the Panchalas setting out to invade the whole earth with their four kinds of troops soon brought the whole earth under their sway. And with their ten Akshauhinis the king of the Panchalas defeated the Bharata prince. Samvarana then with his wife and ministers, sons and relatives, fled in fear, and took shelter in the forest on the banks of the Sindhu extending to the foot of the mountains. There the Bharatas lived for a full thousand years, within their fort. And after they had lived there a thousand years, one day the illustrious Rishi Vasishtha approached the exiled Bharatas, who, on going out, saluted the Rishi and worshipped him by the offer of Arghya. And entertaining him with reverence, they represented everything unto that illustrious Rishi. And after he was seated on his seat, the king himself approached the Rishi and addressed him, saying, 'Be thou our priest, O illustrious one! We will endeavour to regain our kingdom.' And Vasishtha answered the Bharatas by saying, 'Om' (the sign of consent). It hath been heard by us that Vasishtha then installed the Bharata prince in the sovereignty of all the Kshatriyas on earth, making by virtue of his Mantras this descendant of Puru the veritable horns of the wild bull or the tusks of the wild elephants. And the king retook the capital that had been taken away from him and once more made all monarchs pay tribute to him. The powerful Samvarana, thus installed once more in the actual sovereignty of the whole earth, performed many sacrifices at which the presents to the Brahmanas were great.

"Samvarana begat upon his wife, Tapati, the daughter of Surya, a son named Kuru. This Kuru was exceedingly virtuous, and therefore, he was installed on the throne by his people. It is after his name that the field called Kuru-jangala has become so famous in the world. Devoted to asceticism, he made that field (Kurukshetra) sacred by practising asceticism there. And it has been heard by us that Kuru's highly intelligent wife, Vahini, brought forth five sons, viz., Avikshit, Bhavishyanta, Chaitraratha, Muni and the celebrated Janamejaya. And Avikshit begat Parikshit the powerful, Savalaswa, Adhiraja, Viraja, Salmali of great physical strength, Uchaihsravas, Bhangakara and Jitari the eighth. In the race of these were born, as the fruit of their pious acts seven mighty car-warriors with Janamejaya at their head. And unto Parikshit were born sons who were all acquainted with (the secrets of) religion and profit. And they were named Kakshasena and Ugrasena, and Chitrasena endued with great energy, and Indrasena and Sushena and Bhimasena. And the sons of Janamejaya were all endued with great strength and became celebrated all over the world. And they were Dhritarashtra who was the eldest, and Pandu and Valhika, and Nishadha endued with great energy, and then the mighty Jamvunada, and then Kundodara and Padati and then Vasati the eighth. And they were all proficient in morality and profit and were kind to all creatures. Among them Dhritarashtra became king. And Dhritarashtra had eight sons, viz., Kundika, Hasti, Vitarka, Kratha the fifth, Havihsravas, Indrabha, and Bhumanyu the invincible, and Dhritarashtra had many grandsons, of whom three only were famous. They were, O king, Pratipa, Dharmanetra, Sunetra. Among these three, Pratipa became unrivalled on earth. And, O bull in Bharata's race, Pratipa begat three sons, viz., Devapi, Santanu, and the mighty car-warrior Valhika. The eldest Devapi adopted the ascetic course of life, impelled thereto by the desire of benefiting his brothers. And the kingdom was obtained by Santanu and the mighty car-warrior Valhika.

"O monarch, besides, there were born in the race of Bharata numberless other excellent monarchs endued with great energy and like unto the celestial Rishis themselves in virtue and ascetic power. And so also in the race of Manu were born many mighty car-warriors like unto the celestials themselves, who by their number swelled the Aila dynasty into gigantic proportions.'"

SECTION XCV
(Sambhava Parva continued)

"Janamejaya said, 'O Brahmana, I have now heard from thee this great history of my ancestors. I had also heard from thee about the great monarchs that were born in this line. But I have not been gratified, this charming account being so short. Therefore, be pleased, O Brahmana, to recite the delightful narrative just in detail commencing from Manu, the lord of creation. Who is there that will not be charmed with such an account, as it is sacred? The fame of these monarchs increased by their wisdom, virtue, accomplishments, and high character, hath so swelled as to cover the three worlds. Having listened to the history, sweet as nectar, of their liberality, prowess, physical strength, mental vigour, energy, and perseverance, I have not been satiated!'

"Vaisampayana said, 'Hear then, O monarch, as I recite in full the auspicious account of thy own race just as I had heard it from Dwaipayana before.

"Daksha begat Aditi, and Aditi begat Vivaswat, and Vivaswat begat Manu, and Manu begat Ha and Ha begat Pururavas. And Pururavas begat Ayus, and Ayus begat Nahusha, and Nahusha begat Yayati. And Yayati had two wives, viz., Devayani, the daughter of Usanas, and Sarmishtha the daughter of Vrishaparvan. Here occurs a sloka regarding (Yayati's) descendants, 'Devayani gave birth to Yadu and Turvasu; and Vrishaparvan's daughter, Sarmishtha gave birth to Druhyu, Anu, and Puru. And the descendants of Yadu are the Yadavas and of Puru are the Pauravas. And Puru had a wife of the name of Kausalya, on whom he begat a son named Janamejaya who performed three horse-sacrifices and a sacrifice called Viswajit. And then he entered into the woods. And Janamejaya had married Ananta, the daughter of Madhava, and begat upon her a son called Prachinwat. And the prince was so called because he had conquered all the eastern countries up to the very confines of the region where the Sun rises. And Prachinwat married Asmaki, a daughter of the Yadavas and begat upon her a son named Sanyati. And Sanyati married Varangi, the daughter of Drishadwata and begat upon her a son named Ahayanti. And Ahayanti married Bhanumati, the daughter of Kritavirya and begat upon her a son named Sarvabhauma. And Sarvabhauma married Sunanda, the daughter of the Kekaya prince, having obtained her by force. And he begat upon her a son named Jayatsena, who married Susrava, the daughter of the Vidarbha king and begat upon her Avachina. And Avachina also married another princess of Vidarbha, Maryada by name. And he begat on her a son named Arihan. And Arihan married Angi and begat on her Mahabhauma. And Mahabhauma married Suyajna, the daughter of Prasenajit. And of her was born Ayutanayi. And he was so called because he had performed a sacrifice at which the fat of an Ayuta (ten thousands) of male beings was required. And Ayutanayi took for a wife Kama, the daughter of Prithusravas. And by her was born a son named Akrodhana, who took to wife Karambha, the daughter of the king of Kalinga. And of her was born Devatithi, and Devatithi took for his wife Maryada, the princess of Videha. And of her was born a son named Arihan. And Arihan took to wife Sudeva, the princess of Anga, and upon her he begat a son named Riksha. And Riksha married Jwala, the daughter of Takshaka, and he begat upon her a son of the name of Matinara, who performed on the bank of Saraswati the twelve years' sacrifice said to be so efficacious. On conclusion of the sacrifice, Saraswati appeared in person before the king and chose him for husband. And he begat upon her a son named Tansu. Here occurs a sloka descriptive of Tansu's descendants.

"Tansu was born of Saraswati by Matinara. And Tansu himself begat a son named Ilina on his wife, the princess Kalingi.

"Ilina begat on his wife Rathantari five sons, of whom Dushmanta was the eldest. And Dushmanta took to wife Sakuntala, the daughter of Viswamitra. And he begat on her a son named Bharata. Here occurs two slokas about (Dushmanta's) descendants.

"The mother is but the sheath of flesh in which the father begets the son. Indeed the father himself is the son. Therefore, O Dushmanta, support thy son and insult not Sakuntala. O god among men, the father himself becoming the son rescueth himself from hell. Sakuntala hath truly said that thou art the author of this child's being.

"It is for this (i.e., because the king supported his child after hearing the above speech of the celestial messenger) that Sakuntala's son came to be called Bharata (the supported). And Bharata married Sunanda, the daughter of Sarvasena, the king of Kasi, and begat upon her the son named Bhumanyu. And Bhumanyu married Vijaya, the daughter of Dasarha. And he begat upon her a son Suhotra who married Suvarna, the daughter of Ikshvaku. To her was born a son named Hasti who founded this city, which has, therefore, been called Hastinapura. And Hasti married Yasodhara, the princess of Trigarta. And of her was born a son named Vikunthana who took for a wife Sudeva, the princess of Dasarha. And by her was born a son named Ajamidha. And Ajamidha had four wives named Raikeyi, Gandhari, Visala and Riksha. And he begat on them two thousand and four hundred sons. But amongst them all, Samvarana became the perpetuator of the dynasty. And Samvarana took for his wife Tapati, the daughter of Vivaswat. And of her was born Kuru, who married Subhangi, the princess of Dasarha. And he begat on her a son named Viduratha, who took to wife Supriya, the daughter of the Madhavas. And he begat upon her a son named Anaswan. And Anaswan married Amrita, the daughter of the Madhavas. And of her was born a son named Parikshit, who took for his wife Suvasa, the daughter of the Vahudas, and begat upon her a son named Bhimasena. And Bhimasena married Kumari, the princess of Kekaya and begat upon her Pratisravas whose son was Pratipa. And Pratipa married Sunanda, the daughter of Sivi, and begat upon her three sons, viz., Devapi, Santanu and Valhika. And Devapi, while still a boy, entered the woods as a hermit. And Santanu became king. Here occurs a sloka in respect of Santanu.

"Those old men that were touched by this monarch not only felt an indescribable sensation of pleasure but also became restored to youth. Therefore, this monarch was called Santanu.

THE MAHABHARATA

"And Santanu married Ganga, who bore him a son Devavrata who was afterwards called Bhishma. And Bhishma, moved by the desire of doing good to his father, got him married to Satyavati who was also called Gandhakali. And in her maidenhood she had a son by Parasara, named Dwaipayana. And upon her Santanu begat two other sons named Chitrangada and Vichitravirya. And before they attained to majority, Chitrangada had been slain by the Gandharvas. But Vichitravirya became king, and married the two daughters of the king of Kasi, named Amvika and Amvalika. But Vichitravirya died childless. Then Satyavati began to think as to how the dynasty of Dushmanta might be perpetuated. Then she recollected the Rishi Dwaipayana. The latter coming before her, asked, 'What are thy commands?' She said, 'Thy brother Vichitravirya hath gone to heaven childless. Beget virtuous children for him.' Dwaipayana, consenting to this, begat three children, viz., Dhritarashtra, Pandu, and Vidura. King Dhritarashtra had a hundred sons by his wife, Gandhari in consequence of the boon granted by Dwaipayana. And amongst those hundred sons of Dhritarashtra, four became celebrated. They are Duryodhana, Duhsasana, Vikarna, and Chitrasena. And Pandu had two jewels of wives, viz., Kunti, also called Pritha, and Madri. One day Pandu, while out a-hunting, saw a deer covering its mate. That was really a Rishi in the form of a deer. Seeing the deer in that attitude, he killed it with his arrows, before its desire was gratified. Pierced with the king's arrow, the deer quickly changed its form and became a Rishi, and said unto Pandu, 'O Pandu, thou art virtuous and acquainted also with the pleasure derived from the gratification of one's desire. My desire unsatisfied, thou hast slain me! Therefore, thou also, when so engaged and before thou art gratified, shalt die!' Pandu, hearing this curse, became pale, and from that time would not go in unto his wives. And he told them these words, 'Through my own fault, I have been cursed! But I have heard that for the childless there are no regions hereafter.' Therefore, he solicited Kunti to have offspring raised for him. And Kunti said, 'Let it be.' So she raised up offspring. By Dharma she had Yudhishthira; by Maruta, Bhima: and by Sakra, Arjuna. And Pandu, well-pleased with her, said, 'This thy co-wife is also childless. Therefore, cause her also to bear children.' Kunti saying, 'So be it,' imparted unto Madri the mantra of invocation. And on Madri were raised by the twin Aswins, the twins Nakula and Sahadeva. And (one day) Pandu, beholding Madri decked with ornaments, had his desire kindled. And, as soon as he touched her, he died. Madri ascended the funeral pyre with her lord. And she said unto Kunti, 'Let these twins of mine be brought up by thee with affection.' After some time those five Pandavas were taken by the ascetics of the woods to Hastinapura and there introduced to Bhishma and Vidura. And after introducing them, the ascetics disappeared in the very sight of all. And after the conclusion of the speech of those ascetics, flowers were showered down upon the spot, and the celestial drums also were beaten in the skies. The Pandavas were then taken (by Bhishma). They then represented the death of their father and performed his last honours duly. And as they were brought up there, Duryodhana became exceedingly jealous of them. And the sinful Duryodhana acting like Rakshasa tried various means to drive them away. But what must be can never be frustrated. So all Duryodhana's efforts proved futile. Then Dhritarashtra sent them, by an act of deception to Varanavata, and they went there willingly. There an endeavour was made to burn them to death; but it proved abortive owing to the warning counsels of Vidura. After that the Pandavas slew Hidimva, and then they went to a town called Ekachakra. There also they slew a Rakshasa of the name of Vaka and then went to Panchala. And there obtaining Draupadi for a wife they returned to Hastinapura. And there they dwelt for some time in peace and begat children. And Yudhishthira begat Prativindhya; Bhima, Sutasoma; Arjuna, Srutakriti; Nakula, Satanika; and Sahadeva, Srutakarman. Besides these, Yudhishthira, having obtained for his wife Devika, the daughter of Govasana of the Saivya tribe, in a self-choice ceremony, begat upon her a son named Yaudheya. And Bhima also obtaining for a wife Valandhara, the daughter of the king of Kasi, offered his own prowess as dower and begat upon her a son named Sarvaga. And Arjuna also, repairing to Dwaravati, brought away by force Subhadra, the sweet-speeched sister of Vasudeva, and returned in happiness to Hastinapura. And he begat upon her a son named Abhimanyu endued with all accomplishments and dear to Vasudeva himself. And Nakula obtaining for his wife Karenumati, the princess of Chedi, begat upon her a son named Niramitra. And Sahadeva also married Vijaya, the daughter of Dyutimat, the king of Madra, obtaining her in a self-choice ceremony and begat upon her a son named Suhotra. And Bhimasena had some time before begat upon Hidimva a son named Ghatotkacha. These are the eleven sons of the Pandavas. Amongst them all, Abhimanyu was the perpetuator of the family. He married Uttara, the daughter of Virata, who brought forth a dead child whom Kunti took up on her lap at the command of Vasudeva who said, 'I will revive this child of six months.' And though born before time, having been burnt by the fire of Aswatthaman's weapon and, therefore, deprived of strength and energy he was revived by Vasudeva and endued with strength, energy and prowess. And after reviving him, Vasudeva said, 'Because this child hath been born in an extinct race, therefore, he shall be called Parikshit.' And Parikshit married Madravati, thy mother, O king, and thou art born to her, O Janamejaya! Thou hast also begotten two sons on thy wife Vapushtama, named Satanika and Sankukarna. And Satanika also hath begotten one son named Aswamedhadatta upon the princess of Videha.

"Thus have I, O king, recited the history of the descendants of Puru and of the Pandavas. This excellent, virtue-increasing, and sacred history should ever be listened to by vow-observing Brahmanas, by Kshatriyas devoted to the practices of their order and ready to protect their subjects; by Vaisyas with attention, and by Sudras with reverence, whose chief occupation is to wait upon the three other orders. Brahmanas conversant in the Vedas and other persons, who with attention and reverence recite this sacred history or listen to it when recited, conquer the heavens and attain to the abode of the blessed. They are also always respected and adored by the gods, Brahamanas, and other men. This holy history of Bharata hath been composed by the sacred and illustrious Vyasa. Veda-knowing Brahmanas and other persons who with reverence and without malice hear it recited, earn great religious merits and conquer the heavens. Though sinning, they are not disregarded by any one. Here occurs a sloka, 'This (Bharata) is equal unto the Vedas: it is holy and excellent. It bestoweth wealth, fame, and life. Therefore, it should be listened to by men with rapt attention.'"

SECTION XCVI
(Sambhava Parva continued)

"Vaisampayana said, 'There was a king known by the name of Mahabhisha born in the race of Ikshvaku. He was the lord of all the earth, and was truthful (in speech) and of true prowess. By a thousand horse-sacrifices and a hundred Rajasuyas he had gratified the chief of the celestials and ultimately attained to heaven.

"One day the celestials had assembled together and were worshipping Brahman. Many royal sages and king Mahabhisha also were present on the spot. And Ganga, the queen of rivers, also came there to pay her adorations to the Grandsire. And her garments white as the beams of the moon was displaced by the action of the wind. And as her person became exposed, the celestials bent down their heads. But the royal sage Mahabhisha rudely stared at the queen of rivers. And Mahabhisha was for this cursed by Brahman, who said, 'Wretch, as thou hast forgotten thyself at the sight of Ganga, thou shalt be re-born on earth. But thou shall again and again attain to these regions. And she, too, shall be born in the world of men and shall do thee injuries. But when thy wrath shall be provoked, thou shalt then be freed from my curse.'

"Vaisampayana continued, 'King Mahabhisha then recollecting all the monarchs and ascetics on earth, wished to be born as son to Pratipa of great prowess. And the queen of rivers, too, seeing king Mahabhisha lose his firmness, went away, thinking of him wishfully. And on her way, she saw those dwellers in heaven, the Vasus, also pursuing the same path. And the queen of rivers beholding them in the predicament, asked them, 'Why look ye so dejected? Ye dwellers in heaven, is everything right with you?' Those celestials, the Vasus, answered her, saying, 'O queen of rivers, we have been cursed, for a venial fault, by the illustrious Vasishtha in anger. The foremost of excellent Rishis, Vasishtha, had been engaged in his twilight adorations and seated as he was, he could not be seen by us. We crossed him in ignorance. Therefore, in wrath he hath cursed us, saying, Be ye born among men!' It is beyond our power to frustrate what hath been said by that utterance of Brahma. Therefore, O river, thyself becoming a human female make us the Vasus, thy children. O amiable one, we are unwilling to enter the womb of any human female.' Thus addressed, the queen of rivers told them, 'Be it so and asked them, 'On earth, who is that foremost of men whom ye will make your father?'

"The Vasus replied, 'On earth, unto Pratipa shall be born a son, Santanu, who will be a king of world-wide fame.' Ganga then said, 'Ye celestials, that is exactly my wish which ye sinless ones have expressed. I shall, indeed, do good to that Santanu. That is also your desire as just expressed.' The Vasus then said, 'It behoveth thee to throw thy children after birth, into the water, so that, O thou of three courses (celestial, terrestrial, and subterranean) we may be rescued soon without having to live on earth for any length of time.' Ganga then answered, 'I shall do what ye desire. But in order that his intercourse with me may not be entirely fruitless, provide ye that one son at least may live.' The Vasus then replied, 'We shall each contribute an eighth part of our respective energies. With the sum thereof, thou shall have one son according to thy and his wishes. But this son shall not begat any children on earth. Therefore, that son of thine endued with great energy, shall be childless.'

"The Vasus, making this arrangement with Ganga, went away without waiting to the place they liked.'"

SECTION XCVII
(Sambhava Parva continued)

"Vaisampayana said. 'There was a king of the name of Pratipa, who was kind to all creatures. He spent many years in ascetic penances at the source of the river Ganga. The accomplished and lovely Ganga, one day, assuming the form of a beautiful female, and rising from the waters, made up to the monarch. The celestial maiden, endued with ravishing beauty, approached the royal sage engaged in ascetic austerities, and sat upon his right thigh that was, for manly strength, a veritable Sala tree. When the maiden of handsome face had so sat upon his lap, the monarch said unto her, 'O amiable one, what dost thou desire? What shall I do?' The damsel answered, 'I desire thee, O king, for my husband! O foremost one of the Kurus, be mine! To refuse a woman coming of her own accord is never applauded by the wise.' Pratipa answered, 'O thou of the fairest complexion, moved by lust, I never go in unto others' wives or women that are not of my order. This, indeed, is my virtuous vow.' The maiden rejoined, 'I am not inauspicious or ugly. I am every way worthy of being enjoyed. I am a celestial maiden of rare beauty; I desire thee for my husband. Refuse me not, O king.' To this Pratipa answered, 'I am, O damsel, abstaining from that course to which thou wouldst incite me. If I break my vow, sin will overwhelm and kill me. O thou of the fairest complexion, thou hast embraced me, sitting on my right thigh. But, O timid one, know that this is the seat for daughters and daughters-in-law. The left lap is for the wife, but thou hast not accepted that. Therefore, O best of women, I cannot enjoy thee as an object of desire. Be my daughter-in-law. I accept thee for my son!'

"The damsel then said, 'O virtuous one, let it be as thou sayest. Let me be united with thy son. From my respect for thee, I shall be a wife of the celebrated Bharata race. Ye (of the Bharata race) are the refuge of all the monarchs on earth! I am incapable of numbering the virtues of this race even within a hundred years. The greatness and goodness of many celebrated monarchs of this race are limitless. O lord of all, let it be understood now that when I become thy daughter-in-law, thy son shall not be able to judge of the propriety of my acts. Living thus with thy son, I shall do good to him and increase his happiness. And he shall finally attain to heaven in consequence of the sons I shall bear him, and of his virtues and good conduct.'

"Vaisampayana continued, 'O king, having said so, the celestial damsel disappeared then and there. And the king, too, waited for the birth of his son in order to fulfil his promise.'

"About this time Pratipa, that light of the Kuru race, that bull amongst Kshatriyas, was engaged, along with his wife, in austerities from desire of offspring. And when they had grown old, a son was born unto them. This was no other than Mahabhisha. And the child was called Santanu because he was born when his father had controlled his passions by ascetic penances. And the best of Kurus, Santanu, knowing that region of indestructible bliss can be acquired by one's deeds alone, became devoted to virtue. When Santanu grew up into a youth, Pratipa addressed him and said, 'Some time ago, O Santanu, a celestial damsel came to me for thy good. If thou meetest that fair-complexioned one in secret and if she solicit thee for children, accept her as thy wife. And, O sinless one, judge not of the propriety or impropriety of her action and ask not who she is, or whose or whence, but accept her as thy wife at my command!'" Vaisampayana continued, "Pratipa, having thus commanded his son Santanu and installed him on his throne, retired into the woods. And king Santanu endued with great intelligence and equal unto Indra himself in splendour, became addicted to hunting and passed much of his time in the woods. And the best of monarchs always slew deer and buffaloes. And one day, as he was wandering along the bank of the Ganges, he came upon a region frequented by Siddhas and Charanas. And there he saw a lovely maiden of blazing beauty and like unto another Sri herself; of faultless and pearly teeth and decked with celestial ornaments, and attired in garments of fine texture that resembled in splendour the filaments of the lotus. And the monarch, on beholding that damsel, became surprised, and his raptures produced instant horripilation. With steadfast gaze he seemed to be drinking her charms, but repeated draughts failed to quench his thirst. The damsel also beholding the monarch of blazing splendour moving about in great agitation, was moved herself and experienced an affection for him. She gazed and gazed and longed to gaze on him evermore. The monarch then in soft words addressed her and said, 'O slender-waisted one, be thou a goddess or the daughter of a Danava, be thou of the race of the

Gandharvas, or Apsaras, be thou of the Yakshas or the Nagas, or be thou of human origin, O thou of celestial beauty, I solicit thee to be my wife!'"

SECTION XCVIII
(Sambhava Parva continued)

"Vaisampayana said, 'The maiden then, hearing those soft and sweet words of the smiling monarch, and remembering her promise to the Vasus, addressed the king in reply. Of faultless features, the damsel sending a thrill of pleasure into the heart by every word she uttered, said, 'O king, I shall become thy wife and obey thy commands. But, O monarch, thou must not interfere with me in anything I do, be it agreeable or disagreeable. Nor shall thou ever address me unkindly. As long as thou shalt behave kindly I promise to live with thee. But I shall certainly leave thee the moment thou interferest with me or speakest to me an unkind word.' The king answered, 'Be it so.' And thereupon the damsel obtaining that excellent monarch, that foremost one of the Bharata race for her husband, became highly pleased. And king Santanu also, obtaining her for his wife, enjoyed to the full the pleasure of her company. And adhering to his promise, he refrained from asking her anything. And the lord of earth, Santanu, became exceedingly gratified with her conduct, beauty, magnanimity, and attention to his comforts. And the goddess Ganga also, of three courses (celestial, terrestrial, and subterranean) assuming a human form of superior complexion and endued with celestial beauty, lived happily as the wife of Santanu, having as the fruit of her virtuous acts, obtained for her husband, that tiger among kings equal unto Indra himself in splendour. And she gratified the king by her attractiveness and affection, by her wiles and love, by her music and dance, and became herself gratified. And the monarch was so enraptured with his beautiful wife that months, seasons, and years rolled on without his being conscious of them. And the king, while thus enjoying himself with his wife, had eight children born unto him who in beauty were like the very celestials themselves. But, O Bharata, those children, one after another, as soon as they were born, were thrown into the river by Ganga who said, 'This is for thy good.' And the children sank to rise no more. The king, however, could not be pleased with such conduct. But he spoke not a word about it lest his wife should leave him. But when the eighth child was born, and when his wife as before was about to throw it smilingly into the river, the king with a sorrowful countenance and desirous of saving it from destruction, addressed her and said, 'Kill it not! Who art thou and whose? Why dost thou kill thy own children? Murderess of thy sons, the load of thy sins is great!'" His wife, thus addressed, replied, 'O thou desirous of offspring, thou hast already become the first of those that have children. I shall not destroy this child of thine. But according to our agreement, the period of my stay with thee is at an end. I am Ganga, the daughter of Jahnu. I am ever worshipped by the great sages; I have lived with thee so long for accomplishing the purposes of the celestials. The eight illustrious Vasus endued with great energy had, from Vasishtha's curse, to assume human forms. On earth, besides thee, there was none else to deserve the honour of being their begetter. There is no woman also on earth except one like me, a celestial of human form, to become their mother. I assumed a human form to bring them forth. Thou also, having become the father of the eight Vasus, hast acquired many regions of perennial bliss. It was also agreed between myself and the Vasus that I should free them from their human forms as soon as they would be born. I have thus freed them from the curse of the Rishi Apava. Blest be thou; I leave thee, O king! But rear thou this child of rigid vows. That I should live with thee so long was the promise I gave to the Vasus. And let this child be called Gangadatta.'"

THE MAHABHARATA

SECTION XCIX
(Sambhava Parva continued)

"Santanu asked, 'What was the fault of the Vasus and who was Apava, through whose curse the Vasus had to be born among men? What also hath this child of thine, Gangadatta, done for which he shall have to live among men? Why also were the Vasus, the lords of the three worlds, condemned to be born amongst men? O daughter of Jahnu, tell me all.'

"Vaisampayana continued, 'Thus addressed, the celestial daughter of Jahnu, Ganga, then replied unto the monarch, her husband, that bull amongst men, saying, 'O best of Bharata's race, he who was obtained as son by Varuna was called Vasishtha, the Muni who afterwards came to be known as Apava. He had his asylum on the breast of the king of mountains called Meru. The spot was sacred and abounded with birds and beasts. And there bloomed at all times of the year flowers of every season. And, O best of Bharata's race, that foremost of virtuous men, the son of Varuna, practised his ascetic penances in those woods abounding with sweet roots and water.

"Daksha had a daughter known by the name of Surabhi, who, O bull of Bharata's race, for benefiting the world, brought forth, by her connection with Kasyapa, a daughter (Nandini) in the form of a cow. That foremost of all kine, Nandini, was the cow of plenty (capable of granting every desire). The virtuous son of Varuna obtained Nandini for his Homa rites. And Nandini, dwelling in that hermitage which was adored by Munis, roamed about fearlessly in those sacred and delightful woods.

"One day, O bull of Bharata's race, there came into those woods adored by the gods and celestial Rishis, the Vasus with Prithu at their head. And wandering there with their wives, they enjoyed themselves in those delightful woods and mountains. And as they wandered there, the slender- waisted wife of one of the Vasus, O thou of the prowess of Indra, saw in those woods Nandini, the cow of plenty. And seeing that cow possessing the wealth of all accomplishments, large eyes, full udders, fine tail, beautiful hoofs, and every other auspicious sign, and yielding much milk, she showed the animal to her husband Dyu. O thou of the prowess of the first of elephants, when Dyu was shown that cow, he began to admire her several qualities and addressing his wife, said, 'O black-eyed girl of fair thighs, this excellent cow belongeth to that Rishi whose is this delightful asylum. O slender-waisted one, that mortal who drinketh the sweet milk of this cow remaineth in unchanged youth for ten thousand years.' O best of monarchs, hearing this, the slender-waisted goddess of faultless features then addressed her lord of blazing splendour and said, 'There is on earth a friend of mine, Jitavati by name, possessed of great beauty and youth. She is the daughter of that god among men, the royal sage Usinara, endued with intelligence and devoted to truth. I desire to have this cow, O illustrious one, with her calf for that friend of mine. Therefore, O best of celestials, bring that cow so that my friend drinking of her milk may alone become on earth free from disease and decrepitude. O illustrious and blameless one, it behoveth thee to grant me this desire of mine. There is nothing that would be more agreeable to me.' On hearing these words of his wife, Dyu, moved by the desire of humouring her, stole that cow, aided by his brothers Prithu and the others. Indeed, Dyu, commanded by his lotus-eyed wife, did her bidding, forgetting at the moment the high ascetic merits of the Rishi who owned her. He did not think at the time that he was going to fall by committing the sin of stealing the cow.

"When the son of Varuna returned to his asylum in the evening with fruits he had collected, he beheld not the cow with her calf there. He began to search for them in the woods, but when the great ascetic of superior intelligence found not his cow on search, he saw by his ascetic vision that she had been stolen by the Vasus. His wrath was instantly kindled and he cursed the Vasus, saying, 'Because the Vasus have stolen my cow of sweet milk and handsome tail, therefore, shall they certainly be born on earth!'

"O thou bull of Bharata's race, the illustrious Rishi Apava thus cursed the Vasus in wrath. And having cursed them, the illustrious one set his heart once more on ascetic meditation. And after that Brahmarshi of great power and ascetic wealth had thus in wrath cursed the Vasus, the latter, O king, coming to know of it, speedily came into his asylum. And addressing the Rishi, O bull among kings, they endeavoured to pacify him. But they failed, O tiger among men, to obtain grace from Apava—that Rishi conversant, with all rules of virtue. The virtuous Apava, however, said, 'Ye Vasus, with Dhava and others, ye have been cursed by me. But ye shall be freed from my curse within a year of your birth among men. But he for whose deed ye have been cursed by me he, viz., Dyu, shall for his sinful act, have to dwell on earth for a length of time. I shall not make futile the words I have uttered in wrath. Dyu, though dwelling on Earth, shall not beget children. He shall, however, be virtuous and conversant with the scriptures. He shall be an obedient son to his father, but he shall have to abstain from the pleasure of female companionship.'

"Thus addressing the Vasus, the great Rishi went away. The Vasus then together came to me. And, O king, they begged of me the boon that as soon as they would be born, I should throw them into the water. And, O best of kings, I did as they desired, in order to free them from their earthly life. And O best of kings, from the Rishi's curse, this one only, viz., Dyu, himself, is to live on earth for some time.'

"Vaisampayana continued, 'Having said this, the goddess disappeared then and there. And taking with her the child, she went away to the region she chose. And that child of Santanu was named both Gangeya and Devavrata and excelled his father in all accomplishments.

"Santanu, after the disappearance of his wife, returned to his capital with a sorrowful heart. I shall now recount to thee the many virtues and the great good fortune of the illustrious king Santanu of the Bharata race. Indeed, it is this splendid history that is called the Mahabharata.'"

SECTION C
(Sambhava Parva continued)

"Vaisampayana said, 'The monarch Santanu, the most adored of the gods and royal sages, was known in all the worlds for his wisdom, virtues, and truthfulness (of speech). The qualities of self-control, liberality, forgiveness, intelligence, modesty, patience and superior energy ever dwelt in that bull among men, viz., Santanu, that great being endued with these accomplishments and conversant with both religion and profit, the monarch was at once the protector of the Bharata race and all human beings. His neck was marked with (three) lines, like a conch-shell; his shoulders were broad, and he resembled in prowess an infuriated elephant. It would seem that all the auspicious signs of royalty dwelt in his person, considering that to be their fittest abode. Men, seeing the behaviour of that monarch of great achievements came to know that virtue was ever superior to pleasure and profit. These were the attributes that dwelt in that great being—that bull among men—Santanu. And truly there was never a king like Santanu. All the kings of the earth, beholding him devoted to virtue, bestowed upon that foremost of virtuous men the title of King of kings. And all the kings of the earth during the time of that lord- protector of the Bharata race, were without woe and fear and anxiety of any kind. And they all slept in peace, rising from bed every morning after happy dreams. And owing to that monarch of splendid achievements resembling Indra himself in energy, all the kings of the earth became virtuous and devoted to liberality, religious acts and sacrifices. And when the earth was ruled by Santanu and other monarchs like him, the religious merits of every order increased very greatly. The Kshatriyas served the Brahmanas; the Vaisyas waited upon the Kshatriyas, and the Sudras adoring the Brahmanas and the Kshatriyas, waited upon the Vaisyas. And Santanu residing in Hastinapura, the delightful capital of the Kurus, ruled the whole earth bounded by seas. He was truthful and guileless, and like the king of the celestials himself conversant with the dictates of virtue. And from the combination in him of liberality, religion and asceticism, he acquired a great good fortune. He was free from anger and malice, and was handsome in person like Soma himself. In splendour he was like the Sun and in impetuosity of valour like Vayu. In wrath he was like Yama, and in patience like the Earth. And, O king, while Santanu ruled the earth, no deer, boars, birds, or other animals were needlessly slain. In his dominions the great virtue of kindness to all creatures prevailed, and the king himself, with the soul of mercy, and void of desire and wrath, extended equal protection unto all creatures. Then sacrifices in honour of the gods, the Rishis, and Pitris commenced, and no creature was deprived of life sinfully. And Santanu was the king and father of all— of those that were miserable and those that had no protectors, of birds and beasts, in fact, of every created thing. And during the rule of the best of Kurus— of that king of kings— speech became united with truth, and the minds of men were directed towards liberality and virtue. And Santanu, having enjoyed domestic felicity for six and thirty years, retired into the woods.

"And Santanu's son, the Vasu born of Ganga, named Devavrata resembled Santanu himself in personal beauty, in habits and behaviour, and in learning. And in all branches of knowledge worldly or spiritual his skill was very great. His strength and energy were extraordinary. He became a mighty car-warrior. In fact he was a great king.

"One day, while pursuing along the banks of the Ganges a deer that he had struck with his arrow, king Santanu observed that the river had become shallow. On observing this, that bull among men, viz., Santanu, began to reflect upon this strange phenomenon. He mentally asked why that first of rivers ran out so quickly as before. And while seeking for a cause, the illustrious monarch beheld that a youth of great comeliness, well-built and amiable person, like Indra himself, had, by his keen celestial weapon, checked the flow of the river. And the king, beholding this extraordinary feat of the river Ganga having been checked in her course near where that youth stood, became very much surprised. This youth was no other than Santanu's son himself. But as Santanu had seen his son only once a few moments after his birth, he had not sufficient recollection to identify that infant with the youth before his eyes. The youth, however, seeing his father, knew him at once, but instead of disclosing himself, he clouded the king's perception by his celestial powers of illusion and disappeared in his very sight.

"King Santanu, wondering much at what he saw and imagining the youth to be his own son then addressed Ganga and said, 'Show me that child.' Ganga thus addressed, assuming a beautiful form, and holding the boy decked with ornaments in her right arm, showed him to Santanu. And Santanu did not recognise that beautiful female bedecked with ornaments and attired in fine robes of white, although he had known her before. And Ganga said, 'O tiger among men, that eighth son whom thou hadst some time before begat upon me is this. Know that this excellent child is conversant with all weapons, O monarch, take him now. I have reared him with care. And go home, O tiger among men, taking him with thee. Endued with superior intelligence, he has studied with Vasishtha the entire Vedas with their branches. Skilled in all weapons and a mighty bowman, he is like Indra in battle. And, O Bharata, both the gods and the Asuras look upon him with favour. Whatever branches of knowledge are known to Usanas, this one knoweth completely. And so is he the master of all those Sastras that the son of Angiras (Vrihaspati) adored by the gods and the Asuras, knoweth. And all the weapons known to the powerful and invincible Rama, the son of Jamadagni are known to this thy son of mighty arms. O king of superior courage, take this thy own heroic child given unto thee by me. He is a mighty bowman and conversant with the interpretation of all treatises on the duties of a king.' Thus commanded by Ganga, Santanu took his child resembling the Sun himself in glory and returned to his capital. And having reached his city that was like unto the celestial capital, that monarch of Puru's line regarded himself greatly fortunate. And having summoned all the Pauravas together, for the protection of his kingdom he installed his son as his heir-apparent. And O bull of Bharata's race, the prince soon gratified by his behaviour his father and the other members of the Paurava race: in fact, all the subjects of the kingdom. And the king of incomparable prowess lived happily with that son of his.

"Four years had thus passed away, when the king one day went into the woods on the bank of the Yamuna. And while the king was rambling there, he perceived a sweet scent coming from an unknown direction. And the monarch, impelled by the desire of ascertaining the cause, wandered hither and thither. And in course of his ramble, he beheld a black-eyed maiden of celestial beauty, the daughter of a fisherman. The king addressing her, said, 'Who art thou, and whose daughter? What dost thou do here, O timid one?' She answered, 'Blest be thou! I am the daughter of the chief of the fishermen. At his command, I am engaged for religious merit, in rowing passengers across this river in my boat.' And Santanu, beholding that maiden of celestial form endued with beauty, amiableness, and such fragrance, desired her for his wife. And repairing unto her father, the king solicited his consent to the proposed match. But the chief of the fishermen replied to the monarch, saying, 'O king, as soon as my daughter of superior complexion was born, it was of course, understood that she should be bestowed upon a husband. But listen to the desire I have cherished all along in my heart. O sinless one, thou art truthful: if thou desirest to obtain this maiden as a gift from me, give, me then this pledge. If, indeed, thou givest the pledge, I will of course bestow my daughter upon thee for truly I can never obtain a husband for her equal to thee.'

"Santanu, hearing this, replied, 'When I have heard of the pledge thou askest, I shall then say whether I would be able to grant it. If it is capable of being granted, I shall certainly grant it. Otherwise how shall I grant it.' The fisherman said, 'O king, what I ask of thee is this: the son born of this maiden shall be installed by thee on thy throne and none else shall thou make thy successor.'

"Vaisampayana continued, 'O Bharata, when Santanu heard this, he felt no inclination to grant such a boon, though the fire of desire sorely burnt him within. The king with his heart afflicted by desire returned to Hastinapura, thinking all the way of the fisherman's daughter. And having returned home, the monarch passed his time in sorrowful meditation. One day, Devavrata approaching his afflicted father said, 'All is prosperity with thee; all chiefs obey thee; then how is it that thou grievest thus? Absorbed in thy own thoughts, thou speakest not a word to me in reply. Thou goest not out on horse-back now; thou lookest pale and emaciated, having lost all animation. I wish to know the disease thou sufferest from, so that I may endeavour to apply a remedy.' Thus addressed by his son, Santanu answered, 'Thou sayest truly, O son, that I have become melancholy. I will also tell thee why I am so. O thou of Bharata's line, thou art the only scion of this our large race. Thou art always engaged in sports of arms and achievements of prowess. But, O son, I am always thinking of the instability of human life. If any danger overtake thee, O child of Ganga, the result is that we become sonless. Truly thou alone art to me as a century of sons. I do not, therefore, desire to wed again. I only desire and pray that prosperity may ever attend thee so that our dynasty may be perpetuated. The wise say that he that hath one son hath no son. Sacrifices before fire and the knowledge of the three Vedas yield, it is true, everlasting religious merit, but all these, in point of religious merit, do not come up to a sixteenth part of the religious merit attainable on the birth of a son. Indeed, in this respect, there is hardly any difference between men and the lower animals. O wise one, I do not entertain a shadow of doubt that one attains to heaven in consequence of his having begotten a son. The Vedas which constitute the root of the Puranas and are regarded as authoritative even by the gods, contain numerous proof of this. O thou of Bharata's race, thou art a hero of excitable temper, who is always engaged in the exercise of arms. It is very probable that thou wilt be slain on the field of battle. If it so happen, what then will be the state of the Bharata dynasty, It is this thought that hath made me so melancholy. I have now told thee fully the causes of my sorrow.'

"Vaisampayana continued, 'Devavrata who was endued with great intelligence, having ascertained all this from the king, reflected within himself for a while. He then went to the old minister devoted to his father's welfare and asked him about the cause of the king's grief. O bull of Bharata's race, when the prince questioned the minister, the latter told him about the boon that was demanded by the chief of the fishermen in respect of his daughter Gandhavati. Then Devavrata, accompanied by many Kshatriya chiefs of venerable age, personally repaired to the chief of the fishermen and begged of him his daughter on behalf of the king. The chief of the fishermen received him with due adorations, and, O thou of Bharata's race, when the prince took his seat in the court of the chief, the latter addressed him and said, 'O bull among the Bharatas, thou art the first of all wielders of weapons and the only son of Santanu. Thy power is great. But I have something to tell thee. If the bride's father was Indra himself, even then he would have to repent of rejecting such an exceedingly honourable and desirable proposal of marriage. The great man of whose seed this celebrated maiden named Satyavati was born, is, indeed, equal to you in virtue. He hath spoken to me on many occasions of the virtues of thy father and told me that, the king alone is worthy of (marrying) Satyavati. Let me tell you that I have even rejected the solicitations of that best of Brahmarshis—the celestial sage Asita— who, too, had often asked for Satyavati's hand in marriage. I have only one word to say on the part of this maiden. In the matter of the proposed marriage there is one great objection founded on the fact of a rival in the person of a co-wife's son. O oppressor of all foes, he hath no security, even if he be an Asura or a Gandharva, who hath a rival in thee. There is this only objection to the proposed marriage, and nothing else. Blest be thou! But this is all I have to say in the matter of the bestowal or otherwise, of Satyavati.'

"Vaisampayana continued, 'O thou of Bharata's race, Devavrata, having heard these words, and moved by the desire of benefiting his father thus answered in the hearing of the assembled chiefs, 'O foremost of truthful men, listen to the vow I utter! The man has not been or will not be born, who will have the courage to take such a vow! I shall accomplish all that thou demandest! The son that may be born of this maiden shall be our king.' Thus addressed, the chief of the fishermen, impelled by desire of sovereignty (for his daughter's son), to achieve the almost impossible, then said, 'O thou of virtuous soul, thou art come hither as full agent on behalf of thy father Santanu of immeasurable glory; be thou also the sole manager on my behalf in the matter of the bestowal of this my daughter. But, O amiable one, there is something else to be said, something else to be reflected upon by thee. O suppressor of foes, those that have daughters, from the very nature of their obligations, must say what I say. O thou that art devoted to truth, the promise thou hast given in the presence of these chiefs for the benefit of Satyavati, hath, indeed, been worthy of thee. O thou of mighty arms, I have not the least doubt of its ever being violated by thee. But I have my doubts in respect of the children thou mayst beget.'

"Vaisampayana continued, 'O king, the son of Ganga, devoted to truth, having ascertained the scruples of the chief of the fishermen, then said, moved thereto by the desire of benefiting his father, 'Chief of fishermen, thou best of men, listen to what I say in the presence of these assembled kings. Ye kings, I have already relinquished my right to the throne, I shall now settle the matter of my children. O fisherman, from this day I adopt the vow of Brahmacharya (study and meditation in celibacy). If I die sonless, I shall yet attain to regions of perennial bliss in heaven!'

"Vaisampayana continued, 'Upon these words of the son of Ganga, the hair on the fisherman's body stood on end from glee, and he replied, 'I bestow my daughter!' Immediately after, the Apsaras and the gods with diverse tribes of Rishis began to rain down flowers from the firmament upon the head of Devavrata and exclaimed, 'This one is Bhishma (the terrible).' Bhishma then, to serve his father, addressed the illustrious damsel and said, 'O mother, ascend this chariot, and let us go unto our house.'

"Vaisampayana continued, 'Having said this, Bhishma helped the beautiful maiden into his chariot. On arriving with her at Hastinapura, he told Santanu everything as it had happened. And the assembled kings, jointly and individually, applauded his extraordinary act and said, 'He is really Bhishma (the terrible)!' And Santanu also, hearing of the extraordinary achievements of his son, became highly gratified and bestowed upon the high-souled prince the boon of death at will, saying, 'Death shall never come to thee as long as thou desirest to live. Truly death shall approach thee, O sinless one, having first obtained thy command.'"

SECTION CI
(Sambhava Parva continued)

"Vaisampayana said, 'O monarch, after the nuptials were over, king Santanu established his beautiful bride in his household. Soon after was born of Satyavati an intelligent and heroic son of Santanu named Chitrangada. He was endued with great energy and became an eminent man. The lord Santanu of great prowess also begat upon Satyavati another son named Vichitravirya, who became a mighty bowman and who became king after his father. And before that bull among men, viz., Vichitravirya, attained to majority, the wise king Santanu realised the inevitable influence of Time. And after Santanu had ascended to heaven, Bhishma, placing himself under the command of Satyavati, installed that suppressor of foes, viz., Chitrangada, on the throne, who, having soon vanquished by his prowess all monarchs, considered not any man as his equal. And beholding that he could vanquish men, Asuras, and the very gods, his namesake, the powerful king of the Gandharvas, approached him for an encounter. Between that Gandharva and that foremost one of the Kurus, who were both very powerful, there occurred on the field of Kurukshetra a fierce combat which lasted full three years on the banks of the Saraswati. In that terrible encounter characterised by thick showers of weapons and in which the combatants ground each other fiercely, the Gandharva, who had greater prowess or strategic deception, slew the Kuru prince. Having slain Chitrangada—that first of men and oppressor of foes—the Gandharva ascended to heaven. When that tiger among men endued with great prowess was slain, Bhishma, the son of Santanu, performed, O king, all his obsequies. He then installed the boy Vichitravirya of mighty arms, still in his minority, on the throne of the Kurus. And Vichitravirya, placing himself under the command of Bhishma, ruled the ancestral kingdom. And he adored Santanu's son Bhishma who was conversant with all the rules of religion and law; so, indeed, Bhishma also protected him that was so obedient to the dictates of duty.'"

SECTION CII
(Sambhava Parva continued)

"Vaisampayana said, 'O thou of Kuru's race, after Chitrangada was slain, his successor Vichitravirya being a minor, Bhishma ruled the kingdom, placing himself under the command of Satyavati. When he saw that his brother, who was the foremost of intelligent men, attained to majority, Bhishma set his heart upon marrying Vichitravirya. At this time he heard that the three daughters of the king of Kasi, all equal in beauty to the Apsaras themselves, would be married on the same occasion, selecting their husbands at a self-choice ceremony. Then that foremost of car-warriors, that vanquisher of all foes, at the command of his mother, went to the city of Varanasi in a single chariot. There Bhishma, the son of Santanu, saw that innumerable monarchs had come from all directions; and there he also saw those three maidens that would select their own husbands. And when the (assembled) kings were each being mentioned by name, Bhishma chose those maidens (on behalf of his brother). And taking them upon his chariot, Bhishma, that first of smiters in battle, addressed the kings, O monarch, and said in a voice deep as the roar of the clouds, 'The wise have directed that when an accomplished person has been invited, a maiden may be bestowed on him, decked with ornaments and along with many valuable presents. Others again may bestow their daughters by accepting a couple of kine. Some again bestow their daughters by taking a fixed sum, and some take away maidens by force. Some wed with the consent of the maidens, some by drugging them into consent, and some by going unto the maidens' parents and obtaining their sanction. Some again obtain wives as presents for assisting at sacrifices. Of these, the learned always applaud the eighth form of marriage. Kings, however, speak highly of the Swyamvara (the fifth form as above) and themselves wed according to it. But the sages have said that, that wife is dearly to be prized who is taken away by force, after the slaughter of opponents, from amidst the concourse of princes and kings invited to a self-choice ceremony. Therefore, ye monarchs, I bear away these maidens hence by force. Strive ye, to the best of your might, to vanquish me or to be vanquished. Ye monarchs, I stand here resolved to fight!' Kuru prince, endued with great energy, thus addressing the assembled monarchs and the king of Kasi, took upon his car those maidens. And having taken them up, he sped his chariot away, challenging the invited kings to a fight.

"The challenged monarchs then all stood up, slapping their arms and biting their nether lips in wrath. And loud was the din produced, as, in a great hurry, they began to cast off their ornaments and put on their armour. And the motion of their ornaments and armour, O Janamejaya, brilliant as these were, resembled meteoric flashes in the sky. And with brows contracted and eyes red with rage, the monarchs moved in impatience, their armour and ornaments dazzling or waving with their agitated steps. The charioteers soon brought handsome cars with fine horses harnessed thereto. Those splendid warriors then, equipped with all kinds of weapons, rode on those cars, and with uplifted weapons pursued the retreating chief of the Kurus. Then, O Bharata, occurred the terrible encounter between those innumerable monarchs on one side and the Kuru warrior alone on the other. And the assembled monarchs threw at their foe ten thousand arrows at the same time. Bhishma, however speedily checked those numberless arrows before they could come at him by means of a shower of his own arrows as innumerable as the down on the body. Then those kings surrounded him from all sides and rained arrows on him like masses of clouds showering on the mountain-breast. But Bhishma, arresting with his shafts the course of that arrowy downpour, pierced each of the monarchs with three shafts. The latter, in their turn pierced Bhishma, each with five shafts. But, O king, Bhishma checked those by his prowess and pierced each of the contending kings with two shafts. The combat became so fierce with that dense shower of arrows and other missiles that it looked very much like the encounter between the celestials and the Asuras of old, and men of courage who took no part in it were struck with fear even to look at the scene. Bhishma cut off, with his arrows, on the field of battle, bows, and flagstaffs, and coats of mail, and human heads by hundreds and thousands. And such was his terrible prowess and extraordinary lightness of hand, and such the skill with which he protected himself, that the contending car-warriors, though his enemies, began to applaud him loudly. Then that foremost of all wielders of weapons having vanquished in battle all those monarchs, pursued his way towards the capital of the Bharatas, taking those maidens with him.

"It was then, O king, that mighty car-warrior, king Salya of immeasurable prowess, from behind summoned Bhishma, the son of Santanu, to an encounter. And desirous of obtaining the maidens, he came upon Bhishma like a mighty leader of a herd of elephants rushing upon another of his kind, and tearing with his tusks at the latter's hips at the sight of a female elephant in heat. And Salya of mighty arms, moved by wrath addressed Bhishma and said, 'Stay, Stay.' Then Bhishma, that tiger among men, that grinder of hostile armies, provoked by these words, flamed up in wrath like a blazing fire. Bow in hand, and brow furrowed into wrinkles, he stayed on his car, in obedience to Kshatriya usage having checked its course in expectation of the enemy. All the monarchs seeing him stop, stood there to become spectators of the coming encounter between him and Salya. The two then began to exhibit their prowess (upon each other) like roaring bulls of great strength at the sight of a cow in rut. Then that foremost of men, king Salya covered Bhishma, the son of Santanu with hundreds and thousands of swift-winged shafts. And those monarchs seeing Salya thus covering Bhishma at the outset with innumerable shafts, wondered much and uttered shouts of applause. Beholding his lightness of hand in combat, the crowd of regal spectators became very glad and applauded Salya greatly. That subjugator of hostile towns, Bhishma, then, on hearing those shouts of the Kshatriyas, became very angry and said, 'Stay, Stay'. In wrath, he commanded his charioteer, saying, 'Lead thou my car to where Salya is, so that I may slay him instantly as Garuda slays a serpent.' Then the Kuru chief fixed the Varuna weapon on his bow-string, and with it afflicted the four steeds of king Salya. And, O tiger among kings, the Kuru chief, then, warding off with his weapons those of his foe, slew Salya's charioteer. Then that first of men, Bhishma, the son of Santanu, fighting for the sake of those damsels, slew with the Aindra weapon the noble steeds of his adversary. He then vanquished that best of monarchs but left him with his life. O bull of Bharata's race, Salya, after his defeat, returned to his kingdom and continued to rule it virtuously. And O conqueror of hostile towns, the other kings also, who had come to witness the self-choice ceremony returned to their own kingdoms.

"That foremost of smiters, viz., Bhishma, after defeating those monarchs, set out with those damsels, for Hastinapura whence the virtuous Kuru prince Vichitravirya ruled the earth like that best of monarchs, viz., his father Santanu. And, O king, passing through many forests, rivers, hills, and woods abounding with trees, he arrived (at the capital) in no time. Of immeasurable prowess in battle, the son of the ocean-going Ganga, having slain numberless foes in battle without a scratch on his own person, brought the daughters of the king of Kasi unto the Kurus as tenderly if they were his daughters-in-law, or younger sisters, or daughters. And Bhishma of mighty arms, impelled by the desire of benefiting his brother, having by his prowess brought them thus, then offered those maidens possessing every accomplishment unto Vichitravirya. Conversant with the dictates of virtue, the son of Santanu, having achieved such an extraordinary feat according to (kingly) custom, then began to make preparations for his brother's wedding. And when everything about the wedding had been settled by Bhishma in consultation with Satyavati, the eldest daughter of the king of Kasi, with a soft smile, told him these words, 'At heart I had chosen the king of Saubha for my husband. He had, in his heart, accepted me for his wife. This was also approved by my father. At the self-choice ceremony also I would have chosen him as my lord. Thou art conversant with all the dictates of virtue, knowing all this, do as thou likest.' Thus addressed by that maiden in the presence of the Brahmanas, the heroic Bhishma began to reflect as to what should be done. As he was conversant with the rules of virtue, he consulted with the Brahmanas who had mastered the Vedas, and permitted Amba, the eldest daughter of the ruler of Kasi to do as she liked. But he bestowed with due rites the two other daughters, Ambika and Ambalika on his younger brother Vichitravirya. And though Vichitravirya was virtuous and abstemious, yet, proud of youth and beauty, he soon became lustful after his marriage. And both Ambika and Ambalika were of tall stature, and of the complexion of molten gold. And their heads were covered with black curly hair, and their finger-nails were high and red; their hips were fat and round, and their breasts full and deep. And endued with every auspicious mark, the amiable young ladies considered themselves to be wedded to a husband who was every way worthy of themselves, and extremely loved and respected Vichitravirya. And Vichitravirya also, endued with the prowess of the celestials and the beauty of the twin Aswins, could steal the heart of any beautiful woman. And the prince passed seven years uninterruptedly in the company of his wives. He was attacked while yet in the prime of youth, with phthisis. Friends and relatives in consultation with one another tried to effect a cure. But in spite of all efforts, the Kuru prince died, setting like the evening sun. The virtuous Bhishma then became plunged into anxiety and grief, and in consultation with Satyavati caused the obsequial rites of the deceased to be performed by learned priests and the several of the Kuru race.'"

SECTION CIII
(Sambhava Parva continued)

"Vaisampayana said, 'The unfortunate Satyavati then became plunged in grief on account of her son. And after performing with her daughters-in- law the funeral rites of the deceased, consoled, as best she could, her weeping daughters-in-law and Bhishma, that foremost of all wielders of weapons. And turning her eyes to religion, and to the paternal and maternal lines (of the Kurus), she addressed Bhishma and said 'The funeral cake, the achievements, and the perpetuation of the line of the virtuous and celebrated Santanu of Kuru's race, all now depend on thee. As the attainment of heaven is inseparable from good deeds, as long life is inseparable from truth and faith, so is virtue inseparable from thee. O virtuous one, thou art well-acquainted, in detail and in the abstract, with the dictates of virtue, with various Srutis, and with all the branches of the Vedas; know very well that thou art equal unto Sukra and Angiras as regards firmness in virtue, knowledge of the particular customs of families, and readiness of inventions under difficulties. Therefore, O foremost of virtuous men, relying on thee greatly, I shall appoint thee in a certain matter. Hearing me, it behoveth thee to do my bidding. O bull among men, my son and thy brother, endued with energy and dear unto thee, hath gone childless to heaven while still a boy. These wives of thy brother, the amiable daughters of the ruler of Kasi, possessing beauty and youth, have become desirous of children. Therefore, O thou of mighty arms, at my command, raise offspring on them for the perpetuation of our line. It behoveth thee to guard virtue against loss. Install thyself on the throne and rule the kingdom of the Bharatas. Wed thou duly a wife. Plunge not thy ancestors into hell.'

"Vaisampayana continued, 'Thus addressed by his mother and friends and relatives, that oppressor of foes, the virtuous Bhishma, gave this reply conformable to the dictates of virtue, 'O mother, what thou sayest is certainly sanctioned by virtue. But thou knowest what my vow is in the matter of begetting children. Thou knowest also all that transpired in connection with thy dower. O Satyavati, I repeat the pledge I once gave, viz., I would renounce three worlds, the empire of heaven, anything that may be greater than that, but truth I would never renounce. The earth may renounce its scent, water may renounce its moisture, light may renounce its attribute of exhibiting forms, air may renounce its attribute of touch, the sun may renounce his glory, fire, its heat, the moon, his cooling rays, space, its capacity of generating sound, the slayer of Vritra, his prowess, the god of justice, his impartiality; but I cannot renounce truth.' Thus addressed by her son endued wealth of energy, Satyavati said unto Bhishma, 'O thou whose prowess is truth, I know of thy firmness in truth. Thou canst, if so minded, create, by the help of thy energy, three worlds other than those that exist. I know what thy vow was on my account. But considering this emergency, bear thou the burden of the duty that one oweth to his ancestors. O punisher of foes, act in such a way that the lineal link may not be broken and our friends and relatives may not grieve.' Thus urged by the miserable and weeping Satyavati speaking such words inconsistent with virtue from grief at the loss of her son, Bhishma addressed her again and said, 'O Queen, turn not thy eyes away from virtue. O, destroy us not. Breach of truth by a Kshatriya is never applauded in our treatises on religion. I shall soon tell thee, O Queen, what the established Kshatriya usage is to which recourse may be had to prevent Santanu's line becoming extinct on earth. Hearing me, reflect on what should be done in consultation with learned priests and those that are acquainted with practices allowable in times of emergency and distress, forgetting not at the same time what the ordinary course of social conduct is.'"

SECTION CIV
(Sambhava Parva continued)

"Bhishma continued, 'In olden days, Rama, the son of Jamadagni, in anger at the death of his father, slew with his battle axe the king of the Haihayas. And Rama, by cutting off the thousand arms of Arjuna (the Haihaya king), achieved a most difficult feat in the world. Not content with this, he set out on his chariot for the conquest of the world, and taking up his bow he cast around his mighty weapons to exterminate the Kshatriyas. And the illustrious scion of Bhrigu's race, by means of his swift arrows annihilated the Kshatriya tribe one and twenty times.

"And when the earth was thus deprived of Kshatriyas by the great Rishi, the Kshatriya ladies all over the land had offspring raised by Brahmanas skilled in the Vedas. It has been said in the Vedas that the sons so raised belongeth to him that had married the mother. And the Kshatriya ladies went in unto the Brahamanas not lustfully but from motives of virtue. Indeed, it was thus that the Kshatriya race was revived.

"In this connection there is another old history that I will recite to you. There was in olden days a wise Rishi of the name of Utathya. He had a wife of the name Mamata whom he dearly loved. One day Utathya's younger brother Vrihaspati, the priest of the celestials, endued with great energy, approached Mamata. The latter, however, told her husband's younger brother— that foremost of eloquent men—that she had conceived from her connection with his elder brother and that, therefore, he should not then seek for the consummation of his wishes. She continued, 'O illustrious Vrihaspati, the child that I have conceived hath studied in his mother's womb the Vedas with the six Angas, Semen tuum frustra perdi non potest. How can then this womb of mine afford room for two children at a time? Therefore, it behoveth thee not to seek for the consummation of thy desire at such a time.' Thus addressed by her, Vrihaspati, though possessed of great wisdom, succeeded not in suppressing his desire. Quum auten jam cum illa coiturus esset, the child in the womb then addressed him and said, 'O father, cease from thy attempt. There is no space here for two. O illustrious one, the room is small. I have occupied it first. Semen tuum perdi non potest. It behoveth thee not to afflict me.' But Vrihaspati without listening to what that child in the womb said, sought the embraces of Mamata possessing the most beautiful pair of eyes. Ille tamen Muni qui in venture erat punctum temporis quo humor vitalis jam emissum iret providens, viam per quam semen intrare posset pedibus obstruxit. Semen ita exhisum, excidit et in terram projectumest. And the illustrious Vrihaspati, beholding this, became indignant, and reproached Utathya's child and cursed him, saying, 'Because thou hast spoken to me in the way thou hast at a time of pleasure that is sought after by all creatures, perpetual darkness shall overtake thee.' And from this curse of the illustrious Vrishaspati Utathya's child who was equal unto Vrihaspati in energy, was born blind and came to be called Dirghatamas (enveloped in perpetual darkness). And the wise Dirghatamas, possessed of a knowledge of the Vedas, though born blind, succeeded yet by virtue of his learning, in obtaining for a wife a young and handsome Brahmana maiden of the name of Pradweshi. And having married her, the illustrious Dirghatamas, for the expansion of Utathya's race, begat upon her several children with Gautama as their eldest. These children, however, were all given to covetousness and folly. The virtuous and illustrious Dirghatamas possessing complete mastery over the Vedas, soon after learnt from Surabhi's son the practices of their order and fearlessly betook himself to those practices, regarding them with reverence. (For shame is the creature of sin and can never be where there is purity of intention). Then those best of Munis that dwelt in the same asylum, beholding him transgress the limits of propriety became indignant, seeing sin where sin was not. And they said, 'O, this man, transgresseth the limit of propriety. No longer doth he deserve a place amongst us. Therefore, shall we all cast this sinful wretch off.' And they said many other things regarding the Muni Dirghatamas. And his wife, too, having obtained children, became indignant with him.

"The husband then addressing his wife Pradweshi, said, 'Why is it that thou also hast been dissatisfied with me?' His wife answered, 'The husband is called the Bhartri because he supporteth the wife. He is called Pati because he protecteth her. But thou art neither, to me! O thou of great ascetic merit, on the other hand, thou hast been blind from birth, it is I who have supported thee and thy children. I shall not do so in future.'

"Hearing these words of his wife, the Rishi became indignant and said unto her and her children, 'Take me unto the Kshatriyas and thou shalt then be rich.' His wife replied (by saying), 'I desire not wealth that may be procured by thee, for that can never bring me happiness. O best of Brahmanas, do as thou likest. I shall not be able to maintain thee as before.' At these words of his wife, Dirghatamas said, 'I lay down from this day as a rule that every woman shall have to adhere to one husband for her life. Be the husband dead or alive, it shall not be lawful for a woman to have connection with another. And she who may have such connection shall certainly be regarded as fallen. A woman without husband shall always be liable to be sinful. And even if she be wealthy she shall not be able to enjoy that wealth truly. Calumny and evil report shall ever dog her.' Hearing these words of her husband Pradweshi became very angry, and commanded her sons, saying, 'Throw him into the waters of Ganga!' And at the command of their mother, the wicked Gautama and his brothers, those slaves of covetousness and folly, exclaiming, 'Indeed, why should we support this old man?—'tied the Muni to a raft and committing him to the mercy of the stream returned home without compunction. The blind old man drifting along the stream on that raft, passed through the territories of many kings. One day a king named Vali conversant with every duty went to the Ganges to perform his ablutions. And as the monarch was thus engaged, the raft to which the Rishi was tied, approached him. And as it came, the king took the old man. The virtuous Vali, ever devoted to truth, then learning who the man was that was thus saved by him, chose him for raising up offspring. And Vali said, 'O illustrious one, it behoveth thee to raise upon my wife a few sons that shall be virtuous and wise.' Thus addressed, the Rishi endued with great energy, expressed his willingness. Thereupon king Vali sent his wife Sudeshna unto him. But the queen knowing that the latter was blind and old went not unto him, she sent unto him her nurse. And upon that Sudra woman the virtuous Rishi of passions under full control begat eleven children of whom Kakshivat was the eldest. And beholding those eleven sons with Kakshivat as the eldest, who had studied all the Vedas and who like Rishis were utterers of Brahma and were possessed of great power, king Vali one day asked the Rishi saying, 'Are these children mine?' The Rishi replied, 'No, they are mine. Kakshivat and others have been begotten by me upon a Sudra woman. Thy unfortunate queen Sudeshna, seeing me blind and old, insulted me by not coming herself but sending unto me, instead, her nurse.' The king then pacified that best of Rishis and sent unto him his queen Sudeshna. The Rishi by merely touching her person said to her, 'Thou shalt have five children named Anga, Vanga, Kalinga, Pundra and Suhma, who shall be like unto Surya (Sun) himself in glory. And after their names as many countries shall be known on earth. It is after their names that their dominions have come to be called Anga, Vanga, Kalinga, Pundra and Suhma.'

"It was thus that the line of Vali was perpetuated, in days of old, by a great Rishi. And it was thus also that many mighty bowmen and great car-warriors wedded to virtue, sprung in the Kshatriya race from the seed of Brahmanas. Hearing this, O mother, do as thou likest, as regards the matter in hand.'"

SECTION CV
(Sambhava Parva continued)

"Bhishma, continued, 'Listen, O mother, to me as I indicate the means by which the Bharata line may be perpetuated. Let an accomplished Brahmana be invited by an offer of wealth, and let him raise offspring upon the wives of Vichitravirya.'

"Vaisampayana continued, 'Satyavati, then, smiling softly and in voice broken in bashfulness, addressed Bhishma saying, 'O Bharata of mighty arms, what thou sayest is true. From my confidence in thee I shall now indicate the means of perpetuating our line. Thou shall not be able to reject it, being conversant, as thou art, with the practices permitted in seasons of distress. In our race, thou art Virtue, and thou art Truth, and thou art, too, our sole refuge. Therefore hearing what I say truly, do what may be proper.

"My father was a virtuous man. For virtue's sake he had kept a (ferry) boat. One day, in the prime of my youth, I went to ply that boat. It so happened that the great and wise Rishi Parasara, that foremost of all virtuous men, came, and betook himself to my boat for crossing the Yamuna. As I was rowing him across the river, the Rishi became excited with desire and began to address me in soft words. The fear of my father was uppermost in my mind. But the terror of the Rishi's curse at last prevailed. And having obtained from him a precious boon, I could not refuse his solicitations. The Rishi by his energy brought me under his complete control, and gratified his desire then and there, having first enveloped the region in a thick fog. Before this there was a revolting fishy odour in my body; but the Rishi dispelled it and gave me my present fragrance. The Rishi also told me that by bringing forth his child in an island of the river, I would still continue (to be) a virgin. And the child of Parasara so born of me in my maidenhood hath become a great Rishi endued with large ascetic powers and known by the name of Dwaipayana (the island-born). That illustrious Rishi having by his ascetic power divided the Vedas into four parts hath come to be called on earth by the name of Vyasa (the divider or arranger), and for his dark colour, Krishna (the dark). Truthful in speech, free from passion, a mighty ascetic who hath burnt all his sins, he went away with his father immediately after his birth. Appointed by me and thee also, that Rishi of incomparable splendour will certainly beget good children upon the wives of thy brother. He told me when he went away, 'Mother, think of me when thou art in difficulty.' I will now call him up, if thou, O Bhishma of mighty arms so desirest. If thou art willing, O Bhishma, I am sure that great ascetic will beget children upon Vichitravirya's field.'

"Vaisampayana continued, 'Mention being made of the great Rishi, Bhishma with joined palms said, 'That man is truly intelligent who fixes his eyes judiciously on virtue, profit, and pleasure, and who after reflecting with patience, acteth in such a way that virtue may lead to future virtue, profit to future profit and pleasure to future pleasure. Therefore, that which hath been said by thee and which, besides being beneficial to us, is consistent with virtue, is certainly the best advice and hath my full approval.' And when Bhishma had said this, O thou of Kuru's race, Kali (Satyavati) thought of the Muni Dwaipayana and Dwaipayana who was then engaged in interpreting the Vedas, learning that he was being called up by his mother, came instantly unto her without anybody's knowing it. Satayavati then duly greeted her son and embraced him with arms, bathing him in her tears, for the daughter of the fisherman wept bitterly at the sight of her son after so long a time. And her first son, the great Vyasa, beholding her weeping, washed her with cool water, and bowing unto her, said, 'I have come, O mother, to fulfil thy wishes. Therefore, O virtuous one, command me without delay. I shall accomplish thy desire.' The family priest of the Bharatas then worshipped the great Rishi duly, and the latter accepted the offerings of worship, uttering the usual mantras. And gratified with the worship he received, he took his seat. Satyavati, beholding him seated at his ease, after the usual inquiries, addressed him and said, 'O learned one, sons derive their birth both from the father and the mother. They are, therefore, the common property of both parents. There cannot be the least doubt about it that the mother hath as much power over them as the father. As thou art, indeed, my eldest son according to the ordinance, O Brahmarshi, so is Vichitravirya my youngest son. And as Bhishma is Vichitravirya's brother on the father's side, so art thou his brother on the same mother's side. I do not know what you may think, but this is what, O son, I think. This Bhishma, the son of Santanu, devoted to truth, doth not, for the sake of truth, entertain the desire of either begetting children or ruling the kingdom. Therefore, from affection for thy brother Vichitravirya, for the perpetuation of our dynasty, for the sake of this Bhishma's request and my command, for kindness to all creatures, for the protection of the people and from the liberality of thy heart, O sinless one, it behoveth thee to do what I say. Thy younger brother hath left two widows like unto the daughters of the celestials themselves, endued with youth and great beauty. For the sake of virtue and religion, they have become desirous of offspring. Thou art the fittest person to be appointed. Therefore beget upon them children worthy of our race and for the continuance of our line.'

"Vyasa, hearing this, said, 'O Satyavati, thou knowest what virtue is both in respect of this life and the other. O thou of great wisdom, thy affections also are set on virtue. Therefore, at thy command, making virtue my motive, I shall do what thou desirest. Indeed, this practice that is conformable to the true and eternal religion is known to me. I shall give unto my brother children that shall be like unto Mitra and Varuna. Let the ladies then duly observe for one full year the vow I indicate. They shall then be purified. No women shall ever approach me without having observed a rigid vow.'

"Satyavati then said, 'O sinless one, it must be as thou sayest. Take such steps that the ladies may conceive immediately. In a kingdom where there is no king, the people perish from want of protection; sacrifices and other holy acts are suspended; the clouds send no showers; and the gods disappear. How can a kingdom be protected that hath no king? Therefore, see thou that the ladies conceive. Bhishma will watch over the children as long as they are in their mother's wombs.

"Vyasa replied, 'If I am to give unto my brother children so unseasonably, then let the ladies bear my ugliness. That in itself shall, in their case, be the austerest of penances. If the princess of Kosala can bear my strong odour, my ugly and grim visage, my attire and body, she shall then conceive an excellent child.'"

"Vaisampayana continued, 'Having spoken thus unto Satyavati, Vyasa of great energy addressed her and said, 'Let the princess of Kosala clad in clean attire and checked with ornaments wait for me in her bed-chamber.' Saying this, the Rishi disappeared, Satyavati then went to her daughter-in- law and seeing her in private spoke to her these words of beneficial and virtuous import, 'O princess of Kosala, listen to what I say. It is consistent with virtue. The dynasty of the Bharatas hath become extinct from my misfortune. Beholding my affliction and the extinction of his paternal line, the wise Bhishma, impelled also by the desire of perpetuating our race, hath made me a suggestion, which suggestion, however, for its accomplishment is dependent on thee. Accomplish it, O daughter, and restore the lost line of the Bharatas. O thou of fair hips, bring thou forth a child equal in splendour unto the chief of the celestials. He shall bear the onerous burden of this our hereditary kingdom.'

"Satyavati having succeeded with great difficulty in procuring the assent of her virtuous daughter-in-law to her proposal which was not inconsistent with virtue, then fed Brahmanas and Rishis and numberless guests who arrived on the occasion.'"

SECTION CVI
(Sambhava Parva continued)

"Vaisampayana said, 'Soon after the monthly season of the princess of Kosala had been over, Satyavati, purifying her daughter-in-law with a bath, led her into the sleeping apartment. There seating her upon a luxurious bed, she addressed her, saying, 'O Princess of Kosala, thy husband hath an elder brother who shall this day enter thy womb as thy child. Wait for him tonight without dropping off to sleep.' Hearing these words of her mother- in-law, the amiable princess, as she lay on her bed, began to think of Bhishma and the other elders of the Kuru race. Then the Rishi of truthful speech, who had given his promise in respect of Amvika (the eldest of the princesses) in the first instance, entered her chamber while the lamp was burning. The princess, seeing his dark visage, his matted locks of copper hue, blazing eyes, his grim beard, closed her eyes in fear. The Rishi, from desire of accomplishing his mother's wishes, however knew her. But the latter, struck with fear, opened not her eyes even once to look at him. And when Vyasa came out, he was met by his mother, who asked him, 'Shall the princess have an accomplished son?' Hearing her, he replied, 'The son of the princess she will bring forth shall be equal in might unto ten thousand elephants. He will be an illustrious royal sage, possessed of great learning and intelligence and energy. The high-souled one shall have in his time a century of sons. But from the fault of his mother he shall be blind.' At these words of her son, Satyavati said, 'O thou of ascetic wealth, how can one that is blind become a monarch worthy of the Kurus? How can one that is blind become the protector of his relatives and family, and the glory of his father's race? It behoveth thee to give another king unto the Kurus.' Saying, 'So be it,' Vyasa went away. And the first princess of Kosala in due time brought forth a blind son.

"Soon after Satyavati, O chastiser of foes, summoned Vyasa, after having secured the assent of her daughter-in-law. Vyasa came according to his promise, and approached, as before, the second wife of his brother. And Ambalika beholding the Rishi, became pale with fear. And, O Bharata, beholding her so afflicted and pale with fear, Vyasa addressed her and said, 'Because thou hast been pale with fear at the sight of my grim visage, therefore, thy child shall be pale in complexion. O thou of handsome face, the name also thy child shall bear will be Pandu (the pale).' Saying this, the illustrious and best of Rishis came out of her chamber. And as he came out, he was met by his mother who asked him about the would-be-child. The Rishi told her that the child would be of pale complexion and known by the name of Pandu. Satyavati again begged of the Rishi another child, and the Rishi told her in reply, 'So be it.' Ambalika, then, when her time came, brought forth a son of pale complexion. Blazing with beauty the child was endued with all auspicious marks. Indeed, it was this child who afterwards became the father of those mighty archers, the Pandavas.

"Some time after, when the oldest of Vichitravirya's widows again had her monthly season, she was solicited by Satyavati to approach Vyasa once again. Possessed of beauty like a daughter of a celestial, the princess refused to do her mother-in-law's bidding, remembering the grim visage and strong odour of the Rishi. She, however, sent unto him a maid of hers, endued with the beauty of an Apsara and decked with her own ornaments. And when the Vyasa arrived, the maid rose up and saluted him. And she waited upon him respectfully and took her seat near him when asked. And, O king, the great Rishi of rigid vows, was well-pleased with her, and when he rose to go away, he addressed her and said, 'Amiable one, thou shalt no longer be a slave. Thy child also shall be greatly fortunate and virtuous, and the foremost of all intelligent men on earth!' And, O king, the son thus begotten upon her by Krishna-Dwaipayana was afterwards known by the name of Vidura. He was thus the brother of Dhritarashtra and the illustrious Pandu. And Vidura was free from desire and passion and was conversant with the rules of government, and was the god of justice born on earth under the curse of the illustrious Rishi Mandavya. And Krishna-Dwaipayana, when he met his mother as before, informed her as to how he had been deceived by the seniormost of the princesses and how he had begotten a son upon a Sudra woman. And having spoken thus unto his mother the Rishi disappeared from her sight.

"Thus were born, in the field of Vichitravirya, even of Dwaipayana those sons of the splendour of celestial children, those propagators of the Kuru race.'"

SECTION CVII
(Sambhava Parva continued)

"Janamejaya said, 'What did the god of justice do for which he was cursed? And who was the Brahmana ascetic from whose curse the god had to be born in the Sudra caste?'

"Vaisampayana said, 'There was a Brahmana known by the name of Mandavya. He was conversant with all duties and was devoted to religion, truth and asceticism. The great ascetic used to sit at the entrance of his hermitage at the foot of a tree, with his arms upraised in the observance of the vow of silence. And as he sat there for years together, one day there came into his asylum a number of robbers laden with spoil. And, O bull in Bharata's race, those robbers were then being pursued by a superior body as guardians of the peace. The thieves, on entering that asylum, hid their booty there, and in fear concealed themselves thereabout before the guards came. But scarcely had they thus concealed themselves when the constables in pursuit came to the spot. The latter, observing the Rishi sitting under the tree, questioned him, O king, saying, 'O best of Brahmanas, which way have the thieves taken? Point it out to us so that we may follow it without loss of time.' Thus questioned by the guardians of peace the ascetic, O king, said not a word, good or otherwise, in reply. The officers of the king, however, on searching that asylum soon discovered the thieves concealed thereabout together with the plunder. Upon this, their suspicion fell upon the Muni, and accordingly they seized him with the thieves and brought him before the king. The king sentenced him to be executed along with his supposed associates. And the officers, acting in ignorance, carried out the sentence by impaling the celebrated Rishi. And having impaled him, they went to the king with the booty they had recovered. But the virtuous Rishi, though impaled and kept without food, remained in that state for a long time without dying. And the Rishi by his ascetic power not only preserved his life but summoned other Rishi to the scene. And they came there in the night in the forms of birds, and beholding him engaged in ascetic meditation though

THE MAHABHARATA

fixed on that stake, became plunged into grief. And telling that best of Brahmanas who they were, they asked him saying, 'O Brahmana, we desire to know what hath been thy sin for which thou hast thus been made to suffer the tortures of impalement!'"

SECTION CVIII
(Sambhava Parva continued)

"Vaisampayana said, 'Thus asked, the tiger among Munis then answered those Rishis of ascetic wealth, 'Whom shall I blame for this? In fact, none else (than my own self) hath offended against me!' After this, O monarch, the officers of justice, seeing him alive, informed the king of it. The latter hearing what they said, consulted with his advisers, and came to the place and began to pacify the Rishi, fixed on the stake. And the king said, 'O thou best of Rishis, I have offended against thee in ignorance. I beseech thee to pardon me for the same. It behoveth thee not to be angry with me.' Thus addressed by the king, the Muni was pacified. And beholding him free from wrath, the king took him up with the stake and endeavoured to extract it from his body. But not succeeding therein, he cut it off at the point just outside the body. The Muni, with a portion of the stake within his body, walked about, and in that state practised the austerest of penances and conquered numberless regions unattainable by others. And for the circumstances of a part of the stake being within his body, he came to be known in the three worlds by the name of Ani-Mandavya (Mandavya with the stake within). And one day that Brahamana acquainted with the highest truth of religion went unto the abode of the god of justice. And beholding the god there seated on his throne, the Rishi reproached him and said, 'What, pray, is that sinful act committed by me unconsciously, for which I am bearing this punishment? O, tell me soon, and behold the power of my asceticism.'

"The god of justice, thus questioned, replied, 'O thou of ascetic wealth, a little insect was once pierced by thee on a blade of grass. Thou bearest now the consequence of the act. O Rishi, as a gift, however small, multiplieth in respect of its religious merits, so a sinful act multiplieth in respect of the woe it bringeth in its train.' On hearing this, Ani-Mandavya asked, 'O tell me truly when this act was committed by me.' Told in reply by the god of justice that he had committed it when a child, the Rishi said, 'That shall not be a sin which may be done by a child up to the twelfth year of his age from birth. The scriptures shall not recognise it as sinful. The punishment thou hast inflicted on me for such a venial offence hath been disproportionate in severity. The killing of a Brahmana involves a sin that is heavier than the killing of any other living being. Thou shall, therefore, O god of justice, have to be born among men even in the Sudra order. And from this day I establish this limit in respect of the consequence of acts that an act shall not be sinful when committed by one below the age of fourteen. But when committed by one above that age, it shall be regarded as sin.'

"Vaisampayana continued, 'Cursed for this fault by that illustrious Rishi, the god of justice had his birth as Vidura in the Sudra order. And Vidura was well-versed in the doctrines of morality and also politics and worldly profit. And he was entirely free from covetousness and wrath. Possessed of great foresight and undisturbed tranquillity of mind, Vidura was ever devoted to the welfare of the Kurus.'"

SECTION CIX
(Sambhava Parva continued)

"Vaisampayana said, 'Upon the birth of those three children, Kurujangala, Kurukshetra, and the Kurus grew in prosperity. The earth began to yield abundant harvest, and the crops also were of good flavour. And the clouds began to pour rain in season and trees became full of fruits and flowers. And the draught cattle were all happy and the birds and other animals rejoiced exceedingly. And the flowers became fragrant and the fruits became sweet; the cities and towns became filled with merchants, artisans, traders and artists of every description. And the people became brave, learned, honest and happy. And there were no robbers then, nor anybody who was sinful. And it seemed that the golden age had come upon every part of the kingdom. And the people devoted to virtuous acts, sacrifices and truth, and regarding one another with love and affection grew in prosperity. And free from pride, wrath and covetousness, they rejoiced in perfectly innocent sports. And the capital of the Kurus, full as the ocean, was a second Amaravati, teeming with hundreds of palaces and mansions, and possessing gates and arches dark as the clouds. And men in great cheerfulness sported constantly on rivers, lakes and tanks, and in fine groves and charming woods. And the southern Kurus, in their virtuous rivalry with their northern kinsmen, walked about in the company of Siddhas and Charanas and Rishis. And all over that delightful country whose prosperity was thus increased by the Kurus, there were no misers and no widowed women. And the wells and lakes were ever full; the groves abounded with trees, and the houses and abodes of Brahmanas were full of wealth and the whole kingdom was full of festivities. And, O king, virtuously ruled by Bhishma, the kingdom was adorned with hundreds of sacrificial stakes. And the wheel of virtue having been set in motion by Bhishma, and the country became so contented that the subjects of other kingdoms, quitting their homes, came to dwell there and increase its population. And the citizens and the people were filled with hope, upon seeing the youthful acts of their illustrious princes. And, O king, in the house of the Kuru chiefs as also of the principal citizens, 'give', 'eat' were the only words constantly heard. And Dhritarashtra and Pandu and Vidura of great intelligence were from their birth brought up by Bhishma, as if they were his own sons. And the children, having passed through the usual rites of their order, devoted themselves to vows and study. And they grew up into fine young men skilled in the Vedas and all athletic sports. And they became well-skilled in the practice of bow, in horsemanship, in encounters with mace, sword and shield, in the management of elephants in battle, and in the science of morality. Well-read in history and the Puranas and various branches of learning, and acquainted with the truths of the Vedas and their branches they acquired knowledge, which was versatile and deep. And Pandu, possessed of great prowess, excelled all men in archery while Dhritarashtra excelled all in personal strength, while in the three worlds there was no one equal to Vidura in devotion to virtue and in the knowledge of the dictates of morality. And beholding the restoration of the extinct line of Santanu, the saying became current in all countries that among mothers of heroes, the daughters of the king of Kasi were the first; that among countries Kurujangala was the first; that among virtuous men, Vidura was the first; that among cities Hastinapura was the first. Pandu became king, for Dhritarashtra, owing to the blindness, and Vidura, for his birth by a Sudra woman, did not obtain the kingdom. One day Bhishma, the foremost of those acquainted with the duties of a statesman and dictates of morality, properly addressing Vidura conversant with the truth of religion and virtue, said as follows."

SECTION CX
(Sambhava Parva continued)

"Bhishma said, 'This our celebrated race, resplendent with every virtue and accomplishment, hath all along sovereignty over all other monarchs on earth. Its glory maintained and itself perpetuated by many virtuous and illustrious monarchs of old, the illustrious Krishna (Dwaipayana) and Satyavati and myself have raised you (three) up, in order that it may not be extinct. It behoveth myself and thee also to take such steps that this our dynasty may expand again as the sea. It hath been heard by me that there are three maidens worthy of being allied to our race. One is the daughter of (Surasena of) the Yadava race; the other is the daughter of Suvala; and the third is the princess of Madra. O son, all these maidens are of course of blue blood. Possessed of beauty and pure blood, they are eminently fit for an alliance with our family. O thou foremost of intelligent men, I think we should choose them for the growth of our race. Tell me what thou thinkest.' Thus addressed, Vidura replied, 'Thou art our father and thou art our mother, too. Thou art our respected spiritual instructor. Therefore, do thou what may be best for us in thy eyes.'

"Vaisampayana continued, 'Soon after Bhishma heard from the Brahmanas that Gandhari, the amiable daughter of Suvala, having worshipped Hara (Siva) had obtained from the deity the boon that she should have a century of sons. Bhishma, the grandfather of the Kurus, having heard this, sent messengers unto the king of Gandhara. King Suvala at first hesitated on account of the blindness of the bridegroom, but taking into consideration the blood of the Kurus, their fame and behaviour, he gave his virtuous daughter unto Dhritarashtra and the chaste Gandhari hearing that Dhritarashtra was blind and that her parents had consented to marry her to him, from love and respect for her future husband, blindfolded her own eyes.

Sakuni, the son of Suvala, bringing unto the Kurus his sister endued with youth and beauty, formally gave her away unto Dhritarashtra. And Gandhari was received with great respect and the nuptials were celebrated with great pomp under Bhishma's directions. And the heroic Sakuni, after having bestowed his sister along with many valuable robes, and having received Bhishma's adorations, returned to his own city. And, O thou of Bharata's race, the beautiful Gandhari gratified all the Kurus by her behaviour and respectful attentions. And Gandhari, ever devoted to her husband, gratified her superiors by her good conduct; and as she was chaste, she never referred even by words to men other than her husband or such superiors.'"

SECTION CXI
(Sambhava Parva continued)

"Vaisampayana continued, 'There was amongst the Yadavas a chief named Sura. He was the father of Vasudeva. And he had a daughter called Pritha, who was unrivalled for beauty on earth. And, O thou of Bharata's race, Sura, always truthful in speech, gave from friendship this his firstborn daughter unto his childless cousin and friend, the illustrious Kuntibhoja— the son of his paternal aunt—pursuant to a former promise. And Pritha in the house of her adoptive father was engaged in looking after the duties of hospitality to Brahmanas and other guests. Once she gratified by her attentions the terrible Brahmana of rigid vows, who was known by the name of Durvasa and was well-acquainted with the hidden truths of morality. Gratified with her respectful attentions, the sage, anticipating by his spiritual power the future (season of) distress (consequent upon the curse to be pronounced upon Pandu for his unrighteous act of slaying a deer while serving its mate) imparted to her a formula of invocation for summoning any of the celestials she liked to give her children. And the Rishi said, 'Those celestials that thou shall summon by this Mantra shall certainly approach thee and give thee children.' Thus addressed by the Brahmana, the amiable Kunti (Pritha) became curious, and in her maidenhood summoned the god Arka (Sun). And as soon as he pronounced the Mantra, she beheld that effulgent deity—that beholder of everything in the world— approaching her. And beholding that extraordinary sight, the maiden of faultless features was overcome with surprise. But the god Vivaswat (Sun) approaching her, said, 'Here I am, O black-eyed girl! Tell me what I am to do for thee.'

"Hearing this, Kunti said, 'O slayer of foes, a certain Brahamana gave me this formula of invocation as a boon, and, O lord, I have summoned thee only to test its efficacy. For this offence I bow to thee. A woman, whatever be her offence, always deserveth pardon.' Surya (Sun) replied, 'I know that Durvasa hath granted this boon. But cast off thy fears, timid maiden, and grant me thy embraces. Amiable one, my approach cannot be futile; it must bear fruit. Thou hast summoned me, and if it be for nothing, it shall certainly be regarded as thy transgression.'

"Vaisampayana continued, 'Vivaswat thus spoke unto her many things with a view to allay her fears, but, O Bharata, the amiable maiden, from modesty and fear of her relatives, consented not to grant his request. And, O bull of Bharata's race, Arka addressed her again and said, 'O princess, for my sake, it shall not be sinful for thee to grant my wish.' Thus speaking unto the daughter of Kuntibhoja, the illustrious Tapana—the illuminator of the universe—gratified his wish. And of this connection there was immediately born a son known all over the world as Karna accountred with natural armour and with face brightened by ear-rings. And the heroic Karna was the first of all wielders of weapons, blessed with good fortune, and endued with the beauty of a celestial child. And after the birth of this child, the illustrious Tapana granted unto Pritha her maidenhood and ascended to heaven. And the princess of the Vrishni race beholding with sorrow that son born of her, reflected intently upon what was then the best for her to do. And from fear of her relatives she resolved to conceal that evidence of her folly. And she cast her offspring endued with great physical strength into the water. Then the well-known husband of Radha, of the Suta caste, took up the child thus cast into the water, and he and his wife brought him up as their own son. And Radha and her husband bestowed on him the name of Vasusena (born with wealth) because he was born with a natural armour and ear-rings. And endued as he was born with great strength, as he grew up, he became skilled in all weapons. Possessed of great energy, he used to adore the sun until his back was heated by his rays (i.e., from dawn to midday), and during the hours of worship, there was nothing on earth that the heroic and intelligent Vasusena would not give unto the Brahmanas. And Indra desirous of benefiting his own son Phalguni (Arjuna), assuming the form of a Brahmana, approached Vasusena on one occasion and begged of him his natural armour. Thus

141

asked Karna took off his natural armour, and joining his hands in reverence gave it unto Indra in the guise of a Brahmana. And the chief of the celestials accepted the gift and was exceedingly gratified with Karna's liberality. He therefore, gave unto him a fine dart, saying, 'That one (and one only) among the celestials, the Asuras, men, the Gandharvas, the Nagas, and the Rakshasas, whom thou desirest to conquer, shall be certainly slain with this dart.'

"The son of Surya was before this known by the name of Vasusena. But since he cut off his natural armour, he came to be called Karna (the cutter or peeler of his own cover)."'

SECTION CXII
(Sambhava Parva continued)

"Vaisampayana said. 'The large-eyed daughter of Kuntibhoja, Pritha by name, was endued with beauty and every accomplishment. Of rigid vows, she was devoted to virtue and possessed of every good quality. But though endued with beauty and youth and every womanly attribute, yet it so happened that no king asked for her hand. Her father Kuntibhoja seeing this, invited, O best of monarchs, the princes and kings of other countries and desired his daughter to select her husband from among her guests. The intelligent Kunti, entering the amphitheatre, beheld Pandu—the foremost of the Bharatas—that tiger among kings—in that concourse of crowned heads. Proud as the lion, broad-chested, bull-eyed, endued with great strength, and outshining all other monarchs in splendour, he looked like another Indra in that royal assemblage. The amiable daughter of Kuntibhoja, of faultless features, beholding Pandu—that best of men—in that assembly, became very much agitated. And advancing with modesty, all the while quivering with emotion, she placed the nuptial garland about Pandu's neck. The other monarchs, seeing Kunti choose Pandu for her lord, returned to their respective kingdoms on elephants, horses and cars, as they had come. Then, O king, the bride's father caused the nuptial rites to be performed duly. The Kuru prince blessed with great good fortune and the daughter of Kuntibhoja formed a couple like Maghavat and Paulomi (the king and queen of the celestials). And, O best of Kuru monarchs, king Kuntibhoja, after the nuptials were over, presented his son-in-law with much wealth and sent him back to his capital. Then the Kuru prince Pandu, accompanied by a large force bearing various kinds of banners and pennons, and eulogised by Brahmanas and great Rishis pronouncing benedictions, reached his capital. And after arriving at his own palace, he established his queen therein."'

SECTION CXIII
(Sambhava Parva continued)

"Vaisampayana continued, 'Some time after, Bhishma the intelligent son of Santanu set his heart upon getting Pandu married to a second wife. Accompanied by an army composed of four kinds of force, and also by aged councillors and Brahmanas and great Rishis, he went to the capital of the king of Madra. And that bull of the Valhikas—the king of Madra—hearing that Bhishma had arrived, went out to receive him. And having received him with respect, he got him to enter his palace. Arriving there, the king of Madra offered unto Bhishma a white carpet for a seat; water to wash his feet with, and usual oblation of various ingredients indicative of respect. And when he was seated at ease, the king asked him about the reason of his visit. Then Bhishma—the supporter of the dignity of the Kurus—addressed the king of Madra and said, 'O oppressor of all foes, know that I have come for the hand of a maiden. It hath been heard by us that thou hast a sister named Madri celebrated for her beauty and endued with every virtue; I would chose her for Pandu. Thou art, O king, in every respect worthy of an alliance with us, and we also are worthy of thee. Reflecting upon all this, O king of Madra, accept us duly.' The ruler of Madra, thus addressed by Bhishma, replied, 'To my mind, there is none else than one of thy family with whom I can enter into an alliance. But there is a custom in our family observed by our ancestors, which, be it good or bad, I am incapable of transgressing. It is well-known, and therefore is known to thee as well, I doubt not. Therefore, it is not proper for thee to say to me,—Bestow thy sister. The custom to which I allude is our family custom. With us that is a virtue and worthy of observance. It is for this only, O slayer of foes, I cannot give thee any assurance in the matter of thy request.' On hearing this, Bhishma answered the king of Madra, saying, 'O king, this, no doubt, is a virtue. The self-create himself hath said it. Thy ancestors were observant of custom. There is no fault to find with it. It is also well-known, O Salya, that this custom in respect of family dignity hath the approval of the wise and the good.' Saying this Bhishma of great energy gave unto Salya much gold both coined and uncoined, and precious stones of various colours by thousands, and elephants and horses and cars, and much cloth and many ornaments, and gems and pearls and corals. And Salya accepting with a cheerful heart those precious gifts then gave away his sister decked in ornaments unto that bull of the Kuru race. Then the wise Bhishma, the son of the oceangoing Ganga, rejoiced at the issue of his mission, took Madri with him, and returned to the Kuru capital named after the elephant.

"Then selecting an auspicious day and moment as indicated by the wise for the ceremony, King Pandu was duly united with Madri. And after the nuptials were over, the Kuru king established his beautiful bride in handsome apartments. And, O king of kings, that best of monarchs then gave himself up to enjoyment in the company of his two wives as best he liked and to the limit of his desires. And after thirty days had elapsed, the Kuru king, O monarch, started from his capital for the conquest of the world. And after reverentially saluting and bowing to Bhishma and the other elders of the Kuru race, and with adieus to Dhritarashtra and others of the family, and obtaining their leave, he set out on his grand campaign, accompanied by a large force of elephants, horses, and cars, and well- pleased with the blessings uttered by all around and the auspicious rites performed by the citizens for his success. And Pandu, accompanied by such a strong force marched against various foes. And that tiger among men— that spreader of the fame of the Kurus—first subjugated the robber tribes of asarna. He next turned his army composed of innumerable elephants, cavalry, infantry, and charioteers, with standards of various colours against Dhirga—the ruler of the kingdom of Maghadha who was proud of his strength, and offended against numerous monarchs. And attacking him in his capital, Pandu slew him there, and took everything in his treasury and also vehicles and draught animals without number. He then marched into Mithila and subjugated the Videhas. And then, O bull among men, Pandu led his army against Kasi, Sumbha, and Pundra, and by the strength and prowess of his arms spread the fame of the Kurus. And Pandu, that oppressor of foes, like unto a mighty fire whose far-reaching flames were represented by his arrows and splendour by his weapons, began to consume all kings that came in contact with him. These with their forces, vanquished by Pandu at the head of his army, were made the vassals of the Kurus. And all kings of the world, thus vanquished by him, regarded him as the one single hero on earth even as the celestials regard Indra in heaven. And the kings of earth with joined palms bowed to him and waited on him with presents of various kinds of gems and wealth, precious stones and pearls and corals, and much gold and silver, and first-class kine and handsome horses and fine cars and elephants, and asses and camels and buffaloes, and goats and sheep, and blankets and beautiful hides, and cloths woven out of furs. And the king of Hastinapura accepting those offerings retraced his steps towards his capital, to the great delight of his subjects. And the citizens and others filled with joy, and kings and ministers, all began to say, 'O, the fame of the achievements of Santanu, that tiger among kings, and of the wise Bharata, which were about to die, hath been revived by Pandu. They who robbed before the Kurus of both territory and wealth have been subjugated by Pandu—the tiger of Hastinapura—and made to pay tribute.' And all the citizens with Bhishma at their head went out to receive the victorious king. They had not proceeded far when they saw the attendants of the king laden with much wealth, and the train of various conveyances laden with all kinds of wealth, and of elephants, horses, cars, kine, camels and other animals, was so long that they saw not its end. Then Pandu, beholding Bhishma, who was a father to him, worshipped his feet and saluted the citizens and others as each deserved. And Bhishma, too, embracing Pandu as his son who had returned victorious after grinding many hostile kingdoms, wept tears of joy. And Pandu, instilling joy into the hearts of his people with a flourish of trumpets and conchs and kettle- drums, entered his capital.'"

SECTION CXIV
(Sambhava Parva continued)

"Vaisampayana said, 'Pandu, then, at the command of Dhritarashtra, offered the wealth he had acquired by the prowess of his arms to Bhishma, their grand-mother Satyavati and their mothers. And he sent portion of his wealth to Vidura also. And the virtuous Pandu gratified his other relatives also with similar presents. Then Satyavati and Bhishma and the Kosala princes were all gratified with the presents Pandu made out of the acquisitions of his prowess. And Ambalika in particular, upon embracing her son of incomparable prowess, became as glad as the queen of heaven upon embracing Jayanta. And with the wealth acquired by that hero Dhritarashtra performed five great sacrifices that were equal unto a hundred great horse-sacrifices, at all of which the offerings to Brahmanas were by hundreds and thousands.

"A little while after, O bull of Bharata's race, Pandu who had achieved a victory over sloth and lethargy, accompanied by his two wives, Kunti and Madri, retired into the woods. Leaving his excellent palace with its luxurious beds, he became a permanent inhabitant of the woods, devoting the whole of his time to the chase of the deer. And fixing his abode in a delightful and hilly region overgrown with huge sala trees, on the southern slope of the Himavat mountains, he roamed about in perfect freedom. The handsome Pandu with his two wives wandered in those woods like Airavata accompanied by two she-elephants. And the dwellers in those woods, beholding the heroic Bharata prince in the company of his wives, armed with sword, arrows, and bow, clad with his beautiful armour, and skilled in all excellent weapons, regarded him as the very god wandering amongst them.

"And at the command of Dhritarashtra, people were busy in supplying Pandu in his retirement with every object of pleasure and enjoyment.

"Meanwhile the son of the ocean-going Ganga heard that king Devaka had a daughter endued with youth and beauty and begotten upon a Sudra wife. Bringing her from her father's abode, Bhishma married her to Vidura of great wisdom. And Vidura begot upon her many children like unto himself in accomplishments.'"

SECTION CXV
(Sambhava Parva continued)

"Vaisampayana said, 'Meanwhile, O Janamejaya, Dhritarashtra begat upon Gandhari a hundred sons, and upon a Vaisya wife another besides those hundred. And Pandu had, by his two wives Kunti and Madri, five sons who were great charioteers and who were all begotten by the celestials for the perpetuation of the Kuru line.'

"Janamejaya said, 'O best of Brahmanas, how did Gandhari bring forth those hundred sons and in how many years? What were also the periods of life allotted to each? How did Dhritarashtra also beget another son in a Vaisya wife? How did Dhritarashtra behave towards his loving obedient, and virtuous wife Gandhari? How were also begotten the five sons of Pandu, those mighty charioteers, even though Pandu himself laboured under the curse of the great Rishi (he slew)? Tell me all this in detail, for my thirst for hearing everything relating to my own ancestor hath not been slaked.'

"Vaisampayana said, 'One day Gandhari entertained with respectful attention the great Dwaipayana who came to her abode, exhausted with hunger and fatigue. Gratified with Gandhari's hospitality, the Rishi gave her the boon she asked for, viz., that she should have a century of sons each equal unto her lord in strength and accomplishments. Some time after Gandhari conceived and she bore the burden in her womb for two long years without being delivered. And she was greatly afflicted at this. It was then that she heard that Kunti had brought forth a son whose splendour was like unto the morning sun. Impatient of the period of gestation which had prolonged so long, and deprived of reason by grief, she struck her womb with great violence without the knowledge of her husband. And thereupon came out of her womb, after two years' growth, a hard mass of flesh like unto an iron ball. When she was about to throw it away, Dwaipayana, learning everything by his spiritual powers, promptly came there, and that first of ascetics beholding that ball of flesh, addressed the daughter of Suvala thus, 'What hast thou done?' Gandhari, without endeavouring to disguise her feelings, addressed the Rishi and said, 'Having heard that Kunti had brought forth a son like unto Surya in splendour, I struck in grief at my womb. Thou hadst, O Rishi, granted me the boon that I should have a hundred sons, but here is only a ball of flesh for those hundred sons!' Vyasa then said, 'Daughter of Suvala, it is even so. But my words can never be futile. I have not spoken an untruth even in jest. I need not speak of other occasions. Let a hundred pots full of clarified butter be brought instantly, and let them be placed at a concealed spot. In the meantime, let cool water be sprinkled over this ball of flesh.'

"Vaisampayana continued, 'That ball of flesh then, sprinkled over with water, became, in time, divided into a hundred and one parts, each about the size of the thumb. These were then put into those pots full of clarified butter that had been placed at a concealed spot and were watched with care. The illustrious Vyasa then said unto the daughter of Suvala that she should open the covers of the pots after full two years. And having said this and made these arrangements, the wise Dwaipayana went to the Himavat mountains for devoting himself to asceticism.

"Then in time, king Duryodhana was born from among those pieces of the ball of flesh that had been deposited in those pots. According to the order of birth, king Yudhishthira was the oldest. The news of Duryodhana's birth was carried to Bhishma and the wise Vidura. The day that the haughty Duryodhana was born was also the birth-day of Bhima of mighty arms and great prowess.

"As soon as Duryodhana was born, he began to cry and bray like an ass. And hearing that sound, the asses, vultures, jackals and crows uttered their respective cries responsively. Violent winds began to blow, and there were fires in various directions. Then king Dhritarashtra in great fear, summoning Bhishma and Vidura and other well-wishers and all the Kurus, and numberless Brahmanas, addressed them and said, 'The oldest of those princes, Yudhishthira, is the perpetuator of our line. By virtue of his birth he hath acquired the kingdom. We have nothing to say to this. But shall this my son born after him become king? Tell me truly what is lawful and right under these circumstances.' As soon as these words were spoken, O Bharata, jackals and other carnivorous animals began to howl ominously. And marking those frightful omens all around, the assembled Brahmanas and the wise Vidura replied, 'O king, O bull among men, when these frightful omens are noticeable at the birth of thy eldest son, it is evident that he shall be the exterminator of thy race. The prosperity of all dependeth on his abandonment. Calamity there must be in keeping him. O king, if thou abandonest him, there remain yet thy nine and ninety sons. If thou desirest the good of thy race, abandon him, O Bharata! O king, do good to the world and thy own race by casting off this one child of thine. It hath been said that an individual should be cast off for the sake of the family; that a family should be cast off for the sake of a village; that a village may be abandoned for the sake of the whole country; and that the earth itself may be abandoned for the sake of the soul.' When Vidura and those Brahmanas had stated so, king Dhritarashtra out of affection for his son had not the heart to follow that advice. Then, O king, within a month, were born a full hundred sons unto Dhritarashtra and a daughter also in excess of this hundred. And during the time when Gandhari was in a state of advanced pregnancy, there was a maid servant of the Vaisya class who used to attend on Dhritarashtra. During that year, O king, was begotten upon her by the illustrious Dhritarashtra a son endued with great intelligence who was afterwards named Yuyutsu. And because he was begotten by a Kshatriya upon a Vaisya woman, he came to be called Karna.

"Thus were born unto the wise Dhritarashtra a hundred sons who were all heroes and mighty chariot-fighters, and a daughter over and above the hundred, and another son Yuyutsu of great energy and prowess begotten upon a Vaisya woman.'"

SECTION CXVI
(Sambhava Parva continued)

"Janamejaya said, 'O sinless one, thou hast narrated to me from the beginning all about the birth of Dhritarashtra's hundred sons owing to the boon granted by the Rishi. But thou hast not told me as yet any particulars about the birth of the daughter. Thou hast merely said that over and above the hundred sons, there was another son named Yuyutsu begotten upon a Vaisya woman, and a daughter. The great Rishi Vyasa of immeasurable energy said unto the daughter of the king of Gandhara that she would become the mother of a hundred sons. Illustrious one, how is that thou sayest Gandhari had a daughter over and above her hundred sons? If the ball of flesh was distributed by the great Rishi only into a hundred parts, and if

Gandhari did not conceive on any other occasion, how was then Duhsala born. Tell me this, O Rishi! my curiosity hath been great."

"Vaisampayana said, 'O descendant of the Pandavas, thy question is just, and I will tell thee how it happened. The illustrious and great Rishi himself, by sprinkling water over that ball of flesh, began to divide it into parts. And as it was being divided into parts, the nurse began to take them up and put them one by one into those pots filled with clarified butter. While this process was going on, the beautiful and chaste Gandhari of rigid vows, realising the affection that one feeleth for a daughter, began to think within herself, 'There is no doubt that I shall have a hundred sons, the Muni having said so. It can never be otherwise. But I should be very happy if a daughter were born of me over and above these hundred sons and junior to them all. My husband then may attain to those worlds that the possession of a daughter's sons conferreth. Then again, the affection the women feel for their sons-in-law is great. If, therefore, I obtain a daughter over and above my hundred sons, then, surrounded by sons and daughter's sons, I may feel supremely blest. If I have ever practised ascetic austerities, if I have ever given anything in charity, if I have ever performed the homa (through Brahamanas), if I have ever gratified my superiors by respectful attentions, then (as the fruit of those acts) let a daughter be born unto me.' All this while that illustrious and best of Rishis, Krishna-Dwaipayana himself was dividing the ball of flesh; and counting a full hundred of the parts, he said unto the daughter of Suvala, 'Here are thy hundred sons. I did not speak aught unto thee that was false. Here, however, is one part in excess of the hundred, intended for giving thee a daughter's son. This part shall develop into an amiable and fortunate daughter, as thou hast desired.' Then that great ascetic brought another pot full of clarified butter, and put the part intended for a daughter into it.

"Thus have I, O Bharata, narrated unto thee all about the birth of Duhsala. Tell me, O sinless one, what more I am now to narrate.'"

SECTION CXVII
(Sambhava Parva continued)

"Janamejaya said, 'Please recite the names of Dhritarashtra's sons according to the order of their birth.'

"Vaisampayana said, 'Their names, O king, according to the order of birth, are Duryodhana, Yuyutsu, Duhsasana, Duhsaha, Duhsala, Jalasandha, Sama, Saha, Vinda and Anuvinda, Durdharsha, Suvahu, Dushpradharshana, Durmarshana and Durmukha, Dushkarna, and Karna; Vivinsati and Vikarna, Sala, Satwa, Sulochana, Chitra and Upachitra, Chitraksha, Charuchitra, Sarasana, Durmada and Durvigaha, Vivitsu, Vikatanana; Urnanabha and Sunabha, then Nandaka and Upanandaka; Chitravana, Chitravarman, Suvarman, Durvimochana; Ayovahu, Mahavahu, Chitranga, Chitrakundala, Bhimavega, Bhimavala, Balaki, Balavardhana, Ugrayudha; Bhima, Karna, Kanakaya, Dridhayudha, Dridhavarman, Dridhakshatra, Somakitri, Anudara; Dridhasandha, Jarasandha, Satyasandha, Sada, Suvak, Ugrasravas, Ugrasena, Senani, Dushparajaya, Aparajita, Kundasayin, Visalaksha, Duradhara; Dridhahasta, Suhasta, Vatavega, and Suvarchas; Adityaketu, Vahvashin, Nagadatta, Agrayayin; Kavachin, Krathana, Kunda, Kundadhara, Dhanurdhara; the heroes, Ugra and Bhimaratha, Viravahu, Alolupa; Abhaya, and Raudrakarman, and Dridharatha; Anadhrishya, Kundabhedin, Viravi, Dhirghalochana Pramatha, and Pramathi and the powerful Dhirgharoma; Dirghavahu, Mahavahu, Vyudhoru, Kanakadhvaja; Kundasi and Virajas. Besides these hundred sons, there was a daughter named Duhsala. All were heroes and Atirathas, and were well-skilled in warfare. All were learned in the Vedas, and all kinds of weapons. And, O, king, worthy wives were in time selected for all of them by Dhritarashtra after proper examination. And king Dhritarashtra, O monarch, also bestowed Duhsala, in proper time and with proper rites, upon Jayadratha (the king of Sindhu).'"

THE MAHABHARATA

SECTION CXVIII
(Sambhava Parva continued)

"Janamejaya said, 'O utterer of Brahma, thou hast recited (everything about) the extraordinary birth among men, of the sons of Dhritarashtra in consequence of the Rishi's grace. Thou hast also said what their names are, according to the order of their birth. O Brahmana, I have heard all these from thee. But tell me now all about the Pandavas. While reciting the incarnations on earth of the celestial, the Asuras, and the beings of other classes, thou saidst that the Pandavas were all illustrious and endued with the prowess of gods, and that they were incarnate portion of the celestials themselves. I desire, therefore, to hear all about those beings of extraordinary achievements beginning from the moment of their birth. O Vaisampayana, recite thou their achievements.'

"Vaisampayana said, 'O king, one day Pandu, while roaming about in the woods (on the southern slopes of the Himavat) that teemed with deer and wild animals of fierce disposition, saw a large deer, that seemed to be the leader of a herd, serving his mate. Beholding the animals, the monarch pierced them both with five of his sharp and swift arrows winged with golden feathers. O monarch, that was no deer that Pandu struck at, but a Rishi's son of great ascetic merit who was enjoying his mate in the form of a deer. Pierced by Pandu, while engaged in the act of intercourse, he fell down to the ground, uttering cries that were of a man and began to weep bitterly.

"The deer then addressed Pandu and said, 'O king, even men that are slaves to lust and wrath, and void of reason, and ever sinful, never commit such a cruel act as this. Individual judgment prevaileth not against the ordinance, the ordinance prevaileth against individual judgment. The wise never sanction anything discountenanced by the ordinance. Thou art born, O Bharata, in a race that hath ever been virtuous. How is it, therefore, that even thou, suffering thyself to be overpowered by passion and wrath losest thy reason?' Hearing this, Pandu replied, 'O deer, kings behave in the matter of slaying animals of thy species exactly as they do in the matter of slaying foes. It behoveth thee not, therefore, to reprove me thus from ignorance. Animals of thy species are slain by open or covert means. This, indeed, is the practice of kings. Then why dost thou reprove me? Formerly, the Rishi Agastya, while engaged in the performance of a grand sacrifice, chased the deer, and devoted every deer in the forest unto the gods in general. Thou hast been slain, pursuant to the usage sanctioned by such precedent. Wherefore reprovest us then? For his especial sacrifices Agastya performed the homa with fat of the deer.'

"The deer then said, 'O king, men do not let fly their arrows at their enemies when the latter are unprepared. But there is a time for doing it (viz., after declaration of hostilities). Slaughter at such a time is not censurable.'

"Pandu replied, 'It is well-known that men slay deer by various effective means without regarding whether the animals are careful or careless. Therefore, O deer, why dost thou reprove me?'

"The deer then said, 'O, king, I did not blame thee for thy having killed a deer, or for the injury thou hast done to me. But, instead of acting so cruelly, thou shouldst have waited till the completion of my act of intercourse. What man of wisdom and virtue is there that can kill a deer while engaged in such an act? The time of sexual intercourse is agreeable to every creature and productive of good to all. O king, with this my mate I was engaged in the gratification of my sexual desire. But that effort of mine hath been rendered futile by thee. O king of the Kurus, as thou art born in the race of the Pauravas ever noted for white (virtuous) deeds, such an act hath scarcely been worthy of thee. O Bharata, this act must be regarded as extremely cruel, deserving of universal execration, infamous, and sinful, and certainly leading to hell. Thou art acquainted with the pleasures of sexual intercourse. Thou art acquainted also with the teaching of morality and dictates of duty. Like unto a celestial as thou art, it behoveth thee not to do such an act as leadeth to hell. O best of kings, thy duty is to chastise all who act cruelly, who are engaged in sinful practices and who have thrown to the winds religion, profit, and pleasure as explained in the scriptures. What hast thou done, O best of men, in killing me who have given thee no offence? I am, O king, a Muni who liveth on fruits and roots, though disguised as a deer. I was living in the woods in peace with all. Yet thou hast killed me, O king, for which I will curse thee certainly. As thou hast been cruel unto a couple of opposite sexes, death shall certainly overtake thee as soon as thou feelest the influence of sexual desire. I am a Muni of the name of Kindama, possessed of ascetic merit. I was engaged in sexual intercourse with this deer, because my feelings of modesty did not permit me to indulge in such an act in human society. In the form of a deer I rove in the deep woods in the company of other deer. Thou hast slain me without knowing that I am a Brahmana, the sin of having slain a Brahmana shall not, therefore, be thine. But senseless man, as you have killed me,

147

disguised as a deer, at such a time, thy fate shall certainly be even like mine. When, approaching thy wife lustfully, thou wilt unite with her even as I had done with mine, in that very state shalt thou have to go to the world of the spirits. And that wife of thine with whom thou mayst be united in intercourse at the time of thy death shall also follow thee with affection and reverence to the domains of the king of the dead. Thou hast brought me grief when I was happy. So shall grief come to thee when thou art in happiness.'

"Vaisampayana continued, 'Saying this, that deer, afflicted with grief gave up the ghost; and Pandu also was plunged in woe at the sight.'"

SECTION CXIX
(Sambhava Parva continued)

"Vaisampayana said, 'After the death of that deer, king Pandu with his wives was deeply afflicted and wept bitterly. And he exclaimed, 'The wicked, even if born in virtuous families, deluded by their own passions, become overwhelmed with misery as the fruit of their own deeds. I have heard that my father, though begotten by Santanu of virtuous soul, was cut off while still a youth, only because he had become a slave to his lust. In the soil of that lustful king, the illustrious Rishi Krishna-Dwaipayana himself, of truthful speech, begot me. A son though I am of such a being, with my wicked heart wedded to vice, I am yet leading a wandering life in the woods in the chase of the deer. Oh, the very gods have forsaken me! I shall seek salvation now. The great impediments to salvation are the desire to beget children, and other concerns of the world. I shall now adopt the Brahmacharya mode of life and follow in the imperishable wake of my father. I shall certainly bring my passions under complete control by severe ascetic penances. Forsaking my wives and other relatives and shaving my head, alone shall I wander over the earth, begging for my subsistence from each of these trees standing here. Forsaking every object of affection and aversion, and covering my body with dust, I shall make the shelter of trees or deserted houses my home. I shall never yield to influence of sorrow or joy, and I shall regard slander and eulogy in the same light. I shall not seek benedictions or bows. I shall be at peace with all, and shall not accept gifts. I shall not mock anybody, nor shall I knit my brows at any one, but shall be ever cheerful and devoted to the good of all creatures. I shall not harm any of the four orders of life gifted with power of locomotion or otherwise, viz., oviparous and viviparous creatures and worms and vegetables. But on the contrary, preserve an equality of behaviour towards all, as if they were, my own children. Once a day shall I beg of five or ten families at the most, and if I do not succeed in obtaining alms, I shall then go without food. I shall rather stint myself than beg more than once of the same person. If I do not obtain anything after completing my round of seven or ten houses, moved by covetousness, I shall not enlarge my round. Whether I obtain or fail to obtain alms. I shall be equally unmoved like a great ascetic. One lopping off an arm of mine with a hatchet, and one smearing another arm with sandal-paste, shall be regarded by me equally. I shall not wish prosperity to the one or misery to the other. I shall not be pleased with life or displeased with death. I shall neither desire to live nor to die. Washing my heart of all sins, I shall certainly transcend those sacred rites productive of happiness, that men perform in auspicious moments, days, and periods. I shall also abstain from all acts of religion and profit and also those that lead to the gratification of the senses. Freed from all sins and snares of the world, I shall be like the wind subject to none. Following the path of fearlessness and bearing myself in this way I shall at last lay down my life. Destitute of the power of begetting children, firmly adhering to the line of duty I shall not certainly deviate therefrom in order to tread in the vile path of the world that is so full of misery. Whether respected or disrespected in the world that man who from covetousness casteth on others a begging look, certainly behaveth like a dog. (Destitute as I am of the power of procreation, I should not certainly, from desire of offspring, solicit others to give me children.)'

"Vaisampayana continued, 'The king, having thus wept in sorrow, with a sigh looked at his two wives Kunti and Madri, and addressing them said, 'Let the princess of Kosala (my mother), Vidura, the king with our friends, the venerable Satyavati, Bhishma, the priests of our family, illustrious Soma-drinking Brahmanas of rigid vows and all elderly citizens depending on us be informed, after being prepared for it, that Pandu hath retired into the woods to lead a life of asceticism.' Hearing these words of their lord who had set his heart on a life of asceticism in the woods, both Kunti and Madri addressed him in these proper words, 'O bull of Bharata's race, there are many other modes of life which thou canst adopt and in which thou canst undergo the severest penances along with us, thy wedded wives—in which for the salvation of thy body (freedom from re-birth), thou mayest obtain heaven. We also, in the company of our lord, and for his benefit, controlling our passions and bidding adieu to all luxuries, shall subject ourselves to the severest austerities. O king, O thou of great wisdom, if thou abandonest us, we shall then this very day truly depart from this world.'

Pandu replied, 'If, indeed, this your resolve springeth from virtue, then with you both I shall follow the imperishable path of my fathers. Abandoning the luxuries of cities and towns, clad in barks of trees, and living on fruits and roots, I shall wander in deep woods, practising the severest penances. Bathing morning and evening, I shall perform the homa. I shall reduce my body by eating very sparingly and shall wear rags and skins and knotted locks on my head. Exposing myself to heat and cold and disregarding hunger and thirst, I shall reduce my body by severe ascetic penances, I shall live in solitude and I shall give myself up to contemplation; I shall eat fruit, ripe or green, that I may find. I shall offer oblations to the Pitris (manes) and the gods with speech, water and the fruits of the wilderness. I shall not see, far less harm, any of the denizens of the woods, or any of my relatives, or any of the residents of cities and towns. Until I lay down this body, I shall thus practise the severe ordinances of the Vanaprastha scriptures, always searching for severer ones that they may contain.'

"Vaisampayana continued, 'The Kuru king, having said this unto his wives, gave away to Brahmanas the big jewel in his diadem, his necklace of precious gold, his bracelets, his large ear-rings, his valuable robes and all the ornaments of his wives. Then summoning his attendants, he commended them, saying, 'Return ye to Hastinapura and proclaim unto all that Pandu with his wives hath gone into the woods, foregoing wealth, desire, happiness, and even sexual appetite.' Then those followers and attendants, hearing these and other soft words of the king, set up a loud wail, uttering, 'Oh, we are undone!' Then with hot tears trickling down their cheeks they left the monarch and returned to Hastinapura with speed carrying that wealth with them (that was to be distributed in charity). Then Dhritarashtra, that first of men, hearing from them everything that had happened in the woods, wept for his brother. He brooded over his affliction continually, little relishing the comfort of beds and seats and dishes.

"Meanwhile, the Kuru prince Pandu (after sending away his attendants) accompanied by his two wives and eating fruits and roots went to the mountains of Nagasata. He next went to Chaitraratha, and then crossed the Kalakuta, and finally, crossing the Himavat, he arrived at Gandhamadana. Protected by Mahabhutas, Siddhas, and great Rishis, Pandu lived, O king, sometimes on level ground and sometimes on mountain slopes. He then journeyed on to the lake of Indradyumna, whence crossing the mountains of Hansakuta, he went to the mountain of hundred peaks (Sata-sringa) and there continued to practise ascetic austerities.'"

SECTION CXX
(Sambhava Parva continued)

"Vaisampayana said, 'Pandu, possessed of great energy, then devoted himself to asceticism. Within a short time he became the favourite of the whole body of the Siddhas and Charanas residing there. And, O Bharata, devoted to the service of his spiritual masters, free from vanity, with mind under complete control and the passions fully subdued, the prince, becoming competent to enter heaven by his own energy, attained to great (ascetic) prowess. Some of the Rishis would call him brother, some friend, while others cherished him as their son. And, O bull of Bharata's race, having acquired after a long time great ascetic merit coupled with complete singleness, Pandu became even like a Brahmarshi (though he was a Kshatriya by birth).

"On a certain day of the new moon, the great Rishis of rigid vows assembled together, and desirous of beholding Brahman were on the point of starting on their expedition. Seeing them about to start, Pandu asked those ascetics, saying, 'Ye first of eloquent men, where shall we go?' The Rishis answered, 'There will be a great gathering today, in the abode of Brahman, of celestials, Rishis and Pitris. Desirous of beholding the Self- create we shall go there today.'

"Vaisampayana continued, 'Hearing this, Pandu rose up suddenly, desirous of visiting heaven along with the great Rishis. Accompanied by his two wives, when he was on the point of following the Rishis in the northerly direction from the mountain of hundred peaks, those ascetics addressed him saying, 'In our northward march, while gradually ascending the king of mountains, we have seen on its delightful breast many regions inaccessible to ordinary mortals; retreats also of the gods, and Gandharvas and Apsaras, with palatial mansions by hundreds clustering thick around and resounding with the sweet notes of celestial music, the gardens of Kuvera laid out on even and uneven grounds, banks of mighty rivers, and deep caverns. There are many regions also on those heights that are covered with perpetual snow and are utterly destitute of vegetable and animal existence. In some places the downpour of rain is so heavy that they are perfectly inaccessible and incapable of being utilised for habitation. Not to speak of other animals, even winged creatures cannot cross them. The only thing that can go there is air, and the only beings, Siddhas and great Rishis. How shall these princesses ascend those heights of the king of mountains? Unaccustomed to pain, shall they not droop in affliction? Therefore, come not with us, O bull of Bharata's race!'

"Pandu replied, 'Ye fortunate ones, it is said that for the sonless there is no admittance into heaven. I am sonless! In affliction I speak unto you! I am afflicted because I have not been able to discharge the debt I owe to my ancestors. It is certain that with the dissolution of this my body my ancestors perish! Men are born on this earth with four debts, viz. those due unto the (deceased) ancestors, the gods, the Rishis, and other men. In justice these must be discharged. The wise have declared that no regions of bliss exist for them that neglect to pay these debts in due time. The gods are paid (gratified) by sacrifices, the Rishis, by study, meditation, and asceticism, the (deceased) ancestors, by begetting children and offering the funeral cake, and, lastly other men, by leading a humane and inoffensive life. I have justly discharged my obligations to the Rishis, the gods, and other men. But those others than these three are sure to perish with the dissolution of my body! Ye ascetics, I am not yet freed from the debt I owe to my (deceased) ancestors. The best of men are born in this world to beget children for discharging that debt. I would ask you, should children be begotten in my soil (upon my wives) as I myself was begotten in the soil of my father by the eminent Rishi?'

"The Rishis said, 'O king of virtuous soul, there is progeny in store for thee, that is sinless and blest with good fortune and like unto the gods. We behold it all with our prophetic eyes. Therefore, O tiger among men, accomplish by your own acts that which destiny pointeth at. Men of intelligence, acting with deliberation, always obtain good fruits; it behoveth thee, therefore, O king, to exert thyself. The fruits thou wouldst obtain are distinctly visible. Thou wouldst really obtain accomplished and agreeable progeny.'

"Vaisampayana continued, 'Hearing these words of the ascetics, Pandu, remembering the loss of his procreative powers owing to the curse of the deer, began to reflect deeply. And calling his wedded wife the excellent Kunti, unto him, he told her in private, 'Strive thou to raise offspring at this time of distress. The wise expounders of the eternal religion declare that a son, O Kunti, is the cause of virtuous fame in the three worlds. It is said that sacrifices, charitable gifts, ascetic penances, and vows observed most carefully, do not confer religious merit on a sonless man. O thou of sweet smiles, knowing all this, I am certain that as I am sonless, I shall not obtain regions of true felicity. O timid one, wretch that I was and addicted to cruel deeds, as a consequence of the polluted life I led, my power of procreation hath been destroyed by the curse of the deer. The religious institutes mention six kinds of sons that are heirs and kinsmen, and six other kinds that are not heirs but kinsmen. I shall speak of them presently. O Pritha, listen to me. They are: 1st, the son begotten by one's own self upon his wedded wife; 2nd, the son begotten upon one's wife by an accomplished person from motives of kindness; 3rd, the son begotten upon one's wife by a person for pecuniary consideration; 4th, the son begotten upon the wife after the husband's death; 5th, the maiden-born son; 6th, the son born of an unchaste wife; 7th, the son given; 8th, the son bought for a consideration; 9th, the son self-given; 10th, the son received with a pregnant bride; 11th, the brother's son; and 12th, the son begotten upon a wife of lower caste. On failure of offspring of a prior class, the mother should desire to have offspring of the next class. In times of distress, men solicit offspring from accomplished younger brothers. The self-born Manu hath said that men failing to have legitimate offspring of their own may have offspring begotten upon their wives by others, for sons confer the highest religious merit. Therefore, O Kunti, being destitute myself of the power of procreation, I command thee to raise good offspring through some person who is either equal or superior to me. O Kunti, listen to the history of the daughter of Saradandayana who was appointed by her lord to raise offspring. That warrior-dame, when her monthly season arrived, bathed duly and in the night went out and waited on a spot where four roads met. She did not wait long when a Brahmana crowned with ascetic success came there. The daughter of Saradandayana solicited him for offspring. After pouring libations of clarified butter on the fire (in the performance of the sacrifice known by the name of Punsavana) she brought forth three sons that were mighty car-warriors and of whom Durjaya was the eldest, begotten upon her by that Brahmana. O thou of good fortune, do thou follow that warrior-dame's example at my command, and speedily raise offspring out of the seed of some Brahmana of high ascetic merit.'"

SECTION CXXI
(Sambhava Parva continued)

"Vaisampayana said, 'Thus addressed, Kunti replied unto her heroic lord, king Pandu, that bull amongst the Kurus, saying, 'O virtuous one, it behoveth thee not to say so unto me. I am, O thou lotus-eyed one, thy wedded wife, devoted to thee. O, Bharata of mighty arms, thyself shalt, in righteousness, beget upon me children endued with great energy. Then I shall ascend to heaven with thee; O prince of Kuru's race, receive me in thy embrace for begetting children. I shall not certainly, even in imagination, accept any other man except thee in my embraces. What other man is there in this world superior to thee? O virtuous one, listen to this Pauranic narrative that hath been, O thou of large eyes, heard by me, and that I shall presently narrate.

"There was, in ancient times, a king in the race of Puru, known by the name of Vyushitaswa. He was devoted to truth and virtue. Of virtuous soul and mighty arms, on one occasion, while he was performing a sacrifice the gods with Indra and the great Rishis came to him, and Indra was so intoxicated with the Soma juice he drank and the Brahmanas with the large presents they received, that both the gods and the great Rishis began themselves to perform everything appertaining to that sacrifice of the illustrious royal sage. And thereupon Vyushitaswa began to shine above all men like the Sun appearing in double splendour after the season of frost is over. And the powerful Vyushitaswa, who was endued with the strength of ten elephants very soon performed the horse-sacrifice, overthrowing, O best of monarchs, all the kings of the East, the North, the West and the South, and exacted tributes from them all. There is an anecdote, O best of the Kurus, that is sung by all reciters of the Puranas, in connection with that first of all men, the illustrious Vyushitaswa.—Having conquered the whole Earth up to the coast of the sea, Vyushitaswa protected every class of his subjects as a father does his own begotten sons.—Performing many great sacrifices he gave away much wealth to the Brahmanas. After collecting unlimited jewels and precious stones he made arrangements for performing still greater ones. And he performed also the Agnishtoma, and other special Vedic sacrifices, extracting great quantities of Soma juice. And, O king, Vyushitaswa had for his dear wife, Bhadra, the daughter of Kakshivat, unrivalled for beauty on earth. And it hath been heard by us that the couple loved each other deeply. King Vyushitaswa was seldom separated from his wife. Sexual excess, however, brought on an attack of phthisis and the king died within a few days, sinking like the Sun in his glory. Then Bhadra, his beautiful queen, was plunged into woe, and as she was sonless, O tiger among men, she wept in great affliction. Listen to me, O king, as I narrate to you all that Bhadra said with bitter tears trickling down her cheeks. 'O virtuous one', she said, 'Women serve no purpose when their husbands are dead. She who liveth after her husband is dead, draggeth on a miserable existence that can hardly be called life. O bull of the Kshatriya order, death is a blessing to women without husbands. I wish to follow the way thou hast gone. Be kind and take me with thee. In thy absence, I am unable to bear life even for a moment. Be kind to me, O king and take me hence pretty soon. O tiger among men, I shall follow thee over the even and uneven ground. Thou hast gone away, O lord, never to return. I shall follow thee, O king, as thy own shadow. O tiger among men, I will obey thee (as thy slave) and will ever do what is agreeable to thee and what is for thy good. O thou of eyes like lotus-petals, without thee, from this day, mental agonies will overwhelm me and eat into my heart. A wretch that I am, some loving couple had doubtless been separated by me in a former life, for which, in this life, I am made to suffer the pangs of separation from thee. O king, that wretched woman who liveth even for a moment separated from her lord, liveth in woe and suffereth the pangs of hell even here. Some loving couple had doubtless been separated by me in a former life, for which sinful act I am suffering this torture arising from my separation from thee. O king, from this day I will lay myself down on a bed of Kusa grass and abstain from every luxury, hoping to behold thee once more. O tiger among men, show thyself to me. O king, O lord, command once more thy wretched and bitterly weeping wife plunged in woe.'

"Kunti continued, 'It was thus, O Pandu, that the beautiful Bhadra wept over the death of her lord. And the weeping Bhadra clasped in her arms the corpse in anguish of heart. Then she was addressed by an incorporeal voice in these words, "Rise up, O Bhadra, and leave this place. O thou of sweet smiles, I grant thee this boon. I will beget offspring upon thee. Lie thou down with me on thy own bed, after the catamenial bath, on the night of the eighth or the fourteenth day of the moon.' Thus addressed by the incorporeal voice, the chaste Bhadra did, as she was directed, for obtaining offspring. And, O bull of the Bharatas, the corpse of her husband begat upon her seven children viz., three Salwas and four Madras. O bull of the Bharatas, do thou also beget offspring upon me, like the illustrious Vyushitaswa, by the exercise of that ascetic power which thou possessest.'"

SECTION CXXII
(Sambhava Parva continued)

"Vaisampayana said, 'Thus addressed by his loving wife, king Pandu, well-acquainted with all rules of morality, replied in these words of virtuous import, 'O Kunti, what thou hast said is quite true. Vyushitaswa of old did even as thou hast said. Indeed he was equal unto the celestials themselves. But I shall now tell thee about the practices of old indicated by illustrious Rishis, fully acquainted with every rule of morality. O thou of handsome face and sweet smiles, women formerly were not immured within houses and dependent on husbands and other relatives. They used to go about freely, enjoying themselves as best as they liked. O thou of excellent qualities, they did not then adhere to their husbands faithfully, and yet, O handsome one, they were not regarded sinful, for that was the sanctioned usage of the times. That very usage is followed to this day by birds and beasts without any (exhibition of) jealousy. That practice, sanctioned by precedent, is applauded by great Rishis. O thou of taper thighs, the practice is yet regarded with respect amongst the Northern Kurus. Indeed, that usage, so lenient to women, hath the sanction of antiquity. The present practice, however (of women's being confined to one husband for life) hath been established but lately. I shall tell thee in detail who established it and why.

"It hath been heard by us that there was a great Rishi of the name of Uddalaka, who had a son named Swetaketu who also was an ascetic of merit. O thou of eyes like lotus-petals, the present virtuous practice hath been established by that Swetaketu from anger. Hear thou the reason. One day, in the presence of Swetaketu's father a Brahmana came and catching Swetaketu's mother by the hand, told her, 'Let us go.' Beholding his mother seized by the hand and taken away apparently by force, the son was greatly moved by wrath. Seeing his son indignant, Uddalaka addressed him and said, 'Be not angry. O son! This is the practice sanctioned by antiquity. The women of all orders in this world are free, O son; men in this matter, as regards their respective orders, act as kine.' The Rishi's son, Swetaketu, however, disapproved of the usage and established in the world the present practice as regards men and women. It hath been heard by us, O thou of great virtue, that the existing practice dates from that period among human beings but not among beings of other classes. Accordingly, since the establishment of the present usage, it is sinful for women not to adhere to their husbands. Women transgressing the limits assigned by the Rishi became guilty of slaying the embryo. And, men, too, violating a chaste and loving wife who hath from her maidenhood observed the vow of purity, became guilty of the same sin. The woman also who, being commanded by her husband to raise offspring, refuses to do his bidding, becometh equally sinful.

"Thus, O timid one, was the existing usage established of old by Swetaketu, the son of Uddalaka, in defiance of antiquity. O thou of taper thighs, it hath also been heard by us that Madayanti, the wife of Saudasa, commanded by her husband to raise offspring went unto Rishi Vasishtha. And on going in unto him, the handsome Madayanti obtained a son named Asmaka. She did this, moved by the desire of doing good to her husband. O thou of lotus-eyes, thou knowest, O timid girl, how we ourselves, for the perpetuation of the Kuru race, were begotten by Krishna-Dwaipayana. O faultless one, beholding all these precedents it behoveth thee to do my bidding, which is not inconsistent with virtue, O princess, who is devoted to her husband, it hath also been said by those acquainted with the rules of morality that a wife, when her monthly season cometh, must ever seek her husband, though at other times she deserveth liberty. The wise have declared this to be the ancient practice. But, be the act sinful or sinless, those acquainted with the Vedas have declared that it is the duty of wives to do what their husbands bid them do. Especially, O thou of faultless features, I, who am deprived of the power of procreation, having yet become desirous of beholding offspring, deserve the more to be obeyed by thee. O amiable one, joining my palms furnished with rosy fingers, and making of them a cup as of lotus leaves, I place them on my head to propitiate thee. O thou of lair looks, it behoveth thee to raise offspring, at my command, through some Brahmana possessed of high ascetic merit. For then, owing to thee, O thou of fair hips, I may go the way that is reserved for those that are blessed with children.'

"Vaisampayana continued, 'Thus addressed by Pandu, that subjugator of hostile cities, the handsome Kunti, ever attentive to what was agreeable and beneficial to her lord, then replied unto him, saying, 'In my girlhood, O lord, I was in my father's house engaged in attending upon all guests. I used to wait respectfully upon Brahmanas of rigid vows and great ascetic merit. One day I gratified with my attentions that Brahmana whom people call Durvasa, of mind under full control and possessing knowledge of all the mysteries of religion. Pleased with my services, that Brahmana gave me a boon in the form of a mantra (formula of invocation) for calling into my presence any one of the celestials I liked. And the Rishi, addressing me, said,

'Anyone among the celestials whom thou callest by this shall, O girl, approach thee and be obedient to thy will, whether he liketh it or not. And, O princess, thou shall also have offspring through his grace.' O Bharata, that Brahmana told me this when I lived in my father's house. The words uttered by the Brahmana can never be false. The time also hath come when they may yield fruit. Commanded by thee, O royal sage, I can by that mantra summon any of the celestials, so that we may have good children. O foremost of all truthful men, tell me which of the celestials I shall summon. Know that, as regards this matter, I await your commands.'

"Hearing this, Pandu replied, 'O handsome one, strive duly this very day to gratify our wishes. Fortunate one, summon thou the god of justice. He is the most virtuous of the celestials. The god of justice and virtue will never be able to pollute us with sin. The world also, O beautiful princess, will then think that what we do can never be unholy. The son also that we shall obtain from him shall in virtue be certainly the foremost among the Kurus. Begotten by the god of justice and morality, he would never set his heart upon anything that is sinful or unholy. Therefore, O thou of sweet smiles, steadily keeping virtue before thy eyes, and duly observing holy vows, summon thou the god of justice and virtue by the help of thy solicitations and incantations.'

"Vaisampayana continued, 'Then Kunti, that best of women, thus addressed by her lord, said, 'So be it.' And bowing down to him and reverently circumambulating his person, she resolved to do his bidding.'"

SECTION CXXIII
(Sambhava Parva continued)

"Vaisampayana said, 'O Janamejaya, when Gandhari's conception had been a full year old, it was then that Kunti summoned the eternal god of justice to obtain offspring from him. And she offered without loss of time, sacrifices unto the god and began to duly repeat the formula that Durvasa had imparted to her some time before. Then the god, overpowered by her incantations, arrived at the spot where Kunti was seated in his car resplendent as the Sun. Smiling, he asked, 'O Kunti, what am I to give thee?' And Kunti too smiling in her turn, replied, 'Thou must even give me offspring.' Then the handsome Kunti was united (in intercourse) with the god of justice in his spiritual form and obtained from him a son devoted to the good of all creatures. And she brought his excellent child, who lived to acquire a great fame, at the eighth Muhurta called Abhijit, of the hour of noon of that very auspicious day of the seventh month (Kartika), viz., the fifth of the lighted fortnight, when the star Jyeshtha in conjunction with the moon was ascendant. And as soon as the child was born, an incorporeal voice (from the skies) said, 'This child shall be the best of men, the foremost of those that are virtuous. Endued with great prowess and truthful in speech, he shall certainly be the ruler of the earth. And this first child of Pandu shall be known by the name of Yudhishthira. Possessed of prowess and honesty of disposition, he shall be a famous king, known throughout the three worlds.'

"Pandu, having obtained that virtuous son, again addressed his wife and said, 'The wise have declared that a Kshatriya must be endued with physical strength, otherwise he is no Kshatriya.' Therefore, ask thou for an offspring of superior strength.' Thus commanded by her lord, Kunti then invoked Vayu. And the mighty god of wind, thus invoked, came unto her, riding upon a deer, and said, 'What, O Kunti, am I to give thee? Tell me what is in thy heart.' Smiling in modesty, she said to him, 'Give me, O best of celestials, a child endued with great strength and largeness of limbs and capable of humbling the pride of every body.' The god of wind thereupon begat upon her the child afterwards known as Bhima of mighty arms and fierce prowess. And upon the birth of that child endued with extraordinary strength, an incorporeal voice, O Bharata, as before, said, 'This child shall be the foremost of all endued with strength.' I must tell you, O Bharata, of another wonderful event that occurred after the birth of Vrikodara (Bhima). While he fell from the lap of his mother upon the mountain breast, the violence of the fall broke into fragments the stone upon which he fell without his infant body being injured in the least. And he fell from his mother's lap because Kunti, frightened by a tiger, had risen up suddenly, unconscious of the child that lay asleep on her lap. And as she had risen, the infant, of body hard as the thunderbolt, falling down upon the mountain breast, broke into a hundred fragments the rocky mass upon which he fell. And beholding this, Pandu wondered much. And it so happened that that very day on which Vrikodara was born, was also, O best of Bharatas, the birthday of Duryodhana who afterwards became the ruler of the whole earth.'

153

"After the birth of Vrikodara, Pandu again began to think, 'How am I to obtain a very superior son who shall achieve world-wide fame? Every thing in the world dependeth on destiny and exertion. But destiny can never be successful except by timely exertion. We have heard it said that Indra is the chief of the gods. Indeed, he is endued with immeasurable might and energy and prowess and glory. Gratifying him with my asceticism, I shall obtain from him a son of great strength. Indeed, the son he giveth me must be superior to all and capable of vanquishing in battle all men and creatures other than men. I shall, therefore, practise the severest austerities, with heart, deed and speech.'

"After this, the Kuru king Pandu, taking counsel with the great Rishis commanded Kunti to observe an auspicious vow for one full year, while he himself commenced, O Bharata, to stand upon one leg from morning to evening, and practise other severe austerities with mind rapt in meditation, for gratifying the lord of the celestials.

"It was after a long time that Indra (gratified with such devotion) approached Pandu and, addressing him, said, 'I shall give thee, O king, a son who will be celebrated all over the three worlds and who will promote the welfare of Brahmanas, kine and all honest men. The son I shall give thee will be the smiter of the wicked and the delight of friends and relatives. Foremost of all men, he will be an irresistible slayer of all foes.' Thus addressed by Vasava (the king of the celestials), the virtuous king of the Kuru race, well-recollecting those words, said unto Kunti, 'O fortunate one, thy vow hath become successful. The lord of the celestials hath been gratified, and is willing to give thee a son such as thou desirest, of superhuman achievements and great fame. He will be the oppressor of all enemies and possessed of great wisdom. Endued with a great soul, in splendour equal unto the Sun, invincible in battles, and of great achievements, he will also be extremely handsome. O thou of fair hips and sweet smiles, the lord of the celestials hath become gracious to thee. Invoking him, bring thou forth a child who will be the very home of all Kshatriya virtues.'

"Vaisampayana continued, 'The celebrated Kunti, thus addressed by her lord, invoked Sakra (the king of the gods) who thereupon came unto her and begat him that was afterwards called Arjuna. And as soon as this child was born, an incorporeal voice, loud and deep as that of the clouds and filling the whole welkin, distinctly said, addressing Kunti in the hearing of every creature dwelling in that asylum, 'This child of thine, O Kunti, will be equal unto Kartavirya in energy and Siva in prowess. Invincible like Sakra himself he will spread thy fame far and wide. As Vishnu (the youngest of Aditi's sons) had enhanced Aditi's joy, so shall this child enhance thy joy. Subjugating the Madras, the Kurus along with the Somakas, and the people of Chedi, Kasi and Karusha, he will maintain the prosperity of the Kurus. (Surfeited with libations at the sacrifice of king Swetaketu), Agni will derive great gratification from the fat of all creatures dwelling in the Khandava woods (to be burnt down) by the might of this one's arms. This mighty hero, vanquishing all the monarchs of the earth, will with his brothers perform three great sacrifices. In prowess, O Kunti, he will be even as Jamadagnya or Vishnu. The foremost of all men endued with prowess, he will achieve great fame. He will gratify in battle (by his heroism) Sankara, the god of gods (Mahadeva), and will receive from him the great weapon named Pasupata. This thy son of mighty arms will also slay, at the command of Indra, those Daityas called the Nivatakavachas who are the enemies of the gods. He will also acquire all kinds of celestial weapons, and this bull among men will also retrieve the fortunes of his race.'

"Kunti heard these extraordinary words, while lying in the room. And hearing those words uttered so loudly, the ascetics dwelling on the mountain of a hundred peaks, and the celestials with Indra sitting in their cars, became exceedingly glad. The sounds of the (invisible) drum filled the entire welkin. There were shouts of joy, and the whole region was covered with flowers showered down by invisible agents. The various tribes of celestials assembled together, began to offer their respectful adorations to the son of Pritha. The sons of Kadru (Nagas), the son of Vinata, the Gandharvas, the lords of the creation, and the seven great Rishis, viz., Bharadwaja, Kasyapa, Gautama, Viswamitra, Jamadagni, Vasishtha, and the illustrious Atri who illumined the world of old when the Sun was lost, all came there. And Marichi, Angiras, Pulastya, Pulaha, Kratu, Daksha the lord of creation, the Gandharvas, and Apsaras, came there also. The various tribes of Apsaras, decked with celestial garlands and every ornament, and attired in fine robes, came there and danced in joy, chanting the praises of Vibhatsu (Arjuna). All around, the great Rishis began to utter propitiatory formulas. And Tumvuru accompanied by the Gandharvas began to sing in charming notes. And Bhimasena and Ugrasena, Urnayus and Anagha, Gopati and Dhritarashtra and Suryavarchas the eighth, Yugapa and Trinapa, Karshni, Nandi, and Chitraratha, Salisirah the thirteenth, Parjanya the fourteenth, Kali the fifteenth, and Narada the sixteenth in this list, Vrihatta, Vrihaka, Karala of great soul, Brahmacharin, Vahuguna, Suvarna of great fame, Viswavasu, Bhumanyu, Suchandra, Sam and the celebrated tribes of Haha and Huhu gifted with wonderful melody of voice,—these celestial Gandharvas, O king, all went there. Many illustrious Apsaras also of large eyes, decked with every ornament came there to dance and sing. And Anuchana and Anavadya, Gunamukhya and Gunavara, Adrika and Soma, Misrakesi and Alambusha, Marichi and Suchika, Vidyutparna and Tilottama and Ambika, Lakshmana, Kshema Devi, Rambha, Manorama, Asita, Suvahu, Supriya, Suvapuh, Pundarika, Sugandha, Surasa, Pramathini, Kamya and Saradwati, all danced there together. And Menaka, Sahajanya, Karnika, Punjikasthala, Ritusthala, Ghritachi, Viswachi, Purvachiti, the celebrated Umlocha, Pramlocha the tenth and Urvasi the eleventh,—these large-eyed dancing girls of heaven,—came there and sang in chorus. And Dharti and Aryaman and Mitra and Varuna, Bhaga and Indra, Vivaswat, Pushan, Tvastri and Parjanya or Vishnu, these twelve Adityas came there to glorify Pandu's son. And, O king, Mrigavyadha, Sarpa, the celebrated Niriti, Ajaikapada, Ahivradhna, Pinakin, Dahana, Iswara, Kapalin, Sthanu and the illustrious Bhaga—these eleven Rudras,—also came there. And the twin Aswins, the eight Vasus, the mighty Maruts, the Viswedevas, and the Sadhyas, also came there. And Karkotaka, Vasuki, Kachchhapa, Kunda and the great Naga Takshaka,—these mighty and wrathful snakes possessed of high ascetic merit also came there. And Tarkshya, Arishtanemi, Garuda, Asitadvaja,—these and many other Nagas, came there, so also Aruna and Aruni of Vinata's race also came there. And only great Rishis crowned with ascetic success and not others saw those celestials and other beings seated in their cars or waiting on the mountain peaks. Those best of Munis beholding that wonderful sight, became amazed, and their love and affection for the children of Pandu was in consequence enhanced.

"The celebrated Pandu, tempted by the desire of having more children wished to speak again unto his wedded wife (for invoking some other god). But Kunti addressed him, saying, 'The wise do not sanction a fourth delivery even in a season of distress. The woman having intercourse with four different men is called a Swairini (wanton), while she having intercourse with five becometh a harlot. Therefore, O learned one, as thou art well-acquainted with the scripture on this subject, why dost thou, beguiled by desire of offspring, tell me so in seeming forgetfulness of the ordinance?'"

SECTION CXXIV
(Sambhava Parva continued)

"Vaisampayana said, 'After the birth of Kunti's sons and also of the hundred sons of Dhritarashtra the daughter of the king of the Madras privately addressed Pandu, saying, 'O slayer of foes, I have no complaint even if thou beest unpropitious to me. I have, O sinless one, also no complaint that though by birth I am superior to Kunti yet I am inferior to her in station. I do not grieve, O thou of Kuru's race, that Gandhari hath obtained a hundred sons. This, however, is my great grief that while Kunti and I are equal, I should be childless, while it should so chance that thou shouldst have offspring by Kunti alone. If the daughter of Kuntibhoja should so provide that I should have offspring, she would then be really doing me a great favour and benefiting thee likewise. She being my rival, I feel a delicacy in soliciting any favour of her. If thou beest, O king, propitiously disposed to me, then ask her to grant my desire.'

"Hearing her, Pandu replied, 'O Madri, I do revolve this matter often in my own mind, but I have hitherto hesitated to tell thee anything, not knowing how thou wouldst receive it. Now that I know what your wishes are, I shall certainly strive after that end. I think that, asked by me, Kunti will not refuse.'

"Vaisampayana continued, 'After this, Pandu addressed Kunti in private, saying, 'O Kunti, grant me some more offspring for the expansion of my race and for the benefit of the world. O blessed one, provide thou that I myself, my ancestors, and thine also, may always have the funeral cake offered to us. O, do what is beneficial to me, and grant me and the world what, indeed, is the best of benefits. O, do what, indeed, may be difficult for thee, moved by the desire of achieving undying fame. Behold, Indra, even though he hath obtained the sovereignty of the celestials, doth yet, for fame alone, perform sacrifices. O handsome one, Brahmanas, well-acquainted with the Vedas, and having achieved high ascetic merit, do yet, for fame alone, approach their spiritual masters with reverence. So also all royal sages and Brahmanas possessed of ascetic wealth have achieved, for fame only, the most difficult of ascetic feat. Therefore, O blameless one, rescue this Madri as by a raft (by granting her the means of obtaining offspring), and achieve thou imperishable fame by making her a mother of children.'

"Thus addressed by her lord, Kunti readily yielded, and said unto Madri, 'Think thou, without loss of time, of some celestial, and thou shall certainly obtain from him a child like unto him.' Reflecting for a few moments. Madri thought of the twin Aswins, who coming unto her with speed begat upon her two sons that were twins named Nakula and Sahadeva, unrivalled on earth for personal beauty. And as soon as they were born, an incorporeal voice said, 'In energy and beauty these twins shall transcend even the twin Aswins themselves.' Indeed possessed of great energy and beauty, they illumined the whole region.

"O king, after all the children were born the Rishis dwelling on the mountain of a hundred peaks uttering blessings on them and affectionately performing the first rites of birth, bestowed appellations on them. The eldest of Kunti's children was called Yudhishthira, the second Bhimasena, and the third Arjuna, and of Madri's sons, the first-born of the twins was called Nakula and the next Sahadeva. And those foremost sons born at an interval of one year after one another, looked like an embodied period of five years. And king Pandu, beholding his children of celestial beauty and of super-abundant energy, great strength and prowess, and of largeness of soul, rejoiced exceedingly. And the children became great favourites of the Rishis, as also of their wives, dwelling on the mountain of a hundred peaks.

"Some time after, Pandu again requested Kunti on behalf of Madri. Addressed, O king, by her lord in private, Kunti replied, 'Having given her the formula of invocation only once, she hath, O king, managed to obtain two sons. Have I not been thus deceived by her, I fear, O king, that she will soon surpass me in the number of her children. This, indeed, is the way of all wicked women. Fool that I was, I did not know that by invoking the twin gods I could obtain at one birth twin children. I beseech thee, O king, do not command me any further. Let this be the boon granted (by thee) to me.'

"Thus, O king, were born unto Pandu five sons who were begotten by celestials and were endued with great strength, and who all lived to achieve great fame and expand the Kuru race. Each bearing every auspicious mark on his person, handsome like Soma, proud as the lion, well-skilled in the use of the bow, and of leonine tread, breast, heart, eyes, neck and prowess, those foremost of men, resembling the celestials themselves in might, began to grow up. And beholding them and their virtues growing with years, the great Rishis dwelling on that snowcapped sacred mountain were filled with wonder. And the five Pandavas and the hundred sons of Dhritarashtra—that propagator of the Kuru race—grew up rapidly like a cluster of lotuses in a lake.'"

SECTION CXXV
(Sambhava Parva continued)

"Vaisampayana said, "Beholding his five handsome sons growing up before him in that great forest on the charming mountain slope, Pandu felt the last might of his arms revive once more. One day in the season of spring which maddens every creature the king accompanied by his wife (Madri), began to rove in the woods where every tree had put forth new blossoms. He beheld all around Palasas and Tilakas and Mangoes and Champakas and Parihadrakas and Karnikaras, Asokas and Kesaras and Atimuktas and Kuruvakas with swarms of maddened bees sweetly humming about. And there were flowers of blossoming Parijatas with the Kokilas pouring forth their melodies from under every twig echoing with the sweet hums of the black bees. And he beheld also various other kinds of trees bent down with the weight of their flowers and fruits. And there were also many fine pools of water overgrown with hundreds of fragrant lotuses. Beholding all these, Pandu felt the soft influence of desire. Roving like a celestial with a light heart amidst such scenery, Pandu was alone with his wife Madri in semi-transparent attire. And beholding the youthful Madri thus attired, the king's desire flamed up like a forest-fire. And ill-able to suppress his desire thus kindled at the sight of his wife of eyes like lotus-petals, he was completely overpowered. The king then seized her against her will, but Madri trembling in fear resisted him to the best of her might. Consumed by desire, he forgot everything about his misfortune. And, O thou of Kuru's race unrestrained by the fear of (the Rishi's) curse and impelled by fate, the monarch, overpowered by passion, forcibly sought the embraces of Madri, as if he wished to put an end to his own life. His reason, thus beguiled by the great Destroyer himself by intoxicating his senses, was itself lost with his life. And the Kuru king Pandu, of virtuous soul, thus succumbed to the inevitable influence of Time, while united in intercourse with his wife.

"Then Madri, clasping the body of her senseless lord, began to weep aloud. And Kunti with her sons and the twins of Madri, hearing those cries of grief, came to the spot where the king lay in that state. Then, O king, Madri addressing Kunti in a piteous voice, said, 'Come hither alone, O Kunti, and let the children stay there.' Hearing these words, Kunti, the children stay, ran with speed, exclaiming, 'Woe to me!' And beholding both Pandu and Madri lying prostrate on the ground she went in grief and affliction, saying, 'Of passions under complete control, this hero, O Madri, had all along been watched by me with care. How did he then forgetting the Rishi's curse, approach thee with enkindled desire? O Madri, this foremost of men should have been protected by thee. Why didst thou tempt him into solitude? Always melancholy at the thought of the Rishi's curse, how came he to be merry with thee in solitude? O princess of Valhika, more fortunate than myself, thou art really to be envied, for thou hast seen the face of our lord suffused with gladness and joy.'

"Madri then replied, saying, 'Revered sister, with tears in my eyes, I resisted the king, but he could not control himself, bent on, as it were making the Rishi's curse true.'

"Kunti then said, 'I am the older of his wedded wives; the chief religious merit must be mine. Therefore, O Madri, prevent me not from achieving that which must be achieved. I must follow our lord to the region of the dead. Rise up, O Madri, and yield me his body. Rear thou these children.' Madri replied, saying, 'I do clasp our lord yet, and have not allowed him to depart; therefore, I shall follow him. My appetite hath not been appeased. Thou art my older sister, O let me have thy sanction. This foremost one of the Bharata princes had approached me, desiring to have intercourse. His appetite unsatiated, shall I not follow him in the region of Yama to gratify him? O revered one, if I survive thee, it is certain I shall not be able to rear thy children as if they were mine. Will not sin touch me on that account? But, thou O Kunti, shall be able to bring my sons up as if they were thine. The king, in seeking me wishfully, hath gone to the region of spirits; therefore, my body should be burnt with his. O revered sister, withhold not thy sanction to this which is agreeable to me. Thou wilt certainly bring up the children carefully. That indeed, would be very agreeable to me. I have no other direction to give!'

"Vaisampayana continued, 'Having said this, the daughter of the king of Madras, the wedded wife of Pandu, ascended the funeral pyre of her lord, that bull among men.'"

SECTION CXXVI
(Sambhava Parva continued)

"Vaisampayana said, 'The godlike Rishis, wise in counsels, beholding the death of Pandu, consulted with one another, and said, 'The virtuous and renowned king Pandu, abandoning both sovereignty and kingdom came hither for practising ascetic austerities and resigned himself to the ascetics dwelling on this mountain. He hath hence ascended to heaven, leaving his wife and infant sons as a trust in our hands. Our duty now is to repair to his kingdom with these his offspring, and his wife.'

"Vaisampayana continued, 'Then those godlike Rishis of magnanimous hearts, and crowned with ascetic success, summoning one another, resolved to go to Hastinapura with Pandu's children ahead, desiring to place them in the hands of Bhishma and Dhritarashtra. The ascetics set out that very moment, taking with them those children and Kunti and the two dead bodies. And though unused to toil all her life, the affectionate Kunti now regarded as very short the really long journey she had to perform. Having arrived at Kurujangala within a short time, the illustrious Kunti presented herself at the principal gate. The ascetics then charged the porters to inform the king of their arrival. The men carried the message in a trice to the court. And the citizens of Hastinapura, hearing of the arrival of thousands of Charanas and Munis, were filled with wonder. And it was soon after sunrise that they began to come out in numbers with their wives and children to behold those ascetics. Seated in all kinds of cars and conveyances by thousands, vast numbers of Kshatriyas with their wives, and Brahmanas with theirs came out. And the concourse of Vaisyas and Sudras too was as large on the occasion. The vast assemblage was very peaceful, for every heart then was inclined to piety. And there also came out Bhishma, the son of Santanu, and Somadatta or Valhika and the royal sage (Dhritarashtra) endued with the vision of knowledge and Vidura himself and the venerable Satyavati and the illustrious princess of Kosala and Gandhari accompanied by the other ladies of the royal household. And the hundred sons of Dhritarashtra, decked with various ornaments, also came out.

"The Kauravas, then, accompanied by their priest, saluted the Rishis by lowering their heads, and took their seats before them. The citizens also saluting the ascetics and bowing down unto them with touching the ground, took their seats there. Then Bhishma, setting that vast concourse perfectly still, duly worshipped, O king, those ascetics by offering them water to wash their feet with and the customary Arghya. And having done this, he spoke unto them about the sovereignty and the kingdom. Then the oldest of the ascetics with matted locks on head and loins covered with animal skin, stood up, and with the concurrence of the other Rishis, spoke as follows, 'You all know that that possessor of the sovereignty of the Kurus who was called king Pandu, had, after abandoning the pleasures of the world, repaired hence to dwell on the mountain of a hundred peaks. He adopted the Brahmacharya mode of life, but for some inscrutable purpose the gods have in view, this his eldest son, Yudhishthira, was born there, begotten by Dharma himself. Then that illustrious king obtained from Vayu this other son—the foremost of all mighty men—called Bhima. This other son, begotten upon Kunti by Indra, is Dhananjaya whose achievements will humble all bowmen in the world. Look here again at these tigers among men, mighty in the use of the bow, the twin children begotten upon Madri by the twin Aswins. Leading in righteousness the life of a Vanaprastha in the woods, illustrious Pandu hath thus revived the almost extinct line of his grandfather. The birth, growth, and Vedic studies of these children of Pandu, will, no doubt, give you great pleasure. Steadily adhering to the path of the virtuous and the wise, and leaving behind him these children, Pandu departed hence seventeen days ago. His wife Madri, beholding him placed in the funeral pyre and about to be consumed, herself ascended the same pyre, and sacrificing her life thus, hath gone with her lord to the region reserved for chaste wives. Accomplish now whatever rites should be performed for their benefit. These are (the unburnt portions of) their bodies. Here also are their children—these oppressors of foes—with their mother. Let these be now received with due honours. After the completion of the first rites in honour of the dead, let the virtuous Pandu, who had all along been the supporter of the dignity of the Kurus, have the first annual Sraddha (sapindakarana) performed with a view to installing him formally among the Pitris.'

"Vaisampayana continued, 'The ascetics with Guhyakas, having said this unto the Kurus, instantly disappeared in the very sight of the people. And beholding the Rishis and the Siddhas thus vanish in their sight like vapoury forms appearing and disappearing in the skies, the citizens filled with wonder returned to their homes.'"

SECTION CXXVII
(Sambhava Parva continued)

"Vaisampayana continued, 'Dhritarashtra then said, 'O Vidura, celebrate the funeral ceremonies of that lion among kings viz., Pandu, and of Madri also, in right royal style. For the good of their souls, distribute cattle, cloths, gems and diverse kinds of wealth, every one receiving as much as he asketh for. Make arrangements also for Kunti's performing the last rites of Madri in such a style as pleaseth her. And let Madri's body be so carefully wrapped up that neither the Sun nor Vayu (god of wind) may behold it. Lament not for the sinless Pandu. He was a worthy king and hath left behind him five heroic sons equal unto the celestials themselves.'

"Vaisampayana continued, 'Then Vidura, O Bharata, saying, 'So be it,' in consultation with Bhishma, fixed upon a sacred spot for the funeral rites of Pandu. The family priests went out of the city without loss of time, carrying with them the blazing sacred fire fed with clarified butter and rendered fragrant therewith. Then friends, relatives, and adherents, wrapping it up in cloth, decked the body of the monarch with the flowers of the season and sprinkled various excellent perfumes over it. And they also decked the hearse itself with garlands and rich hangings. Then placing the covered body of the king with that of his queen on that excellent bier decked out so brightly, they caused it to be carried on human shoulders. With the white umbrella (of state) held over the hearse with waving yak-tails and sounds of various musical instruments, the whole scene looked bright and grand. Hundreds of people began to distribute gems among the crowd on the occasion of the funeral rites of the king. At length some beautiful robes, and white umbrellas and larger yak-tails, were brought for the great ceremony. The priests clad in white walked in the van of the procession pouring libations of clarified butter on the sacred fire blazing in an ornamental vessel. And Brahmanas, and Kshatriyas, and Vaisyas, and Sudras by thousands followed the deceased king, loudly wailing in these accents, 'O prince, where dost thou go, leaving us behind, and making us forlorn and wretched for ever?' And Bhishma, and Vidura, and the Pandavas, also all wept aloud. At last they came to a romantic wood on the banks of the Ganga. There they laid down the hearse on which the truthful and lion-hearted prince and his spouse lay. Then they brought water in many golden vessels, washed the prince's body besmeared before with several kinds of fragrant paste, and again smeared it over with sandal paste. They then dressed it in a white dress made of indigenous fabrics. And with the new suit on, the king seemed as if he was living and only sleeping on a costly bed.

"When the other funeral ceremonies also were finished in consonance with the directions of the priests, the Kauravas set fire to the dead bodies of the king and the queen, bringing lotuses, sandal-paste, and other fragrant substances to the pyre.

"Then seeing the bodies aflame, Kausalya burst out, 'O my son, my son!'— and fell down senseless on the ground. And seeing her down the citizens and the inhabitants of the provinces began to wail from grief and affection for their king. And the birds of the air and the beasts of the field were touched by the lamentations of Kunti. And Bhishma, the son of Santanu, and the wise Vidura, and the others also that were there, became disconsolate.

"Thus weeping, Bhishma, Vidura, Dhritarashtra, the Pandavas and the Kuru ladies, all performed the watery ceremony of the king. And when all this was over, the people, themselves filled with sorrow, began to console the bereaved sons of Pandu. And the Pandavas with their friends began to sleep on the ground. Seeing this the Brahmanas and the other citizens also renounced their beds. Young and old, all the citizens grieved on account of the sons of king Pandu, and passed twelve days in mourning with the weeping Pandavas.'"

SECTION CXXVIII
(Sambhava Parva continued)

"Vaisampayana said, 'Then Bhishma and Kunti with their friends celebrated the Sraddha of the deceased monarch, and offered the Pinda. And they feasted the Kauravas and thousands of Brahmanas unto whom they also gave gems and lands. Then the citizens returned to Hastinapura with the sons of Pandu, now that they had been cleansed from the impurity incident to the demise of their father. All then fell to weeping for the departed king. It seemed as if they had lost one of their own kin.

"When the Sraddha had been celebrated in the manner mentioned above, the venerable Vyasa, seeing all the subjects sunk in grief, said one day to his mother Satyavati, 'Mother, our days of happiness have gone by and days of calamity have succeeded. Sin beginneth to increase day by day. The world hath got old. The empire of the Kauravas will no longer endure because of wrong and oppression. Go thou then into the forest, and devote thyself to contemplation through Yoga. Henceforth society will be filled with deceit and wrong. Good work will cease. Do not witness the annihilation of thy race, in thy old age.'

"Acquiescing in the words of Vyasa, Satyavati entered the inner apartments and addressed her daughter-in-law, saying, 'O Ambika, I hear that in consequence of the deeds of your grandsons, this Bharata dynasty and its subjects will perish. If thou permit, I would go to the forest with Kausalya, so grieved at the loss of her son.' O king, saying this the queen, taking the permission of Bhishma also, went to the forest. And arriving there with her two daughters-in-law, she became engaged in profound contemplation, and in good time leaving her body ascended to heaven.'

"Vaisampayana continued, 'Then the sons of king Pandu, having gone through all the purifying rites prescribed in the Vedas, began to grow up in princely style in the home of their father. Whenever they were engaged in play with the sons of Dhritarashtra, their superiority of strength became marked. In speed, in striking the objects aimed at, in consuming articles of food, and scattering dust, Bhimasena beat all the sons of Dhritarashtra. The son of the Wind-god pulled them by the hair and made them fight with one another, laughing all the while. And Vrikodara easily defeated those hundred and one children of great energy as if they were one instead of being a hundred and one. The second Pandava used to seize them by the hair, and throwing them down, to drag them along the earth. By this, some had their knees broken, some their heads, and some their shoulders. That youth, sometimes holding ten of them, drowned them in water, till they were nearly dead. When the sons of Dhritarashtra got up to the boughs of a tree for plucking fruits, Bhima used to shake that tree, by striking it with his foot, so that down came the fruits and the fruitpluckers at the same time. In fact, those princes were no match for Bhima in pugilistic encounters, in speed, or in skill. Bhima used to make a display of his strength by thus tormenting them in childishness but not from malice.

"Seeing these wonderful exhibitions of the might of Bhima, the powerful Duryodhana, the eldest son of Dhritarashtra, began to conceive hostility towards him. And the wicked and unrighteous Duryodhana, through ignorance and ambition, prepared himself for an act of sin. He thought, 'There is no other individual who can compare with Bhima, the second son of Pandu, in point of prowess. I shall have to destroy him by artifice. Singly, Bhima dares a century of us to the combat. Therefore, when he shall sleep in the garden, I shall throw him into the current of the Ganga. Afterwards, confining his eldest brother Yudhishthira and his younger brother Arjuna, I shall reign sole king without molestation.' Determined thus, the wicked Duryodhana was ever on the watch to find out an opportunity for injuring Bhima. And, O Bharata, at length at a beautiful place called Pramanakoti on the banks of the Ganga, he built a palace decorated with hangings of broad-cloth and other rich stuffs. And he built this palace for sporting in the water there, and filled it with all kinds of entertaining things and choice viands. Gay flags waved on the top of this mansion. The name of the house was 'the water-sport house.' Skilful cooks prepared various kinds of viands. When all was ready, the officers gave intimation to Duryodhana. Then the evil-minded prince said unto the Pandavas, 'Let us all go to the banks of the Ganga graced with trees and crowned with flowers and sport there in the water.' And upon Yudhishthira agreeing to this, the sons of Dhritarashtra, taking the Pandavas with them, mounted country-born elephants of great size and cars resembling towns, and left the metropolis.

"On arriving at the place, the princes dismissed their attendants, and surveying the beauty of the gardens and the groves, entered the palace, like lions entering their mountain caves. On entering they saw that the architects had handsomely plastered the walls and the ceilings and that painters had painted them beautifully. The windows looked very graceful, and the artificial fountains were splendid. Here and there were tanks of pellucid water in which bloomed forests of lotuses. The banks were decked with various flowers whose fragrance filled the atmosphere. The Kauravas and the Pandavas sat down and began to enjoy the things provided for them. They became engaged in play and began to exchange morsels of food with one another. Meanwhile the wicked Duryodhana had mixed a powerful poison with a quantity of food, with the object of making away with Bhima. That wicked youth who had nectar in his tongue and a razor in his heart, rose at length, and in a friendly way fed Bhima largely with that poisoned food, and thinking himself lucky in having compassed his end, was exceedingly glad at heart. Then the sons of Dhritarashtra and Pandu together became cheerfully engaged in sporting in the water. Their sport having been finished, they dressed themselves in white habiliments, and decked themselves with various ornaments. Fatigued with play, they felt inclined in the evening to rest in the pleasurehouse belonging to the garden. Having made the other youths take exercise in the waters, the powerful second Pandava was excessively fatigued. So that on rising from the water, he lay down on the ground. He was weary and under the influence of the poison. And the cool air served to spread the poison over all his frame, so that he lost his senses at once. Seeing this Duryodhana bound him with chords of shrubs, and threw him into the water. The insensible son of Pandu sank down till he reached the Naga kingdom. Nagas, furnished with fangs containing virulent venom, bit him by thousands. The vegetable poison, mingled in the blood of the son of the Wind god, was neutralised by the snake-poison. The serpents had bitten all over his frame, except his chest, the skin of which was so tough that their fangs could not penetrate it.

"On regaining consciousness, the son of Kunti burst his bands and began to press the snakes down under the ground. A remnant fled for life, and going to their king Vasuki, represented, 'O king of snakes, a man drowned under the water, bound in chords of shrubs; probably he had drunk poison. For when he fell amongst us, he was insensible. But when we began to bite him, he regained his senses, and bursting his fetters, commenced laying at us. May it please Your Majesty to enquire who is.'

"Then Vasuki, in accordance with the prayer of the inferior Nagas, went to the place and saw Bhimasena. Of the serpents, there was one, named Aryaka. He was the grandfather of the father of Kunti. The lord of serpents saw his relative and embraced him. Then, Vasuki, learning all, was pleased with Bhima, and said to Aryaka with satisfaction, 'How are we to please him? Let him have money and gems in profusion."

"On hearing the words of Vasuki, Aryaka said, 'O king of serpents, when Your Majesty is pleased with him, no need of wealth for him! Permit him to drink of rasakunda (nectar-vessels) and thus immeasurable strength. There is the strength of a thousand elephants in each one of those vessels. Let this prince drink as much as he can.'

"The king of serpents gave his consent. And the serpents thereupon began auspicious rites. Then purifying himself carefully, Bhimasena facing the east began to drink nectar. At one breath, he quaffed off the contents of a whole vessel, and in this manner drained off eight successive jars, till he was full. At length, the serpents prepared an excellent bed for him, on which he lay down at ease.'"

SECTION CXXIX
(Sambhava Parva continued)

"Vaisampayana said, 'Meanwhile the Kauravas and the Pandavas, after having thus sported there, set out, without Bhima, for Hastinapura, some on horses, some on elephants, while others preferred cars and other conveyances. And on their way they said to one another, 'Perhaps, Bhima hath gone before us.' And the wicked Duryodhana was glad at heart to miss Bhima, and entered the city with his brothers in joy.

"The virtuous Yudhishthira, himself unacquainted with vice and wickedness, regarded others to be as honest as himself. The eldest son of Pritha, filled with fraternal love, going unto his mother, said, after making obeisance to her, 'O mother, hath Bhima come? O good mother, I don't find him here. Where may he have gone? We long sought for him everywhere in the gardens and the beautiful woods; but found him nowhere. At length, we thought that the heroic Bhima preceded us all. O illustrious dame, we came hither in great anxiety. Arrived here, where hath he gone? Have you sent him anywhere? O tell me, I am full of doubts respecting the mighty Bhima. He had been asleep and hath not come. I conclude he is no more.'

"Hearing these words of the highly intelligent Yudhishthira, Kunti shrieked, in alarm, and said, 'Dear son, I have not seen Bhima. He did not come to me. O, return in haste, and with your brothers search for him.'

"Having said this in affliction to her eldest son, she summoned Vidura, and said, 'O illustrious Kshattri, Bhimasena is missing! Where has he gone? The other brothers have all come back from the gardens, only Bhima of mighty arms does not come home! Duryodhana likes him not. The Kaurava is crooked and malicious and low-minded and imprudent. He coveteth the throne openly. I am afraid he may have in a fit of anger slain my darling. This afflicts me sorely, indeed, it burns my heart.'

"Vidura replied, 'Blessed dame, say not so! Protect thy other sons with care. If the wicked Duryodhana be accused, he may slay thy remaining sons. The great sage hath said that all thy sons will be long-lived. Therefore, Bhima will surely return and gladden thy heart.'

"Vaisampayana continued, 'The wise Vidura, having said this unto Kunti, returned to his abode, while Kunti, in great anxiety, continued to stay at home with her children.

"Meanwhile, Bhimasena awoke from that slumber on the eighth day, and felt strong beyond measure in consequence of the nectar he had taken having been all digested. Seeing him awake, the Nagas began to console and cheer him, saying, 'O thou of mighty arms, the strength-giving liquor thou hast drunk will give thee the might of ten thousand elephants! No one now will be able to vanquish thee in fight. O bull of Kuru's race, do thou bath in this holy and auspicious water and return home. Thy brothers are disconsolate because of thee.'

"Then Bhima purified himself with a bath in those waters, and decked in white robes and flowery garlands of the same hue, ate of the paramanna (rice and sugar pudding) offered to him by the Nagas. Then that oppressor of all foes, decked in celestial ornaments, received the adorations and blessings of the snakes, and saluting them in return, rose from the nether region. Bearing up the lotus-eyed Pandava from under the waters, the Nagas placed him in the selfsame gardens wherein he had been sporting, and vanished in his very sight.

"The mighty Bhimasena, arrived on the surface of the earth, ran with speed to his mother. And bowing down unto her and his eldest brother, and smelling the heads of his younger brothers, that oppressor of all foes was himself embraced by his mother and every one of those bulls among men. Affectionate unto one another, they all repeatedly exclaimed, 'What is our joy today, O what joy!'

"Then Bhima, endued with great strength and prowess, related to his brothers everything about the villainy of Duryodhana, and the lucky and unlucky incidents that had befallen him in the world of the Serpents. Thereupon Yudhishthira said, 'Do thou observe silence on this. Do not speak of this to any one. From this day, protect ye all one another with care.' Thus cautioned by the righteous Yudhishthira, they all, with Yudhishthira himself, became very vigilant from that day. And lest negligence might occur on the part of the sons of Kunti, Vidura continually offered them sage advice.

"Some time after, Duryodhana again mixed in the food of Bhima a poison that was fresh, virulent, and very deadly. But Yuyutsu (Dhritarashtra's son by a Vaisya wife), moved by his friendship for the Pandavas, informed them of this. Vrikodara, however, swallowed it without any hesitation, and digested it completely. And, though virulent the poison produced no effects on Bhima.

"When that terrible poison intended for the destruction of Bhima failed of its effect, Duryodhana, Karna and Sakuni, without giving up their wicked design had recourse to numerous other contrivances for accomplishing the death of the Pandavas. And though every one of these contrivances was fully known to the Pandavas, yet in accordance with the advice of Vidura they suppressed their indignation.

"Meanwhile, the king (Dhritarashtra), beholding the Kuru princes passing their time in idleness and growing naughty, appointed Gautama as their preceptor and sent them unto him for instruction. Born among a clump of heath, Gautama was well-skilled in the Vedas and it was under him (also called Kripa) that the Kuru princes began to learn the use of arms.'"

SECTION CXXX
(Sambhava Parva continued)

"Janamejaya said, 'O Brahmana, it behoveth thee to relate to me everything about the birth of Kripa. How did he spring from a clump of heath? Whence also did he obtain his weapons?'

"Vaisampayana said, 'O king, the great sage Gautama had a son named Saradwat. This Saradwat was born with arrows (in hand). O oppressor of foes, the son of Gautama exhibited great aptitude for the study of the science of weapons, but none for the other sciences. Saradwat acquired all his weapons by those austerities by which Brahmanas in student life acquire the knowledge of Vedas. Gautama (the son of Gotama) by his aptitude for the science of weapons and by his austerities made Indra himself greatly afraid of him. Then, O thou of Kuru's race, the chief of the gods summoned a celestial damsel named Janapadi and sent her unto Gautama, saying, 'Do thy best to disturb the austerities of Gautama.' Repairing unto the charming asylum of Saradwat, the damsel began to tempt the ascetic equipped with bow and arrows. Beholding that Apsara, of figure unrivalled on earth for beauty, alone in those woods and clad in a single piece of cloth, Saradwat's eyes expanded with delight. At the sight of the damsel, his bow and arrows slipped from his hand and his frame shook all over with emotion; but possessed of ascetic fortitude and strength of soul, the sage mustered sufficient patience to bear up against the temptation. The suddenness, however, of his mental agitation, caused an unconscious emission of his vital fluid. Leaving his bow and arrows and deer-skin behind, he went away, flying from the Apsara. His vital fluid, however, having fallen upon a clump of heath, was divided into two parts, whence sprang two children that were twins.

"And it happened that a soldier in attendance upon king Santanu while the monarch was out a-hunting in the woods, came upon the twins. And seeing the bow and arrows and deer-skin on the ground, he thought they might be the offspring of some Brahmana proficient in the science of arms. Deciding thus, he took up the children along with the bow and arrows, and showed what he had to the king. Beholding them the king was moved with pity, and saying, 'Let these become my children,' brought them to his palace. Then that first of men, Santanu, the son of Pratipa having brought Gautama's twins into his house, performed in respect of them the usual rites of religion. And he began to bring them up and called them Kripa and Kripi, in allusion to the fact that he brought them up from motives of pity (Kripa). The son of Gotama having left his former asylum, continued his study of the science of arms in right earnest. By his spiritual insight he learnt that his son and daughter were in the palace of Santanu. He thereupon went to the monarch and represented everything about his lineage. He then taught Kripa the four branches of the science of arms, and various other branches of knowledge, including all their mysteries and recondite details. In a short time Kripa became an eminent professor of the science (of arms). And the hundred sons of Dhritarashtra, and the Pandavas along with the Yadavas, and the Vrishnis, and many other princes from various lands, began to receive lessons from him in that science.'"

SECTION CXXXI
(Sambhava Parva continued)

"Vaisampayana said, 'Desirous of giving his grandsons a superior education, Bhishma was on the look-out for a teacher endued with energy and well- skilled in the science of arms. Deciding, O chief of the

Bharatas, that none who was not possessed of great intelligence, none who was not illustrious or a perfect master of the science of arms, none who was not of godlike might, should be the instructor of the Kuru (princes), the son of Ganga, O tiger among men, placed the Pandavas and the Kauravas under the tuition of Bharadwaja's son, the intelligent Drona skilled in all the Vedas. Pleased with the reception given him by the great Bhishma, that foremost of all men skilled in arms, viz., illustrious Drona of world-wide fame, accepted the princes as his pupils. And Drona taught them the science of arms in all its branches. And, O monarch, both the Kauravas and the Pandavas endued with immeasurable power, in a short time became proficient in the use of all kinds of arms.'

"Janamejaya asked, 'O Brahmana, how was Drona born? How and whence did he acquire his arms? How and why came he unto the Kurus? Whose son also was endued with such energy? Again, how was his son Aswatthaman, the foremost of all skilled in arms born? I wish to hear all this! Please recite them in detail.'

"Vaisampayana said, 'There dwelt at the source of the Ganga, a great sage named Bharadwaja, ceaselessly observing the most rigid vows. One day, of old, intending to celebrate the Agnihotra sacrifice he went along with many great Rishis to the Ganga to perform his ablutions. Arrived at the bank of the stream, he saw Ghritachi herself, that Apsara endued with youth and beauty, who had gone there a little before. With an expression of pride in her countenance, mixed with a voluptuous languor of attitude, the damsel rose from the water after her ablutions were over. And as she was gently treading on the bank, her attire which was loose became disordered. Seeing her attire disordered, the sage was smitten with burning desire. The next moment his vital fluid came out, in consequence of the violence of his emotion. The Rishi immediately held it in a vessel called a drona. Then, O king, Drona sprang from the fluid thus preserved in that vessel by the wise Bharadwaja. And the child thus born studied all the Vedas and their branches. Before now Bharadwaja of great prowess and the foremost of those possessing a knowledge of arms, had communicated to the illustrious Agnivesa, a knowledge of the weapon called Agneya. O foremost one of Bharata's race, the Rishi (Agnivesa) sprung from fire now communicated the knowledge of that great weapon to Drona the son of his preceptor.

"There was a king named Prishata who was a great friend of Bharadwaja. About this time Prishata had a son born unto him, named Drupada. And that bull among Kshatriyas, viz., Drupada, the son of Prishata, used every day to come to the hermitage of Bharadwaja to play with Drona and study in his company. O monarch, when Prishata was dead, this Drupada of mighty arms became the king of the northern Panchalas. About this time the illustrious Bharadwaja also ascended to heaven. Drona continuing to reside in his father's hermitage devoted himself to ascetic austerities. Having become well-versed in the Vedas and their branches and having burnt also all his sins by asceticism, the celebrated Drona, obedient to the injunctions of his father and moved by the desire of offspring married Kripi, the daughter of Saradwat. And this woman, ever engaged in virtuous acts and the Agnihotra, and the austerest of penances, obtained a son named Aswatthaman. And as soon as Aswatthaman was born, he neighed like the (celestial) steed Ucchaihsravas. Hearing that cry, an invisible being in the skies said, 'The voice of this child hath, like the neighing of a horse, been audible all around. The child shall, therefore, be known by the name of Aswatthaman, (the horse-voiced).' The son of Bharadwaja (Drona) was exceedingly glad at having obtained that child. Continuing to reside in that hermitage he devoted himself to the study of the science of arms.

"O king, it was about this time that Drona heard that the illustrious Brahmana Jamadagnya, that slayer of foes, that foremost one among all wielders of weapons, versed in all kinds of knowledge, had expressed a desire of giving away all his wealth to Brahmanas. Having heard of Rama's knowledge of arms and of his celestial weapons also, Drona set his heart upon them as also upon the knowledge of morality that Rama possessed. Then Drona of mighty arms, endued with high ascetic virtues, accompanied by disciples who were all devoted to vows ascetic austerities, set out for the Mahendra mountains. Arrived at Mahendra, the son of Bharadwaja possessed of high ascetic merit, beheld the son of Bhrigu, the exterminator of all foes, endued with great patience and with mind under complete control. Then, approaching with his disciples that scion of the Bhrigu race Drona, giving him his name, told him of his birth in the line of Angiras. And touching the ground with his head, he worshipped Rama's feet. And beholding the illustrious son of Jamadagni intent upon retiring into the woods after having given away all his wealth, Drona said, 'Know me to have sprung from Bharadwaja, but not in any woman's womb! I am a Brahmana of high birth, Drona by name, come to thee with the desire of obtaining thy wealth.'

"On hearing him, that illustrious grinder of the Kshatriya race replied, 'Thou art welcome, O best of regenerate ones! Tell me what thou desirest.' Thus addressed by Rama, the son of Bharadwaja replied unto that foremost of all smiters, desirous of giving away the whole of his wealth, 'O thou of multifarious vows, I am a candidate for thy eternal wealth.' 'O thou of ascetic wealth, returned Rama, 'My gold and whatever other wealth I had, have all been given away unto Brahmanas! This earth also, to the verge of the sea, decked with towns and cities, as with a garland of flowers, I have given unto Kasyapa. I have now my body only and my various valuable weapons left. I am prepared to give either my body or my weapons. Say, which thou wouldst have! I would give it thee! Say quickly!'

"Drona answered, O son of Bhrigu, it behoveth thee to give me all thy weapons together with the mysteries of hurling and recalling them.'

"Saying, 'So be it,' the son of Bhrigu gave all his weapons unto Drona,— indeed, the whole science of arms with its rules and mysteries. Accepting them all, and thinking himself amply rewarded that best of Brahmanas then, glad at heart, set out, for (the city of) his friend Drupada.'"

SECTION CXXXII
(Sambhava Parva continued)

"Vaisampayana said, 'Then, O king, the mighty son of Bharadyaja presented himself before Drupada, and addressing that monarch, said, 'Know me for thy friend.' Thus addressed by his friend, the son of Bharadwaja, with a joyous heart, the lord of the Panchalas was ill-able to bear that speech. The king, intoxicated with the pride of wealth, contracted his brows in wrath, and with reddened eyes spake these words unto Drona, 'O Brahmana, thy intelligence is scarcely of a high order, inasmuch as thou sayest unto me, all on a sudden, that thou art my friend! O thou of dull apprehension, great kings can never be friends with such luckless and indigent wights as thou! It is true there had been friendship between thee and me before, for we were then both equally circumstanced. But Time that impaireth everything in its course, impaireth friendship also. In this world, friendship never endureth for ever in any heart. Time weareth it off and anger destroyeth it too. Do not stick, therefore, to that worn-off friendship. Think not of it any longer. The friendship I had with thee, O first of Brahmanas, was for a particular purpose. Friendship can never subsist between a poor man and a rich man, between a man of letters and an unlettered mind, between a hero and a coward. Why dost thou desire the continuance of our former friendship? There may be friendship or hostility between persons equally situated as to wealth or might. The indigent and the affluent can neither be friends nor quarrel with each other. One of impure birth can never be a friend to one of pure birth; one who is not a car-warrior can never be a friend to one who is so; and one who is not a king never have a king for his friend. Therefore, why dost thou desire the continuance of our former friendship?'

"Vaisampayana continued, 'Thus addressed by Drupada, the mighty son of Bharadwaja became filled with wrath, and reflecting for a moment, made up his mind as to his course of action. Seeing the insolence of the Panchala king, he wished to check it effectually. Hastily leaving the Panchala capital Drona bent his steps towards the capital of the Kurus, named after the elephant.'"

SECTION CXXXIII
(Sambhava Parva continued)

"Vaisampayana said, 'Arrived at Hastinapura, that best of Brahmanas, the son of Bharadwaja, continued to live privately in the house of Gautama (Kripa). His mighty son (Aswatthaman) at intervals of Kripa's teaching, used to give the sons of Kunti lessons in the use of arms. But as yet none knew of Aswatthaman's prowess.

"Drona had thus lived privately for some time in the house of Kripa when one day the heroic princes, all in a company, came out of Hastinapura. And coming out of the city, they began to play with a ball and roam about in gladness of heart. And it so happened that the ball with which they had been playing fell into a well. And thereupon the princes strove their best to recover it from the well. But all the efforts the princes made to recover it proved futile. They then began to eye one another bashfully, and not knowing how to recover it, their anxiety became great. Just at this time they beheld a Brahmana near enough unto them, of darkish hue, decrepit and lean, sanctified by the performance of the Agnihotra and who had finished his daily rites of worship. And beholding that illustrious Brahmana, the princes who had despaired of success surrounded him immediately. Drona (for that Brahmana was no other), seeing the princes unsuccessful, and conscious of his own skill, smiled a little, and addressing them said, 'Shame on your Kshatriya might, and shame also on your skill in arms! You have been born in the race of Bharata! How is it that ye cannot recover the ball (from the bottom of this well)? If ye promise me a dinner today, I will, with these blades of grass, bring up not only the ball ye have lost but this ring also that I now throw down!' Thus saying, Drona that oppressor of foes, taking off his ring, threw it down into the dry well. Then Yudhishthira, the son of Kunti, addressing Drona, said, 'O Brahmana (thou askest for a trifle)! Do thou, with Kripa's permission, obtain of us that which would last thee for life!' Thus addressed, Drona with smiles replied unto the Bharata princes, saying, 'This handful of long grass I would invest, by my mantras, with the virtue of weapons. Behold these blades possess virtues that other weapons, have not! I will, with one of these blades, pierce the ball, and then pierce that blade with another, and that another with a third, and thus shall I, by a chain, bring up the ball.'

"Vaisampayana continued, 'Then Drona did exactly what he had said. And the princes were all amazed and their eyes expanded with delight. And regarding what they had witnessed to be very extraordinary, they said, O learned Brahmana, do thou bring up the ring also without loss of time.'

"Then the illustrious Drona, taking a bow with an arrow, pierced the ring with that arrow and brought it up at once. And taking the ring thus brought up from the well still pierced with his arrow, he coolly gave it to the astonished princes. Then the latter, seeing the ring thus recovered, said, 'We bow to thee, O Brahmana! None else owneth such skill. We long to know who thou art and whose son. What also can we do for thee?'

"Thus addressed, Drona replied unto the princes, saying, 'Do ye repair unto Bhishma and describe to him my likeness and skill. The mighty one will recognize me.' The princes then saying, 'So be it,' repaired unto Bhishma and telling him of the purport of that Brahmana's speech, related everything about his (extraordinary) feat. Hearing everything from the princes, Bhishma at once understood that the Brahmana was none else than Drona, and thinking that he would make the best preceptor for the princes, went in person unto him and welcoming him respectfully, brought him over to the place. Then Bhishma, that foremost of all wielders of arms, adroitly asked him the cause of his arrival at Hastinapura. Asked by him, Drona represented everything as it had happened, saying, 'O sir, in times past I went to the great Rishi Agnivesa for obtaining from him his weapons, desirous also of learning the science of arms. Devoted to the service of my preceptor, I lived with him for many years in the humble guise of a Brahmacharin, with matted locks on my head. At that time, actuated by the same motives, the prince of Panchala, the mighty Yajnasena, also lived in the same asylum. He became my friend, always seeking my welfare. I liked him much. Indeed, we lived together for many, many years. O thou of Kuru's race, from our earliest years we had studied together and, indeed, he was my friend from boyhood, always speaking and doing what was agreeable to me. For gratifying me, O Bhishma, he used to tell me, 'O Drona, I am the favourite child of my illustrious father. When the king installeth me as monarch of the Panchalas, the kingdom shall be thine. O friend, this, indeed, is my solemn promise. My dominion, wealth and happiness, shall all be dependent on thee.' At last the time came for his departure. Having finished his studies, he bent his steps towards his country. I offered him my regards at the time, and, indeed, I remembered his words ever afterwards.

"Some time after, in obedience to the injunctions of my father and tempted also by the desire of offspring, I married Kripi of short hair, who gifted with great intelligence, had observed many rigid vows, and was ever engaged in the Agnihotra and other sacrifices and rigid austerities. Gautami, in time, gave birth to a son named Aswatthaman of great prowess and equal in splendour unto the Sun himself. Indeed, I was pleased on having obtained Aswatthaman as much as my father had been on obtaining me.

"And it so happened that one day the child Aswatthaman observing some rich men's sons drink milk, began to cry. At this I was so beside myself that I lost all knowledge of the point of the compass. Instead of asking him who had only a few kine (so that if he gave me one, he would no longer be able to perform his sacrifices and thus sustain a loss of virtue), I was desirous of obtaining a cow from one who had many, and for that I wandered from country to country. But my wanderings proved unsuccessful, for I failed to obtain a milch cow. After I had come back unsuccessful, some of my son's playmates gave him water mixed with powdered rice. Drinking this, the poor boy, was deceived into the belief that he had taken milk, and began to dance in joy, saying, 'O, I have taken milk. I have taken milk!' Beholding him dance with joy amid these playmates smiling at his simplicity, I was exceedingly touched. Hearing also the derisive speeches of busy-bodies who said, 'Fie upon the indigent Drona, who strives not to earn wealth, whose son drinking water mixed with powdered rice mistaketh it for milk and danceth with joy, saying, 'I have taken milk,—I have taken milk!'—I was quite beside myself. Reproaching myself much, I at last resolved that even if I should have to live cast off and censured by Brahmanas, I would not yet, from desire of wealth, be anybody's servant, which is ever hateful. Thus resolved, O Bhishma, I went, for former friendship, unto the king of the Somakas, taking with me my dear child and wife. Hearing that he had been installed in the sovereignty (of the Somakas), I regarded myself as blessed beyond compare. Joyfully I went unto that dear friend of mine seated on the throne, remembering my former friendship with him and also his own words to me. And, O illustrious one, approaching Drupada, I said, 'O tiger among men, know me for thy friend!'— Saying this, I approached him confidently as a friend should. But Drupada, laughing in derision cast me off as if I were a vulgar fellow. Addressing me he said, 'Thy intelligence scarcely seemeth to be of a high order inasmuch as approaching me suddenly, thou sayest thou art my friend! Time that impaireth everything, impaireth friendship also. My former friendship with thee was for a particular purpose. One of impure birth can never be a friend of one who is of pure birth. One who is not a car-warrior can never be a friend of one who is such. Friendship can only subsist between persons that are of equal rank, but not between those that are unequally situated. Friendship never subsisteth for ever in my heart. Time impaireth friendships, as also anger destroyeth them. Do thou not stick, therefore, to that worn-off friendship between us. Think not of it any longer. The friendship I had with thee, O best of Brahmanas, was for a special purpose. There cannot be friendship between a poor man and a rich man, between an unlettered hind and a man of letters, between a coward and a hero. Why dost thou, therefore, desire the revival of our former friendship? O thou of simple understanding, great kings can never have friendship with such indigent and luckless wight as thou. One who is not a king can never have a king for his friend. I do not remember ever having promised thee my kingdom. But, O Brahmana, I can now give thee food and shelter for one night.'—Thus addressed by him, I left his presence quickly with my wife, vowing to do that which I will certainly do soon enough. Thus insulted by Drupada, O Bhishma, I have been filled with wrath, I have come to the Kurus, desirous of obtaining intelligent and docile pupils. I come to Hastinapura to gratify thy wishes. O, tell me what I am to do.'

"Vaisampayana continued, 'Thus addressed by the son of Bharadwaja, Bhishma said unto him, 'String thy bow, O Brahmana, and make the Kuru princes accomplished in arms. Worshipped by the Kurus, enjoy with a glad heart to thy fill every comfort in their abode. Thou art the absolute lord, O Brahmana, of what ever wealth the Kurus have and of their sovereignty and kingdom! The Kurus are thine (from this day). Think that as already accomplished which may be in thy heart. Thou art, O Brahmana, obtained by us as the fruit of our great good luck. Indeed, the favour thou hast conferred upon me by thy arrival is great.'

SECTION CXXXIV
(Sambhava Parva continued)

"Vaisampayana said, 'Thus worshipped by Bhishma, Drona, that first of men, endued with great energy, took up his quarters in the abode of the Kurus and continued to live there, receiving their adorations. After he had rested a while, Bhishma, taking with him his grandsons, the Kaurava princes, gave them unto him as pupils, making at the same time many valuable presents. And the mighty one (Bhishma) also joyfully gave unto the son of Bharadwaja a house that was tidy and neat and well-filled with paddy and every kind of wealth. And that first of archers, Drona, thereupon joyfully accepted the Kauravas, viz., the sons of Pandu and Dhritarashtra, as his pupils. And having accepted them all as his pupils, one day Drona called them apart and making them touch his feet, said to them with a swelling heart, 'I have in my heart a particular purpose. Promise me truly, ye sinless ones, that when ye have become skilled in arms, ye will accomplish it.'

"Vaisampayana continued, 'Hearing these words, the Kuru princes remained silent. But Arjuna, O king, vowed to accomplish it whatever it was. Drona then cheerfully clasped Arjuna to his bosom and took the scent of his head repeatedly, shedding tears of joy all the while. Then Drona endued with great prowess taught the sons of Pandu (the use of) many weapons both celestial and human. And, O bull of the Bharata race, many other princes also flocked to that best of Brahmanas for instruction in arms. The Vrishnis and the Andhakas, and princes from various lands, and the (adopted) son of Radha of the Suta caste, (Karna), all became pupils of Drona. But of them all, the Suta child Karna, from jealousy, frequently defied Arjuna, and supported by Duryodhana, used to disregard the Pandavas. Arjuna, however, from devotion to the science of arms, always stayed by the side of his preceptor, and in skill, strength of arms, and perseverance, excelled all (his class-fellows). Indeed, although the instruction the preceptor gave, was the same in the case of all, yet in lightness and skill Arjuna became the foremost of all his fellow-pupils. And Drona was convinced that none of his pupils would (at any time) be able to be equal to that son of Indra.

"Thus Drona continued giving lessons to the princes in the science of weapons. And while he gave unto every one of his pupils a narrow-mouthed vessel (for fetching water) in order that much time may be spent in filling them, he gave unto his own son Aswatthaman a broad-mouthed vessel, so that, filling it quickly, he might return soon enough. And in the intervals so gained, Drona used to instruct his own son in several superior methods (of using weapons). Jishnu (Arjuna) came to know of this, and thereupon filling his narrow-mouthed vessel with water by means of the Varuna weapon he used to come unto his preceptor at the same time with his preceptor's son. And accordingly the intelligent son of Pritha, that foremost of all men possessing a knowledge of weapons, had no inferiority to his preceptor's son in respect of excellence. Arjuna's devotion to the service of his preceptor as also to arms was very great and he soon became the favourite of his preceptor. And Drona, beholding his pupil's devotion to arms, summoned the cook, and told him in secret, 'Never give Arjuna his food in the dark, nor tell him that I have told thee this.' A few days after, however, when Arjuna was taking his food, a wind arose, and thereupon the lamp that had been burning went out. But Arjuna, endued with energy, continued eating in the dark, his hand, from habit, going to his mouth. His attention being thus called to the force of habit, the strong- armed son of Pandu set his heart upon practising with his bow in the night. And, O Bharata, Drona, hearing the twang of his bowstring in the night, came to him, and clasping him, said, 'Truly do I tell thee that I shall do that unto thee by which there shall not be an archer equal to thee in this world.'

"Vaisampayana continued, 'Thereafter Drona began to teach Arjuna the art of fighting on horse-back, on the back of elephants, on car, and on the ground. And the mighty Drona also instructed Arjuna in fighting with the mace, the sword, the lance, the spear, and the dart. And he also instructed him in using many weapons and fighting with many men at the same time. And hearing reports of his skill, kings and princes, desirous of learning the science of arms, flocked to Drona by thousands. Amongst those that came there, O monarch, was a prince named Ekalavya, who was the son of Hiranyadhanus, king of the Nishadas (the lowest of the mixed orders). Drona, however, cognisant of all rules of morality, accepted not the prince as his pupil in archery, seeing that he was a Nishada who might (in time) excel all his high-born pupils. But, O oppressor of all enemies, the Nishada prince, touching Drona's feet with bent head, wended his way into the forest, and there he made a clay-image of Drona, and began to worship it respectfully, as if it was his real preceptor, and practised weapons before it with the most rigid regularity. In consequence of his exceptional reverence for his preceptor and his devotion to his purpose, all the three processes of fixing arrows on the bowstring, aiming, and letting off became very easy for him.

"And one day, O grinder of foes, the Kuru and the Pandava princes, with Drona's leave, set out in their cars on a hunting excursion. A servant, O king, followed the party at leisure, with the usual implements and a dog. Having come to the woods, they wandered about, intent on the purpose they had in view. Meanwhile, the dog also, in wandering alone in the woods, came upon the Nishada prince (Ekalavya). And beholding the Nishada of dark hue, of body besmeared with filth, dressed in black and bearing matted locks on head, the dog began to bark aloud.

"Thereupon the Nishada prince, desirous of exhibiting his lightness of hand, sent seven arrows into its mouth (before it could shut it). The dog, thus pierced with seven arrows, came back to the Pandavas. Those heroes, who beheld that sight, were filled with wonder, and, ashamed of their own skill, began to praise the lightness of hand and precision of aim by auricular precision (exhibited by the unknown archer). And they thereupon began to seek in those woods for the unknown dweller therein that had shown such skill. And, O king, the Pandavas soon found out the object of their search ceaselessly discharging arrows from the bow. And beholding that man of grim visage, who was totally a stranger to them, they asked, 'Who art thou and whose son?' Thus questioned, the man replied, 'Ye heroes, I am the son of Hiranyadhanus, king of the Nishadas. Know me also for a pupil of Drona, labouring for the mastery of the art of arms.'

"Vaisampayana continued, 'The Pandavas then, having made themselves acquainted with everything connected with him, returned (to the city), and going unto Drona, told him of that wonderful feat of archery which they had witnessed in the woods. Arjuna, in particular, thinking all the while, O king, Ekalavya, saw Drona in private and relying upon his preceptor's affection for him, said, 'Thou hadst lovingly told me, clasping me, to thy bosom, that no pupil of thine should be equal to me. Why then is there a pupil of thine, the mighty son of the Nishada king, superior to me?'

"Vaisampayana continued, 'On hearing these words, Drona reflected for a moment, and resolving upon the course of action he should follow, took Arjuna with him and went unto the Nishada prince. And he beheld Ekalavya with body besmeared with filth, matted locks (on head), clad in rags, bearing a bow in hand

and ceaselessly shooting arrows therefrom. And when Ekalavya saw Drona approaching towards him, he went a few steps forward, and touched his feet and prostrated himself on the ground. And the son of the Nishada king worshipping Drona, duly represented himself as his pupil, and clasping his hands in reverence stood before him (awaiting his commands). Then Drona, O king, addressed Ekalavya, saying, 'If, O hero, thou art really my pupil, give me then my fees.' On hearing these words, Ekalavya was very much gratified, and said in reply, 'O illustrious preceptor, what shall I give? Command me; for there is nothing, O foremost of all persons conversant with the Vedas, that I may not give unto my preceptor.' Drona answered, 'O Ekalavya, if thou art really intent on making me a gift, I should like then to have the thumb of thy right hand.'

"Vaisampayana continued, 'Hearing these cruel words of Drona, who had asked of him his thumb as tuition-fee, Ekalavya, ever devoted to truth and desirous also of keeping his promise, with a cheerful face and an unafflicted heart cut off without ado his thumb, and gave it unto Drona. After this, when the Nishada prince began once more to shoot with the help of his remaining fingers, he found, O king, that he had lost his former lightness of hand. And at this Arjuna became happy, the fever (of jealousy) having left him.

"Two of Drona's pupils became very much accomplished in the use of mace. These were Druvodhana and Bhima, who were, however, always jealous of each other. Aswatthaman excelled everyone (in the mysteries of the science of arms). The twins (Nakula and Sahadeva) excelled everybody in handling the sword. Yudhishthira surpassed everybody as a car-warrior; but Arjuna, however, outdistanced everyone in every respect—in intelligence, resourcefulness, strength and perseverance. Accomplished in all weapons, Arjuna became the foremost of even the foremost of car-warriors; and his fame spread all over the earth to the verge of the sea. And although the instruction was the same, the mighty Arjuna excelled all (the princes in lightness of hand). Indeed, in weapons as in devotion to his preceptor, he became the foremost of them all. And amongst all the princes, Arjuna alone became an Atiratha (a car-warrior capable of fighting at one time with sixty thousand foes). And the wicked sons of Dhritarashtra, beholding Bhimasena endued with great strength and Arjuna accomplished in all arms, became very jealous of them.

"O bull among men, one day Drona desirous of testing the comparative excellence of all his pupils in the use of arms, collected them all together after their education had been completed. And before assembling them together, he had caused an artificial bird, as the would be aim, to be placed on the top of a neighbouring tree. And when they were all together, Drona said unto them, 'Take up your bows quickly and stand here aiming at that bird on the tree, with arrows fixed on your bowstrings; shoot and cut off the bird's head, as soon as I give the order. I shall give each of you a turn, one by one, my children.'

"Vaisampayana continued, 'Then Drona, that foremost of all Angira's sons first addressed Yudhishthira saying, 'O irrepressible one, aim with thy arrow and shoot as soon as I give the order.' Yudhishthira took up the bow first, as desired, O king, by his preceptor, and stood aiming at the bird. But, O bull of Bharata's race, Drona in an instant, addressing the Kuru prince standing with bow in hand, said, 'Behold, O prince, that bird on top of the tree.' Yudhishthira replied unto his preceptor, saying, 'I do.' But the next instant Drona again asked him, 'What dost thou see now, O prince? Seest thou the tree, myself or thy brothers?' Yudhishthira answered, 'I see the tree, myself, my brothers, and the bird.' Drona repeated his question, but was answered as often in the same words. Drona then, vexed with Yudhishthira, reproachingly said, 'Stand thou apart. It is not for thee to strike the aim.' Then Drona repeated the experiment with Duryodhana and the other sons of Dhritarashtra, one after another, as also with his other pupils, Bhima and the rest, including the princes that had come unto him from other lands. But the answer in every case was the same as Yudhishthira's viz., 'We behold the tree, thyself, our fellow- pupils, and the bird.' And reproached by their preceptor, they were all ordered, one after another, to stand apart.'"

SECTION CXXXV
(Sambhava Parva continued)

"Vaisampayana said, 'When everyone had failed, Drona smilingly called Arjuna and said unto him, 'By thee the aim must be shot; therefore, turn thy eyes to it. Thou must let fly the arrow as soon as I give the order. Therefore, O son, stand here with bow and arrow for an instant.' Thus addressed, Arjuna stood aiming at the bird as desired by his preceptor, with his bow bent. An instant after Drona asked him as in the case of others, 'Seest thou, O Arjuna, the bird there, the tree, and myself?' Arjuna replied, 'I see the bird only, but nor the tree, or thyself.' Then the irrepressible Drona, well-pleased with Arjuna, the instant after, again said unto that mighty car-warrior amongst the Pandavas, 'If thou seest the vulture, then describe it to me.' Arjuna said, 'I see only the head of the vulture, not its body.' At these words of Arjuna, the hair (on Drona's body) stood on end from delight. He then said to Partha, 'Shoot.' And the latter instantly let fly (his arrow) and with his sharp shaft speedily struck off the head of the vulture on the tree and brought it down to the ground. No sooner was the deed done than Drona clasped Phalguna to his bosom and thought Drupada with his friends had already been vanquished in fight.

"Some time after, O bull of Bharata's race, Drona, accompanied by all of his pupils, went to the bank of the Ganga to bathe in that sacred stream. And when Drona had plunged into the stream, a strong alligator, sent as it were, by Death himself seized him by the thigh. And though himself quite capable, Drona in a seeming hurry asked his pupil to rescue him. And he said, 'O, kill this monster and rescue me.' Contemporaneously with this speech, Vibhatsu (Arjuna) struck the monster within the water with five sharp arrows irresistible in their course, while the other pupils stood confounded, each at his place. Beholding Arjuna's readiness, Drona considered him to be the foremost of all his pupils, and became highly pleased. The monster, in the meantime cut into pieces by the arrows of Arjuna, released the thigh of illustrious Drona and gave up the ghost. The son of Bharadwaja then addressed the illustrious and mighty car-warrior Arjuna and said, 'Accept, O thou of mighty arms, this very superior and irresistible weapon called Brahmasira with the methods of hurling and recalling it. Thou must not, however, ever use it against any human foe, for if hurled at any foe endued with inferior energy, it might burn the whole universe. It is said, O child, that this weapon hath not a peer in the three worlds. Keep it, therefore, with great care, and listen to what I say. If ever, O hero, any foe, not human, contendeth against thee thou mayst then employ it against him for compassing his death in battle.' Pledging himself to do what he was bid, Vibhatsu then, with joined hands, received that great weapon.

The preceptor then, addressing him again, said, 'None else in this world will ever become a superior bowman to thee. Vanquished thou shall never be by any foe, and thy achievements will be great.'"

SECTION CXXXVI
(Sambhava Parva continued)

"Vaisampayana said, 'O thou of Bharata's race, beholding the sons of Dhritarashtra and Pandu accomplished in arms, Drona, O monarch, addressed king Dhritarashtra, in the presence of Kripa, Somadatta, Valhika, the wise son of Ganga (Bhishma), Vyasa, and Vidura, and said, 'O best of Kuru kings, thy children have completed their education. With thy permission, O king, let them now show their proficiency.' Hearing him, the king said with a gladdened heart, 'O best of Brahmanas, thou hast, indeed, accomplished a great deed. Command me thyself as to the place and the time where and when and the manner also in which the trial may be held. Grief arising from my own blindness maketh me envy those who, blessed with sight, will behold my children's prowess in arm. O Kshatri (Vidura), do all that Drona sayeth. O thou devoted to virtue, I think there is nothing that can be more agreeable to me.' Then Vidura, giving the necessary assurance to the king, went out to do what he was bid. And Drona endued with great wisdom, then measured out a piece of land that was void of trees and thickets and furnished with wells and springs. And upon the spot of land so measured out, Drona, that first of eloquent men, selecting a lunar day when the star ascendant was auspicious, offered up sacrifice unto the gods in the presence of the citizens assembled by proclamation to witness the same. And then, O bull among men, the artificers of the king built thereon a large and elegant stage according to the rules laid down in the scriptures, and it was furnished with all kinds of weapons. They also built another elegant hall for the lady-spectators. And the citizens constructed many platforms while the wealthier of them pitched many spacious and high tents all around.

"When the day fixed for the Tournament came, the king accompanied by his ministers, with Bhishma and Kripa, the foremost of preceptors, walking ahead, came unto that theatre of almost celestial beauty constructed of pure gold, and decked with strings of pearls and stones of lapis lazuli. And, O first of victorious men, Gandhari blessed with great good fortune and Kunti, and the other ladies of the royal household, in gorgeous attire and accompanied by their waiting women, joyfully ascended the platforms, like celestial ladies ascending the Sumeru mountain. And the four orders including the Brahmanas and Kshatriyas, desirous of beholding the princes' skill in arms, left the city and came running to the spot. And so impatient was every one to behold the spectacle, that the vast crowd assembled there in almost an instant. And with the sounds of trumpets and drums and the noise of many voices, that vast concourse appeared like an agitated ocean.

"At last, Drona accompanied by his son, dressed in white (attire), with a white sacred thread, white locks, white beard, white garlands, and white sandal-paste rubbed over his body, entered the lists. It seemed as if the Moon himself accompanied by the planet Mars appeared in an unclouded sky. On entering Bharadwaja performed timely worship and caused Brahmanas versed in mantras to celebrate the auspicious rites. And after auspicious and sweet-sounding musical instruments had been struck up as a propitiatory ceremony, some persons entered, equipped with various arms. And then having girded up their loins, those mighty warriors, those foremost ones of Bharata's race (the princes) entered, furnished with finger-protectors (gauntlet), and bows, and quivers. And with Yudhishthira at their head, the valiant princes entered in order of age and began to show wonderful skill with their weapons. Some of the spectators lowered their heads, apprehending fall of arrows while others fearlessly gazed on with wonder. And riding swiftly on horses and managing them 'dexterously' the princes began to hit marks with shafts engraved with their respective names. And seeing the prowess of the princes armed with bows and arrows, the spectators thought that they were beholding the city of the Gandharvas, became filled with amazement. And, O Bharata, all on a sudden, some hundreds and thousands, with eyes wide open in wonder, exclaimed, 'Well done! Well done!' And having repeatedly displayed their skill and dexterity in the use of bows and arrows and in the management of cars, the mighty warriors took up their swords and bucklers, and began to range the lists, playing their weapons. The spectators saw (with wonder) their agility, the symmetry of their bodies, their grace, their calmness, the firmness of their grasp and their deftness in the use of sword and buckler. Then Vrikodara and Suyodhana, internally delighted (at the prospect of fight), entered the arena, mace in hand, like two single-peaked mountains. And those mighty-armed warriors braced their loins, and summoning all their energy, roared like two infuriate elephants contending for a cow- elephant; and like two infuriated elephants those mighty heroes faultlessly (in consonance with the dictates of the science of arm) careered right and left, circling the lists. And Vidura described to Dhritarashtra and the mother of the Pandavas (Kunti) and Gandhari, all the feats of the princes.'"

SECTION CXXXVII
(Sambhava Parva continued)

"Vaisampayana continued, 'Upon the Kuru king and Bhima, the foremost of all endued with strength, having entered the arena, the spectators were divided into two parties in consequence of the partiality swaying their affections. Some cried, 'Behold the heroic king of the Kurus!'—some— 'Behold Bhima!'—And on account of these cries, there was, all on a sudden, a loud uproar. And seeing the place become like a troubled ocean, the intelligent Bharadwaja said unto his dear son, Aswatthaman, 'Restrain both these mighty warriors so proficient in arms. Let not the ire of the assembly be provoked by this combat of Bhima and Duryodhana.'

"Vaisampayana continued, 'Then the son of the preceptor of the princes restrained those combatants with their maces uplifted and resembling two swollen oceans agitated by the winds that blow at the universal dissolution. And Drona himself entering the yard of the arena commanded the musicians to stop, and with a voice deep as that of the clouds addressed these words, 'Behold ye now that Partha who is dearer to me than my own son, the master of all arms, the son of Indra himself, and like unto the younger brother of Indra, (Vishnu)! And having performed the propitiatory rites, the youthful Phalguna, equipped with the finger protector (gauntlet) and his quiver full of shafts and bow in hand, donning his golden mail, appeared in the lists even like an evening cloud reflecting the rays of the setting sun and illumined by the hues of the rainbow and flashes of lightning.

"On seeing Arjuna, the whole assembly were delighted and conchs began to be blown all around with other musical instruments. And there arose a great uproar in consequence of the spectators' exclaiming,— 'This is the graceful son of Kunti!'—'This is the middle (third) Pandava!'—'This is the son of the mighty

Indra!'—'This is the protector of the Kurus'—'This is the foremost of those versed in arms!'—'This is the foremost of all cherishers of virtue!'—'This is the foremost of the persons of correct behaviour, the great repository of the knowledge of manners!' At those exclamations, the tears of Kunti, mixing with the milk of her breast, wetted her bosom. And his ears being filled with that uproar, that first of men, Dhritarashtra, asked Vidura in delight, 'O Kshatri, what is this great uproar for, like unto that of the troubled ocean, arising all on a sudden and rending the very heavens?' Vidura replied, 'O mighty monarch, the son of Pandu and Pritha, Phalguna, clad in mail hath entered the lists. And hence this uproar!' Dhritarashtra said, 'O thou of soul so great, by the three fires sprung from Pritha who is even like the sacred fuel, I have, indeed, been blessed, favoured and protected!'

"Vaisampayana continued, 'When the spectators, excited with delight, had somewhat regained their equanimity, Vibhatsu began to display his lightness in the use of weapons. By the Agneya weapon, he created fire, and by the Varuna weapon he created water, by the Vayavya weapon, he created air, and by the Parjanya weapon he created clouds. And by the Bhauma weapon, he created land, and by the Parvatya weapon, he brought mountains into being. By the Antardhana weapon all these were made to disappear. Now the beloved one of his preceptor (Arjuna) appeared tall and now short; now he was seen on the yoke of his car, and now on the car itself; and the next moment he was on the ground. And the hero favoured by his practised dexterity, hit with his various butts—some tender, some fine and some of thick composition. And like one shaft, he let fly at a time into the mouth of a moving iron-boar five shafts together from his bow-string. And that hero of mighty energy discharged one and twenty arrows into the hollow of a cow's horn hung up on a rope swaying to and fro. In this manner, O sinless one, Arjuna showed his profound skill in the use of sword, bow, and mace, walking over the lists in circles.

"And, O Bharata, when the exhibition had well-nigh ended, the excitement of the spectators had cooled, and the sounds of instruments had died out there was heard proceeding from the gate, the slapping of arms, betokening might and strength, and even like unto the roar of the thunder. And, O king, as soon as this sound was heard, the assembled multitude instantly thought, 'Are the mountains splitting or is the earth itself rending asunder, or is the welkin resounding with the roar of gathering clouds?' And then all the spectators turned their eyes towards the gate. And Drona stood, surrounded by the five brothers, the sons of Pritha, and looked like the moon in conjunction with the five-starred constellation Hasta. And Duryodhana, that slayer of foes, stood up in haste and was surrounded by his century of haughty brothers with Aswatthaman amongst them. And that prince, mace in hand, thus surrounded by his hundred brothers with uplifted weapons appeared like Purandara in days of yore, encircled by the celestial host on the occasion of the battle with the Danavas.'"

SECTION CXXXVIII
(Sambhava Parva continued)

"Vaisampayana continued, 'When the spectators, with eyes expanded with wonder, made way for that subjugator of hostile cities, Karna, that hero with his natural mail and face brightened with ear-rings, took up his bow and girded on his sword, and then entered the spacious lists, like a walking cliff. That far-famed destroyer of hostile hosts, the large-eyed Karna, was born of Pritha in her maidenhood. He was a portion of the hot-beamed Sun and his energy and prowess were like unto those of the lion, or the bull, or the leader of a herd of elephants. In splendour he resembled the Sun, in loveliness the Moon, and in energy the fire. Begotten by the Sun himself, he was tall in stature like a golden palm tree, and, endued with the vigour of youth, he was capable of slaying a lion. Handsome in features, he was possessed of countless accomplishments. The mighty-armed warrior, eyeing all around the arena, bowed indifferently to Drona and Kripa. And the entire assembly, motionless and with steadfast gaze, thought, 'Who is he?' And they became agitated in their curiosity to know the warrior. And that foremost of eloquent men, the offspring of the Sun, in a voice deep as that of the clouds, addressed his unknown brother, the son of the subduer of the Asura, Paka (Indra), saying, 'O Partha, I shall perform feats before this gazing multitude; excelling all thou hast performed! Beholding them, thou shall be amazed.' And, O thou best of those blest with speech, he had hardly done when the spectators stood up all at once, uplifted by some instrument, as it were. And, O tiger among men, Duryodhana was filled with delight, while Vibhatsu was instantly all abashment and anger.

Then with the permission of Drona, the mighty Karna, delighting in battle, there did all that Partha had done before. And, O Bharata, Duryodhana with his brothers thereupon embraced Karna in joy and then addressed him saying, 'Welcome O mighty-armed warrior! I have obtained thee by good fortune, O polite one! Live thou as thou pleasest, and command me, and the kingdom of the Kurus.' Karna replied, 'When thou hast said it, I regard it as already accomplished. I only long for thy friendship. And, O lord, my wish is even for a single combat with Arjuna.' Duryodhana said, 'Do thou with me enjoy the good things of life! Be thou the benefactor of thy friend, and, O represser of enemies, place thou thy feet on the heads of all foes.'

"Arjuna, after this, deeming himself disgraced, said unto Karna stationed amidst the brothers like unto a cliff, 'That path which the unwelcome intruder and the uninvited talker cometh to, shall be thine, O Karna, for thou shall be slain by me.' Karna replied, 'This arena is meant for all, not for thee alone, O Phalguna! They are kings who are superior in energy; and verily the Kshatriya regardeth might and might alone. What need of altercation which is the exercise of the weak? O Bharata, speak then in arrows until with arrows I strike off thy head today before the preceptor himself!'

"Vaisampayana continued, 'Hastily embraced by his brothers, Partha that subduer of hostile cities, with the permission of Drona, advanced for the combat. On the other side, Karna, having been embraced by Duryodhana with his brothers, taking up his bow and arrows, stood ready for the fight. Then the firmament became enveloped in clouds emitting flashes of lightning, and the coloured bow of Indra appeared shedding its effulgent rays. And the clouds seemed to laugh on account of the rows of white cranes that were then on the wing. And seeing Indra thus viewing the arena from affection (for his son), the sun too dispersed the clouds from over his own offspring. And Phalguna remained deep hid under cover of the clouds, while Karna remained visible, being surrounded by the rays of the Sun. And the son of Dhritarashtra stood by Karna, and Bharadwaja and Kripa and Bhishma remained with Partha. And the assembly was divided, as also the female spectators. And knowing the state of things, Kunti the daughter of Bhoja, swooned away. And by the help of female attendants, Vidura, versed in the lore of all duties, revived the insensible Kunti by sprinkling sandal-paste and water on her person. On being restored to consciousness, Kunti, seeing her two sons clad in mail, was seized with fear, but she could do nothing (to protect them). And beholding both the warriors with bows strung in their hands the son of Saradwat, viz., Kripa, knowing all duties and cognisant of the rules regulating duels, addressed Karna, saying 'This Pandava, who is the youngest son of Kunti, belongeth to the Kaurava race: he will engage in combat with thee. But, O mighty-armed one, thou too must tell us thy lineage and the names of thy father and mother and the royal line of which thou art the ornament. Learning all this, Partha will fight with thee or not (as he will think fit). Sons of kings never fight with men of inglorious lineage.'

"Vaisampayana continued, 'When he was thus addressed by Kripa, Karna's countenance became like unto a lotus pale and torn with the pelting showers in the rainy season. Duryodhana said, 'O preceptor, verily the scriptures have it that three classes of persons can lay claim to royalty, viz., persons of the blood royal, heroes, and lastly, those that lead armies. If Phalguna is unwilling to fight with one who is not a king, I will install Karna as king of Anga.'

"Vaisampayana said, 'At that very moment, seated on a golden seat, with parched paddy and with flowers and water-pots and much gold, the mighty warrior Karna was installed king by Brahmanas versed in mantras. And the royal umbrella was held over his head, while Yak-tails waved around that redoubtable hero of graceful mien. And the cheers, having ceased, king (Karna) said unto the Kaurava Duryodhana, 'O tiger among monarchs, what shall I give unto thee that may compare with thy gift of a kingdom? O king, I will do all thou biddest!' And Suyodhana said unto him, 'I eagerly wish for thy friendship.' Thus spoken to, Karna replied, 'Be it so.' And they embraced each other in joy, and experienced great happiness.'"

SECTION CXXXIX
(Sambhava Parva continued)

"Vaisampayana said, 'After this, with his sheet loosely hanging down, Adhiratha entered the lists, perspiring and trembling, and supporting himself on a staff.

"Seeing him, Karna left his bow and impelled by filial regard bowed down his head still wet with the water of inauguration. And them the charioteer, hurriedly covering his feet with the end of his sheet, addressed Karna crowned with success as his son. And the charioteer embraced Karna and from excess of affection bedewed his head with tears, that head still wet with the water sprinkled over it on account of the coronation as king of Anga. Seeing the charioteer, the Pandava Bhimasena took Karna for a charioteer's son, and said by way of ridicule, 'O son of a charioteer, thou dost not deserve death in fight at the hands of Partha. As befits thy race take thou anon the whip. And, O worst of mortals, surely thou art not worthy to sway the kingdom of Anga, even as a dog doth not deserve the butter placed before the sacrificial fire.' Karna, thus addressed, with slightly quivering lips fetched a deep sigh, looked at the God of the day in the skies. And even as a mad elephant riseth from an assemblage of lotuses, the mighty Duryodhana rose in wrath from among his brothers, and addressed that performer of dreadful deeds, Bhimasena, present there, 'O Vrikodara, it behoveth thee not to speak such words. Might is the cardinal virtue of a Kshatriya, and even a Kshatriya of inferior birth deserveth to be fought with. The lineage of heroes, like the sources of a lordly river, is ever unknown. The fire that covereth the whole world riseth from the waters. The thunder that slayeth the Danavas was made of a bone of (a mortal named) Dadhichi. The illustrious deity Guha, who combines in his composition the portions of all the other deities is of a lineage unknown. Some call him the offspring of Agni; some, of Krittika, some, of Rudra, and some of Ganga. It hath been heard by us that persons born in the Kshatriya order have become Brahmanas. Viswamitra and others (born Kshatriyas) have obtained the eternal Brahma. The foremost of all wielders of weapons, the preceptor Drona hath been born in a waterpot and Kripa of the race of Gotama hath sprung from a clump of heath. Your own births, ye Pandava princes, are known to me. Can a she-deer bring forth a tiger (like Karna), of the splendour of the Sun, and endued with every auspicious mark, and born also with a natural mail and ear-rings? This prince among men deserveth the sovereignty of the world, not of Anga only, in consequence of the might of his arm and my swearing to obey him in everything. If there be anybody here to whom all that I have done unto Karna hath become intolerable, let him ascend his chariot and bend his bow with the help of his feet.'

"Vaisampayana continued, 'Then there arose a confused murmur amongst the spectators approving of Duryodhana's speech. The sun, however, went down, but prince Duryodhana taking Karna's hand led him out of the arena lighted with countless lamps. And, O king, the Pandavas also, accompanied by Drona and Kripa and Bhishma, returned to their abodes. And the people, too, came away, some naming Arjuna, some Karna, and some Duryodhana (as the victor of the day). And Kunti, recognising her son in Karna by the various auspicious marks on his person and beholding him installed in the sovereignty of Anga, was from motherly affection, very pleased. And Duryodhana, O monarch, having obtained Karna (in this way), banished his fears arising out of Arjuna's proficiency in arms. And the heroic Karna, accomplished in arms, began to gratify Duryodhana by sweet speeches, while Yudhishthira was impressed with the belief that there was no warrior on earth like unto Karna.'"

SECTION CXL
(Sambhava Parva continued)

"Vaisampayana continued, 'Beholding the Pandavas and the son of Dhritarashtra accomplished in arms, Drona thought the time had come when he could demand the preceptorial fee. And, O king, assembling his pupils one day together, the preceptor Drona asked of them the fee, saying, 'Seize Drupada, the king of Panchala in battle and bring him unto me. That shall be the most acceptable fee.' Those warriors then answering, 'So be it', speedily mounted up on their chariots, and for bestowing upon their preceptor the fee he had demanded, marched out, accompanied by him. Those bulls among men, smiting the Panchalas on their way, laid siege to the capital of the great Drupada. And Duryodhana and Karna and the mighty Yuyutsu, and Duhsasana and Vikarna and Jalasandha and Sulochana,—these and many other foremost of Kshatriya princes of great prowess, vied with one another in becoming the foremost in the attack. And the princes, riding in first class chariots and following the cavalry, entered the hostile capital, and proceeded along the streets.

"Meanwhile, the king of Panchala, beholding that mighty force and hearing its loud clamour, came out of his palace, accompanied by his brothers. Though king Yajnasena was well-armed, the Kuru army assailed him with a shower of arrows, uttering their war-cry. Yajnasena, however, not easy to be subdued in battle, approaching the Kurus upon his white chariot, began to rain his fierce arrows around.

"Before the battle commenced, Arjuna, beholding the pride of prowess displayed by the princes, addressed his preceptor, that best of Brahmanas, Drona, and said, 'We shall exert ourselves after these have displayed their prowess. The king of Panchala can never be taken on the field of the battle by any of these.' Having said this, the sinless son of Kunti surrounded by his brothers, waited outside the town at a distance of a mile from it. Meanwhile Drupada beholding the Kuru host, rushed forward and pouring a fierce shower of arrows around, terribly afflicted the Kuru ranks. And such was his lightness of motion on the field of battle that, though he was fighting unsupported on a single chariot, the Kurus from panic supposed that there were many Drupadas opposed to them. And the fierce arrows of that monarch fell fast on all sides, till conchs and trumpets and drums by thousands began to be sounded by the Panchalas from their houses (giving the alarm). Then there arose from the mighty Panchala host a roar terrible as that of the lion, while the twang of their bow- strings seemed to rend the very heavens. Then Duryodhana and Vikarna, Suvahu and Dirghalochana and Duhsasana becoming furious, began to shower their arrows upon the enemy. But the mighty bowman, Prishata's son, invincible in battle, though very much pierced with the arrows of the enemy, instantly began, O Bharata, to afflict the hostile ranks with greater vigour. And careering over the field of battle like a fiery wheel, king Drupada with his arrows smote Duryodhana and Vikarna and even the mighty Karna and many other heroic princes and numberless warriors, and slaked their thirst for battle. Then all the citizens showered upon the Kurus various missiles like clouds showering rain-drops upon the earth. Young and old, they all rushed to battle, assailing the Kurus with vigour. The Kauravas, then, O Bharata, beholding the battle become frightful, broke and fled wailing towards the Pandavas.

"The Pandavas, hearing the terrible wail of the beaten host, reverentially saluted Drona and ascended their chariots. Then Arjuna hastily bidding Yudhishthira not to engage in the fight, rushed forward, appointing the sons of Madri (Nakula and Sahadeva) the protectors of his chariot-wheels, while Bhimasena ever fighting in the van, mace in hand, ran ahead. The sinless Arjuna, thus accompanied by his brothers, hearing the shouts of the enemy, advanced towards them, filling the whole region with the rattle of his chariot-wheels. And like a Makara entering the sea, the mighty- armed Bhima, resembling a second Yama, mace in hand, entered the Panchala ranks, fiercely roaring like the ocean in a tempest. And Bhima, mace in hand, first rushed towards the array of elephants in the hostile force, while Arjuna, proficient in battle, assailed that force with the prowess of his arms. And Bhima, like the great Destroyer himself, began to slay those elephants with his mace. Those huge animals, like unto mountains, struck with Bhima's mace, had their heads broken into pieces. Covered with stream of blood, they began to fall upon the ground like cliffs loosened by thunder. And the Pandavas prostrated on the ground elephants and horses and cars by thousands and slew many foot-soldiers and many car-warriors. Indeed, as a herdsman in the woods driveth before him with his staff countless cattle with ease, so did Vrikodara drive before him the chariots and elephants of the hostile force.

"Meanwhile, Phalguna, impelled by the desire of doing good unto Bharadwaja's son, assailed the son of Prishata with a shower of arrows and felled him from the elephant on which he was seated. And, O monarch, Arjuna, like unto the terrible fire that consumeth all things at the end of the Yuga, began to prostrate on the ground horses and cars and elephants by thousands. The Panchalas and the Srinjayas, on the other hand, thus assailed by the Pandava, met him with a perfect shower of weapons of various kinds. And they sent up a loud shout and fought desperately with Arjuna. The battle became furious and terrible to behold. Hearing the enemy's shouts, the son of Indra was filled with wrath and assailing the hostile host with a thick shower of arrows, rushed towards it furiously afflicting it with renewed vigour. They who observed the illustrious Arjuna at that time could not mark any interval between his fixing the arrows on the bowstring and letting them off. Loud were the shouts that rose there, mingled with cheers of approval. Then the king of the Panchalas, accompanied by (the generalissimo of his forces) Satyajit, rushed with speed at Arjuna like the Asura Samvara rushing at the chief of the celestials (in days of yore). Then Arjuna covered the king of Panchala with a shower of arrows. Then there arose a frightful uproar among the Panchala host like unto the roar of a mighty lion springing at the leader of a herd of elephants. And beholding Arjuna rushing at the king of Panchala to seize him, Satyajit of great prowess rushed at him. And the two warriors, like unto Indra and the Asura Virochana's son (Vali), approaching each other for combat, began to grind each other's ranks. Then Arjuna with great force pierced Satyajit with ten keen shafts at which feat the spectators were all amazed. But Satyajit, without losing any time, assailed Arjuna with a hundred shafts. Then that mighty car-warrior, Arjuna, endued with remarkable lightness of motion, thus covered by that shower of arrows, rubbed his bow-string to increase the force and velocity of his shafts. Then cutting in twain his antagonist's bow, Arjuna rushed at the king of the Panchalas, but Satyajit, quickly taking up a tougher bow, pierced with his arrows Partha, his chariot, charioteer, and horses. Arjuna, thus assailed in battle by the Panchala warrior, forgave not his foe. Eager to slay him at once, he pierced with a number of arrows his antagonist's horses, flags, bow, clenched (left) fist, charioteer, and the attendant at his back. Then Satyajit, finding his bows repeatedly cut in twain and his horses slain, desisted from the fight.

"The king of the Panchalas, beholding his general thus discomfited in the encounter, himself began to shower his arrows upon the Pandava prince. Then Arjuna, that foremost of warriors, crowned with success, began to fight furiously, and quickly cutting his enemy's bow in twain as also his flagstaff which he caused to fall down, pierced his antagonist's horses, and charioteer also with five arrows. Then throwing aside his bow Arjuna took his quiver, and taking out a scimitar and sending forth a loud shout, leaped from his own chariot upon that of his foe. And standing there with perfect fearlessness he seized Drupada as Garuda seizeth a huge snake after agitating the waters of the ocean. At the sight of this, the Panchala troops ran away in all directions.

"Then Dhananjaya, having thus exhibited the might of his arm in the presence of both hosts, sent forth a loud shout and came out of the Panchala ranks. And beholding him returning (with his captive), the princes began to lay waste Drupada's capital. Addressing them Arjuna said, 'This best of monarchs, Drupada, is a relative of the Kuru heroes. Therefore, O Bhima, slay not his soldiers. Let us only give unto our preceptor his fee.'

"Vaisampayana continued, 'O king, thus prevented by Arjuna, the mighty Bhimasena, though unsatiated with the exercise of battle, refrained from the act of slaughter. And, O bull of the Bharata race, the princes then, taking Drupada with them after having seized him on the field of battle along with his friends and counsellors, offered him unto Drona. And Drona beholding Drupada thus brought under complete control—humiliated and deprived of wealth—remembered that monarch's former hostility and addressing him said, 'Thy kingdom and capital have been laid waste by me. But fear not for thy life, though it dependeth now on the will of thy foe. Dost thou now desire to revive thy friendship (with me)?' Having said this, he smiled a little and again said, 'Fear not for thy life, brave king! We, Brahmanas, are ever forgiving. And, O bull among Kshatriyas, my affection and love for thee have grown with me in consequence of our having sported together in childhood in the hermitage. Therefore, O king, I ask for thy friendship again. And as a boon (unasked), I give thee half the kingdom (that was thine). Thou toldest me before that none who was not a king could be a king's friend. Therefore is it, O Yajnasena, that I retain half thy kingdom. Thou art the king of all the territory lying on the southern side of the Bhagirathi, while I become king of all the territory on the north of that river. And, O Panchala, if it pleaseth thee, know me hence for thy friend.'

"On hearing these words, Drupada answered, 'Thou art of noble soul and great prowess. Therefore, O Brahmana, I am not surprised at what thou doest. I am very much gratified with thee, and I desire thy eternal friendship.'

"Vaisampayana continued, 'After this, O Bharata, Drona released the king of Panchala, and cheerfully performing the usual offices of regard, bestowed upon him half the kingdom. Thenceforth Drupada began to reside sorrowfully in (the city of) Kampilya within (the province of) Makandi on the banks of the Ganga filled with many towns and cities. And after his defeat by Drona, Drupada also ruled the southern Panchalas up to the bank of the Charmanwati river. And Drupada from that day was well-convinced that he could not, by Kshatriya might alone, defeat Drona, being very much his inferior in Brahma (spiritual) power. And he, therefore, began to wander over the whole earth to find out the means of obtaining a son (who would subjugate his Brahmana foe).

"Meanwhile Drona continued to reside in Ahicchatra. Thus, O king, was the territory of Ahicchatra full of towns and cities, obtained by Arjuna, and bestowed upon Drona."

SECTION CXLI
(Sambhava Parva continued)

"Vaisampayana continued, 'After the expiration, O king, of a year from this, Dhritarashtra, moved by kindness for the people, installed Yudhishthira, the son of Pandu, as the heir-apparent of the kingdom on account of his firmness, fortitude, patience, benevolence, frankness and unswerving honesty (of heart). And within a short time Yudhishthira, the son of Kunti, by his good behaviour, manners and close application to business, overshadowed the deeds of his father. And the second Pandava, Vrikodara, began to receive continued lessons from Sankarshana (Valarama) in encounters with the sword and the mace and on the chariot. And after Bhima's education was finished, he became in strength like unto Dyumatsena himself and continuing to live in harmony with his brothers, he began to exert his prowess. And Arjuna became celebrated for the firmness of his grasp (of weapons), for his lightness of motion, precision of aim, and his proficiency in the use of the Kshura, Naracha, Vala and Vipatha weapons, indeed, of all weapons, whether straight or crooked or heavy. And Drona certified that there was none in the world who was equal to Arjuna in lightness of hand and general proficiency.

"One day, Drona, addressing Arjuna before the assembled Kaurava princes, said, 'There was a disciple of Agastya in the science of arms called Agnivesa. He was my preceptor and I, his disciple. By ascetic merit I obtained from him a weapon called Brahmasira which could never be futile and which was like unto thunder itself, capable of consuming the whole earth. That weapon, O Bharata, from what I have done, may now pass from disciple to disciple. While imparting it to me, my preceptor said, 'O son of Bharadwaja, never shouldst thou hurl this weapon at any human being, especially at one who is of poor energy. Thou hast, O hero, obtained that celestial weapon. None else deserveth it. But obey the command of the Rishi (Agnivesa).' And, look here, Arjuna, give me now the preceptorial fee in the presence of these thy cousins and relatives.' When Arjuna, on hearing this, pledged his word that he would give what the preceptor demanded, the latter said, 'O sinless one, thou must fight with me when I fight with thee.' And that bull among the Kuru princes thereupon pledged his word unto Drona and touching his feet, went away northward. Then there arose a loud shout covering the whole earth bounded by her belt of seas to the effect that there was no bowman in the whole world like unto Arjuna. And, indeed, Dhananjaya, in encounters with the mace and the sword and on the chariot as also with the bow, acquired wonderful proficiency. Sahadeva obtained the whole science of morality and duties from (Vrihaspati) the spiritual chief of celestials, and continued to live under the control of his brothers. And Nakula, the favourite of his brothers taught by Drona, became known as a skilful warrior and a great car-warrior (Ati-ratha). Indeed, Arjuna and the other Pandava princes became so powerful that they slew in battle the great Sauvira who had performed a sacrifice extending over three years, undaunted by the raids of the Gandharvas. And the king of the Yavanas himself whom the powerful Pandu even had failed to bring under subjection was brought by Arjuna under control. Then again Vipula, the king of the Sauviras, endued with great prowess, who had always shown a disregard for the Kurus, was made by the intelligent Arjuna to feel the edge of his power. And Arjuna also repressed by means of his arrows (the pride of) king Sumitra of Sauvira, also known by the name of Dattamitra who had resolutely sought an encounter with him. The third of the Pandava princes, assisted by Bhima, on only a single car subjugated all the kings of the East backed by ten thousand cars. In the same way, having conquered on a single car the whole of the south, Dhananjaya sent unto the kingdom of the Kurus a large booty.

"Thus did those foremost of men, the illustrious Pandavas, conquering the territories of other kings, extend the limits of their own kingdom. But beholding the great prowess and strength of those mighty bowmen, king Dhritarashtra's sentiments towards the Pandavas became suddenly poisoned, and from that day the monarch became so anxious that he could hardly sleep."

SECTION CXLII
(Sambhava Parva continued)

"Vaisampayana continued, 'On hearing that the heroic sons of Pandu endued with excess of energy had become so mighty, king Dhritarashtra became very miserable with anxiety. Then summoning unto his side Kanika, that foremost of minister, well-versed in the science of politics and an expert in counsels the king said, 'O best of Brahmanas, the Pandavas are daily overshadowing the earth. I am exceedingly jealous of them. Should I have peace or war with them? O Kanika, advise me truly, for I shall do as thou biddest.

"Vaisampayana continued, 'That best of Brahmanas, thus addressed by the king, freely answered him in these pointed words well-agreeing with the import of political science."

"Listen to me, O sinless king, as I answer thee. And, O best of Kuru kings, it behoveth thee not to be angry with me after hearing all I say. Kings should ever be ready with uplifted maces (to strike when necessary), and they should ever increase their prowess. Carefully avoiding all faults themselves they should ceaselessly watch over the faults of their foes and take advantage of them. If the king is always ready to strike, everybody

THE MAHABHARATA

feareth him. Therefore the king should ever have recourse to chastisement in all he doeth. He should so conduct himself that, his foe may not detect any weak side in him. But by means of the weakness he detecteth in his foe he should pursue him (to destruction). He should always conceal, like the tortoise concealing its body, his means and ends, and he should always keep back his own weakness from the sight of others. And having begun a particular act, he should ever accomplish it thoroughly. Behold, a thorn, if not extracted wholly, produceth a festering sore. The slaughter of a foe who doeth thee evil is always praiseworthy. If the foe be one of great prowess, one should watch for the hour of his disaster and then kill him without any scruples. If he should happen to be a great warrior, his hour of disaster also should be watched and he should then be induced to fly. O sire, an enemy should never be scorned, however contemptible. A spark of fire is capable of consuming an extensive forest if only it can spread from one object to another in proximity. Kings should sometimes feign blindness and deafness, for if impotent to chastise, they should pretend not to notice the faults that call for chastisement. On occasions, such as these, let them regard their bows as made of straw. But they should be always on the alert like a herd of deer sleeping in the woods. When thy foe is in thy power, destroy him by every means open or secret. Do not show him any mercy, although he seeketh thy protection. A foe, or one that hath once injured thee, should be destroyed by lavishing money, if necessary, for by killing him thou mayest be at thy ease. The dead can never inspire fear. Thou must destroy the three, five and seven (resources) of thy foes. Thou must destroy thy foes root and branch. Then shouldst thou destroy their allies and partisans. The allies and partisans can never exist if the principal be destroyed. If the root of the tree is torn up, the branches and twigs can never exist as before. Carefully concealing thy own means and ends, thou shouldst always watch thy foes, always seeking their flaws. Thou shouldst, O king, rule thy kingdom, always anxiously watching thy foes. By maintaining the perpetual fire by sacrifices, by brown cloths, by matted locks, and by hides of animals for thy bedding, shouldst thou at first gain the confidence of thy foes, and when thou has gained it thou shouldst then spring upon them like a wolf. For it hath been said that in the acquisition of wealth even the garb of holiness might be employed as a hooked staff to bend down a branch in order to pluck the fruits that are ripe. The method followed in the plucking of fruits should be the method in destroying foes, for thou shouldst proceed on the principle of selection. Bear thy foe upon thy shoulders till the time cometh when thou canst throw him down, breaking him into pieces like an earthen pot thrown down with violence upon a stony surface. The foe must never be let off even though he addresseth thee most piteously. No pity thou show him but slay him at once. By the arts of conciliation or the expenditure of money should the foe be slain. By creating disunion amongst his allies, or by the employment of force, indeed by every means in thy power shouldst thou destroy thy foe.'

"Dhritarashtra said, 'Tell me truly how a foe can be destroyed by the arts of conciliation or the expenditure of money, or by producing disunion or by the employment of force.'

"Kanika replied, 'Listen, O monarch, to the history of a jackal dwelling in days of yore in the forest and fully acquainted with the science of politics. There was a wise jackal, mindful of his own interests who lived in the company of four friends, viz., a tiger, a mouse, a wolf, and a mongoose. One day they saw in the woods a strong deer, the leader of a herd, whom, however, they could not seize for his fleetness and strength. They thereupon called a council for consultation. The jackal opening the proceedings said, 'O tiger, thou hast made many an effort to seize this deer, but all in vain simply because this deer is young, fleet and very intelligent. Let now the mouse go and eat into its feet when it lieth asleep. And when this is done, let the tiger approach and seize it. Then shall we all, with great pleasure feast on it.' Hearing these words of the jackal, they all set to work very cautiously as he directed. And the mouse ate into the feet of the deer and the tiger killed it as anticipated. And beholding the body of the deer lying motionless on the ground, the jackal said unto his companions, 'Blessed be ye! Go and perform your ablutions. In the meantime I will look after the deer.' Hearing what the jackal said, they all went into a stream. And the jackal waited there, deeply meditating upon what he should do. The tiger endued with great strength, returned first of all to the spot after having performed his ablutions. And he saw the jackal there plunged in meditation. The tiger said, 'Why art thou so sorrowful, O wise one! Thou art the foremost of all intelligent beings. Let us enjoy ourselves today by feasting on this carcass.' The jackal said, 'Hear, O mighty-armed one, what the mouse hath said. He hath even said, 'O, fie on the strength of the king of the beasts! This deer hath been slain by me. By might of my arm he will today gratify his hunger.' When he hath boasted in such a language, I, for my part, do not wish to touch this food.' The tiger replied, 'If, indeed, the mouse hath said so, my sense is now awakened. I shall, from this day, slay with the might of my own arms, creatures ranging the forest and then feast on their flesh.' Having said this, the tiger went away.

"And after the tiger had left the spot, the mouse came. And seeing the mouse come, the jackal addressed him and said, 'Blest be thou, O mouse, but listen to what the mongoose hath said. He hath even said, The carcass of this deer is poison (the tiger having touched it with his claws). I will not eat of it. On the other hand, if thou, O jackal, permittest it, I will even slay the mouse and feast on him.' Hearing this the mouse became alarmed and quickly entered his hole. And after the mouse had gone, the wolf, O king, came there having performed his ablutions. And seeing the wolf come, the jackal said unto him, 'The king of the beasts hath been angry with thee. Evil is certain to overtake thee. He is expected here with his wife. Do as thou pleasest.' Thus was the wolf also, fond of animal flesh, got rid of by the jackal. And the wolf fled, contracting his body into the smallest dimensions. It was then that the mongoose came. And, O king, the jackal, seeing him come, said, 'By the might of my arm have I defeated the others who have already fled. Fight with me first and then eat of this flesh as you please.' The mongoose replied, 'When, indeed, the tiger, the wolf, and the intelligent mouse have all been defeated by thee, heroes as they are, thou seemest to be a greater hero still. I do not desire to fight with thee.' Saying this, the mongoose also went away.

"Kanika continued, 'When they all had thus left the place, the jackal, well-pleased with the success of his policy, alone ate up that flesh. If kings always act in this way, they can be happy. Thus should the timid by exciting their fears, the courageous by the arts of conciliation, the covetous by gift of wealth, and equals and inferiors by exhibition of prowess be brought under thy sway. Besides all this, O king, that I have said, listen now to something else that I say.'

"Kanika continued, 'If thy son, friend, brother, father, or even the spiritual preceptor, anyone becometh thy foe, thou shouldst, if desirous of prosperity, slay him without scruples. By curses and incantations, by gift of wealth, by poison, or by deception, the foe should be slain. He should never be neglected from disdain. If both the parties be equal and success uncertain, then he that acteth with diligence groweth in prosperity. If the spiritual preceptor himself be vain, ignorant of what should be done and what left undone, and vicious in his ways, even he should be chastised. If thou art angry, show thyself as if thou art not so, speaking even then with a smile on thy lips. Never reprove any one with indications of anger (in thy speech). And O Bharata, speak soft words before thou smitest and even while thou art smiting! After the smiting is over, pity the victim, and grieve for him, and even shed tears. Comforting thy foe by conciliation, by gift of wealth, and smooth behaviour, thou must smite him when he walketh not aright. Thou shouldst equally smile the heinous offender who liveth by the practice of virtue, for the garb of virtue simply covereth his offences like black clouds covering the mountains. Thou shouldst burn the house of that person whom thou punishest with death. And thou shouldst never permit beggars and atheists and thieves to dwell in thy kingdom. By a sudden sally or pitched battle by poison or by corrupting his allies, by gift of wealth, by any means in thy power, thou shouldst destroy thy foe. Thou mayest act with the greatest cruelty. Thou shouldst make thy teeth sharp to give a fatal bite. And thou should ever smite so effectually that thy foe may not again raise his head. Thou shouldst ever stand in fear of even one from whom there is no fear, not to speak of him from whom there is such. For if the first be ever powerful he may destroy thee to the root (for thy unpreparedness). Thou shouldst never trust the faithless, nor trust too much those that are faithful, for if those in whom thou confidest prove thy foes, thou art certain to be annihilated. After testing their faithfulness thou shouldst employ spies in thy own kingdom and in the kingdoms of others. Thy spies in foreign kingdoms should be apt deceivers and persons in the garb of ascetics. Thy spies should be placed in gardens, places of amusement, temples and other holy places, drinking halls, streets, and with the (eighteen) tirthas (viz., the minister, the chief priest, the heir- presumptive, the commander-in-chief, the gate-keepers of the court, persons in the inner apartments, the jailor, the chief surveyor, the head of the treasury, the general executant of orders, the chief of the town police, the chief architect, the chief justice, the president of the council, the chief of the punitive department, the commander of the fort, the chief of the arsenal, the chief of the frontier guards, and the keeper of the forests), and in places of sacrifice, near wells, on mountains and in rivers, in forests, and in all places where people congregate. In speech thou shouldst ever be humble, but let thy heart be ever sharp as razor. And when thou art engaged in doing even a very cruel and terrible act, thou shouldst talk with smiles on thy lips. If desirous of prosperity, thou shouldst adopt all arts—humility, oath, conciliation, worshipping the feet of others by lowering thy head, inspiring hope, and the like. And, a person conversant with the rules of policy is like a tree decked with flowers but bearing no fruit; or, if bearing fruit, these must be at a great height not easily attainable from the ground; and if any of these fruits seem to be ripe care must be taken to make it appear raw. Conducting himself in such a way, he shall never fade. Virtue, wealth and pleasure have both their evil and good effects closely knit together. While extracting the effects that are good, those that are evil should be avoided. Those that practise virtue (incessantly) are made unhappy for want of wealth and the neglect of pleasure. Those again in pursuit of wealth are made unhappy for the neglect of two others. And so those who pursue pleasure suffer for their inattention to virtue and wealth. Therefore, thou shouldst pursue virtue, wealth and pleasure, in such a way

THE MAHABHARATA

that thou mayest not have to suffer therefrom. With humiliation and attention, without jealousy and solicitous of accomplishing thy purpose, shouldst thou, in all sincerity, consult with the Brahmanas. When thou art fallen, thou shouldst raise thyself by any means, gentle or violent; and after thou hast thus raised thyself thou shouldst practise virtue. He that hath never been afflicted with calamity can never have prosperity. This may be seen in the life of one who surviveth his calamities. He that is afflicted with sorrow should be consoled by the recitation of the history of persons of former times (like those of Nala and Rama). He whose heart hath been unstrung by sorrow should be consoled with hopes of future prosperity. He again who is learned and wise should be consoled by pleasing offices presently rendered unto him. He who, having concluded a treaty with an enemy, reposeth at ease as if he hath nothing more to do, is very like a person who awaketh, fallen down from the top of a tree whereon he had slept. A king should ever keep to himself his counsels without fear of calumny, and while beholding everything with the eyes of his spies, he should take care to conceal his own emotions before the spies of his enemies. Like a fisherman who becometh prosperous by catching and killing fish, a king can never grow prosperous without tearing the vitals of his enemy and without doing some violent deeds. The might of thy foe, as represented by his armed force, should ever be completely destroyed, by ploughing it up (like weeds) and mowing it down and otherwise afflicting it by disease, starvation, and want of drink. A person in want never approacheth (from love) one in affluence; and when one's purpose hath been accomplished, one hath no need to approach him whom he had hitherto looked to for its accomplishment. Therefore, when thou doest anything never do it completely, but ever leave something to be desired for by others (whose services thou mayest need). One who is desirous of prosperity should with diligence seek allies and means, and carefully conduct his wars. His exertions in these respects should always be guided by prudence. A prudent king should ever act in such a way that friends and foes may never know his motive before the commencement of his acts. Let them know all when the act hath been commenced or ended, and as long as danger doth not come, so long only shall thou act as if thou art afraid. But when it hath overtaken thee, thou must grapple with it courageously. He who trusteth in a foe who hath been brought under subjection by force, summoneth his own death as a crab by her act of conception. Thou shouldst always reckon the future act as already arrived (and concert measures for meeting it), else, from want of calmness caused by haste, thou mayest overlook an important point in meeting it when it is before thee. A person desirous of prosperity should always exert with prudence, adopting his measures to time and place. He should also act with an eye to destiny as capable of being regulated by mantras and sacrificial rites; and to virtue, wealth, and pleasure. It is well-known that time and place (if taken into consideration) always produce the greatest good. If the foe is insignificant, he should not yet be despised, for he may soon grow like a palmyra tree extending its roots or like a spark of fire in the deep woods that may soon burst into an extensive conflagration. As a little fire gradually fed with faggots soon becometh capable of consuming even the biggest blocks, so the person who increaseth his power by making alliances and friendships soon becometh capable of subjugating even the most formidable foe. The hope thou givest unto thy foe should be long deferred before it is fulfilled; and when the time cometh for its fulfilment, invent some pretext for deferring it still. Let that pretext be shown as founded upon some reason, and let that reason itself be made to appear as founded on some other reason. Kings should, in the matter of destroying their foes, ever resemble razors in every particular; unpitying as these are sharp, hiding their intents as these are concealed in their leathern cases, striking when the opportunity cometh as these are used on proper occasions, sweeping off their foes with all their allies and dependants as these shave the head or the chin without leaving a single hair. O supporter of the dignity of the Kurus, bearing thyself towards the Pandavas and others also as policy dictateth, act in such a way that thou mayest not have to grieve in future. Well do I know that thou art endued with every blessing, and possessed of every mark of good fortune. Therefore, O king, protect thyself from the sons of Pandu! O king, the sons of Pandu are stronger than their cousins (thy sons); therefore, O chastiser of foes, I tell thee plainly what thou shouldst do. Listen to it, O king, with thy children, and having listened to it, exert yourselves (to do the needful). O king, act in such a way that there may not be any fear for thee from the Pandavas. Indeed, adopt such measures consonant with the science of policy that thou mayest not have to grieve in the future.'

"Vaisampayana continued, 'Having delivered himself thus Kanika returned to his abode, while the Kuru king Dhritarashtra became pensive and melancholy."

SECTION CXLIII
(Jatugriha Parva)

"Vaisampayana said, 'Then the son of Suvala (Sakuni), king Duryodhana, Duhsasana and Karna, in consultation with one another, formed an evil conspiracy. With the sanction of Dhritarashtra, the king of the Kurus, they resolved to burn to death Kunti and her (five) sons. But that wise Vidura, capable of reading the heart by external signs, ascertained the intention of these wicked persons by observing their countenances alone. Then the sinless Vidura, of soul enlightened by true knowledge, and devoted to the good of the Pandavas, came to the conclusion that Kunti with her children should fly away from her foes. And providing for that purpose a boat strong enough to withstand both wind and wave, he addressed Kunti and said, 'This Dhritarashtra hath been born for destroying the fame and offspring of the (Kuru) race. Of wicked soul, he is about to cast off eternal virtue. O blessed one, I have kept ready on the stream a boat capable of withstanding both wind and wave. Escape by it with thy children from the net that death hath spread around you.'

"Vaisampayana continued, 'Hearing these words, the illustrious Kunti was deeply grieved, and with her children, O bull of Bharata's race, stepped into the boat and went over the Ganges. Then leaving the boat according to the advice of Vidura, the Pandavas took with them the wealth that had been given to them (while at Varanavata) by their enemies and safely entered the deep woods. In the house of lac, however, that had been prepared for the destruction of the Pandavas, an innocent Nishada woman who had come there for some purpose, was, with her children burnt to death. And that worst of Mlechchhas, the wretched Purochana (who was the architect employed in building the house of lac) was also burnt in the conflagration. And thus were the sons of Dhirtarashtra with their counsellors deceived in their expectations. And thus also were the illustrious Pandavas, by the advice of Vidura, saved with their mother. But the people (of Varanavata) knew not of their safety. And the citizens of Varanavata, seeing the house of lac consumed (and believing the Pandavas to have been burnt to death) became exceedingly sorry. And they sent messengers unto king Dhritarashtra to represent everything that had happened. And they said to the monarch, 'Thy great end hath been achieved! Thou hast at last burnt the Pandavas to death! Thy desire fulfilled, enjoy with thy children. O king of the Kurus, the kingdom.' Hearing this, Dhritarashtra with his children, made a show of grief, and along with his relatives, including Kshattri (Vidura) and Bhishma the foremost of the Kurus, performed the last honours of the Pandavas.'

"Janamejaya said, 'O best of Brahmanas, I desire to hear in full this history of the burning of the house of lac and the escape of the Pandavas there from. That was a cruel act of theirs (the Kurus), acting under the counsels of the wicked (Kanika). Recite the history to me of all that happened. I am burning with curiosity to hear it.'

"Vaisampayana said, 'O chastiser of all foes, listen to me, O monarch, as I recite the (history of the) burning of the house of lac and the escape of the Pandavas. The wicked Duryodhana, beholding Bhimasena surpass (everybody) in strength and Arjuna highly accomplished in arms became pensive and sad. Then Karna, the offspring of the Sun, and Sakuni, the son of Suvala, endeavoured by various means to compass the death of the Pandavas. The Pandavas too counteracted all those contrivances one after another, and in obedience to the counsels of Vidura, never spoke of them afterwards. Then the citizens, beholding the son of Pandu possessed of accomplishments, began, O Bharata, to speak of them in all places of public resort. And assembled in courtyards and other places of gathering, they talked of the eldest son of Pandu (Yudhishthira) as possessed of the qualifications for ruling the kingdom. And they said, 'Dhritarashtra, though possessed of the eye of knowledge, having been (born) blind, had not obtained the kingdom before. How can he (therefore) become king now? Then Bhishma, the son of Santanu, of rigid vows and devoted to truth, having formerly relinquished the sovereignty would never accept it now. We shall, therefore, now install (on the throne) with proper ceremonies the eldest of the Pandavas endued with youth, accomplished in battle, versed in the Vedas, and truthful and kind. Worshipping Bhishma, the son of Santanu and Dhritarashtra conversant with the rules of morality, he will certainly maintain the former and the latter with his children in every kind of enjoyment.'

"The wretched Duryodhana, hearing these words of the parting partisans of Yudhishthira, became very much distressed. Deeply afflicted, the wicked prince could not put up with those speeches. Inflamed with jealousy, he went unto Dhritarashtra, and finding him alone he saluted him with reverence and distressed at (the sight of) the partiality of the citizens for Yudhishthira, he addressed the monarch and said, 'O father, I have heard the parting citizens utter words of ill omen. Passing thee by, and Bhishma too, they desire the son of Pandu to be their king. Bhishma will sanction this, for he will not rule the kingdom. It seems, therefore,

THE MAHABHARATA

that the citizens are endeavouring to inflict a great injury on us. Pandu obtained of old the ancestral kingdom by virtue of his own accomplishments, but thou, from blindness, didst not obtain the kingdom, though fully qualified to have it. If Pandu's son now obtaineth the kingdom as his inheritance from Pandu, his son will obtain it after him and that son's son also, and so on will it descend in Pandu's line. In that case, O king of the world, ourselves with our children, excluded from the royal line, shall certainly be disregarded by all men. Therefore, O monarch, adopt such counsels that we may not suffer perpetual distress, becoming dependent on others for our food. O king, if thou hadst obtained the sovereignty before, we would certainly have succeeded to it, however much the people might be unfavourable to us.'"

SECTION CXLIV
(Jatugriha Parva continued)

"Vaisampayana continued, "King Dhritarashtra whose knowledge only was his eyes, on hearing these words of his son and recollecting everything that Kanika had, said unto him, became afflicted with sorrow, and his mind also thereupon began to waver. Then Duryodhana and Karna, and Sakuni, the son of Suvala, and Duhsasana as their fourth, held a consultation together. Prince Duryodhana said unto Dhritarashtra, 'Send, O father, by some clever contrivance, the Pandavas to the town of Varanavata. We shall then have no fear of them.' Dhritarashtra, on hearing these words uttered by his son, reflected for a moment and replied unto Duryodhana, saying, 'Pandu, ever devoted to virtue, always behaved dutifully towards all his relatives but particularly towards me. He cared very little for the enjoyments of the world, but devotedly gave everything unto me, even the kingdom. His son is as much devoted to virtue as he, and is possessed of every accomplishment. Of world-wide fame, he is again the favourite of the people. He is possessed of allies; how can we by force exile him from his ancestral kingdom? The counsellors and soldiers (of the state) and their sons and grandsons have all been cherished and maintained by Pandu. Thus benefited of old by Pandu, shall not, O child, the citizens slay us with all our friends and relatives now on account of Yudhishthira?'

"Duryodhana replied, 'What thou sayest, O father, is perfectly true. But in view of the evil that is looming on the future as regards thyself, if we conciliate the people with wealth and honours, they would assuredly side with us for these proofs of our power. The treasury and the ministers of state, O king, are at this moment under our control. Therefore, it behoveth thee now to banish, by some gentle means, the Pandavas to the town of Varanavata; O king, when the sovereignty shall have been vested in me, then, O Bharata, may Kunti with her children come back from that place.'

"Dhritarashtra replied, 'This, O Duryodhana, is the very thought existing in my mind. But from its sinfulness I have never given expression to it. Neither Bhishma, nor Drona, nor Kshattri, nor Gautama (Kripa) will ever sanction the exile of the Pandavas. In their eyes, O dear son, amongst the Kurus ourselves and the Pandavas are equal. Those wise and virtuous persons will make no difference between us. If therefore, we behave so towards the Pandavas, shall we not, O son, deserve death at the hands of the Kurus, of these illustrious personages, and of the whole world?'

"Duryodhana answered, 'Bhishma hath no excess of affection for either side, and will, therefore, be neutral (in case of dispute). The son of Drona (Aswatthaman) is on my side. There is no doubt that where the son is, there the father will be. Kripa, the son of Saradwat, must be on the side on which Drona and Aswatthaman are. He will never abandon Drona and his sister's son (Aswatthaman). Kshattri (Vidura) is dependent on us for his means of life, though he is secretly with the foe. If he sides the Pandavas, he alone can do us no injury, Therefore, exile thou the Pandavas to Varanavata without any fear. And take such steps that they may go thither this very day. By this act, O father, extinguish the grief that consumeth me like a blazing fire, that robbeth me of sleep, and that pierces my heart even like a terrible dart.'"

SECTION CXLV
(Jatugriha Parva continued)

"Vaisampayana said, 'Then prince Duryodhana, along with his brothers began to gradually win over the people to his side by grants of wealth and honours. Meanwhile, some clever councillors, instructed by Dhritarashtra, one day began to describe (in court) the town of Varanavata as a charming place. And they said, The festival of Pasupati (Siva) hath commenced in the town of Varanavata. The concourse of people is great and the procession is the most delightful of all ever witnessed on earth. Decked with every ornament, it charmed the hearts of all spectators.' Thus did those councillors, instructed by Dhritarashtra, speak of Varanavata, and whilst they were so speaking, the Pandavas, O king, felt the desire of going to that delightful town. And when the king (Dhritarashtra) ascertained that the curiosity of the Pandavas had been awakened, the son of Ambika addressed them, saying, 'These men of mine often speak of Varanavata as the most delightful town in the world. If therefore, ye children, ye desire to witness that festival, go to Varanavata with your followers and friends and enjoy yourselves there like the celestials. And give ye away pearls and gems unto the Brahmanas and the musicians (that may be assembled there). And sporting there for some time as ye please like the resplendent celestials and enjoying as much pleasure as ye like, return ye to Hastinapura again.'

"Vaisampayana continued, 'Yudhishthira, fully understanding the motives of Dhritarashtra and considering that he himself was weak and friendless, replied unto the king, saying, 'So be it.' Then addressing Bhishma, the son of Santanu, the wise Vidura, Drona, Valhika, the Kaurava, Somadatta, Kripa, Aswatthaman, Bhurisravas, and the other councillors, and Brahmanas and ascetics, and the priests and the citizens, and the illustrious Gandhari, he said slowly and humbly, 'With our friends and followers we go to the delightful and populous town of Varanavata at the command of Dhritarashtra. Cheerfully give us your benedictions so that acquiring prosperity, therewith we may not be touched by sin.' Thus addressed by the eldest of Pandu's sons, the Kaurava chiefs all cheerfully pronounced blessings on them, saying, 'Ye sons of Pandu, let all the elements bless you along your way and let not the slightest evil befall you.'

"The Pandavas, having performed propitiatory rites for obtaining (their share of) the kingdom, and finishing their preparations, set out for Varanavata.'"

SECTION CXLVI
(Jatugriha Parva continued)

"Vaisampayana said, 'The wicked Duryodhana became very pleased when the king, O Bharata, had said so unto Pandavas. And, O bull of Bharata's race, Duryodhana, then, summoning his counsellor, Purochana in private, took hold of his right hand and said, 'O Purochana, this world, so full of wealth, is mine. But it is thine equally with me. It behoveth thee, therefore, to protect it. I have no more trustworthy counsellor than thee with whom to consult. Therefore, O sire, keep my counsel and exterminate my foes by a clever device. O, do as I bid thee. The Pandavas have, by Dhritarashtra, been sent to Varanavata, where they will, at Dhritarashtra's command, enjoy themselves during the festivities. Do that by which thou mayest this very day reach Varanavata in a car drawn by swift mules. Repairing thither, cause thou to be erected a quadrangular palace in the neighbourhood of the arsenal, rich in the materials and furniture, and guard thou the mansion well (with prying eyes). And use thou (in erecting that house) hemp and resin and all other inflammable materials that are procurable. And mixing a little earth with clarified butter and oil and fat and a large quantity of lac, make thou a plaster for lining the walls, and scatter thou all around that house hemp and oil and clarified butter and lac and wood in such a way that the Pandavas, or any others, may not, even with scrutiny behold them there or conclude the house to be an inflammable one. And having erected such mansion, cause thou the Pandavas, after worshipping them with great reverence, to dwell in it with Kunti and all their friends. And place thou there seats and conveyances and beds, all of the best workmanship, for the Pandavas, so that Dhritarashtra may have no reason to complain. Thou must also so manage it all that none of Varanavata may know anything till the end we have in view is accomplished. And assuring thyself that the Pandavas are sleeping within in confidence and without fear, thou must then set fire to that mansion beginning at the outer door. The Pandavas thereupon must be burnt to death, but the people will say that they have been burnt in (an accidental) conflagration of their house.'

"Saying, 'So be it' unto the Kuru prince, Purochana repaired to Varanavata in a car drawn by fleet mules. And going thither, O king, without loss of time, obedient to the instructions of Duryodhana, did everything that the prince had bid him do."

SECTION CXLVII
(Jatugriha Parva continued)

"Vaisampayana said, 'Meanwhile the Pandavas got into their cars, yoking thereto some fine horses endued with the speed of wind. While they were on the point of entering their cars, they touched, in great sorrow, the feet of Bhishma, of king Dhritarashtra, of the illustrious Drona, of Kripa, of Vidura and of the other elders of the Kuru race. Then saluting with reverence all the older men, and embracing their equals, receiving the farewell of even the children, and taking leave of all the venerable ladies in their household, and walking round them respectfully, and bidding farewell unto all the citizens, the Pandavas, ever mindful of their vows, set out for Varanavata. And Vidura of great wisdom and the other bulls among the Kurus and the citizens also, from great affliction, followed those tigers among men to some distance. And some amongst the citizens and the country people, who followed the Pandavas, afflicted beyond measure at beholding the sons of Pandu in such distress, began to say aloud, 'King Dhritarashtra of wicked soul seeth no things with the same eye. The Kuru monarch casteth not his eye on virtue. Neither the sinless Yudhishthira, nor Bhima the foremost of mighty men, nor Dhananjaya the (youngest) son of Kunti, will ever be guilty (of the sin of waging a rebellious war). When these will remain quiet, how shall the illustrious son of Madri do anything? Having inherited the kingdom from their father, Dhritarashtra could not bear them. How is that Bhishma who suffers the exile of the Pandavas to that wretched place, sanctions this act of great injustice? Vichitravirya, the son of Santanu, and the royal sage Pandu of Kuru's race both cherished us of old with fatherly care. But now that Pandu that tiger among men, hath ascended to heaven, Dhritarashtra cannot bear with these princes his children. We who do not sanction this exile shall all go, leaving this excellent town and our own homes, where Yudhishthira will go.'

"Unto those distressed citizens talking in this way, the virtuous Yudhishthira, himself afflicted with sorrow, reflecting for a few moments said, 'The king is our father, worthy of regard, our spiritual guide, and our superior. To carry out with unsuspicious hearts whatever he biddeth, is indeed, our duty. Ye are our friends. Walking round us and making us happy by your blessings, return ye to your abodes. When the time cometh for anything to be done for us by you, then, indeed, accomplish all that is agreeable and beneficial to us.' Thus addressed, the citizens walked round the Pandavas and blessed them with their blessings and returned to their respective abodes.

"And after the citizens had ceased following the Pandavas, Vidura, conversant with all the dictates of morality, desirous of awakening the eldest of the Pandavas (to a sense of his dangers), addressed him in these words. The learned Vidura, conversant with the jargon (of the Mlechchhas), addressed the learned Yudhishthira who also was conversant with the same jargon, in the words of the Mlechchha tongue, so as to be unintelligible to all except Yudhishthira. He said, 'He that knoweth the schemes his foes contrive in accordance with the dictates of political science, should, knowing them, act in such a way as to avoid all danger. He that knoweth that there are sharp weapons capable of cutting the body though not made of steel, and understandeth also the means of warding them off, can never be injured by foes. He liveth who protecteth himself by the knowledge that neither the consumer of straw and wood nor the drier of the dew burneth the inmates of a hole in the deep woods. The blind man seeth not his way: the blind man hath no knowledge of direction. He that hath no firmness never acquireth prosperity. Remembering this, be upon your guard. The man who taketh a weapon not made of steel (i.e., an inflammable abode) given him by his foes, can escape from fire by making his abode like unto that of a jackal (having many outlets). By wandering a man may acquire the knowledge of ways, and by the stars he can ascertain the direction, and he that keepeth his five (senses) under control can never be oppressed by his enemies.'

"Thus addressed, Pandu's son, Yudhishthira the just replied unto Vidura, that foremost of all learned men, saying, 'I have understood thee.' Then Vidura, having instructed the Pandavas and followed them (thus far), walked around them and bidding them farewell returned to his own abode. When the citizens and Bhishma and Vidura had all ceased following, Kunti approached Yudhishthira and said, 'The words that

Kshattri said unto thee in the midst of many people so indistinctly as if he did not say anything, and thy reply also to him in similar words and voice, we have not understood. If it is not improper for us to know them I should then like to hear everything that had passed between him and thee.'

"Yudhishthira replied, 'The virtuous Vidura said unto me that we should know that the mansion (for our accommodation at Varanavata) hath been built of inflammable materials. He said unto me, 'The path of escape too shall not be unknown to thee,'—and further,—'Those that can control their senses can acquire the sovereignty of the whole world.'—The reply that I gave unto Vidura was, 'I have understood thee.'

"Vaisampayana continued, 'The Pandavas set out on the eighth day of the month of Phalguna when the star Rohini was in the ascendant, and arriving at they beheld the town and the people.'"

SECTION CXLVIII
(Jatugriha Parva continued)

"Vaisampayana said, 'Then all the citizens (of Varanavata) on hearing that the son of Pandu had come, were filled with joy at the tidings, speedily came out of Varanavata, in vehicles of various kinds numbering by thousands, taking with them every auspicious article as directed by the Sastras, for receiving those foremost of men. And the people of Varanavata, approaching the sons of Kunti blessed them by uttering the Jaya and stood surrounding them. That tiger among men, viz., the virtuous Yudhishthira thus surrounded by them looked resplendent like him having the thunderbolt in his hands (viz., Indra) in the midst of the celestials. And those sinless ones, welcomed by the citizens and welcoming the citizens in return, then entered the populous town of Varanavata decked with every ornament. Entering the town those heroes first went, O monarch, to the abodes of Brahmanas engaged in their proper duties. Those foremost of men then went to the abodes of the officials of the town, and then of the Sutas and the Vaisyas and then to those of even the Sudras, O bull of Bharata's race, thus adored by the citizens, the Pandavas at last went with Purochana going before them, to the palace that had been built for them, Purochana then began to place before them food and drink and beds and carpets, all of the first and most agreeable order. The Pandavas attired in costly robes, continued to live there, adored by Purochana and the people having their homes in Varanavata.

"After the Pandavas had thus lived for ten nights, Purochana spoke to them of the mansion (he had built) called 'The Blessed Home,' but in reality the cursed house. Then those tigers among men, attired in costly dress, entered that mansion at the instance of Purochana like Guhyakas entering the palace (of Siva) on the Kailasa mount. The foremost of all virtuous men, Yudhishthira, inspecting the house, said unto Bhima that it was really built of inflammable materials. Smelling the scent of fat mixed with clarified butter and preparations of lac, he said unto Bhima, 'O chastiser of foes, this house is truly built of inflammable materials! Indeed, it is apparent that such is the case! The enemy, it is evident, by the aid of trusted artists well-skilled in the construction of houses, have finely built this mansion, after procuring hemp, resin, heath, straw, and bamboos, all soaked in clarified butter. This wicked wretch, Purochana, acting under the instruction of Duryodhana, stayeth here with the object of burning me to death when he seeth me trustful. But, O son of Pritha, Vidura of great intelligence, knew of this danger, and, therefore, hath warned me of it beforehand. Knowing it all, that youngest uncle of ours, ever wishing our good from affection hath told us that this house, so full of danger, hath been constructed by the wretches under Duryodhana acting in secrecy.'

"Hearing this, Bhima replied, 'If, sir, you know this house to be so inflammable, it would then be well for us to return thither where we had taken up our quarters first.' Yudhishthira replied, 'It seems to me that we should rather continue to live here in seeming unsuspiciousness but all the while with caution and our senses wide awake and seeking for some certain means of escape. If Purochana findeth from our countenances that we have fathomed designs, acting with haste he may suddenly burn us to death. Indeed, Purochana careth little for obloquy or sin. The wretch stayeth here acting under the instruction of Duryodhana. If we are burnt to death, will our grandfather Bhishma be angry? Why will he, by showing his wrath, make the Kauravas angry with him? Or, perhaps, our grandfather Bhishma and the other bull of Kuru's race, regarding indignation at such a sinful act to be virtuous, may become wrathful. If however, from fear of being burnt, we fly from here, Duryodhana, ambitious of sovereignty will certainly compass our death by means of spies. While we have no rank and power, Duryodhana hath both; while we have no friends and allies, Duryodhana hath both; while we are without wealth, Duryodhana hath at his command a full treasury. Will he not, therefore, certainly destroy us by adopting adequate means? Let us, therefore, by deceiving this wretch (Purochana) and that other wretch Duryodhana, pass our days, disguising ourselves at times. Let us also lead a hunting life, wandering over the earth. We shall then, if we have to escape our enemies, be familiar with all paths. We shall also, this very day, cause a subterranean passage to be dug in our chamber in great secrecy. If we act in this way, concealing what we do from all, fire shall never be able to consume us. We shall live here, actively doing everything for our safety but with such privacy that neither Purochana nor any of the citizens of Varanavata may know what we are after.'"

SECTION CXLIX
(Jatugriha Parva continued)

"Vaisampayana continued, 'A friend of Vidura's, well-skilled in mining, coming unto the Pandavas, addressed them in secret, saying, 'I have been sent by Vidura and am a skilful miner. I am to serve the Pandavas. Tell me what I am to do for ye. From the trust he reposeth in me Vidura hath said unto me, 'Go thou unto the Pandavas and accomplish thou their good.' What shall I do for you? Purochana will set fire to the door of thy house on the fourteenth night of this dark fortnight. To burn to death those tigers among men, the Pandavas, with their mother, is the design of that wicked wretch, the son of Dhritarashtra. O son of Pandu, Vidura also told thee something in the Mlechchha tongue to which thou also didst reply in same language. I state these particulars as my credentials.' Hearing these words, Yudhishthira, the truthful son of Kunti replied, 'O amiable one, I now know thee as a dear and trusted friend of Vidura, true and ever devoted to him. There is nothing that the learned Vidura doth not know. As his, so ours art thou. Make no difference between him and us. We are as much thine as his. O, protect us as the learned Vidura ever protecteth us. I know that this house, so inflammable, hath been contrived for me by Purochana at the command of Dhritarashtra's son. That wicked wretch commanding wealth and allies pursueth us without intermission. O, save us with a little exertion from the impending conflagration. If we are burnt to death here, Duryodhana's most cherished desire will be satisfied. Here is that wretch's well-furnished arsenal. This large mansion hath been built abutting the high ramparts of the arsenal without any outlet. But this unholy contrivance of Duryodhana was known to Vidura from the first, and he it was who enlightened us beforehand. The danger of which Kshattri had foreknowledge is now at our door. Save us from it without Purochana's knowledge thereof.' On hearing these words, the miner said, 'So be it,' and carefully beginning his work of excavation, made a large subterranean passage. And the mouth of that passage was in the centre of that house, and it was on a level with the floor and closed up with planks. The mouth was so covered from fear of Purochana, that wicked wretch who kept a constant watch at the door of the house. The Pandavas used to sleep within their chambers with arms ready for use, while, during the day, they went a-hunting from forest to forest. Thus, O king, they lived (in that mansion) very guardedly, deceiving Purochana by a show of trustfulness and contentment while in reality they were trustless and discontented. Nor did the citizens of Varanavata know anything about these plans of the Pandavas. In fact, none else knew of them except Vidura's friend, that good miner.'"

SECTION CL
(Jatugriha Parva continued)

"Vaisampayana said, 'Seeing the Pandavas living there cheerfully and without suspicion for a full year, Purochana became exceedingly glad. And beholding Purochana so very glad, Yudhishthira, the virtuous son of Kunti, addressing Bhima and Arjuna and the twins (Nakula and Sahadeva) said, 'The cruel-hearted wretch hath been well-deceived. I think the time is come for our escape. Setting fire to the arsenal and burning Purochana to death and letting his body lie here, let us, six persons, fly hence unobserved by all!'

"Vaisampayana continued, 'Then on the occasion of an almsgiving, O king, Kunti fed on a certain night a large number of Brahmanas. There came also a number of ladies who while eating and drinking, enjoyed there as they pleased, and with Kunti's leave returned to their respective homes. Desirous of obtaining food, there came, as though impelled by fate, to that feast, in course of her wanderings, a Nishada woman, the mother of five children, accompanied by all her sons. O king, she, and her children, intoxicated with the wine they drank, became incapable. Deprived of consciousness and more dead than alive, she with all her sons lay down in that mansion to sleep. Then when all the inmates of the house lay down to sleep, there began to blow a violent wind in the night. Bhima then set fire to the house just where Purochana was sleeping. Then the son of Pandu set fire to the door of that house of lac. Then he set fire to the mansion in several parts all around. Then when the sons of Pandu were satisfied that the house had caught fire in several parts those chastisers of foes with their mother, entered the subterranean passage without losing any time. Then the heat and the roar of the fire became intense and awakened the townspeople. Beholding the house in flames, the citizens with sorrowful faces began to say, 'The wretch (Purochana) of wicked soul had under the instruction of Duryodhana built his house for the destruction of his employer's relatives. He indeed hath set fire to it. O, fie on Dhritarashtra's heart which is so partial. He hath burnt to death, as if he were their foe, the sinless heirs of Pandu! O, the sinful and wicked- souled (Purochana) who hath burnt those best of men, the innocent and unsuspicious princes, hath himself been burnt to death as fate would have it.'

"Vaisampayana continued, 'The citizens of Varanavata thus bewailed (the fate of the Pandavas), and waited there for the whole night surrounding that house. The Pandavas, however, accompanied by their mother coming out of the subterranean passage, fled in haste unnoticed. But those chastisers of foes, for sleepiness and fear, could not with their mother proceed in haste. But, O monarch, Bhimasena, endued with terrible prowess and swiftness of motion took upon his body all his brothers and mother and began to push through the darkness. Placing his mother on his shoulder, the twins on his sides, and Yudhishthira and Arjuna on both his arms, Vrikodara of great energy and strength and endued with the speed of the wind, commenced his march, breaking the trees with his breast and pressing deep the earth with his stamp.'"

SECTION CLI
(Jatugriha Parva continued)

"Vaisampayana said, 'About this time, the learned Vidura had sent into those woods a man of pure character and much trusted by him. This person going to where he had been directed, saw the Pandavas with their mother in the forest employed in a certain place in measuring the depth of a river. The design that the wicked Duryodhana had formed had been, through his spies, known to Vidura of great intelligence, and, therefore, he had sent that prudent person unto the Pandavas. Sent by Vidura unto them, he showed the Pandavas on the sacred banks of the Ganga a boat with engines and flags, constructed by trusted artificers and capable of withstanding wind and wave and endued with the speed of the tempest or of thought. He then addressed the Pandavas in these words to show that he had really been sent by Vidura, 'O Yudhishthira,' he said, 'listen to these words the learned Vidura had said (unto thee) as a proof of the fact that I come from him. Neither the consumer of straw and the wood nor the drier of dew ever burneth the inmates of a hole in the forest. He escapeth from death who protecteth himself knowing this, etc. By these credentials know me to be the person who has been truly sent by Vidura and to be also his trusted agent. Vidura, conversant with everything, hath again said, 'O son of Kunti, thou shalt surely defeat in battle Karna, and Duryodhana with his brothers, and Sakuni.' This boat is ready on the waters, and it will glide pleasantly thereon, and shall certainly bear you all from these regions!'

"Then beholding those foremost of men with their mother pensive and sad he caused them to go into the boat that was on the Ganga, and accompanied them himself. Addressing them again, he said, 'Vidura having smelt your heads and embraced you (mentally), hath said again that in commencing your auspicious journey and going alone you should never be careless.'

"Saying these words unto those heroic princes, the person sent by Vidura took those bulls among men over to the other side of the Ganga in his boat. And having taken them over the water and seen them all safe on the opposite bank, he uttered the word 'Jaya' (victory) to their success and then left them and returned to the place whence he had come.

"The illustrious Pandavas also sending through that person some message to Vidura, began, after having crossed the Ganga, to proceed with haste and in great secrecy.'"

THE MAHABHARATA

SECTION CLII
(Jatugriha Parva continued)

"Vaisampayana said, 'Then, when the night had passed away, a large concourse of the townspeople came there in haste to see the sons of Pandu. After extinguishing the fire, they saw that the house just burnt down had been built of lac in materials and that (Duryodhana's) counsellor Purochana had been burnt to death. And the people began to bewail aloud saying, 'Indeed, this had been contrived by the sinful Duryodhana for the destruction of the Pandavas. There is little doubt that Duryodhana hath, with Dhritarashtra's knowledge, burnt to death the heirs of Pandu, else the prince would have been prevented by his father. There is little doubt that even Bhishma, the son of Santanu, and Drona and Vidura and Kripa and other Kauravas have not, any of them, followed the dictates of duty. Let us now send to Dhritarashtra to say, 'Thy great desire hath been achieved! Thou hast burnt to death the Pandavas!'

"They then began to extinguish the members to obtain some trace of the Pandavas, and they saw the innocent Nishada woman with her five sons burnt to death. Then the miner sent by Vidura, while removing the ashes, covered the hole he had dug with those ashes in such a way that it remained unnoticed by all who had gone there.

"The citizens then sent to Dhritarashtra to inform him that the Pandavas along with (Duryodhana's) counsellor Purochana had been burnt to death. King Dhritarashtra, on hearing the evil news of the death of the Pandavas, wept in great sorrow. And he said, 'King Pandu, my brother of great fame, hath, indeed, died today when those heroic sons of his together with their mother have been burnt to death. Ye men, repair quickly to Varanavata and cause the funeral rites to be performed of those heroes and of the daughter of Kuntiraj! Let also the bones of the deceased be sanctified with the usual rites, and let all the beneficial and great acts (usual on such occasions) be performed. Let the friends and relatives of those that have been burnt to death repair thither. Let also all other beneficial acts that ought, under the circumstances, to be performed by us for the Pandavas and Kunti be accomplished by wealth.'

"Having said this, Dhritarashtra, the son of Ambika, surrounded by his relatives, offered oblations of water to the sons of Pandu. And all of them, afflicted with excessive sorrow, bewailed aloud, exclaiming, 'O Yudhishthira! Oh prince of the Kuru race!'—While others cried aloud, 'Oh, Bhima!—O Phalguna!'—while some again,—'Oh, the twins!—Oh, Kunti!'— Thus did they sorrow for the Pandavas and offer oblations of water unto them. The citizens also wept for the Pandavas but Vidura did not weep much, because he knew the truth.

"Meanwhile the Pandavas endued with great strength with their mother forming a company of six going out of the town of Varanavata arrived at the banks of the Ganga. They then speedily reached the opposite bank aided by the strength of the boatmen's arms, the rapidity of the river's current, and a favourable wind. Leaving the boat, they proceeded in the southern direction finding their way in the dark by the light of the stars. After much suffering they at last reached, O king, a dense forest. They were then tired and thirsty; sleep was closing their eyes every moment. Then Yudhishthira, addressing Bhima endued with great energy, said, 'What can be more painful than this? We are now in the deep woods. We know not which side is which, nor can we proceed much further. We do not know whether that wretch Purochana hath or hath not been burnt to death. How shall we escape from these dangers unseen by others? O Bharata, taking us on thyself, proceed thou as before. Thou alone amongst us art strong and swift as the wind.'

"Thus addressed by Yudhishthira the just, the mighty Bhimasena, taking up on his body Kunti and his brothers, began to proceed with great celerity."

SECTION CLIII
(Jatugriha Parva continued)

"Vaisampayana said," As the mighty Bhima proceeded, the whole forest with its trees and their branches seemed to tremble, in consequence of their clash with his breast. The motion of his thighs raised a wind like unto that which blows during the months of Jyaishtha and Ashadha (May and June). And the mighty Bhima proceeded, making a path for himself, but treading down the trees and creepers before him. In fact, he broke (by the pressure of his body) the large trees and plants, with their flowers and fruits, standing on his way. Even so passeth through the woods breaking down mighty trees, the leader of a herd of elephants, of the age of sixty years, angry and endued with excess of energy, during the season of rut when the liquid juice trickle down the three parts of his body. Indeed, so great was the force with which Bhima endued with the speed of Garuda or of Marut (the god of wind), proceeded that the Pandavas seemed to faint in consequence. Frequently swimming across streams difficult of being crossed, the Pandavas disguised themselves on their way from fear of the sons of Dhritarashtra. And Bhima carried on his shoulder his illustrious mother of delicate sensibilities along the uneven banks of rivers. Towards the evening, O bull of Bharata's race, Bhima (bearing his brothers and mother on his back) reached a terrible forest where fruits and roots and water were scarce and which resounded with the terrible cries of birds and beasts. The twilight deepened the cries of birds and beasts became fiercer, darkness shrouded everything from the view and untimely winds began to blow that broke and laid low many a tree large and small and many creepers with dry leaves and fruits. The Kaurava princes, afflicted with fatigue and thirst, and heavy with sleep, were unable to proceed further. They then all sat down in that forest without food and drink. Then Kunti, smitten with thirst, said unto her sons, 'I am the mother of the five Pandavas and am now in their midst. Yet I am burning with thirst!' Kunti repeatedly said this unto her sons. Hearing these words, Bhima's heart, from affection for his mother, was warmed by compassion and he resolved to go (along as before). Then Bhima, proceeding through that terrible and extensive forest without a living soul, saw a beautiful banian tree with widespreading branches. Setting down there his brothers and mother, O bull of Bharata's race, he said unto them, 'Rest you here, while I go in quest of water. I hear the sweet cries of aquatic fowls. I think there must be a large pool here.' Commanded, O Bharata, by his elder brother who said unto him, 'Go', Bhima proceeded in the direction whence the cries of those aquatic fowls were coming. And, O bull of Bharata's race, he soon came upon a lake and bathed and slaked his thirst. And affectionate unto his brothers, he brought for them, O Bharata, water by soaking his upper garments. Hastily retracing his way over those four miles he came unto where his mother was and beholding her he was afflicted with sorrow and began to sigh like a snake. Distressed with grief at seeing his mother and brothers asleep on the bare ground, Vrikodara began to weep, 'Oh, wretch that I am, who behold my brothers asleep on the bare ground, what can befall me more painful than this? Alas, they who formerly at Varanavata could not sleep on the softest and costliest beds are now asleep on the bare ground! Oh, what more painful sight shall I ever behold than that of Kunti—the sister of Vasudeva, that grinder of hostile hosts—the daughter of Kuntiraja,—herself decked with every auspicious mark, the daughter-in- law of Vichitravirya,—the wife of the illustrious Pandu,—the mother of us (five brothers),— resplendent as the filaments of the lotus and delicate and tender and fit to sleep on the costliest bed—thus asleep, as she should never be, on the bare ground! Oh, she who hath brought forth these sons by Dharma and Indra and Maruta—she who hath ever slept within palaces—now sleepeth, fatigued, on the bare ground! What more painful sight shall ever be beheld by me than that of these tigers among men (my brothers) asleep on the ground! Oh, the virtuous Yudhishthira, who deserveth the sovereignty of the three worlds, sleepeth, fatigued, like an ordinary man, on the bare ground! This Arjuna of the darkish hue of blue clouds, and unequalled amongst men sleepeth on the ground like an ordinary person! Oh, what can be more painful than this? Oh the twins, who in beauty are like the twin Aswins amongst the celestials, are asleep like ordinary mortals on the bare ground! He who hath no jealous evil-minded relatives, liveth in happiness in this world like a single tree in a village. The tree that standeth single in a village with its leaves and fruits, from absence of other of the same species, becometh sacred and is worshipped and venerated by all. They again that have many relatives who, however, are all heroic and virtuous, live happily in the world without sorrow of any kind. Themselves powerful and growing in prosperity and always gladdening their friends and relatives, they live, depending on each other, like tall trees growing in the same forest. We, however, have been forced in exile by the wicked Dhritarashtra and his sons having escaped with difficulty, from sheer good fortune, a fiery death. Having escaped from that fire, we are now resting in the shade of this tree. Having already suffered so much, where now are we to go? Ye sons of Dhritarashtra of little foresight, ye wicked fellows, enjoy your temporary success. The gods are certainly auspicious to you. But ye wicked wretches, ye are alive yet, only because Yudhishthira doth not command me to take your lives. Else this very day, filled with wrath, I would send thee, (O Duryodhana), to the of Yama (Pluto) with thy children and friends and brothers, and Karna, and (Sakuni) the son of Suvala! But what can I do, for, ye sinful wretches, the virtuous king Yudhishthira, the eldest of the Pandavas, is not yet angry with you?'

"Having said this, Bhima of mighty arms, fired with wrath, began to squeeze his palms, sighing deeply in affliction. Excited again with wrath like an extinguished fire blazing up all on a sudden, Vrikodara once more beheld his brothers sleeping on the ground like ordinary persons sleeping in trustfulness. And Bhima said unto himself, 'I think there is some town not far off from this forest. These all are asleep, so I will sit awake. And this will slake their thirst after they rise refreshed from sleep.' Saying this, Bhima sat there awake, keeping watch over his sleeping mother and brothers.'"

SECTION CLIV
(Hidimva-vadha Parva)

"Vaisampayana said, 'Not far from the place where the Pandavas were asleep, a Rakshasa by name Hidimva dwelt on the Sala tree. Possessed of great energy and prowess, he was a cruel cannibal of visage that was grim in consequence of his sharp and long teeth. He was now hungry and longing for human flesh. Of long shanks and a large belly, his locks and beard were both red in hue. His shoulders were broad like the neck of a tree; his ears were like unto arrows, and his features were frightful. Of red eyes and grim visage, the monster beheld, while casting his glances around, the sons of Pandu sleeping in those woods. He was then hungry and longing for human flesh. Shaking his dry and grizzly locks and scratching them with his fingers pointed upwards, the large-mouthed cannibal repeatedly looked at the sleeping sons of Pandu yawning wistfully at times. Of huge body and great strength, of complexion like the colour of a mass of clouds, of teeth long and sharp-pointed and face emitting a sort of lustre, he was ever pleased with human flesh. And scenting the odour of man, he addressed his sister, saying, 'O sister, it is after a long time that such agreeable food hath approached me! My mouth waters at the anticipated relish of such food. My eight teeth, so sharp-pointed and incapable of being resisted by any substance, I shall, today, after a long time, put into the most delicious flesh. Attacking the human throat and even opening the veins, I shall (today) drink a plentiful quantity of human blood, hot and fresh and frothy. Go and ascertain who these are, lying asleep in these woods. The strong scent of man pleaseth my nostrils. Slaughtering all these men, bring them unto me. They sleep within my territory. Thou needest have no fear from them. Do my bidding soon, for we shall then together eat their flesh, tearing off their bodies at pleasure. And after feasting to our fill on human flesh we shall then dance together to various measures!'

"Thus addressed by Hidimva in those woods, Hidimva, the female cannibal, at the command of her brother, went, O bull of Bharata's race, to the spot where the Pandavas were. And on going there, she beheld the Pandavas asleep with their mother and the invincible Bhimasena sitting awake. And beholding Bhimasena unrivalled on earth for beauty and like unto a vigorous Sala tree, the Rakshasa woman immediately fell in love with him, and she said to herself, 'This person of hue like heated gold and of mighty arms, of broad shoulders as the lion, and so resplendent, of neck marked with three lines like a conch-shell and eyes like lotus-petals, is worthy of being my husband. I shall not obey the cruel mandate of my brother. A woman's love for her husband is stronger than her affection for her brother. If I slay him, my brother's gratification as well as mine will only be momentary. But if I slay him not, I can enjoy with him for ever and ever.' Thus saying, the Rakshasa woman, capable of assuming form at will, assumed an excellent human form and began to advance with slow steps towards Bhima of mighty arms. Decked with celestial ornaments she advanced with smiles on her lips and a modest gait, and addressing Bhima said, 'O bull among men, whence hast thou come here and who art thou? Who, besides, are these persons of celestial beauty sleeping here? Who also, O sinless one, is this lady of transcendent beauty sleeping so trustfully in these woods as if she were lying in her own chamber? Dost thou not know that this forest is the abode of a Rakshasa. Truly do I say, here liveth the wicked Rakshasa called Hidimva. Ye beings of celestial beauty, I have been sent hither even by that Rakshasa—my brother—with the cruel intent of killing you for his food. But I tell thee truly that beholding thee resplendent as a celestial, I would have none else for my husband save thee! Thou who art acquainted with all duties, knowing this, do unto me what is proper. My heart as well as my body hath been pierced by (the shafts of) Kama (Cupid). O, as I am desirous of obtaining thee, make me thine. O thou of mighty arms, I will rescue thee from the Rakshasa who eateth human flesh. O sinless one, be thou my husband. We shall then live on the breasts of mountains inaccessible to ordinary mortals. I can range the air and I do so at pleasure. Thou mayest enjoy great felicity with me in those regions.'

"Hearing these words of hers, Bhima replied, 'O Rakshasa woman, who can, like a Muni having all his passions under control, abandon his sleeping mother and elder and younger brothers? What man like me would go to gratify his lust, leaving his sleeping mother and brothers as food for a Rakshasa?'

"The Rakshasa woman replied, 'O, awaken all these, I shall do unto you all that is agreeable to thee! I shall certainly rescue you all from my cannibal brother.'

"Bhima then said, 'O Rakshasa woman, I will not, from fear of thy wicked brother, awaken my brothers and mother sleeping comfortably in the woods. O timid one, Rakshasas are never able to bear the prowess of my arms. And, O thou of handsome eyes, neither men, nor Gandharvas, nor Yakshas are able to bear my might. O amiable one, thou mayst stay or go as thou likest, or mayst even send thy cannibal brother, O thou of delicate shape. I care not.'"

SECTION CLV
(Hidimva-vadha Parva continued)

"Vaisampayana said, 'Hidimva, the chief of the Rakshasas, seeing that his sister returned not soon enough, alighted from the tree, proceeded quickly to the spot where the Pandavas were. Of red eyes and strong arms and the arms and the hair of his head standing erect, of large open mouth and body like unto a mass of dark clouds, teeth long and sharp-pointed, he was terrible to behold. And Hidimva, beholding her brother of frightful visage alight from the tree, became very much alarmed, and addressing Bhima said, 'The wicked cannibal is coming hither in wrath. I entreat thee, do with thy brothers, as I bid thee. O thou of great courage, as I am endued with the powers of a Rakshasa, I am capable of going whithersoever I like. Mount ye on my hips, I will carry you all through the skies. And, O chastiser of foes, awaken these and thy mother sleeping in comfort. Taking them all on my body, I will convey you through the skies.'

"Bhima then said, 'O thou of fair hips, fear not anything. I am sure that as long as I am here, there is no Rakshasa capable of injuring any of these, O thou of slender waist. I will slay this (cannibal) before thy very eyes. This worst of Rakshasas, O timid one, is no worthy antagonist of mine, nor can all the Rakshasas together bear the strength of my arms. Behold these strong arms of mine, each like unto the trunk of an elephant. Behold also these thighs of mine like unto iron maces, and this broad and adamantine chest. O beautiful one, thou shall today behold my prowess like unto that of Indra. O thou of fair hips, hate me not, thinking that I am a man.'

"Hidimva replied saying, 'O tiger among men, O thou of the beauty of a celestial, I do not certainly hold thee in contempt. But I have seen the prowess that Rakshasas exert upon men.'

"Vaisampayana continued, 'Then, O Bharata, the wrathful Rakshasa eating human flesh heard these words of Bhima who had been talking in that way. And Hidimva beheld his sister disguised in human form, her head decked with garlands of flowers and her face like the full moon and her eyebrows and nose and eyes and ringlets all of the handsomest description, and her nails and complexion of the most delicate hue, and herself wearing every kind of ornament and attired in fine transparent robes. The cannibal, beholding her in that charming human form, suspected that she was desirous of carnal intercourse and became indignant. And, O best of the Kurus, becoming angry with his sister, the Rakshasa dilated his eyes and addressing her said, 'What senseless creature wishes to throw obstacles in my path now that I am so hungry? Hast thou become so senseless, O Hidimva, that thou fearest not my wrath? Fie on thee, thou unchaste woman! Thou art even now desirous of carnal intercourse and solicitous of doing me an injury. Thou art ready to sacrifice the good name and honour of all the Rakshasas, thy ancestors! Those with whose aid thou wouldst do me this great injury, I will, even now, slay along with thee.' Addressing his sister thus, Hidimva, with eyes red with anger and teeth pressing against teeth, ran at her to kill her then and there. But beholding him rush at his sister, Bhima, that foremost of smiter, endued with great energy, rebuked him and said, 'Stop—Stop!'"

"Vaisampayana continued, 'And Bhima, beholding the Rakshasa angry with his sister, smiled (in derision), and said, addressing him, 'O Hidimva, what need is there for thee to awaken these persons sleeping so comfortably? O wicked cannibal, approach me first without loss of time. Smite me first,— it behoveth thee not to kill a woman, especially when she hath been sinned against instead of sinning. This girl is scarcely responsible for her act in desiring intercourse with me. She hath, in this, been moved by the deity of desire that pervadeth every living form. Thou wicked wretch and the most infamous of Rakshasas, thy sister came here at thy command. Beholding my person, she desireth me. In that the timid girl doth no injury to thee. It is the deity of desire that hath offended. It behoveth thee not to injure her for this offence. O wicked wretch, thou shalt not slay a woman when I am here. Come with me, O cannibal, and fight with myself singly. Singly shall I send thee today to the abode of Yama (Pluto). O Rakshasa, let thy head today, pressed by my might, be pounded to pieces, as though pressed by the tread of a mighty elephant. When thou art slain by me on the field of battle, let herons and hawks and jackals tear in glee thy limbs today on the ground. In a moment I shall today make this forest destitute of Rakshasas,—this forest that had so long been ruled by thee, devourer of human beings! Thy sister, O Rakshasa, shall today behold thyself, huge though thou art like a mountain, like a huge elephant repeatedly dragged by a lion. O worst of Rakshasas, thyself slain by me, men ranging these woods will henceforth do so safely and without fear.'

"Hearing these words, Hidimva said, 'What need is there, O man, for this thy vaunt and this thy boast? Accomplish all this first, and then mayst thou vaunt indeed. Therefore, delay thou not. Thou knowest thyself to be strong and endued with prowess, so thou shalt rightly estimate thy strength today in thy encounter with me. Until that, I will not slay these (thy brothers). Let them sleep comfortably. But I will, as thou art a fool and the utterer of evil speeches, slay thee first. After drinking thy blood, I will slay these also, and then last of all, this (sister of mine) that hath done me an injury.'

"Vaisampayana continued, 'Saying this, the cannibal, extending his arms ran in wrath towards Bhimasena, that chastiser of foes. Then Bhima of terrible prowess quickly seized, as though in sport, with great force, the extended arms of the Rakshasa who had rushed at him. Then seizing the struggling Rakshasa with violence, Bhima dragged him from that spot full thirty-two cubits like a lion dragging a little animal. Then the Rakshasa, thus made to feel the weight of Bhima's strength, became very angry and clasping the Pandava, sent forth a terrible yell. The mighty Bhima then dragged with force the Rakshasa to a greater distance, lest his yells should awaken his brothers sleeping in comfort. Clasping and dragging each other with great force, both Hidimva and Bhimasena put forth their prowess. Fighting like two full-grown elephants mad with rage, they then began to break down the trees and tear the creepers that grew around. And at those sounds, those tigers among men (the sleeping Pandavas) woke up with their mother, and saw Hidimva sitting before them.'"

SECTION CLVI
(Hidimva-vadha Parva continued)

"Vaisampayana said, 'Roused from sleep, those tigers among men, with their mother, beholding the extraordinary beauty of Hidimva, were filled with wonder. And Kunti, gazing at her with wonder at her beauty, addressed her sweetly and gave her every assurance. She asked, 'O thou of the splendour of a daughter of the celestials, whose art thou and who art thou? O thou of the fairest complexion, on what business hast thou come hither and whence hast thou come? If thou art the deity of these woods or an Apsara, tell me all regarding thyself and also why thou stayest here?' Thereupon Hidimva replied, 'This extensive forest that thou seest, of the hue of blue cloud, is the abode of a Rakshasa of the name of Hidimva. O handsome lady, know me as the sister of that chief of the Rakshasa. Revered dame, I had been sent by that brother of mine to kill thee with all thy children. But on arriving here at the command of that cruel brother of mine, I beheld thy mighty son. Then, O blessed lady, I was brought under the control of thy son by the deity of love who pervadeth the nature of every being, and I then (mentally) chose that mighty son of thine as my husband. I tried my best to convey you hence, but I could not (because of thy son's opposition). Then the cannibal, seeing my delay, came hither to kill all these thy children. But he hath been dragged hence with force by that mighty and intelligent son of thine—my husband. Behold now that couple— man and Rakshasa—both endued with great strength and prowess, engaged in combat, grinding each other and filling the whole region with their shouts.'

"Vaisampayana continued, 'Hearing those words of hers, Yudhishthira suddenly rose up and Arjuna also and Nakula and Sahadeva of great energy and they beheld Bhima and the Rakshasa already engaged in fight, eager to overcome each other and dragging each other with great force, like two lions endued with great might. The dust raised by their feet in consequence of that encounter looked like the smoke of a forest-conflagration. Covered with that dust their huge bodies resembled two tall cliffs enveloped in mist. Then Arjuna, beholding Bhima rather oppressed in the fight by the Rakshasa, slowly, said with smiles on his lips, 'Fear not, O Bhima of mighty arms! We (had been asleep and therefore) knew not that thou wast engaged with a terrible Rakshasa and tired in fight. Here do I stand to help thee, let me slay the Rakshasa, and let

Nakula and Sahadeva protect our mother.' Hearing him, Bhima said, 'Look on this encounter, O brother, like a stranger. Fear not for the result. Having come within the reach of my arms, he shall not escape with life.' Then Arjuna said, 'What need, O Bhima, for keeping the Rakshasa alive so long? O oppressor of enemies, we are to go hence, and cannot stay here longer. The east is reddening, the morning twilight is about to set in. The Rakshasa became stronger by break of day, therefore, hasten, O Bhima! Play not (with thy victim), but slay the terrible Rakshasa soon. During the two twilights Rakshasas always put forth their powers of deception. Use all the strength of thy arms.'

"Vaisampayana continued, 'At this speech of Arjuna, Bhima blazing up with anger, summoned the might that Vayu (his father) puts forth at the time of the universal dissolution. And filled with rage, he quickly raised high in the air the Rakshasa's body, blue as the clouds of heaven, and whirled it a hundred times. Then addressing the cannibal, Bhima said, 'O Rakshasa, thy intelligence was given thee in vain, and in vain hast thou grown and thriven on unsanctified flesh. Thou deservest, therefore, an unholy death and I shall reduce thee today to nothing. I shall make this forest blessed today, like one without prickly plants. And, O Rakshasa, thou shalt no longer slay human beings for thy food.' Arjuna at this juncture, said, 'O Bhima, if thou thinkest it a hard task for thee to overcome this Rakshasa in combat, let me render thee help, else, slay him thyself without loss of time. Or, O Vrikodara, let me alone slay the Rakshasa. Thou art tired, and hast almost finished the affair. Well dost thou deserve rest.'

"Vaisampayana continued, 'Hearing these words of Arjuna, Bhima was fired with rage and dashing the Rakshasa on the ground with all his might slew him as if he were an animal. The Rakshasa, while dying, sent forth a terrible yell that filled the whole forest, and was deep as the sound of a wet drum. Then the mighty Bhima, holding the body with his hands, bent it double, and breaking it in the middle, greatly gratified his brothers. Beholding Hidimva slain, they became exceedingly glad and lost no time in offering their congratulations to Bhima, that chastiser of all foes. Then Arjuna worshipping the illustrious Bhima of terrible prowess, addressed him again and said, 'Revered senior, I think there is a town not far off from this forest. Blest be thou, let us go hence soon, so that Duryodhana may not trace us.'

"Then all those mighty car-warriors, those tigers among men, saying, 'So be it,' proceeded along with their mother, followed by Hidimva, the Rakshasa woman.'"

SECTION CLVII
(Hidimva-vadha Parva continued)

"Vaisampayana said, 'Bhima, beholding Hidimva following them, addressed her, saying, 'Rakshasas revenge themselves on their enemies by adopting deceptions that are incapable of being penetrated. Therefore, O Hidimva, go thou the way on which thy brother hath gone.' Then Yudhishthira beholding Bhima in rage, said, 'O Bhima, O tiger among men, however enraged, do not slay a woman. O Pandava, the observance of virtue is a higher duty than the protection of life. Hidimva, who had come with the object of slaying us, thou hast already slain. This woman is the sister of that Rakshasa, what can she do to us even if she were angry?'

"Vaisampayana continued, 'Then Hidimva reverentially saluting Kunti and her son Yudhishthira also, said, with joined palms, 'O revered lady, thou knowest the pangs that women are made to feel at the hands of the deity of love. Blessed dame, these pangs, of which Bhimasena hath been the cause, are torturing me. I had hitherto borne these insufferable pangs, waiting for the time (when thy son could assuage them). That time is now come, when I expected I would be made happy. Casting off my friends and relations and the usage of my race, I have, O blessed lady, chosen this son of thine, this tiger among men, as my husband. I tell thee truly, O illustrious lady, that if I am cast off by that hero or by thee either, I will no longer bear this life of mine. Therefore, O thou of the fairest complexion, it behoveth thee to show me mercy, thinking me either as very silly or thy obedient slave. O illustrious dame, unite me with this thy son, my husband. Endued as he is with the form of a celestial, let me go taking him with me wherever I like. Trust me, O blessed lady, I will again bring him back unto you all. When you think of me I will come to you immediately and convey you whithersoever ye may command. I will rescue you from all dangers and carry you across inaccessible and uneven regions. I will carry you on my back whenever ye desire to proceed with swiftness. O, be gracious unto me and make Bhima accept me. It hath been said that in a season of distress one should protect one's life by any means. He, that seeketh to discharge that duty should not scruple about the means. He, that in a season of distress keepeth his virtue, is the foremost of virtuous men. Indeed, distress is the greatest danger to virtue and virtuous men. It is virtue that protecteth life; therefore is virtue called the giver of life. Hence the means by which virtue or the observance of a duty is secured can never be censurable.'

"Hearing these words of Hidimva, Yudhishthira said. 'It is even so, O Hidimva, as thou sayest. There is no doubt of it. But, O thou of slender waist, thou must act even as thou hast said. Bhima will, after he hath washed himself and said his prayers and performed the usual propitiatory rites, pay his attentions to thee till the sun sets. Sport thou with him as thou likest during the day, O thou that art endued with the speed of the mind! But thou must bring back Bhimasena hither every day at night- fall.'

"Vaisampayana continued, 'Then Bhima, expressing his assent to all that Yudhishthira said, addressed Hidimva, saying, 'Listen to me, O Rakshasa woman! Truly do I make this engagement with thee that I will stay with thee, O thou of slender waist, until thou obtainest a son.' Then Hidimva, saying, 'So be it,' took Bhima upon her body and sped through the skies. On mountain peaks of picturesque scenery and regions sacred to the gods, abounding with dappled herds and echoing with the melodies of feathered tribes, herself assuming the handsomest form decked with every ornament and pouring forth at times mellifluous strains, Hidimva sported with the Pandava and studied to make him happy. So also, in inaccessible regions of forests, and on mountain-breasts overgrown with blossoming trees on lakes resplendent with lotuses and lilies, islands of rivers and their pebbly banks, on sylvan streams with beautiful banks and mountain-currents, in picturesque woods with blossoming trees and creepers in Himalayan bowers, and various caves, on crystal pools smiling with lotuses, on sea-shores shining with gold and pearls, in beautiful towns and fine gardens, in woods sacred to the gods and on hill-sides, in the regions of Guhyakas and ascetics, on the banks of Manasarovara abounding with fruits and flowers of every season Hidimva, assuming the handsomest form, sported with Bhima and studied to make him happy. Endued with the speed of the mind, she sported with Bhima in all these regions, till in time, she conceived and brought forth a mighty son begotten upon her by the Pandava. Of terrible eyes and large mouth and straight arrowy ears, the child was terrible to behold. Of lips brown as copper and sharp teeth and loud roar, of mighty arms and great strength and excessive prowess, this child became a mighty bowman. Of long nose, broad chest, frightfully swelling calves, celerity of motion and excessive strength, he had nothing human in his countenance, though born of man. And he excelled (in strength and prowess) all Pisachas and kindred tribes as well as all Rakshasas. And, O monarch, though a little child, he grew up a youth the very hour he was born. The mighty hero soon acquired high proficiency in the use of all weapons. The Rakshasa women bring forth the very day they conceive, and capable of assuming any forms at will, they always change their forms. And the bald- headed child, that mighty bowman, soon after his birth, bowing down to his mother, touched her feet and the feet also of his father. His parents then bestowed upon him a name. His mother having remarked that his head was (bald) like unto a Ghata (water-pot), both his parents thereupon called him Ghatotkacha (the pot-headed). And Ghatotkacha who was exceedingly devoted to the Pandavas, became a great favourite with them, indeed almost one of them.

"Then Hidimva, knowing that the period of her stay (with her husband) had come to an end, saluted the Pandavas and making a new appointment with them went away whithersoever she liked. And Ghatotkacha also—that foremost of Rakshasas—promising unto his father that he would come when wanted on business, saluted them and went away northward. Indeed, it was the illustrious Indra who created (by lending a portion of himself) the mighty car-warrior Ghatotkacha as a fit antagonist of Karna of unrivalled energy, in consequence of the dart he had given unto Karna (and which was sure to kill the person against whom it would be hurled)."

SECTION CLVIII
(Hidimva-vadha Parva continued)

"Vaisampayana said, 'Those mighty car-warriors, the heroic Pandavas, then went, O king, from forest to forest killing deer and many animals (for their food). And in the course of their wanderings they saw the countries of the Matsyas, the Trigartas, the Panchalas and then of the Kichakas, and also many beautiful woods and lakes therein. And they all had matted locks on their heads and were attired in barks of trees and the skins of animals. Indeed, with Kunti in their company those illustrious heroes were attired in the garbs of ascetics. And those mighty car-warriors sometimes proceeded in haste, carrying their mother on their backs; and sometimes they proceeded in disguise, and sometimes again with great celerity. And they used to study the Rik and the other Vedas and also all the Vedangas as well as the sciences of morals and politics. And the Pandavas, conversant with the science of morals, met, in course of their wanderings their grandfather (Vyasa). And saluting the illustrious Krishna-Dwaipayana, those chastisers of enemies, with their mother, stood before him with joined hands.'

"Vyasa then said, 'Ye bulls of Bharata's race, I knew beforehand of this affliction of yours consisting in your deceitful exile by the son of Dhritarashtra. Knowing this, I have come to you, desirous of doing you some great good. Do not grieve for what hath befallen you. Know that all this is for your happiness. Undoubtedly, the sons of Dhritarashtra and you are all equal in my eye. But men are always partial to those who are in misfortune or of tender years. It is therefore, that my affection for you is greater now. And in consequence of that affection, I desire to do you good. Listen to me! Not far off before you is a delightful town where no danger can overtake you. Live ye there in disguise, waiting for my return.'

"Vaisampayana continued, 'Vyasa, the son of Satyavati, thus comforting the Pandavas, led them into the town of Ekachakra. And the master also comforted Kunti, saying, 'Live, O daughter! This son of thine, Yudhishthira, ever devoted to truth, this illustrious bull among men, having by his justice conquered the whole world, will rule over all the other monarchs of the earth. There is little doubt that, having by means of Bhima's and Arjuna's prowess conquered the whole earth with her belt of seas, he will enjoy the sovereignty thereof. Thy sons as well as those of Madri—mighty car-warriors all—will cheerfully sport as pleaseth them in their dominions. These tigers among men will also perform various sacrifices, such as the Rajasuya and the horse-sacrifice, in which the presents unto the Brahmanas are very large. And these thy sons will rule their ancestral kingdom, maintaining their friends and relatives in luxury and affluence and happiness.'

"Vaisampayana continued, 'With these words Vyasa introduced them into the dwelling of a Brahmana. And the island-born Rishi, addressing the eldest of the Pandavas, said, 'Wait here for me! I will come back to you! By adapting yourselves to the country and the occasion you will succeed in becoming very happy.'

"Then, O king, the Pandavas with joined hands said unto the Rishi, 'So be it.' And the illustrious master, the Rishi Vyasa, then went away to the region whence he had come.'"

SECTION CLIX
(Vaka-vadha Parva)

"Janamejaya asked, 'O first of Brahmanas, what did the Pandavas, those mighty car-warriors, the sons of Kunti, do after arriving at Ekachakra?'

"Vaisampayana said, 'Those mighty car-warriors, the sons of Kunti, on arriving at Ekachakra, lived for a short time in the abode of a Brahmana. Leading an eleemosynary life, they behold (in course of their wanderings) various delightful forests and earthly regions, and many rivers and lakes, and they became great favourites of the inhabitants of that town in consequence of their own accomplishments. At nightfall they placed before Kunti all they gathered in their mendicant tours, and Kunti used to divide the whole amongst them, each taking what was allotted to him. And those heroic chastisers of foes, with their mother, together took one moiety of the whole, while the mighty Bhima alone took the other moiety. In this way, O bull of Bharata's race, the illustrious Pandavas lived there for some time.

"One day, while those bulls of the Bharata race were out on their tour of mendicancy, it so happened that Bhima was (at home) with (his mother) Pritha. That day, O Bharata, Kunti heard a loud and heart-rending wail of sorrow coming from within the apartments of the Brahmana. Hearing the inmates of the Brahmana's house wailing and indulging in piteous lamentations, Kunti, O king, from compassion and the goodness of her heart, could not bear it with indifference. Afflicted with sorrow, the amiable Pritha, addressing Bhima, said these words full of compassion. 'Our woes assuaged, we are, O son, living happily in the house of this Brahmana, respected by him and unknown to Dhritarashtra's son. O son, I always think of the good I should do to this Brahmana, like what they do that live happily in others' abodes! O child, he is a true man upon whom favours are never lost. He payeth back to others more than what he receiveth at their hands. There is no doubt, some affliction hath overtaken this Brahmana. If we could be of any help to him, we should then be requiting his services.'

"Hearing these words of his mother, Bhima said, 'Ascertain, O mother the nature of the Brahmana's distress and whence also it hath arisen. Learning all about it, relieve it I will however difficult may the task prove.'

"Vaisampayana continued 'While mother and son were thus talking with each other, they heard again, O king, another wail of sorrow proceeding from the Brahmana and his wife. Then Kunti quickly entered the inner apartments of that illustrious Brahmana, like unto a cow running towards her tethered calf. She beheld the Brahmana with his wife, son and daughter, sitting with a woeful face, and she heard the Brahmana say, 'Oh, fie on this earthly life which is hollow as the reed and so fruitless after all which is based on sorrow and hath no freedom, and which hath misery for its lot! Life is sorrow and disease; life is truly a record of misery! The soul is one: but it hath to pursue virtue, wealth and pleasure. And because these are pursued at one and the same time, there frequently occurs a disagreement that is the source of much misery. Some say that salvation is the highest object of our desire. But I believe it can never be attained. The acquisition of wealth is hell; the pursuit of wealth is attended with misery; there is more misery after one has acquired it, for one loves one's possessions, and if any mishap befalls them, the possessor becomes afflicted with woe. I do not see by what means I can escape from this danger, nor how I can fly hence, with my wife to some region free from danger. Remember, O wife, that I endeavoured to migrate to some other place where we would be happy, but thou didst not then listen to me. Though frequently solicited by me, thou, O simple woman, said to me, 'I have been born here, and here have I grown old; this is my ancestral homestead.' Thy venerable father, O wife, and thy mother also, have, a long time ago, ascended to heaven. Thy relations also had all been dead. Oh why then didst thou yet like to live here? Led by affection for thy relatives thou didst not then hear what I said. But the time is now come when thou art to witness the death of a relative. Oh, how sad is that spectacle for me! Or perhaps the time is come for my own death, for I shall never be able to abandon cruelly one of my own as long as I myself am alive. Thou art my helpmate in all good deeds, self-denying and always affectionate unto me as a mother. The gods have given thee to me as a true friend and thou art ever my prime stay. Thou hast, by my parents, been made the participator in my domestic concerns. Thou art of pure lineage and good disposition, the mother of children, devoted to me, and so innocent; having chosen and wedded thee with due rites, I cannot abandon thee, my wife, so constant in thy vows, to save my life. How shall I myself be able to sacrifice my son a child of tender years and yet without the hirsute appendages (of manhood)? How shall I sacrifice my daughter whom I have begotten myself, who hath been placed, as a pledge, in my hands by the Creator himself for bestowal on a husband and through whom I hope to enjoy, along with my ancestors, the regions attainable by those only that have daughters' sons? Some people think that the father's affection for a son is greater; others, that his affection for a daughter is greater; mine, however, is equal. How can I be prepared to give up the innocent daughter upon whom rest the regions of bliss obtainable by me in after life and my own lineage and perpetual happiness? If, again, I sacrifice myself and go to the other world, I should scarcely know any peace, for, indeed, it is evident that, left by me these would not be able to support life. The sacrifice of any of these would be cruel and censurable. On the other hand, if I sacrifice myself, these, without me, will certainly perish. The distress into which I have fallen is great; nor do I know the means of escape. Alas, what course shall I take today with my near ones. It is well that I should die with all these, for I can live no longer.'"

SECTION CLX
(Vaka-vadha Parva continued)

"Vaisampayana said, "On hearing these words of the Brahmana, his wife said, 'Thou shouldst not, O Brahmana, grieve like an ordinary man. Nor is this the time for mourning. Thou hast learning; thou knowest that all men are sure to die; none should grieve for that which is inevitable. Wife, son, and daughter, all these are sought for one's own self. As thou art possessed of a good understanding, kill thou thy sorrows. I will myself go there. This indeed, is the highest and the eternal duty of a woman, viz., that by sacrificing her life she should seek the good of her husband. Such an act done by me will make thee happy, and bring me fame in this world and eternal bliss hereafter. This, indeed, is the highest virtue that I tell thee, and thou mayest, by this, acquire both virtue and happiness. The object for which one desireth a wife hath already been achieved by thee through me. I have borne thee a daughter and a son and thus been freed from the debt I had owed thee. Thou art well able to support and cherish the children, but I however, can never support and cherish them like thee. Thou art my life, wealth, and lord; bereft of thee, how shall these children of tender years—how also shall I myself, exist? Widowed and masterless, with two children depending on me, how shall I, without thee, keep alive the pair, myself leading an honest life? If the daughter of thine is solicited (in marriage) by persons dishonourable and vain and unworthy of contracting an alliance with thee, how shall I be able to protect the girl? Indeed, as birds seek with avidity for meat that hath been thrown away on the ground, so do men solicit a woman that hath lost her husband. O best of Brahmanas, solicited by wicked men, I may waver and may not be able to continue in the path that is desired by all honest men. How shall I be able to place this sole daughter of thy house—this innocent girl—in the way along which her ancestors have always walked? How shall I then be able to impart unto this child every desirable accomplishment to make him virtuous as thyself, in that season of want when I shall become masterless? Overpowering myself who shall be masterless, unworthy persons will demand (the hand of) this daughter of thine, like Sudras desiring to hear the Vedas. And if I bestow not upon them this girl possessing thy blood and qualities, they may even take her away by force, like crows carrying away the sacrificial butter. And beholding thy son become so unlike to thee, and thy daughter placed under the control of some unworthy persons, I shall be despised in the world by even persons that are dishonourable, and I will certainly die. These children also, bereft of me and thee, their father, will, I doubt not, perish like fish when the water drieth up. There is no doubt that bereft of thee the three will perish: therefore it behoveth thee to sacrifice me. O Brahmana, persons conversant with morals have said that for women that have borne children, to predecease their lords is an act of the highest merit. Ready am I to abandon this son and this daughter, these my relations, and life itself, for thee. For a woman to be ever employed in doing agreeable offices to her lord is a higher duty than sacrifices, asceticism, vows, and charities of every description. The act, therefore, which I intend to perform is consonant with the highest virtue and is for thy good and that of thy race. The wise have declared that children and relatives and wife and all things held dear are cherished for the purpose of liberating one's self from danger and distress. One must guard one's wealth for freeing one's self from danger, and it is by his wealth that he should cherish and protect his wife. But he must protect his own self both by (means of) his wife and his wealth. The learned have enunciated the truth that one's wife, son, wealth, and house, are acquired with the intention of providing against accidents, foreseen or unforeseen. The wise have also said that all one's relations weighed against one's own self would not be equal unto one's self. Therefore, revered sir, protect thy own self by abandoning me. O, give me leave to sacrifice myself, and cherish thou my children. Those that are conversant with the morals have, in their treatises, said, that women should never be slaughtered and that Rakshasas are not ignorant of the rules of morality. Therefore, while it is certain that the Rakshasa will kill a man, it is doubtful whether he will kill a woman. It behoveth thee, therefore, being conversant with the rules of morality, to place me before the Rakshasa. I have enjoyed much happiness, have obtained much that is agreeable to me, and have also acquired great religious merit. I have also obtained from thee children that are so dear to me. Therefore, it grieveth not me to die. I have borne thee children and have also grown old; I am ever desirous of doing good to thee; remembering all these I have come to this resolution. O revered sir, abandoning me thou mayest obtain another wife. By her thou mayest again acquire religious merit. There is no sin in this. For a man polygamy is an act of merit, but for a woman it is very sinful to betake herself to a second husband after the first. Considering all this, and remembering too that sacrifice of thy own self is censurable, O, liberate today without loss of time thy own self, thy race, and these thy children (by abandoning me).'

"Vaisampayana continued, 'Thus addressed by her, O Bharata, the Brahmana embraced her, and they both began to weep in silence, afflicted with grief.'"

SECTION CLXI
(Vaka-vadha Parva continued)

"Vaisampayana said, 'On hearing these words of her afflicted parents, the daughter was filled with grief, and she addressed them, saying, 'Why are you so afflicted and why do you so weep, as if you have none to look after you? O, listen to me and do what may be proper. There is little doubt that you are bound in duty to abandon me at a certain time. Sure to abandon me once, O, abandon me now and save every thing at the expense of me alone. Men desire to have children, thinking that children would save them (in this world as well as in the region hereafter). O, cross the stream of your difficulties by means of my poor self, as if I were a raft. A child rescueth his parents in this and the other regions; therefore is the child called by the learned Putra (rescuer). The ancestors desire daughter's sons from me (as a special means of salvation). But (without waiting for my children) I myself will rescue them by protecting the life of my father. This my brother is of tender years, so there is little doubt that he will perish if thou diest now. If thou, my father, diest and my brother followeth thee, the funeral cake of the Pitris will be suspended and they will be greatly injured. Left behind by my father and brother, and by my mother also (for she will not survive her husband and son) I shall be plunged deeper and deeper in woe and ultimately perish in great distress. There can be little doubt that if thou escape from this danger as also my mother and infant brother, then thy race and the (ancestral) cake will be perpetuated. The son is one's own self; the wife is one's friend; the daughter, however, is the source of trouble. Do thou save thyself, therefore, by removing that source of trouble, and do thou thereby set me in the path of virtue. As I am a girl, O father, destitute of thee, I shall be helpless and plunged in woe, and shall have to go everywhere. It is therefore that I am resolved to rescue my father's race and share the merit of that act by accomplishing this difficult task. If thou, O best of Brahmanas, goest thither (unto the Rakshasa), leaving me here, then I shall be very much pained. Therefore, O father, be kind to me. O thou best of men, for our sake, for that of virtue and also thy race, save thyself, abandoning me, whom at one time thou shall be constrained to part from. There need be no delay, O father, in doing that which is inevitable. What can be more painful than that, when thou hast ascended to heaven, we shall have to go about begging our food, like dogs, from strangers. But if thou art with thy relations from these difficulties, I shall then live happily in the region of the celestials. It hath been heard by us that if after bestowing thy daughter in this way, thou offerest oblations to the gods and the celestials, they will certainly be propitious.'

"Vaisampayana continued, 'The Brahmana and his wife, hearing these various lamentations of their daughter, became sadder than before and the three began to weep together. Their son, then, of tender years, beholding them and their daughter thus weeping together, lisped these words in a sweet tone, his eyes having dilated with delight, 'Weep not, O father, nor thou, O mother, nor thou O sister!' And smilingly did the child approach each of them, and at last taking up a blade of grass said in glee, 'With this will I slay the Rakshasa who eateth human beings!' Although all of them had been plunged in woe, yet hearing what the child lisped so sweetly, joy appeared on their faces. Then Kunti thinking that to be the proper opportunity, approached the group and said these words. Indeed, her words revived them as nectar reviveth a person that is dead.'"

SECTION CLXII
(Vaka-vadha Parva continued

"Kunti said, 'I desire to learn from you the cause of this grief, for I will remove it, if possible.'

"The Brahmana replied, 'O thou of ascetic wealth, thy speech is, indeed worthy of thee. But this grief is incapable of being removed by any human being. Not far from this town, there liveth a Rakshasa of the name of Vaka, which cannibal is the lord of this country and town. Thriving on human flesh, that wretched Rakshasa endued with great strength ruleth this country. He being the chief of the Asuras, this town and the country in which it is situate are protected by his might. We have no fear from the machinations of any enemy, or indeed from any living soul. The fee, however, fixed for that cannibal is his food, which consists of a cart- load of rice, two buffaloes, and a human being who conveyeth them unto him. One after another, the house-holders have to send him this food. The turn, however, cometh to a particular family at intervals of many long years. If there are any that seek to avoid it, the Rakshasa slayeth them with their children and wives and devoureth them all. There is, in this country, a city called Vetrakiya, where liveth the king of these territories. He is ignorant of the science of government, and possessed of little intelligence, he adopts not with care any measure by which these territories may be rendered safe for all time to come. But we certainly deserve it all, inasmuch as we live within the dominion of that wretched and weak monarch in perpetual anxiety. Brahmanas can never be made to dwell permanently within the dominions of any one, for they are dependent on nobody, they live rather like birds ranging all countries in perfect freedom. It hath been said that one must secure a (good) king, then a wife, and then wealth. It is by the acquisition of these three that one can rescue his relatives and sons. But as regards the acquisition of these three, the course of my actions hath been the reverse. Hence, plunged into a sea of danger, am suffering sorely. That turn, destructive of one's family, hath now devolved upon me. I shall have to give unto the Rakshasa as his fee the food of the aforesaid description and one human being to boot. I have no wealth to buy a man with. I cannot by any means consent to part with any one of my family, nor do I see any way of escape from (the clutches of) that Rakshasa. I am now sunk in an ocean of grief from which there is no escape. I shall go to that Rakshasa today, attended by all my family in order that that wretch might devour us all at once.'"

SECTION CLXIII
(Vaka-vadha Parva continued)

"Kunti said, 'Grieve not at all, O Brahmana, on account of this danger. I see a way by which to rescue thee from that Rakshasa. Thou hast only one son, who, besides, is of very tender years, also only one daughter, young and helpless, so I do not like that any of these, or thy wife, or even thyself should go unto the Rakshasa. I have five sons, O Brahmana, let one of them go, carrying in thy behalf tribute of that Rakshasa.'

"Hearing this, the Brahmana replied, 'To save my own life I shall never suffer this to be done. I shall never sacrifice, to save myself, the life of a Brahmana or of a guest. Indeed, even those that are of low origin and of sinful practices refuse to do (what thou askest me to do). It is said that one should sacrifice one's self and one's offspring for the benefit of a Brahmana. I regard this advice excellent and I like to follow it too. When I have to choose between the death of a Brahmana and that of my own, I would prefer the latter. The killing of a Brahmana is the highest sin, and there is no expiation for it. I think a reluctant sacrifice of one's own self is better than the reluctant sacrifice of a Brahmana. O blessed lady, in sacrificing myself I do not become guilty of self-destruction. No sin can attach to me when another will take my life. But if I deliberately consent to the death of a Brahmana, it would be a cruel and sinful act, from the consequence of which there is no escape. The learned have said that the abandonment of one who hath come to thy house or sought thy protection, as also the killing of one who seeketh death at thy hands, is both cruel and sinful. The illustrious among those conversant with practices allowable in seasons of distress, have before now said that one should never perform an act that is cruel and censurable. It is well for me that I should today perish myself with my wife, but I would never sanction the death of a Brahmana.'

"Kunti said, 'I too am firmly of opinion, O Brahmana, that Brahmanas should ever be protected. As regards myself, no son of mine would be less dear to me even if I had a hundred instead of the five I have. But this Rakshasa will not be able to kill my son, for that son of mine is endued with great prowess and energy, and skilled in mantras. He will faithfully deliver to the Rakshasa his food, but will, I know to a certainty, rescue himself. I have seen before many mighty Rakshasas of huge bodies engaged in combat with my heroic son and killed too by him. But, O Brahmana, do not disclose this fact to anybody, for if it be known, persons desirous of obtaining this power, will, from curiosity, always trouble my sons. The wise have said that if my son imparteth any knowledge, without the assent of his preceptor, unto any person, my son himself will no longer be able to profit by that knowledge.'

"Thus addressed by Pritha, the Brahmana with his wife became exceedingly glad and assented to Kunti's speech, which was unto them as nectar. Then Kunti, accompanied by the Brahmana, went unto the son of Vayu (Bhima) and asked him to accomplish (that difficult task). Bhima replied unto them, saying, 'So be it.'"

SECTION CLXIV
(Vaka-vadha Parva continued)

"Vaisampayana said, 'After Bhima had pledged himself to accomplish the task, saying, 'I will do it,' the Pandavas, O Bharata, returned home with the alms they had obtained during the day. Then Yudhishthira, the son of Pandu from Bhima's countenance alone, suspected the nature of the task he had undertaken to accomplish. Sitting by the side of his mother, Yudhishthira asked her in private, 'What is the task, O mother, that Bhima of terrible prowess seeketh to accomplish? Doth he do so at thy command or of his own accord?' Kunti replied, 'Bhima, that chastiser of foes, will at my command, do this great deed for the good of the Brahmana and the liberation of this town.'

"Yudhishthira said, 'What rash act hast thou done, O mother! It is difficult of being performed and almost amounteth to suicide! The learned never applaud the abandonment of one's own child. Why dost thou, O mother, wish to sacrifice thy own child for the sake of another's? Thou hast, O mother, by this abandonment of thy child, acted not only against the course of human practices but also against the teachings of the Vedas. That Bhima, relying on whose arms we sleep happily in the night and hope to recover the kingdom of which we have been deprived by the covetous son of Dhritarashtra, that hero of immeasurable energy, remembering whose prowess Duryodhana and Sakuni do not sleep a wink during the whole night and by whose prowess we were rescued from the palace of lac and various other dangers, that Bhima who caused the death of Purochana, and relying on whose might we regard ourselves as having already slain the sons of Dhritarashtra and acquired the whole earth with all her wealth, upon what considerations, O mother, hast thou resolved upon abandoning him? Hast thou been deprived of thy reason? Hath thy understanding been clouded by the calamities thou hast undergone?'

"On hearing these words of her son, Kunti said, 'O Yudhishthira, thou needst not be at all anxious on account of Vrikodara. I have not come to this resolve owing to any weakness of understanding. Respected by him, and with our sorrows assuaged, we have, O son, been living in the house of this Brahmana, unknown to the sons of Dhritarashtra. For requiting, O son, that Brahmana, I have resolved to do this. He, indeed, is a man upon whom good offices are never lost. The measure of his requital becometh greater than the measure of the services he receiveth. Beholding the prowess of Bhima on the occasion of (our escape from) the house of lac, and from the destruction also of Hidimva, my confidence in Vrikodara is great. The might of Bhima's arms is equal unto that of ten thousand elephants. It was, therefore, that he succeeded in carrying you all, each heavy as an elephant, from Varanavata. There is no one on earth equal unto Bhima in might; he may even overcome that foremost of warriors, the holder of the thunderbolt himself. Soon after his birth he fell from my lap on the breast of the mountain. By the weight of his body the mass of stone on which he fell down broke in pieces. From this also, O son of Pandu, I have come to know Bhima's might. For this reason have I resolved to set him against the Brahmana's foe. I have not acted in this from foolishness or ignorance or from motive of gain. I have deliberately resolved to do this virtuous deed. By this act, O Yudhishthira, two objects will be accomplished; one is a requital of the services rendered by the Brahmana and the other is the acquisition of high religious merit. It is my conviction that the Kshatriya who rendereth help unto a Brahmana in anything acquireth regions of bliss hereafter. So also a Kshatriya who saveth the life of a Kshatriya achieveth that great fame in this world as in the other. A Kshatriya rendering help unto a Vaisya also on this earth certainly acquires world-wide popularity. One of the kingly tribe should protect even the Sudra who cometh to him for protection. If he doeth so, in his next life he receiveth his birth in a royal line, commanding prosperity and the respect of other kings. O scion of Puru's race, the illustrious Vyasa of wisdom acquired by hard ascetic toil told me so in bygone days. It is therefore, that I have resolved upon accomplishing this.'"

SECTION CLXV
(Vaka-vadha Parva continued)

"Having heard these words of his mother, Yudhishthira said, 'What thou, O mother, hast deliberately done, moved by compassion for the afflicted Brahmana, is, indeed, excellent. Bhima will certainly come back with life, after having slain the cannibal, inasmuch as thou art, O mother, always compassionate unto Brahmanas. But tell the Brahmana, O mother, that he doth not do anything whereby the dwellers in this town may know all about it, and make him promise to keep thy request.'

"Vaisampayana continued, 'Then, when the night passed away, Bhimasena, the son of Pandu, taking with him the Rakshasa's food set out for the place where the cannibal lived. The mighty son of Pandu, approaching the forest where the Rakshasa dwelt, began to eat himself the food he carried, calling loudly to the Rakshasa by name. The Rakshasa, inflamed with anger at Bhima's words, came out and approached the place where Bhima was.

"Of huge body and great strength, of red eyes, red beard, and red hair, he was terrible to behold, and he came, pressing deep the earth with his tread. The opening of his mouth, was from ear to ear and his ears themselves were straight as arrows. Of grim visage, he had a forehead furrowed into three lines. Beholding Bhima eating his food, the Rakshasa advanced, biting his nether lip and expanding his eyes in wrath. And addressing Bhima he said, 'Who is this fool, who desiring to go to the abode of Yama, eateth in my very sight the food intended for me?' Hearing these words, Bhima, O Bharata, smiled in derision and disregarding the Rakshasa, continued eating with averted face. Beholding this, the cannibal uttered a frightful yell and with both arms upraised ran at Bhima desiring to kill him, there and then. Even then disregarding the Rakshasa and casting only a single glance at him, Vrikodara, that slayer of hostile heroes continued to eat the Rakshasa's food. Filled with wrath at this, the Rakshasa struck from behind with both his arms a heavy blow on the back of Vrikodara, the son of Kunti. But Bhima, though struck heavily by the mighty Rakshasa, with both his hands, did not even look up at the Rakshasa but continued to eat as before. Then the mighty Rakshasa, inflamed with wrath, tore up a tree and ran at Bhima for striking him again. Meanwhile the mighty Bhima, that bull among men had leisurely eaten up the whole of that food and washing himself stood cheerfully for fight. Then, O Bharata, possessed of great energy, Bhima, smiling in derision, caught with his left hand the tree hurled at him by the Rakshasa in wrath. Then that mighty Rakshasa, tearing up many more trees, hurled them at Bhima, and the Pandava also hurled as many at the Rakshasa. Then, O king, the combat with trees between that human being and the Rakshasa, became so terrible that the region around soon became destitute of trees. Then the Rakshasa, saying that he was none else than Vaka, sprang upon the Pandava and seized the mighty Bhima with his arms. That mighty hero also clasping with his own strong arms the strong-armed Rakshasa, and exerting himself actively, began to drag him violently. Dragged by Bhima and dragging Bhima also, the cannibal was overcome with great fatigue. The earth began to tremble in consequence of the strength they both exerted, and large trees that stood there broke in pieces. Then Bhima, beholding the cannibal overcome with fatigue, pressed him down on the earth with his knees and began to strike him with great force. Then placing one knee on the middle of the Rakshasa's back, Bhima seized his neck with his right hand and the cloth on his waist with his left, and bent him double with great force. The cannibal then roared frightfully. And, O monarch, he also began to vomit blood while he was being thus broken on Bhima's knee.'"

SECTION CLXVI
(Vaka-vadha Parva continued)

"Vaisampayana said 'Then Vaka, huge as a mountain, thus broken (on Bhima's knee), died, uttering frightful yells. Terrified by these sounds, the relatives of that Rakshasa came out, O king, with their attendants. Bhima, that foremost of smiters, seeing them so terrified and deprived of reason, comforted them and made them promise (to give up cannibalism), saying, 'Do not ever again kill human beings. If ye kill men, ye will have to die even as Vaka.' Those Rakshasas hearing this speech of Bhima, said, 'So be it,' and gave, O king, the desired promise. From that day, O Bharata, the Rakshasas (of the region) were seen by the inhabitants of that town to be very peaceful towards mankind. Then Bhima, dragging the lifeless cannibal, placed him at one of the gates of the town and went away unobserved by any one. The kinsmen of Vaka, beholding him slain by the might of Bhima, became frightened and fled in different directions.

"Meanwhile Bhima, having slain the Rakshasa, returned to the Brahmana's abode and related to Yudhishthira all that had happened, in detail. The next morning the inhabitants of the town in coming out saw the Rakshasa lying dead on the ground, his body covered with blood. Beholding that terrible cannibal, huge as a mountain cliff, thus mangled and lying on the ground, the hair of the spectators stood erect. Returning to Ekachakra, they soon gave the intelligence. Then, O king, the citizens by thousands accompanied by their wives, young and old, all began to come to the spot for beholding the Vaka and they were all amazed at seeing that superhuman feat. Instantly, O monarch, they began to pray to their gods. Then they began to calculate whose turn it had been the day before to carry food to the Rakshasa. And ascertaining this, they all came to that Brahmana and asked him (to satisfy their curiosity). Thus asked by them repeatedly, that bull among Brahmanas, desirous of concealing the Pandavas, said these words unto all the citizens, 'A certain high-souled Brahmana, skilled in mantras, beheld me weeping with my relatives after I had been ordered to supply the Rakshasa's food. Asking me the cause and ascertaining the distress of the town, that first of Brahmanas gave me every assurance and with smiles said, 'I shall carry the food for that wretched Rakshasa today. Do not fear for me.' Saying this he conveyed the food towards the forest of Vaka. This deed, so beneficial unto us all, hath very certainly been done by him.'

"Then those Brahmanas and Kshatriyas (of the city), hearing this, wondered much. And the Vaisyas and the Sudras also became exceedingly glad, and they all established a festival in which the worship of Brahmanas was the principal ceremony (in remembrance of this Brahmana who had relieved them from their fears of Vaka)."

SECTION CLXVII
(Chaitraratha Parva)

"After this citizens returned to their respective houses and the Pandavas continued to dwell at Ekachakra as before."

"Janamejaya said, 'O Brahmana, what did those tigers among men, the Pandavas, do after they had slain the Rakshasa Vaka?'

"Vaisampayana said, 'The Pandavas, O king, after slaying the Rakshasa Vaka, continued to dwell in the abode of that Brahmana, employed in the study of the Vedas. Within a few days there came a Brahmana of rigid vows unto the abode of their host to take up his quarters there. Their host, that bull among Brahmanas, ever hospitable unto all guests, worshipping the newly- arrived Brahmana with due ceremonies, gave him quarters in his own abode. Then those bulls among men, the Pandavas, with their mother Kunti, solicited the new lodger to narrate to them his interesting experiences. The Brahmana spake to them of various countries and shrines and (holy) rivers, of kings and many wonderful provinces and cities. And after this narration was over, that Brahmana, O Janamejaya, also spoke of the wonderful self-choice of Yajnasena's daughter, the princes of Panchala, and of the births of Dhrishtadyumna and Sikhandi, and of the birth, without the intervention of a woman, of Krishna (Draupadi) at the great sacrifice of Drupada.

"Then those bulls among men, the Pandavas, hearing of these extraordinary facts regarding that illustrious monarch (Drupada), and desiring to know the details thereof, asked the Brahmana, after his narration was concluded, to satisfy their curiosity. The Pandavas said, 'How, O Brahmana, did the birth of Dhrishtadyumna the son of Drupada, take place from the (sacrificial) fire? How also did the extraordinary birth of Krishna take place from the centre of the sacrificial platform? How also did Drupada's son learn all weapons from the great bowman Drona? And, O Brahmana, how and for whom and for what reason was the friendship between Drona and Drupada broken off?'

"Vaisampayana continued, 'Thus questioned, O monarch, by those bulls among men, the Brahmana narrated all the particulars about the birth of Draupadi.'"

SECTION CLXVIII
(Chaitraratha Parva continued)

"The Brahmana said, 'At that region where the Ganga entered the plains there lived a great Rishi, devoted to the austerest of penances. Of rigid vows and great wisdom, he bore the name Bharadwaja. One day, on coming to the Ganga to perform his ablutions, the Rishi saw the Apsara Ghritachi, who had come before, standing on the bank after her ablutions were over. And it so happened that a wind arose and disrobed the Apsara standing there. And the Rishi beholding her thus disrobed, felt the influence of desire. Though practising the vow of continence from his very youth, as soon as he felt the influence of desire, the Rishi's vital fluid came out. And as it came out, he held it in a pot (drana), and of that fluid thus preserved in a pot was born a son who came to be called Drona (the pot-born). And Drona studied all the Vedas and their several branches. And Bharadwaja had a friend named Prishata who was the king of Panchalas. And about the time that Drona was born, Prishata also obtained a son named Drupada. And that bull amongst Kshatriyas, Prishata's son, going every day to that asylum of Bharadwaja, played and studied with Drona. And after Prishata's death, Drupada succeeded him on the throne. Drona about this time heard that (the great Brahmana hero) Rama (on the eve of his retiring into the weeds) was resolved to give away all his wealth. Hearing this, the son of Bharadwaja repaired unto Rama who was about to retire into the woods and addressing him, said, 'O best of Brahmanas, know me to be Drona who hath come to thee to obtain thy wealth.' Rama replied, saying, 'I have given away everything. All that I now have is this body of mine and my weapons. O Brahmana, thou mayest ask of me one of these two, either my body or my weapons.' Then Drona said, 'It behoveth thee, sir, to give me all thy weapons together with (the mysteries of) their use and withdrawal.'

"The Brahmana continued, 'Then Rama of Bhrigu's race, saying, 'So be it,' gave all his weapons unto Drona, who obtaining them regarded himself as crowned with success. Drona obtaining from Rama the most exalted of all weapons, called the Brahma weapon, became exceedingly glad and acquired a decided superiority over all men. Then the son of Bharadwaja, endued with great prowess went to king Drupada, and approaching that monarch, that tiger among men, said, 'Know me for thy friend.' Hearing this Drupada said, 'One of low birth can never be the friend of one whose lineage is pure, nor can one who is not a car-warrior have a car-warrior for his friend. So also one who is not a king cannot have a king as his friend. Why dost thou, therefore, desire (to revive our) former friendship?'

"The Brahmana continued, 'Drona, gifted with great intelligence, was extremely mortified at this, and settling in his mind some means of humiliating the king of the Panchala he went to the capital of the Kurus, called after the name of an elephant. Then Bhishma, taking with him his grandsons, presented them unto the wise son of Bharadwaja as his pupils for instruction, along with various kinds of wealth. Then Drona, desirous of humiliating king Drupada, called together his disciples and addressed them, 'Ye sinless ones, it behoveth you, after you have been accomplished in arms, to give me as preceptorial fee something that I cherish in my heart.' Then Arjuna and others said unto their preceptor, 'So be it.'— After a time when the Pandavas became skilled in arms and sure aims, demanding of them his fee, he again told them these words, 'Drupada, the son of Prishata, is the king of Chhatravati. Take away from him his kingdom, and give it unto me.' Then the Pandavas, defeating Drupada in battle and taking him prisoner along with his ministers, offered him unto Drona, who beholding the vanquished monarch, said, 'O king, I again solicit thy friendship; and because none who is not a king deserveth to be the friend of a king, therefore, O Yajnasena, I am resolved to divide thy kingdom amongst ourselves. While thou art the king of the country to the south of Bhagirathi (Ganga), I will rule the country to the north.'

"The Brahmana continued, 'The king of the Panchalas, thus addressed by the wise son of Bharadwaja, told that best of Brahmanas and foremost of all persons conversant with weapons, these words, 'O high-souled son of Bharadwaja, blest be thou, let it be so, let there be eternal friendship between us as thou desirest!' Thus addressing each other and establishing a permanent bond between themselves, Drona and the king of Panchala, both of them chastisers of foes, went away to the places they came from. But the thought of that humiliation did not leave the king's mind for a single moment. Sad at heart, the king began to waste away.'"

THE MAHABHARATA

SECTION CLXIX
(Chaitraratha Parva continued)

"The Brahmana continued, 'King Drupada (after this), distressed at heart, wandered among many asylums of Brahmanas in search of superior Brahmanas well-skilled in sacrificial rites. Overwhelmed with grief and eagerly yearning for children, the king always said, 'Oh, I have no offspring surpassing all in accomplishments.' And the monarch, from great despondency, always said 'Oh, fie on those children that I have and on my relatives!' And ever thinking of revenging himself on Drona, the monarch sighed incessantly. And that best of kings, O Bharata, even after much deliberation, saw no way of overcoming, by his Kshatriya might, the prowess and discipline and training and accomplishment of Drona. Wandering along the banks of the Yamuna and the Ganga, the monarch once came upon a sacred asylum of Brahmanas. There was in that asylum no Brahmana who was not a Snataka, no one who was not of rigid vows, and none who was not virtuous to a high degree. And the king saw there two Brahmana sages named Yaja and Upayaja, both of rigid vows and souls under complete control and belonging to the most superior order. They were both devoted to the study of the ancient institutes and sprung from the race of Kasyapa. And those best of Brahmanas were well able to help the king in the attainment of his object. The king then, with great assiduity and singleness of purpose, began to court this pair of excellent Brahmanas. Ascertaining the superior accomplishments of the younger of the two the king courted in private Upayaja of rigid vows, by the offer of every desirable acquisition. Employed in paying homage to the feet of Upayaja, always addressing in sweet words and offering him every object of human desire, Drupada, after worshipping that Brahmana, addressed him (one day), saying, 'O Upayaja, O Brahmana, if thou, performest those sacrificial rites by (virtue of) which I may obtain a son who may slay Drona, I promise thee ten thousand kine, or whatever else may be agreeable to thee, O first of Brahmanas, truly am I ready to make gifts to thee.' Thus addressed by the king, the Rishi replied, saying, 'I cannot (perform such rites).' But Drupada without accepting this reply as final, once more began to serve and pay homage unto that Brahmana. Then, after the expiration of a year, Upayaja, that first of Brahmanas, O monarch, addressing Drupada in sweet tone, said, 'My elder brother (Yaja), one day, while wandering through the deep woods, took up a fruit that had fallen upon a spot the purity of which he cared not to enquire about. I was following him (at the time) and observed this unworthy act of his. Indeed, he entertains no scruples in accepting things impure. In accepting that (particular) fruit he saw not any impropriety of sinful nature: Indeed, he who observeth not purity (in one instance) is not very likely to observe it in the other instances. When he lived in the house of his preceptor, employed in studying the institutes, he always used to eat (impure) remnants of other people's feasts. He always speaks approvingly of food and entertains no dislike for anything. Arguing from these, I believe that my brother covets earthy acquisitions. Therefore, O king, go unto him; he will perform spiritual offices for thee.' Hearing these words of Upayaja, king Drupada, though entertaining a low opinion of Yaja, nevertheless went to his abode. Worshipping Yaja who was (still) worthy of homage, Drupada said unto him, 'O master, perform thou spiritual offices for me and I will give thee eighty thousand kine! Enmity with Drona burneth my heart; it behoveth thee therefore to cool that heart of mine. Foremost of those conversant with the Vedas, Drona is also skilled in the Brahma weapon and for this, Drona hath overcome me in a contest arising from (impaired) friendship. Gifted with great intelligence, the son of Bharadwaja is (now) the chief preceptor of the Kurus. There is no Kshatriya in this world superior to him. His bow is full six cubits long and looks formidable, and his shafts are capable of slaying every living being. That great bowman, the high-souled son of Bharadwaja, habited as a Brahmana, is destroying the Kshatriya power all over the earth. Indeed, he is like a second Jamadagnya intended for the extermination of the Kshatriya race. There is no man on earth who can overcome the terrible force of his weapons. Like a blazing fire fed with clarified butter, Drona, possessed of Brahma might and uniting it with Kshatriya might, consumeth every antagonist in battle. But (thy) Brahma force is greater in itself than (Drona's) Brahma force united with Kshatriya might. Therefore, as I am inferior (to Drona) in consequence of my possession of Kshatriya might alone, I solicit the aid of thy Brahma force, having obtained thee so superior to Drona in knowledge of Brahma. O Yaja, perform that sacrifice by means of which I may obtain a son invincible in battle and capable of slaying Drona. Ready am I to give thee ten thousand kine.' Hearing these words of Drupada, Yaja said, 'So be it.' Yaja then began to recollect the various ceremonies appertaining to the particular sacrifice. And knowing the affair to be a very grave one, he asked the assistance of Upayaja who coveted nothing. Then Yaja promised to perform the sacrifice for the destruction of Drona. Then the great ascetic Upayaja spoke unto king Drupada of everything required for the grand sacrifice (by aid of fire) from which the king was to obtain offspring. And he said, 'O king, a child shall be born unto thee, endued, as thou desirest, with great prowess, great energy, and great strength.'

"The Brahmana continued, 'Then king Drupada, impelled by the desire of obtaining a son who was to slay Drona, began, for the success of his wish, to make the necessary preparations. (And when everything was complete) Yaja, after having poured libations of clarified butter on the sacrificial fire, commanded Drupada's queen, saying, 'Come hither, O queen, O daughter- in-law of Prishata! A son and a daughter have arrived for thee!' Hearing this, the queen said, 'O Brahmana, my mouth is yet filled with saffron and other perfumed things. My body also beareth many sweet scents; I am hardly fit for accepting (the sanctified butter which is to give me offspring). Wait for me a little, O Yaja! Wait for that happy consummation.' Yaja, however, replied, 'O lady, whether thou comest or waitest, why should not the object of this sacrifice be accomplished when the oblation hath already been prepared by me and sanctified by Upayaja's invocations?'

"The Brahmana continued, 'Having said this, Yaja poured the sanctified libation on the fire, whereupon arose from those flames a child resembling a celestial who possessing the effulgence of fire, was terrible to behold. With a crown on this head and his body encased in excellent armour, sword in hand, and bearing a bow and arrows, he frequently sent forth loud roars. And immediately after his birth, he ascended an excellent chariot and went about in it for some time. Then the Panchalas in great joy shouted, 'Excellent, Excellent.' The very earth seemed at that time unable to bear the weight of the Panchalas mad with joy. Then, marvellous to say, the voice of some invisible spirit in the skies said, 'This prince hath been born for the destruction of Drona. He shall dispel all the fears of the Panchalas and spread their fame. He shall also remove the sorrow of the king.' And there arose, after this from the centre of the sacrificial platform, a daughter also, called Panchali, who, blest with great good fortune, was exceedingly handsome. Her eyes were black, and large as lotus- petals, her complexion was dark, and her locks were blue and curly. Her nails were beautifully convex, and bright as burnished copper; her eye- brows were fair, and bosom was deep. Indeed, she resembled the veritable daughter of a celestial born among men. Her body gave out fragrance like that of a blue lotus, perceivable from a distance of full two miles. Her beauty was such that she had no equal on earth. Like a celestial herself, she could be desired (in marriage) by a celestial, a Danava, or a Yaksha. When this girl of fair hips was born an incorporeal voice said, 'This dark- complexioned girl will be the first of all women, and she will be the cause of the destruction of many Kshatriyas. This slender-waisted one will, in time, accomplish the purpose of the gods, and along with her many a danger will overtake the Kauravas.' On hearing these words, the Panchalas uttered a loud leonine roar, and the earth was unable to bear the weight of that joyous concourse. Then beholding the boy and the girl, the daughter-in-law of Prishata, desiring to have them, approached Yaja and said, 'Let not these know any one else except myself as their mother.' Yaja, desiring to do good unto the king said, 'So be it!' Then the Brahmanas (present there), their expectations fully gratified, bestowed names upon the new-born pair, 'Let this son of king Drupada, they said, be called Dhrishtadyumna, because of his excessive audacity and because of his being born like Dyumna with a natural mail and weapon.' And they also said, 'Because this daughter is so dark in complexion, she should be called Krishna (the dark).'

"The Brahmana continued, 'Thus were born those twins of the great sacrifice of Drupada. And the great Drona, bringing the Panchala prince into his own abode, taught him all weapons in requital of half the kingdom he had formerly taken from Drupada. The high-souled son of Bharadwaja, regarding destiny to be inevitable, did what would perpetuate his own great deeds.'"

SECTION CLXX
(Chaitraratha Parva continued)

"Vaisampayana said, 'Hearing these words of the Brahmana, the sons of Kunti seemed to be, as it were, pierced with darts. Indeed, all those mighty heroes lost their peace of mind. Then the truthful Kunti, beholding all her sons listless and inattentive, addressed Yudhishthira and said, 'We have now lived many nights in the abode of this Brahmana. We have passed our time pleasantly in this town, living on the alms obtained from many honest and illustrious persons. O oppressor of foes, as we have now seen often and often all the agreeable woods and gardens that are in this part of the country, seeing them again would no longer give any pleasure. O heroic scion of Kuru's race, alms also are not now obtainable here as easily as before. If thou wishest it would be well for us now to go to Panchala; we have not seen that country, it will, no doubt, O hero, prove delightful to us. O crusher of foes, it hath been heard by us that alms are obtainable in the country of the Panchala, and that Yajnasena, the king thereof, is devoted to Brahmanas. I am of opinion that it is not good to live long in one place. Therefore, O son, if thou likest, it is good for us to go there.'

"Hearing these words, Yudhishthira said, 'It is our duty to obey thy command, which, besides, must be for our good. I do not, however, know whether my younger brothers are willing to go.'"

SECTION CLXXI
(Chaitraratha Parva continued)

"Vaisampayana continued, 'Then Kunti spoke unto Bhimasena and Arjuna and the twins regarding the journey to Panchala. They all said, 'So be it.' Then, O king, Kunti with her sons saluted the Brahmana (in whose house they had dwelt) and set out for the delightful town of the illustrious Drupada.'

"Vaisampayana said, 'While the illustrious Pandavas were living disguised in the abode of the Brahmana, Vyasa, the son of Satyavati, once went to see them. Those chastisers of foes, beholding him coming rose up and stepped onward to receive him. Saluting him reverentially and worshipping him also the Pandavas stood in silence with joined hands. Thus worshipped by them the sage became gratified. He asked them to be seated, and cheerfully addressing them said, 'Ye slayers of foes, are ye living in the path of virtue and according to the scriptures? Do ye worship the Brahmanas? Ye are not, I hope, backward in paying homage unto those that deserve your homage?' The illustrious Rishi, after this, spoke many words of virtuous import, and after discoursing upon many topics of great interest, he said, 'An illustrious Rishi, living in a certain hermitage, had a daughter of tender waist, fair lips, and fine eye-brows, and possessing every accomplishment. As a consequence of her own acts (in a past life) the fair maid became very unfortunate. Though chaste and beautiful, the damsel obtained not a husband. With a sorrowful heart she thereupon began to practise ascetic penances with the object of obtaining a husband. She soon gratified by her severe the god Sankara (Mahadeva), who became propitious unto her and said unto that illustrious damsel, 'Ask thou the boon thou desirest! Blest be thou! I am Sankara prepared to give thee what thou wilt ask.' Desirous of benefiting herself, the maid repeatedly said unto the supreme lord, 'O give me, a husband endued with every accomplishment.' Then Isana (Mahadeva), that foremost of all speakers, replied unto her, saying, 'O blessed one, thou shall have five husbands from among the Bharata princes.' Thus told, the maiden said unto the god who had given her that boon, 'O lord, I desire to have only one husband through thy grace.' The god then addressed her again and said these excellent words, 'Thou hast, O girl, said full five times, 'Give me (a) husband.' Thou shalt, therefore, in another life have five husbands!' Ye princes of Bharata's line, that damsel of celestial beauty hath been born in the line of Drupada. The faultless Krishna of Prishata's line hath been appointed to be the wife of you all. Ye mighty ones, go therefore, to the capital of the Panchalas and dwell ye there. There is no doubt that having obtained her as wife ye shall be very happy.'

"Vaisampayana continued, 'Having said so unto the Pandavas, the illustrious and blessed grandsire then bade them farewell. The great ascetic then left them and went to the place whence he had come.'"

SECTION CLXXII
(Chaitraratha Parva continued)

"Vaisampayana said, 'After Vyasa had gone away, those bulls among men, the Pandavas, saluted the Brahmana and bade him farewell, and proceeded (towards Panchala) with joyous hearts and with their mother walking before them. Those slayers of all foes, in order to reach their destination, proceeded in a due northerly direction, walking day and night till they reached a sacred shrine of Siva with the crescent mark on his brow. Then those tigers among men, the sons of Pandu, arrived at the banks of the Ganga, Dhananjaya, that mighty car-warrior, walking before them, torch in hand, for showing the way and guarding them (against wild animals). And it so happened that at that time the proud king of the Gandharvas, with his wives, was sporting in that solitary region in the delightful waters of the Ganga. The king of the Gandharvas heard the tread of the Pandavas as they approached the river. On hearing the sounds of their foot-steps, the mighty Gandharvas were inflamed with wrath, and beholding those chastisers of foes, the Pandavas, approach towards him with their mother, he drew his frightful bow to a circle and said, 'It is known that excepting the first forty seconds the grey twilight preceding nightfall hath been appointed for the wandering of the Yakshas, the Gandharvas and the Rakshasas, all of whom are capable of going everywhere at will. The rest of the time hath been appointed for man to do his work. If therefore, men, wandering during those moments from greed of gain, come near us, both we and the Rakshasas slay those fools. Therefore, persons acquainted with the Vedas never applaud those men—not even kings at the head of their troops—who approach any pools of water at such a time. Stay ye at a distance, and approach me not. Know ye not that I am bathing in the waters of the Bhagirathi? Know that I am Angaraparna the Gandharva, ever relying on my own strength! I am proud and haughty and am the friend of Kuvera. This my forest on the banks of the Ganga, where I sport to gratify all my senses, is called Angaraparna after my own name. Here neither gods, nor Kapalikas, nor Gandharvas nor Yakshas, can come. How dare ye approach me who am the brightest jewel on the diadem of Kuvera?'

"Hearing these words of the Gandharva, Arjuna said, 'Blockhead, whether it be day, night, or twilight, who can bar others from the ocean, the sides of the Himalayas, and this river? O ranger of the skies, whether the stomach be empty or full, whether it is night or day, there is no special time for anybody to come to the Ganga—that foremost of all rivers. As regards ourselves endued with might, we care not when we disturb thee. Wicked being, those who are weak in fighting worship thee. This Ganga, issuing out of the golden peaks of Himavat, falleth into the waters of the ocean, being distributed into seven streams. They who drink the waters of these seven streams, viz., Ganga, Yamuna, Saraswati, Vitashta, Sarayu, Gomati, and Gandaki, are cleansed of all their sins. O Gandharva, this sacred Ganga again, flowing through the celestial region is called there the Alakananda. It hath again in the region of the Pitris become the Vaitarani, difficult of being crossed by sinners, and, Krishna-Dwaipayana himself hath said so. The auspicious and celestial river, capable of leading to heaven (them that touch its waters), is free from all dangers. Why dost thou then desire to bar us from it? This act of thine is not in consonance with eternal virtue. Disregarding thy words, why shall we not touch the sacred waters of the Bhagirathi free from all dangers and from which none can bar us?'

"Vaisampayana continued, 'Hearing these words of Arjuna, Angaraparna became inflamed with wrath and drawing his bow to a circle began to shoot his arrows like venomous snakes at the Pandavas. Then Dhananjaya, the son of Pandu, wielding a good shield and the torch he held in his hand, warded off all those arrows and addressing the Gandharva again said, 'O Gandharva, seek not to terrify those that are skilled in weapons, for weapons hurled at them vanish like froth. I think, O Gandharva, that ye are superior (in prowess) to men; therefore shall I fight with thee, using celestial weapons and not with any crooked means. This fiery weapon (that I shall hurl at thee), Vrihaspati the revered preceptor of Indra, gave unto Bharadwaja, from whom it was obtained by Agnivesya, and from Agnivesya by my preceptor, that foremost of Brahmanas, Drona, who gave it away to me.'

"Vaisampayana continued, 'Saying these words, the Pandava wrathfully hurled at the Gandharva that blazing weapon made of fire which burnt the Gandharva's chariot in a trice. Deprived of consciousness by the force of that weapon, the mighty Gandharva was falling, head downward, from his chariot. Dhananjaya seized him by the hair of his head adorned with garlands of flowers and thus dragged the unconscious Gandharva towards his brothers. Beholding this, that Gandharva's wife Kumbhinasi, desirous of saving her husband, ran towards Yudhishthira and sought his protection. The Gandharvi said, 'O exalted one, extend to me thy protection! O, set my husband free! O lord, I am Kumbhinasi by name, the wife of this Gandharva, who seeketh thy protection!' Beholding her (so afflicted), the mighty Yudhishthira addressed Arjuna and said, 'O slayer of foes, O child, who would slay a foe who hath been vanquished in fight, who hath been deprived of fame, who is protected by a woman, and who hath no prowess?' Arjuna replied, saying, 'Keep thou thy life, O Gandharva! Go hence, and grieve not I. Yudhishthira, the king of the Kurus, commandeth me to show thee mercy.'

"The Gandharva replied, 'I have been vanquished by thee. I shall, therefore, abandon my former name Angaraparna (the blazing vehicle). In name alone, O friend, I should not be boastful when my pride in my strength hath been overcome: I have been fortunate in that I have obtained thee; O Arjuna, that wielder of celestial weapons! I like to impart to thee the power of (producing) illusions which Gandharvas alone have. My excellent and variegated chariot hath been burnt by means of thy fiery weapon. I who had formerly been called after my excellent chariot should now be called after my burnt chariot. The science of producing illusions that I have spoken of was formerly obtained by me by ascetic penances. That science I will today impart to the giver of my life—thy illustrious self! What good luck doth he not deserve who, after overcoming a foe by his might, giveth him life when that foe asketh for it? This science is called Chakshushi. It was communicated by Manu unto Soma and by Soma unto Viswavasu, and lastly by Viswavasu unto me. Communicated by my preceptor, that science, having come unto me who am without energy, is gradually becoming fruitless. I have spoken to thee about its origin and transmission. Listen now to its power! One may see (by its aid) whatever one wisheth to see, and in whatever way he liketh (generally or particularly). One can acquire this science only after standing on one leg for six months. I shall however, communicate to thee this science without thyself being obliged to observe any rigid vow. O king, it is for this knowledge that we are superior to men. And as we are capable of seeing everything by spiritual sight, we are equal to the gods. O best of men, I intend to give thee and each of thy brothers a hundred steeds born in the country of the Gandharvas. Of celestial colour and endued with the speed of the mind, those horses are employed in bearing the celestial, and the Gandharvas. They may be lean-fleshed but they tire not, nor doth their speed suffer on that account. In days of yore the thunderbolt was created for the chief of the celestials in order that he might slay (the Asura) Vritra with it. But hurled at Vritra's head it broke in a thousand pieces. The celestials worship with reverence those fragments of the thunderbolt. That which is known in the three worlds as glory is but a portion of the thunderbolt. The hand of the Brahmana with which he poureth libations on the sacrificial fire, the chariot upon which the Kshatriya fighteth, the charity of the Vaisya, and the service of the Sudra rendered unto the three other classes, are all fragments of the thunderbolt. It hath been said that horses, forming as they do a portion of the Kshatriya's chariot, are, on that account, unslayable. Again horses which form a portion of the Kshatriya's chariot, are the offspring of Vadava. Those amongst them that are born in the region of the Gandharvas can go everywhere and assume any hue and speed at the will of their owners. These horses of mine that I give thee will always gratify thy wishes.'

"On hearing these words of the Gandharva, Arjuna said, 'O Gandharva, if from satisfaction for having obtained thy life at my hands in a situation of danger, thou givest me thy science, and these horses, I would not accept thy gift.' The Gandharva replied, saying, 'A meeting with an illustrious person is ever a source of gratification; besides thou hast given me my life. Gratified with thee, I will give thee my science. That the obligation, however, may not all be on one side, I will take from thee, O Vibhatsu, O bull in Bharata's race, thy excellent and eternal weapon of fire!'

"Arjuna said, 'I would accept thy horses in exchange for my weapon. Let our friendship last for ever. O friend, tell us for what we human beings have to stand in fear of the Gandharvas. Chastisers of foes that we are and virtuous and conversant with the Vedas, tell us, O Gandharva, why in travelling in the night-time we have been censured by thee.'

"The Gandharva said, 'Ye are without wives (though ye have completed the period of study). Ye are without a particular Asrama (mode of life). Lastly, ye are out without a Brahmana walking before, therefore, ye sons of Pandu, ye have been censured by me. The Yakshas, Rakshasas, Gandharvas, Pisachas, Uragas and Danavas, are possessed of wisdom and intelligence, and acquainted with the history of the Kuru race. O hero, I have heard too from Narada and other celestial Rishis about the good deeds of your wise ancestors. I myself, too, while roaming over the whole earth bounded by her belt of seas, have witnessed the prowess of thy great race. O Arjuna, I have personal knowledge of thy preceptor, the illustrious son of Bharadwaja, celebrated throughout the three worlds for his knowledge of the Vedas and the science of arms. O tiger in Kuru's race, O son of Pritha, I also know Dharma, Vayu, Sakra, the twin Aswins, and Pandu,—these six perpetuators of Kuru race,—these excellent celestials and human progenitors of you all. I also know that you five brothers are learned and high-souled, that ye are foremost of all wielders of weapons, that ye are brave and virtuous and observant of vows. Knowing that your understanding and hearts are excellent and your behaviour faultless, I have yet censured you. For, O thou of Kuru's race, it behoveth no man endued with might of arms to bear with patience any ill usage in the sight of his wife. Especially as, O son of Kunti, our might increaseth during the hours of darkness, accompanied by my wife I was filled with wrath. O best of vow- observing men, I have, however, been vanquished by thee in battle. Listen to me as I tell thee the reasons that have led to my discomfiture. The Brahmacharya is a very superior mode of life, and as art in that mode now, it is for this, O Partha, that I have been defeated by thee in battle. O chastiser of foes, if any married Kshatriya fight with us at night, he can never escape, with life. But, O Partha, a married Kshatriya, who is sanctified with Brahma, and who hath assigned the cares of his State to a priest, might vanquish all wanderers in the night. O child of Tapati, men should therefore, ever employ learned priests possessing self-command for the acquisition of every good luck they desire. That Brahmana is worthy of being the king's priest who is learned in the Vedas and the six branches thereof, who is pure and truthful, who is of virtuous soul and possessed of self-command. The monarch becometh ever victorious and finally earneth heaven who hath for his priest a Brahmana conversant with the rules of morality, who is a master of words, and is pure and of good behaviour. The king should always select an accomplished priest in order to acquire what he hath not and protect what he hath. He who desireth his own prosperity should ever be guided by his priest, for he may then obtain ever the whole earth surrounded by her belt of seas. O son of Tapati, a king, who is without a Brahmana, can never acquire any land by his bravery or glory of birth alone. Know, therefore, O perpetuator of Kuru's race, that the kingdom lasteth for ever in which Brahmanas have power.'"

SECTION CLXXIII
(Chaitraratha Parva continued)

"Arjuna said, 'Thou hast addressed me (more than once) as Tapatya. I therefore wish to know what the precise significance of this word is, O virtuous Gandharva, being sons of Kunti, we are, indeed, Kaunteyas. But who is Tapati that we should be called Tapatyas?'

"Vaisampayana continued, 'Thus addressed, the Gandharva related to Dhananjaya, the son of Kunti, the (following) story well-known in the three worlds.'

"The Gandharva said, 'O son of Pritha, O foremost of all intelligent men, I will duly recite to you in full this charming narrative. O, listen with attention to what I say in explanation of why I have addressed thee as Tapatya. That one in heaven who pervadeth by his light the whole firmament had a daughter named Tapati equal unto himself. Tapati, the daughter of the god Vivaswat, was the younger sister of Savitri, and she was celebrated throughout the three worlds and devoted to ascetic penances. There was no woman amongst the celestials, the Asuras, the Yakshas, the Rakshasas, the Apsaras, and the Gandharvas, who was equal to her in beauty. Of perfect, and faultless features, of black and large eyes, and in beautiful attire, the girl was chaste and of perfect conduct. And, O Bharata, seeing her Savitri (the sun) thought that there was none in the three worlds who, for his beauty, accomplishments, behaviour, and learning, deserved to be her husband. Beholding her attain the age of puberty and, therefore, worthy of being bestowed on a husband, her father knew no peace of mind, always thinking of the person he should select. At that time, O son of Kunti, Riksha's son, that bull amongst the Kurus, the mighty king Samvarana, was duly worshipping Surya with offerings of Arghya and flower- garlands and scents, and with vows and fasts and ascetic penances of various kinds. Indeed, Samvarana was worshipping Surya constantly in all his glory, with devotion and humility and piety. And beholding Samvarana conversant with all rules of virtue and unequalled on earth for beauty, Surya regarded him as the fit husband for his daughter, Tapati. And, O thou of Kuru's race, Vivaswat then resolved to bestow his daughter on that best of kings, viz., Samvarana, the scion of a race of world-wide fame. As Surya himself in the heavens filleth the firmament with his splendour, so did king Samvarana on earth fill every region with the splendour of his good achievements. And all men, O Partha, except Brahmanas, worshipped Samvarana. Blest with good luck, king Samvarana excelled Soma in soothing the hearts of friends and Surya in scorching the hearts of foes. And, O Kaurava, Tapana (Surya) himself was resolved upon bestowing his daughter Tapati upon king Samvarana, who was possessed of such virtues and accomplishments.

"Once on a time, O Partha, king Samvarana, endued with beauty (of person) and immeasurable prowess, went on a hunting expedition to the under-woods on the mountain-breast. While wandering in quest of deer, the excellent steed the king rode, overcome, O Partha, with hunger, thirst and fatigue, died on the mountains. Abandoning the steed, the king, O Arjuna, began to wander about upon the mountain-breast on foot and in course of his wandering the monarch saw a maiden of large eyes and unrivalled beauty, That grinder of hostile host—that tiger among kings—himself without a companion, beholding there that maiden without a companion, stood motionless gazing at her steadfastly. For her beauty, the monarch for some moment believed her to be (the goddess) Sri herself. Next he regarded her to be the embodiment of the rays emanating from Surya. In splendour of her person she resembled a flame of fire, though in benignity and loveliness she resembled a spotless digit of the moon. And standing on the mountain- breast, the black-eyed maiden appeared like a bright statue of gold. The mountain itself with its creepers and plants, because of the beauty and attire of that damsel, seemed to be converted into gold. The sight of that maiden inspired the monarch with a contempt for all women that he had seen before. By beholding her, the king regarded his eye-sight truly blessed. Nothing the king had seen from the day of his birth could equal, he thought, the beauty of that girl. The king's heart and eyes were captivated by that damsel, as if they were bound with a cord and he remained rooted to that spot, deprived of his senses. The monarch thought that the artificer of so much beauty had created it only after churning the whole world of gods Asuras and human beings. Entertaining these various thoughts, king Samvarana regarded that maiden as unrivalled in the three worlds for wealth of beauty.

"And the monarch of pure descent, beholding the beautiful maiden, was pierced with Kama's (Cupid's) shafts and lost his peace of mind. Burnt with the strong flame of desire the king asked that charming maiden, still innocent, though in her full youth, saying, 'Who art thou and whose? Why also dost thou stay here? O thou of sweet smiles, why dost thou wander alone in these solitary woods? Of every feature perfectly faultless, and decked with every ornament, thou seemest to be the coveted ornament of these ornaments themselves! Thou seemest not to be of celestial or Asura or Yaksha or Rakshasa or Naga or Gandharva or human origin. O excellent lady, the best of women that I have ever seen or heard of would not compare with thee in beauty! O thou of handsome face, at sight of thee lovelier than the moon and graced with eyes like lotus-petals, the god of desire is grinding me.'

"King Samvarana thus addressed that damsel in the forest, who however, spoke not a word unto the monarch burning with desire. Instead, like lightning in the clouds, that large-eyed maiden quickly disappeared in the very sight of the monarch. The king then wandered through the whole forest, like one out of his senses, in search of that girl of eyes like lotus-petals. Failing to find her, that best of monarchs indulged in copious lamentations and for a time stood motionless with grief.'"

SECTION CLXXIV
(Chaitraratha Parva continued)

"The Gandharva continued, 'When that maiden disappeared, that feller of hostile ranks deprived of his senses by Kama (concupiscence) himself fell down on the earth. And as the monarch fell down, that maiden of sweet smiles and prominent and round hips appeared again before him, and smiling sweetly, said unto that perpetuator of Kuru's race these honeyed words, 'Rise, rise, O chastiser of foes! Blest be thou; it behoveth thee not, O tiger among kings, to lose thy reason, a celebrated man as thou art in the world.' Addressed in these honeyed words, the king opened his eyes and saw before him that selfsame girl of swelling hips. The monarch who was burning with the flame of desire then addressed that black-eyed damsel in accents, weak with emotion, and said, 'Blest be thou O excellent woman of black eyes! As I am burning with desire and paying thee court, O, accept me! My life is ebbing away. O thou of large eyes, for thy sake it is, O thou of the splendour of the filaments of the lotus, that Kama is incessantly piercing me with his keen shafts without stopping for a moment! O amiable and cheerful girl, I have been bitten by Kama who is even like a venomous viper. O thou of swelling and large hips, have mercy on me! O thou of handsome and faultless features, O thou of face like unto the lotus-petal or the moon, O thou of voice sweet as that of singing Kinnaras, my life now depends on thee! Without thee, O timid one, I am unable to live! O thou of eyes like lotus-petals, Kama is piercing me incessantly! O large-eyed girl, be merciful unto me! It becometh thee not, O black-eyed maid, to cast me off; O handsome girl, it behoveth thee to relieve me from such affliction by giving me thy love! At first sight thou hast attracted my heart. My mind wandereth! Beholding thee I like not to cast my eyes on any other woman! Be merciful! I am thy obedient slave—thy adorer! O, accept me! O beautiful lady, O large-eyed girl at the sight of thee, the god of desire hath entered my heart, and is piercing me with his shafts! O thou of lotus-eyes, the flame of desire burneth within me! O, extinguish that flame with the water of thy love poured on it! O beautiful lady, by becoming mine, pacify thou the irrepressible god of desire that hath appeared here armed with his deadly bow and arrows and that is piercing me incessantly with those keen shafts of his! O thou of the fairest complexion, wed me according to the Gandharva form, for, O thou of tapering hips, of all forms of marriage the Gandharva hath been said to be the best.'

"The Gandharva continued, 'Hearing those words of the monarch, Tapati made answer, 'O king, I am not the mistress of my own self! Be it known that I am a maiden under the control of my father. If thou really entertainest an affection for me, demand me of my father. Thou sayest, O king, that thy heart hath been robbed by me. But thou also hast, at first sight, robbed me of my heart; I am not the mistress of my body, and therefore, O best of kings, I do not approach thee; women are never independent. What girl is there in the three worlds that would not desire thee for her husband, as thou art kind unto all thy dependents and as thou art born in a pure race? Therefore, when the opportunity comes, ask my father Aditya for my hand with worship, ascetic penances, and vows. If my father bestoweth me upon thee, then, O king, I shall ever be thy obedient wife. My name is Tapati and I am the younger sister of Savitri, and the daughter, O bull amongst Kshatriyas of Savitri, of (Sun) the illuminator of the universe.'"

SECTION CLXXV
(Chaitraratha Parva continued)

"The Gandharva continued, 'Saying this, Tapati of faultless features, ascended the skies. The monarch thereupon again fell down on the earth. His ministers and followers searching for him throughout the forest at length came upon him lying on that solitary spot, and beholding that excellent king, that mighty bowman, thus lying forsaken on the ground like a rainbow dropped from the firmament, his minister-in-chief became like one burnt by a flame of fire. Advancing hastily with affection and respect, the minister raised that best of monarchs lying prostrate on the ground and deprived of his senses by desire. Old in wisdom as in age, old in achievements as in policy, the minister, after having raised the prostrate monarch, became easy (in mind). Addressing the king in sweet words that were also for his good, he said, 'Blest be thou, O sinless one! Fear not, O tiger among kings!' The minister thought that the monarch, that great feller of hostile ranks in battle, had been lying on the ground overcome with hunger, thirst, and fatigue. The old man then sprinkled over the crownless head of the monarch water that was cold and rendered fragrant with lotus-petals. Slowly regaining his consciousness, the mighty monarch sent away all his attendants with the exception of his minister only. After those attendants had retired at his command, the king sat upon the mountain-breast. Having purified himself duly, the king sat upon that chief of mountains, and began, with joined palms and upturned face, to worship Surya. King Samvarana, that smiter of all foes, thought also of his chief priest Vasishtha, that best of Rishis. The king continued to sit there day and night without intermission. The Brahmana sage Vasishtha came there on the twelfth day: that great Rishi of soul under perfect command knew at once by his ascetic power that the monarch had lost his senses in consequence of Tapati. And that virtuous and best of Munis, as soon as he knew this, desirous of benefiting the monarch who was ever observant of vows, addressed him and gave him every assurance. The illustrious Rishi, in the very sight of that monarch, ascended upward to interview Surya, himself possessed of the splendour of that luminary. The Brahmana then approached with joined hands the god of a thousand rays and introduced himself cheerfully unto him, saying, 'I am Vasishtha.' Then Vivaswat of great energy said unto that best of Rishis, 'Welcome art thou, O great Rishi! Tell me what is in thy mind. O thou of great good fortune, whatever thou demandest of me, O foremost of eloquent men, I will confer on thee, however difficult it may be for me!' Thus addressed by Surya, the Rishi of great ascetic merit, bowing unto the god of light, replied, saying, 'O Vibhavasu, this thy daughter, Tapati, the younger sister of Savitri, I ask of thee for Samvarana! That monarch is of mighty achievements, conversant with virtue, and of high soul. O firmament-ranger, Samvarana will make a worthy husband for thy daughter.' Thus addressed by the Rishi Vibhakara, resolved upon bestowing his daughter upon Samvarana, saluted the Rishi, and replied unto him, saying, 'Oh, Samvarana is the best of monarchs, thou art the best of Rishis, Tapati is the best of women. What should we do, therefore, but bestow her on Samvarana?' With these words, the god Tapana, made over his daughter, Tapati, of every feature perfectly faultless, unto the illustrious Vasishtha to bestow her upon Samvarana. And the great Rishi then accepted the girl, Tapati, and taking leave of Surya, came back to the spot, where that bull amongst the Kurus, of celestial achievements, was. King Samvarana, possessed by love and with his heart fixed on Tapati, beholding that celestial maiden of sweet smiles led by Vasishtha, became exceedingly glad. And Tapati of fair eyebrows came down from the firmament like lightning from the clouds, dazzling the ten points of the heavens. And the illustrious Rishi Vasishtha of pure soul approached the monarch after the latter's twelve nights' vow was over. It was thus that king Samvarana obtained a wife after having worshipped with like the full moon. And that mighty bowman, that foremost one in Kuru's race having his curiosity greatly excited by what he heard of Vasishtha's ascetic power, asked the Gandharva, saying, 'I desire to hear of the Rishi whom

THE MAHABHARATA

thou hast mentioned as Vasishtha. O, tell me in full about him! O chief of the Gandharvas, tell me who this illustrious Rishi was that was the priest of our forefathers.' The Gandharva replied, 'Vasishtha is Brahma's spiritual (lit, mind-born) son and Arundhati's husband. Ever difficult of being conquered by the very immortals, Desire and Wrath, conquered by Vasishtha's ascetic penances, used to shampoo his feet. Though his wrath was excited by Viswamitra's offence, that high-souled Rishi did not yet exterminate Kusikas (the tribe whose king Viswamitra was). Afflicted at the loss of his sons, he did not, as though powerless, though really otherwise, do any dreadful act destructive of Viswamitra, Like the ocean transgressing not its continents, Vasishtha transgressed not (the laws of) Yama by bringing back his children from the domains of the king of the dead. It was by obtaining that illustrious one who had conquered his own self that Ikshvaku and other great monarchs acquired the whole earth. And, O prince of Kuru's race, it was by obtaining Vasishtha, that best of Rishis as their priest, that those monarchs performed many grand sacrifices. And, O best of the Pandavas, that regenerate Rishi assisted these monarchs in the performance of their sacrifices like Vrihaspati assisting the immortals. Therefore, look ye for some accomplished and desirable Brahmana conversant with the Vedas and in whose heart virtue prevails, to appoint as your priest. A Kshatriya of good lineage, desirous of extending his dominions by conquering the earth, should, O Partha, first appoint a priest. He who is desirous of conquering the earth should have a Brahmana before him. Therefore, O Arjuna, let some accomplished and learned Brahmana, who has his senses under complete control and who is conversant with religion, profit and pleasure, be your priest.'"

SECTION CLXXVII
(Chaitraratha Parva continued)

"Vaisampayana continued, 'Hearing this, Arjuna said, 'O Gandharva, whence arose the hostility between Viswamitra and Vasishtha both of whom dwelt in a celestial hermitage? O, tell us all about it.'

"The Gandharva replied, 'O Partha, the story of Vasishtha is regarded as a Purana (legend) in all the three worlds. Listen to me as I recite it fully. There was, in Kanyakuvja, O bull of Bharata's race, a great king of worldwide fame named Gadhi, the son of Kusika. The virtuous Gadhi had a son named Viswamitra, that grinder of foes, possessing a large army and many animals and vehicles. And Viswamitra, accompanied by his ministers, used to roam in quest of deer through the deep woods and over picturesque marascetic penances the propitious lord Vivaswat, by the help of Vasishtha's (ascetic power). And Samvarana, that bull among men with due rites took Tapati's hand on that mountain-breast which was resorted to by the celestials and the Gandharvas. The royal sage, with the permission of Vasishtha, desired to sport with his wife on that mountain. And the king caused Vasishtha to be proclaimed his regent in his capital and kingdom, in the woods and gardens. And bidding farewell unto the monarch, Vasishtha left him and went away. Samvarana, who sported on that mountain like a celestial, sported with his wife in the woods and the under-woods on that mountain for twelve full years. And, O best of the Bharatas, the god of a thousand eyes poured no rain for twelve years on the capital and on the kingdom of that monarch. Then, O chastiser of enemies, when that season of drought broke out, the people of that kingdom, as also the trees and lower animals began to die fast. And during the continuance of that dreadful drought, not even a drop of dew fell from the skies and no corn grew. And the inhabitants in despair, and afflicted with the fear of hunger, left their homes and fled away in all directions. And the famished people of the capital and the country began to abandon their wives and children and grew reckless of one another. The people being afflicted with hunger, without a morsel of food and reduced to skeletons, the capital looked very much like the city of the king of the dead, full of only ghostly beings. On beholding the capital reduced to such a state, the illustrious and virtuous and best of Rishis, Vasishtha was resolved upon applying a remedy and brought back unto the city that tiger among kings, Samvarana, along with his wife, after the latter had passed so long a period in solitude and seclusion. After the king had entered his capital, things became as before, for, when that tiger among kings came back to his own, the god of a thousand eyes, the slayer of Asuras, poured rain in abundance and caused corn to grow. Revivified by the foremost of virtuous souls the capital and the country became animated with extreme joy. The monarch, with his wife, Tapati, once more performed sacrifices for twelve years, like the lord Indra (god of rain) performing sacrifices with his wife, Sachi.'

"The Gandharva continued, 'This, O Partha, is the history of Tapati of old, the daughter of Vivaswat. It is for her that thou art (called) Tapatya. King Samvarana begot upon Tapati a son named Kuru, who was the foremost of ascetics. Born in the race of Kuru, thou art, O Arjuna, to be called Tapatya.'"

SECTION CLXXVI
(Chaitraratha Parva continued)

"The Gandharva continued, 'Once on a time, while king Viswamitra went quest of deer, the king became weak with exertion and thirst. The monarch arrived in that state at the asylum of Vasishtha, and the blessed and illustrious Rishi beholding him arrive, reverenced with his homage that best of men, king Viswamitra. And O Bharata, the Rishi saluted the monarch by offering him water to wash his face and feet with, and Arghya, and wild fruits, and clarified butter. For the illustrious Rishi had a cow yielding anything that was desired of her. When she was addressed, saying, 'O give', she always yielded the article that was sought. And she yielded various fruits and corn, wild or grown in gardens and fields, and milk, and many excellent nutritive viands full of six different kinds of juice (taste?) and like unto nectar itself, and various other kinds of enjoyable things, O Arjuna, of ambrosial taste for drinking and eating, and for licking and sucking, and also many precious gems and robes of various kinds. With these desirable objects in profusion the monarch was worshipped. And the king with his minister and troops became highly pleased. And the monarch wondered much, beholding that cow with six elevated limbs and the beautiful flanks and hips, and five limbs that were broad, and eyes prominent like those of the frog and beautiful in size, and high udders, and faultless make, and straight and uplifted ears, and handsome horns, and well-developed head and neck.

"And, O prince, the son of Gadhi, gratified with everything and applauding the cow named Nandini, addressed the Rishi, saying, 'O Brahmana, O great Muni, give me thy Naridini in exchange for ten thousand kine, or my kingdom. Enjoy thou my kingdom (giving me thy cow).'

"Hearing these words of Viswamitra, Vasishtha said, 'O sinless one, this cow hath been kept by me for the sake of the gods, guests, and the Pitris, as also for my sacrifices. I cannot give Nandini in exchange for even thy kingdom.' Viswamitra replied, 'I am a Kshatriya, but thou art a Brahmana devoted to asceticism and study. Is there any energy in Brahmanas who are peaceful and who have their souls under perfect command? When thou givest me not what I desire in exchange even for ten thousand cows, I will not abandon the practice of my order; I will take thy cow even by force!'

"Vasishtha said, 'Thou art a Kshatriya endued with might of arms. Thou art a powerful monarch. O, do in haste what thou desirest; and stop not to consider its propriety.'

"The Gandharva continued, 'Thus addressed by Vasishtha, Viswamitra, O Partha, then forcibly seized Nandini, that cow (white) like the swan or the moon, and attempted to take her away, afflicting her with stripes and persecuting her otherwise. The innocent Nandini then began, O Partha, to low piteously, and approaching the illustrious Vasishtha stood before him with uplifted face. Though persecuted very cruelly, she refused to leave the Rishi's asylum.

"Beholding her in that plight, Vasishtha said, 'O amiable one, thou art lowing repeatedly and I am hearing thy cries. But, O Nandini, even Viswamitra is taking thee away by force, what can I do in this matter, as I am a forgiving Brahmana?'

"The Gandharva continued, 'Then, O bull in Bharata's race, Nandini, alarmed at the sight of Viswamitra's troops and terrified by Viswamitra himself, approached the Rishi still closer, and said, 'O illustrious one, why art thou so indifferent to my poor self afflicted with the stripes of the cruel troops of Viswamitra and crying so piteously as if I were masterless?' Hearing these words of the crying and persecuted Nandini, the great Rishi lost not his patience nor turned from his vow of forgiveness. He replied, 'The Kshatriya's might lies in physical strength, the Brahmana's in forgiveness. Because I cannot give up forgiveness, go thou, O Nandini, if thou choosest.' Nandini answered, 'Castest thou me away, O illustrious one, that thou sayest so? If thou dost not cast me off, I cannot, O Brahmana, be taken away by force.' Vasishtha said, 'O blessed one, I do not cast thee off! Stay if thou canst! O, yonder is thy calf, tied with a stout cord, and even now being weakened by it!'

"The Gandharva continued, 'Then the cow of Vasishtha, hearing the word stay, raised her head and neck upward, and became terrible to behold. With eyes red with rage and lowing repeatedly, she then attacked

Viswamitra's troops on all sides. Afflicted with their stripes and running hither and thither with those red eyes of hers, her wrath increased. Blazing with rage, she soon became terrible to behold like unto the sun in his midday glory. And from her tail she began to rain showers of burning coals all around. And some moments after, from her tail she brought forth an army of Palhavas, and from her udders, an army of Dravidas and Sakas; and from her womb, an army of Yavanas, and from her dung, an army of Savaras; and from her urine, an army of Kanchis; and from her sides, an army of Savaras. And from the froth of her mouth came out hosts of Paundras and Kiratas, Yavanas and Sinhalas, and the barbarous tribes of Khasas and Chivukas and Pulindas and Chinas and Hunas with Keralas, and numerous other Mlechchhas. And that vast army of Mlechchhas in various uniforms, and armed with various weapons, as soon as it sprang into life, deploying in the very sight of Viswamitra, attacked that monarch's soldiers. And so numerous was that Mlechchha host that each particular soldier of Viswamitra was attacked by a band of six or seven of their enemies. Assailed with a mighty shower of weapons, Viswamitra's troops broke and fled, panic-stricken, in all directions, before his very eyes. But, O bull in Bharata's race, the troops of Vasishtha, though excited with wrath, took not the life of any of Viswamitra's troops. Nandini simply caused the monarch's army to be routed and driven off. And driven (from the asylum) twenty-seven full miles, panic-stricken, they shrieked aloud and beheld not anyone that could protect them. Viswamitra, beholding this wonderful feat that resulted from Brahmana prowess, became disgusted with Kshatriya prowess and said, 'O, fie on Kshatriya prowess! Brahmana prowess is true prowess! In judging of strength and weakness, I see that asceticism is true strength.' Saying this, the monarch, abandoning his large domains and regal splendour and turning his back upon all pleasures, set his mind on asceticism. Crowned with success in asceticism and filling the three worlds with the heat of his ascetic penances, he afflicted all creatures and finally became a Brahmana. The son of Kusika at last drank Soma with Indra himself (in Heaven).'"

SECTION CLXXVIII
(Chaitraratha Parva continued)

"The Gandharva continued, 'There was, O Partha, a king in this world, named Kalmashapada, who was of the race of Ikshvaku and was unequalled on earth for prowess. One day the king went from his capital into the woods for purposes of hunting, and this grinder of foes pierced (with his arrows) many deer and wild boars. And in those deep woods the king also slew many rhinoceroses. Engaged in sport for some length of time, the monarch became very much fatigued and at last he gave up the chase, desiring to rest awhile.

"The great Viswamitra, endued with energy, had, a little while ago, desired to make that monarch his disciple. As the monarch, afflicted with hunger and thirst, was proceeding through the woods, he came across that best of Rishis, the illustrious son of Vasishtha, coming along the same path. The king ever victorious in battle saw that Muni bearing the name of Saktri, that illustrious propagator of Vasishtha's race, the eldest of the high-souled Vasishtha's hundred sons, coming along from opposite direction. The king, beholding him said, 'Stand out of our way.' The Rishi, addressing the monarch in a conciliatory manner, said unto him sweetly, 'O king, this is my way. This is the eternal rule of morality indicated in every treatise on duty and religion, viz., that a king should ever make way for Brahmanas.' Thus did they address each other respecting their right of way. 'Stand aside, stand aside', were the words they said unto each other. The Rishi, who was in the right, did not yield, nor did the king yield to him from pride and anger. That best of monarchs, enraged at the Rishi, refusing to yield him the way, acted like a Rakshasa, striking him with his whip. Thus whipped by the monarch, that best of Rishis, the son of Vasishtha, was deprived of his senses by anger, and speedily cursed that first of monarchs, saying, 'O worst of kings, since thou persecutest like a Rakshasa an ascetic, thou shalt from this day, became a Rakshasa subsisting on human flesh! Hence, thou worst of kings! thou shalt wander over the earth, affecting human form!' Thus did the Rishi Sakti, endued with great prowess, speak unto king Kalmashapada. At this time Viswamitra, between whom and Vasishtha there was a dispute about the discipleship of Kalmashapada, approached the place where that monarch and Vasishtha's son were. And, O Partha, that Rishi of severe ascetic penances, viz., Viswamitra of great energy, approached the pair (knowing by his spiritual insight that they had been thus quarrelling with each other). After the curse had been pronounced, that best of monarchs knew that Rishi to be Vasishtha's son and equal unto Vasishtha himself in energy. And, O Bharata, Viswamitra, desirous of benefiting himself, remained on that spot, concealed from the sight of both by making himself invisible. Then that best of monarchs, thus cursed by Saktri, desiring to propitiate the Rishi began to humbly beseech him. And, O chief of the Kurus, Viswamitra, ascertaining the disposition of the king (and fearing that the difference might be made up), ordered a Rakshasa to enter the body of the king. And a Rakshasa of the name of Kinkara then entered the monarch's body in obedience to Saktri's curse and Viswamitra's command. And knowing, O chastiser of foes, that the Rakshasa had possessed himself of the monarch, that best of Rishis, Viswamitra, then left the spot and went away.

"Shortly after, O Partha, the monarch, possessed by the Rakshasa and terribly afflicted by him, lost all his senses. At this time a Brahmana beheld the king in the woods. Afflicted with hunger, that Brahmana begged of the king some food with meat. The royal sage, Kalmashapada, that cherisher of friends, answered the Brahmana, saying, 'Stay thou here, O Brahmana for a moment. On my return, I will give thee whatever food thou desirest.' Having said this, the monarch went away, but the Brahmana stayed on there. The high-minded king having roved for some time at pleasure and according to his will, at last entered his inner apartment. Thus waking at midnight and remembering his promise, he summoned his cook and told him of his promise unto the Brahmana staying in the forest. And he commanded him, saying, 'Hie thee to that forest. A Brahmana waiteth for me in the hope of food. Go and entertain him with food and meat.'

"The Gandharva continued, 'Thus commanded, the cook went out in search of meat. Distressed at not having found any, he informed the king of his failure. The monarch, however, possessed as he was by the Rakshasa, repeatedly said, without scruple of any kind, 'Feed him with human flesh.' The cook, saying, 'So be it,' went to the place where the (king's) executioners were, and thence taking human flesh and washing and cooking it duly and covering it with boiled rice offered it unto that hungry Brahmana devoted to ascetic penances. But that best of Brahmanas, seeing with his spiritual sight that the food was unholy and, therefore, unworthy of being eaten, said these words with eyes red with anger, 'Because that worst of kings offereth me food that is unholy and unworthy of being taken, therefore that wretch shall have himself a fondness for such food. And becoming fond of human flesh as cursed by Saktri of old, the wretch shall wander over the earth, alarming and otherwise troubling all creatures.' The curse, therefore, on that king, thus repeated a second time, became very strong, and the king, possessed by a Rakshasa disposition, soon lost all his senses.

"A little while after, O Bharata, that best of monarchs, deprived of all his senses by the Rakshasa within him, beholding Saktri who had cursed him, said, 'Because thou hast pronounced on me this extraordinary curse, therefore, I shall begin my life of cannibalism by devouring thee.' Having said this, the king immediately slew Saktri and ate him up, like a tiger eating the animal it was fond of. Beholding Saktri thus slain and devoured, Viswamitra repeatedly urged that Rakshasa (who was within the monarch) against the other sons of Vasishtha. Like a wrathful lion devouring small animals, that Rakshasa soon devoured the other sons of the illustrious Vasishtha that were junior to Saktri in age. But Vasishtha, learning that all his sons had been caused to be slain by Viswamitra, patiently bore his grief like the great mountain that bears the earth. That best of Munis, that foremost of intelligent men, was resolved rather to sacrifice his own life than exterminate (in anger) the race of Kusikas. The illustrious Rishi threw himself down from the summit of Meru, but he descended on the stony ground as though on a heap of cotton. And, O son of Pandu, when the illustrious one found that death did not result from that fall, he kindled a huge fire in the forest and entered it with alacrity. But that fire, though burning brightly, consumed him not. O slayer of foes, that blazing fire seemed to him cool. Then the great Muni under the influence of grief, beholding the sea, tied a stony weight to his neck and threw himself into its waters. But the waves soon cast him ashore. At last when that Brahmana of rigid vows succeeded not in killing himself by any means, he returned, in distress of heart, to his asylum.'"

SECTION CLXXIX
(Chaitraratha Parva continued)

"The Gandharva continued, 'Beholding his asylum bereft of his children, the Muni afflicted with great grief left it again. And in course of his wandering he saw, O Partha, a river swollen with the waters of the rainy season, sweeping away numberless trees and plants that had grown on its margin. Beholding this, O thou of Kuru's race, the distressed Muni thinking that he would certainly be drowned if he fell into the waters of that river, he tied himself strongly with several cords and flung himself, under the influence of grief, into the current of that mighty stream. But, O slayer of foes, that stream soon cut those cords and cast the Rishi ashore. And the Rishi rose from the bank, freed from the cords with which he had tied himself. And because his cords were thus broken off by the violence of the current, the Rishi called the stream by the name of Vipasa (the cord-breaker). For his grief the Muni could not, from that time, stay in one place; he began to wander over mountains and along rivers and lakes. And beholding once again a river named Haimavati (flowing from Himavat) of terrible aspect and full of fierce crocodiles and other (aquatic) monsters, the Rishi threw himself into it, but the river mistaking the Brahmana for a mass of (unquenchable) fire, immediately flew in a hundred different directions, and hath been known ever since by the name of the Satadru (the river of a hundred courses). Seeing himself on the dry land even there he exclaimed, 'O, I cannot die by my own hands!' Saying this, the Rishi once more bent his steps towards his asylum. Crossing numberless mountains and countries, as he was about to re-enter his asylum, he was followed by his daughter-in-law named Adrisyanti. As she neared him, he heard the sound from behind of a very intelligent recitation of the Vedas with the six graces of elocution. Hearing that sound, the Rishi asked, 'Who is it that followeth me?' His daughter-in-law then answered, 'I am Adrisyanti, the wife of Saktri. I am helpless, though devoted to asceticism.' Hearing her, Vasishtha said, 'O daughter, whose is this voice that I heard, repeating the Vedas along with the Angas like unto the voice of Saktri reciting the Vedas with the Angas?' Adrisyanti answered, 'I bear in my womb a child by thy son Saktri. He hath been here full twelve years. The voice thou hearest is that of the Muni, who is reciting the Vedas.'

"The Gandharva continued, 'Thus addressed by her the illustrious Vasishtha became exceedingly glad. And saying, 'O, there is a child (of my race)!'— he refrained, O Partha, from self-destruction. The sinless one accompanied by his daughter-in-law, then returned to his asylum. And the Rishi saw one day in the solitary woods (the Rakshasa) Kalmashapada. The king, O Bharata, possessed by fierce Rakshasa, as he saw the Rishi, became filled with wrath and rose up, desiring to devour him. And Adrisyanti beholding before her that the Rakshasa of cruel deeds, addressed Vasishtha in these words, full of anxiety and fear, 'O illustrious one, the cruel Rakshasa, like unto Death himself armed with (his) fierce club, cometh towards us with a wooden club in hand! There is none else on earth, except thee, O illustrious one, and, O foremost of all that are conversant with the Vedas to restrain him today. Protect me, O illustrious one, from this cruel wretch of terrible mien. Surely, the Rakshasa cometh hither to devour us!' Vasishtha, hearing this, said, 'Fear not, O daughter, there is no need of any fear from any Rakshasa. This one is no Rakshasa from whom thou apprehendest such imminent danger. This is king Kalmashapada endued with great energy and celebrated on earth. That terrible man dwelleth in these woods.'

"The Gandharva continued, 'Beholding him advancing, the illustrious Rishi Vasishtha, endued with great energy, restrained him, O Bharata, by uttering the sound Hum. Sprinkling him again with water sanctified with incantations the Rishi freed the monarch from that terrible curse. For twelve years the monarch had been overwhelmed by the energy of Vasishtha's son like Surya seized by the planet (Rahu) during the season of an eclipse. Freed from the Rakshasa the monarch illumined that large forest by his splendour like the sun illumining the evening clouds. Recovering his power of reason, the king saluted that best of Rishis with joined palms and said, 'O illustrious one, I am the son of Sudasa and thy disciple, O best of Munis! O, tell me what is thy pleasure and what I am to do.' Vasishtha replied, saying, 'My desire hath already been accomplished. Return now to thy kingdom and rule thy subjects. And, O chief of men, never insult Brahmanas any more.' The monarch replied, 'O illustrious one, I shall never more insult superior Brahmanas. In obedience to thy command I shall always worship Brahmanas. But, O best of Brahmanas, I desire to obtain from thee that by which, O foremost of all that are conversant with the Vedas, I may be freed from the debt I owe to the race of Ikshvaku! O best of men, it behoveth thee to grant me, for the perpetuation of Ikshvaku's race, a desirable son possessing beauty and accomplishments and good behaviour.'

"The Gandharva continued, 'Thus addressed, Vasishtha, that best of Brahmanas devoted to truth replied unto that mighty bowman of a monarch, saying, 'I will give you.' After some time, O prince of men, Vasishtha, accompanied by the monarch, went to the latter's capital known all over the earth by the name of Ayodhya. The citizens in great joy came out to receive the sinless and illustrious one, like the dwellers in heaven coming out to receive their chief. The monarch, accompanied by Vasishtha, re-entered his auspicious capital after a long time. The citizens of Ayodhya beheld their king accompanied by his priest, as if he were the rising sun. The monarch who was superior to everyone in beauty filled by his splendour the whole town of Ayodhya, like the autumnal moon filling by his splendour the whole firmament. And the excellent city itself, in consequence of its streets having been watered and swept, and of the rows of banners and pendants beautifying it all around, gladdened the monarch's heart. And, O prince of Kuru's race, the city filled as it was with joyous and healthy souls, in consequence of his presence, looked gay like Amaravati with the presence of the chief of the celestials. After the royal sage had entered his capital, the queen, at the king's command, approached Vasishtha. The great Rishi, making a covenant with her, united himself with her according to the high ordinance. And after a little while, when the queen conceived, that best of Rishis, receiving the reverential salutations of the king, went back to his asylum. The queen bore the embryo in her womb for a long time. When she saw that she did not bring forth anything, she tore open her womb by a piece of stone. It was then that at the twelfth year (of the conception) was born Asmaka, that bull amongst men, that royal sage who founded (the city of) Paudanya.'"

SECTION CLXXX
(Chaitraratha Parva continued)

"The Gandharva continued, 'Then, O Partha, Adrisyanti, who had been residing in Vasishtha's asylum, brought forth (when the time came) a son who was the perpetuator of Saktri's race and who was a second Saktri in everything. O foremost of Bharatas, that best of Munis, the illustrious Vasishtha himself performed the usual after-birth ceremonies of his grandson. And, because the Rishi Vasishtha had resolved on self-destruction but had abstained therefrom as soon as he knew of the existence of that child, that child, when born, was called Parasara (the vivifier of the dead). The virtuous Parasara, from the day of his birth, knew Vasishtha for his father and behaved towards the Muni as such. One day, O son of Kunti, the child addressed Vasishtha, that first of Brahmana sages, as father, in the presence of his mother Adrisyanti. Adrisyanti, hearing the very intelligible sound father sweetly uttered by her son, addressed him with tearful eyes and said, 'O child, do not address this thy grandfather as father? Thy father, O son, has been devoured by a Rakshasa in a different forest. O innocent one, he is not thy father whom thou regardest so. The revered one is the father of that celebrated father of thine.' Thus addressed by his mother that best of Rishis of truthful speech, gave way to sorrow, but soon fired up and resolved to destroy the whole creation. Then that illustrious and great ascetic Vasishtha, that foremost of all persons conversant with Brahma, that son of Mitravaruna, that Rishi acquainted with positive truth, addressed his grandson who had set his heart upon the destruction of the world. Hear, O Arjuna, the arguments by which Vasishtha succeeded in driving out that resolution from his grandson's mind.'

"The Gandharva continued, 'Then Vasishtha said, 'There was a celebrated king of the name of Kritavirya. That bull among the kings of the earth was the disciple of the Veda-knowing Bhrigus. That king, O child, after performing the Soma sacrifice, gratified the Brahmanas with great presents of rice and wealth. After that monarch had ascended to heaven, an occasion came when his descendants were in want of wealth. And knowing that the Bhrigus were rich, those princes went unto those best of Brahmanas, in the guise of beggars. Some amongst the Bhrigus, to protect their wealth, buried it under earth; and some from fear of the Kshatriyas, began to give away their wealth unto (other) Brahmanas; while some amongst them duly gave unto the Kshatriyas whatever they wanted. It happened, however, that some Kshatriyas, in digging as they pleased at the house of particular Bhargava, came upon a large treasure. And the treasure was seen by all those bulls among Kshatriyas who had been there. Enraged at what they regarded as the deceitful behaviour of the Bhrigus, the Kshatriyas insulted the Brahmanas, though the latter asked for mercy. And those mighty bowmen began to slaughter the Bhrigus with their sharp arrows. And the Kshatriyas wandered over the earth, slaughtering even the embryos that were in the wombs of the women of the Bhrigu race. And while the Bhrigu race was thus being exterminated, the women of that tribe fled from fear to the inaccessible mountains of Himavat. And one amongst these women, of tapering thighs, desiring to perpetuate her husband's race, held in one of her thighs an embryo endued with great energy. A certain Brahmana woman, however, who came to know this fact, went from fear unto the Kshatriyas and reported the matter unto them. And the Kshatriyas then went to destroy that embryo. Arrived at the place, they beheld the would-be mother blazing with inborn energy, and the child that was in her thigh came out tearing up the thigh and dazzling the eyes of those Kshatriyas like the midday sun. Thus deprived of their eyes, the Kshatriyas began to wander over those inaccessible mountains. And distressed at the loss of sight, the princes were afflicted with woe, and desirous of regaining the use of their eyes they resolved to seek the protection of that faultless woman. Then those Kshatriyas, afflicted with sorrow, and from loss of sight like unto a fire that hath gone out, addressed with anxious hearts that illustrious lady, saying, 'By thy grace. O lady, we wish to be restored to sight. We shall then return to our homes all together and abstain for ever from our sinful practice. O handsome one, it behoveth thee with thy child to show us mercy. It behoveth thee to favour these kings by granting them their eye-sight.'"

SECTION CLXXXI
(Chaitraratha Parva continued)

"Vasishtha continued, 'The Brahmana lady, thus addressed by them, said, 'Ye children, I have not robbed you of your eye-sight, nor am I angry with you. This child, however, of the Bhrigu race hath certainly been angry with you. There is little doubt, ye children, that ye have been robbed of your sight by that illustrious child whose wrath hath been kindled at the remembrance of the slaughter of his race. Ye children, while ye were destroying even the embryos of the Bhrigu race, this child was held by me in my thigh for a hundred years! And in order that the prosperity of Bhrigu's race might be restored, the entire Vedas with their branches came unto this one even while he was in the womb. It is plain that this scion of the Bhrigu race, enraged at the slaughter of his fathers, desireth to slay you! It is by his celestial energy that your eyes have been scorched. Therefore, ye children, pray ye unto this my excellent child born of my thigh. Propitiated by your homage he may restore your eye-sight.'

"Vasishtha continued, 'Hearing those words of the Brahmana lady, all these princes addressed the thigh-born child, saying, 'Be propitious!' And the child became propitious unto them. And that best of Brahmana Rishis, in consequence of his having been born after tearing open his mother's thigh, came to be known throughout the three worlds by the name of Aurva (thigh- born). And those princes regaining their eye-sight went away. But the Muni Aurva of the Bhrigu race resolved upon overcoming the whole world. And the high-souled Rishi set his heart, O child, upon the destruction of every creature in the world. And that scion of the Bhrigu race, for paying homage (as he regarded) unto his slaughtered ancestors, devoted himself to the austerest of penances with the object of destroying the whole world. And desirous of gratifying his ancestors, the Rishi afflicted by his severe asceticism the three worlds with the celestials, the Asuras and human beings. The Pitris, then, learning what the child of their race was about, all came from their own region unto the Rishi and addressing him said:

'Aurva, O son, fierce thou hast been in thy asceticism. Thy power hath been witnessed by us. Be propitious unto the three worlds. O, control thy wrath. O child, it was not from incapacity that the Bhrigus of souls under complete control were, all of them, indifferent to their own destruction at the hands of the murderous Kshatriyas. O child, when we grew weary of the long periods of life alloted to us, it was then that we desired our own destruction through the instrumentality of the Kshatriyas. The wealth that the Bhrigus had placed in their house underground had been placed only with the object of enraging the Kshatriyas and picking a quarrel with them. O thou best of Brahmanas, as we were desirous of heaven, of what use could wealth be to us? The treasurer of heaven (Kuvera) had kept a large treasure for us. When we found that death could not, by any means, overtake us all, it was then, O child, that we regarded this as the best means (of compassing our desire). They who commit suicide never attain to regions that are blessed. Reflecting upon this, we abstained from self- destruction. That which, therefore thou desirest to do is not agreeable to us. Restrain thy mind, therefore, from the sinful act of destroying the whole world. O child, destroy not the Kshatriyas nor the seven worlds. O, kill this wrath of thine that staineth thy ascetic energy.'"

SECTION CLXXXII
(Chaitraratha Parva continued)

"The Gandharva said, 'Vasishtha after this, continued the narration saying, 'Hearing words of the Pitris, Aurva, O child, replied unto them to this effect:

'Ye Pitris, the vow I have made from anger for the destruction of all the worlds, must not go in vain. I cannot consent to be one whose anger and vows are futile. Like fire consuming dry woods, this rage of mine will certainly consume me if I do not accomplish my vow. The man that represseth his wrath that hath been excited by (adequate) cause, becometh incapable of duly compassing the three ends of life (viz., religion, profit and pleasure). The wrath that kings desirous of subjugating the whole earth exhibit, is not without its uses. It serveth to restrain the wicked and to protect the honest. While lying unborn within my mother's thigh, I heard the doleful cries of my mother and other women of the Bhrigu race who were then being exterminated by the Kshatriyas. Ye Pitris, when those wretches of Kshatriyas began to exterminate the Bhrigus together with unborn children of their race, it was then that wrath filled my soul. My mother and the other women of our race, each in an advanced state of pregnancy, and my father, while terribly alarmed, found not in all the worlds a single protector. Then when the Bhrigu women found not a single protector, my mother held me in one of her thighs. If there be a punisher of crimes in the worlds no one in all the worlds would dare commit a crime; if he findeth not a punisher, the number of sinners becometh large. The man who having the power to prevent or punish sin doth not do so knowing that a sin hath been committed, is himself defiled by that sin. When kings and others, capable of protecting my fathers, protect them not, postponing that duty preferring the pleasures of life, I have just cause to be enraged with them. I am the lord of the creation, capable of punishing its iniquity. I am incapable of obeying your command. Capable of punishing this crime, if I abstain from so doing, men will once more have to undergo a similar persecution. The fire of my wrath too that is ready to consume the worlds, if repressed, will certainly consume by its own energy my own self. Ye masters, I know that ye ever seek the good of the worlds: direct me, therefore, as to what may benefit both myself and the worlds.'

"Vasishtha continued, 'The Pitris replied saying, O, throw this fire that is born of thy wrath and that desireth to consume the worlds, into the waters. That will do thee good. The worlds, indeed, are all dependent on water (as their elementary cause). Every juicy substance containeth water, indeed the whole universe is made of water. Therefore, O thou best of Brahmanas, cast thou this fire of thy wrath into the waters. If, therefore, thou desirest it, O Brahmana, let this fire born of thy wrath abide in the great ocean, consuming the waters thereof, for it hath been said that the worlds are made of water. In this way, O thou sinless one, thy word will be rendered true, and the worlds with the gods will not be destroyed.'

"Vasishtha continued, 'Then, O child, Aurva cast the fire of his wrath into the abode of Varuna. And that fire which consumeth the waters of the great ocean, became like unto a large horse's head which persons conversant with the Vedas call by the name of Vadavamukha. And emitting itself from that mouth it consumeth the waters of the mighty ocean. Blest be thou! It behoveth not thee, therefore, to destroy the worlds. O thou Parasara, who art acquainted with the higher regions, thou foremost of wise men!'"

SECTION CLXXXIII
(Chaitraratha Parva continued)

"The Gandharva continued, 'The Brahmana sage (Parasara) thus addressed by the illustrious Vasishtha restrained his wrath from destroying the worlds. But the Rishi Parasara endued with great energy—the son of Saktri—the foremost of all persons acquainted with the Vedas—performed a grand Rakshasa sacrifice. And remembering the slaughter of (his father) Saktri, the great Muni began to consume the Rakshasas, young and old, in the sacrifice he performed. And Vasishtha did not restrain him from this slaughter of the Rakshasa, from the determination of not obstructing this second vow (of his grandson). And in that sacrifice the great Muni Parasara sat before three blazing fires, himself like unto a fourth fire. And the son of Saktri, like the Sun just emerging from the clouds, illuminated the whole firmament by that stainless sacrifice of his into which large were the libations poured of clarified butter. Then Vasishtha and the other Rishis regarded that Muni blazing with his own energy as if he were the second Sun. Then the great Rishi Atri of liberal soul desirous of ending that sacrifice, an achievement highly difficult for others,— came to that place. And there also came, O thou slayer of all foes, Pulastya and Pulaha, and Kratu the performer of many great sacrifices, all influenced by the desire of saving the Rakshasas. And, O thou bull of the Bharata race, Pulastya then, seeing that many Rakshasas had already been slain, told these words unto Parasara that oppressor of all enemies:

'There is no obstruction, I hope, to this sacrifice of thine, O child! Takest thou any pleasure, O child, in this slaughter of even all those innocent Rakshasas that know nothing of thy father's death. It behoveth thee not to destroy any creatures thus. This, O child, is not the occupation of a Brahmana devoted to asceticism. Peace is the highest virtue. Therefore, O Parasara, establish thou peace. How hast thou, O Parasara, being so superior, engaged thyself in such a sinful practice? It behoveth not thee to transgress against Saktri himself who was well- acquainted with all rules of morality. It behoveth not thee to extirpate any creatures. O descendant of Vasishtha's race, that which befell thy father was brought about by his own curse. It was for his own fault that Saktri was taken hence unto heaven. O Muni, no Rakshasa was capable of devouring Saktri; he himself provided for his own death. And, O Parasara, Viswamitra was only a blind instrument in that matter. Both Saktri and Kalmashapada, having ascended to heaven are enjoying great happiness. And, the other sons also of the great Rishi Vasishtha who were younger than Saktri, are even now enjoying themselves with the celestials. And, O child, O offspring of Vasishtha's son, thou hast also been, in this sacrifice, only an instrument in the destruction of these innocent Rakshasas. O, blest be thou! Abandon this sacrifice of thine. Let it come to an end.'

"The Gandharva continued, 'Thus addressed by Pulastya, as also by the intelligent Vasishtha, that mighty Muni—the son of Saktri then brought that sacrifice to an end. And the Rishi cast the fire that he had ignited for the purpose of the Rakshasas' sacrifice into the deep woods on the north of the Himavat. And that fire may be seen to this day consuming Rakshasas and trees and stones in all seasons.'"

SECTION CLXXXIV
(Chaitraratha Parva continued)

"Arjuna asked, 'What for, O Gandharva, did king Kalmashapada command his queen to go unto that foremost of all persons conversant with the Vedas— the master Vasishtha? Why also did that illustrious and great Rishi Vasishtha himself who was acquainted with every rule of morality know a woman he should not have known? O friend, was this an act of sin on the part of Vasishtha? It behoveth thee to remove the doubts I entertain and refer to thee for solution.'

"The Gandharva replied, saying, 'O irrepressible Dhananjaya, listen to me as I answer the question thou hast asked in respect of Vasishtha and king Kalmashapada that cherisher of friends. O thou best of the Bharatas, I have told thee all about the curse of king Kalmashapada by Saktri, the illustrious son of Vasishtha. Brought under the influence of the curse, that smiter of all foes—king Kalmashapada—with eyes whirling in anger went out of his capital accompanied by his wife. And entering with his wife the solitary woods the king began to wander about. And one day while the king under the influence of the curse was wandering through that forest abounding in several kinds of deer and various other animals and overgrown with numerous large trees and shrubs and creepers and resounding with terrible cries, he became exceedingly hungry. And the monarch thereupon began to search for some food. Pinched with hunger, the king at last saw, in a very solitary part of the woods, a Brahmana and his wife enjoying each other. Alarmed at beholding the monarch the couple ran away, their desire ungratified. Pursuing the retreating pair, the king forcibly seized the Brahmana. Then the Brahmani, beholding her lord seized, addressed the monarch, saying, 'Listen to what I say, O monarch of excellent vows! It is known all over the world that thou art born in the solar race, and that thou art ever vigilant in the practice of morality and devoted to the service of thy superiors. It behoveth thee not to commit sin, O thou irrepressible one, deprived though thou hast been of thy senses by (the Rishi's) curse. My season hath come, and wishful of my husband's company I was connected with him. I have not been gratified yet. Be propitious unto us, O thou best of kings! Liberate my husband.' The monarch, however, without listening to her cries cruelly devoured her husband like a tiger devouring its desirable prey. Possessed with wrath at this sight, the tears that that woman shed blazed up like fire and consumed everything in that place. Afflicted with grief at the calamity that overtook her lord, the Brahmani in anger cursed the royal sage Kalmashapada, 'Vile wretch, since thou hast today cruelly devoured under my very nose my illustrious husband dear unto me, even before my desires have been gratified, therefore shall thou, O wicked one afflicted by my curse, meet with instant death when thou goest in for thy wife in season. And thy wife, O wretch, shall bring forth a son uniting herself with that Rishi Vasishtha whose children have been devoured by thee. And that child, O worst of kings, shall be the perpetuator of thy race.' And cursing the monarch thus, that lady of Angira's house bearing every auspicious mark, entered the blazing fire in the very sight of the monarch. And, O thou oppressor of all foes, the illustrious and exalted Vasishtha by his ascetic power and spiritual insight immediately knew all. And long after this, when the king became freed from his curse, he approached his wife Madayanati when her season came. But Madayanati softly sent him away. Under the influence of passion the monarch had no recollection of that curse. Hearing, however, the words of his wife, the best of kings became terribly alarmed. And recollecting the curse he repented bitterly of what he had done. It was for this reason, O thou best of men, that the monarch infected with the Brahmani's curse, appointed Vasishtha to beget a son upon his queen.'"

SECTION CLXXXV
(Chaitraratha Parva continued)

"Arjuna asked, 'O Gandharva, thou art acquainted with everything. Tell us, therefore, which Veda-knowing Brahmana is worthy to be appointed as our priest.'

"The Gandharva replied, 'There is in these woods a shrine of the name of Utkochaka. Dhaumya, the younger brother of Devala is engaged there in ascetic penances. Appoint him, if ye desire, your priest.'"

"Vaisampayana said, 'Then Arjuna, highly pleased with everything that had happened, gave unto that Gandharva, his weapon of fire with befitting ceremonies. And addressing him, the Pandava also said, 'O thou best of Gandharvas, let the horses thou givest us remain with thee for a time. When the occasion cometh, we will take them from thee. Blest be thou.' Then the Gandharva and the Pandavas, respectfully saluting each other, left the delightful banks of the Bhagirathi and went wheresoever they desired. Then, O Bharata, the Pandavas going to Utkochaka, the sacred asylum of Dhaumya installed Dhaumya as their priest. And Dhaumya, the foremost of all conversant with the Vedas, receiving them with presents of wild fruits and (edible) roots, consented to become their priest. And the Pandavas with their mother forming the sixth of the company, having obtained that Brahmana as their priest regarded their sovereignty and kingdom as already regained and the daughter of the Panchala king as already obtained in the Swayamavara. And those bulls of the Bharata race, having obtained the master Dhaumya as their priest, also regarded themselves as placed under a powerful protector. And the high-souled Dhaumya, acquainted with the true meaning of the Vedas and every rule of morality, becoming the spiritual preceptor of the virtuous Pandavas, made them his Yajamanas (spiritual disciples). And that Brahmana, beholding those heroes endued with intelligence and strength and perseverance like unto the celestials, regarded them as already restored, by virtue of their own accomplishments to their sovereignty and kingdom. Then those kings of men, having had benedictions uttered upon them by that Brahmana, resolved to go, accompanied by him, to the Swayamvara of the Princess of Panchala.'"

SECTION CLXXXVI
(Swayamvara Parva)

"Vaisampayana said, 'Then those tigers among men—those brothers—the five Pandavas, set out for Panchala to behold that country and Draupadi and the festivities (in view of her marriage). And those tigers among men—those oppressors of all enemies—in going along with their mother, saw on the way numerous Brahmanas proceeding together. And those Brahmanas who were all Brahmacharis beholding the Pandavas, O king, asked them, 'Where are ye going to? Whence also are ye come?' And Yudhishthira replied unto them, saying, 'Ye bulls among Brahmanas, know ye that we are uterine brothers proceeding together with our mother. We are coming even from Ekachakra.' The Brahmanas then said, 'Go ye this very day to the abode of Drupada in the country of the Panchalas. A great Swayamvara takes place there, on which a large sum of money will be spent. We also are proceeding thither. Let us all go together. Extraordinary festivities will take place (in Drupada's abode). The illustrious Yajnasena, otherwise called Drupada, had a daughter risen from the centre of the sacrificial altar. Of eyes like lotus-petals and of faultless features endued with youth and intelligence, she is extremely beautiful. And the slender-waisted Draupadi of every feature perfectly faultless, and whose body emitteth a fragrance like unto that of the blue lotus for two full miles around, is the sister of the strong-armed Dhrishtadyumna gifted with great prowess—the (would-be) slayer of Drona—who was born with natural mail and sword and bow and arrows from the blazing fire, himself like unto the second Fire. And that daughter of Yajnasena will select a husband from among the invited princes. And we are repairing thither to behold her and the festivities on the occasion, like unto the festivities of heaven. And to that Swayamvara will come from various lands kings and princes who are performers of sacrifices in which the presents to the Brahmanas are large: who are devoted to study, are holy, illustrious, and of rigid vows; who are young and handsome; and who are mighty car-warriors and accomplished in arms. Desirous of winning (the hand of) the maiden those monarchs will all give away much wealth and kine and food and other articles of enjoyment. And taking all they will give away and witnessing the Swayamvara, and enjoying the festivities, we shall go wheresoever we like. And there will also come unto that Swayamvara, from various countries, actors, and bards singing the panegyrics of kings, and dancers, and reciters of Puranas, and heralds, and powerful athletes. And beholding all these sights and taking what will be given away to illustrious ones, ye will return with us. Ye are all handsome and like unto the celestials! Beholding you, Krishna may, by chance, choose some one amongst you superior to the rest. This thy brother of mighty arms and handsome and endued with beauty also, engaged in (athletic) encounters, may, by chance, earn great wealth.'

"On hearing these words of the Brahmanas, Yudhishthira replied, 'Ye Brahmanas, we will all go with you to witness that maiden's Swayamvara— that excellent jubilee.'"

SECTION CLXXXVII
(Swayamvara Parva continued)

"Vaisampayana said, 'Thus addressed by the Brahmanas, the Pandavas, O Janamejaya, proceeded towards the country of the southern Panchalas ruled over by the king Drupada. And on their way those heroes beheld the illustrious Dwaipayana—that Muni of pure soul, and perfectly sinless. And duly saluting the Rishi and saluted by him, after their conversation was over, commanded by him they proceeded to Drupada's abode. And those mighty chariot-fighters proceeded by slow stages staying for some time within those beautiful woods and by fine lakes that they beheld along their way. Devoted to study, pure in their practices, amiable, and sweet-speeched, the Pandavas at last entered the country of the Panchalas. And beholding the capital, as also the fort, they took up their quarters in the house of a potter. Adopting the Brahmanical profession, they began to lead an eleemosynary life. And no men recognised those heroes during their stay in Drupada's capital.

"Yajnasena always cherished the desire of bestowing his daughter on Kiriti (Arjuna), the son of Pandu. But he never spoke of it to anybody. And, O Janamejaya, the king of Panchala thinking of Arjuna caused a very stiff bow to be made that was incapable of being bent by any except Arjuna. Causing some machinery to be erected in the sky, the king set up a mark attached to that machinery. And Drupada said, 'He that will string this bow and with these well-adorned arrows shoot the mark above the machine shall obtain my daughter.'

"Vaisampayana continued, 'With these words king Drupada proclaimed the Swayamvara. On hearing of them, O Bharata, the kings of other lands came to his capital. And there came also many illustrious Rishis desirous of beholding the Swayamvara. And there came also, O king, Duryodhana and the Kurus accompanied by Karna. There also came many superior Brahmanas from every country. And the monarchs who came there were all received with reverence by the illustrious Drupada. Desirous of beholding the Swayamvara, the citizens, roaring like the sea, all took their seats on the platforms that were erected around the amphitheatre. The monarch entered the grand amphitheatre by the north-eastern gate. And the amphitheatre which itself had been erected on an auspicious and level plain to the north-east of Drupada's capital, was surrounded by beautiful mansions. And it was enclosed on all sides with high walls and a moat with arched doorways here and there. The vast amphitheatre was also shaded by a canopy of various colours. And resounding with the notes of thousands of trumpets, it was scented with black aloes and sprinkled all over with water mixed with sandal-paste and decorated with garlands of flowers. It was surrounded with high mansions perfectly white and resembling the cloud-kissing peaks of Kailasa. The windows of those mansions were covered with net works of gold; the walls were set with diamonds and precious costly carpets and cloths. All those mansions adorned with wreaths and garlands of flowers and rendered fragrant with excellent aloes, were all white and spotless, like unto the necks of swans. And the fragrance therefrom could be perceived from the distance of a Yojana (eight miles). And they were each furnished with a hundred doors wide enough to admit a crowd of persons; they were adorned with costly beds and carpets, and beautified with various metals; they resembled the peaks of the Himavat. And in those seven-storied houses of various sizes dwelt the monarchs invited by Drupada whose persons were adorned with every ornament and who were possessed with the desire of excelling one another. And the inhabitants of the city and the country who had come to behold Krishna and taken their seats on the excellent platforms erected around, beheld seated within those mansions those lions among kings who were all endued with the energy of great souls. And those exalted sovereigns were all adorned with the fragrant paste of the black aloe. Of great liberality, they were all devoted to Brahma and they protected their kingdoms against all foes. And for their own good deeds they were loved by the whole world.

"The Pandavas, too, entering that amphitheatre, sat with the Brahmanas and beheld the unequalled affluence of the king of the Panchalas. And that concourse of princes, Brahmanas, and others, looking gay at the performances of actors and dancers (large presents of every kind of wealth being constantly made), began to swell day by day. And it lasted, O king, several days, till on the sixteenth day when it was at its full, the daughter of Drupada, O thou bull of the Bharata race, having washed herself clean entered the amphitheatre, richly attired and adorned with every ornament and bearing in her hand a dish of gold (whereon were the usual offerings of Arghya) and a garland of flowers. Then the priest of the lunar race—a holy Brahmana conversant with all mantras—ignited the sacrificial fire and poured on it with due rites libations of clarified butter. And gratifying Agni by these libations and making the Brahmanas utter the auspicious formula of benediction, stopped the musical instruments that were playing all around. And when that vast amphitheatre, O monarch, became perfectly still, Dhrishtadyumna possessed of a voice deep as the sound of the kettledrum or the clouds, taking hold of his sister's arm, stood in the midst of that concourse, and said, with a voice loud and deep as the roar of the clouds, these charming words of excellent import, 'Hear ye assembled kings, this is the bow, that is the mark, and these are the arrows. Shoot the mark through the orifice of the machine with these five sharpened arrows. Truly do I say that, possessed of lineage, beauty of persons, and strength whoever achieveth this great feat shall obtain today this my sister, Krishna for his wife.' Having thus spoken unto the assembled monarchs Drupada's son then addressed his sister, reciting unto her the names and lineages and achievements of those assembled lords of the earth.'"

SECTION CLXXXVIII
(Swayamvara Parva continued)

"Dhrishtadyumna said, 'Duryodhana, Durvisaha, Durmukha and Dushpradharshana, Vivinsati, Vikarna, Saha, and Duhsasana; Yuyutsu and Vayuvega and Bhimavegarava; Ugrayudha, Valaki, Kanakayu, and Virochana, Sukundala, Chitrasena, Suvarcha, and Kanakadhwaja; Nandaka, and Vahusali, and Tuhunda, and Vikata; these, O sister, and many other mighty sons of Dhritarashtra—all heroes—accompanied by Karna, have come for thy hand. Innumerable other illustrious monarchs all bulls among Kshatriyas—have also come for thee. Sakuni, Sauvala, Vrisaka, and Vrihadvala,—these sons of the king Gandhara—have also come. Foremost of all wielders of weapons —the illustrious Aswatthaman and Bhoja, adorned with every ornament have also come for thee. Vrihanta, Manimana, Dandadhara, Sahadeva, Jayatsena, Meghasandhi, Virata with his two sons Sankha and Uttara, Vardhakshemi, Susarma, Senavindu, Suketu with his two sons Sunama and Suvarcha, Suchitra, Sukumara, Vrika, Satyadhriti, Suryadhwaja, Rochamana, Nila, Chitrayudha, Agsuman, Chekitana, the mighty Sreniman, Chandrasena the mighty son of Samudrasena, Jarasandha, Vidanda, and Danda—the father and son, Paundraka, Vasudeva, Bhagadatta endued with great energy, Kalinga, Tamralipta, the king of Pattana, the mighty car-warrior Salya, the king of Madra, with his son, the heroic Rukmangada, Rukmaratha, Somadatta of the Kuru race with his three sons, all mighty chariot-fighters and heroes, viz., Bhuri, Bhurisrava, and Sala, Sudakshina, Kamvoja of the Puru race,

Vrihadvala, Sushena, Sivi, the son of Usinara, Patcharanihanta, the king of Karusha, Sankarshana (Valadeva), Vasudeva (Krishna) the mighty son of Rukmini, Samva, Charudeshna, the son of Pradyumna with Gada, Akrura, Satyaki, the high-souled Uddhava, Kritavarman, the son of Hridika, Prithu, Viprithu, Viduratha, Kanka, Sanku with Gaveshana, Asavaha, Aniruddha, Samika, Sarimejaya, the heroic Vatapi Jhilli Pindaraka, the powerful Usinara, all these of the Vrishni race, Bhagiratha, Vrihatkshatra, Jayadratha the son of Sindhu, Vrihadratha, Valhika, the mighty charioteer Srutayu, Uluka, Kaitava, Chitrangada and Suvangada, the highly intelligent Vatsaraja, the king of Kosala, Sisupala and the powerful Jarasandha, these and many other great kings—all Kshatriyas celebrated throughout the world—have come, O blessed one, for thee. Endued with prowess, these will shoot the mark. And thou shalt choose him for thy husband who amongst these will shoot the mark.'"

SECTION CLXXXXIX
(Swayamvara Parva continued)

"Vaisampayana said, 'Then those youthful princes adorned with ear-rings, vying with one another and each regarding himself accomplished in arms and gifted with might, stood up brandishing their weapons. And intoxicated with pride of beauty, prowess, lineage, knowledge, wealth, and youth, they were like Himalayan elephants in the season of rut with crowns split from excess of temporal juice. And beholding each other with jealousy and influenced by the god of desire, they suddenly rose up from their royal seats, exclaiming 'Krishna shall be mine.' And the Kshatriyas assembled in that amphitheatre, each desirous of winning the daughter of Drupada, looked like the celestial (of old) standing round Uma, the daughter of the King of mountains. Afflicted with the shafts of the god of the flowery bow and with hearts utterly lost in the contemplation of Krishna, those princes descended into the amphitheatre for winning the Panchala maiden and began to regard even their best friends with jealousy. And there came also the celestials on their cars, with the Rudras and the Adityas, the Vasus and the twin Aswins, the Swadhas and all the Marutas, and Kuvera with Yama walking ahead. And there came also the Daityas and the Suparnas, the great Nagas and the celestial Rishis, the Guhyakas and the Charanas and Viswavasu and Narada and Parvata, and the principal Gandharvas with Apsaras. And Halayudha (Valadeva) and Janardana (Krishna) and the chief of the Vrishni, Andhaka, and Yadava tribes who obeyed the leadership of Krishna were also there, viewing the scene. And beholding those elephants in rut—the five (Pandavas)—attracted towards Draupadi like mighty elephants towards a lake overgrown with lotuses, or like fire covered with ashes, Krishna the foremost of Yadu heroes began to reflect. And he said unto Rama (Valadeva), 'That is Yudhishthira; that is Bhima with Jishnu (Arjuna); and those are the twin heroes.' And Rama surveying them slowly cast a glance of satisfaction at Krishna. Biting their nether lips in wrath, the other heroes there—sons and grandsons of kings—with their eyes and hearts and thoughts set on Krishna, looked with expanded eyes on Draupadi alone without noticing the Pandavas. And the sons of Pritha also, of mighty arms, and the illustrious twin heroes, beholding Draupadi, were all likewise struck by the shafts of Kama. And crowded with celestial Rishis and Gandharvas and Suparnas and Nagas and Asuras and Siddhas, and filled with celestial perfumes and scattered over with celestial flowers, and resounding with the kettle-drum and the deep hum of infinite voices, and echoing with the softer music of the flute, the Vina, and the tabor, the cars of the celestials could scarcely find a passage through the firmament. Then those princes—Karna, Duryodhana, Salwa, Salya, Aswatthaman, Kratha, Sunitha, Vakra, the ruler of Kalinga and Banga, Pandya, Paundra, the ruler of Videha, the chief of the Yavanas, and many other sons and grandsons of kings,—sovereigns of territories with eyes like lotus-petals,—one after another began to exhibit prowess for (winning) that maiden of unrivalled beauty. Adorned with crowns, garlands, bracelets, and other ornaments, endued with mighty arms, possessed of prowess and vigour and bursting with strength and energy, those princes could not, even in imagination, string that bow of extraordinary stiffness.

"And (some amongst) those kings in exerting with swelling lips each according to his strength, education, skill, and energy,—to string that bow, were tossed on the ground and lay perfectly motionless for some time. Their strength spent and their crowns and garlands loosened from their persons, they began to pant for breath and their ambition of winning that fair maiden was cooled. Tossed by that tough bow, and their garlands and bracelets and other ornaments disordered, they began to utter exclamations of woe. And that assemblage of monarchs, their hope of obtaining Krishna gone, looked sad and woeful. And beholding the plight of those monarchs, Karna that foremost of all wielders of the bow went to where the bow was, and quickly raising it strung it and placed the arrows on the string. And beholding the son of Surya—Karna of the Suta tribe—like unto fire, or Soma, or Surya himself, resolved to shoot the mark, those foremost of bowmen—the sons of Pandu—regarded the mark as already shot and brought down upon the ground. But seeing Karna, Draupadi loudly said, 'I will not select a Suta for my lord.' Then Karna, laughing in vexation and casting glance at the Sun, threw aside the bow already drawn to a circle.

"Then when all those Kshatriyas gave up the task, the heroic king of the Chedis—mighty as Yama (Pluto) himself—the illustrious and determined Sisupala, the son of Damaghosa, in endeavouring to string the bow, himself fell upon his knees on the ground. Then king Jarasandha endued with great strength and powers, approaching the bow stood there for some moment, fixed and motionless like a mountain. Tossed by the bow, he too fell upon his knees on the ground, and rising up, the monarch left the amphitheatre for (returning to) his kingdom. Then the great hero Salya, the king of Madra, endued with great strength, in endeavouring to string the bow fell upon his knees on the ground. At last when in that assemblage consisting of highly respectable people, all the monarchs had become subjects of derisive talk that foremost of heroes—Jishnu, the son of Kunti—desired to string the bow and placed the arrows on the bow-string.'"

SECTION CLXL
(Swayamvara Parva continued)

"Vaisampayana continued, 'When all the monarchs had desisted from stringing that bow, the high-souled Jishnu arose from among the crowd of Brahmanas seated in that assembly. And beholding Partha possessing the complexion of Indra's banner, advancing towards the bow, the principal Brahmanas shaking their deer-skins raised a loud clamour. And while some were displeased, there were others that were well-pleased. And some there were, possessed of intelligence and foresight, who addressing one another said, 'Ye Brahmanas, how can a Brahmana stripling unpractised in arms and weak in strength, string that bow which such celebrated Kshatriyas as Salya and others endued with might and accomplished in the science and practice of arms could not? If he doth not achieve success in this untried task which he hath undertaken from a spirit of boyish unsteadiness, the entire body of Brahmanas here will be rendered ridiculous in the eyes of the assembled monarchs. Therefore, forbid this Brahmana that he may not go to string the bow which he is even now desirous of doing from vanity, or mere childish daring.' Others replied, 'We shall not be made ridiculous, nor shall we incur the disrespect of anybody or the displeasure of the sovereigns. Some remarked, 'This handsome youth is even like the trunk of a mighty elephant, whose shoulders and arms and thighs are so well-built, who in patience looks like the Himavat, whose gait is even like that of the lion, and whose prowess seems to be like that of an elephant in rut, and who is so resolute, that it is probable that he will accomplish this feat. He has strength and resolution. If he had none, he would never go of his own accord. Besides, there is nothing in the three worlds that Brahmanas of all mortal men cannot accomplish. Abstaining from all food or living upon air or eating of fruits, persevering in their vows, and emaciated and weak, Brahmanas are ever strong in their own energy. One should never disregard a Brahmana whether his acts be right or wrong, by supposing him incapable of achieving any task that is great or little, or that is fraught with bliss or woe. Rama the son of Jamadagni defeated in battle, all the Kshatriyas. Agastya by his Brahma energy drank off the fathomless ocean. Therefore, say ye, 'Let this youth bend the bow and string it with ease' (and many said), 'So be it.' And the Brahmanas continued speaking unto one another these and other words. Then Arjuna approached the bow and stood there like a mountain. And walking round that bow, and bending his head unto that giver of boons—the lord Isana—and remembering Krishna also, he took it up. And that bow which Rukma, Sunitha, Vakra, Radha's son, Duryodhana, Salya, and many other kings accomplished in the science and practice of arms, could not even with great exertion, string, Arjuna, the son of Indra, that foremost of all persons endued with energy and like unto the younger brother of Indra (Vishnu) in might, strung in the twinkling of an eye. And taking up the five arrows he shot the mark and caused it to fall down on the ground through the hole in the machine above which it had been placed. Then there arose a loud uproar in the firmament, and the amphitheatre also resounded with a loud clamour. And the gods showered celestial flowers on the head of Partha the slayer of foes. And thousands of Brahmanas began to wave their upper garments in joy. And all around, the monarchs who had been unsuccessful, uttered exclamations of grief and despair. And flowers were rained from the skies all over the amphitheatre. And the musicians struck up in concert. Bards and heralds began to chant in sweet tones the praises (of the hero who accomplished the feat). And beholding Arjuna, Drupada—that slayer of foes,— was filled with joy. And the monarch desired to assist with his forces the hero if the occasion arose. And when the uproar was at its height, Yudhishthira, the foremost of all virtuous men, accompanied by those first of men the twins, hastily left the amphitheatre for returning to his temporary home. And Krishna beholding the mark shot and beholding Partha also like unto Indra himself, who had shot the mark, was filled with joy, and approached the son of Kunti with a white robe and a garland of flowers. And Arjuna the accomplisher of inconceivable feats, having won Draupadi by his success in the amphitheatre, was saluted with reverence by all the Brahmanas. And he soon after left the lists followed close by her who thus became his wife.'"

SECTION CLXLI
(Swayamvara Parva continued)

"Vaisampayana said, 'When the king (Drupada) expressed his desire of bestowing his daughter on that Brahmana (who had shot the mark), all those monarchs who had been invited to the Swayamvara, looking at one another, were suddenly filled with wrath. And they said, 'Passing us by and treating the assembled monarchs as straw this Drupada desireth to bestow his daughter—that first of women,—on a Brahmana! Having planted the tree he cutteth it down when it is about to bear fruit. The wretch regardeth us not: therefore let us slay him. He deserveth not our respect nor the veneration due to age. Owing to such qualities of his, we shall, therefore, slay this wretch that insulteth all kings, along with his son. Inviting all the monarchs and entertaining them with excellent food, he disregardeth us at last. In this assemblage of monarchs like unto a conclave of the celestials, doth he not see a single monarch equal unto himself? The Vedic declaration is well-known that the Swayamvara is for the Kshatriyas. The Brahmanas have no claim in respect of a selection of husband by a Kshatriya damsel. Or, ye kings, if this damsel desireth not to select any one of us as her lord, let us cast her into the fire and return to our kingdoms. As regards this Brahmana, although he hath, from officiousness or avarice, done this injury to the monarchs, he should not yet be slain; for our kingdoms, lives, treasures, sons, grandsons, and whatever other wealth we have, all exist for Brahmanas. Something must be done here (even unto him), so that from fear of disgrace and the desire of maintaining what properly belongeth unto each order, other Swayamvaras may not terminate in this way.'

"Having addressed one another thus, those tigers among monarchs endued with arms like unto spiked iron maces, took up their weapons and rushed at Drupada to slay him then and there. And Drupada beholding those monarchs all at once rushing towards him in anger with bows and arrows, sought, from fear, the protection of the Brahmanas. But those mighty bowmen (Bhima and Arjuna) of the Pandavas, capable of chastising all foes, advanced to oppose those monarchs rushing towards them impetuously like elephants in the season of rut. Then the monarchs with gloved fingers and upraised weapons rushed in anger at the Kuru princes, Bhima and Arjuna, to slay them. Then the mighty Bhima of extraordinary achievements, endued with the strength of thunder, tore up like an elephant a large tree and divested it of its leaves. And with that tree, the strong-armed Bhima, the son of Pritha, that grinder of foes, stood, like unto the mace-bearing king of the dead (Yama) armed with his fierce mace, near Arjuna that bull amongst men. And beholding that feat of his brother, Jishnu of extraordinary intelligence, himself also of inconceivable feats, wondered much. And equal unto Indra himself in achievements, shaking off all fear he stood with his bow ready to receive those assailants. And beholding those feats of both Jishnu and his brother, Damodara (Krishna) of superhuman intelligence and inconceivable feats, addressing his brother, Halayudha (Valadeva) of fierce energy, said, 'That hero there, of tread like that of a mighty lion, who draweth the large bow in his hand four full cubits in length, is Arjuna! There is no doubt, O Sankarshana, about this, if I am Vasudeva. That other hero who having speedily torn up the tree hath suddenly become ready to drive off the monarchs is Vrikodara! For no one in the world, except Vrikodara, could today perform such a feat in the field of battle. And that other youth of eyes like unto lotus-petals, of full four cubits height, of gait like that of a mighty lion, and humble withal, of fair complexion and prominent and shining nose, who had, a little before, left the amphitheatre, is Dharma's son (Yudhishthira). The two other youths, like unto Kartikeya, are, I suspect, the sons of the twin

Aswins. I heard that the sons of Pandu along with their mother Pritha had all escaped from the conflagration of the house of lac.' Then Halayudha of complexion like unto that of clouds uncharged with rain, addressing his younger brother (Krishna), said with great satisfaction, 'O, I am happy to hear, as I do from sheer good fortune, that our father's sister Pritha with the foremost of the Kaurava princes have all escaped (from death)!'"

SECTION CLXLII
(Swayamvara Parva continued)

"Vaisampayana said, 'Then those bulls among Brahmanas shaking their deer- skins and water-pots made of cocoanut-shells exclaimed, 'Fear not, we will fight the foe!' Arjuna smilingly addressing those Brahmanas exclaiming thus, said, 'Stand ye aside as spectators (of the fray). Showering hundreds of arrows furnished with straight points even I shall check, like snakes with mantras, all those angry monarchs.' Having said this, the mighty Arjuna taking up the bow he had obtained as dower accompanied by his brother Bhima stood immovable as a mountain. And beholding those Kshatriyas who were ever furious in battle with Karna ahead, the heroic brothers rushed fearlessly at them like two elephants rushing against a hostile elephant. Then those monarchs eager for the fight fiercely exclaimed, 'The slaughter in battle of one desiring to fight is permitted.' And saying this, the monarchs suddenly rushed against the Brahmanas. And Karna endued with great energy rushed against Jishnu for fight. And Salya the mighty king of Madra rushed against Bhima like an elephant rushing against another for the sake of a she-elephant in heat; while Duryodhana and others engaged with the Brahmanas, skirmished with them lightly and carelessly. Then the illustrious Arjuna beholding Karna, the son of Vikartana (Surya), advancing towards him, drew his tough bow and pieced him with his sharp arrows. And the impetus of those whetted arrows furnished with fierce energy made Radheya (Karna) faint. Recovering consciousness Karna attacked Arjuna with greater care than before. Then Karna and Arjuna, both foremost of victorious warriors, desirous of vanquishing each other, fought madly on. And such was the lightness of hand they both displayed that (each enveloped by the other's shower of arrows) they both became invisible (unto the spectators of their encounter). 'Behold the strength of my arms.'— 'Mark, how I have counteracted that feat,'—those were the words—intelligible to heroes alone—in which they addressed each other. And incensed at finding the strength and energy of Arjuna's arms unequalled on the earth, Karna, the son of Surya, fought with greater vigour. And parrying all those impetuous arrows shot at him by Arjuna, Karna sent up a loud shout. And this feat of his was applauded by all the warriors. Then addressing his antagonist, Karna said, 'O thou foremost of Brahmanas, I am gratified to observe the energy of thy arms that knoweth no relaxation in battle and thy weapons themselves fit for achieving victory. Art thou the embodiment of the science of weapons, or art thou Rama that best of Brahmanas, or Indra himself, or Indra's younger brother Vishnu called also Achyuta, who for disguising himself hath assumed the form of a Brahmana and mustering such energy of arms fighteth with me? No other person except the husband himself of Sachi or Kiriti, the son of Pandu, is capable of fighting with me when I am angry on the field of battle.' Then hearing those words of his, Phalguna replied, saying, 'O Karna, I am neither the science of arms (personified), nor Rama endued with superhuman powers. I am only a Brahmana who is the foremost of all warriors and all wielders of weapons. By the grace of my preceptor I have become accomplished in the Brahma and the Paurandara weapons. I am here to vanquish thee in battle. Therefore, O hero, wait a little.'

"Vaisampayana continued, 'Thus addressed (by Arjuna), Karna the adopted son of Radha desisted from the fight, for that mighty chariot-fighter thought that Brahma energy is ever invincible. Meanwhile on another part of the field, the mighty heroes Salya and Vrikodara, well-skilled in battle and possessed of great strength and proficiency, challenging each other, engaged in fight like two elephants in rut. And they struck each other with their clenched fists and knees. And sometimes pushing each other forward and sometimes dragging each other near, sometimes throwing each other down; face downward, and sometimes on the sides, they fought on, striking, each other at times with their clenched fists. And encountering each other with blows hard as the clash of two masses of granite, the lists rang with the sounds of their combat. Fighting with each other thus for a few seconds, Bhima the foremost of the Kuru heroes taking up Salya on his arms hurled him to a distance. And Bhimasena, that bull amongst men, surprised all (by the dexterity of his feat) for though he threw Salya on the ground he did it without hurting him much. And when Salya was thus thrown down and Karna was struck with fear, the other monarchs were all alarmed. And they hastily surrounded Bhima and exclaimed, 'Surely these bulls amongst Brahmanas are excellent (warriors)! Ascertain in what race they have been born and where they abide. Who can encounter Karna, the son of Radha, in fight, except Rama or Drona, or Kiriti, the son of Pandu? Who also can encounter Duryodhana in battle except Krishna, the son of Devaki, and Kripa, the son of Saradwan? Who also can overthrow in battle Salya, that first of mighty warriors, except the hero Valadeva or Vrikodara, the son of Pandu, or the heroic Duryodhana? Let us, therefore, desist from this fight with the Brahmanas. Indeed, Brahmanas, however offending, should yet be ever protected. And first let us ascertain who these are; for after we have done that we may cheerfully fight with them.'

"Vaisampayana continued, 'And Krishna, having beheld that feat of Bhima, believed them both to be the son of Kunti. And gently addressing the assembled monarchs, saying, 'This maiden hath been justly acquired (by the Brahmana),' he induced them to abandon the fight. Accomplished in battle, those monarchs then desisted from the fight. And those best of monarchs then returned to their respective kingdoms, wondering much. And those who had come there went away saying, 'The festive scene hath terminated in the victory of the Brahmanas. The princess of Panchala hath become the bride of a Brahmana.' And surrounded by Brahmanas dressed in skins of deer and other wild animals, Bhima and Dhananjaya passed with difficulty out of the throng. And those heroes among men, mangled by the enemy and followed by Krishna, on coming at last out of that throng, looked like the full moon and the sun emerging from the clouds.

"Meanwhile Kunti seeing that her sons were late in returning from their eleemosynary round, was filled with anxiety. She began to think of various evils having overtaken her sons. At one time she thought that the sons of Dhritarashtra having recognised her sons had slain them. Next she feared that some cruel and strong Rakshasas endued with powers of deception had slain them. And she asked herself, 'Could the illustrious Vyasa himself (who had directed my sons to come to Panchala) have been guided by perverse intelligence?' Thus reflected Pritha in consequence of her affection for her offspring. Then in the stillness of the late afternoon, Jishnu, accompanied by a body of Brahmanas, entered the abode of the potter, like the cloud-covered sun appearing on a cloudy day.'"

SECTION CLXLIII
(Swayamvara Parva continued)

"Vaisampayana said, 'Then those illustrious sons of Pritha, on returning to the potter's abode, approached their mother. And those first of men represented Yajnaseni unto their mother as the alms they had obtained that day. And Kunti who was there within the room and saw not her sons, replied, saying, 'Enjoy ye all (what ye have obtained).' The moment after, she beheld Krishna and then she said, 'Oh, what have I said?' And anxious from fear of sin, and reflecting how every one could be extricated from the situation, she took the cheerful Yajnaseni by the hand, and approaching Yudhishthira said, 'The daughter of king Yajnasena upon being represented to me by thy younger brothers as the alms they had obtained, from ignorance, O king, I said what was proper, viz., 'Enjoy ye all what hath been obtained.' O thou bull of the Kuru race, tell me how my speech may not become untrue; how sin may not touch the daughter of the king of Panchala, and how also she may not become uneasy.'

"Vaisampayana continued, 'Thus addressed by his mother that hero among men, that foremost scion of the Kuru race, the intelligent king (Yudhishthira), reflecting for a moment, consoled Kunti, and addressing Dhananjaya, said, 'By thee, O Phalguna, hath Yajnaseni been won. It is proper, therefore, that thou shouldst wed her. O thou withstander of all foes, igniting the sacred fire, take thou her hand with due rites.'

"Arjuna, hearing this, replied, 'O king, do not make me a participator in sin. Thy behest is not conformable to virtue. That is the path followed by the sinful. Thou shouldst wed first, then the strong-armed Bhima of inconceivable feats, then myself, then Nakula, and last of all, Sahadeva endued with great activity. Both Vrikodara and myself, and the twins and this maiden also, all await, O monarch, thy commands. When such is the state of things, do that, after reflection, which would be proper, and conformable virtue, and productive of fame, and beneficial unto the king of Panchala. All of us are obedient to thee. O, command us as thou likest.'

"Vaisampayana continued, 'Hearing these words of Jishnu, so full of respect and affection, the Pandavas all cast their eyes upon the princess of Panchala. And the princess of Panchala also looked at them all. And casting their glances on the illustrious Krishna, those princes looked at one another. And taking their seats, they began to think of Draupadi alone. Indeed, after those princes of immeasurable energy had looked at Draupadi, the God of Desire invaded their hearts and continued to crush all their senses. As the lavishing beauty of Panchali who had been modelled by the Creator himself, was superior to that of all other women on earth, it could captivate the heart of every creature. And Yudhishthira, the son of Kunti, beholding his younger brothers, understood what was passing in their minds. And that bull among men immediately recollected the words of Krishna-Dwaipayana. And the king, then, from fear of a division amongst the brothers, addressing all of them, said, 'The auspicious Draupadi shall be the common wife of us all.'

"Vaisampayana continued, 'The sons of Pandu, then, hearing those words of their eldest brother, began to revolve them in their minds in great cheerfulness. The hero of the Vrishni race (Krishna suspecting the five persons he had seen at the Swayamvara to be none else than the heroes of the Kuru race), came accompanied by the son of Rohini (Valadeva), to the house of the potter where those foremost of men had taken up their quarters. On arriving there, Krishna and Valadeva beheld seated in that potter's house Ajatasanu (Yudhishthira) of well developed and long arms, and his younger brothers passing the splendour of fire sitting around him. Then Vasudeva approaching that foremost of virtuous men—the son of Kunti— and touching the feet of that prince of the Ajamida race, said, 'I am Krishna.' And the son of Rohini (Valadeva) also approaching Yudhishthira, did the same. And the Pandavas, beholding Krishna and Valadeva, began to express great delight. And, O thou foremost of the Bharata race, those heroes of the Yadu race thereafter touched also the feet of Kunti, their father's sister. And Ajatasatru, that foremost of the Kuru race, beholding Krishna, enquired after his well-being and asked, 'How, O Vasudeva, hast thou been able to trace us, as we are living in disguise?' And Vasudeva, smilingly answered, 'O king, fire, even if it is covered, can be known. Who else among men than the Pandavas could exhibit such might? Ye resisters of all foes, ye sons of Pandu, by sheer good fortune have ye escaped from that fierce fire. And it is by sheer good fortune alone that the wicked son of Dhritarashtra and his counsellors have not succeeded in accomplishing their wishes. Blest be ye! And grow ye in prosperity like a fire in a cave gradually growing and spreading itself all around. And lest any of the monarchs recognise ye, let us return to our tent.' Then, obtaining Yudhishthira's leave, Krishna of prosperity knowing no decrease, accompanied by Valadeva, hastily went away from the potter's abode.'"

SECTION CLXLIV
(Swayamvara Parva continued)

"Vaisampayana said, 'When the Kuru princes (Bhima and Arjuna) were wending towards the abode of the potter, Dhrishtadyumna, the Panchala prince followed them. And sending away all his attendants, he concealed himself in some part of the potter's house, unknown to the Pandavas. Then Bhima, that grinder of all foes, and Jishnu, and the illustrious twins, on returning from their eleemosynary round in the evening, cheerfully gave everything unto Yudhishthira. Then the kind-hearted Kunti addressing the daughter of Drupada said, 'O amiable one, take thou first a portion from this and devote it to the gods and give it away to Brahmanas, and feed those that desire to eat and give unto those who have become our guests. Divide the rest into two halves. Give one of these unto Bhima, O amiable one, for this strong youth of fair complexion— equal unto a king of elephants—this hero always eateth much. And divide the other half into six parts, four for these youths, one for myself, and one for thee.' Then the princess hearing those instructive words of her mother-in-law cheerfully did all that she had been directed to do. And those heroes then all ate of the food prepared by Krishna. Then Sahadeva, the son of Madri, endued with great activity, spread on the ground a bed of kusa grass. Then those heroes, each spreading thereon his deer-skin, laid themselves down to sleep. And those foremost of the Kuru princes lay down with heads towards the south. And Kunti laid herself down along the line of their heads, and Krishna along that of their feet. And Krishna though she lay with the sons of Pandu on that bed of kusa grass along the line of their feet as if she were their nether pillow, grieved not in her heart nor thought disrespectfully of those bulls amongst the Kurus. Then those heroes began to converse with one another. And the conversations of those princes, each worthy to lead an army, was exceedingly interesting, they being upon celestial cars and weapons and elephants, and swords and arrows, and battle-axes. And the son of the Panchala king listened (from his place of concealment) unto all they said. And all those who were with him beheld Krishna in that state.

"When morning came, the prince Dhristadyumna set out from his place of concealment with great haste in order to report to Drupada in detail all that had happened at the potter's abode and all that he had heard those heroes speak amongst themselves during the night. The king of Panchala had been sad because he knew not the Pandavas as those who had taken away his daughter. And the illustrious monarch asked Dhristadyumna on his return, 'Oh, where hath Krishna gone? Who hath taken her away? Hath any Sudra or anybody of mean descent, or hath a tribute-paying Vaisya by taking my daughter away, placed his dirty foot on my head? O son, hath that wreath of flowers been thrown away on a grave-yard? Hath any Kshatriya of high birth, or any one of the superior order (Brahmana) obtained my daughter? Hath any one of mean descent, by having won Krishna, placed his left foot on my head? I would not, O son, grieve but feel greatly happy, if my daughter hath been united with Partha that foremost of men! O thou exalted one, tell me truly who hath won my daughter today? O, are the sons of that foremost of Kurus, Vichitravirya's son alive? Was it Partha (Arjuna) that took up the bow and shot the mark?'"

SECTION CLXLV
(Vaivahika Parva)

"Vaisampayana said, 'Thus addressed Dhrishtadyumna, that foremost of the Lunar princes, cheerfully said unto his father all that had happened and by whom Krishna had been won. And the prince said, 'With large, red eyes, attired in deer-skin, and resembling a celestial in beauty, the youth who strung that foremost of bows and brought down to the ground the mark set on high, was soon surrounded by the foremost of Brahmanas who also offered him their homage for the feat he had achieved. Incapable of bearing the sight of a foe and endued with great activity, he began to exert his prowess. And surrounded by the Brahmanas he resembled the thunder-wielding Indra standing in the midst of the celestials, and the Rishis. And like a she-elephant following the leader of a herd, Krishna cheerfully followed that youth catching hold of his deer-skin. Then when the assembled monarchs incapable of bearing that sight rose up in wrath and advanced for fight, there rose up another hero who tearing up a large tree rushed at that concourse of kings, felling them right and left like Yama himself smiting down creatures endued with life. Then, O monarch, the assembled kings stood motionless and looked at that couple of heroes, while they, resembling the Sun and the Moon, taking Krishna with them, left the amphitheatre and went into the abode of a potter in the suburbs of the town, and there at the potter's abode sat a lady like unto a flame of fire who, I think, is their mother. And around her also sat three other foremost of men each of whom was like unto fire. And the couple of heroes having approached her paid homage unto her feet, and they said unto Krishna also to do the same. And keeping Krishna with her, those foremost of men all went the round of eleemosynary visits. Some time after when they returned, Krishna taking from them what they had obtained as alms, devoted a portion thereof to the gods, and gave another portion away (in gift) to Brahmanas. And of what remained after this, she gave a portion to that venerable lady, and distributed the rest amongst those five foremost of men. And she took a little for herself and ate it last of all. Then, O monarch, they all laid themselves down for sleep, Krishna lying along the line of their feet as their nether pillow. And the bed on which they lay was made of kusa grass upon which was spread their deer-skins. And before going to sleep they talked on diverse subjects in voices deep as of black clouds. The talk of those heroes indicated them to be neither Vaisyas nor Sudras, nor Brahmanas. Without doubt, O monarch, they are bulls amongst Kshatriyas, their discourse having been on military subjects. It seems, O father, that our hope hath been fructified, for we have heard that the sons of Kunti all escaped from the conflagration of the house of lac. From the way in which the mark was shot down by that youth, and the strength with which the bow was strung by him, and the manner in which I have heard them talk with one another proves conclusively, O monarch, that they are the sons of Pritha wandering in disguise.'

"Hearing these words of his son, king Drupada became exceedingly glad, and he sent unto them his priest directing him to ascertain who they were and whether they were the sons of the illustrious Pandu. Thus directed, the king's priest went unto them and applauding them all, delivered the king's message duly, saying, 'Ye who are worthy of preference in everything, the boon-giving king of the earth—Drupada—is desirous of ascertaining who ye are. Beholding this one who hath shot down the mark, his joy knoweth no bounds. Giving us all particulars of your family and tribe, place ye your feet on the heads of your foes and gladden the hearts of the king of Panchala mid his men and mine also. King Pandu was the dear friend of Drupada and was regarded by him as his counterself. And Drupada had all along cherished the desire of bestowing this daughter of his upon Pandu as his daughter-in-law. Ye heroes of features perfectly faultless, king Drupada hath all along cherished this desire in his heart that Arjuna of strong and long arms might wed this daughter of his according to the ordinance. If that hath become possible, nothing could be better; nothing more beneficial; nothing more conducive to fame and virtue, so far as Drupada is concerned.'

"Having said this, the priest remained silent and humbly waited for an answer. Beholding him sitting thus, the king Yudhishthira commanded Bhima who sat near, saying, 'Let water to wash his feet with and the Arghya be offered unto this Brahmana. He is king Drupada's priest and, therefore, worthy of great respect. We should worship him with more than ordinary reverence.' Then, O monarch, Bhima did as directed. Accepting the worship thus offered unto him, the Brahmana with a joyous heart sat at his ease. Then Yudhishthira addressed him and said, 'The king of the Panchalas hath, by fixing a special kind of dower, given away his daughter according to the practice of his order and not freely. This hero hath, by satisfying that demand, won the princess. King Drupada, therefore, hath nothing now to say in regard to the race, tribe, family and disposition of him who hath performed that feat. Indeed, all his queries have been answered by the stringing of the bow and the shooting down of the mark. It is by doing what he had directed that this illustrious hero hath brought away Krishna from among the assembled monarchs. In these circumstances, the king of the Lunar race should not indulge in any regrets which can only make him unhappy without mending matters in the least. The desire that king Drupada hath all along cherished will be accomplished for his handsome princess who beareth, I think, every auspicious mark. None that is weak in strength could string that bow, and none of mean birth and unaccomplished in arms could have shot down the mark. It behoveth not, therefore, the king of the Panchalas to grieve for his daughter today. Nor can anybody in the world undo that act of shooting down the mark. Therefore the king should not grieve for what must take its course.'

"While Yudhishthira was saying all this, another messenger from the king of the Panchalas, coming thither in haste, said, 'The (nuptial) feast' is ready.'"

SECTION CLXLVI
(Vaivahika Parva continued)

"Vaisampayana continued, 'The messenger said, 'King Drupada hath, in view of his daughter's nuptials prepared a good feast for the bride-groom's party. Come ye thither after finishing your daily rites. Krishna's wedding will take place there. Delay ye not. These cars adorned with golden lotuses drawn by excellent horses are worthy of kings. Riding on them, come ye into the abode of the king of the Panchalas.'

"Vaisampayana continued, 'Then those bulls among the Kurus, dismissing the priest and causing Kunti and Krishna to ride together on one of those cars, themselves ascended those splendid vehicles and proceeded towards Drupada's place. Meanwhile, O Bharata, hearing from his priest the words that Yudhishthira had said, king Drupada, in order to ascertain the order to which those heroes belonged, kept ready a large collection of articles (required by the ordinance for the wedding of each of the four orders). And he kept ready fruits, sanctified garlands, and coats of mail, and shields, and carpets, and kine, and seeds, and various other articles and implements of agriculture. And the king also collected, O monarch, every article appertaining to other arts, and various implements and apparatus of every kind of sport. And he also collected excellent coats of mail and shining shields, and swords and scimitars, of fine temper, and beautiful chariots and horses, and first-class bows and well-adorned arrows, and various kinds of missiles ornamented with gold. And he also kept ready darts and rockets and battle-axes and various utensils of war. And there were in that collection beds and carpets and various fine things, and cloths of various sorts. When the party went to Drupada's abode, Kunti taking with her the virtuous Krishna entered the inner apartments of the king. The ladies of the king's household with joyous hearts worshipped the queen of the Kurus. Beholding, O monarch, those foremost of men, each possessing the sportive gait of the lion, with deer-skins for their upper garments, eyes like unto those of mighty bulls, broad shoulders, and long- hanging arms like unto the bodies of mighty snakes, the king, and the king's ministers, and the king's son, and the king's friends and attendants, all became exceedingly glad. Those heroes sat on excellent seats, furnished with footstools without any awkwardness and hesitation. And those foremost of men sat with perfect fearlessness on those costly seats one after another according to the order of their ages. After those heroes were seated, well-dressed servants male and female, and skilful cooks brought excellent and costly viands worthy of kings on gold and silver plates. Then those foremost of men dined on those dishes and became well-pleased. And after the dinner was over, those heroes among men, passing over all other articles, began to observe with interest the various utensils of war. Beholding this, Drupada's son and Drupada himself, along with all his chief ministers of state, understanding the sons of Kunti to be all of royal blood became exceedingly glad.'"

SECTION CLXLVII
(Vaivahika Parva continued)

"Vaisampayana said, 'Then the illustrious king of Panchala, addressing prince Yudhishthira in the form applicable to Brahmanas, cheerfully enquired of that illustrious son of Kunti, saying, 'Are we to know you as Kshatriyas, or Brahamanas, or are we to know you as celestials who disguising themselves as Brahmanas are ranging the earth and come hither for the hand of Krishna? O tell us truly, for we have great doubts! Shall we not be glad when our doubts have been removed? O chastiser of enemies, have the fates been propitious unto us? Tell us the truth willingly! Truth becometh monarchs better than sacrifices and dedications of tanks. Therefore, tell us not what is untrue. O thou of the beauty of a celestial, O chastiser of foes, hearing thy reply I shall make arrangements for my daughter's wedding according to the order to which ye belong.'

"Hearing these words of Drupada, Yudhishthira answered, saying 'Be not cheerless, O king; let joy fill thy heart! The desire cherished by thee hath certainly been accomplished. We are Kshatriyas, O king, and sons of the illustrious Pandu. Know me to be the eldest of the sons of Kunti and these to be Bhima and Arjuna. By these, O king, was thy daughter won amid the concourse of monarchs. The twins (Nakula and Sahadeva) and Kunti wait where Krishna is. O bull amongst men, let grief be driven from thy heart, for we are Kshatriyas. Thy daughter, O monarch, hath like a lotus been transferred only from one lake into another. O king, thou art our revered superior and chief refuge. I have told thee the whole truth.'

"Vaisampayana continued, 'Hearing those words, the king Drupada's eyes rolled in ecstasy. And filled with delight the king could not, for some moments answer Yudhishthira. Checking his emotion with great effort, that chastiser of foes at last replied unto Yudhishthira in proper words. The virtuous monarch enquired how the Pandavas had escaped from the town of Varanavata. The son of Pandu told the monarch every particular in detail of their escape from the burning palace of lac. Hearing everything that the son of Kunti said, king Drupada censured Dhritarashtra, that ruler of men. And the monarch gave every assurance unto Yudhishthira, the son of Kunti. And that foremost of eloquent men then and there vowed to restore Yudhishthira to his paternal throne.

"Then Kunti and Krishna and Bhima and Arjuna and the twins, commanded by the king, to reside there, treated by Yajnasena with due respect. Then king Drupada with his sons, assured by all that had happened, approaching Yudhishthira, said, 'O thou of mighty arms, let the Kuru prince Arjuna take with due rites, the hand of my daughter on this auspicious day, and let him, therefore, perform the usual initiatory rites of marriage.'

"Vaisampayana continued, 'Hearing these words of Drupada, the virtuous king Yudhishthira replied, saying, 'O great king, I also shall have to marry.' Hearing him, Drupada said, 'If it pleaseth thee, take thou the hand of my daughter thyself with due rites. Or, give Krishna in marriage unto whomsoever of thy brothers thou likest.' Yudhishthira said, 'Thy daughter, O king, shall be the common wife of us all! Even thus it hath been ordered, O monarch, by our mother. I am unmarried still, and Bhima also is so amongst the sons of Pandu. This thy jewel of a daughter hath been won by Arjuna. This, O king, is the rule with us; to ever enjoy equally a jewel that we may obtain. O best of monarchs, that rule of conduct we cannot now abandon. Krishna, therefore, shall become the wedded wife of us all. Let her take our hands, one after another before the fire.'

'Drupada answered, 'O scion of Kuru's race, it hath been directed that one man may have many wives. But it hath never been heard that one woman may have many husbands! O son of Kunti, as thou art pure and acquainted with the rules of morality, it behoveth thee not to commit an act that is sinful and opposed both to usage and the Vedas. Why, O prince, hath thy understanding become so?' Yudhishthira said in reply, 'O monarch, morality is subtle. We do not know its course. Let us follow the way trodden by the illustrious ones of former ages. My tongue never uttered an untruth. My heart also never turneth to what is sinful. My mother commandeth so; and my heart also approveth of it. Therefore, O king, that is quite conformable to virtue. Act according to it, without any scruples. Entertain no fear, O king, about this matter.'

"Drupada said, 'O son of Kunti thy mother, and my son Dhrishtadyumna and thyself, settle amongst yourselves as to what should be done. Tell me the result of your deliberations and tomorrow I will do what is proper.'

"Vaisampayana continued, 'After this, O Bharata, Yudhishthira, Kunti and Dhrishtadyumna discoursed upon this matter. Just at that time, however, the island-born (Vyasa), O monarch, came there in course of his wanderings.'"

SECTION CLXLVIII
(Vaivahika Parva continued)

"Vaisampayana said, 'Then all the Pandavas and the illustrious king of the Panchalas and all others there present stood up and saluted with reverence the illustrious Rishi Krishna (Dwaipayana). The high-souled Rishi, saluting them in return and enquiring after their welfare, sat down on a carpet of gold. And commanded by Krishna (Dwaipayana) of immeasurable energy, those foremost of men all sat down on costly seats. A little after, O monarch, the son of Prishata in sweet accents asked the illustrious Rishi about the wedding of his daughter. And he said, 'How, O illustrious one, can one woman become the wife of many men without being defiled by sin? O, tell me truly all about this.' Hearing these words Vyasa replied, 'This practice, O king, being opposed to usage and the Vedas, hath become obsolete. I desire, however, to hear what the opinion of each of you is upon this matter.'

"Hearing these words of the Rishi, Drupada spoke first, saying, 'The practice is sinful in my opinion, being opposed to both usage and the Vedas. O best of Brahmanas, nowhere have I seen many men having one wife. The illustrious ones also of former ages never had such a usage amongst them. The wise should never commit a sin. I, therefore, can never make up mind to act in this way. This practice always appeareth to me to be of doubtful morality.

"After Drupada had ceased, Dhrishtadyumna spoke, saying 'O bull amongst Brahmanas, O thou of ascetic wealth, how can, O Brahmana, the elder brother, if he is of a good disposition, approach the wife of his younger brother? The ways of morality are ever subtle, and, therefore, we know them not. We cannot, therefore, say what is conformable to morality and what not. We cannot do such a deed, therefore, with a safe conscience. Indeed, O Brahmana, I cannot say, 'Let Draupadi become the common wife of five brothers.'

"Yudhishthira then spoke, saying, 'My tongue never uttereth an untruth and my heart never inclineth to what is sinful. When my heart approveth of it, it can never be sinful. I have heard in the Purana that a lady of name Jatila, the foremost of all virtuous women belonging to the race of Gotama had married seven Rishis. So also an ascetic's daughter, born of a tree, had in former times united herself in marriage with ten brothers all bearing the same name of Prachetas and who were all of souls exalted by asceticism. O foremost of all that are acquainted with the rules of morality, it is said that obedience to superior is ever meritorious. Amongst all superiors, it is well-known that the mother is the foremost. Even she hath commanded us to enjoy Draupadi as we do anything obtained as alms. It is for this, O best of Brahmanas, that I regard the (proposed) act as virtuous.'

"Kunti then said, 'The act is even so as the virtuous Yudhishthira hath said. I greatly fear, O Brahmana, lest my speech should become untrue. How shall I be saved from untruth?'

"When they had all finished speaking, Vyasa said, 'O amiable one, how shall thou be saved from the consequence of untruth? Even this is eternal virtue! I will not, O king of the Panchalas, discourse on this before you all. But thou alone shalt listen to me when I disclose how this practice hath been established and why it is to be regarded as old and eternal. There is no doubt that what Yudhishthira hath said is quite conformable to virtue.'

"Vaisampayana continued, 'Then the illustrious Vyasa—the master Dwaipayana—rose, and taking hold of Drupada's hand led him to a private apartment. The Pandavas and Kunti and Dhrishtadyumna of Prishata's race sat there, waiting for the return of Vyasa and Drupada. Meanwhile, Dwaipayana began his discourse with illustrious monarch for explaining how the practice of polyandry could not be regarded as sinful.'"

SECTION CLXLIX
(Vaivahika Parva continued)

"Vaisampayana said, 'Vyasa continued, 'In days of yore, the celestials had once commenced a grand sacrifice in the forest of Naimisha. At that sacrifice, O king, Yama, the son of Vivaswat, became the slayer of the devoted animals. Yama, thus employed in that sacrifice, did not (during that period), O king, kill a single human being. Death being suspended in the world, the number of human beings increased very greatly. Then Soma and Sakra and Varuna and Kuvera, the Sadhyas, the Rudras, the Vasus, the twin Aswins,—these and other celestials went unto Prajapati, the Creator of the universe. Struck with fear for the increase of the human population of the world they addressed the Master of creation and said, 'Alarmed, O lord, at the increase of human beings on earth, we come to thee for relief. Indeed, we crave thy protection.' Hearing those words the Grandsire said, 'Ye have little cause to be frightened at this increase of human beings. Ye all are immortal. It behoveth you not to take fright at human beings.' The celestials replied, 'The mortals have all become immortal. There is no distinction now between us and them. Vexed at the disappearance of all distinction, we have come to thee in order that thou mayest distinguish us from them.' The Creator then said, 'The son of Vivaswat is even now engaged in the grand sacrifice. It is for this that men are not dying. But when Yama's work in connection with the sacrifice terminates, men will again begin to die as before. Strengthened by your respective energies, Yama will, when that time comes, sweep away by thousands the inhabitants on earth who will scarcely have then any energy left in them.'

"Vyasa continued, 'Hearing these words of the first-born deity, the celestials returned to the spot where the grand sacrifice was being performed. And the mighty one sitting by the side of the Bhagirathi saw a (golden) lotus being carried along by the current. And beholding that (golden) lotus, they wondered much. And amongst them, that foremost of celestials, viz., Indra, desirous of ascertaining whence it came, proceeded up along the course of the Bhagirathi. And reaching that spot whence the goddess Ganga issues perennially, Indra beheld a woman possessing the splendour of fire. The woman who had come there to take water was washing in the stream, weeping all the while. The tear-drops she shed, falling on the stream, were being transformed into golden lotuses. The wielder of the thunderbolt, beholding that wonderful sight, approached the woman and asked her, 'Who art thou, amiable lady? Why dost thou weep? I desire to know the truth. O, tell me everything.'

"Vyasa continued, 'The woman thereupon answered, 'O Sakra, thou mayest know who I am and why, unfortunate that I am, I weep, if only, O chief of the celestials, thou comest with me as I lead the way. Thou shall then see what it is I weep for." Hearing these words of the lady, Indra followed her as she led the way. And soon he saw, not far off from where he was, a handsome youth with a young lady seated on a throne placed on one of the peaks of Himavat and playing at dice. Beholding that youth, the chief of the celestials said, 'Know, intelligent youth, that this universe is under my sway.' Seeing, however, that the person addressed was so engrossed in dice that he took no notice of what he said, Indra was possessed by anger and repeated, 'I am the lord of the universe.' The youth who was none else than the god Mahadeva (the god of the gods), seeing Indra filled with wrath, only smiled, having cast a glance at him. At that glance, however, the chief of the celestials was at once paralysed and stood there like a stake. When the game at dice was over, Isana addressing the weeping woman said, 'Bring Sakra hither, for I shall soon so deal with him that pride may not again enter his heart.' As soon as Sakra was touched by that woman, the chief of the celestials with limbs paralysed by that touch, fell down on the earth. The illustrious Isana of fierce energy then said unto him, 'Act not, O Sakra, ever again in this way. Remove this huge stone, for thy strength and energy are immeasurable, and enter the hole (it will disclose) where await some others possessing the splendour of the sun and who are all like unto thee.' Indra, then, on removing that stone, beheld a cave in the breast of that king of mountains, within which were four others resembling himself. Beholding their plight, Sakra became seized with grief and exclaimed, 'Shall I be even like these?' Then the god Girisha, looking full at Indra with expanded eyes, said in anger, 'O thou of a hundred sacrifices, enter this cave without loss of time, for thou hast from folly insulted me.' Thus addressed by the lord Isana, the chief of the celestials, in consequence of that terrible imprecation, was deeply pained, and with limbs weakened by fear trembled like the wind-shaken leaf of a Himalayan fig. And cursed unexpectedly by the god owning a bull for his vehicle, Indra, with joined hands and shaking from head to foot, addressed that fierce god of multi-form manifestations, saying, 'Thou art, O Bhava, the over-looker of the infinite Universe!' Hearing these words the god of fiery energy smiled and said, 'Those that are of disposition like thine never obtain my grace. These others (within the cave) had at one time been like thee. Enter thou this cave, therefore, and lie there for some time. The fate of you all shall certainly be the same. All of you shall have to take your birth in the world of men, where, having achieved many difficult feats and slaying a large number of men, ye shall again by the merits of your respective deeds, regain the valued region of Indra. Ye shall accomplish all I have said and much more besides, of other kinds of work.' Then those Indras, of their shorn glory said, 'We shall go from our celestial regions even unto the region of men where salvation is ordained to be difficult of acquisition. But let the gods Dharma, Vayu, Maghavat, and the twin Aswins beget us upon our would-be mother. Fighting with men by means of both celestial and human weapons, we shall again come back into the region of Indra.'

"Vyasa continued, 'Hearing these words of the former Indras, the wielder of the thunderbolt once more addressed that foremost of gods, saying, 'Instead of going myself, I shall, with a portion of my energy, create from myself a person for the accomplishment of the task (thou assignest) to form the fifth among these!' Vishwabhuk, Bhutadhaman, Sivi of great energy, Santi the fourth, and Tejaswin, these it is said were the five Indras of old. And the illustrious god of the formidable bow, from his kindness, granted unto the five Indras the desire they cherished. And he also appointed that woman of extraordinary beauty, who was none else than celestial Sri (goddess of grace) herself, to be their common wife in the world of men. Accompanied by all those Indras, the god Isana then went unto Narayana of immeasurable energy, the Infinite, the Immaterial, the Uncreate, the Old, the Eternal, and the Spirit of these universes without limits. Narayana approved of everything. Those Indras then were born in the world of men. And Hari (Narayana) took up two hairs from his body, one of which hairs was black and the other white. And those two hairs entered the wombs of two of the Yadu race, by name Devaki and Rohini. And one of these hairs viz., that which was white, became Valadeva. And the hair that was black was born as Kesava's self, Krishna. And those Indras of old who had been confined in the cave on the Himavat are none else than the sons of Pandu, endued with great energy. And Arjuna amongst the Pandavas, called also Savyasachin (using both hands with equal dexterity) is a portion of Sakra.'

"Vyasa continued, 'Thus, O king, they who have been born as the Pandavas are none else than those Indras of old. And the celestial Sri herself who had been appointed as their wife is this Draupadi of extraordinary beauty. How could she whose effulgence is like that of the sun or the moon, whose fragrance spreads for two miles around, take her birth in any other than an extraordinary way, viz., from within the earth, by virtue of the sacrificial rites? Unto thee, O king, I cheerfully grant this other boon in the form of spiritual sight. Behold now the sons of Kunti endued with their sacred and celestial bodies of old!'

"Vaisampayana continued, 'Saying this, that sacred Brahmana Vyasa of generous deeds, by means of his ascetic power, granted celestial sight unto the king. Thereupon the king beheld all the Pandavas endued with their former bodies. And the king saw them possessed of celestial bodies, with golden crowns and celestial garlands, and each resembling Indra himself, with complexions radiant as fire or the sun, and decked with every ornament, and handsome, and youthful, with broad chests and statures measuring about five cubits. Endued with every accomplishment, and decked with celestial robes of great beauty and fragrant garlands of excellent making the king beheld them as so many three-eyed gods (Mahadeva), or Vasus, or Rudras, or Adityas themselves. And observing the Pandavas in the forms of those Indras of old, and Arjuna also in the form of Indra sprung from Sakra himself, king Drupada was highly pleased. And the monarch wondered much on beholding that manifestation of celestial power under deep disguise. The king looking at his daughter, that foremost of women endued with great beauty, like unto a celestial damsel and possessed of the splendour of fire or the moon, regarded her as the worthy wife of those celestial beings, for her beauty, splendour and fame. And beholding that wonderful sight, the monarch touched the feet of Satyavati's son, exclaiming, 'O great Rishi, nothing is miraculous in thee!' The Rishi then cheerfully continued, 'In a certain hermitage there was an illustrious Rishi's daughter, who, though handsome and chaste, obtained not a husband. The maiden gratified, by severe ascetic penances, the god Sankara (Mahadeva). The lord Sankara, gratified at her penances, told her himself, 'Ask thou the boon thou desirest.' Thus addressed, the maiden repeatedly said unto the boon-giving Supreme Lord, 'I desire to obtain a husband possessed of every accomplishment.' Sankara, the chief of the gods, gratified with her, gave her the boon she asked, saying, 'Thou shall have, amiable maiden, five husbands.' The maiden, who had succeeded in gratifying the god, said again, 'O Sankara, I desire to have from thee only one husband possessed of every virtue?' The god of gods, well-pleased with her, spake again, saying, 'Thou hast, O maiden, addressed me five full times, repeating, 'Give me a husband.' Therefore, O amiable one, it shall even be as thou hast asked. Blessed be thou. All this, however, will happen in a future life of thine!'

"Vyasa continued, 'O Drupada, this thy daughter of celestial beauty is that maiden. Indeed, the faultless Krishna sprung from Prishata's race hath been pre-ordained to become the common wife of five husbands. The celestial Sri, having undergone severe ascetic penances, hath, for the sake of the Pandavas, had her birth as thy daughter, in the course of thy grand sacrifice. That handsome goddess, waited upon by all the celestials, as a consequence of her own acts becomes the (common) wife of five husbands. It is for this that the self-create had created her. Having listened to all this, O king Drupada, do what thou desirest.'"

SECTION CC
(Vaivahika Parva continued)

"Vaisampayana said, 'Drupada, on hearing this, observed, O great Rishi, it was only when I had not heard this from thee that I had sought to act in the way I told thee of. Now, however, that I know all, I cannot be indifferent to what hath been ordained by the gods. Therefore do I resolve to accomplish what thou hast said. The knot of destiny cannot be untied. Nothing in this world is the result of our own acts. That which had been appointed by us in view of securing one only bridegroom hath now terminated in favour of many. As Krishna (in a former life) had repeatedly said, 'O, give me a husband!' the great god himself even gave her the boon she had asked. The god himself knows the right or wrong of this. As regards myself, when Sankara hath ordained so, right or wrong, no sin can attach to me. Let these with happy hearts take, as ordained, the hand of Krishna with the rites.'

"Vaisampayana continued, 'Then the illustrious Vyasa, addressing Yudhishthira the just, said, 'This day is an auspicious day, O son of Pandu! This day the moon has entered the constellation called Pushya. Take thou the hand of Krishna today, thyself first before thy brothers!' When Vyasa had said so, king Yajnasena and his son made preparations for the wedding. And the monarch kept ready various costly articles as marriage presents. Then he brought out his daughter Krishna, decked, after a bath, with many jewels and pearls. Then there came to witness the wedding all the friends and relatives of the king, ministers of state, and many Brahmanas and citizens. And they all took their seats according to their respective ranks. Adorned with that concourse of principal men, with its yard decked with lotuses and lilies scattered thereupon, and beautified with lines of troops, king Drupada's palace, festooned around with diamonds and precious stones, looked like the firmament studded with brilliant stars. Then those princes of the Kuru line, endued with youth and adorned with ear-rings, attired in costly robes and perfumed with sandal-paste, bathed and performed the usual religious rites and accompanied by their priest Dhaumya who was possessed of the splendour of fire, entered the wedding hall one after another in due order, and with glad hearts, like mighty bulls entering a cow-pen. Then Dhaumya, well- conversant with the Vedas, igniting the sacred fire, poured with due mantras libations of clarified butter into that blazing element. And calling Yudhishthira there, Dhaumya, acquainted with mantras, united him with Krishna. Walking round the fire the bridegroom and the bride took each other's hand. After their union was complete, the priest Dhaumya, taking leave of Yudhishthira, that ornament of battles, went out of the palace. Then those mighty car-warriors,—those perpetuators of the Kuru line,—those princes attired in gorgeous dresses, took the hand of that best of women, day by day in succession, aided by that priest. O king, the celestial Rishi told me of a very wonderful and extraordinary thing in connection with these marriages, viz., that the illustrious princess of slender waist regained her virginity every day after a previous marriage. After the weddings were over, king Drupada gave unto those mighty car- warriors diverse kinds of excellent wealth. And the king gave unto them one hundred cars with golden standards, each drawn by four steeds with golden bridles. And he gave them one hundred elephants all possessing auspicious marks on their temples and faces and like unto a hundred mountains with golden peaks. He also gave them a hundred female servants all in the prime of youth and clad in costly robes and ornaments and floral wreaths. And the illustrious monarch of the Lunar race gave unto each of those princes of celestial beauty, making the sacred fire a witness of his gifts, much wealth and many costly robes and ornaments of great splendour. The sons of Pandu endued with great strength, after their wedding were over, and after they had obtained Krishna like unto a second Sri along with great wealth, passed their days in joy and happiness, like so many Indras, in the capital of the king of the Panchalas,'"

SECTION CCI
(Vaivahika Parva continued)

"Vaisampayana said, 'King Drupada, after his alliance with the Pandavas, had all his fears dispelled. Indeed, the monarch no longer stood in fear even of the gods. The ladies of the illustrious Drupada's household approached Kunti and introduced themselves unto her, mentioning their respective names, and worshipped her feet with heads touching the ground. Krishna also, attired in red silk and her wrists still encircled with the auspicious thread, saluting her mother-in-law with reverence, stood contentedly before her with joined palms. Pritha, out of affection, pronounced a blessing upon her daughter-in-law endued with great beauty and every auspicious mark and possessed of a sweet disposition and good character, saying, 'Be thou unto thy husband as Sachi unto Indra, Swaha unto Vibhavasu, Rohini unto Soma, Damayanti unto Nala, Bhadra unto Vaisravana, Arundhati unto Vasishtha, Lakshmi unto Narayana! O amiable one, be thou the mother of long-lived and heroic children, and possessed of everything that can make thee happy! Let luck and prosperity ever wait on thee! Wait thou ever on husbands engaged in the performance of grand sacrifices. Be thou devoted to thy husbands. And let thy days be ever passed in duly entertaining and reverencing guests and strangers arrived at thy abode, and the pious and the old; children and superiors. Be thou installed as the Queen of the kingdom and the capital of Kurujangala, with thy husband Yudhishthira the just! O daughter, let the whole earth, conquered by the prowess of thy husbands endued with great strength, be given away by thee unto Brahmanas at horse-sacrifice! O accomplished one whatever gems there are on earth possessed of superior virtues, obtain them, O lucky one, and be thou happy for a full hundred years! And, O daughter-in-law, as I rejoice today beholding thee attired in red silk, so shall I rejoice again, when, O accomplished one, I behold thee become the mother of a son!'

"Vaisampayana continued, 'After the sons of Pandu had been married, Hari (Krishna) sent unto them (as presents) various gold ornaments set with pearls and black gems (lapis lazuli). And Madhava (Krishna) also sent unto them costly robes manufactured in various countries, and many beautiful and soft blankets and hides of great value, and many costly beds and carpets and vehicles. He also sent them vessels by hundreds, set with gems and diamonds. And Krishna also gave them female servants by thousands, brought from various countries, and endued with beauty, youth and accomplishments and decked with every ornament. He also gave them many well-trained elephants brought from the country of Madra, and many excellent horses in costly harness, cars drawn by horses of excellent colours and large teeth. The slayer of Madhu, of immeasurable soul, also sent them coins of pure gold by crores upon crores in separate heaps. And Yudhishthira the just, desirous of gratifying Govinda, accepted all those presents with great joy.'"

SECTION CCII
(Viduragamana Parva)

"Vaisampayana said, 'The news was carried unto all the monarchs (who had come to the Self-choice of Draupadi) by their trusted spies that the handsome Draupadi had been united in marriage with the sons of Pandu. And they were also informed that the illustrious hero who had bent the bow and shot the mark was none else than Arjuna, that foremost of victorious warriors and first of all wielders of the bow and arrows. And it became known that the mighty warrior who had dashed Salya, the king of Madra, on the ground, and who in wrath had terrified the assembled monarchs by means of the tree (he had uprooted), and who had taken his stand before all foes in perfect fearlessness, was none else than Bhima, that feller of hostile ranks, whose touch alone was sufficient to take the lives out of all foes. The monarchs, upon being informed that the Pandavas had assumed the guise of peaceful Brahmanas, wondered much. They even heard that Kunti with all her sons had been burnt to death in the conflagration of the house of lac. They, therefore, now regarded the Pandavas in the light of persons who had come back from the region of the dead. And recollecting the cruel scheme contrived by Purochana, they began to say, 'O, fie on Bhishma, fie on Dhritarashtra of the Kuru race!'

"After the Self-choice was over, all the monarchs (who had come thither), hearing that Draupadi had been united with the Pandavas, set out for their own dominions. And Duryodhana, hearing that Draupadi had selected the owner of white steeds (Arjuna) as her lord, became greatly depressed. Accompanied by his brothers, Aswatthaman, his uncle (Sakuni), Karna and Kripa the prince set out with a heavy heart for his capital. Then Duhsasana, blushing with shame, addressed his brother softly and said, 'If Arjuna had not disguised himself as a Brahmana, he could never have succeeded in obtaining Draupadi. It was for this disguise, O king, that no one could recognise him as Dhananjaya. Fate, I ween, is ever supreme. Exertion is fruitless; fie on our exertions, O brother! The Pandavas are still alive!' Speaking unto one another thus and blaming Purochana (for his carelessness), they then entered the city of Hastinapura, with cheerless and sorrowful hearts. Beholding the mighty sons of Pritha, escaped from the burning house of lac and allied with Drupada, and thinking of Dhrishtadyumna and Sikhandin and the other sons of Drupada all accomplished in fight, they were struck with fear and overcome with despair.

"Then Vidura, having learnt that Draupadi had been won by the Pandavas and that the sons of Dhritarashtra had come back (to Hastinapura) in shame, their pride humiliated, became filled with joy. And, O king, approaching Dhritarashtra, Kshattri said, 'The Kurus are prospering by good luck!' Hearing those words of Vidura, the son of Vichitravirya, wondering, said in great glee, 'What good luck, O Vidura! What good luck!' From ignorance, the blind monarch understood that his eldest son Duryodhana had been chosen by Drupada's daughter as her lord. And the king immediately ordered various ornaments to be made for Draupadi. And he commanded that both Draupadi and his son Duryodhana should be brought with pomp to Hastinapura. It was then that Vidura told the monarch that Draupadi had chosen the Pandavas for her lords, and that those heroes were all alive and at peace, and that they had been received with great respect by king Drupada. And he also informed Dhritarashtra that the Pandavas had been united with the many relatives and friends of Drupada, each owning large armies, and with many others who had come to that self-choice.

"Hearing these words of Vidura, Dhritarashtra said, 'Those children are to me as dear as they were to Pandu. Nay, more. O listen to me why my affection for them now is even greater! The heroic sons of Pandu are well and at ease. They have obtained many friends. Their relatives, and others whom they have gained as allies, are all endued with great strength. Who amongst monarchs in prosperity or adversity would not like to have Drupada with his relatives as an ally?'

"Vaisampayana continued, 'Having heard these words of the monarch, Vidura said, 'O king, let thy understanding remain so without change for a hundred years!' Having said this Vidura returned to his own abode. Then, O monarch, there came unto Dhritarashtra, Duryodhana and the son of Radha, Karna. Addressing the monarch, they said, 'We cannot, O king, speak of any transgression in the presence of Vidura! We have now found thee alone, and will, therefore, say all we like! What is this that thou hast, O monarch, desired to do? Dost thou regard the prosperity of thy foes as if it were thy own, that thou hast been applauding the Pandavas, O foremost of men, in the presence of Vidura? O sinless one, thou actest not, O king, in the way thou shouldst! O father, we should now act every day in such a way as to weaken (the strength of) the Pandavas. The time hath come, O father, for us to take counsel together, so that the Pandavas may not swallow us all with our children and friends and relatives.'"

SECTION CCIII
(Viduragamana Parva continued)

"Vaisampayana said, 'Dhritarashtra replied saying, I desire to do exactly what you would recommend. But I do not wish to inform Vidura of it even by a change of muscle. It was, therefore, O son, that I was applauding the Pandavas in Vidura's presence, so that he might not know even by a sign what is in my mind. Now that Vidura hath gone away, this is the time, O Suyodhana (Duryodhana), for telling me what thou hast hit upon, and what, O Radheya (Karna), thou too hast hit upon.'

"Duryodhana said. 'Let us, O father, by means of trusted and skilful and adroit Brahmanas, seek to produce dissensions between the sons of Kunti and Madri. Or, let king Drupada and his sons, and all his ministers of state, be plied with presents of large wealth, so that they may abandon the cause of Yudhishthira, the son of Kunti. Or, let our spies induce the Pandavas to settle in Drupada's dominions, by describing to them, separately, the inconvenience of residing in Hastinapura, so that, separated from as, they may permanently settle in Panchala. Or, let some clever spies, full of resources, sowing the seeds of dissension among the Pandavas, make them jealous of one another. Or, let them incite Krishna against her husbands. She has many lords and this will not present any difficulty. Or, let some seek to make the Pandavas themselves dissatisfied with Krishna, in which case Krishna also will be dissatisfied with them. Or, let, O king, some clever spies, repairing thither, secretly compass the death of Bhimasena. Bhima is the strongest of them all. Relying upon Bhima alone, the Pandavas used to disregard us, of old. Bhima is fierce and brave and the (sole) refuge of the Pandavas. If he be slain, the others will be deprived of strength and energy. Deprived of Bhima who is their sole refuge, they will no longer strive to regain their kingdom. Arjuna, O king, is invincible in battle, if Bhima protecteth him from behind. Without Bhima, Arjuna is not equal to even a fourth part of Radheya. Indeed, O king, the Pandavas conscious of their own feebleness without Bhima and of our strength would not really strive to recover the kingdom. Or, if, O monarch, coming hither, they prove docile and obedient to us, we would then seek to repress them according to the dictates of political science (as explained by Kanika). Or, we may tempt them by means of handsome girls, upon which the princess of Panchala will get annoyed with them. Or, O Radheya, let messengers be despatched to bring them hither, so that, when arrived, we may through trusted agents, by some of the above methods, cause them to be slain. Strive, O father, to employ any of these (various) methods that may appear to thee faultless. Time passeth. Before their confidence in king Drupada—that bull amongst kings—is established we may succeed, O monarch, to encounter them. But after their confidence hath been established in Drupada, we are sure to fail. These, O father, are my views for the discomfiture of the Pandavas. Judge whether they be good or bad. What, O Karna, dost thou think?'"

SECTION CCIV
(Viduragamana Parva continued)

"Vaisampayana said, 'Thus addressed by Duryodhana, Karna said, 'It doth not seem to me, O Duryodhana, that thy reasoning is well-founded. O perpetuator of the Kuru race, no method will succeed against the Pandavas. O brave prince, thou hast before, by various subtle means, striven to carry out thy wishes. But ever hast thou failed to slay thy foes. They were then living near thee, O king! They were then unfledged and of tender years, but thou couldst not injure them then. They are now living at a distance, grown up, full-fledged. The sons of Kunti, O thou of firm resolution, cannot now be injured by any subtle contrivances of thine. This is my opinion. As they are aided by the very Fates, and as they are desirous of regaining their ancestral kingdom, we can never succeed in injuring them by any means in our power. It is impossible to create disunion amongst them. They can never be disunited who have all taken to a common wife. Nor can we succeed in estranging Krishna from the Pandavas by any spies of ours. She chose them as her lords when they were in adversity. Will she abandon them now that they are in prosperity? Besides women always like to have many husbands, Krishna hath obtained her wish. She can never be estranged from the Pandavas. The king of Panchala is honest and virtuous; he is not avaricious. Even if we offer him our whole kingdom he will not abandon the Pandavas. Drupada's son also possesseth every accomplishment, and is attached to the Pandavas. Therefore, I do not think that the Pandavas can now be injured by any subtle means in thy power. But, O bull amongst men, this is what is good and advisable for us now, viz., to attack and smite them till they are exterminated. Let this course recommend itself to thee. As long as our party is strong and that of the king of the Panchalas is weak, so long strike them without any scruple. O son of Gandhari, as long as their innumerable vehicles and animals, friends, and friendly tribes are not mustered together, continue, O king, to exhibit thy prowess. As long as the king of the Panchalas together with his sons gifted with great prowess, setteth not his heart upon fighting with us, so long, O king, exhibit thy prowess. And, O king, exert thy prowess before he of the Vrishni race (Krishna) cometh with the Yadava host into the city of Drupada, carrying everything before him, to restore the Pandavas to their paternal kingdom. Wealth, every article of enjoyment, kingdom, there is nothing that Krishna may not sacrifice for the sake of the Pandavas. The illustrious Bharata had acquired the whole earth by his prowess alone. Indra hath acquired sovereignty of the three worlds by prowess alone. O king, prowess is always applauded by the Kshatriyas. O bull amongst Kshatriyas, prowess is the cardinal virtue of the brave. Let us, therefore, O monarch, with our large army consisting of four kinds of forces, grind Drupada without loss of time, and bring hither the Pandavas. Indeed, the Pandavas are incapable of being discomfited by any policy of conciliation, of gift, of wealth and bribery, or of disunion. Vanquish them, therefore, by thy prowess. And vanquishing them by thy prowess, rule thou this wide earth. O monarch, I see not any other means by which we may accomplish our end.'

"Vaisampayana continued, 'Hearing these words of Radheya, Dhritarashtra, endued with great strength, applauded him highly. The monarch then addressed him and said, 'Thou, O son of a Suta, art gifted with great wisdom and accomplished in arms. This speech, therefore, favouring the exhibition of prowess suiteth thee well. But let Bhishma, and Drona, and Vidura, and you two, take counsel together and adopt that proposal which may lead to our benefit.'

Vaisampayana continued, '"Then king Dhritarashtra called unto him, all those celebrated ministers and took counsel with them.'"

SECTION CCV
(Viduragamana Parva continued)

"Vaisampayana said, 'Asked by Dhritarashtra to give his opinion, Bhishma replied, 'O Dhritarashtra, a quarrel with the Pandavas is what I can never approve of. As thou art to me, so was Pandu without doubt. And the sons of Gandhari are to me, as those of Kunti. I should protect them as well as I should thy sons, O Dhritarashtra! And, O king, the Pandavas are as much near to me as they are to prince Duryodhana or to all the other Kurus. Under these circumstances a quarrel with them is what I never like. Concluding a treaty with those heroes, let half the land be given unto them. This is without doubt, the paternal kingdom of those foremost ones of the Kuru race. And, O Duryodhana, like thee who lookest upon this kingdom as thy paternal property, the Pandavas also look upon it as their paternal possession. If the renowned sons of Pandu obtain not the kingdom, how can it be thine, or that of any other descendant of the Bharata race? If thou regardest thyself as one that hath lawfully come into the possession of the kingdom, I think they also may be regarded to have lawfully come into the possession of this kingdom before thee. Give them half the kingdom quietly. This, O tiger among men, is beneficial to all. If thou actest otherwise, evil will befall us all. Thou too shall be covered with dishonour. O Duryodhana, strive to maintain thy good name. A good name is, indeed, the source of one's strength. It hath been said that one liveth in vain whose reputation hath gone. A man, O Kaurava, doth not die so long as his fame lasteth. One liveth as long as one's fame endureth, and dieth when one's fame is gone. Follow thou, O son of Gandhari, the practice that is worthy of the Kuru race. O thou of mighty arms, imitate thy own ancestors. We are fortunate that the Pandavas have not perished. We are fortunate that Kunti liveth. We are fortunate that the wretch Purochana without being able to accomplish his purpose hath himself perished. From that time when I heard that the sons of Kuntibhoja's daughter had been burnt to death, I was, O son of Gandhari, ill able to meet any living creature. O tiger among men, hearing of the fate that overtook Kunti, the world doth not regard Purochana so guilty as it regardeth thee. O king, the escape, therefore, of the sons of Pandu with life from that conflagration and their re-appearance, do away with thy evil repute. Know, O thou of Kuru's race, that as long as those heroes live, the wielder of the thunder himself cannot deprive them of their ancestral share in the kingdom. The Pandavas are virtuous and united. They are being wrongly kept out of their equal share in the kingdom. If thou shouldst act rightly, if thou shouldst do what is agreeable to me, if thou shouldst seek the welfare of all, then give half the kingdom unto them.'"

SECTION CCVI
(Viduragamana Parva continued)

"Vaisampayana said, 'After Bhishma had concluded, Drona spoke, saying, 'O king Dhritarashtra, it hath been heard by us that friends summoned for consultation should always speak what is right, true, and conductive to fame. O sire, I am of the same mind in this matter with the illustrious Bhishma. Let a share of the kingdom be given unto the Pandavas. This is eternal virtue. Send, O Bharata, unto Drupada without loss of time some messenger of agreeable speech, carrying with him a large treasure for the Pandavas. And let the man go unto Drupada carrying costly presents for both the bridegrooms and the bride, and let him speak unto that monarch of thy increase of power and dignity arising from this new alliance with him. And, O monarch, let the man know also that both thyself and Duryodhana have become exceedingly glad in consequence of what hath happened. Let him say this repeatedly unto Drupada and Dhrishtadyumna. And let him speak also about the alliance as having been exceedingly proper, and agreeable unto thee, and of thyself being worthy of it. And let the man repeatedly propitiate the sons of Kunti and those of Madri (in proper words). And at thy command, O king, let plenty of ornaments of pure gold be given unto Draupadi. And let, O bull of Bharata's race, proper presents be given unto all the sons of Drupada. Let the messenger then propose the return of the Pandavas to Hastinapura. After the heroes will have been permitted (by Drupada), to come hither, let Duhsasana and Vikarna go out with a handsome train to receive them. And when they will have arrived at Hastinapura, let those foremost of men be received with affection by thee. And let them then be installed on their paternal throne, agreeably to the wishes of the people of the realm. This, O monarch of Bharata's race, is what I think should be thy behaviour towards the Pandavas who are to thee even as thy own sons.'

"Vaisampayana continued, 'After Drona had ceased, Karna spake again, 'Both Bhishma and Drona have been pampered with wealth that is thine and favours conferred by thee! They are also always regarded by thee as thy trusted friends! What can therefore be more amusing than that they both should give thee advice which is not for thy good? How can the wise approve that advice which is pronounced good by a person speaking with wicked intent but taking care to conceal the wickedness of his heart? Indeed, in a season of distress, friends can neither benefit nor injure. Every one's happiness or the reverse dependeth on destiny. He that is wise and he that is foolish, he that is young (in years) and he that is old, he that hath allies and he that hath none, all become, it is seen everywhere, happy or unhappy at times. It hath been heard by us that there was, of old, a king by name Amvuvicha. Having his capital at Rajagriha, he was the king of all the Magadha chiefs. He never attended to his affairs. All his exertion consisted in inhaling the air. All his affairs were in the hands of his minister. And his minister, named Mahakarni, became the supreme authority in the state. Regarding himself all powerful, he began to disregard the king. And the wretch himself appropriated everything belonging unto the king, his queens and treasures and sovereignty. But the possession of all these, instead of satisfying his avarice, only served to inflame him the more. Having appropriated everything belonging to the king, he even coveted the throne. But it hath been heard by us that with all his best endeavours he succeeded not in acquiring the kingdom of the monarch, his master, even though the latter was inattentive to business and content with only breathing the air. What else can be said, O king, than that monarch's sovereignty was dependent on destiny? If, therefore, O king, this kingdom be established in thee by destiny, it will certainly continue in thee, even if the whole world were to become thy enemy! If, however, destiny hath ordained otherwise, howsoever mayest thou strive, it will not last in thee! O learned one, remembering all this, judge of the honesty or otherwise of thy advisers. Ascertain also who amongst them are wicked and who have spoken wisely and well.'

"Vaisampayana continued, 'Hearing these words of Karna, Drona replied, 'As thou art wicked it is evident thou sayest so in consequence of the wickedness of thy intent. It is for injuring the Pandavas that thou findest fault with us. But know, O Karna, what I have said is for the good of all and the prosperity of the Kuru race. If thou regardest all this as productive of evil, declare thyself what is for our good. If the good advice I have given be not followed, I think the Kurus will be exterminated in no time.'"

SECTION CCVII
(Viduragamana Parva continued)

"Vaisampayana said, 'After Drona had ceased, Vidura spoke, saying, 'O monarch, thy friends without doubt, are saying unto thee what is for thy good. But as thou art unwilling to listen to what they say, their words scarcely find a place in thy ears. What that foremost one of Kuru's race, viz., Bhishma, the son of Santanu, hath said, is excellent and is for thy good. But thou dost not listen to it. The preceptor Drona also hath said much that is for thy good which however Karna, the son of Radha, doth not regard to be such. But, O king, reflecting hard I do not find any one who is better a friend to thee than either of these two lions among men (viz., Bhishma and Drona), or any one who excels either of them in wisdom. These two, old in years, in wisdom, and in learning, always regard thee, O king, and the sons of Pandu with equal eyes. Without doubt, O king of Bharata's race, they are both, in virtue and truthfulness, not inferior to Rama, the son of Dasaratha, and Gaya. Never before did they give thee any evil advice. Thou also, O monarch, hast never done them any injury. Why should, therefore, these tigers among men, who are ever truthful, give thee wicked advice, especially when thou hast never injured them? Endued with wisdom these foremost of men, O king, will never give thee counsels that are crooked. O scion of Kuru's rate, this is my firm conviction that these two, acquainted with all rules of morality, will never, tempted by wealth, utter anything betraying a spirit of partisanship. What they have said, O Bharata, I regard highly beneficial to thee. Without doubt, O monarch, the Pandavas are thy sons as much as Duryodhana and others are. Those ministers, therefore, that give thee any counsel fraught with evil unto the Pandavas, do not really look to thy interests. If there is any partiality in thy heart, O king, for thy own children, they who by their counsel seek to bring it out, certainly do thee no good. Therefore, O king, these illustrious persons endued with great splendour, have not I think, said anything that leadeth to evil. Thou, however, dost not understand it. What these bulls among men have said regarding the invincibility of the Pandavas is perfectly true. Think not otherwise of it, O tiger among men. Blest be thou! Can the handsome Dhananjaya, the son of Pandu, using the right and the left hand with equal activity, be vanquished in battle even by Maghavat himself? Can the great Bhimasena of strong arms possessing the might of ten thousand elephants, be vanquished in battle by the immortals themselves? Who also that desireth to live can overcome in battle the twins (Nakula and Sahadeva) like unto the sons of Yama himself, and well- skilled in fight? How too can the eldest one of the Pandavas in whom patience, mercy, forgiveness, truth, and prowess always live together, be vanquished? They who have Rama (Valadeva) as their ally, and Janardana (Krishna) as their counsellor, and Satyaki as their partisan, have already defeated everybody in war. They who have Drupada for their father-in-law, and Drupada's sons—the heroic brothers, viz., Dhristadyumna and others of Prishata's race for their brothers-in-law, are certainly invincible. Remembering this, O monarch, and knowing that their claim to the kingdom is even prior to thine, behave virtuously towards them. The stain of calumny is on thee, O monarch, in consequence of that act of Purochana. Wash thyself of it now, by a kindly behaviour towards the Pandavas. This kindly behaviour of thine, O monarch, towards the Pandavas will be an act of great benefit to us, protecting the lives of us all that belong to Kuru's race, and leading to the growth of the whole Kshatriya order! We had formerly warred with king Drupada; if we can now secure him as an ally, it will strengthen our party. The Dasarhas, O king, are numerous and strong. Know where Krishna is, all of them must be, and where Krishna is, there victory also must be! O king, who, unless cursed by the gods, would seek, to effect that by means of war which can be effected by conciliation? Hearing that the sons of Pritha are alive, the citizens and other subjects of the realm have become exceedingly glad and eager for beholding them. O monarch, act in a way that is agreeable to them. Duryodhana and Karna and Sakuni, the son of Suvala, are sinful, foolish and young; listen not to them. Possessed of every virtue thou art I long ago told thee, O monarch that for Duryodhana's fault, the subjects of this kingdom would be exterminated.'"

SECTION CCVIII
(Viduragamana Parva continued)

"Vaisampayana said, 'Hearing these various speeches, Dhritarashtra said, 'The learned Bhishma, the son of Santanu, and the illustrious Rishi Drona, and thyself also (O Vidura), have said the truth and what also is most beneficial to me. Indeed, as those mighty car-warriors, the heroic sons of Kunti, are the children of Pandu, so are they, without doubt, my children according to the ordinance. And as my sons are entitled to this kingdom, so are the sons of Pandu certainly entitled to it. Therefore, hasten to bring hither the Pandavas along with their mother, treating them with affectionate consideration. O thou of Bharata's race, bring also Krishna of celestial beauty along with them. From sheer good fortune the sons of Pritha are alive; and from good fortune alone those mighty car-warriors have obtained the daughter of Drupada. It is from good fortune alone that our strength hath increased, and it is from good fortune alone that Purochana hath perished. O thou of great splendour, it is from good fortune that my great grief hath been killed!'

"Vaisampayana continued, 'Then Vidura, at the command of Dhritarashtra, repaired, O Bharata, unto Yajnasena and the Pandavas. And he repaired thither carrying with him numerous jewels and various kinds of wealth for Draupadi and the Pandavas and Yajnasena also. Arrived at Drupada's abode, Vidura conversant with every rule of morality and deep in every science, properly accosted the monarch and waited upon him. Drupada received Vidura in proper form and they both enquired after each other's welfare. Vidura then saw there the Pandavas and Vasudeva. As soon as he saw them he embraced them from affection and enquired after their well being. The Pandavas also along with Vasudeva, in due order, worshipped Vidura of immeasurable intelligence. But Vidura, O king, in the name of Dhritarashtra repeatedly enquired with great affection after their welfare. He then gave, O monarch, unto the Pandavas and Kunti and Draupadi, and unto Drupada and Drupada's sons, the gems and various kinds of wealth that the Kauravas had sent through him. Possessed of immeasurable intelligence, the modest Vidura then, in the presence of the Pandavas and Keshava, addressed the well-behaved Drupada thus:

"With thy ministers and sons, O monarch, listen to what I say. King Dhritarashtra, with ministers, sons, and friends, hath with a joyous heart, O king, repeatedly enquired after thy welfare. And, O monarch, he hath been highly pleased with this alliance with thee. So also, O king, Bhishma of great wisdom, the son of Santanu, with all the Kurus, enquired after thy welfare in every respect. Drona also of great wisdom the son of Bharadwaja and thy dear friend, embracing thee mentally, enquired of thy happiness. And, O king of Panchalas, Dhritarashtra and all the Kurus, in consequence of this alliance with thee regard themselves supremely blest. O Yajnasena, the establishment of this alliance with thee hath made them happier than if they had acquired a new kingdom. Knowing all this, O monarch, permit the Pandavas to re-visit their ancestral kingdom. The Kurus are exceedingly eager to behold the sons of Pandu. These bulls among men have been long absent (from their kingdom). They as well as Pritha must be very eager to behold their city. And all the Kuru ladies and the citizens and our subjects are eagerly waiting to behold Krishna the Panchala Princess. This, therefore, is my opinion, O monarch, that thou shouldst, without delay, permit the Pandavas to go thither with their wife. And after the illustrious Pandavas, O king, will have received thy permission to go thither, I shall send information unto Dhritarashtra by quick messengers. Then, O king, will the Pandavas set out with Kunti and Krishna.'"

SECTION CCIX
(Viduragamana Parva continued)

"Vaisampayana said, 'Hearing these words of Vidura, Drupada said, 'It is even so as thou, O Vidura of great wisdom, hast said. Venerable one, I too have been exceedingly happy in consequence of this alliance. It is highly proper that these illustrious princes should return to their ancestral kingdom. But it is not proper for me to say this myself. If the brave son of Kunti viz., Yudhishthira, if Bhima and Arjuna, if these among men, viz., the twins, themselves desire to go and if Rama (Valadeva) and Krishna, both acquainted with every rule of morality, be of the same mind, then let the Pandavas go thither. For these tigers among men (Rama and Krishna) are ever engaged in doing what is agreeable and beneficial to the sons of Pandu.'

"Hearing this, Yudhishthira said, 'We are now, O monarch, with all our younger brothers, dependent on thee. We shall cheerfully do what thou art pleased to command.'

"Vaisampayana continued, 'Then Vasudeva said, 'I am of opinion that the Pandavas should go. But we should all abide by the opinion of king Drupada who is conversant with every rule of morality.'

"Drupada then spoke, 'I certainly agree with what this foremost of men, thinketh, having regard to the circumstances. For the illustrious sons of Pandu now are to me as they are, without doubt, to Vasudeva. Kunti's son Yudhishthira himself doth not seek the welfare of the Pandavas so earnestly as, Kesava, that tiger among men.'

"Vaisampayana continued, 'Commanded by the illustrious Drupada, the Pandavas, then, O king, and Krishna and Vidura, taking with them Krishna, the daughter of Drupada, and the renowned Kunti, journeyed towards the city called after the elephant, stopping at various places along the way for purposes of pleasure and enjoyment. King Dhritarashtra, hearing that those heroes had neared the capital sent out the Kauravas to receive them. They who were thus sent out were, O Bharata, Vikarna of the great bow, and Chitrasena, and Drona that foremost of warriors, and Kripa of Gautama's line. Surrounded by these, those mighty heroes, their splendour enhanced by that throng slowly entered the city of Hastinapura. The whole city became radiant, as it were, with the gay throng of sight-seers animated by curiosity. Those tigers among men gladdened the hearts of all who beheld them. And the Pandavas, dear unto the hearts of the people, heard, as they proceeded, various exclamations with the citizens, ever desirous of obeying the wishes of those princes, loudly uttered. Some exclaimed, 'Here returns that tiger among men, conversant with all the rules of morality and who always protects us as if we were his nearest relatives.' And elsewhere they said, 'It seems that king Pandu—the beloved of his people— returneth today from the forest, doubtless to do what is agreeable to us.' And there were some that said, 'What good is not done to us today when the heroic sons of Kunti come back to our town? If we have ever given away in charity, if we have ever poured libations of clarified butter on the fire, if we have any ascetic merit, let the Pandavas, by virtue of all those acts stay in town for a hundred years.'

"At last the Pandavas, on arriving at the place, worshipped the feet of Dhritarashtra, as also those of the illustrious Bhishma. They also worshipped the feet of everybody else that deserved that honour. And they enquired after the welfare of every citizen (there present). At last, at the command of Dhritarashtra they entered the chambers that had been assigned to them.

"After they had rested there for some time, they were summoned (to the court) by king Dhritarashtra and Bhishma, the son of Santanu. When they came, king Dhritarashtra addressing Yudhishthira, said, 'Listen, O son of Kunti, with thy brothers, to what I say. Repair ye to Khandavaprastha so that no difference may arise again (between you and your cousins). If you take up your quarters there no one will be able to do you any injury. Protected by Partha (Arjuna), like the celestials by the thunderbolt, reside ye at Khandavaprastha, taking half of the kingdom.'

"Vaisampayana continued, 'Agreeing to what Dhritarashtra said, those bulls among men worshipping the king set out from Hastinapura. And content with half the kingdom, they removed to Khandavaprastha, which was in unreclaimed desert. Then those heroes of unfading splendour, viz., the Pandavas, with Krishna at their head, arriving there, beautified the place and made it a second heaven. And those mighty car-warriors, selecting with Dwaipayana's assistance a sacred and auspicious region, performed certain propitiatory ceremonies and measured out a piece of land for their city. Then surrounded by a trench wide as the sea and by walls reaching high up to the heavens and white as the fleecy clouds or the rays of the moon, that foremost of cities looked resplendent like Bhogavati (the capital of the nether kingdom) decked with the Nagas. And it stood adorned with palatial mansions and numerous gates, each furnished with a couple of panels resembling the out-stretched wings of Garuda. And it was protected with gateways looking like the clouds and high as the Mandara mountains. And well-furnished with numerous weapons of attack the missiles of the foes could not make slightest impression on them. And they were almost covered with darts and other missiles like double-tongued snakes. The turrets along the walls were filled with armed men in course of training; and the walls were lined with numerous warriors along their whole length. And there were thousands of sharp hooks and Sataghnis (machines slaying a century of warriors) and numerous other machines on the battlements. There were also large iron wheels planted on them. And with all these was that foremost of cities adorned. The streets were all wide and laid out excellently; and there was no fear in them of accident. And decked with innumerable mansions, the city became like unto Amaravati and came to be called Indraprastha (like unto Indra's city). In a delightful and auspicious part of the city rose the palace of the Pandavas filled with every kind of wealth and like unto the mansion of the celestial treasurer (Kuvera) himself. And it looked like a mass of clouds charged with lightning.

"When the city was built, there came, O king, numerous Brahmanas well- acquainted with all the Vedas and conversant with every language, wishing to dwell there. And there came also unto that town numerous merchants from every direction, in the hope of earning wealth. There also came numerous persons well-skilled in all the arts, wishing to take up their abode there. And around the city were laid out many delightful gardens adorned with numerous trees bearing both fruits and flowers. There were Amras (mango trees) and Amaratakas, and Kadamvas and Asokas, and Champakas; and Punnagas and Nagas and Lakuchas and Panasas; and Salas and Talas (palm trees) and Tamalas and Vakulas, and Ketakas with their fragrant loads; beautiful and blossoming and grand Amalakas with branches bent down with the weight of fruits and Lodhras and blossoming Ankolas; and Jamvus (blackberry trees) and Patalas and Kunjakas and Atimuktas; and Karaviras and Parijatas and numerous other kinds of trees always adorned with flowers and fruits and alive with feathery creatures of various species. And those verdant groves always resounded with the notes of maddened peacocks and Kokilas (blackbirds). And there were various pleasure-houses, bright as mirrors, and numerous bowers of creepers, and charming and artificial hillocks, and many lakes full to the brim of crystal water, and delightful tanks fragrant with lotuses and lilies and adorned with swans and ducks and chakravakas (brahminy ducks). And there were many delicious pools overgrown with fine aquatic plants. And there were also diverse ponds of great beauty and large dimension. And, O king, the joy of the Pandavas increased from day to day, in consequence of their residence in that large kingdom that was peopled with pious men.

"Thus in consequence of the virtuous behaviour of Bhishma and king Dhritarashtra towards them, the Pandavas took up their abode in Khandavaprastha. Adorned with those five mighty warriors, each equal unto Indra himself, that foremost of cities looked like Bhogavati (the capital of the nether kingdom) adorned with the Nagas. And, O monarch, having settled the Pandavas there, the heroic Krishna, obtaining their leave, came back with Rama to Dwaravati.'"

SECTION CCX
(Rajya-labha Parva)

"Janamejaya said, 'O thou possessed of ascetic wealth, what did those high- souled ones, my grandsires, the illustrious Pandavas, do, after obtaining the kingdom of Indraprastha? How did their wife Draupadi obey them all? How is it also that no dissensions arose amongst those illustrious rulers of men, all attached to one wife, viz., Krishna? O thou of the wealth of asceticism, I wish to hear everything in detail regarding the behaviour towards one another of those rulers of men after their union with Krishna.'

"Vaisampayana said, 'Those scorchers of foes, the Pandavas, having obtained their kingdom, at the command of Dhritarashtra, passed their days in joy and happiness at Khandavaprastha with Krishna. And Yudhishthira. endued with great energy and ever adhering to truth, having obtained the sovereignty, virtuously ruled the land, assisted by his brothers. And the sons of Pandu, endued with great wisdom and devoted to truth and virtue, having vanquished all their foes, continued to live there in great happiness. And those bulls among men, seated on royal seats of great value, used to discharge all the duties of government. And one day, while all those illustrious heroes were so seated, there came unto them the celestial Rishi Narada, in course of his wanderings. Beholding the Rishi, Yudhishthira offered him his own handsome seat. And after the celestial Rishi had been seated, the wise Yudhishthira duly offered him the Arghya with his own hands. And the king also informed the Rishi of the state of his kingdom. The Rishi accepting the worship, became well-pleased, and eulogising him with benedictions, commanded the king to take his seat. Commanded by the Rishi, the king took his seat. Then the king sent word unto Krishna (in the inner apartments) of the arrival of the illustrious one. Hearing of the Rishi's arrival Draupadi, purifying herself properly, came with a respectful attitude to where Narada was with the Pandavas. The virtuous princess of Panchala, worshipping the celestial Rishi's feet, stood with joined hands before him, properly veiled. The illustrious Narada, pronouncing various benedictions on her, commanded the princess to retire. After Krishna had retired, the illustrious Rishi, addressing in private all the Pandavas with Yudhishthira at their head, said, 'The renowned princess of Panchala is the wedded wife of you all. Establish a rule amongst yourselves so that disunion may not arise amongst you. There were, in former days, celebrated throughout the three worlds, two brothers named Sunda and Upasunda living together and incapable of being slain by anybody unless each slew the other. They ruled the same kingdom, lived in the same house, slept on the same bed, sat on the same seat, and ate from the same dish. And yet they killed each for the sake of Tilottama. Therefore, O Yudhishthira, preserve your friendship for one another and do that which may not produce disunion amongst you.'

"On hearing this, Yudhishthira asked, 'O great Muni, whose sons were Asuras called Sunda and Upasunda? Whence arose that dissension amongst them, and why did they slay each other? Whose daughter also was this Tilottama for whose love the maddened brothers killed each other? Was she an Apsara (water nymph) or the daughter of any celestial? O thou whose wealth is asceticism, we desire, O Brahmana, to hear in detail everything as it happened. Indeed, our curiosity hath become great.'"

SECTION CCXI
(Rajya-labha Parva continued)

"Vaisampayana said, 'Hearing these words of Yudhishthira, Narada replied, 'O son of Pritha, listen with thy brothers to me as I recite this old story, O Yudhishthira, exactly as everything happened. In olden days, a mighty Daitya named Nikumbha, endued with great energy and strength was born in the race of the great Asura, Hiranyakasipu. Unto this Nikumbha, were born two sons called Sunda and Upasunda. Both of them were mighty Asuras endued with great energy and terrible prowess. The brothers were both fierce and possessed of wicked hearts. And those Daityas were both of the same resolution, and ever engaged in achieving the same tasks and ends. They were ever sharers with each other in happiness as well as in woe. Each speaking and doing what was agreeable to the other, the brothers never were unless they were together, and never went anywhere unless together. Of exactly the same disposition and habits, they seemed to be one individual divided into two parts. Endued with great energy and ever of the same resolution in everything they undertook, the brothers gradually grew up. Always entertaining the same purpose, desirous of subjugating the three worlds, the brothers, after due initiation, went to the mountains of Vindhya. And severe were the ascetic penances they performed there. Exhausted with hunger and thirst, with matted locks on their heads and attired in barks of trees, they acquired sufficient ascetic merit at length. Besmearing themselves with dirt from head to foot, living upon air alone, standing on their toes, they threw pieces of the flesh of their bodies into the fire. Their arms upraised, and eye fixed, long was the period for which they observed their vows. And during the course of their ascetic penances, a wonderful incident occurred there. For the mountains of Vindhya, heated for a long course of years by the power of their ascetic austerities, began to emit vapour from every part of their bodies. And beholding the severity of their austerities, the celestials became alarmed. The gods began to cause numerous obstructions to impede the progress of their asceticism. The celestials repeatedly tempted the brothers by means of every precious possession and the most beautiful girls. The brothers broke not their vows. Then the celestials once more manifested, before the illustrious brothers, their powers of illusion. For it seemed their sisters, mothers, wives, and other relatives, with disordered hair and ornaments and robes, were running towards them in terror, pursued and struck by a Rakshasa with a lance in hand. And it seemed that the women implored the help of the brothers crying, 'O save us!' But all this went for nothing, for firmly wedded thereto, the brothers did not still break their vows. And when it was found that all this produced not the slightest impression on any of the two, both the women and the Rakshasa vanished from sight. At last the Grandsire himself, the Supreme Lord ever seeking the welfare of all, came unto those great Asuras and asked them to solicit the boon they desired. Then the brothers Sunda and Upasunda, both of great prowess, beholding the Grandsire, rose from their seats and waited with joined palms. And the brothers both said unto the God, 'O Grandsire, if thou hast been pleased with these our ascetic austerities, and art, O lord, propitious unto us, then let us have knowledge of all weapons and of all powers of illusion. Let us be endued with great strength, and let us be able to assume any form at will. And last of all, let us also be immortal.' Hearing these words of theirs, Brahman said, 'Except the immortality you ask for, you shall be given all that you desire. Solicit you some form of death by which you may still be equal unto the immortals. And since you have undergone these severe ascetic austerities from desire of sovereignty alone I cannot confer on you the boon of immortality. You have performed your ascetic penances even for the subjugation of the three worlds. It is for this, O mighty Daityas, that I cannot grant you what you desire.'

"Narada continued, 'Hearing these words of Brahman, Sunda and Upasunda said, 'O Grandsire, let us have no fear then from any created thing, mobile or immobile, in the three worlds, except only from each other!' The Grandsire then said, 'I grant you what you have asked for, even this your desire'. And granting them this boon, the Grandsire made them desist from their asceticism, and returned to his own region. Then the brothers, those mighty Daityas, having received those several boons became incapable of being slain by anybody in the universe. They then returned to their own abode. All their friends and relatives, beholding those Daityas of great intelligence, crowned with success in the matter of the boons they had obtained, became exceedingly glad. And Sunda and Upasunda then cut off their matted locks and wore coronets on their heads. Attired in costly robes and ornaments, they looked exceedingly handsome. They caused the moon to rise over their city every night even out of his season. And friends and relatives gave themselves up to joy and merriment with happy hearts. Eat, feed, give, make merry, sing, drink—these were the sounds heard everyday in every house. And here and there arose loud uproars of hilarity mixed with clappings of hands which filled the whole city of the Daityas, who being capable of assuming any form at will, were engaged in every kind of amusement and sport and scarcely noticed the flight of time, even regarding a whole year as a single day.'"

SECTION CCXII
(Rajya-labha Parva continued)

'Narada continued, 'As soon as those festivities came to an end, the brothers Sunda and Upasunda, desirous of the Sovereignty of the three worlds, took counsel and commanded their forces to be arranged. Obtaining the assent of their friends and relatives, of the elders of the Daitya race and of their ministers of state, and performing the preliminary rites of departure, they set out in the night when the constellation Magha was in the ascendant. The brothers set out with a large Daitya force clad in mail and armed with maces and axes and lances and clubs. The Daitya heroes set out on their expedition with joyous hearts, the charanas (bards) chanting auspicious panegyrics indicative of their future triumphs. Furious in war, the Daitya brothers, capable of going everywhere at will, ascended the skies and went to the region of the celestials. The celestials knowing they were coming and acquainted also with the boons granted unto them by the Supreme Deity left heaven and sought refuge in the region of Brahman. Endued with fierce prowess, the Daitya heroes soon subjugated the region of Indra, and vanquishing the diverse tribes of Yakshas and Rakshasas and every creature ranging the skies, came away. Those mighty car-warriors next subjugated the Nagas of the nether region, and then the inmates of the ocean and then all the tribes of the Mlechchhas. Desirous next of subjugating the whole earth, those heroes of irresistible sway, summoning their soldiers, issued these cruel commands. 'Brahmanas and royal sages (on earth) with their libations and other food offered at grand sacrifices, increase the energy and strength of the gods, as also their prosperity. Engaged in such acts, they are the enemies of the Asuras. All of us, therefore, mustering together should completely slaughter them off the face of the earth!' Ordering their soldiers thus on the eastern shore of the great ocean, and entertaining such a cruel resolution, the Asura brothers set out in all directions. And those that were performing sacrifices and the Brahmanas that were assisting at those sacrifices, the mighty brothers instantly slew. And slaughtering them with violence they departed for some other place. Whilst their soldiers threw into the water the sacrificial fires that were in the asylums of Munis with souls under complete control, the curses uttered by the illustrious Rishis in wrath, rendered abortive by the boons granted (by Brahman), affected not the Asura brothers. When the Brahmanas saw that their curses produced not the slightest effect like shafts shot at stones they fled in all directions, forsaking their rites and vows. Even those Rishis on earth that were crowned with ascetic success, and had their passions under complete control and were wholly engrossed in meditation of the Deity, from fear of the Asura brothers, fled like snakes at the approach of Vinata's son (Garuda the snake-eater). The sacred asylums were all trodden down and broken. The sacrificial jars and vessels being broken, their (sacred) contents were scattered over the ground. The whole universe became empty, as if its creatures had all been stricken down during the season of general dissolution. And, O king, after the Rishis had all disappeared and made themselves invisible both the great Asuras, resolved upon their destruction, began to assume various forms. Assuming the forms of maddened elephants with temples rent from excess of juice, the Asura pair, searching out the Rishis who had sheltered themselves in caves, sent them to the region of Yama. Sometimes becoming as lions and again as tigers and disappearing the next moment, by these and other methods the cruel couple, seeing the Rishis, slew them instantly. Sacrifice and study ceased, and kings and Brahmanas were exterminated. The earth became utterly destitute of sacrifices and festivals. And the terrified people uttered cries of Oh and Alas and all buying and selling were stopped. All religious rites ceased, and the earth became destitute of sacred ceremonies and marriages. Agriculture was neglected and cattle were no longer tended. Towns and asylums became desolate. And scattered over with bones and skeletons, the earth assumed a frightful aspect. All ceremonies in honour of the Pitris were suspended, and the sacred sound of Vashat and the whole circle of auspicious rites ceased. The earth became frightful to behold. The Sun and the Moon, the Planets and Stars, and Constellations, and the other dwellers in the firmament, witnessing these acts of Sunda and Upasunda, grieved deeply. Subjugating all the points of heaven by means of such cruel acts, the Asura brothers took up their abode in Kurukshetra, without a single rival.'"

SECTION CCXIII
(Rajya-labha Parva continued)

"Narada continued, 'Then the celestial Rishis, the Siddhas, and the high- souled Rishis possessing the attributes of tranquillity and self-restraint, beholding that act of universal slaughter, were afflicted with great grief. With passions and senses and souls under complete control, they then went to the abode of the Grandsire, moved by compassion for the universe. Arrived there, they beheld the Grandsire seated with gods, Siddhas, and Brahmarshis around him. There were present that God of gods, viz., Mahadeva, and Agni, accompanied by Vayu, and Soma and Surya and Sakra, and Rishis devoted to the contemplation of Brahma, and the Vaikhanasas, the Valakhilyas, the Vanaprasthas, the Marichipas, the Ajas, the Avimudas, and other ascetics of great energy. All those Rishis were sitting with the Grandsire, when the celestial and other Rishis, approaching Brahman with sorrowful hearts, represented unto him all the acts of Sunda and Upasunda. And they told the Grandsire in detail everything that the Asura brothers had done, and how they had done it, and in what order. Then all the celestials and the great Rishis pressed the matter before the Grandsire. The Grandsire, hearing everything they said, reflected for a moment and settled in his mind what he should do. Resolving to compass the destruction of the Asura brothers, he summoned Viswakarman (the celestial architect). Seeing Viswakarman before him, the Grandsire possessed of supreme ascetic merit commanded him, saying, 'Create thou a damsel capable of captivating all hearts.' Bowing down unto the Grandsire and receiving his command with reverence, the great artificer of the universe created a celestial maiden with careful attention. Viswakrit first collected all handsome features upon the body of the damsel he created. Indeed, the celestial maiden that he created was almost a mass of gems. And created with great care by Viswakarman, the damsel, in beauty, became unrivalled among the women of the three worlds. There was not even a minute part of her body which by its wealth of beauty could not attract the gaze of beholders. And like unto the embodied Sri herself, that damsel of extraordinary beauty captivated the eyes and hearts of every creature. And because she had been created with portions of every gem taken in minute measures, the Grandsire bestowed upon her the name of Tilottama. And as soon as he started it into life, the damsel bowed to Brahman and with joined palms said, 'Lord of every created thing, what task am I to accomplish and what have I been created for?' The Grandsire answered, 'Go, O Tilottama, unto the Asuras, Sunda and Upasunda. O amiable one, tempt them with thy captivating beauty. And, O damsel, conduct thyself there in such a way that the Asura brothers may, in consequence of the wealth of thy beauty, quarrel with each other as soon as they cast their eyes upon thee.'

"Narada continued, 'Bowing unto the Grandsire and saying, 'So be it,'—the damsel walked round the celestial conclave. The illustrious Brahman was then sitting with face turned eastwards, and Mahadeva with face also towards the east, and all the celestials with faces northwards, and the Rishis with faces towards all directions. While Tilottama walked round the conclave of the celestials, Indra and the illustrious Sthanu (Mahadeva) were the only ones that succeeded in preserving their tranquillity of mind. But exceedingly desirous as Mahadeva was (of beholding Tilottama) when the damsel (in her progress round the celestial conclave) was at his side, another face like a full-blown lotus appeared on the southern side of his body. And when she was behind him, another face appeared on the west. And when the damsel was on the northern side of the great god, a fourth face appeared on the northern side of his body. Mahadeva (who was eager to behold the damsel) came also to have a thousand eyes, each large and slightly reddish, before, behind and on his flanks. And it was thus that Sthanu the great god came to have four faces, and the slayer of Vala, a thousand eyes. And as regards the mass of the celestials and the Rishis, they turned their faces towards all directions as Tilottama walked round them. Except the divine Grandsire himself, the glances of those illustrious personages, even of all of them fell upon Tilottama's body. And when Tilottama set out (for the city of the Asuras) with the wealth of her beauty, all regarded the task as already accomplished. After Tilottama had gone away, the great god who was the First Cause of the Universe, dismissed all the celestials and the Rishis.'"

SECTION CCXIV
(Rajya-labha Parva continued)

"Narada continued, 'Meanwhile the Asura brothers having subjugated the earth were without a rival. The fatigue of exertion gone, they, having brought the three worlds under equal sway, regarded themselves as persons that had nothing more to do. Having brought all the treasures of the gods, the Gandharvas, the Yakshas, the Nagas, the Rakshasas, and the kings of the earth, the brothers began to pass their days in great happiness. When they saw they had no rivals (in the three worlds), they gave up all exertion and devoted their time to pleasure and merriment, like the celestials. They experienced great happiness by giving themselves up to every kind of enjoyment, such as women, and perfumes and floral wreaths and viands, and drinks and many other agreeable objects all in profusion. In houses and woods and gardens, on hills and in forests, wherever they liked they passed their time in pleasure and amusement, like the immortals. And it so happened that one day they went for purposes of pleasure to a tableland of the Vindhya range, perfectly level and stony, and overgrown with blossoming trees. After every object of desire, all of the most agreeable kind, had been brought, the brothers sat on an excellent seat, with happy hearts and accompanied by handsome women. And those damsels, desirous of pleasing the brothers, commenced a dance in accompaniment to music, and sweetly chanted many a song in praise of the mighty pair.'

"Meanwhile Tilottama attired in a single piece of red silk that exposed all her charms, came along, plucking wild flowers on her way. She advanced slowly to where those mighty Asuras were. The Asura brothers, intoxicated with the large portions they had imbibed, were smitten upon beholding that maiden of transcendent beauty. Leaving their seats they went quickly to where the damsel was. Both of them being under the influence of lust, each sought the maiden for himself. And Sunda seized that maid of fair brows by her right hand. Intoxicated with the boons they had obtained, with physical might, with the wealth and gems they had gathered from every quarter, and with the wine they had drunk, maddened with all these, and influenced by wishful desire, they addressed each other, each contracting his brow in anger. 'She is my wife, and therefore your superior,' said Sunda. 'She is my wife, and therefore your sister-in-law', replied Upasunda. And they said unto each other, 'She is mine not yours.' And soon they were under the influence of rage. Maddened by the beauty of the damsel, they soon forgot their love and affection for each other. Both of them, deprived of reason by passion, then took up their fierce maces. Each repeating, 'I was the first, I was the first,' (in taking her hand) struck the other. And the fierce Asuras, struck by each other with the mace, fell down upon the ground, their bodies bathed in blood, like two suns dislodged from the firmament. And beholding this, the women that had come there, and the other Asuras there present, all fled away trembling in grief and fear, and took refuge in the nether regions. The Grandsire himself of pure soul, then came there, accompanied by the celestials, and the great Rishis. And the illustrious Grandsire applauded Tilottama and expressed his wish of granting her a boon. The Supreme Deity, before Tilottama spoke, desirous of granting her a boon, cheerfully said, 'O beautiful damsel, thou shalt roam in the region of the Adityas. Thy splendour shall be so great that nobody will ever be able to look at thee for any length of time!' The Grandsire of all creatures, granting this boon unto her, establishing the three worlds in Indra as before, returned to his own region.

"Narada continued, 'It was thus that Asuras, ever united and inspired by the same purpose slew each other in wrath for the sake of Tilottama. Therefore, from affection I tell you, ye foremost ones of Bharata's line, that if you desire to do anything agreeable to me, make some such arrangements that you may not quarrel with one another for the sake of Draupadi.'

"Vaisampayana continued, 'The illustrious Pandavas, thus addressed by the great Rishi Narada, consulting with one another, established a rule amongst themselves in the presence of the celestial Rishi himself endued with immeasurable energy. And the rule they made was that when one of them would be sitting with Draupadi, any of the other four who would see that one thus must retire into the forest for twelve years, passing his days as a Brahmacharin. After the virtuous Pandavas had established that rule amongst themselves, the great Muni Narada, gratified with them, went to the place he wished. Thus, O Janamejaya, did the Pandavas urged by Narada, established a rule amongst themselves in regard to their common wife. And it was for this, O Bharata, that no dispute ever arose between them.'"

SECTION CCXV
(Arjuna-vanavasa Parva)

"Vaisampayana said, 'The Pandavas, having established such a rule, continued to reside there. By the prowess of their arms they brought many kings under their sway. And Krishna became obedient unto all the five sons of Pritha, those lions among men, of immeasurable energy. Like the river Saraswati decked with elephants, which again take pleasure in that stream, Draupadi took great delight in her five heroic husbands and they too took delight in her. And in consequence of the illustrious Pandavas being exceedingly virtuous in their practice, the whole race of Kurus, free from sin, and happy, grew in prosperity.

"After some time, O king, it so happened that certain robbers lifted the cattle of a Brahmana, and while they were carrying away the booty, the Brahmana, deprived of his senses by anger, repaired to Khandavaprastha, and began to reprove the Pandavas in accents of woe. The Brahmana said, 'Ye Pandavas, from this your dominion, my kine are even now being taken away by force by despicable and wicked wretches! Pursue ye the thieves. Alas, the sacrificial butter of a peaceful Brahmana is being taken away by crows! Alas, the wretched jackal invadeth the empty cave of a lion! A king that taketh the sixth part of the produce of the land without protecting the subject, hath been called by the wise to be the most sinful person in the whole world. The wealth of a Brahmana is being taken away by robbers! Virtue itself is sustaining a diminution! Take me up by the hand, ye Pandavas for I am plunged in grief!"

"Vaisampayana continued, 'Dhananjaya, the son of Kunti, heard those accents of the Brahmana weeping in bitter grief. As soon as he heard those accents, he loudly assured the Brahmana, saying, 'No fear!' But it so happened that the chamber where the illustrious Pandavas had their weapons was then occupied by Yudhishthira the just with Krishna. Arjuna, therefore, was incapable of entering it or, going alone with the Brahmana, though repeatedly urged (to do either) by the weeping accents of the Brahmana. Summoned by the Brahmana, Arjuna reflected, with a sorrowful heart, 'Alas, this innocent Brahmana's wealth is being robbed! I should certainly dry up his tears. He hath come to our gate, and is weeping even now. If I do not protect him, the king will be touched with sin in consequence of my indifference; our own irreligiousness will be cited throughout the kingdom, and we shall incur a great sin. If, disregarding the king, I enter the chamber, without doubt I shall be behaving untruthfully towards the monarch without a foe. By entering the chamber, again, I incur the penalty of an exile in the woods. But I must overlook everything. I care not if I have to incur sin by disregarding the king. I care not if I have to go to the woods and die there. Virtue is superior to the body and lasteth after the body hath perished!' Dhananjaya, arriving at this resolution, entered the chamber and talked with Yudhishthira. Coming out with the bow, he cheerfully told the Brahmana, 'Proceed, O Brahmana, with haste, so that those wretched robbers may not go much ahead of us. I shall accompany thee and restore unto thee thy wealth that hath fallen into the hands of the thieves.' Then Dhananjaya, capable of using both his arms with equal skill, armed with the bow and cased in mail and riding in his war-chariot decked with a standard, pursued the thieves, and piercing them with his arrows, compelled them to give up the booty. Benefiting the Brahmana thus by making over to him his kine, and winning great renown, the hero returned to the capital. Bowing unto all the elders, and congratulated by everybody, Partha at last approached Yudhishthira, and addressing him, said, 'Give me leave, O lord, to observe the vow I took. In beholding thee sitting with Draupadi, I have violated the rule established by ourselves. I shall therefore go into the woods, for this is even our understanding.' Then Yudhishthira, suddenly hearing those painful words, became afflicted with grief, and said in an agitated voice, 'Why!' A little while after, king Yudhishthira in grief said unto his brother Dhananjaya of curly hair who never departed from his vows, these words, 'O sinless one, if I am an authority worthy of regard, listen to what I say. O hero, full well do I know the reason why thou hadst entered my chamber and didst what thou regardest to be an act disagreeable to me. But there is no displeasure in my mind. The younger brother may, without fault, enter the chamber where the elder brother sitteth with his wife. It is only the elder brother that acts against the rules of propriety by entering the room where the younger brother sitteth with his wife. Therefore, O thou of mighty arms, desist from thy purpose. Do what I say. Thy virtue hath sustained no diminution. Thou hast not disregarded me.'

"Arjuna, hearing this, replied, 'I have heard, even from thee, that quibbling is not permitted in the discharge of duty. I cannot waver from truth. Truth is my weapon.'

"Vaisampayana continued, 'Obtaining then the king's permission, Arjuna prepared himself for a forest-life; and he went to the forest to live there for twelve years.'"

SECTION CCXVI
(Arjuna-vanavasa Parva continued)

"Vaisampayana said, 'When that spreader of the renown of Kuru's race, the strong-armed Arjuna, set out (for the forest), Brahmanas conversant with the Vedas walked behind that illustrious hero to a certain distance. Followed by Brahmanas conversant with the Vedas and their branches and devoted to the contemplation of the Supreme Spirit, by persons skilled in music, by ascetics devoted to the Deity, by reciters of Puranas, by narrators of sacred stories by devotees leading celibate lives, by Vanaprasthas, by Brahmanas sweetly reciting celestial histories, and by various other classes of persons of sweet speeches, Arjuna journeyed like Indra followed by the Maruts. And, O thou of Bharata's race, that bull among the Bharatas saw, as he journeyed, many delightful and picturesque forests, lakes, rivers, seas, provinces, and waters. At length, on arriving at the source of the Ganges the mighty hero thought of settling there.

"Listen now, O Janamejaya, to a wonderful feat which that foremost of the sons of Pandu, of high soul, did, while living there. When that son of Kunti, O Bharata, and the Brahmanas who had followed him, took up their residence in that region, the latter performed innumerable Agnihotras (sacrificial rites by igniting the sacred fire). And, O king, in consequence of those learned vow-observing, and illustrious Brahmanas, who never deviated from the right path, daily establishing and igniting with mantras on the banks of that sacred stream, after the performance of their ablutions, fires for their sacrifices, and pouring libations of clarified butter into the same, and worshipping those fires with offerings of flowers, that region itself where the Ganges entered the plains became exceedingly beautiful. One day that bull amongst the Pandavas, while residing in that region in the midst of those Brahmanas, descended (as usual) into the Ganges to perform his ablutions. After his ablutions had been over, and after he had offered oblations of water unto his deceased ancestors, he was about to get up from the stream to perform his sacrificial rites before the fire, when the mighty-armed hero, O king, was dragged into the bottom of the water by Ulupi, the daughter of the king of the Nagas, urged by the god of desire. And it so happened that the son of Pandu was carried into the beautiful mansion of Kauravya, the king of the Nagas. Arjuna saw there a sacrificial fire ignited for himself. Beholding that fire, Dhananjaya, the son of Kunti performed his sacrificial rites with devotion. And Agni was much gratified with Arjuna for the fearlessness with which that hero had poured libations into his manifest form. After he had thus performed his rites before the fire, the son of Kunti, beholding the daughter of the king of the Nagas, addressed her smilingly and said, 'O handsome girl, what an act of rashness hast thou done, O timid one! Whose is this beautiful region, who art thou and whose daughter?'

"Hearing these words of Arjuna, Ulupi answered, 'There is a Naga of the name of Kauravya, born in the line of Airavata. I am, O prince, the daughter of that Kauravya, and my name is Ulupi. O tiger among men, beholding thee descend into the stream to perform thy ablutions, I was deprived of reason by the god of desire. O sinless one, I am still unmarried. Afflicted as I am by the god of desire on account of thee, O thou of Kuru's race, gratify me today by giving thyself up to me.'

"Arjuna replied, 'Commanded by king Yudhishthira, O amiable one, I am undergoing the vow of Brahmacharin for twelve years. I am not free to act in any way I like. But, O ranger of the waters, I am still willing to do thy pleasure (if I can). I have never spoken an untruth in my life. Tell me, therefore, O Naga maid, how I may act so that, while doing thy pleasure, I may not be guilty of any untruth or breach of duty.'

"Ulupi answered, 'I know, O son of Pandu, why thou wanderest over the earth, and why thou hast been commanded to lead the life of a Brahmacharin by the superior. Even this was the understanding to which all of you had been pledged, viz., that amongst you all owning Drupada's daughter as your common wife, he who would from ignorance enter the room where one of you would be sitting with her, should lead the life of a Brahmacharin in the woods for twelve years. The exile of any one amongst you, therefore, is only for the sake of Draupadi. Thou art but observing the duty arising from that vow. Thy virtue cannot sustain any diminution (by acceding to my solicitation). Then again, O thou of large eyes, it is a duty to relieve the distressed. Thy virtue suffereth no diminution by relieving me. Oh, if (by this act), O Arjuna, thy virtue doth suffer a small diminution, thou wilt acquire great merit by saving my life. Know me for thy worshipper, O Partha! Therefore, yield thyself up to me! Even this, O lord, is the opinion of the wise (viz., that one should accept a woman that wooeth). If thou do not act in this way, know that I will destroy myself. O thou of mighty arms, earn great merit by saving my life. I seek thy shelter, O best of men! Thou protectest always, O son of Kunti, the afflicted and the masterless. I seek thy protection, weeping in sorrow. I woo thee, being filled with desire. Therefore, do what is agreeable to me. It behoveth thee to gratify my wish by yielding thy self up to me.'

"Vaisampayana said, 'Thus addressed by the daughter of the king of the Nagas, the son of Kunti did everything she desired, making virtue his motive. The mighty Arjuna, spending the night in the mansion of the Naga rose with the sun in the morning. Accompanied by Ulupi he came back from the palace of Kauravya to the region where the Ganges entereth the plains. The chaste Ulupi, taking her leave there, returned to her own abode. And, O Bharata, she granted unto Arjuna a boon making him invincible in water, saying, 'Every amphibious creature shall, without doubt, be vanquishable by thee.'"

SECTION CCXVII
(Arjuna-vanavasa Parva continued)

"Vaisampayana said, 'Then the son of the wielder of the thunderbolt narrated everything unto those Brahmanas (residing with him there), set out for the breast of Himavat. Arriving at the spot called Agastyavata, he next went to Vasishtha's peak. Thence the son of Kunti proceeded to the peak of Bhrigu. Purifying himself with ablutions and rites there, that foremost of the Kurus gave away unto Brahmanas many thousands of cows and many houses. Thence that best of men proceeded to the sacred asylum called Hiranyavindu. Performing his ablutions there, that foremost of the sons of Pandu saw many holy regions. Descending from those heights that chief of men, O Bharata, accompanied by the Brahmanas, journeyed towards the east, desiring to behold the regions that lay in that direction. That foremost one of Kuru's race saw many regions of sacred waters one after another. And beholding in the forest of Naimisha the delightful river Utpalini (full of lotuses) and the Nanda and the Apara Nanda, the far-famed Kausiki, and the mighty rivers Gaya and Ganga, and all the regions of sacred water, he purified himself, O Bharata, (with the usual rites), and gave away many cows unto Brahmanas. Whatever regions of sacred waters and whatever other holy palaces there were in Vanga and Kalinga, Arjuna visited all of them. Seeing them all and performing proper ceremonies, he gave away much wealth. Then, O Bharata, all those Brahmanas following the son of Pandu, bade him farewell at the gate of the kingdom of Kalinga and desisted from proceeding with him any further. The brave Dhananjaya, the son of Kunti, obtaining their leave, went towards the ocean, accompanied by only a few attendants. Crossing the country of the Kalingas, the mighty one proceeded, seeing on his way diverse countries and sacred spots and diverse delightful mansions and houses. Beholding the Mahendra mountain adorned with the ascetics (residing there), he went to Manipura, proceeding slowly along the sea-shore. Beholding all the sacred waters and other holy places in that province, the strong-armed son of Pandu at last went, O king, to the virtuous Chitravahana, the ruler of Manipura. The king of Manipura had a daughter of great beauty named Chitrangada. And it so happened that Arjuna beheld her in her father's palace roving at pleasure. Beholding the handsome daughter of Chitravahana, Arjuna desired to possess her. Going unto the king (her father), he represented unto him what he sought. He said, 'Give away unto me thy daughter, O king! I am an illustrious Kshatriya's son.' Hearing this, the king asked him, 'Whose son art thou?' Arjuna replied, 'I am Dhananjaya, the son of Pandu and Kunti.' The king, hearing this, spoke unto him these words in sweet accents, 'There was in our race a king of the name of Prabhanjana, who was childless. To obtain a child, he underwent severe ascetic penances. By his severe asceticism, O Partha, he gratified that god of gods, Mahadeva, the husband of Uma, that supreme Lord holding (the mighty bow called) Pinaka. The illustrious Lord granted him the boon that each successive descendant of his race should have one child only. In consequence of that boon only one child is born unto every successive descendant of this race. All my ancestors (one after another) had each a male child. I, however, have only a daughter to perpetuate my race. But, O bull amongst men, I ever look upon this daughter of mine as my son. O bull of Bharata's race, I have duly made her a Putrika. Therefore, one amongst the sons that may be begotten upon her by thee, O Bharata, shall be the perpetuator of my race. That son is the dower for which I may give away my daughter. O son of Pandu, if thou choosest, thou canst take her upon this understanding.' Hearing these words of the king, Arjuna accepted them all, saying, 'So be it.' Taking Chitravahana's daughter (as his wife), the son of Kunti resided in that city for three years. When Chitrangada at last gave birth to a son, Arjuna embraced that handsome princess affectionately. And taking leave of the king (her father), he set out on his wanderings again.'"

SECTION CCXVIII
(Arjuna-vanavasa Parva continued)

"Vaisampayana said, 'Then that bull of Bharata's race went to the sacred waters on the banks of the southern ocean, all adorned with the ascetics residing there. And there lay scattered five such regions where also dwelt many ascetics. But those five waters themselves were shunned by all of them. Those sacred waters were called Agastya, and Saubhadra and Pauloma of great holiness, and Karandhama of great propitiousness yielding the fruits of a horse-sacrifice unto those that bathed there, and Bharadwaja, that great washer of sins. That foremost one among the Kurus, beholding those five sacred waters, and finding them uninhabited, and ascertaining also that they were shunned by the virtuous ascetics dwelling around, asked those pious men with joined hands, saying, 'Why O ascetics, are these five sacred waters shunned by utterers of Brahma?' Hearing him, the ascetics replied, 'There dwell in these waters five large crocodiles which take away the ascetics that may happen to bathe in them. It is for this, O son of Kuru's race, that these waters are shunned.'

"Vaisampayana continued, 'Hearing these words of the ascetics, that foremost of men endued with mighty arms, though dissuaded by them went to behold those waters. Arrived at the excellent sacred water called Saubhadra after a great Rishi, the brave scorcher of all foes suddenly plunged into it to have a bath. As soon as that tiger among men had plunged into the water a great crocodile (that was in it) seized him by the leg. But the strong-armed Dhananjaya the son of Kunti, that foremost of all men endued with might, seized that struggling ranger of the water and dragged it forcibly to the shore. But dragged by the renowned Arjuna to the land, that crocodile became (transformed into) a beautiful damsel bedecked with ornament. O king, that charming damsel of celestial form seemed to shine for her beauty and complexion. Dhananjaya, the son of Kunti, beholding that strange sight, asked that damsel with a pleased heart, 'Who art thou, O beautiful one? Why hast thou been a ranger of the waters? Why also didst thou commit such a dreadful sin?' The damsel replied, saying, 'I am, O mighty-armed one, an Apsara that sported in the celestial woods. I am, O mighty one, Varga by name, and ever dear unto the celestial treasurer (Kuvera). I have four other companions, all handsome and capable of going everywhere at will. Accompanied by them I was one day going to the abode of Kuvera. On the way we beheld a Brahmana of rigid vows, and exceedingly handsome, studying the Vedas in solitude. The whole forest (in which he was sitting) seemed to be covered with his ascetic splendour. He seemed to have illuminated the whole region like the Sun himself. Beholding his ascetic devotion of that nature and his wonderful beauty, we alighted in that region, in order to disturb his meditations. Myself and Saurabheyi and Samichi and Vudvuda and Lata, that Brahmana, O Bharata, at the same time. We began to sing and smile and otherwise tempt that Brahmana. But, O hero, that Brahmana (youth) set not his heart even once upon us. His mind fixed on pure meditation, that youth of great energy suffered not his heart to waver, O bull among Kshatriyas, the glance he cast upon us was one of wrath. And he said, staring at us, 'Becoming crocodiles, range ye the waters for a hundred years.'"

SECTION CCXIX
(Arjuna-vanavasa Parva continued)

"Vaisampayana said, 'Varga continued, 'We were then, O foremost one of Bharata's race, deeply distressed at this curse. We sought to propitiate that Brahmana of ascetic wealth that departed not from his vow. Addressing him, we said, 'Inflated with a sense of our beauty and youth, and urged by the god of desire, we have acted very improperly. It behoveth thee, O Brahmana, to pardon us! Truly, O Brahmana, it was death to us that we had at all come hither to tempt thee of rigid vows and ascetic wealth. The virtuous, however, have said that women should never be slain. Therefore grow thou in virtue. It behoveth thee not to slay us so. O thou that art conversant with virtue, it hath been said that a Brahmana is ever the friend of every creature. O thou of great prosperity, let this speech of the wise become true. The eminent always protect those that seek protection at their hands. We seek thy protection. It behoveth thee to grant us pardon.'

"Vaisampayana continued, 'Thus addressed, that Brahmana of virtuous soul and good deeds and equal in splendour, O hero, unto the sun or the moon, became propitious unto them. And the Brahmana said, 'The words hundred and hundred thousand are all indicative of eternity. The word hundred, however, as employed by me is to be understood as a limited period and not indicative of a period without end. Ye shall, therefore, becoming crocodiles, seize and take away men (for only a hundred years as explained by me). At the end of that period, an exalted individual will drag you all from water to the land. Then ye will resume your real forms. Never have I spoken an untruth even in jest. Therefore, all that I have said must come to pass. And those sacred waters (within which I assign you your places), will, after you will have been delivered by that individual, become known all over the world by the name of Nari-tirthas (or sacred waters connected with the sufferings and the deliverance of females), and all of them shall become sacred and sin cleansing in the eyes of the virtuous and the wise.'

"Vaisampayana continued, 'Varga then addressing Arjuna, finished her discourse, saying, 'Hearing these words of the Brahmana, we saluted him with reverence and walked round him. Leaving that region we came away with heavy hearts, thinking as we proceeded, 'Where shall we all soon meet with that man who will give us back our own shapes (after our transformation)?' As we were thinking of it, in almost a moment, O Bharata, we beheld even the eminent celestial Rishi Narada. Beholding that Rishi of immeasurable energy, our hearts were filled with joy. Saluting him with reverence, O Partha, we stood before him, with blushing faces. He asked of us the cause of our sorrow and we told him all. Hearing what had happened the Rishi said, 'In the low-lands bordering on the southern ocean, there are five regions of sacred water. They are delightful and eminently holy. Go ye thither without delay. That tiger among men, Dhananjaya, the son of Pandu of pure soul, will soon deliver you, without doubt, from this sad plight.' O hero, hearing the Rishi's words, all of us came hither. O sinless one, true it is that I have today been delivered by thee. But those four friends of mine are still within the other waters here. O hero, do a good deed by delivering them also.'

"Vaisampayana continued, 'Then, O monarch, that foremost of the Pandavas, endued with great prowess, cheerfully delivered all of them from that curse. Rising from the waters they all regained their own forms. Those Apsaras then, O king, all looked as before. Freeing those sacred waters (from the danger for which they had been notorious), and giving the Apsaras leave to go where they chose, Arjuna became desirous of once more beholding Chitrangada. He, therefore, proceeded towards the city of Manipura. Arrived there, he beheld on the throne the son he had begotten upon Chitrangada, and who was called by the name of Vabhruvahana. Seeing Chitrangada once more, Arjuna proceeded, O monarch, towards the spot called Gokarna.'"

SECTION CCXX
(Arjuna-vanavasa Parva continued)

"Vaisampayana said, 'Then Arjuna of immeasurable prowess saw, one after another, all the sacred waters and other holy places that were on the shores of the western ocean. Vibhatsu reached the sacred spot called Prabhasa. When the invisible Arjuna arrived at that sacred and delightful region, the slayer of Madhu

(Krishna) heard of it. Madhava soon went there to see his friend, the son of Kunti. Krishna and Arjuna met together and embracing each other enquired after each other's welfare. Those dear friends, who were none else than the Rishis Nara and Narayana of old, sat down. Vasudeva asked Arjuna about his travels, saying, 'Why, O Pandava art thou wandering over the earth, beholding all the sacred waters and other holy places?' Then Arjuna told him everything that had happened. Hearing everything, that mighty hero of Vrishni's race said, 'This is as it should be.' And Krishna and Arjuna having sported as they liked, for some time at Prabhasa, went to the Raivataka mountain to pass some days there. Before they arrived at Raivataka, that mountain had, at the command of Krishna been well-adorned by many artificers. Much food also had, at Krishna's command, been collected there. Enjoying everything that had been collected there for him, Arjuna sat with Vasudeva to see the performances of the actors and the dancers. Then the high-souled Pandava, dismissing them all with proper respect, laid himself down on a well-adorned and excellent bed. As the strong-armed one lay on that excellent bed, he described unto Krishna everything about the sacred waters, the lakes and the mountains, the rivers and the forests he had seen. While he was speaking of these, stretched upon that celestial bed, sleep, O Janamejaya, stole upon him. He rose in the morning, awakened, by sweet songs and melodious notes of the Vina (guitar) and the panegyrics and benedictions of the bards. After he had gone through the necessary acts and ceremonies, he was affectionately accosted by him of the Vrishni race. Riding upon a golden car, the hero then set out for Dwaraka, the capital of the Yadavas. And, O Janamejaya, for honouring the son of Kunti, the city of Dwaraka, was well-adorned, even all the gardens and houses within it. The citizens of Dwaraka, desirous of beholding the son of Kunti, began to pour eagerly into the public thoroughfares by hundreds of thousands. In the public squares and thoroughfares, hundreds and thousands of women, mixing with the men, swelled the great crowd of the Bhojas, the Vrishnis, and the Andhakas, that had collected there. Arjuna was welcomed with respect by all the sons of Bhojas, the Vrishnis, and the Andhakas. And he, in his turn, worshipped those that deserved his worship, receiving their blessings. The hero was welcomed with affectionate reception by all the young men of the Yadava tribe. He repeatedly embraced all that were equal to him in age. Wending then to the delightful mansion of Krishna that was filled with gems and every article of enjoyment, he took up his abode there with Krishna for many days.'"

SECTION CCXXI
(Subhadra-harana Parva)

"Vaisampayana said, 'O best of monarchs, within a few days after this, there commenced on the Raivataka mountain, a grand festival of the Vrishnis and the Andhakas. At the mountain-festival of the Bhojas, the Vrishnis and the Andhakas, the heroes of those tribes began to give away much wealth unto Brahmanas by thousands. The region around that hill, O king was adorned with many a mansion decked with gems and many an artificial tree of gaudy hue. The musicians struck up in concert and the dancers began to dance and the vocalists to sing. And the youth of the Vrishni race, endued with great energy, adorned with every ornament, and riding in their gold-decked cars, looked extremely handsome. The citizens, some on foot and some in excellent cars, with their wives and followers were there by hundreds and thousands. And there was the lord Haladhara (Valarama), roving at will, hilarious with drink, accompanied by (his wife) Revati, and followed by many musicians and vocalists. There came Ugrasena also, the powerful king of the Vrishni race, accompanied by his thousand wives and followed by sweet singers. And Raukmineya and Shamva also, ever furious in battle, roved there, excited with drink and adorned with floral wreaths of great beauty and with costly attires, and disported themselves like a pair of celestials. And Akrura and Sarana and Gada, and Vabhru, and Nisatha, and Charudeshna, and Prithu, Viprithu, and Satyaka, and Satyaki, and Bhangakara, and Maharava, and Hardikya, and Uddhava, and many others whose names are not given, accompanied by their wives that followed by bands of singers, adorned that mountain-festival. When that delightful festival of immense grandeur commenced, Vasudeva and Partha went about, together, beholding everything around. While wandering there, they saw the handsome daughter of Vasudeva, Bhadra by name, decked with every ornament, in the midst of her maids. As soon as Arjuna beheld her he was possessed by the god of desire. Then, O Bharata, that tiger among men, Krishna, observing Partha contemplate her with absorbed attention, said with a smile, 'How is this? Can the heart of one that rangeth the woods be agitated by the god of desire? This is my sister, O Partha, and the uterine sister of Sarana. Blest be thou, her name is Bhadra and she is the favourite daughter of my father. Tell me if thy heart is fixed upon her, for I shall then speak to my father myself.'

"Arjuna answered, 'She is Vasudeva's daughter and Vasudeva's (Krishna) sister; endued with so much beauty, whom can she not fascinate? If this thy sister, this maid of the Vrishni race, becometh my wife, truly may I win prosperity in everything. Tell me, O Janardana, by what means I may obtain her. To get her I will achieve anything that is achievable by man.'

"Vasudeva answered, 'O bull amongst men, self-choice hath been ordained for the marriage of Kshatriyas. But that is doubtful (in its consequences), O Partha, as we do not know this girl's temper and disposition. In the case of Kshatriyas that are brave, a forcible abduction for purposes of marriage is applauded, as the learned have said. Therefore O Arjuna, carry away this my beautiful sister by force, for who knows what she may do at a self-choice.' Then Krishna and Arjuna, having thus settled as to what should be done sent some speedy messengers unto Yudhishthira at Indraprastha, informing him of everything. The strong-armed Yudhishthira, as soon as he heard it, gave his assent to it.'"

SECTION CCXXII
(Subhadra-harana Parva continued)

"'Then Dhananjaya, informed of the assent of Yudhishthira, and ascertaining, O Janamejaya, that the maiden had gone to the Raivataka hill, obtained the assent of Vasudeva also, after having settled in consultation with him all that required to be done. Then that bull of Bharata's race, that foremost of men, with Krishna's assent, riding in his well-built car of gold equipped with rows of small bells and with every kind of weapon and the clatter of whose wheels resembled the roar of the clouds and whose splendour was like unto that of a blazing fire and which struck terror into the hearts of all foes and unto which were yoked the steeds Saivya and Sugriva, himself accoutred in mail and armed with sword and his fingers encased in leathern gloves, set out, as it were, on a hunting expedition. Meanwhile Subhadra, having paid her homage unto that prince of hills, Raivataka and having worshipped the deities and made the Brahmanas utter benedictions upon her, and having also walked round the hill, was coming towards Dwaravati. The son of Kunti, afflicted with the shafts of the god of desire, suddenly rushed towards that Yadava girl of faultless features and forcibly took her into his car. Having seized that girl of sweet smiles, that tiger among men proceeded in his car of gold towards his own city (Indraprastha). Meanwhile, the armed attendants of Subhadra, beholding her thus seized and taken away, all ran, crying towards the city of Dwaraka. Reaching all together the Yadava court called by the name of Sudharma, they represented everything about the prowess of Partha unto the chief officer of the court. The chief officer of the court, having heard everything from those messengers, blew his gold-decked trumpet of loud blare, calling all to arms. Stirred up by that sound, the Bhojas, the Vrishnis, and the Andhakas began to pour in from all sides. Those that were eating left their food, and those that were drinking left their drink. Those tigers among men, those great warriors of the Vrishni and the Andhaka tribes, took their seats upon their thousand thrones of gold covered with excellent carpets and variegated with gems and corals and possessed of the lustre of blazing fire. Indeed they took their seats upon those thrones, like blazing fires receiving faggots to increase their splendour. And after they were seated in that court which was like unto a conclave of the celestials themselves, the chief officer of the court, assisted by those that stood at his back, spoke of the conduct of Jishnu. The proud Vrishni heroes, of eyes red with wine, as soon as they heard of it, rose up from their seats, unable to brook what Arjuna had done. Some amongst them said, 'Yoke our cars', and some, 'Bring our weapons' and some said, 'Bring our costly bows and strong coats of mail,' and some loudly called upon their charioteers to harness their cars, and some, from impatience, themselves yoked their horses decked with gold unto their cars. And while their cars and armours and standards were being brought, loud became the uproar of those heroes. Then Valadeva, white and tall as the peak of Kailasa, decked with garlands of wild flowers and attired in blue robes, and proud and intoxicated with drink, said these words:

'Ye senseless men, what are ye doing, when Janardana sitteth silent? Without knowing what is in his mind, vainly do we roar in wrath! Let the high-souled Krishna give out what he proposeth. Accomplish promptly what he desireth to do.' Then all of them, hearing those words of Halayudha that deserved to be accepted, exclaimed, 'Excellent! Excellent!' They then all became silent. Silence having been restored by the words of the intelligent Valadeva, they took their seats once more in that assembly. Then Rama, that oppressor of foes, spoke unto Vasudeva, saying, 'Why, O Janardana, sittest thou, gazing silently? O Achyuta, it was for thy sake that the son of Pritha had been welcomed and honoured by us. It seemeth, however, that that vile wretch deserved not our homage. What man is there born of a respectable family that would break the plate after having dined from it! Even if one desireth to make such an alliance, yet remembering all the services he hath received, who is there, desirous of happiness, that acts so rashly? That Pandava disregarding us and thee too hath today outraged Subhadra, desiring (to compass) his own death. He hath placed his foot on the crown of my head. How shall I, O Govinda, tamely bear it? Shall I not resent it, even like a snake that is trodden upon? Alone shall I today make the earth destitute of Kauravas! Never shall I put up with this transgression by Arjuna.' Then all the Bhojas, Vrishnis, and Andhakas, present there, approved of everything that Valadeva had said, deeply roaring like unto a kettle-drum or the clouds.'"

SECTION CCXXIII
(Haranaharana Parva)

"Vaisampayana said, 'When the heroes of the Vrishni race began to speak repeatedly in this strain, Vasudeva uttered these words pregnant with deep import and consistent with true morality. 'Gudakesa (the conqueror of sleep or he of the curly hair), by what he hath done, hath not insulted our family. He hath without doubt, rather enhanced our respect. Partha knoweth that we of the Satwata race are never mercenary. The son of Pandu also regardeth a self-choice as doubtful in its results. Who also would approve of accepting a bride in gift as if she were an animal? What man again is there on earth that would sell his offspring? I think Arjuna, seeing these faults in all the other methods took the maiden away by force, according to the ordinance. This alliance is very proper. Subhadra is a renowned girl. Partha too possesseth renown. Perhaps, thinking of all this, Arjuna hath taken her away by force. Who is there that would not desire to have Arjuna for a friend, who is born in the race of Bharata and the renowned Santanu, and the son also of the daughter of Kuntibhoja? I do not see, in all the worlds with Indra and the Rudras, the person that can by force vanquish Partha in battle, except the three-eyed god Mahadeva. His car is well-known. Yoked thereunto are those steeds of mine. Partha as a warrior is well-known; and his lightness of hand is well-known. Who shall be equal to him? Even this is my opinion: go ye cheerfully after Dhananjaya and by conciliation stop him and bring him back. If Partha goes to his city after having vanquished us by force, our fame will be gone. There is no disgrace, however, in conciliation.' Hearing, O monarch, those words of Vasudeva, they did as he directed. Stopped by them, Arjuna returned to Dwaraka and was united in marriage with Subhadra. Worshipped by the sons of Vrishni's race, Arjuna, sporting there as he pleased, passed a whole year in Dwaraka. The last year of his exile the exalted one passed at the sacred region of Pushkara. After the twelve years were complete he came back to Khandavaprastha. He approached the king first and then worshipped the Brahmanas with respectful attention. At last the hero went unto Draupadi. Draupadi, from jealousy, spoke unto him, saying, 'Why tarriest thou here, O son of Kunti? Go where the daughter of the Satwata race is!' And Krishna lamented much in this strain. But Dhananjaya pacified her repeatedly and asked for her forgiveness. And returning soon unto where Subhadra, attired in red silk, was staying, Arjuna, sent her into the inner apartments dressed not as a queen but in the simple garb of a cowherd woman. But arrived at the palace, the renowned Subhadra looked handsomer in that dress. The celebrated Bhadra of large and slightly red eyes first worshipped Pritha. Kunti from excess of affection smelt the head of that girl of perfectly faultless features, and pronounced infinite blessing upon her. Then that girl of face like the full moon hastily went unto Draupadi and worshipped her, saying, 'I am thy maid!' Krishna rose hastily and embraced the sister of Madhava from affection, and said, 'Let thy husband be without a foe!' Bhadra then, with a delighted heart, said unto Draupadi, 'So be it!' From that time, O Janamejaya, those great warriors, the Pandavas, began to live happily, and Kunti also became very happy.'

"Vaisampayana continued, 'When that scorcher of foes, viz., Kesava of pure soul and eyes, like lotus-petals, heard that the foremost of the Pandavas, viz., Arjuna, had reached his own excellent city of Indraprastha, he came thither accompanied by Rama and the other heroes and great warriors of the Vrishni and the Andhaka tribes, and by his brothers and sons and many other brave warriors. And Saurin came accompanied by a large army that protected him. And there came with Saurin, that oppressor of foes, viz., the exceedingly liberal Akrura of great intelligence and renown, the generalissimo of the brave Vrishni host. And there also came Anadhrishti of great prowess, and Uddhava of great renown, of great intelligence, of great soul, and a disciple of Vrihaspati himself. And there also came Satyaka and Salyaka and Kritavarman and Satwata; and Pradyumna and Samva and Nisatha and Sanku; and Charudeshna, and Jhilli of great prowess, and Viprithu also and Sarana of mighty arms and Gada, the foremost of learned men. These and many other Vrishnis and Bhojas, and Andhakas came to Indraprastha, bringing with them many nuptial presents. King Yudhishthira, hearing that Madhava had arrived, sent the twins out to receive him. Received by them, the Vrishni host of great prosperity entered Khandavaprastha well-adorned with flags and ensigns. The streets were well- swept and watered and decked with floral wreaths and bunches. These were, again, sprinkled over with sandalwood water that was fragrant and cooling. Every part of the town was filled with the sweet scent of burning aloes. And the city was full of joyous and healthy people and adorned with merchants and traders. That best of men, viz., Kesava of mighty arms, accompanied by Rama and many of the Vrishnis, Andhakas and Bhojas, having entered the town, was worshipped by the citizens and Brahmanas by thousands. At last Kesava entered the palace of the king which was like unto the mansion of Indra himself. Beholding Rama, Yudhishthira received him with due ceremonies. The king smelt the head of Kesava and embraced him. Govinda, gratified with the reception, humbly worshipped Yudhishthira. He also paid homage unto Bhima, that tiger among men. Yudhishthira the son of Kunti then received the other principal men of the Vrishni and the Andhaka tribes with due ceremonies. Yudhishthira reverentially worshipped some as his superiors, and welcomed others as equals. And some he received with affection and by some he was worshipped with reverence. Then Hrishikesa of great renown gave unto the party of the bridegroom much wealth. And unto Subhadra he gave the nuptial presents that had been given to her by her relatives. Krishna gave unto the Pandavas a thousand cars of gold furnished with rows of bells, and unto each of which were put four steeds driven by well-trained charioteers. He also gave unto them ten thousand cows belonging to the country of Mathura, and yielding much milk and all of excellent colour. Well-pleased, Janardana also gave them a thousand mares with gold harnesses and of colour white as the beams of the moon. He also gave them a thousand mules, all well-trained and possessing the speed of the wind, of white colour with black manes. And he of eyes like lotus-petals also gave unto them a thousand damsels well-skilled in assisting at bathing and at drinking, young in years and virgins all before their first-season, well-attired and of excellent complexion, each wearing a hundred pieces of gold around her neck, of skins perfectly polished, decked with every ornament, and well-skilled in every kind of personal service. Janardana also gave unto them hundreds of thousands of draft horses from the country of the Valhikas as Subhadra's excellent dower. That foremost one of Dasarha's race also gave unto Subhadra as her peculium ten carrier-loads of first class gold possessing the splendour of fire, some purified and some in a state of ore. And Rama having the plough for his weapon and always loving bravery gave unto Arjuna, as a nuptial present, a thousand elephants with secretions flowing in three streams from the three parts of their bodies (the temple, the ears, and the anus) each large as a mountain summit, irresistible in battle, decked with coverlets and bells, well-adorned with other golden ornaments, and equipped with excellent thrones on their backs. And that large wave of wealth and gems that the Yadavas presented, together with the cloths and blankets that represented its foam, and the elephants its alligators and sharks, and the flags its floating weeds swelling into large proportions, mingled with the Pandu ocean and filled it to the brim, to the great sorrow of all foes. Yudhishthira accepted all those presents and worshipped all those great warriors of the Vrishni and the Andhaka races. Those illustrious heroes of the Kuru, the Vrishni, and the Andhaka races passed their days in pleasure and merriment there like virtuous men (after death) in the celestial regions. The Kurus and the Vrishnis with joyous hearts amused themselves there, setting up at times loud shouts mingled with clappings of the hand. Spending many days in sports and merriment there, and worshipped by the Kurus all the while, the Vrishni heroes endued with great energy then returned to the city of Dwaravati. And the great warriors of the Vrishni and the Andhaka races set out with Rama in the van, carrying with them those gems of the purest rays that had been given them by those foremost ones of Kuru's race. And, O Bharata, the high- souled Vasudeva remained there with Arjuna in the delightful city of Indraprastha. And the illustrious one wandered over the banks of the Yamuna in search of deer. And he sported with Arjuna piercing with his shafts deer and wild boars. Then Subhadra, the favourite sister of Kesava, gave birth to an illustrious son, like Puloma's daughter, (the queen of heaven) bringing forth Jayanta. And the son that Subhadra brought forth was of long arms, broad chest, and eyes as large as those of a bull. That hero and oppressor of foes came to be called Abhimanyu. And the son of Arjuna, that grinder of foes and bull among men, was called Abhimanyu because he was fearless and wrathful. And that great warrior was begotten upon the daughter of the Satwata race by Dhananjaya, like fire produced in a sacrifice from within the sami wood by the process of rubbing. Upon the birth of this child, Yudhishthira, the powerful son of Kunti, gave away unto Brahmanas ten thousand cows and coins of gold. The child from his earliest years became the favourite of Vasudeva and of his father and uncles, like the moon of all the people of the world. Upon his birth, Krishna performed the usual rites of infancy. The child began to grow up like the Moon of the bright fortnight. That grinder of foes soon became conversant with the Vedas and acquired from his father the science of weapon both celestial and human, consisting of four branches and ten divisions.

"Endued with great strength, the child also acquired the knowledge of counteracting the weapons hurled at him by others, and great lightness of hand and fleetness of motion forward and backward and transverse and wheeling. Abhimanyu became like unto his father in knowledge of the scriptures and rites of religion. And Dhananjaya, beholding his son, became filled with joy. Like Maghavat beholding Arjuna, the latter beheld his son Abhimanyu and became exceedingly happy. Abhimanyu possessed the power of slaying every foe and bore on his person every auspicious mark. He was invisible in battle and broad-shouldered as the bull. Possessing a broad face as (the hood of) the snake, he was proud like the lion. Wielding a large bow, his prowess was like that of an elephant in rut. Possessed of a face handsome as the full-moon, and of a voice deep as the sound of the drum or the clouds, he was equal unto Krishna in bravery and energy, in beauty and in features. The auspicious Panchali also, from her five husbands, obtained five sons all of whom were heroes of the foremost rank and immovable in battle like the hills. Prativindhya by Yudhishthira, Sutasoma by Vrikodara, Srutakarman by Arjuna, Satanika by Nakula, and Srutasena by Sahadeva,—these were the five heroes and great warriors that Panchali brought forth, like Aditi bringing forth the Adityas. And the Brahmanas, from their foreknowledge, said unto Yudhishthira that as the son of his would be capable of bearing like the Vindhya mountains the weapons of the foe, he should be called Prativindhya. And because the child that Draupadi bore to Bhimasena was born after Bhima had performed a thousand Soma sacrifices, he came to be called Sutasoma. And because Arjuna's son was born upon his return from exile during which he had achieved many celebrated feats, that child came to be called Srutakarman. While Nakula named his son Satanika after a royal sage of that name, in the illustrious race of Kuru. Again the son that Draupadi bore to Sahadeva was born under the constellation called Vahni-daivata (Krittika), therefore was he called after the generalissimo of the celestial host, Srutasena (Kartikeya). The sons of Draupadi were born, each at the interval of one year, and all of them became renowned and much attached to one another. And, O monarch, all their rites of infancy and childhood, such as Chudakarana and Upanayana (first shave of the head and investiture with the sacred threads) were performed by Dhaumya according to the ordinance. All of them, of excellent behaviour and vows, after having studied the Vedas, acquired from Arjuna a knowledge of all the weapons, celestial and human. And, O tiger among kings, the Pandavas, having obtained sons all of whom were equal unto the children of the celestials and endued with broad chests, and all of whom became great warriors, were filled with joy.'"

SECTION CCXXIV
(Khandava-daha Parva)

"Vaisampayana said, 'The Pandavas, after they had taken up their abode at Indraprastha at the command of Dhritarashtra and Bhishma began to bring other kings under their sway. All the subjects (of the kingdom) lived most happily depending upon Yudhishthira the just, like a soul living happily depending upon a body blest with auspicious marks and pious deeds. And, O bull in Bharata's race, Yudhishthira paid homage unto virtue, pleasure, and profit, in judicious proportion, as if each were a friend dear unto him as his own self. It seemed as if the three pursuits—virtue, pleasure, and profit—became personified on earth, and amongst them the king shone as a fourth. The subjects having obtained Yudhishthira as their king, obtained in their monarch one that was devoted to the study of the Vedas, one that was performer of the great sacrifices, and one that was protector of all good people. In consequence of Yudhishthira's influence, the good fortune of all the monarchs of the earth became stationary, and their hearts became devoted to the meditation of the Supreme Spirit, and virtue itself began to grow every way all round. And in the midst of and assisted by his four brothers, the king looked more resplendent (than he would have done if he were alone), like a great sacrifice depending upon and assisted by the four Vedas. Many learned Brahmanas with Dhananjaya at their head, each like unto Vrihaspati, waited upon the monarch, like the celestials waiting upon the Lord of the creation. From excess of affection, the eyes and hearts of all the people equally took great delight in Yudhishthira who was even as the full moon without a stain. The people took delight in him not only because he was their king but also from sincere affection. The king always did what was agreeable to them. The sweet-speeched Yudhishthira of great intelligence never uttered anything that was improper or untrue or unbearable or disagreeable. The best of monarchs of the Bharata race, endued with great energy, passed his days happily for the welfare of all as his own. His brothers also bringing by their energy other kings under their sway, passed their days in happiness, without a foe to disturb their peace.

"After a few days, Vibhatsu, addressing Krishna, said, 'The summer days have set in, O Krishna! Therefore, let us go to the banks of the Yamuna. O slayer of Madhu, sporting there in the company of friends, we will, O Janardana, return in the evening'. Thereupon Vasudeva said, 'O son of Kunti, this is also my wish. Let us, O Partha, sport in the waters as we please, in the company of friends.'

"Vaisampayana continued, 'Then, O Bharata, having consulted thus with each other, Partha and Govinda, with Yudhishthira's leave, set out, surrounded by friends. Reaching a fine spot (on the banks of the Yamuna) suitable for purposes of pleasure, overgrown with numerous tall trees and covered with several high mansions that made the place look like the celestial city and within which had been collected for Krishna and Partha numerous costly and well-flavoured viands and drinks and other articles of enjoyment and floral wreaths and various perfumes, the party entered without delay the inner apartments adorned with many precious gems of pure rays. Entering those apartments, everybody, O Bharata, began to sport, according to his pleasure. The women of the party, all of full rotund hips and deep bosoms and handsome eyes, and gait unsteady with wine began to sport there at the command of Krishna and Partha. Some amongst the women sported as they liked in the woods, some in the waters, and some within the mansions, as directed by Partha and Govinda. Draupadi and Subhadra, exhilarated with wine, began to give away unto the women so sporting, their costly robes and ornaments. And some amongst those women began to dance in joy, and some began to sing; and some amongst them began to laugh and jest, and some to drink excellent wines. Some began to obstruct one another's progress and some to fight with one another, and to discourse with one another in private. Those mansions and the woods, filled with the charming music of flutes and guitars and kettledrums, became the scene of Prosperity personified.

"When such was the state of things there, Arjuna and Vasudeva went to a certain charming spot (in those woods) not far from the place where the others were. O monarch, the high-souled Krishna, and that subjugator of hostile cities, viz., Arjuna, going thither, sat down upon two very costly seats. Vasudeva and Partha amused themselves there with discoursing upon many past achievements of prowess and other topics. Unto Vasudeva and Dhananjaya happily sitting there like the Aswins in heaven, a certain Brahmana came. The Brahmana that came there looked like a tall Sala tree. His complexion was like unto molten gold; his beard was bright yellow tinged with green; and the height and the thickness of the body were in just proportion. Of matted locks and dressed in rags, he resembled the morning sun in splendour. Of eyes like lotus-petals and of a tawny hue, he seemed to be blazing with effulgence. Beholding that foremost of Brahmanas blazing with splendour approach towards them both Arjuna and Vasudeva, hastily rising from their seats, stood, waiting (for his commands).'"

SECTION CCXXV
(Khandava-daha Parva continued)

"Vaisampayana said, 'Then that Brahmana addressed Arjuna and Vasudeva of the Satwata race, saying, 'Ye who are now staying so near unto Khandava are the two foremost of heroes on earth. I am a voracious Brahmana that always eateth much. O thou of the Vrishni race, and O Partha, I solicit you to gratify me by giving me sufficient food.' Thus addressed by the Brahmana, Krishna and the son of Pandu answered him, saying, 'O, tell us what kind of food will gratify thee so that we may endeavour to give it thee.' The illustrious Brahmana, thus replied to, said unto those heroes who were enquiring after the kind of food he sought, 'I do not desire to eat ordinary food. Know that I am Agni! Give me that food which suiteth me. This forest of Khandava is always protected by Indra. And as it is protected by the illustrious one, I always fail to consume it. In that forest dwelleth, with his followers and family, a Naga, called Takshaka, who is the friend of Indra.

It is for him that the wielder of the thunderbolt protecteth this forest. Many other creatures also are thus protected here for the sake of Takshaka. Desiring to consume the forest I succeed not in my attempts in consequence of Indra's prowess. Beholding me blazing forth, he always poureth upon me water from the clouds. Therefore, I succeed not in consuming the forest of Khandava, although I desire very much to do so. I have now come to you—you who are both skilled in weapons! If you help me I will surely consume this forest: for even this is the food that is desired by me! As ye are conversant with excellent weapons, I pray you to prevent those showers from descending and any of the creatures from escaping, when I begin to consume this forest!'

"Janamejaya said, 'Why did the illustrious Agni desire to consume the forest of Khandava that was filled with various living creatures and protected by the chief of the celestials? When Agni consumed in wrath the forest of Khandava, it is evident there was a grave cause. I desire, O Brahmana, to hear all this in detail from thee. Tell me, O sage, how the Khandava forest was consumed in days of yore.'

"Vaisampayana said, 'O chief of men, I will narrate to you the story of the conflagration of Khandava as told by Rishis in the Purana. It hath been heard, O king, in the Purana that there was a celebrated king of the name of Swetaki who was endued with strength and prowess and who was equal unto Indra himself. No one on earth has equalled him in sacrifices, charity, and intelligence. Swetaki performed the five great sacrifices and many others, at all of which the presents unto Brahmanas were large. The heart of that monarch, O king, was always set upon sacrifices, religious rites, and gifts of all kinds. And king Swetaki of great intelligence, assisted by his Ritwiks performed sacrifices for many long years, till those sacrificial priests with eyes afflicted by the continued smoke and becoming very weak, left that monarch, wishing never more to assist at his sacrifices. The king, however, repeatedly asked those Ritwiks to come to him. But they came not to his sacrifice in consequence of the painful state of their eyes. The king, therefore, invited at the command of his own Ritwiks, others like unto them, and completed the sacrifice that he had begun. After some days had elapsed, king Swetaki desired to perform another sacrifice which should extend for a hundred years. But the illustrious monarch obtained not any priest to assist him in it. The celebrated king then, with his friends and relatives, casting off all sloth, repeatedly courted his priests with great persistence, by bowing down unto them, by conciliatory speeches, and by gifts of wealth. All of them, however, refused to accomplish the purpose which that king of immeasurable energy had in view. Then that royal sage, getting angry, addressed those Brahmanas sitting in their asylums, and said, 'If, ye Brahmanas, I were a fallen person, or, if, I were wanting in homage and service to you, I should then deserve to be abandoned without scruple by you and by other Brahmanas at the same time. But as I am neither degraded nor wanting in homage to you, it behoveth you not to obstruct the performance by me of my sacrifice or to abandon me thus, ye foremost of Brahmanas, without adequate reason. I seek, ye Brahmanas, your protection! It behoveth you to be propitious unto me. But, ye foremost of Brahmanas, if you abandon me from enmity alone or any improper motive, I shall go unto other priests for their assistance in this sacrifice of mine, and conciliating them by sweet words and gifts, I shall represent unto them the business I have on hand, so that they may accomplish it.' Having said this, the monarch became silent. And, O chastiser of foes, when those priests well knew that they could not assist at the king's sacrifice, they pretended to be angry, and addressing that best of monarchs said, 'O best of kings, thy sacrifices are incessant! By assisting thee always, we have all been fatigued. And as we have been wearied in consequence of these labours, it behoveth thee to give us leave. O sinless one, from loss of judgment thou canst not wait (but urgest us repeatedly). Go unto Rudra! He will assist at thy sacrifice!' Hearing those words of censure and wrath, king Swetaki became angry. And the monarch wending to the mountains of Kailasa, devoted himself to asceticism there. And, O king, the monarch began to worship Mahadeva, with fixed attention, and by observing the most rigid vows. And foregoing all food at times, he passed a long period. The monarch ate only fruits and roots sometimes at the twelfth and sometimes at the sixteenth hour of the whole day. King Swetaki stood for six months, rapt in attention, with arms upraised and steadfast eyes, like the trunk of a tree or a column rooted to the ground. And, O Bharata, Sankara at last gratified with that tiger among kings, who was undergoing such hard penances, showed himself unto him. And the god spake unto the monarch in a calm and grave voice, saying, 'O tiger among kings, O chastiser of foes, I have been gratified with thee for thy asceticism! Blest be thou! Ask now the boon that thou, O king, desirest.' Hearing these words of Rudra of immeasurable energy, the royal sage bowed unto that deity and replied, saying, 'O illustrious one, O thou that art worshipped by the three worlds, if thou hast been gratified with me, then, O god of gods, assist me thyself, O lord of the celestials, in my sacrifice!' Hearing these words spoken by the monarch, the illustrious god was gratified, and smilingly said, 'We do not ourselves assist at sacrifices: but as thou, O king, hast undergone severe penances, desirous of obtaining a boon, I will, O chastiser of foes, assist at thy sacrifice, upon, O king, this condition.' And Rudra continued, 'If, O king of kings, thou canst, for twelve years, pour without intermission libations of clarified butter into the fire, thyself leading all the while the life of a Brahmacharin with rapt attention, then thou shalt obtain from me what thou askest.' King Swetaki, thus addressed by Rudra, did all that he was directed to do by the wielder of the trident. And after twelve years had elapsed, he again came unto Maheswara. And Sankara, the Creator of the worlds upon seeing Swetaki, that excellent monarch, immediately said, in great gratification, 'I have been gratified by thee, O best of kings, with this thy own act! But, O chastiser of foes, the duty of assisting at sacrifices properly belongeth to Brahmanas. Therefore, O oppressor of foes, I will not myself assist at thy sacrifice today. There is on earth an exalted Brahmana who is even a portion of my own self. He is known by the name of Durvasa. Even that Brahmana endued with great energy will assist you in thy sacrifice. Let, therefore, every preparation be made.' Hearing these words uttered by Rudra, the king, returning to his own capital, began to collect all that was necessary. After everything had been collected, the monarch again presented himself before Rudra and said, 'Every necessary article hath been collected, and all my preparations are complete, through thy grace, O god of gods! Let me, therefore, be installed at the sacrifice tomorrow.' Having heard these words of that illustrious king, Rudra summoned Durvasa before him and said. 'This, O Durvasa, is that best of monarchs called Swetaki. At my command, O best of Brahmanas, assist even this king in his sacrifice.' And the Rishi Durvasa said unto Rudra, 'So be it.' Then the sacrifice for which king Swetaki had made those preparations, took place. And the illustrious monarch's sacrifice was performed according to the ordinance and in proper season. And the gifts, on that occasion, unto the Brahmanas were large. And after that monarch's sacrifice had come to an end, all the other priests who had come to assist at it went away with Durvasa's leave. All other Sadasyas also of immeasurable energy, who had been installed at that sacrifice, then went away. That exalted monarch then entered his own palace, worshipped by exalted Brahmanas conversant with the Vedas, eulogised by chanters of panegyrical hymns and congratulated by the citizens.

"Such was the history of that best of monarchs, the royal sage Swetaki, who, when the time came, ascended to heaven, having won great renown on earth, and accompanied by the Ritwiks and the Sadasyas that had helped him in life.'

"Vaisampayana continued, 'At that sacrifice of Swetaki, Agni had drunk clarified butter for twelve years. Indeed, clarified butter had been poured into Agni's mouth in a continuous stream for that period. Having drunk so much butter, Agni, satiated, desired not to drink butter again from the hand of anybody else at any other sacrifice. Agni became pale, having lost his colour, and he could not shine as before. He felt a loss of appetite from surfeit, and his energy itself decreased and sickness afflicted him. Then when the drinker of sacrificial libations perceived that his energy was gradually diminishing, he went to the sacred abode of Brahman that is worshipped by all. Approaching the great Deity seated on his seat, Agni said, 'O exalted one, Swetaki hath (by his sacrifice) gratified me to excess. Even now I am suffering from surfeit which I cannot dispel. O Lord of the universe, I am being reduced both in splendour and strength. I desire to regain, through thy grace, my own permanent nature.' Hearing these words from Hutavaha, the illustrious Creator of all things smilingly replied unto him, saying, 'O exalted one, thou hast eaten, for twelve years, a continuous stream of sacrificial butter poured into thy mouth! It is for this that illness hath seized thee. But, O Agni, grieve not for it. Thou shalt soon regain thy own nature. I shall dispel this surfeit of thine and the time for it is even come. The dreadful forest Khandava, that abode of the enemies of the gods, which thou hadst of old once consumed to ashes at the request of the gods, hath now become the home of numerous creatures. When thou will have eaten the fat of those creatures, thou shalt regain thy own nature. Proceed thither in haste to consume that forest with its living population. Thou wilt then be cured of thy malady.' Hearing the words that fell from the lips of the Supreme Deity, Hutasana proceeded with great speed and soon reached the forest of Khandava in great vigour. Arrived there, he suddenly blazed forth in anger, assisted by Vayu. Beholding Khandava on fire the dwellers (in the forest) that were there, made great efforts to extinguish the conflagration. Elephants by hundreds of thousands, speeding in anger, brought water in their trunks and scattered it upon the fire. Thousands of many-hooded snakes, mad with anger, hastily began to scatter upon fire much water from those many hoods of theirs. And so, O bull of Bharata's race, the other creatures dwelling in that forest, by various appliances and efforts, soon extinguished the fire. In this way, Agni blazed forth in Khandava repeatedly, even for seven times. And it was in this way that the blazing fire was extinguished there as often by the denizens of that forest.'"

SECTION CCXXVI
(Khandava-daha Parva continued)

"Vaisampayana said, 'Then Havyavahana (Agni) in anger and disappointment, with his ailment uncured, went to the Grandsire. And he represented unto Brahman all that had happened: The illustrious deity, reflecting for a moment, said unto him, 'O sinless one, I see a way by which thou mayest consume the forest of Khandava today in the very sight of Indra. Those old deities, Nara and Narayana, have become incarnate in the world of men to accomplish the business of the celestials. They are called on earth Arjuna and Vasudeva. They are even now staying in the forest of Khandava. Solicit them for aiding thee in consuming that forest. Thou shalt then consume the forest even if it be protected by the celestials. They will certainly prevent the population of Khandava from escaping, and thwart Indra also (in aiding any one in the escape). I have no doubt of this!' Hearing these words, Agni came in haste unto Krishna and Partha. O king, I have already told thee what he said, having approached the illustrious pair. O tiger among kings, hearing those words of Agni who was desirous of consuming the forest of Khandava against the will of Indra, Vibhatsu said unto him these words well-suited to the occasion, 'I have numberless excellent celestial weapons with which I can fight even many wielders of the thunderbolt. But, O exalted one, I have no bow suited to the strength of my arms, and capable of bearing the might I may put forth in battle. In consequence of the lightness of my hands also I require arrows that must never be exhausted. My car also is scarcely able to bear the load of arrows that I would desire to keep by me. I desire celestial steeds of pure white, possessing the speed of the wind; and a car possessing the splendour of the sun and the clatter of whose wheels should resemble the roar of the clouds. Then, there is no weapon suited to Krishna's energy and with which Madhava can slay Nagas and Pisachas. O exalted one, it behoveth thee to give us the means by which success may be achieved and by which we may thwart Indra in pouring his showers upon that extensive forest. O Pavaka, we are ready to do all that manliness and prowess can do. But, O exalted one, it behoveth thee to give us the adequate means.'"

SECTION CCXXVII
(Khandava-daha Parva continued)

"Vaisampayana, said, 'Thus addressed by Arjuna, the smoke-bannered Hutasana, desirous of an interview with Varuna, recollected that son of Aditi,—that deity protecting one of the points of the heavens and having his home in the water and ruling that element. Varuna, knowing that he was thought of by Pavaka, immediately appeared before that deity. The smoke- bannered celestial welcoming with reverence the ruler of the waters, that fourth of the Lokapalas, said unto that eternal god of gods, 'Give me without loss of time that bow and quiver, and that ape-bannered car also, which were obtained from king Soma. Partha will achieve a great task with Gandiva, and Vasudeva also with the discus! Give both, therefore, unto me today.' Hearing these words, Varuna replied unto Pavaka, saying, 'Well, I am giving them.' He then gave that wonderful jewel of a bow that was endued with great energy. That bow was the enhancer of fame and achievements, and was incapable of being injured by any weapon. It was the chief of all weapons, and the grinder of them all. And it was the smiter of hostile armies and was alone equal to a hundred thousand bows. It was the multiplier of kingdoms, and was variegated with excellent colours. It was well-adorned, and beautiful to behold, and without a mark of weakness or injury anywhere. And it was always worshipped both by the celestials and the Gandharvas. Varuna also gave two inexhaustible quivers, and he also gave a car furnished with celestial weapons and whose banner bore a large ape. Yoked unto that car were steeds white as silver of the fleecy clouds, and born in the region of the Gandharvas, and decked with golden harness, and resembling in fleetness the wind or the mind. And it was equipped with implement of war, and was incapable of being vanquished by the celestials or the Asuras. Its splendour was great and the sounds of its wheels was tremendous. It delighted the heart of every creature that looked at it. It had been made by Viswakarman, the architect of the universe and one of the lords of creation, after severe ascetic meditation. Its splendour, like that of the sun, was so great that no one could gaze at it. It was the very car from which the lord Soma had vanquished the Danavas. Resplendent with beauty, it looked like an evening cloud reflecting the effulgence of the setting sun. It was furnished with an excellent flag-staff of golden colour and great beauty. And there sat upon that flag-staff a celestial ape of form fierce like that of a lion or a tiger. Stationed on high, the ape seemed bent upon burning everything it beheld. And upon the (other) flags were various creatures of large size, whose roars and yells caused the enemy's soldiers to faint. Then Arjuna, accoutred in mail and armed with the sword, and his fingers cased in leathern gloves, walking round that excellent car adorned with numerous flags and bowing unto the gods, ascended it like a virtuous man riding in the celestial car that bears him to heaven. And taking up that celestial and first of bows created by Brahman of old and called Gandiva, Arjuna was filled with joy. And bowing unto Hutasana, Partha endued with great energy, took up the bow and strung it forcibly. Those who heard the noise that was made while the mighty Pandava strung that bow, quaked with fear. And having obtained that car and that bow, and the two inexhaustible quivers, the son of Kunti became glad and thought himself competent to assist at the task. And Pavaka then gave unto Krishna a discus with an iron pole attached to a hole in the centre. And it was a fiery weapon and became his favourite. Having obtained that weapon, Krishna also became equal to the task. Pavaka then, addressing Krishna, said, 'With this, O slayer of Madhu, thou shalt be able without doubt to vanquish in battle even foes that are not human. With this weapon, without doubt, thou shalt be superior in battle to men and gods, and Rakshasas and Pisachas, and Daityas and Nagas. And thou shalt certainly be able with this to smite all. And, O Madhava, hurled by thee in battle at thy foes, this weapon will irresistibly slay the enemy and again come back into thy hands.' And the lord Varuna, after this, gave unto Krishna a mace, of name Kaumodaki, capable of slaying every Daitya and producing, when hurled, a roar like that of the thunder. Then Arjuna and Achyuta, filled with joy said unto Pavaka, 'O exalted one, furnished with weapons and knowing their use, possessed of cars with flags and flagstaffs, we are now able to fight with even all the celestials and the Asuras (together), let alone the wielder of the thunderbolt desirous of fighting for the sake of the Naga (his friend Takshaka).' Arjuna also said, 'O Pavaka, while Hrishikesa, endued with abundant energy, moves on the field of battle with this discus in hand, there is nothing in the three worlds that he will not be able to consume by hurling this weapon. Having obtained the bow Gandiva and this couple of inexhaustible quivers I also am ready to conquer in battle the three worlds. Therefore, O lord, blaze thou forth as thou likest, surrounding this large forest on every side. We are quite able to help thee.'

"Vaisampayana continued, 'Thus addressed both by Dasarha and Arjuna, the illustrious god then put forth his most energetic form, and prepared to consume the forest. Surrounding it on all sides with his seven flames, he began to consume the forest of Khandava, exhibiting his all-consuming form like that at the end of the Yuga (cycle). And, O bull of Bharata's race, surrounding that forest and catching it from all sides with a roar like that of the clouds, Agni made every creature within it tremble. And, O Bharata, that burning forest then looked resplendent like the king of mountains, Meru, blazing with the rays of the sun fallen thereupon.'"

SECTION CCXXVIII
(Khandava-daha Parva continued)

"Vaisampayana said, 'Then those foremost of car-warriors (Krishna and Arjuna), riding in their cars and placing themselves on opposite sides of that forest, began a great slaughter, on all sides, of the creatures dwelling in Khandava. At whatever point any of the creatures residing in Khandava could be seen attempting to escape, thither rushed those mighty heroes (to prevent its flight). Indeed those two excellent cars seemed to be but one, and the two warriors also therein but one individual. And while the forest was burning, hundreds and thousands of living creatures, uttering frightful yells, began to run about in all directions. Some had particular limbs burnt, some were scorched with excessive heat, and some came out, and some ran about from fear. And some clasping their children and some their parents and brothers, died calmly without, from excess of affection, being able to abandon these that were dear to them. And many there were who biting their nether lips rose upwards and soon fell whirling into the blazing element below. And some were seen to roll on the ground with wings, eyes, and feet scorched and burnt. These creatures were all seen to perish there almost soon enough. The tanks and ponds within that forest, heated by the fire around, began to boil; the fishes and the tortoises in them were all seen to perish. During that great slaughter of living creatures in that forest, the burning bodies of various animals looked as if fire itself had assumed many forms. The birds that took wings to escape from that conflagration were pierced by Arjuna with his shafts, and cut into pieces, they fell down into the burning element below. Pierced all over with Arjuna's shafts, the birds dropped down into the burning forest, uttering loud cries. The denizens of the forest, struck with those shafts, began to roar and yell. The clamour they raised was like unto the frightful uproar heard during the churning of the ocean (in days of yore). The mighty flames of the blazing fire reaching the firmament, caused great anxiety to the celestials themselves. Then all the illustrious dwellers in heaven went in a body unto him of a hundred sacrifices and thousand eyes, viz., their chief, that grinder of Asuras. Approaching Indra, the celestial said, 'Why, O lord of immortals, doth Agni burn these creatures below? Hath the time come for the destruction of the world?'

"Vaisampayana continued, 'Hearing these words of the gods, and himself beholding what Agni was doing, the slayer of Vritra set out for the protection of the forest of Khandava. And Vasava, the chief of the celestials soon covering the sky with masses of clouds of every kind began to shower upon the burning forest. Those masses of clouds by hundreds and thousands, commanded by Indra began to pour rain upon Khandava in showers thick as the flag-staffs of battle-cars. But the showers were all dried up in the sky itself by the heat of the fire and could not, therefore, reach the fire at all! Then the slayer of Namuchi, getting angry with Agni, collected huge masses of clouds and caused them to yield a heavy downpour. Then with the flames contending with those heavy showers, and with masses of clouds overhead, that forest, filled with smoke and flashes of lightning, became terrible to behold.'"

SECTION CCXXIX
(Khandava-daha Parva continued)

"Vaisampayana said, 'Then Vibhatsu, the son of Pandu, invoking his excellent weapons, prevented that shower of rain by Indra, by means of a shower of his own weapons. And Arjuna of immeasurable soul soon covered the forest of Khandava with innumerable arrows like the moon covering the atmosphere with a thick fog. When the sky above that forest was thus covered with the arrows of Arjuna no living creature could then escape from below. And it so happened that while that forest was burning, Takshaka, the chief of the Nagas, was not there, having gone at that time to the field of Kurukshetra. But Aswasena, the mighty son of Takshaka, was there. He made great efforts to escape from that fire; but confined by Arjuna's shafts he succeeded not in finding a way. It was then that his mother, the daughter of a snake, determined to save him by swallowing him first. His mother first swallowed his head and then was swallowing his tail. And desirous of saving her son, the sea-snake rose (up from the earth) while still employed in swallowing her son's tail. But Arjuna as soon as he beheld her escaping, severed her head from her body by means of a sharp and keen-edged arrow. Indra saw all this, and desiring to save his friend's son, the wielder of the thunderbolt, by raising a violent wind, deprived Arjuna of consciousness. During those few moments, Aswasena succeeded in effecting his escape. Beholding that manifestation of the power of illusion, and deceived by that snake, Arjuna was much enraged. He forthwith cut every animal seeking to escape by the skies, into two, three, or more pieces. And Vibhatsu in anger, and Agni, and Vasudeva also, cursed the snake that had escaped so deceitfully, saying, 'Never shalt thou be famous!' And Jishnu remembering the deception practised upon him, became angry, and covering the firmament with a cloud of arrows, sought to fight with him of a thousand eyes. The chief of the celestials also, seeing Arjuna in anger, sought to fight with him, and hurled his own fierce weapons, covering the wide expanse of the firmament. Then the winds, making a loud roar and agitating all the oceans, brought together masses of clouds in the sky, charged with torrents of rain. Those masses of clouds began to vomit thunder and terrible flashes of lightning charged with the thunderclap. Then Arjuna possessing a knowledge of means, hurled the excellent weapon called Vayavya with proper mantras to dispel those clouds. With that weapon the energy and force of Indra's thunderbolt and of those clouds were destroyed. And the torrents of rain with which those clouds were charged were all dried up, and the lightning that played amongst them was also destroyed. Within a moment the sky was cleared of dust and darkness, and a delicious, cool breeze began to blow and the disc of the sun resumed its normal state. Then the eater of clarified butter (Agni), glad because none could baffle him, assumed various forms, and sprinkled over with the fat exuded by the bodies of creatures, blazed forth with all his flames, filling the universe with his roar. Then numerous birds of the Garuda tribe bearing excellent feathers, beholding that the forest was protected by Krishna and Arjuna, descended filled with pride, from the upper skies, desirous of striking those heroes with their thunderlike wings, beaks and claws. Innumerable Nagas also, with faces emitting fire descending from high, approached Arjuna, vomiting the most virulent poison all the while. Beholding them approach, Arjuna cut them into pieces by means of arrows steeped in the fire of his own wrath. Then those birds and snakes, deprived of life, fell into the burning element below. And there came also, desirous of battle, innumerable Asuras with Gandharvas and Yakshas and Rakshasas and Nagas sending forth terrific yells. Armed with machines vomiting from their throats (mouths) iron balls and bullets, and catapults for propelling huge stones, and rockets, they approached to strike Krishna and Partha, their energy and strength increased by wrath. But though they rained a perfect shower of weapons, Vibhatsu, addressing them reproachfully, struck off their heads with his own sharp arrows. That slayer of foes, Krishna, also, endued with great energy, made a great slaughter of the Daitya and the Danava with his discus. Many Asuras of immeasurable might, pierced with Krishna's arrows and smitten with the force of his discus, became motionless like waifs and strays stranded on the bank by the violence of the waves. Then Sakra the lord of the celestials, riding on his white elephant, rushed at those heroes, and taking up his thunderbolt which could never go in vain, hurled it with great force. And the slayer of Asuras said unto the gods, 'These two are slain.' Beholding the fierce thunderbolt about to be hurled by their chief, the celestials all took up their respective weapons. Yama, O king, took up the death-dealing mace, and Kuvera his spiked club, and Varuna his noose and beautiful missile. And Skanda (Kartikeya) took up his long lance and stood motionless like the mountain of Meru. The Aswins stood there with resplendent plants in their hands. Dhatri stood, bow in hand, and Jaya with a thick club. Tvashtri of great strength took up in wrath, a huge mountain and Surya stood with a bright dart, and Mrityu with a battle-axe. Aryaman stalked about with a terrible bludgeon furnished with sharp spikes, and Mitra stood there with a discus sharp as a razor. And, O monarch, Pusha and Bhaga and Savitri, in wrath, rushed at Krishna and Partha with bows and scimitars in hand. And Rudras and the Vasus, the mighty Maruts and the Viswedevas and the Sadhyas, all resplendent with their own energy,—these and many other celestials, armed with various weapons rushed against those exalted of men, Krishna and Partha, for smiting them down. Then were seen in that great conflict wonderful portents all around robbing every creature of his sense, and resembling those that appeared at the time of the universal dissolution. But Arjuna and Krishna, fearless and invincible in battle, beholding Sakra and the other celestials prepared for fight, calmly waited, bows in hands. Skilled in battle, those heroes in wrath assailed the advancing host of celestials with their own thunderlike arrows. The celestials repeatedly routed by Krishna and Arjuna, at last left the field of battle for fear and sought the protection of Indra. The Munis who were witnessing the battle from the skies, beholding the celestials defeated by Madhava and Arjuna, were filled with wonder. Sakra also repeatedly witnessing their prowess in battle, became exceedingly gratified, and once more rushed to the assault. The chastiser of Paka then caused a heavy shower of stones, desiring to ascertain the prowess of Arjuna who was able to draw the bow even with his left hand. Arjuna, in great wrath, dispelled with his arrows that thick shower. Then he of a hundred sacrifices beholding that shower baffled, once more caused a thicker shower of stones. But the son of the chastiser of Paka (viz., Arjuna) gratified his father by baffling that shower also with his swift arrows. Then Sakra, desirous of smiting down the son of Pandu, tore up with his hands a large peak from Mandara, with tall trees on it, and hurled it against him. But Arjuna divided that mountain-peak into a thousand pieces by his swift-going and fire-mouthed arrows. The fragments of that mountain, in falling through the skies, looked as if the sun and the moon and the planets, displaced from their positions fell down on earth. That huge peak fell down upon that forest and by its fall killed numerous living creatures that dwelt in Khandava.'"

SECTION CCXXX
(Khandava-daha Parva continued)

"Vaisampayana said, 'Then the inhabitants of the forest of Khandava, the Danavas and Rakshasas and Nagas and wolves and bears and other wild animals, and elephants with rent temples, and tigers, and lions with manes and deer and buffaloes by hundreds, and birds, and various other creatures, frightened at the falling stones and extremely anxious, began to fly in all directions. They saw the forest (burning all around) and Krishna and Arjuna also ready with their weapons. Frightened at the terrible sounds that were audible there those creatures lost their power of movement. Beholding the forest burning in innumerable places and

Krishna also ready to smite them down with his weapons, they all set up a frightful roar. With that terrible clamour as also with the roar of fire, the whole welkin resounded, as it were, with the voice of portentous clouds. Kesava of dark hue and mighty arms, in order to compass their destruction, hurled at them his large and fierce discus resplendent with its own energy. The forest- dwellers including the Danavas and the Rakshasas, afflicted by that weapon, were cut in hundreds of pieces and fell unto the mouth of Agni. Mangled by Krishna's discus, the Asuras were besmeared with blood and fat and looked like evening clouds. And, O Bharata, he of the Vrishni race moved able like death itself, slaying Pisachas and birds and Nagas and other creatures by thousands. The discus itself, repeatedly hurled from the hands of Krishna, that slayer of all foes, came back to his hands after slaughtering numberless creatures. The face and form of Krishna that soul of every created thing became fierce to behold while he was thus employed in the slaughter of the Pisachas, Nagas and Rakshasas. No one among the celestials, who had mustered there could vanquish in battle Krishna and Arjuna. When the celestials saw that they could not protect that forest from the might of Krishna and Arjuna by extinguishing that conflagration, they retired from the scene. Then, O monarch, he of a hundred sacrifices (Indra), beholding the immortals retreat, became filled with joy and applauded Krishna and Arjuna. And when the celestials gave up the fight, an incorporeal voice, deep and loud, addressing him of a hundred sacrifices, said, 'Thy friend Takshaka, that chief of snakes, hath not been slain! Before the conflagration commenced in Khandava he had journeyed to Kurukshetra. Know from my words, O Vasava, that Vasudeva and Arjuna are incapable of being vanquished in battle by any one! They are Nara and Narayana—those gods of old heard of in heaven! Thou knowest what their energy is and what their prowess. Invincible in battle, these best of old Rishis are unconquerable by any one in all the worlds! They deserve the most reverential worship of all the celestials and Asuras; of Yakshas and Rakshasas and Gandharvas, of human beings and Kinnaras and Nagas. Therefore, O Vasava, it behoveth thee to go hence with all the celestials. The destruction of Khandava hath been ordained by Fate!' Then the chief of the immortals, ascertaining those words to be true abandoned his wrath and jealousy, and went back to heaven. The dwellers in heaven, O monarch, beholding the illustrious Indra abandon the fight, followed him with all their soldiers. Then those heroes, Vasudeva and Arjuna, when they saw the chief of the celestials retreat accompanied by all the gods, set up a leonine roar. And, O monarch, Kesava and Arjuna, after Indra had left the scene, became exceedingly glad. Those heroes then fearlessly assisted at the conflagration of the forest. Arjuna scattered the celestials like the wind scattering the clouds, and slew with showers of his arrows, numberless creatures that dwelt in Khandava. Cut off by Arjuna's arrows, no one amongst the innumerable creatures could escape from the burning forest. Far from fighting with him, none amongst even the strongest creatures mustered there could look at Arjuna whose weapons were never futile. Sometimes piercing hundred creatures with one shaft and sometimes a single creature with hundred shafts, Arjuna moved about in his car. The creatures themselves, deprived of life, began to fall into the mouth of Agni (god of fire), struck down as it were by death itself. On the banks of rivers or on uneven plains or on crematoriums, go where they did, the creatures (dwelling in Khandava) found no ease, for wherever they sought shelter there they were afflicted by the heat. And hosts of creatures roared in pain, and elephants and deer and wolves set up cries of affliction. At that sound the fishes of the Ganges and the sea, and the various tribes of Vidyadharas dwelling in that forest all became frightened. O thou of mighty arms, let alone battling with them, no one, could even gaze at Arjuna and Janardana of dark hue. Hari slew with his discus those Rakshasas and Danavas and Nagas that rushed at him in bands. Of huge bodies, their heads and trunks were cut off by the swift motion of the discus, and deprived of life they fell down into the blazing fire. Gratified with large quantities of flesh, blood, and fat, the flames rose up to a great height without a curling wreath of smoke. Hutasana (fire- god) with blazing and coppery eyes, and flaming tongue and large mouth, and the hair on the crown of his head all fiery, drinking, with the help of Krishna and Arjuna, that nectar-like stream of animal fat, became filled with joy. Gratified greatly, Agni derived much happiness.

"And it so happened that the slayer of Madhu suddenly beheld an Asura of the name of Maya escaping from the abode of Takshaka. Agni having Vayu for his car-driver, assuming a body with matted locks on head, and roaring like the clouds, pursued the Asura, desirous of consuming him. Beholding the Asura, Vasudeva stood with his weapon upraised, ready to smite him down, seeing the discus uplifted and Agni pursuing from behind to burn him, Maya said 'Run to me, O Arjuna, and protect me!' Hearing his affrighted voice Arjuna said, 'Fear not!' That voice of Arjuna, O Bharata, seemed to give Maya his life. As the merciful son of Pritha said unto Maya that there was nothing to fear, he of the Dasarha race no longer desired to slay Maya who was the brother of Namuchi, and Agni also burned him not.'

"Vaisampayana continued, 'Protected from Indra by Krishna and Partha, Agni gifted with great intelligence, burned that forest for five and ten days. And while the forest burned Agni spared only six of its dwellers, viz., Aswasena, Maya, and four birds called Sarngakas.'"

SECTION CCXXXI
(Khandava-daha Parva continued)

"Janamejaya said, 'O Brahmana, tell me why and when that forest burnt in that way, Agni consumed not the birds called Sarngakas? Thou hast, O Brahmana, recited (to us) the cause of Aswasena and the Danava Maya not having been consumed. But thou hast not as yet said what the cause was of the escape of the Sarngakas? The escape of those birds, O Brahmana, appeareth to me to be wonderful. Tell us why they were not destroyed in that dreadful conflagration.'

"Vaisampayana said, 'O slayer of all foes, I shall tell thee all as to why Agni did not burn up those birds during the conflagration. There was, O king, a great Rishi known by the name of Mandapala, conversant with all the shastras, of rigid vows, devoted to asceticism, and the foremost of all virtuous persons. Following in the wake of Rishis that had drawn up their virile fluid, that ascetic, O monarch, with every sense under complete control, devoted himself to study and virtue. Having reached the opposite shores of asceticism, O Bharata, he left his human form and went to the region of the Pitris. But going thither he failed to obtain the (expected) fruit of his acts. He asked the celestials that sat around the king of the dead as to the cause of his treatment, saying, 'Why have these regions become unattainable by me,—regions that I had thought had been acquired by me by my ascetic devotions? Have I not performed those acts whose fruits are these regions? Ye inhabitants of heaven, tell me why these regions are shut against me! I will do that which will give me the fruit of my ascetic penances.'

"The celestials answered, 'Hear, O Brahmana, of those acts and things on account of which men are born debtors. Without doubt, it is for religious rites, studies according to the ordinance, and progeny, that men are born debtors. These debts are all discharged by sacrifices, asceticism, and offspring. Thou art an ascetic and hast also performed sacrifices; but thou hast no offspring. These regions are shut against thee only for want of children. Beget children, therefore! Thou shalt then enjoy multifarious regions of felicity. The Vedas declared that the son rescueth the father from a hell called Put. Then, O best of Brahmanas, strive to beget offspring.'

"Vaisampayana continued, 'Mandapala, having heard these words of the dwellers in heaven, reflected how best he could obtain the largest number of offspring within the shortest period of time. The Rishi, after reflection, understood that of all creatures birds alone were blest with fecundity. Assuming the form of a Sarngaka the Rishi had connection with a female bird of the same species called by the name of Jarita. And he begat upon her four sons who were all reciters of the Vedas. Leaving all those sons of his with their mother in that forest, while they were still within eggs, the ascetic went to (another wife called by the name of) Lapita. And, O Bharata, when the exalted sage went away for the company of Lapita, moved by affection for her offspring, Jarita became very thoughtful. Though forsaken by their father in the forest of Khandava, Jarita, anxious in her affection for them, could not forsake her offspring, those infant Rishis encased in eggs. Moved by parental affection, she brought up these children born of her, herself following the pursuits proper to her own species. Some time after, the Rishi, in wandering over that forest in the company of Lapita, saw Agni coming towards Khandava to burn it down. Then the Brahmana Mandapala, knowing the intention of Agni and remembering also that his children were all young moved by fear, gratified the god, of the burning element, that regent of the universe, endued with great energy. And he did this, desiring to put in a word for his unfledged offspring. Addressing Agni, the Rishi said, 'Thou art, O Agni, the mouth of all the worlds! Thou art the carrier of the sacrificial butter! O purifier (of all sins), thou movest invisible with the frame of every creature! The learned have spoken of thee as an One, and again as possessed of triple nature. The wise perform their sacrifices before thee, taking thee as consisting of eight (mouths). The great Rishis declare that this universe hath been created by thee. O thou that feedest on sacrificial butter, without thee this whole universe would be destroyed in a single day. Bowing to thee, the Brahmanas, accompanied by their wives and children, go to eternal regions won by them by help of their own deeds. O Agni, the learned represent thee as the clouds in the heavens charged with lightning. O Agni, the flames put forth by thee consume every creature. O thou of great splendour, this universe hath been created by thee. The Vedas are thy word. All creatures, mobile and immobile, depend upon thee. Water primarily dependeth on thee, so also the whole of this universe. All offerings of clarified butter and oblations of food to the pitris have been established in thee. O god, thou art the consumer, and thou art the creator and thou art Vrihaspati himself (in intelligence). Thou art the twin Aswins; thou art Surya; thou art Soma; thou art Vayu.

"Vaisampayana continued, 'O monarch, thus praised by Mandapala, Agni was gratified with that Rishi of immeasurable energy; and the god, well- pleased, replied, 'What good can I do to thee?' Then Mandapala with joined palms said unto the carrier of clarified butter, 'While thou burnest the forest of Khandava, spare my children.' The illustrious bearer of clarified butter replied, 'So be it.' It was, therefore, O monarch, that he blazed not forth, while consuming the forest of Khandava, for the destruction of Mandapala's children.'"

SECTION CCXXXII
(Khandava-daha Parva continued)

"Vaisampayana said, 'When the fire blazed forth in the forest of Khandava, the infant birds became very much distressed and afflicted. Filled with anxiety, they saw not any means of escape. Their mother, the helpless Jarita, knowing that they were too young to escape, was filled with sorrow and wept aloud. And she said, 'Oh, the terrible, illuminating the whole universe and burning the forest down, approacheth towards us, increasing my woe. These infants with immature understanding, without feathers and feet, and the sole refuge of our deceased ancestors, afflict me. Oh, this fire approacheth, spreading fear all around, and licking with its tongue the tallest trees. But my unfledged children are incapable of effecting their escape. I myself am not capable of escaping, taking all these with me. Nor am I capable of abandoning them, for my heart is distressed on their account. Whom amongst my sons, shall I leave behind, and whom shall I carry with me? What (act) should I do now that is consistent with duty? What also do you, my infant sons, think? I do not, even by reflection, see any way of escape for you. I shall even cover you with my wings and die with you. Your cruel father left me some time before, saying, 'Upon this Jaritari, because he is the eldest of my sons, will my race depend. My second Sarisrikka will beget progeny for the expansion of my ancestors' race. My third, Stamvamitra, will be devoted to asceticism, and my youngest, Drona, will become the foremost of those acquainted with the Vedas.' But how hath this terrible calamity overtaken us! Whom shall I take with me? As I am deprived of judgment what should I do that is consistent with duty? I do not see, by the exercise of my own judgment, the escape of my children from the fire!'

"Vaisampayana said, 'Unto their mother indulging in these lamentations, the infant ones said. 'O mother, relinquishing thy affection for us, go thou to a place where there is no fire. If we are killed here, thou mayest have other children born to thee. If thou, O mother be killed, we can have no more children in our race. Reflecting upon both these calamities, the time hath come for thee, O mother, to do that which is beneficial to our race. Do not be influenced by affection for thy offspring, which promises to destroy both us and thee. If thou savest thyself, our father, who is even desirous of winning regions of felicity, may have his wishes gratified.'

"Hearing what the infants said. Jarita replied, 'There is a hole here in the ground near to this tree, belonging to a mouse. Enter this hole without loss of time. You shall have then no fear of fire. After ye have entered it, I shall, ye children, cover its mouth with dust. This is the only means of escape that I see from the blazing fire. Then when the fire will be put out, I shall return hither to remove the dust. Follow my advice if you are to escape from the conflagration.'

"The infant birds replied, 'Without feathers we are but so many balls of flesh. If we enter the hole, certain it is that the carnivorous mouse will destroy us all. Beholding this danger before us, we cannot enter this hole. Alas, we do not see any means by which we may escape from the fire or from the mouse. We do not see how our father's act of procreation may be prevented from becoming futile, and how also our mother may be saved. If we enter the hole, the mouse will destroy us; we remain where we are and the sky-ranging fire will destroy us. Reflecting upon both the calamities, a death by fire is preferable to a death by being eaten up. If we are devoured by the mouse within the hole, that death is certainly ignoble, whereas the destruction of the body in fire is approved by the wise.'"

SECTION CCXXXIII
(Khandava-daha Parva continued)

"Vaisampayana said, 'Hearing those words of her sons Jarita continued, "The little mouse that had come out of this hole was seized by a hawk with his claws and carried away hence. Therefore, ye may fearlessly enter this hole now.' The young ones replied, 'We are not by any means certain of that mouse having been taken away by the hawk. There may be other mice living here. From them we have every fear. Whereas it is doubtful whether fire will at all approach us here. Already we see an adverse wind blowing the flames away. If we enter the hole, death is certain at the hands of the dwellers in the hole. But if we remain where we are, death is uncertain. O mother, a position in which death is uncertain is better than that in which it is certain. It is thy duty, therefore, to escape thyself, for, if thou livest thou mayest obtain other children as good.'

"Their mother then said, 'Ye children, I myself saw the mighty hawk, that best of birds, swoop down and fly away with the mouse from the hole. And while he was flying away swiftly, I followed him behind and pronounced blessing on him for his having taken away the mouse from the hole. I said unto him. 'O king of hawks, because thou art flying away with our enemy, the mouse, in thy claws, mayest thou, without a foe, live in heaven with a golden body.' Afterwards when that hawk devoured the mouse, I came away, obtaining his leave. Therefore, ye children, enter this hole trustfully. Ye have nothing to fear. The mouse that was its inmate was seized and taken away by the hawk in my sight.' The young ones again said, 'O mother, we do not by any means know that the mouse hath been carried away by the hawk. We cannot enter this hole in the ground without being certain of the fact.' Their mother said, 'I know to a certainty that the mouse hath been carried away by the hawk. Therefore, ye children, ye have nothing to fear; do what I say.' The young ones again said, 'We do not, O mother, say that thou art dispelling our fears with a false story. For whatever is done by a person when his reason hath been disturbed can scarcely be said to be that person's deliberate act. Thou hast not been benefited by us, nor dost thou know who we are. Why dost thou, therefore, strive to protect us at so much cost to thyself? Who are we to thee? Thou art young and handsome, and capable of seeking out thy husband. Go unto thy husband. Thou shalt obtain good children again. Let us by entering the fire attain to regions of felicity. If, however, the fire consume us not, thou mayest come back and obtain us again.'

"Vaisampayana said, 'The parent bird then, thus addressed by her sons, left them in Khandava and hastily went to the spot where there was no fire and there was safety. Then Agni in haste and with fierce flames approached the spot where the sons of Mandapala were. The young birds saw the blazing fire come towards them. Then Jaritari, the eldest of the four, in the hearing of Agni, began to speak.'"

SECTION CCXXXIV
(Khandava-daha Parva continued)

"Jaritari said, 'The person that is wise remaineth wakeful in view of death. Accordingly, when the hour of death approacheth, he feeleth no pangs. But the person of perplexed soul, who remaineth not awake, when the hour of death comes, feeleth the pangs of death and never attaineth salvation.'

"The second brother Sarisrikka, said, 'Thou art patient and intelligent. The time is come when our lives are threatened. Without doubt, one only amongst many becometh wise and brave.'

"The third brother, Stamvamitra, said, 'The eldest brother is called the protector. It is the eldest brother that rescueth (the younger ones) from danger. If the eldest himself faileth to rescue them, what can the younger ones do?'

"The fourth and the youngest brother, Drona said, 'The cruel god of fire, with seven tongues and seven mouths quickly cometh towards our habitation, blazing forth in splendour and licking up everything in his path.'

"Vaisampayana continued, 'Having addressed one another thus, the sons of Mandapala then each devotedly addressed an eulogistic hymn to Agni. Listen now, O monarch, to those hymns as I recite them.'

"Jaritari said, 'Thou art, O fire, the soul of air! Thou art the body of the Earth's vegetation! O Sukra, water is thy parent as thou art the parent of water! O thou of great energy, thy flames, like the rays of the sun, extend themselves above, below, behind, and on each side.'

"Sarisrikka said, 'O smoke-bannered god, our mother is not to be seen, and we know not our father! Our feathers have not grown as yet. We have none to protect us save thee. Therefore, O Agni, infants that we are protect us! O Agni, as we are distressed, protect us with that auspicious form thou hast and with those seven flames of thine! We seek protection at thy hands. Thou alone, O Agni, art the giver of heat (in the universe). O lord, there is none else (save thee) that giveth heat to the rays of the sun. O, protect us who are young and who are Rishis. O Havyavaha (carrier of sacrificial butter), be pleased to go hence by some other route.'

"Stamvamitra said, 'Thou alone, O Agni, art everything! This whole universe is established in thee! Thou sustainest every creature, and thou supportest the universe! Thou art the carrier of the sacrificial butter, and thou art the excellent sacrificial butter itself! The wise know thee to be one (as cause) and many (as effects)! Having created the three worlds, thou, O Havyavaha, again destroyest them when the time cometh, swelling thyself forth! Thou art the productive cause of the whole universe, and thou also art the essence in which the universe dissolveth itself!'

"Drona said, 'O lord of the universe, growing in strength and remaining within their bodies, thou causest the food that living creatures eat to be digested. Everything therefore, is established in thee. O Sukra, O thou from whose mouth the Vedas have sprung, it is thou who assumest the form of the sun, and sucking up the waters of the earth and every liquid juice that the earth yields, givest them back in time in the form of rain and causest everything to grow! From thee, O Sukra, are these plants and creepers with green foliage! From thee have sprung these tanks and pools, and the great ocean also that is ever blessed! O thou of fierce rays, this our (human) body dependeth on Varuna (the water-god)! We are unable to bear thy heat. Be thou, therefore, our auspicious protector! O, destroy us not! O thou of copper-hued eyes, O thou of red neck, O thou whose path is marked by a black colour, save us by going along any remote route, as indeed, the ocean saveth the house on its banks!'

"Vaisampayana continued, 'Thus addressed by Drona—that utterer of Brahma— Agni, well-pleased at what he heard, and remembering also the promise he had made to Mandapala, replied unto him, saying, 'Thou art a Rishi, O Drona! For what thou hast said is Brahma (Vedic truth). I shall do your pleasure. Fear not! Indeed, Mandapala had spoken to me of you to the effect that I should spare his sons, while consuming the forest. The words he spoke and thy speech also are entitled to great weight to me. Say what I am to do. O best of Brahmanas, I have been greatly pleased with thy hymn. Blest be thou, O Brahmana!'

"Drona said, 'O Sukra, these cats trouble us every day. O Hutasana; consume them with their friends and relatives.'

"Vaisampayana continued, 'Then Agni did what the Sarngakas asked him to do, telling them of his intentions. And, O Janamejaya, growing in strength, he began then to consume the forest of Khandava.'"

SECTION CCXXXV
(Khandava-daha Parva continued)

"Vaisampayana said, 'O thou of Kuru's race, the Rishi Mandapala became very anxious about his children, although he had spoken of them to the god of fierce rays. Indeed, his mind was not in peace. Distressed on account of his sons, he addressed Lapita (his second wife with whom he then was), saying, 'O Lapita, as my children are incapable of the power of moving, how are they? When the fire will grow in strength and the wind begin to blow violently, my children will scarcely be able to save themselves. How will their mother be able to rescue them? That innocent woman will be afflicted with great sorrow when she will find herself unable to save her offspring. Oh, how will she compose herself, uttering various lamentations on account of my children who are all incapable of taking wing or rising up into the air. Oh, how is Jaritari, my son, and how is Sarisrikka, and how is Stamvamitra, and how is Drona, and how also is their helpless mother?'

"Unto the Rishi Mandapala thus weeping in the forest, Lapita, O Bharata, thus replied, under the influence of jealousy, 'Thou need not worry for thy children who, as thou hast assured me, are all Rishis endued with energy and prowess! They can have no fear from fire. Didst thou not speak to Agni in my presence, in their behalf? Has not the illustrious deity promised to save them? One of the regents of the universe as Agni is, he will never falsify his speech. Thou hast no anxiety, nor is thy heart inclined towards benefiting friends. It is only by thinking of her—my rival (Jarita) that thou art so distracted! Certain it is that the love thou bearest to me is not equal to what thou hadst for her at first. He that hath two parties dividing his attention, can easily behold one of those suffer all sorts of pangs; but he should not disregard the party that is next to his heart. Then go thou to Jarita, for whom thy heart is sorrowing! As for myself, I shall henceforth wander alone, as a fit reward for my having attached myself to a wicked person.'

"Hearing these words, Mandapala replied, 'I do not wander over the earth with such intentions as thou conceivest. It is only for the sake of progeny that I am here. And even those that I have are in danger. He who casteth off what he hath for the sake of what he may acquire, is a wicked person. The world disregardeth and insulteth him. (Therefore, go I must). As for thyself thou art free to do what thou choosest. This blazing fire that licketh up the trees causeth sorrow in my anxious heart and raiseth therein evil presentiments.'

"Vaisampayana continued, 'Meanwhile, after the fire had left the spot where the Sarngakas dwelt, Jarita, much attached to her children, hastily came thither to see how they were. She found that all of them had escaped from the fire and were perfectly well. Beholding their mother, they began to weep, though safe and sound. She too shed tears upon beholding them alive. And she embraced, one by one, all her weeping children. Just at that time, O Bharata, the Rishi Mandapala arrived there. But none of his sons expressed joy, upon beholding him. The Rishi, however, began to speak to them one after another and unto Jarita also, repeatedly. But neither his sons nor Jarita spoke anything well or ill unto him in return.'

"Mandapala then said, 'Who amongst these is thy first born, and who the next after him? And who is the third, and who the youngest? I am speaking unto thee woefully; why dost thou not reply to me? I left thee, it is true, but I was not happy where I was.'

"Jarita then said, 'What hast thou to do with the eldest of these, and what with him that is next? And what with the third and what with the youngest? Go now unto that Lapita of sweet smiles and endued with youth, unto whom thou didst go of old, beholding me deficient in everything!' Mandapala replied, 'As regards females, there is nothing so destructive of their happiness whether in this or the other world as a co-wife and a clandestine lover. There is nothing like these two that inflames the fire of hostility and causes such anxiety. Even the auspicious and well-behaved Arundhati, celebrated amongst all creatures, had been jealous of the illustrious Vasishtha of great purity of mind and always devoted to the good of his wife. Arundhati insulted even the wise Muni amongst the (celestial) seven. In consequence of such insulting thoughts of hers, she has become a little star, like fire mixed with smoke, sometimes visible and sometimes invisible, like an omen portending no good (amongst a constellation of seven bright stars representing the seven Rishis). I look to thee for the sake of children. I never wronged thee, like Vasishtha who never wronged his wife. Thou hast, therefore, by thy jealousy behaved towards me like Arundhati of old towards Vasishtha. Men should never trust women even if they be wives. Women, when they have become mothers, do not much mind serving their husbands.'

"Vaisampayana continued, 'After this, all his children came forward to worship him. And he also began to speak kindly towards them all, giving them every assurance.'"

SECTION CCXXXVI
(Khandava-daha Parva continued)

"Vaisampayana said, 'Mandapala then addressed his children, saying, 'I had spoken unto Agni for the safety of you all. The illustrious deity had assured me that he would grant my wish. At those words of Agni, and knowing the virtuous disposition of your mother, as also the great energy that is in yourselves, I came not here earlier. Therefore, ye sons, do not harbour in your hearts any resentment towards me. Ye are all Rishis acquainted with the Vedas. Even Agni knoweth you well.'

"Vaisampayana continued, 'Having given such assurances unto his sons, the Brahmana Mandapala took with him his wife and sons, and leaving that region, went away to some other country.

"It thus that the illustrious god of fierce rays, having grown in strength consumed the forest of Khandava with the help of Krishna and Arjuna, for the good of the world. And Agni having drunk several rivers of fat and marrow, became highly gratified, and showed himself to Arjuna. Then Purandara, surrounded by the Maruts, descended from the firmament and addressing Partha and Kesava said, 'Ye have achieved a feat that a celestial even could not. Ask ye each a boon that is not obtainable by any man. I have been gratified with you.'

"Vaisampayana continued, 'Then Partha asked from Indra all his weapons. At this Sakra of great splendour, having fixed the time for giving them, said, 'When the illustrious Madhava becomes pleased with thee, then, O son of Pandu, I will give thee all my weapons! O prince of Kuru's race, I shall know when the time cometh. Even for thy austere asceticism I will give thee all my weapons of fire and all my Vayavya weapons, and thou also wilt accept them all of me.' Then Vasudeva asked that his friendship with Arjuna might be eternal. The chief of the celestials granted unto the intelligent Krishna the boon he desired. And having granted these boons unto Krishna and Arjuna, the lord of the Maruts, accompanied by the celestials, ascended to heaven, having also spoken to Hutasana (one whose food is sacrificial butter). Agni also, having burnt that forest with its animals and birds for five and ten days, became gratified and ceased to burn. Having eaten flesh in abundance and drunk fat and blood, he became highly gratified, and addressing Achyuta and Arjuna said, 'I have been gratified by you two tigers among men. At my command, ye heroes, ye shall be competent to go wheresoever ye choose!' Thus addressed by the illustrious Agni, Arjuna and Vasudeva and the Danava Maya also—these three,—having wandered a little at last sat themselves down on the delightful banks of a river.'"

Printed in Great Britain
by Amazon.co.uk, Ltd.,
Marston Gate.